GANguides

1

2

1 Buddhist temple, Sri Aman, Sarawak
2 Kinarut, Sabah

3

3 Puu Jih Shih temple, Sandakan, Sabah
4 Cheong Fatt Tze Mansion, Penang
5 Banana fronds, Kedah
6 Langkawi, Kedah

7 Kampung Ayer, Brunei
8 Banana leaf, Perak
9 Detail of fishing boat, Terengganu
10 Batang-Ai River, Sarawak

11

12

14

13

11 Mount Kinabalu, Sabah
12 Pulau Tioman, Pahang
13 Petronas Towers, Kuala Lumpur
14 Kiarong Mosque, Brunei

16

17

18

19

15 Fah Cheong's *First Generation*, Singapore River
16 Bandar Seri Begawan, Brunei
17 Shopfront, Melaka
18 Rainforest canopy, Taman Negara, Pahang
19 Semelai canoes, Tasek Bera, Pahang

20 Bako National Park, Sarawak
21 Church of St Francis, Kampung Seling, Sarawak
22 Wet market, Terengganu

20

21

22

23 Lantern beetles, Niah Caves National Park, Sarawak
24 Tasek Merimbun Heritage Park, Brunei
25 Pulau Redang, Terengganu
26 Omar Ali Saifuddien Mosque, Brunei

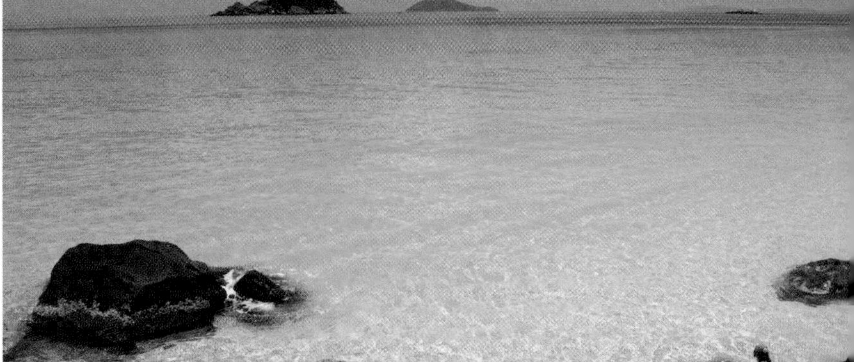

27

27 Kinabalu National Park, Sabah

About the author

James Alexander spent his early childhood in Southeast Asia and has since jumped at any excuse to return to these parts. He has written and contributed to a range of guidebooks covering destinations across Europe and Asia. When not on the move, he works as a copywriter and editor. He lives in Hastings with his wife and two young children.

Author's acknowledgements

I owe an obvious debt of gratitude to the many people who provided help and advice during my time in Southeast Asia. However, my main thanks go to my wife, Caroline, who played an equal part in the research of this book, giving up a year of her life for its cause. It wouldn't have happened without her.

For my parents and in memory of Patricia

Contents

Cadogan Guides
2nd Floor, 233 High Holborn,
London WC1 7DN
info@cadoganguides.co.uk
www.cadoganguides.com

The Globe Pequot Press
246 Goose Lane, PO Box 480, Guilford,
Connecticut 06437–0480

Cover photographs: © Andy Caulfield/ James Alexander
Photo essay: © James Alexander
Maps © Cadogan Guides, drawn by Maidenhead Cartographic Services Ltd.

Art direction: Sarah Gardner
Managing Editor: Natalie Pomier
Editor: Nicola Jessop
Proofreader: Elspeth Anderson
Indexing: Isobel McLean

Printed in Italy by Legoprint
A catalogue record for this book is available from the British Library
ISBN 10: 1-86011-309-5
ISBN 13: 978-1-86011-309-3

Please help us to keep this guide up to date. We have done our best to ensure that the information in this guide is correct at the time of going to press. But places and facilities are constantly changing, and standards and prices in hotels and restaurants fluctuate. We would be delighted to receive any comments concerning existing entries or omissions. Authors of the best letters will receive a copy of the Cadogan Guide of their choice.

Introduction

01

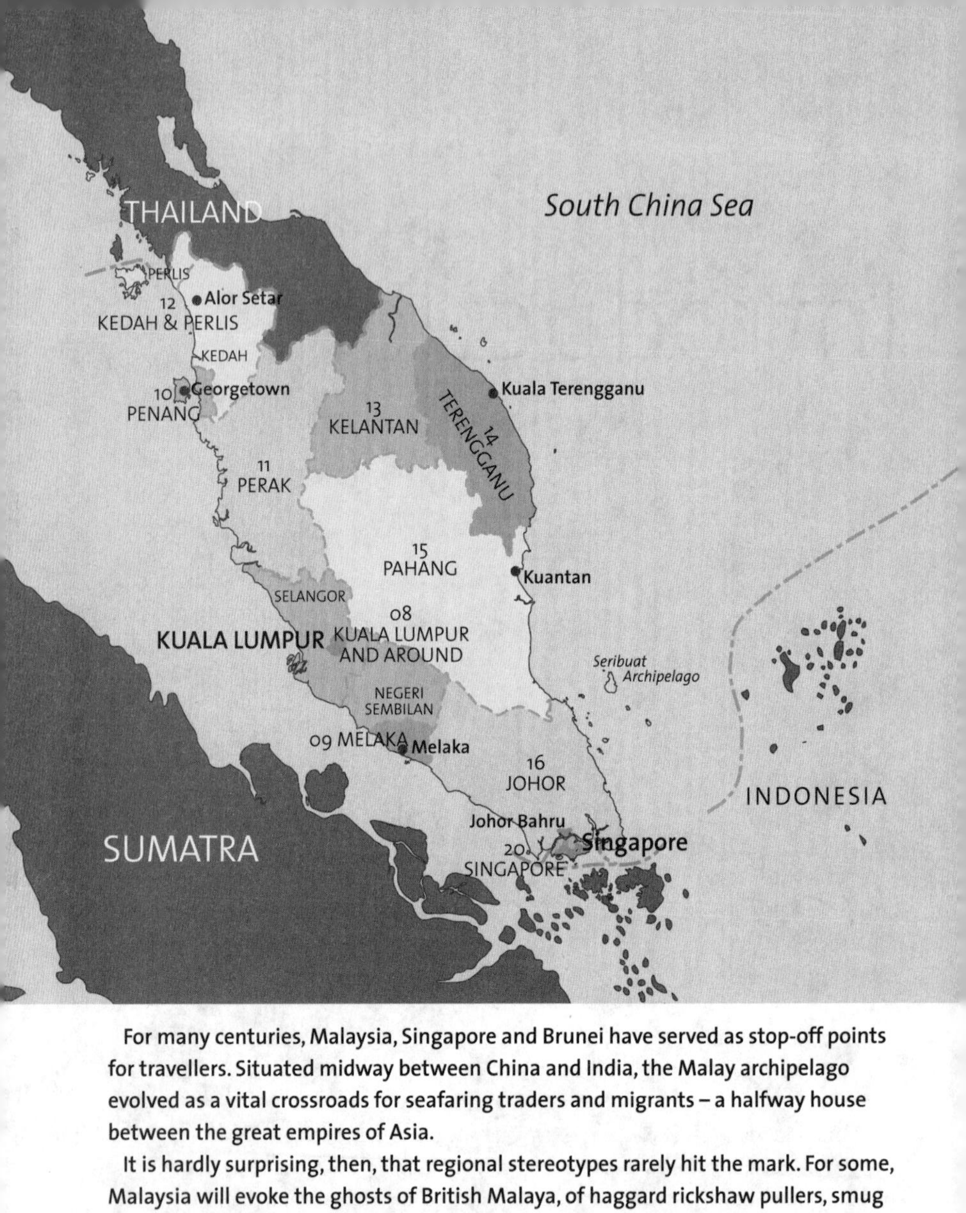

For many centuries, Malaysia, Singapore and Brunei have served as stop-off points for travellers. Situated midway between China and India, the Malay archipelago evolved as a vital crossroads for seafaring traders and migrants – a halfway house between the great empires of Asia.

It is hardly surprising, then, that regional stereotypes rarely hit the mark. For some, Malaysia will evoke the ghosts of British Malaya, of haggard rickshaw pullers, smug colonials and opium-dazed coolies. But this world has long disappeared. As the nation surges towards first-world status, its peoples are as diverse as they ever were.

In the cities, wealthy office workers move between glass-and-steel skyscrapers, Indian *mamak* chefs fling dough above their heads, and Chinese *towkays* play mahjong in backstreet doorways. In Malaysian Borneo, Kadazan porters trudge up and down Mount Kinabalu with supplies for tourists, while on coastal waters, Bajau Laut families dry sea slugs on the decks of *lepa-lepa* – impossibly small houseboats with attap roofs. In the rainforests of Sarawak, the Orang Ulu ('upriver people') live out their lives in the manner of their distant ancestors; old tattooed men, their

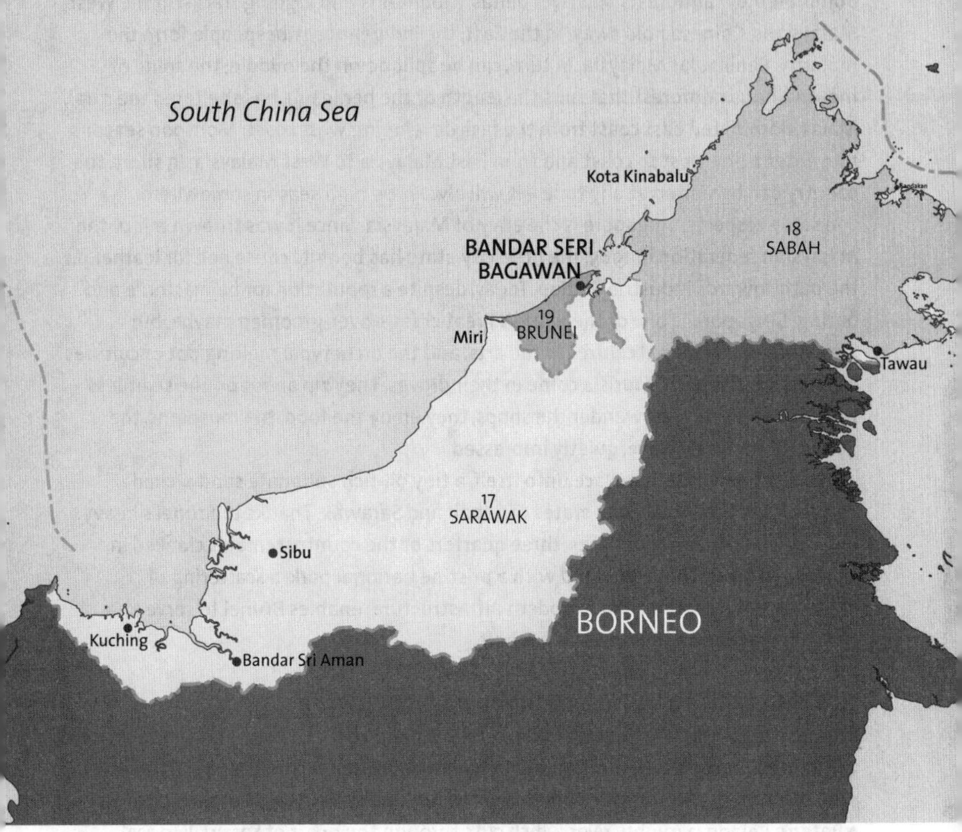

hunting days behind them, stay home to thresh rice, caulk longboats and mind the grandchildren, who race barefoot on the longhouse verandah between dips in the river. All these various peoples – and there are dozens more besides – are Malaysians, each of them heir to as broad an ancestry as any place in the world.

Malaysia's scenery is equally diverse. In spite of logging and the encroachment of oil palm plantations, many visitors are surprised to learn that over half of the Malaysian landmass remains cloaked in rainforest, patches of which are contenders for the most biodiverse spot on Earth. Stunning national parks shelter endangered wildlife; tigers prowl the interior jungles of Peninsular Malaysia; orang-utans survive in the national parks of Malaysian Borneo; in remote lowland rainforests, the world's largest flower, the Rafflesia, spreads its fleshy petals, and in heath forests, pitcher plants trap their six-legged prey. Meanwhile, the coral-rich seas, the world-class dive sites and the islands are equal to anyone's vision of a tropical paradise.

Modern Malaysia wears two faces, its geography split between east and west. Peninsular Malaysia (or West Malaysia) is the political and industrial heartland of the country, home to the federal capital and the bulk of the nation's populace. Malaysian Borneo (or East Malaysia), separated from the peninsula by 500 miles of ocean, is dominated by rainforests and river deltas, mountains and logging tracks. In the West, Malays and Chinese hold sway; in the East, the indigenous tribespeople form the majority. Peninsular Malaysia, in turn, can be split down the middle; the spine of mountainous rainforest that runs the length of the peninsula has sheltered the rural, Malay-dominated east coast from the fast-developing west coast. Monsoon seasons, too, differ from coast to coast and from East Malaysia to West Malaysia. In short, the country can be visited at any time – it will always be high season somewhere.

In some respects, Singapore is the envy of Malaysia. Since it was thrown out of the Malaysian federation in 1965, the little city-state has bent its cause hell for leather on the path towards industrialization. Today, despite a reputation for being sterile and boring, Singapore is one of the world's great cities – over-groomed maybe, but nevertheless a regional centre for the arts, and the archetypal melting pot of cultures and cuisines. As such, tourists come in their droves. They zip about on the seamless transport system, they wander the shops, they enjoy the food, the museums, the gardens. Then they leave, quietly impressed.

Brunei, meanwhile, is a place unto itself, a tiny oil-rich sultanate sandwiched between the East Malaysian states of Sabah and Sarawak. Thanks to Brunei's heavy reliance on oil in modern times, three quarters of the country remains cloaked in virgin rainforest. This, combined with a pristine national park, a scattering of indigenous longhouses and a modern infrastructure, enables Brunei to serve as a gentle introduction to Borneo as a whole.

20 Things Not to be Missed (in no particular order...)

1 Taman Negara, Malaysia's flagship national park (p.267)
2 Gunung Kinabalu, tallest mountain between New Guinea and the Himalayas (p.372)
3 Pulau Tioman, a beautiful, mountainous island cloaked in virgin jungle (p.259)
4 Batang Rejang, a mighty river which cuts through the heart of Sarawak (p.333)
5 Pulau Sipadan, a world-class dive site with a 680m vertical drop-off (p.391)
6 Gunung Mulu National Park, rainforest trails and magnificent caves (p.347)
7 Kuala Kangsar, a sleepy royal town that is a vision of old Malaya (p.192)
8 Sepilok, a popular orang-utan rehabilitation centre in Sabah (p.382)
9 Cameron Highlands, an old colonial hill station with rolling tea plantations (p.286)
10 Melaka, a city combining a colonial heritage with Peranakan architecture (p.123)
11 Jungle Railway, cutting through the heart of rural Malaysia (p.281)
12 Bario, Kelabit Highlands, the highest settled community in Borneo (p.352)
13 Kinabatangan Wetlands, one of Southeast Asia's wildlife hot spots (p.386)
14 Perhentian Islands, white-sand beaches and wonderful snorkelling (p.237)
15 Ulu Temburong National Park, Brunei's biggest draw (p.408)
16 Raffles Hotel, still the iconic symbol of colonial Singapore (p.426)
17 Cheong Fatt Tze Mansion, Penang's heritage showpiece (p.168)
18 Tasek Bera, a remote freshwater lake, home to the Semelai tribe (p.284)
19 Langkawi, Malaysia's leading beach destination (p.207)
20 Kuala Terengganu, home to a thriving cottage industry in Malay crafts (p.233)

History

02

Early History

After hacking through eight feet of petrified bat guano in Sarawak's Niah Caves, archaeologists were rewarded in 1958 with the discovery of a 43,000-year-old skull – the oldest human remains to be found in Southeast Asia (Java Man, though older, is classified as Homo erectus). This find marks the beginning of Malaysia's patchwork history. Further finds within the cave complex provide evidence of an unbroken succession of inhabitants up to 1,500 bc. In West Malaysia, a meagre haul of Stone Age tools, and the discovery of a human skeleton in 1990 (named Perak Man), suggest a similar timeline.

Although recent advances in archaeological methodology have provided historians with a working backbone, Malaysia's distant past is seen as something of a black hole in Asian history. The dank tropical climate has done little to preserve archaeological clues about the region's distant past: only artefacts fashioned from durable stones and metals have survived. Exactly who inhabited the region's tangled jungles and swampy plains, and what they were up to several millennia back, is left largely to speculation. What we do know has been pieced together with the help of visitors' accounts recorded in early Indian, Chinese and Arab sources.

The ebb and flow of migrants from southern China and Indochina between 2500 bc and 200 bc is reflected in the the great variety of ethnic groups that share citizenship of modern Malaysia. These settlers, along with the indigenous tribes who were pushed deeper into the jungle, are generally seen as the primary ancestors of the modern Malays. They were an adaptable people, ready to share ideas and take advantage of the great natural resources of their environment. Even in these early times, a common cultural heritage can be seen to extend its influence from Sumatra to Borneo, with universal animist beliefs (*see* p.40) surviving intact to this very day. In an animist world view every element of nature – every rock, every bird, every plant – has its own spirit. Complex rituals have evolved over the centuries to placate these spirits (including the gory Iban practice of hacking off the heads of enemies, binding them in rattan and hanging them from the rafters of their longhouses). This spiritual dialogue with the natural world is combined with an encyclopaedic knowledge of the jungle and its resources: by adolescence a modern-day Orang Asli ('original man') can identify by name several hundred plant species.

As early as 300 bc, traders from India and China were frequenting the shores of the Peninsula and Borneo, drawn by jungle treasures offered up by the indigenous peoples. In exchange for cloth, ceramics and metalwork, the local tribes plundered the forests for birds' nests, aromatic woods, resins, tortoiseshell, and rhinoceros and hornbill ivory. Gliding about the mangrove swamps in their dugouts, the seagoing tribes (Orang Laut) harvested mangrove bark for its tannin and sent divers to the sea bed for shells, used as currency, and *teripang* (sea slug), used in Chinese cooking and medicine.

A Legendary Kingdom

Over time, the Strait of Melaka became a vital crossroads for traders and their incumbent cultures – a halfway house between the great empires of Asia. Blown across the Indian Ocean by the southwest monsoon, seafarers on the trade route between India and China sought shelter in the calm waters of the Strait, where they would wait for the winds to turn and blow them up across the South China Sea. Others would pack up their goods and cross the isthmus on foot to avoid the pirate-infested waters of the lower Strait.

The Peninsula soon developed a reputation for its tin deposits and for its gold; throughout Asia the region was touted as Suvarnabhumi, or 'Land of Gold', while fair-skinned explorers from the Greek world returned home with stories of a rich, distant land, named 'Golden Chersonese'. By the 2nd century AD the legendary kingdom of **Langkasuka** had sprung up, led by a king who paraded the pavilions of his capital astride an elephant, shaded by a white parasol and adorned with gold. It is likely that the Indianized kingdom spanned the Peninsula with settlements on either coast: 7th-century Chinese sources place Langkasuka somewhere along the east coast, while early Malay literature places the kingdom on the west coast in modern-day Kedah.

Early contact with India had a profound effect on the development of Malay culture. As more Indian traders dropped by to barter for gold, or stock up on ivory, the locals adopted elements of Indian culture and assimilated them into their own traditions. For a start, Malays owe their notions of kingship to the Indian model, with many of the ceremonies still preserved in today's Malay courts. Out in the kampungs, villagers incorporated Hindu gods into their pantheon of spirits, while Indian epics, such as the Ramayana, became staples of Malay heritage. Even today, tales from the Ramayana are ever-present in the traditional shadow plays, known as *wayang kulit* (see p.32). Indianized states sprung up along either side of the Strait, each vying for dominance of this vital trade route. The struggle between growing entrepôt states for control of maritime trade became the defining theme of Malaysia's early history.

Six Centuries of Srivijaya

Through the cunning of its leaders, one state emerged as the dominant force in the Malay archipelago between the 7th and 13th centuries. **Srivijaya**, whose influence crept across much of the Southeast Asian world over this period, was situated directly in the path of the northeast monsoon, on the coast of Sumatra. This meant that trading junks from China were swept directly into the hands of Srivijaya's opportunistic merchants. By this time trade with China had grown in leaps and bounds, and Srivijaya was quick to realize the benefits of developing a special relationship with the Chinese emperors, who they buttered up with extravagant gifts. As a result of these, and other, connections Srivijaya became a renowned centre of learning, attracting Buddhist scholars to its state-sponsored religious foundations.

Another reason for Srivijaya's success was its ability to bully harbour chiefs into submitting to the state's authority. For many centuries, ports along the length of the Strait grudgingly accepted Srivijaya's overlordship – at least then they could take a slice of Srivijaya's trade, as well as earn protection against roving bands of pirates. However, intimidation played a large role in maintaining allegiance throughout Srivijaya's suzerainty. *Derhaka* ('treason to the ruler') was hyped as the most heinous of crimes and carried spine-chilling consequences: according to the *Sejarah Melayu* (the 17th-century 'Malay Annals'), a man guilty of *derhaka* would be tortured to death, as would his immediate family, while his house would be uprooted and the soil upon which it stood thrown into the sea.

The strict laws of the land were policed by the rulers' henchmen, drafted from the formidable Orang Laut, a seagoing people who inhabited the mangrove-fringed estuaries of the Malay archipelago. Lurking among the shoals and secluded bays, these tribes had long held a reputation as fearsome raiders, plucking exotic goods from passing ships and flogging them at local markets. As such they made the perfect seabound police force, annihilating would-be pirates and plundering any ship that tried to bypass Srivijaya's port.

For six centuries these masters of the sea helped Srivijaya maintain its trade monopoly over the Strait. But as the lure of independence became increasingly irresistible for smaller states in the region, Srivijaya came to rely more and more heavily on the Orang Laut, until many of them turned to out-and-out piracy once again. This loosening of control over the seas – combined with a new rush of private Chinese traders who were prepared to head straight for the source of supply – signalled the decline of Srivijaya. Smaller trading ports, notably on the east coast of the Peninsula, took advantage of their new-found breathing space and developed independent relations with traders. Meanwhile in Borneo, the port of Boni (possibly the forerunner to Brunei) began attracting international respect as a wealthy trading state. As 600-year-old Srivijaya declined, its cultural momentum was transferred bit by bit onto a new settlement called Melaka.

The Rise of Melaka

The founding of **Melaka** in 1400 is the common starting point for Malay histories (*see* pp.127–30 for a detailed history of Melaka). It is no coincidence that this is the very period when Islam first became an integral part of Malay culture. In 1414 Melaka's founder, Parameswara, a royal fugitive from crumbling Srivijaya, married a princess from the Muslim state of Pasai in north Sumatra. It was a shrewd political move which drew Melaka into close relations with one of the region's liveliest ports. Muslim traders from India and Java began to visit Melaka, where they were able to barter their goods in exchange for luxuries from China. Parameswara further bonded relations with Pasai by adopting Islam at the court and establishing Melaka as a centre of learning. Theological questions were passed between Melaka and Pasai by elephant and with great pomp. When Muzaffar Shah came to the throne in 1445, he took the title of Sultan, and the Sultanate of Melaka was officially born.

While Parameswara's adopted religion helped transform Melaka from a small estuarine settlement into an international marketplace, it was also a handy form of self-aggrandisement; Muslim leaders were held to be Allah's representatives on Earth, and this way, the king could reinforce his demigod status. The court, meanwhile, was a magnificent spectacle, adorned throughout in gold, while the dapper sultan instigated a long list of privileges designed to set himself apart from his earthly subjects. The wearing of gold or yellow, for example, was banned for anyone but the sultan himself. Though fronted with pomp, the court structure instigated by Melaka's first sultans became the model for a system of government that lasted five centuries. Fifteenth-century Melaka came to be viewed as the golden age of Malay history, a time when music and the Arts were allowed to flourish, and a time of wealth and prestige.

Despite Melaka's official conversion to Islam, its community was a gathering of races, a maelstrom of creeds and customs. With its deep, sheltered harbour and efficient market administration, Melaka quickly became the region's leading entrepôt. Traders from around the world stopped by in increasing numbers. From India, there were Bengalis, Tamils, Klings and Gujaratis; from China, Hokkien, Cantonese, Hakkas and Hainanese. All the races of Southeast Asia had representatives in Melaka, as did the Arabs, Jews and Japanese. Malay became the common means of communication among merchants of different nationality, and before long, it was the lingua franca of Southeast Asia. Thereafter, the term Malay itself came to be applied to those who practised Islam and spoke the Malay language, whatever their ancestral roots.

By the reign of Sultan Mahmud (1488–1528), Melaka had gained suzerainty over much of the west coast of the Penisula and a large swathe of Sumatra's east coast. Melaka was, by now, too large and wealthy to escape the notice of Europe.

Melaka Falls to the Portuguese

The Portuguese were the first of the Europeans to forage about for a trading base in Southeast Asia. Their navigators had spent much of the late 15th century experimenting with sea routes to the Orient via the Cape of Good Hope. The prize? Control of the hugely lucrative spice trade, which at that time was in the hands of the Arabs. Muslim rulers controlled the trade hubs on the Red Sea and the Persian Gulf, where Arab merchants made a healthy living trading produce from India and the East Indies with Venetian merchants, who carried the goods on to the European market. The Portuguese aim was to bypass the middlemen and bring the wealth of the Orient straight home.

It was not only the riches of the Orient that drew the Portuguese eastwards. Contemporary accounts are full of the strangely conceived kingdom of John the

Priest, or 'Prester John', a legendary priest-king much talked about in medieval Europe and said to rule over a Christian kingdom somewhere in the East. With their missionary zeal, this myth was a further driving force for Portuguese forays across the Indian Ocean.

Diogo Lopes de Sequeira was the first Portuguese navigator to anchor off Melaka. He arrived in 1509 with a fleet of five ships and gifts from King Manuel of Portugal. Melaka's *bendahara* (chief minister) welcomed the newcomers with open arms, inviting them to land their goods and begin trading. Melaka's resident Gujeratis were not so enthralled. They saw the arrival of these 'white Bengalis' as a threat to their livelihood. Resentments soon festered and, before long, Melaka's inhabitants woke up to the threat posed by a Portuguese intrusion into their economic affairs. Within a matter of months, Sequeira and his men were driven forcibly from the port.

When Afonso de Albuquerque arrived in Melaka two years later, he was more pugnacious in his approach. Armed to the hilt with a cutting edge arsenal of cannon, the Portuguese soon took control of the port. The bewilderment of the Melakan defenders is recorded in the *Sejarah Melayu* (Malay Annals): 'What may be this round weapon that is sharp enough to kill us?'.

Albuquerque went on to build 'A Famosa', a formidable fortress of stone and mortar, parts of which still stand today. Within the stone ramparts, the Portuguese transformed Melaka into a medieval town of stone, in the European style. The Captain of the Fortress was installed as head of government, a system which remained in place for 60 years, until a Governor of Melaka was appointed in 1571.

Unfortunately for the Portuguese, things didn't go quite to plan. Mastery of the Melaka Strait – always Portugal's primary aim – was something that eluded the colonizers throughout the 16th century. Importantly, the Portuguese underestimated the strength of the Orang Laut, seagoing tribes who were traditionally employed by local rulers to police the seas. To add to Melaka's troubles, Portuguese officials soon gained a reputation for avarice, corruption and gluttony. Consigned to a life in the steamy, malaria-ridden tropics, they compensated for the risks by living in unapologetic splendour. In European circles, Melaka became known as the 'Babylon of the Orient'. None of this went down well with the traders on whom the port relied, particularly the Muslims, many of whom sought alternative ports in which to do their business.

Crucible of Sultanates

While Melaka began to falter as the Malay world's leading entrepôt, the newly emerging sultanates of Johor, Kedah, Aceh and Brunei began to syphon off many of its trading functions. Situated at the mouths of rivers, these sultanates became access points to the indigenous tribes of the interior – the Orang Asli of the Malay Peninsula, and the longhouse-dwelling tribes of Borneo – providing further trading opportunities for seafaring merchants.

Muslim traders were among the first to abandon Melaka for the new sultanates. Many headed for **Brunei**, whose Rajah had converted to Islam (and thus become a sultan) sometime around 1520. The influx of Muslim traders led to the conversion of many of the coastal peoples of northwest Borneo. Brunei boomed in the mid-16th century, at which time the sultan laid claim to the entire north and west coast of Borneo, Mindanao and the Sulu Archipelago. Even before this time, Brunei was a major port; it served as a vassal state to successive Ming Emperors of China, and when the Magellan expedition stopped by in 1521, the crew was shocked to find what chronicler Pigafetta described as a 'large and wealthy city'.

Despite the territorial claims of the Sultan of Brunei, the riverine communities of the interior were a law unto themselves, with the head-hunting Iban pushing into the region now known as **Sarawak**. Intertribal warfare dominated the following three centuries in the interior regions of present-day Sabah and Sarawak. On the coast, meanwhile, the Malays kept themselves to themselves, fearful that their own skulls might end up hanging from the rafters of an Iban longhouse.

Back on the Malay Peninsula, **Johor** was hopeful of succeeding as the rightful heir to Melaka. When the Portuguese razed Melaka in 1511, Sultan Mahmud Shah fled south to the island of Bintan (off Singapore), where he established the first court of Johor. The court was later moved to the upper reaches of the Johor River, where it began to prosper. Meanwhile, descendants of Mahmud Shah established a sultanate in Perak, taking advantage of the region's rich tin fields and adopting Melaka's traditional system of governance. All the while, the power struggle between the Malays and the Portuguese remained unresolved.

Further north, it was the powerful kingdom of Siam which laid nominal claim to new Malay territory. Three times a year, the Siamese demanded tribute from the Malay states of Kedah, Kelantan and Terengganu. Bizarrely, this consisted of two small trees fashioned from gold and silver. Weapons, cloth and a couple of slaves were usually thrown in too, for good measure. The Malays liked to see these more as friendship gifts than as symbols of their vassal status. When, in the mid-17th century, the ruler of Kedah was summoned to a prostration ceremony, he feigned illness rather than undergo the humiliation. In response, the Siamese king sent a statue of himself along with instructions that the court pay homage to his image twice daily. Bar occasional humiliations such as this, the northern Malay states were left largely to their own devices.

Of all the centres of Malay power, it was **Aceh** that benefited most from the downfall of Melaka. Until the 16th century, Aceh was little more than an outpost for piracy on the north tip of Sumatra. When Melaka fell to the Portuguese, Aceh became a centre of resistance against the Christian intruders. Muslim traders flocked to the port, which soon became one of the region's most powerful entrepôts and a rival to Johor. With the rise of Aceh, many of the local Minangkabau people were converted to Islam. Others migrated to the Malay Peninsula where they founded **Negeri Sembilan**, or 'Land of the Nine Territories'. Over the centuries, the Minangkabau people of Negeri Sembilan clung fiercely to their cultural heritage, which is remarkable for two things: its distinctive buffalo-horn architecture and its matrilineal society.

Other influential immigrants from this period include the Buginese, maritime traders from Celebes (Sulawesi) who soon gained dominance in Johor. As with the Minangkabau and the immigrant Javanese, many of their customs were assimilated into Malay culture.

The Dutch East India Company

By the beginning of the 17th century, European maritime dominance had begun to shift from the Portuguese to the Dutch. In 1602, spurred by the growing importance of the spice trade, particularly pepper, the Dutch consolidated their naval supremacy by founding the all-powerful **Dutch East India Company** (VOC). In many ways, this government-backed company was a mini-state in itself, with the power to sign treaties and appoint regional governors. In 1617, the VOC founded Batavia (now Jakarta) as its seat of government, and for the next two decades Dutch influence seeped steadily across the region. Before long they had gained monopolies over pepper exports from Sumatra and the tin trade in Perak.

Unlike their predecessors, the Dutch made little cultural impact on the Malay world. Their sole concern was trade and they made no attempt to spread the Protestant religion. The Portuguese, on the other hand, had worked hard at spreading Catholicism and had encouraged intermarriages between Portuguese officials and Malay women. Their descendants live on today in Melaka's Eurasian quarter.

With their sights set on displacing the Portuguese from their stronghold in Melaka, the Dutch went to great pains to woo Melaka's rivals in Johor and Aceh. By the 1630s it was apparent that the sultanate of Johor would benefit most from the Dutch presence. A Dutch-Johor treaty was signed in 1637 and four years later, with Johor's backing, the Dutch laid siege to Melaka. The siege was devastating, stretching over six months and wiping out around 90% of Melaka's population.

With the Portuguese ousted from Melaka, Johor stood to benefit even further. The Dutch allowed Johor trading privileges at Melaka and assured them protection against the Acehnese. Thanks to Dutch intervention, Johor emerged as the foremost patron of Malay culture and the sultanate soon displaced Melaka as the trading hub of the Melaka Strait.

As Johor rose to prominence, it was the Laksama (head of the military administration) and not the *Bendahara* (chief minister), who found himself wielding most of the power. The sultan, meanwhile, was resigned to playing more of a ceremonial role. When, in 1677, Sultan Ibrahim sought to muffle the powers of the *Laksama*, he paid with his life, dying under suspicious circumstances. His son and heir Mahmud, then a child, was adopted by the *Laksama* family as a means of further consolidating their power. This proved the final straw for many members of Johor's administration, who managed to persuade the *Laksama*'s armed following to turn on their leader. The *Laksama* fled and the traditional roles of government were restored.

The unsettling effect of these squabbles for power in Johor was further exarcerbated when Sultan Mahmud came of age. As a child, Mahmud had established a reputation for cruelty, and when he came to power he gave free rein to his sadistic tendencies. When adventurer Alexander Hamilton presented the young sultan with a pair of English pistols, Mahmud tested the weapons on the first Malay he met outside the palace. His cruelty reached its peak in 1699, when he ordered a pregnant woman to be disemboweled because she had taken a jackfruit from his garden. The Malay chiefs were outraged and supported the woman's husband when he proposed to get his revenge. The sultan was stabbed to death a few days later as he passed through the market.

The regicide marked the beginning of Johor's decline. Many of the state's outposts declared their independence, now that they had no official sultan to pay tribute to (the *Bendahara* had declared himself sultan, but he was not readily accepted as such). Large parts of the Malay world entered a period of relative anarchy. Princes struck out on their own to set up private kingdoms or seek fortunes as pirates. And yet, trade at this time was burgeoning. A new surge of immigrants from India, China and the Arab world descended on the region, drawn by economic opportunities. Europe had just acquired its taste for tea, and the Melaka Strait became a staging post for the tea trade with China. On the east coast, meanwhile, **Terengganu** began to prosper like never before, exporting gold, textiles and pepper.

With the decline of Johor, the west-coast state of **Perak** was soon regarded as the sole heir to Melaka. This was thanks in part to the Dutch East India Company, which signed a treaty with the Sultan of Perak allowing for a VOC monopoly on tin in return for Dutch protection. This triggered a period of peace and stability in Perak, during which time the state thrived on the proceeds of tin and jungle produce.

Arrival of the British

Up until the late 18th century, the Dutch East India Company (VOC) had the Malay world virtually to itself. The **English East India Company** (EIC), founded two years before the VOC in 1600, had spent the intervening period carving its own niche in India. The only EIC base in Southeast Asia during this time was located at Bencoolen, a small and inefficient outlet-port for pepper plantations on Sumatra's west coast. By the mid-18th century, however, trade in opium and tea was booming and the British were keen to establish a greater presence in the region: a port midway between India and China would help refit laden cargo ships, while a navy presence would protect the eastern approach to the Bay of Bengal.

The opportunity for establishing such a port came when Francis Light, an English 'country trader', met with Sultan Abdullah of Kedah, who had been forced to flee his capital after attacks from the Bugis and the Siamese. Desperate for support, the sultan offered Francis Light trading privileges in return for military protection. Light was in the region to negotiate trade deals for various firms based in Madras. He was also on the lookout for a suitable base for the East India Company and had set his sights on the island of **Penang**, with its sheltered bay and deep channel. Entrusted with negotiations by the EIC, Light secured possession of the island from the sultan, in return for the provision of security. The year was 1786.

With the founding of Georgetown on Penang (or Prince of Wales Island, as it was named by the British), the EIC began chipping away at Dutch control of the region. By the end of the century, British supremacy in the region was complete. Back in Europe, William of Orange was on the run from Napoleon: in 1795 he ordered Dutch colonies to open their doors to British troops as protection against the French. The British could hardly believe their luck, and in 1795 a force of 2,000 British soldiers breezed into Melaka without firing a shot. A 'joint' Anglo-Dutch administration was established under control of a British Resident.

By the turn of the 19th century, Penang had grown to become a thriving port, and the EIC made the decision to divert most of Melaka's trade to the island, which gained the status of 'Presidency' alongside Bombay, Calcutta and Madras in India. In 1807 Melaka's old fort was demolished and there was talk of abandoning the port altogether. Among the new officials in Penang was **Stamford Raffles**, a talented and outspoken 25-year-old, who put together a report in favour of the retention of Melaka. Though trade in Penang was thriving, he argued that the island was too far north to succeed long term as the regional entrepôt.

Raffles began to formulate the theory that a port at the entrance to the Strait would succeed in drawing trade from Java and the surrounding islands. In 1819 he struck a deal with a local chieftain in Johor and landed on the sparsely inhabited island of **Singapore**. Immediately, he declared Singapore a free port and laid down a town plan. Within a single year, Singapore's revenue exceeded its administrative costs. Immigrants from China, Malaya, India, Thailand, Java and the Arab world flocked to the island, lured by its free-port status and by Raffles' policy of equality for all before the law.

The Straits Settlements

Just months after the founding of Singapore, the 'free port' was already draining trade from the region's floundering Dutch ports, where heavy taxes and harsh laws prevailed. Soon enough the Dutch felt obliged to concede territory to the British. The Anglo-Dutch Treaty of 1824 was to prove a defining moment in the shaping of modern Malaysia. The parties agreed to a split the Malay world down the Melaka Strait – a division which laid the basis for contemporary boundaries between Malaysia and Indonesia.

Two years later, the British united Singapore, Penang and Melaka into one administrative entity which came to be known as the **Straits Settlements** (1826). At this stage, the British had no plans to extend their influence across the Malay states. Their sole concern was to protect the various staging posts on the trade route between China and India. But as the years passed, the British found themselves interfering to an ever greater extent, as the economic importance of the region became more apparent. Tin was suddenly in high demand and the tin-mining areas of Perak and Selangor boomed over the following decades.

This period of Malaya's history saw a radical shift in the ethnic make-up of the Peninsula, as wave after wave of immigrant Chinese arrived in search of a better life. The Chinese were soon a major presence in the region and came to dominate plantation agriculture as well as mining. Secret societies, guilds and *kongsis* (clan houses) offered protection and networking opportunities for new arrivals. Many of the immigrants arrived penniless, and the existence of the *kongsis* provided the support network they needed to survive the first months. With so much at stake, however, feuds between clan members were common, and as the various secret societies gained in power and influence, these feuds came to be more of a threat to the general stability of the region.

By the 1860s, infighting between secret societies was endemic. Re-establishment of law and order became the British rationale for greater involvement in the region. At least, it was a decent excuse: greater control of the tin mines of Perak and Selangor carried obvious economic advantages. When the Suez Canal opened in 1869, the British began to fear that European commercial interest in the East would mean further threats to their monopoly of the tin trade. So when Rajah Abdullah of Perak invited the British to appoint a 'Resident', in exchange for recognition of his own status as Sultan, the British jumped at the offer. Political intervention by the British was formalised by the **Pangkor Treaty** of 1874, and JWW Birch was appointed Resident of Perak, with the powers to oversee collection of taxes and run the administration of the state.

British Malaya

It was during the decade or so following the Pangkor Treaty that the term 'British Malaya' first came into common currency. Bit by bit, the British extended their authority across the Malay Peninsula, appointing Residents to the states of Selangor, Negeri Sembilan and Pahang during the 1880s. Unsurprisingly, the British met with resistance at every corner. Within a year of JWW Birch's appointment as Resident of Perak, he had been assassinated by furious Malay chiefs – Birch had attempted to centralize the judicial system, ignoring centuries-old traditions and slighting members of the Malay nobility along the way.

Not all of the Residents were unsympathetic to Malay tradition. Frank Swettenham, who became Resident of Selangor in 1886, endorsed the concept of 'indirect rule', whereby the accepted traditions and customs of the Malays were preserved. Both Hugh Low (third Resident of Perak) and Hugh Clifford (Resident of Pahang) studied

Malay culture, learned the language and ran the state in what they hoped was a respectful manner. But it was to be many decades before the British role in Malay affairs was accepted by the old ruling élite. It is an interesting fact that British histories barely mention the rebel Mat Kilau, who led a rebellion against the Pahang Residency in the 1890s, while to schoolchildren across Malaysia he is known as a hero of Malay nationalism.

The British administration of Malaya served to reinforce the division of ethnic groups and emphasize class difference. The Malays, the Chinese and the small population of Indians generally kept themselves to themselves. However, by the time the British appeared on the scene, there had already been a certain degree of merging of cultures. The most striking example of this was the 'Peranakan' culture of the Straits Chinese (descendants of mixed Chinese-Malay blood, *see* pp.137–8), which had its golden age in the late 19th century. The British valued the Straits Chinese as intermediaries between the races, and many rose to prominence within the administration. Influential members of the Straits Chinese community became Anglophiles, adopting the traits of Victorian Britain and joining the highbrow colonial clubs. They were soon known among British administrators as 'the Queen's Chinese'.

In 1896, Selangor, Perak, Negeri Sembilan and Pahang were brought together as the **Federated Malay States**, with the new boom town of Kuala Lumpur as their capital. Slowly, the entire Peninsula fell into British hands. In 1897 Siam was impelled to concede the east-coast states of Kelantan and Terengganu to the British (that year King Edward VII received, to his astonishment, the traditional Malay tribute of two little trees fashioned from gold and silver). In 1909 the north Malay states of Kedah and Perlis followed suit, while the once-mighty state of Johor finally accepted a British Resident in 1914.

Borneo and the Brooke Dynasty

As British Malaya was finding its feet, the northern slice of Borneo also began to come under British influence. Not that this was ever the British intention. By the 19th century, Brunei's influence had dwindled: it was no longer the trading heavyweight of past centuries and its territorial claims were slipping. In British eyes, Borneo was not worth the effort: it was thought of as little more than an uninhabited expanse of rainforest.

This impression, however, missed the hidden dynamic of north Borneo's interior population, which consisted of indigenous tribes vying for control of riverine territories. By the mid-18th century, the Iban people were migrating north in large numbers into modern-day Sarawak. As with all of Borneo's indigenous tribespeople, the Iban were masters of the rainforest and skilled boatmen, but they were particularly feared for their aggression and head-hunting skills. They fought bitterly with local tribes over prime stretches of river, clashing most often with the Bidayuh and the upriver Kayan. When the Iban reached coastal areas, they clashed with the

Mad Sailors

To most Malaysians, the words 'Mat Salleh' have nothing to do with the legendary Bajau leader. They mean *orang putih*, or 'white man'. Around the turn of the 20th century, European boat crews were a common sight in the Port Klang area, where they crowded the drinking houses and gained a reputation for drunken sing-alongs and rowdiness. To local Malays, they were the 'mad sailors'. Over the years 'mad sailor' was Malayanized to become 'Mat Salleh' and broadened in meaning to apply to white people in general.

Among the Chinese, particularly the Hokkien, a white person is often referred to as 'Ang Moh' (red hair) or, occasionally, the less flattering 'Gwai Loh' (devil).

Malays and other Muslim converts such as the Melanau. Some Iban took to the seas as pirates, and it was this that earned them the name 'Sea Dyaks'.

The threat posed by Sea Dyaks on the Muslim populations of northwest Borneo was what first drew English adventurer **James Brooke** onto the scene. Impressed with the Englishman's heavily armed schooner, the Sultan of Brunei enlisted Brooke's help to quell a series of uprisings. In return, Brooke managed to secure land rights in the area around the present-day capital of Sarawak. As well as having the clear military upper hand, Brooke was a skilled diplomat, and it wasn't long before he had silenced disputes among the fighting factions. The sultan was so impressed that, in 1841, he conferred the title 'Rajah of Sarawak' upon the Englishman.

Brooke at once sought the protection of the British Crown, but he met with a negative response and was forced to go it alone. For the best part of a century, he and his successors – who became known as the 'white rajahs' – went on to rule as 'benevolent' dictators over their own private kingdom. Though Sarawak was not given formal British protection until the end of the century, the state was run in the spirit of the other Malay protectorates, with 'indirect rule' as the guiding principle. Brooke gave Malays and local tribesmen (mainly Bidayuh) positions within his administration, while from the Sea Dyaks (Iban) he created a special fighting force known as the Sarawak Rangers. Brooke's guiding principle was one he had learnt from Stamford Raffles (who he visited in Singapore en route to Brunei): to nurture trade while fostering native welfare. It was a formula that worked for the white rajahs, and their territory expanded steadily during the latter decades of the 19th century. By 1905, Sarawak had attained its present-day dimensions.

Meanwhile, in the territory known as North Borneo (present-day Sabah), things weren't going so well for British interests. English businessman Alfred Dent had secured the territory from the sultans of Brunei and Sulu in 1878, before going on to found the **British North Borneo Company** (which, to the Brookes' chagrin, gained the immediate protection of the British Crown).

Unlike the Brookes, principle players within the British North Borneo Company took little heed of local customs and ancestral land rights. Growing hatred of the

European intruders was further stoked by underhand recruitment tactics – unwary tribespeople often found themselves locked into contracts as indentured labourers on tobacco and rubber estates. Before long, the Company had a rebellion on its hands, led by the competent **Mat Salleh**, a Muslim Bajau leader. In 1895 he sacked the Company's two military bases and, despite the hefty price on his head, managed to elude the grasp of Company forces until 1900, when he and his supporters were rounded up and killed. Like Mat Kilau, he lives on in Sabahan history as a martyr to the cause. In a strange twist of irony, Mat Salleh's name has become the common term for 'white man' (*see* above).

In 1888, North Borneo, Sarawak and Brunei became protectorates of the British Crown, surrendering foreign policy in exchange for protection from foreign attack (the British were beginning to worry that the Dutch might snap up their early gains in Borneo). A couple of years later, the Dutch and British signed a further treaty to define the boundary between Dutch and British Borneo – a boundary which serves today as the border between Malaysia and Indonesia.

Malaya's Economy Booms

The last decades of the 19th century, and first of the 20th, saw Malaya's economy boom. With industrial advance in the West and an ever-increasing demand for raw materials, cash crops became the obvious way forward. Across British Malaya, huge tracts of jungle were cleared to make way for plantation estates, while hundreds of thousands of Chinese and Indian labourers made their way to Malaya to take advantage of the new glut of opportunities.

Across the Malay states, the British offered incentives for the planting of cash crops, such as pepper, tobacco, gambier and rubber. A huge push to develop the infrastructure of the Malay Peninsula saw tin exports boom. A new rail and road network soon linked the tin fields with the ports of the west coast. The other major success story was rubber production. The idea was first pioneered in the 1870s by the first director of the Singapore Botanic Gardens, Henry Ridley, whose fervour soon earned him the nickname 'Mad Ridley' (*see* p.432). By the end of the 19th century, Malaya had become the world's leading exporter of rubber, thanks largely to the advent of the pneumatic tyre. Meanwhile, a worldwide demand for railway sleepers in the first decades of the 20th century saw increased logging activity across the Malay world, most notably in North Borneo, where Sandakan became one of the world's largest timber ports.

As well as economic upturn, British rule brought profound social change to the Malay states. While the sultans retained their positions at the head of the age-old aristocratic social system, the influence they were able to exert had been nullified and their roles were merely symbolic. Immigrant labourers posed the greatest threat to the old order, and by the early years of the 20th century, the social landscape of Malaya had turned on its head. (In 1800, Malays constituted more than 90% of the population. By 1930 the indigenous population found itself outnumbered by immigrants.)

Malaya had become a truly pluralistic society, a fact that sparked a greater consciousness of race difference and the first rumblings of nationalist sentiment. Policies adopted by the British as a means of dealing with the society they had created only served to reinforce the race divide. As a general trend, Malays lived in the rural kampungs, Chinese in the towns and Indians on the plantations. Economic development was left to the immigrants, while the Malay élite were appeased by being offered lucrative positions within the civil service of the new order. Many benefited from the system, but just as many found themselves worse off; government-sanctioned opium dens became an important revenue earner and those at the bottom of the social rung all too often became opium wrecks.

After the 1911 Republican Revolution in China, there was a growing commitment to the notion of a Chinese nation among overseas Chinese; up until this point, identity had been conceived along clan lines. The Malays, likewise, were beginning to debate what it meant to be Malay. The Great Depression and further economic slumps of the interwar years led to the questioning of official policy across the races. Resentments began to fester, both towards British rule and between the races. By the time of World War II and the Japanese Occupation, Malaya had become politicized along ethnic lines.

The Japanese Occupation

With the Japanese occupation in late 1941, the Malay world was once more turned on its head. The initial reaction of the populace was one of stunned dismay that the British had retreated without giving proper fight. Betrayal was on the lips of many and trust in British protection was lost for good. By early 1942, the Japanese had total control of the Malay Peninsula, Singapore and Borneo. They established military governments in all of the British territories and plans were announced to integrate the region into a proposed 'Greater East Asia'. Singapore was renamed Syonan-To (Light of the South), local time across the Malay world was advanced to match Tokyo time and the calendar was changed to match the Japanese year.

From the start, the Japanese set about wooing the Malays with talk of a road map towards independence. For the Chinese, however, the Japanese occupation was bad news: China was the traditional enemy of Japan, and in the weeks following the invasion, tens of thousands of Chinese were slaughtered. In response, scattered groups of pro-communist guerrillas took to the rainforest to wage resistance. British POWs, meanwhile, were herded into prison camps, where many met their ends. Some were shipped away to work on Burma's 'Death Railway'. POWs in North Borneo – many of them Australian – suffered the worst outrages, culminating in the 'Death March' from Sandakan to Ranau in September 1944. Of the 2,400 POWs who set out, only six survived. The event has gone down in Australian history as the nation's greatest military tragedy.

In Sarawak, the Japanese established control of the coastal ports and oilfields. However, the state's harsh topography provided the perfect cover for insurgents, the most famous of whom rallied behind Major Tom Harrisson (who would later become Curator of the Sarawak Museum and go on to make ground-breaking archaeological discoveries at the Niah Caves; *see* pp.433–5). In 1944 he parachuted into the remote Kelabit Highlands with a small team of British and Australian commandos, where he rallied support from among the local tribespeople (some of whom are alive today to tell the tale).

The Japanese surrender came in September 1945, after atomic bombs were dropped on Hiroshima and Nagasaki. When the British returned, tails between their legs, they proposed the **Malayan Union**, whereby all of the Malay territories, with the exception of Singapore, North Borneo and Sarawak, would be united as one. Sarawak and North Borneo, meanwhile, became official Crown Colonies for the first time in their history.

On its inauguration in 1946, the Malayan Union aroused immediate opposition among the Malays. Under the Union, the sultans retained their positions as symbolic figureheads, but sovereignty was transferred to the British Crown. More disconcertingly – to the Malays at any rate – citizenship within the Malayan Union was widened to include non-Malays. In response, the Malays formed UMNO (United Malays National Organization) and set about getting the Union revoked. With such widespread support, they succeeded, and in 1948 the British declared the **Federation of Malaya**, in which sovereignty was returned to the sultans and individual states regained a level of autonomy.

This time, it was the non-indigenous population who were unhappy, most of whom would not qualify for citizenship. The response of communist sympathizers was altogether more threatening to the stability of the region.

The Emergency Years

With the declaration of the Federation of Malaya in 1948, the Chinese felt alienated. For centuries, Chinese immigrants had been left to their own devices in the Malay states, keeping the economy afloat and largely steering clear of political involvement. Subordination to the Malays, it was felt, would undermine their position. Radical elements of the Chinese community were particularly alarmed, and they turned to the Malayan Communist Party (MCP) for answers.

The MCP was first formed in 1930 and gained in popularity during the war years, when it served as the backbone of anti-Japanese resistance. Their experience as wartime resistance fighters encouraged radical members of the MCP to return to the jungles to wage guerrilla insurgency on the new colonial government. Supported by only a minority of communist sympathizers, the MCP guerrillas nevertheless sparked a period of major unrest which came to be known as **The Emergency** (1948–60).

To all intents and purposes, this was civil war, but for the insurance purposes of British interests, 'emergency' sounded much better. The communist insurgents operated from secret jungle bases, staging roadblocks and employing terror tactics. Planters and plantation labourers were most at risk: garrottings, guttings and beheadings became commonplace. For two years the British sat on the fence, underestimating the staying power of the insurgents, who relied on impressionable Chinese squatters for their supply line. The squatters consisted of new immigrants and those Chinese who had relocated to remote areas to avoid Japanese victimization during the occupation.

In 1949 the British appointed the experienced General Harold Briggs as Director of Operations, and he at once set about trying to cut off communist supply lines. Around half a million Chinese squatters were forcibly moved to hundreds of 'New Villages'. Though this succeeded in cutting supply lines, it also worked as a recruitment drive for the insurgents (the tightly controlled New Villages were more akin to prison camps than housing estates). British morale reached its lowest ebb in October 1949, when High Commissioner Sir Henry Gurney was assassinated by guerrillas on the road to Fraser's Hill.

It was only when the British began addressing economic grievances that the conflict turned in their favour. In 1953, communist-free areas were declared 'white areas', where rationing and curfews were lifted. This had the effect of alienating the insurgents, many of whom surrendered or were killed. By 1954, only small MCP cells remained in operation, working from hide-outs deep in the jungle. Though communist strikes on plantations continued for a number of years, they slowly began to fizzle out. Meanwhile, the British rallied public opinion firmly against the insurgents by promising independence for Malaya. Talks were held with leading organizations such as UMNO, the MCA (Malayan Chinese Association) and the MIC (Malayan Indian Congress). Independence was declared in 1957, and the state of emergency was officially lifted in July 1960.

Merdeka, finally

To cries of '*Merdeka!*' (freedom), the Federation of Malaya declared its **independence** on 31st August 1957. Tunku Abdul Rahman, leader of UMNO, became Malaya's first Prime Minister under the UMNO Alliance, a democratically elected coalition of leading parties (UMNO, the MCA and the MIC). Kuala Lumpur was declared federal capital and a constitution was signed: kingship was to rotate among the Malay sultans and a two-tiered parliament was established. Though the new government clearly favoured the Malays, the Chinese were given liberal citizenship rights and continued to wield economic power in the region.

Singapore, Sarawak and North Borneo remained Crown Colonies for the time being, though the British allowed Singapore to elect an assembly. Two years later, in 1959, Singapore was granted self-government with Lee Kuan Yew, leader of the People's Action Party (PAP), as Prime Minister. The British then mooted plans to grant Singapore full independence, but Lee Kuan Yew had other designs: he began negotiations with Tunku Abdul Rahman to include Singapore in the Federation of Malaya.

As deliberations over enlargement of the federation continued, eyes turned to Borneo. The success of rubber and timber exports in Sarawak and North Borneo, and the discovery of offshore oil reserves, had sparked a post-war economic boom in the region. Though these states were historically distinct from Peninsular Malaya, the UMNO Alliance was attracted by the idea of balancing Singapore's Chinese majority with the indigneous majorities of Sarawak and North Borneo.

In September 1963, Singapore, Sarawak and North Borneo officially joined the federation. Brunei, jealously guarding its oil reserves, decided to retain independence. North Borneo was renamed Sabah, and the federation itself became known collectively as **Malaysia**.

Malaysia's first steps

Malaysia's first steps as a nation were hampered by fierce conflicts of opinion. Newly independent Indonesia, for one, was not happy with the cosy arrangement of its old neighbour states. The Indonesian government staked immediate claim to Sarawak (with which it shares a long border) and sent government troops across the border. Warfare between Indonesian troops and the ill-equipped armed forces of Sarawak became known as the **Konfrontasi** (Confrontation). Fighting continued until 1966, when the British sent Gurkha troops to the region to settle the conflict.

The Philippines jumped on the bandwagon too. They claimed jurisdiction of Sabah, pointing out that it had once been a part of the Sulu Sultanate. Fortunately for the stability of the region, they backed down from threats to take military action. These external worries only helped to fuel differences between **Singapore**'s Lee Kuan Yew and the UMNO Alliance. When Lee Kuan Yew called for greater racial equality and an end to positive discrimination of Malays, extremists in KL voiced fears that he was plotting to seize control of Malaysia. Then, in 1964, race riots broke out on the island. This proved the final straw for the Alliance, and after several months of deliberation, Singapore was expelled from the Federation in 1965.

Singapore's new status as an independent republic was viewed as a potential disaster by Lee Kuan Yew, who famously shed tears on a televised statement following the expulsion. With no natural resources to fall back on, economic growth became a matter of urgency. Incentives were offered to private capital, industrial estates were built and state-controlled social policies were rigorously pursued. Within a decade, to the surprise of many, the city-state had become an economic heavyweight.

With Singapore out of the way, the Alliance had hoped that racial tensions would fizzle out. But Chinese-Malay resentments already had a long history, and after Chinese gains in the 1969 elections, violent **race riots** broke out in Kuala Lumpur. Hundreds were killed and parts of the city were sacked. Prime Minister Tunku Abdul Rahman found his authority severely undermined. He placed Malaysia under a state of emergency and implemented the unpopular Internal Security Act as a means of detaining activists without trial. He was soon forced to step down as leader.

The 'New Economic Policy'

With the resignation of Tunku Abdul Rahman, the role of Prime Minister fell to Tun Abdul Razak. He was impelled to formulate radical new political and economic strategies to deal with the race divide. One of his first moves was to set about broadening the government coalition to form the **Badisan Nasional** (National Front), an alliance which has remained in power to this day.

Tun Abdul Razak's main concern, however, was the fact that the Malays had virtually no stake in the economy, despite accounting for more than half the nation's population. In 1970, the **New Economic Policy** (NEP) was announced, a policy designed to implement a redistribution of wealth in favour of the Malays. Under the terms of the policy, Malays, now termed *bumiputras* ('sons of the soil'), were to receive special privileges to help them on their way. *Bumiputras* were offered subsidized housing, grants for higher education and low-interest loans. Malay became the official language of instruction in all schools. Public companies were forced to take on Malays at board level and free up shares for new *bumiputra* shareholders.

The inevitable outcries from the Chinese and Indian quarters were muted by government claims that, although the NEP was clearly designed to grant Malays a stake in the economy, these gains were not intended to come at the expense of the Chinese or Indians. Indeed, disingenuous as these claims may have been, the Chinese managed to maintain their prosperity in the years that followed, and the economy expanded to meet the growth of a Malay middle class.

Another aim of the NEP was to introduce a manufacturing sector to Malaysia's economy: until independence, the Malaysian economy had relied almost exclusively on the export of cash crops such as tin, rubber, palm oil, timber and tea. Twenty years later, and the export of manufactured goods had outstripped that of cash crops. The same period saw the rapid industrialization of Malaysia, with the trebling of GDP and the poverty rate slashed from 50 per cent to 15 per cent. As the years progressed, and standards of living steadily improved, former critics of the NEP were forced to bite their tongues.

The Mahathir Era

If one person can be credited with Malaysia's recent economic successes, then it is Dr Mahathir Mohamad – though he has made plenty of enemies along the way. In 1981 Mahathir succeeded Hussein Onn to become leader of the Badisan Nasional (National Front) and Malaysia's fourth Prime Minister. He was the nation's first 'home-grown' PM, born in a modest stilted house on the outskirts of Alor Setar and educated in Malaysia and Singapore (as opposed to Britain, where his predecessors all studied).

Mahathir's rise to power ushered in a new era in Malaysian politics, with self-reliance as the keynote. His slogan '*Malaysia boleh*!' ('Malaysia can do it') perfectly sums up his message to the people. He tightened government control of the media

Historical Timeline

41,000 BC: Earliest known habitation of the region, prompted by the discovery of 'Deep Skull' in Sarawak's Niah Caves.

2,500 BC: Distant ancestors of the Malays begin to migrate south from southern China and Indochina.

300 BC: Traders from India and China begin frequenting the shores of Borneo and the Malay Peninsula.

***c.*150:** Emergence of the legendary kingdom of Langkasuka, an Indianized realm which spanned the Malay Peninsula.

***c.*650:** Founding of Srivijaya, the state which dominated the Malay world until the emergence of Melaka.

1400: Founding of Melaka by Prince Parameswara.

1445: When Muzaffar Shah comes to the throne, he takes the title of sultan, and the Sultanate of Melaka is born.

1488: Beginning of the reign of Sultan Mahmud, a period viewed as Melaka's Golden Age.

1511: Afonso de Albuquerque claims Melaka for the Portuguese.

1512: First court of Johor founded on the island of Bintan by Mahmud Shah, Melaka's deposed sultan.

1520: Brunei's rajah converts to Islam to become the first Sultan of Brunei.

***c.*1550:** Aceh rises to become the regional power at the expense of Melaka.

1602: Founding of the Dutch East India Company.

1637: Dutch-Johor Treaty, in preparation for the assault on Melaka.

1641: Dutch siege of Melaka. Start of Dutch dominance in the Malay world.

1699: Assassination of the cruel Sultan Mahmud of Johor.

1786: Francis Light founds Georgetown on the island of Penang, marking the arrival of the British.

1795: British take control of Melaka.

1819: Stamford Raffles founds Singapore.

1824: Anglo-Dutch Treaty forms the basis for contemporary boundaries between Malaysia and Indonesia.

1826: The British combine Penang, Singapore and Melaka to form the Straits Settlements.

1841: British adventurer James Brooke becomes 'Rajah of Sarawak'.

1874: Pangkor Treaty is signed, signalling the beginning of British intervention across the peninsula.

1875: Assassination of JWW Birch, first British Resident of Perak.

1877: Henry Ridley, Director of the Singapore Botanic Garden, pioneers rubber production in Malaya.

1881: Founding of the British North Borneo Company, which established itself in what is now Sabah.

1888: Sarawak, Brunei and North Borneo become protectorates of the British Crown.

1891: Start of the Pahang Rebellion, led by rebel Mat Kilau.

1895: Start of the Mat Salleh rebellion against the British North Borneo Company.
1896: Selangor, Perak, Pahang and Negeri Sembilan brought together to form the Federated Malay States, with Kuala Lumpur as their capital.
1897: Siam concedes Kelantan and Terengganu to the British.
1909: Siam concedes Kedah and Perlis to the British.
1914: Johor falls under British control and accepts a Resident.
1930: Indigenous Malayans are outnumbered by immigrant Chinese and Indians.
1941: Japanese occupation of Malaya and Borneo.
1945: Japanese surrender.
1946: British introduce the Malayan Union. Opposition to the union sparks the formation of UMNO. Sarawak and North Borneo become Crown Colonies.
1948: Malayan Union replaced by the Federation of Malaya. Start of the period of unrest known as The Emergency, which lasted until 1960.
1949: British High Commissioner Hugh Gurney assassinated by communist insurgents.
1953: Formation of the UMNO Alliance, which went on to become the ruling coalition.
1957: Malaya declares independence.
1959: Singapore granted self-government with Lee Kuan Yew as leader.
1963: Singapore, Sarawak and Sabah join the federation to form Malaysia. Three-year Konfrontasi (Confrontation) with Indonesia begins in Sarawak.
1965: Singapore expelled from the Federation of Malaysia.
1969: Race riots in Kuala Lumpur between Malays/Chinese in the wake of elections.
1970: New Economic Policy announced, designed to redistribute wealth in favour of the Malays. Ruling coalition broadened to become the Badisan Nasional.
1981: Mahathir Mohamad becomes prime minister.
1985: The national car, the Proton, is launched.
1991: National Economic Policy (NEP) is updated to become the National Development Policy (NDP).
1997: Asian economic crisis. The Petronas Towers, tallest buildings in the world at the time, are completed in Kuala Lumpur.
1998: Malaysia hosts the Commonwealth Games. Deputy Prime Minister Anwar Ibrahim is sacked and charged with corruption and sodomy.
1999: Anwar sentenced to nine years imprisonment. General election in which Islamic PAS party make gains at the expense of the ruling coalition.
2000: Anwar sentenced to a further six years in prison.
2001: In the wake of September 11th, Mahathir rounds up dozens of radical Islamists and holds them under the Internal Security Act.
2003: Mahathir steps down as Prime Minister, handing power to Abdullah Badawi.
2004: Abdullah Badawi wins a landslide victory in the general election. Anwar is released from prison on appeal.
2006: Abdullah Badawi unveils the Ninth Malaysia Plan, a five-year blueprint to reduce rural poverty and steer Malaysia back on track towards developed world status by 2020.

and urged Malaysia to 'Look East', rather than turning to Britain and the West for inspiration. His great ambition was to instil pride in Malay values and to put the nation on the world map in its own right. He set about doing so with a series of ambitious 'mega-projects', designed to raise the profile of the country. These initial plans came to fruition in the form of the mighty Petronas Towers, the Multimedia Super Corridor and the vastly improved infrastructure which enabled Malaysia to host the 1998 Commonwealth Games.

Throughout his term in office, Mahathir was an outspoken critic of the West, loosening Malaysian ties with the Commonwealth when it suited him (he loathed anything that smacked of neocolonialism) and turning towards the economies of Japan, Taiwan and South Korea as examples. He soon soured relations with Western leaders, launching a 'Buy British Last' Campaign in 1982 (after Britain raised university tuition fees for foreign students) and, a decade later, engaging in a public spat with then-PM of Australia, Paul Keating (who, with characteristic spite, went on to describe Mahathir as a 'recalcitrant').

One of Mahathir's great successes was his programme of privatization. True to form, the programme was paired off with yet another slogan: 'Malaysia Inc.'. Malaysia's national car, the Proton, began rolling off production lines in 1985 and has since dominated the market. Tax incentives and cheap labour succeeded in drawing foreign investment, and within a decade, Malaysia was one of the world's leading producers of electronic goods.

In 1991, Mahathir updated the NEP to form the National Development Policy (NDP). His main incentive was to tone down the Malay-centric terms of the NEP, which had attracted continual criticism from non-Malay lobbies. In practice, there was little to differentiate the two policies.

The NAP (National Agricultural Policy) was another significant Mahathir policy, introduced to tackle rural poverty and encourage greater efficiency of land use. In practice this meant encouraging the indigenous Orang Asli and Penan to abandon their nomadic lifestyles, exchanging slash-and-burn for sedentary farming techniques. Whatever the motivation, their ancestral lands were being chipped away at year by year, as trees were felled for timber or to make way for high-yielding palm oil plantations. As these people were forced from the forests that supported them, they left behind a culture and system of beliefs that stretch back millennia, exchanging the animist spirit world for gods appropriate to their new environment – the gods of Islam and Christianity. The loss of ancient cultures has become one of the inevitable sacrifices of economic development.

In East Malaysia especially, ecotourism has become an important factor in the preservation of the ancient forests and of indigenous traditions. Indeed, even as the forests retreat year on year, both Sarawak and Sabah present themselves to the world as adventure destinations rich in natural wonders and tribal cultures. In political terms, East Malaysia receives a raw deal from the federal government. Despite large oil reserves, Sarawak and Sabah are some of Malaysia's poorest states, with 95 per cent of their oil profits claimed by federal government. The other major cause for gripes is the Muslim propaganda directed at the largely Christian population of Sabah by the Badisan Nasional. In past years Christians were offered cash rewards for converting to Islam.

Economic Crisis and the Anwar Affair

With the millennium fast approaching, Mahathir began to focus on his vision for the future, 'Wawasan 2020' (Vision 2020), which outlined Malaysia's aim to achieve the status of Newly Industrialized Country (NIC) by the year 2020. After rounding up an impressive advisory board including the likes of Bill Gates, Mahathir decided that the way forward was to concentrate on global IT markets. The result was Malaysia's very own Silicon Valley, a massive IT-friendly industrial park known as the Multimedia Super Corridor (MSC), situated in the Klang Valley.

Then the Asian Economic Crisis of 1997 came along to dampen the mood. In characteristic manner, Mahathir ignored the advice of the International Monetary Fund (IMF), blaming Western speculation for the crisis. His own measures for dealing with the crisis shocked people at home and abroad: to reverse major devaluation of Malaysian currency, he pegged the ringgit to the US dollar and forced banks to merge. Viewed as a no-no by economists, these tactics were expected to end in disaster. To everyone's surprise, Malaysia recovered faster than all of its neighbours.

However, the crisis also revealed an uglier face to the Mahathir premiership. Bolstered by his success, Mahathir decided to deal once and for all with what he perceived to be a threat to his leadership. Then-Deputy Prime Minister and heir-apparent Anwar Ibrahim had fallen out with Mahathir over methods of dealing with the economic crisis. He was unexpectedly sacked in September 1998. A few days later, Anwar was arrested and charged with corruption and sodomy (on paper, homosexual sex is a crime in largely Muslim Malaysia, though charges are rarely pressed). On Anwar's second court appearance, he arrived with a black eye, accusing the police of beating him. Despite a public outcry and a series of demonstrations in favour of Anwar, he was found guilty on both counts and sentenced in total to 15 years imprisonment.

The Anwar affair played its part in the elections of 1999, with Anwar's wife heading Keadilan ('Justice'), a newly formed opposition party which campaigned in alliance with other opposition parties. However, it was the fundamentalist Pan-Malaysia Islamic Party (PAS) that made the greatest gains in the election, taking control of the east-coast state of Terengganu. While some observers read the election results as a swing towards Islamic revivalism, most recognised the PAS successes as a protest vote in the aftermath of the Anwar affair.

A New Era

The attacks of September 11th 2001 prompted Mahathir, and Malaysians in general, to promulgate a more liberal verion of Islam to the rest of the world. In the ensuing months, Mahathir made use of the draconian Internal Security Act to round up dozens of radical Islamists, mainly members of the militant group Jemaah Islamiyah.

On a domestic level, the sudden demonization of militant Islamists across the world played directly into Mahathir's hands in his dealings with the Islamic opposition party PAS. The groundswell of allegiance, particularly that of Malaysia's growing middle class, shifted further away from association with PAS (a shift confirmed in the elections of March 2004 when, to the surprise of Western pundits, the ruling coalition boosted its majority over PAS).

In October 2003, after 22 years in power, Mahathir finally stepped down as Prime Minister, handing power to his deputy, **Abdullah Badawi**. Despite the crises of recent years, and the concerns that Mahathir's parting would signal a breakdown of the ruling coalition, Abdullah Badawi today finds himself in a stable position, winning a landslide victory in the national elections of 2004. He appears to have taken careful heed of the public outcry following the Anwar affair by cracking down on corruption and cutting bureaucratic red tape. More symbolically, in September 2004 he secured the release of Anwar on appeal, putting an end to the six-year saga. Under the new leader, international investors are showing renewed interest in Malaysia, and the economic outlook looks positive once more.

In March 2006 Abdullah Badawi unveiled the Ninth Malaysia Plan, a five-year, multi-billion-dollar blueprint aimed at steering Malaysia back on track towards 'Vision 2020' – Mahathir's original plan to achieve developed world status by 2020. The plan represents a clear shift away from Mahathir's grand projects for technological and industrial development, and a move towards a redistribution of wealth. The new strategy will take the focus off Kuala Lumpur and deal instead with education, agriculture and reducing rural poverty.

For detailed histories of **Brunei** and **Singapore**, *see* pp.**395–8** and pp.**416–20**, respectively.

Art and Architecture

03

Arts and Crafts

Textiles

The weaving of traditional textiles was once integral to kampung life for the Malays. Unlike textile production in India and China, all aspects of weaving on the Malay Peninsula were carried out by women. As well as weaving the cloth on hand looms, the women also bought and sold textiles at the local and coastal markets. The weavers of the east-coast peninsula were generally considered to be the most skilled in the Malay world. And that remains the case today. The highest status was attributed to the ***songket*** weavers. Malay *songket* was a symbol of prestige among the royal courts of the Malay Peninsula. *Songket* is a richly woven silk-and-cotton textile, usually embellished with gold thread brocade (hence the term 'cloth of gold'). Masterpieces commissioned by past sultans took many months to make.

Batik probably has the highest profile among the textiles produced in Malaysia, despite the fact that it is not a native craft; batik became popular in the 1930s as a cottage industry imported from Indonesia. Today batik has been more or less adopted as the traditional Malay dress, and is a common technique in the production of sarongs. Hand-painted batiks are crafted with the use of a special pen filled with molten wax. The colours are then painted on with brushes, with the wax preventing them from mixing.

Textile weaving is also an important part of culture among the indigenous tribes of Malaysian Borneo. ***Pua kumbu***, for instance, is the ceremonial cloth woven by the Iban women of Sarawak. The designs are the inspiration of dreams. Traditionally, a woman's status within the tribe was defined by her skill as a weaver. Other distinctive textiles in Malaysian Borneo include the traditional dress of the Rungus tribe, made from rectangular pieces of woven, indigo-dyed cotton and decorated with geometric patterns. The colourful pieces of cloth, which use a lot of black, are used as sarongs, breast cloths or shawls.

Woodcarving

Among the indigenous peoples of both Peninsular Malaysia and Borneo, wood carving is a much-revered skill. In the past, carvings were an important part of ritual, and many pieces came to be regarded as sacred. Elaborate wooden **masks** were worn during ceremonies as a means of representing spirits. The Iban of Sarawak specialize in ceremonial carvings of the **hornbill**, a bird much revered by the tribe.

It is the upriver tribes of the Kayan and Kenyah who are generally acknowledged to be the most skilled wood carvers. They are best known for their massive burial poles, known as ***klirieng***, each carved from a single *belian* tree and embellished with elaborate designs. The bones of aristocrats are stored inside a hollow chamber within the *klirieng*. Mythological figures – strange anthropomorphic creatures – are sculpted from hardwood by many of Malaysia's indigenous tribes.

Indigneous wood carvings have become popular souvenirs for tourists, and there is now a degree of commercialization in the production of masks and figures, as is the case with rattan mats, basketry and other handicrafts. Items available on the Malay Peninsula include beautiful boat-shaped *congkak* boards, Koran lecterns and coconut scrapers carved into the form of dragons or tigers. Other popular east-coast crafts include **spinning tops** (*gasing*), beautiful objects carved from *afzelia* hardwood, and traditional **kites** (*layang-layang* or *wau*) framed with bamboo. See 'Kampung Games' below for more on these.

In Terengganu, the **boat-builders** of Pulau Duyong have made a name for themselves for their beautiful, handcrafted, hardwood fishing boats, which can be seen along the whole east coast of the penisula. The boats are crafted from local hardwood, without the use of plans and without nails. These methods, though painstaking, have earned the craftsmen wide renown, and commissions now come in from round the world.

Metalwork and Jewellery

Though it is not much in evidence today, the Malay world has a long tradition of metalwork. In the first centuries AD, the region was touted throughout Asia as Suvarnabhumi, or '**Land of Gold**', while the first European explorers returned home with tales of a rich land named 'Golden Chersonese'. The court of the kingdom of Langkasuka, which was said to have sprung up on the Malay Peninsula during the 2nd century AD, was legendary for its ostentatious display of gold (the king was known to parade astride an elephant that was adorned from head to toe in gold). Throughout Southeast Asia, gold is the colour of royalty and for centuries has been used in religious ceremonies. In Malaysia, gold also plays an important part in Hindu and Islamic iconography.

Today the Malays more commonly work in **silver**, though it is only in the Kelantanese capital of Kota Bharu that silversmiths still thrive, producing intricate pieces of filigree jewellery alongside functional items such as tea sets. In the days when betel-nut chewing was fashionable with everyone, from Malay royalty to villagers, the Malay silversmiths did a roaring trade in silver betel sets, examples of which can still be found in antique shops.

Just south of Kelantan, in Terengganu, **brasswork** is a traditional skill, though it is not much in evidence today. Selangor **pewter** has made a name for itself in recent decades. Pewter-making was introduced from China in the 19th century, and the cottage industry soon thrived on the west coast of the peninsula, with its profusion of tin fields (pewter is a tin alloy).

Performance Arts

Wayang kulit (shadow puppets) are one of Malaysia's most popular handicrafts. The puppets are carved from aged buffalo hide and painted with natural dyes. The rods used to manipulate the puppets are fashioned from buffalo horn. Each puppet represents a character from Indian epic tales, such as *The Ramayana*. Earliest records of *wayang kulit* performances go back almost a millennium. Shadow plays were once a common form of entertainment in the Malay kampungs. The best performances were reserved for the sultans' courts, where the epic tales were acted out by jewel-studded puppets. *Wayang* theatre is a refined, highbrow version of Punch and Judy – only it is the shadows you watch, rather than the puppets themselves. The shadows are projected onto a screen of white cotton with the use of coconut-oil lamps. Behind the screen, the *dalang*, or puppeteer, manipulates his puppets to the accompaniment of a gamelan orchestra (see 'Music' below). The audience is often free to wander behind the screen to see the puppets in action.

Visitors to Malaysia are more likely to come across Chinese street theatre. In its grandest incarnation, this takes the form of **Chinese opera** – lengthy interpretations of popular Chinese classics, with extravagant costumes and stylized fights and gestures. Otherwise, the stories are acted out with string puppets (also known as *wayang*). More appealing are the dramatic **lion dances**, which take to the streets during Chinese festivals (in Penang, there are performances on the first day and the midpoint of every lunar month). Though the lion dance was introduced from China, it originated in India, where live lions were once paraded at festivals. Under the Tang Dynasty, the lion dance developed into a ceremony for the purging of demons and evil spirits. During Chinese New Year, troupes of lion dancers, backed by cymbals and booming drums, parade in and out of shops and businesses to signal an auspiscious (and hopefully profitable) year ahead.

The Malay martial art of ***silat*** (also known as *persilat*) is a common feature of cultural shows in modern Malaysia. This highly disciplined art originated in 15th-century Melaka. Over the centuries, *silat* has become so stylized that it is now as much a dance as it is a martial art. It is usually performed by two young men or boys, who 'fight' and defend themselves in fluid, graceful movements, with the backing of an orchestra of percussionists.

Music

Thanks to Malaysia's geography at the confluence of trade routes between China and the Middle East, the nation's musical traditions have eclectic roots, with influences drawn from many parts of the globe. With the fast pace of development, however, these traditions have largely fallen by the wayside; the only place you are likely to come across traditional music is at the cultural shows laid on for tourists.

In keeping with tradition, most of the old royal courts on Peninsular Malaysia have hung on to their ceremonial orchestras, known as ***nobat***. At least, they have hung on to the instruments. On the rare occasions when the instruments are aired – usually private ceremonies – the few musicians who can still play them are rounded up to form an orchestra. The *nobat* consists of a series of drums and gongs, and variations on the flute, the oboe and the trumpet. The nobat always play on the inauguration of a new sultan in the states of Kedah, Perak, Terengganu and Selangor.

Elsewhere traditional music borrows from other cultures. The Javanese **gamelan** orchestra is one example; this consists of a range of gongs and xylophones accompanied by a large drum. There are more than a dozen different types of traditional drum in Malaysia. The ***rebana ubi*** ('giant drum') is the largest of them, and one of the best places to see these in action is at Kelantan's Giant Drum Festival (usually held in early June). Contestants come from across the state to compete in teams of twelve; judges award points for tone, rhythm and unity. Traditionally, *rebana* drums were used as a means of communicating various messages between villages – an invitation to a ceremony, perhaps, or a declaration of war.

In Sabah, the Rungus tribe make use of **ceremonial bronze gongs**, all of which are hand-beaten at Kampung Sumangkap (*see* p.372). Such gongs form the basis for most tribal music in East Malaysia, though more sophisticated instruments are also still in use. The ***sapé*** is a type of guitar, or lute, played by the upriver Orang Ulu tribes. It is usually accompanied by a wooden **xylophone**, and occasionally a bamboo **nose-flute**.

Architecture

Malaysia's geographical location at the crossroads of Asia has left the region open to influences from both East and West, a fact reflected in the nation's architecture. In many ways, the most interesting buildings are those most easily overlooked: the Malay house, the indigenous dwelling and the Chinese shophouse – each of which is perfectly suited to its environment and function.

The emergence of Indianized states in the 2nd–6th century AD left some of the first architectural marks on the Malay world, though very little evidence of these structures has survived to this day. The oldest remains can be found in the Kedah's Bujang Valley (*see* pp.204–5), where there are ruins of Buddhist-Hindu shrines, thought to have been built from around AD 500. Because of the perishable building materials used by the early Malays and indigenous tribes, very little else survives until the arrival of the Portuguese in the early 16th century. By then, the Malays had developed an architectural style characterized by pitched roofs, stilts and jungle timber. Ventilation and protection from flooding were the principle concerns of these construction techniques, which were also employed in the building of palaces and mosques, and in the longhouses of indigenous tribes.

The succession of colonial influences has left its mark on the urban architecture of Malaysia, particularly in cities such as Kuala Lumpur, Georgetown, Melaka (and Singapore). The Portuguese and Dutch influence today is barely noticeable, except in Melaka. But the more recent British presence is evident across the board from mosques to shophouses. The British 'Raj' style (imported from India) was deemed appropriate for Malaya and was employed in the construction of both public and religious buildings. Between the wars, urban architecture in Malaysia reflected the trends of the West, with Art Deco and Modernist influences creeping into most new buildings.

Since independence, Malaysia has attempted to express its nationhood in a new architecture, blending indigenous motifs with the International Style. By the end of the 20th century, the mighty Petronas Towers – then the tallest buildings in the world – stood proud as a symbol of a fast-developing nation.

The Malay House

The styles of Malay houses vary from state to state, with the adoption of both foreign and home-grown influences. However, the basic construction methods are similar across Malaysia. First and foremost, the Malay house is seen not as a single unit, but as a part of the kampung (village) community. As such, every house has provision for both public and private spaces, with a large covered porch area for entertaining guests. The back portion of the house provides the private space for cooking, washing and sleeping. The five traditional sections of a Malay house are the *anjung* (covered porch), the *serambi* (verandah), the *rumah ibu* (main living quarters), the *selang* (passageway between the communal porch and living quarters) and the *rumah dapur* (kitchen). Despite these separate spaces, the Malay house is largely open-plan in layout, with large open spaces for improved ventilation. Malay houses are generally seen as organic structures, with extensions added when families increase in size.

The traditional Malay house makes use of readily available local materials, with a timber frame and thatch roof. The gables are fitted with screens, which protect from driving rains while allowing for ventilation. Malay houses are always raised on posts; it is common to find Malay houses beside rivers and along the coastline, where flooding is a constant threat. The traditional use of woven bamboo for walls, and bertram palm for roofing has been replaced in modern houses by the use of timber and galvanized iron.

Indigenous Dwellings

Many of Malaysia's indigenous dwellings are not dissimilar to the Malay house in construction methods and materials. The primary difference between the two is that indigenous dwellings, on the whole, are temporary structures, which from time to time will need to be rebuilt from scratch – a reflection of the nomadic and semi-nomadic lifestyles of traditional indigenous cultures in Malaysia. Many indigenous dwellings share common features across Southeast Asia; the roof forms, for example, have been used by tribal peoples for as long as 6,000 years.

Building materials are gathered from the immediate surroundings – hardwoods, bamboo, palm thatch and rattan are all used. Some dwellings, such as those of

Sabah's Kadazan tribe, are constructed exclusively from bamboo. The Orang Asli of Peninsular Malaysia build small functional buildings which serve as basic, temporary shelters and storage spaces for materials and goods. Symmetry and finish take second place to functionality in these buildings. The common house form in East Malaysia is the longhouse, a tribal village under one roof (some of which are several hundred metres in length). A covered gallery known as the *ruai* runs the length of the building, backed by a long line of living quarters. Behind the *ruai* is the open verandah, where pepper, rice or other crops are left to dry. Different tribes build longhouses according to their own traditions, and to suit their particular environment – though all are raised on piles and constructed (traditionally) of local materials such as rattan, bamboo, *belian* hardwood and *attap*. For more on longhouse construction *see* 'The Longhouse Experience', pp.328–9.

The Chinese Shophouse

Any visitor to Malaysia or Singapore will soon become familiar with the Chinese shophouse, which dominates the older commercial centres of towns and cities. On first impressions, these simple terraced buildings appear to be of little architectural interest, but there are many styles with subtle ornamental differences.

Shophouse architecture in Malaysia can be traced back to the influx of Chinese immigrants, which began in the early 19th century. Urban construction techniques were imported from China and adapted for the new environment. The first shophouses were built of timber and thatch, but these proved to be major fire hazards and were soon replaced with masonry buildings. Because owners were taxed according to the width of their shopfronts, they built their houses narrow, with fronts often measuring as little as five metres across, while extending up to 60 metres in depth. The brick walls were plastered and roofs were tiled.

The front room of a traditional shophouse serves as the shop, with a central courtyard or air well to the rear. Living quarters are situated on the first floor, while kitchens and bathrooms are located at the rear of the shophouse. Running along the front of all shophouses in Malaysia and Singapore is the so-called 'five-foot way', a covered pavement introduced in 1822 by Stamford Raffles, founder of Singapore. As a means of protecting the shopper from sun and rain, he decreed that all shophouses should be fronted by a minimum five-foot-wide verandah on the ground floor, which has since served as an arcade linking the shops. To Raffles' annoyance, shop owners soon took advantage of the extra space to display their wares. These five-foot ways are unique to the region.

Shophouses are characterized by the decorative styles of their facades. Nouveau riche immigrants were drawn to the Western decorative styles with which they decorated their windows and capitals. Neogothic, Baroque and Palladian styles were all experimented with. Windows were often framed with classical-style columns, while fanlights were made from imported Venetian glass. During the 1920s and 1930s these styles flourished, with the adoption of Grecian pediments and neoclassical parapets along the tops of shophouses. The Art Deco movement of the 1930s also made its impression on the façades of shophouses, with the adoption of geometric shapes and straight lines. Modern shophouses take a utilitarian approach to the design of their façades, which tend to be devoid of ornament, harking back to the original shophouse design.

Places of Worship

After the arrival of Islam in Southeast Asia in the 13th century, the first **mosques** developed as simple timber buildings, similar in design to early kampung houses. The following centuries saw the development of what has become known as the Southeast Asian Great Mosque, which borrowed from the pagoda design of Buddhist architecture. These were originally simple prayer halls, raised on timber piles and square in shape. The roof rose in three tiers to a pinnacle, each tier admitting light and ventilation into the interior of the mosque, while protecting from rain. These mosques were notable for the absence of a minaret; in those days the call to prayers was achieved with the help of a large wooden drum. Pagoda-style minarets were introduced in the 17th century: one of the earliest surviving examples can be seen at the Kampung Kling Mosque in Melaka (*see* pp.140–1).

Mosque design developed further with the arrival of the British, who actively promoted trade between their various colonies. These new links saw the arrival of growing numbers of Indian Muslim traders and the deployment of British architects from India. They drew on the Indian Mogul tradition, combining this with elements of Moorish design to create elaborate and ornate mosques with one central onion-shaped dome, a series of sub-domes and minarets topped with Mogul-style *chatris*. The Ubadiah Mosque in Kuala Kangsar (*see* p192) is a stunning example of this Mogul-Moorish mix.

The eclectic evolution of mosque design in Malaysia has culminated in the wonderful Modernist-Islamic Masjid Negara of Kuala Lumpur, which was completed in 1965. Above the prayer hall, which can seat 10,000, is a giant aluminium-plated 'dome' which fans outwards like a giant bright-blue cocktail umbrella.

Malaysia's early Chinese immigrants built their **Buddhist temples** according to the ancient architectural traditions of their home provinces in the south of China. Today there are thousands of Buddhist temples in varying styles across the country. The most distinctive element of these temples is their exposed structure, with pillars and open walls or large, open entrances, which allow air to circulate the incense-filled halls and shrines. All Buddhist temples are dominated by the auspicious colour red, which symbolizes the sun, represents the traditional 'element' of fire and suggests joy and prosperity. There are plenty of other colours too, each of which represents the other four elements: earth (yellow), metal (white), wood (green) and water (black). Temples are laid out and designed according to the traditions of the different clans, so that Cantonese, Hokkien, Teochew and Hakka temples are all distinguishable from one another. Hokkien and Hakka temples traditionally have prominent curved roofs, while all Buddhist temples in Malaysia incorporate roof ridges which are decorated with auspicious animals and mythological figures. Pillars are often decorated in this manner too. If you look carefully at the mid-point of the roof ridge, you should be able to see the 'celestial pearl', which represents the Yang force and the sun. Statues of lions are placed in the porch area to ward off evil.

Chinese temples in Malaysia may be colourful, but most cannot compete with bombardment of colour at a **Hindu temple**. There are almost 20,000 Indian temples and shrines scattered across Malaysia, each dedicated to a specific Hindu deity. Many were built in the wake of the rubber boom, which drew Indian plantation labourers to British Malaya in the thousands. As a result, there are many temples located in rural areas as well as in the major towns and cities. The construction of many Hindu temples conforms to the requirements of the ancient Agamic texts, which stipulate the use of iconic symbols and define temple ritual. The basic plan of a Hindu temple incorporates four elements: the inner sanctum where the main image or statue of the deity is kept; the 'vehicle' (an animal associated with the deity, which faces the inner sanctum); the sacrificial altar, where devotees kneel to pray and where priests lay flowers; and the flagstaff, which points in the direction of the inner sanctum, and in front of which devotees prostrate themselves. The most distinctive element of Hindu temples is the *gopuram* (entrance tower), which range from the simple three-tiered tower of Melaka's Chitti Temple (with three deities in relief), to the resplendent, almost anarchic, *gopuram* of the Sri Maha Mariamman Temple in Kuala Lumpur, where hundreds of statuettes combine to form one colourful sculpted mass.

Modern Architecture

In the search for a specifically Malaysian architectural identity in the last decades of the 20th century, the authorities looked to a monumental symbolism which combines cutting-edge construction techniques with Islamic motifs. One of the most striking examples of this is the 35-storey Dayabumi Complex in Kuala Lumpur. Built in 1984, the building combines Islamic symbolism with the principles of tropical architecture. The facade of the building, which rises from a series of Islamic-style pillars at the base, is covered in a white grill of geometric Islamic motifs, which functions on a practical level as a shading device.

Other examples of tropical architecture in the region include the futuristic Menara UMNO in Penang, which is designed to maximize ventilation and natural light (thereby minimizing the use of air conditioning); the Sabah Foundation Building outside Kota Kinabalu, whose structure has been likened to that of a tree, with each floor 'dangling' off a central support of high-tensile steel rods; and more recently, in Singapore, the eye-catching Theatres on the Bay complex (2002), where a theatre and concert hall are sealed within domes of glass, which are in turn clad in an armour of aluminium plates angled to reflect the full glare of the sun as it makes its path across the sky (*see* p.429).

In Malaysia, such fast-paced architectural development hit its peak with the construction of the Petronas Towers (1996), which for a time held the record as the tallest buildings in the world (*see* p.113). Then, in 1997, the Asian Economic Crisis came along and put a dampener on what seemed all of a sudden to be blatant over-ambition. The huge scale of ex-Prime Minister Mahathir's aptly named 'mega-projects' was put in perspective and construction work along the Multimedia Super Corridor (*see* p.27) was temporarily halted. However, despite negative forecasts, recovery was speedy and work was soon under way once again. The brand new paperless cities of Putrajaya and Cyberjaya have become a new focus for modern architecture and development in Malaysia.

Topics

04

Indigenous Tribes of Malaysia

The distant ancestors of the Malays – migrants from India, China and Indochina – began settling Peninsular Malaysia and Borneo as long ago as 2500 BC. But they were not the first to arrive. A healthy population of indigenous tribespeople already inhabited the rainforests, which in those days stretched uninhibited from shore to shore. Remarkably, these people had been around for an estimated 50,000 years. Despite racial differences, they all shared a common cultural heritage, much of which is still in evidence today (though it is fast disappearing).

Traditionally, these diverse peoples have two fundamental things in common: their animist world-view and their mastery of the rainforest. Animism is centred on the belief that every element of nature is endowed with a spirit, or soul. Trees, birds, rocks, rivers, fish, mountains – all have spirits which need to be placated through complex rituals, the origins of which go back millennia. Bird augury (interpreting birdsong) is a common feature of animism, as is the interpretation of bird sightings; the Kelabit, for example, rely upon the annual migration of the yellow wagtail as a signal for the sowing and the harvesting of their rice crop. Some rituals are shared among the various tribes, while others are unique. The gory ritual of head-hunting, once practised by tribes in Borneo, represents the greatest extreme.

With the arrival of outside influences, animism has in many cases been supplanted (or supplemented) by Islam and Christianity. But even among those communities which consider themselves staunchly Christian (or staunchly Muslim), traditional animist ceremonies remain an important part of their culture. Many indigenous peoples would say that their old beliefs have not been supplanted at all, only enriched: with its pluralistic outlook, animism is well adapted to absorb outside influences. The animist spirit world, which is not an exclusive domain, can happily make room for the gods or 'spirits' of other religions. The Melanau people of Sarawak provide an excellent example of this. Their modern-day homeland is the coastal village of Mukah, which is split into separate kampungs for the Catholic Melanau and the Muslim Melanau. One has a church, the other a mosque. Despite these new religions, the ritual elements of their traditional beliefs are performed to this day; the annual Kaul festival (*see* p.44) remains the biggest event in the Melanau calendar for Muslims and Catholics alike.

Animism itself evolved out of the relationship of tribal peoples with their environment. At one time, all of Malaysia's indigenous peoples were hunter-gatherers, the jungle providing them with their every need. They fished the rivers and tributaries using rattan fish traps and the juice of the *tam-tam* plant, which was dropped into the water to momentarily stun the fish, allowing them to be harvested by hand. Among virtually every tribe, the blowpipe was considered the weapon best suited to hunting in the rainforest. Even today it remains the weapon of choice among many tribespeople, despite the availability of firearms.

Making a blowpipe is a highly skilled craft, with each blowpipe taking months to perfect (if the hole bored through the centre of the pipe is not dead straight and perfectly smoothed, the weapon is useless). Most blowpipes are constructed from local hardwoods, though the Senoi tribe of Peninsular Malaysia make theirs from *buluh sewor*, a species of bamboo with unusually long internodes. The latter consist of an inner and outer barrel which fit snugly together and a hornbill-ivory mouthpiece. Darts are commonly made from the midrib of the bertam palm tipped with the poisonous resin of the *ipoh* tree. The darts are embedded into conical 'pith heads' carved so that they precisely match the diameter of the blowpipe barrel. The dart is expelled with a short, sharp puff of air. Silent, accurate and deadly, the blowpipe can kill prey as large as a sambar deer within a range of 40 metres (130ft).

Past studies have revealed that when it comes to botanical knowledge, your average Orang Asli is a walking encyclopaedia. Even today, semi-nomadic tribal members can identify by name (and corresponding property) hundreds of plant species. These remarkable skills – which represent a heritage common to us all – have not gone unnoticed by the corporate world. Multinational pharmaceutical companies have begun to exploit indigenous knowledge for medical purposes, sparking an ethical debate and the introduction of new legislation (*see* 'Bioprospecting and the Bintangor Tree', p.50).

The biggest threat to the indigenous cultures of Malaysia – and one which has almost succeeded in wiping out semi-nomadic lifestyles for good – is land clearance. For decades now, loggers have taken full advantage of the indigenous ethos of non-ownership. Over the years, tribespeople have been shunted to and from ever-shrinking corners of rainforest. In many instances, they made way for loggers on the assumption that they could return to the same land once the foliage had returned. But more commonly the land was transformed into palm oil plantations – and tribal homelands were lost for good.

Under the terms of the Malaysia's National Agricultural Policy (NAP), the Orang Asli of Peninsular Malaysia and the Penan of Malaysian Borneo are encouraged to abandon their nomadic lifestyles, exchanging slash-and-burn for sedentary farming techniques. Government incentives have encouraged them to settle in makeshift villages, where they are ensured a supply of rice and access to health clinics. Many Orang Asli now turn to forest medicines only as a second resort. The reaction to resettlement has been mixed. The young find it easier to adapt and integrate into modern society, but the older Orang Asli are resentful; they look back to a time when they could wander freely from Johor as far as the border with Thailand.

In Sarawak, the Penan have had an even harder time, suffering poverty and disease in their new settlements. Lack of training is a principle concern; agricultural techniques do not come instinctively to a people who have survived until now as nomads. The standard compensation offered to Penan who have been forced from their homelands is a pile of raw building materials – useless without the necessary construction skills. In the late 1980s, the plight of the Penan made international headlines when blockades were erected to prevent logging on traditional lands. Coverage was boosted by the involvement of Swiss activist Bruno Manser, who spent six years living among the Penan and became an accepted member of their community. Manser's heroic (or foolhardy) attempts to gain support from the international community earned him the ironic title of 'Swiss Tarzan' from the Malaysian authorities. Determined to end Manser's anti-logging activities, a government bounty was placed on the activist, who subsequently fled. In May 2000 Manser slipped back into Sarawak. Several weeks later he disappeared. He has not been seen since.

However sad the loss of indigenous culture may be, the Malaysian government has been quick to pounce on the inherent hypocrisy of Western sympathies with the plight of indigenous peoples. The phrase 'white man's burden' has raised its head on more than one occasion, with the government pointing out that nobody should be denied the right to economic development, especially if that denial is motivated by the nostalgia of industrialized nations (who wiped out their own indigenous roots centuries ago).

Today, indigenous peoples make up approximately ten per cent of Malaysia's population, with most of them found in the East Malaysian states of Sarawak and Sabah, where indigenous tribes form the majority. Indigenous peoples on Peninsular Malaysia are known collectively as Orang Asli, which is Malay for 'original man' or aborigine. The Orang Asli comprise dozens of separate tribes which fall into three groupings: the Senoi, the Negrito and the Melayu Proto. In total they number less than 100,000. In Malaysian Borneo there are dozens more tribal groups. Of all Malaysia's states, Sarawak has the greatest ethnic mix; the 'divide and rule' policy of the Brooke dynasty (see pp.309–10) helped slow down the intermingling of tribal cultures, though nowadays intermarriages are blurring the boundaries. The Iban and the Kadazan are the largest tribes in Sarawak and Sabah respectively, each forming around one third of their state's population. The most prominent of Malaysia's indigenous tribes are described below, alphabetically.

Bajau

Known to some as 'sea gypsies', the Bajau were originally a seagoing tribe, living exclusively on little houseboats and returning to the Borneo mainland only to bury their dead. They are expert skin-divers and harvest the sea for *teripang* (sea slug) and a wide variety of fish. At night families lash their boats together to form a stable flotilla. A few 'Bajau Laut' (*laut* means sea) continue to live in this way off the east coast of Sabah. However, most have settled on land to become farmers. The settled Bajau have a long tradition as horse and buffalo breeders, and are often referred to as 'Cowboys of the East'. Their largest community is around Kota Belud in Sabah.

Bidayuh

The Bidayuh, once known as 'Land Dyaks', are farmers of hill paddy, whose traditional homeland is the region around Kuching in Sarawak, particularly to its west. These were the first tribal people to come under the influence of Rajah Brooke in the 1840s. Though they took heads when they could, the Bidayuh were thought of as a peace-loving tribe. They usually settled in the hills for protection from their traditional enemies, the Iban. They are highly skilled at rattan basketry and with bamboo (the hills are scattered with their bamboo bridges). The Bidayuh longhouse is often a series of smaller buildings connected by walkways. They are the only tribe to build a *baruk*, a ceremonial house where enemy skulls were hung and where the young men/warriors still sleep at night. Today the Bidayuh form 8% of Sarawak's population.

Iban

The Iban, known in the past as 'Sea Dyaks', are the largest ethnic group in Sarawak, forming 35% of the population. Though many Iban now inhabit the towns and cities, they traditionally live along the rivers of the interior and are expert boatmen. The Iban are known for their hospitality, and no visit to Sarawak is complete without tasting *tuak*, Iban rice wine. The Iban developed a fearsome reputation as headhunters: taking an enemy head was an important token of manhood. Though most Iban are now Christian, animist beliefs still form an important part of Iban culture. Decision making is influenced by bird augury (interpreting birdsong), while dreams are the inspiration behind the design of textiles. The *pua kumbu* is the ceremonial cloth woven by the women (whose status was defined by their skill as weavers, just as men were judged by the number of heads they had taken). Woodcarving is a much-revered skill among the Iban men.

Kadazan (or Dusun)

The many sub-tribes of the Kadazan (or Dusun or Kadasandusun, as they are also known) form the largest ethnic group in Sabah. They farm both wet and hill paddy and originally came from the plains of the interior. The Kadazan take the ritual element of their animist beliefs very seriously, with the *bobohizan*, or high priestess, preciding over events such as the harvest festival. The priestess recites incantations in a language known only to herself (and others with her powers), in attempts to appease the rice spirit. Those Kadazan who have not turned to Christianity believe in a Creator who sacrificed his only daughter, Huminodun, so that the people would have food.

Kayan and Kenyah

Two of the tribes known collectively as Orang Ulu (upriver people), found on the tributaries of the Baram River, and near the upper reaches of the Rejang River in Sarawak. Though the Kayan and Kenyah speak different dialects, they are closely related and both are known for their ornate beadwork, wood carving and basketry. They live the hunter-gather lifestyle supplemented by the cultivation of cash crops such as rice, pepper, tobacco, rubber and sugar cane. Spears and hunting dogs are used for larger game, blowpipes for smaller prey such as monkeys. Like the Iban, their old foe, the Kayan and Kenyah are known for their hospitality. Guests are welcomed with song and dance accompanied by the *sape*, a traditional stringed instrument. Kayan and Kenyah longhouses are often painted with colourful murals in elegant swirling designs. As with other tribes, tattoos are used to denote particular achievements.

Kelabit

Another of the Orang Ulu tribes, the Kelabit live up on a remote and idyllic mountain plateau in Sarawak, an area known as the Kelabit Highlands (*see* p.352). The Kelabit are farmers who use buffalo and sophisticated methods of irrigation. Bario rice (Bario is the heartland of the Kelabit Highlands) is renowned for its delicate flavour. The Kelabit are also known for their great strength and for their culture of building megaliths, such as dolmens in honour of ancestors. The one thing a Kelabit is most likely to boast of is the intelligence of his people. And it is no idle boast: the Kelabit have been proven to have unusually high IQs.

Melanau

The Melanau are a coastal people from the area around Mukah (*see* p.338) in Sarawak. They are skilled fishermen, supplementing their income by sago production (pulp extracted from the sago palm and ground into a flour). They build their longhouses high off the ground on hardwood stilts. The Melanau are closely associated with the Malays through decades of intermarriage and most have turned to Islam (though some are Catholic). However, animist festivals are still observed with gusto. Each year in April the Melanau appease the spirits of the sea at the Kaul Festival, which involves acrobatic games on the beach and offerings to a totemic symbol of the Kaul.

Melayu Proto

This tribal group represents almost half of the Orang Asli population of Peninsular Malaysia. They were the first of the peninsula's indigenous peoples to be introduced to a cash economy, and many have become farmers and fishermen. Despite giving up their semi-nomadic lifestyles, the Melayu Proto tribes have clung fiercely to their traditions and animist religion. The Semelai tribe still paddle the shallow waters of Tasek Bera (Malaysia's largest freshwater lake), setting fish traps and hunting deer and boar, as do the Jakun of Lake Chini. They supplement their income by tapping rubber, cultivating hill paddy and hosting visits by adventurous tourists.

Murut

The Murut are one of the largest indigenous groups in Sabah, with numerous sub-tribes who speak 15 different languages between them. They traditionally inhabit the interior of Sabah (Murut means 'hill people'). The Murut are famous for being the last tribe to abandon the practice of headhunting. Jars, or *sampa*, denote prominent status within Murut society and are used – among other things – as coffins for the dead, who are laid to rest in the foetal position. Like the Iban, the Murut work hard and play hard: one custom prohibits parties from finishing before dawn (though they often last a week).

Negrito

The Negritos are traditionally hunter-gatherers, with possible ancestral links to the aborigines of Australia. They form just seven per cent of Peninsular Malaysia's Orang Asli population. The most commonly seen tribe are the Batek, who are given free rein to subsistence-hunt in Malaysia's largest national park, the Taman Negara. The Batek lifestyle has remained virtually unchanged for 2,000 years. Other tribes sell jungle produce at local markets or work as labourers.

Penan (or Punan)

Small numbers of Penan still live exactly as they always have done – as nomadic hunter-gatherers living exclusively off the resources of Sarawak's jungle. However, many have been forced into ramshackle settlements by logging activities. Their expertise with blowpipes and poison darts is second to none, while their knowledge of the medicinal properties of jungle plants has yet to be fully tapped. The Penan are thought to be the descendants of Borneo's first inhabitants.

Rungus

The Rungus are a small tribe of 40,000 who live at the northern tip of Sabah, around Kudat. They are known for their beautiful costumes made from black cloth hand-stitched with colourful patterns and hung with antique beads. As a modern tribal people, the Rungus are particularly keen to keep their customs and traditions alive. The ancient art of gong-making, for example, has been re-established in recent years (the gong is a valuable commodity within the Rungus community and has a central role within animist ritual).

Senoi

Half of the Orang Asli people of Peninsular Malaysia fall into this tribal grouping. They live predominantly in the central and northern interior of the peninsula. They work mainly as shifting cultivators and are skilled in the use of bamboo. Like the Melayu Proto, they have largely clung on to their traditional customs.

The Natural World

Situated upon the Equator, and bathed by the tepid water of the great tropical oceans, this region enjoys a climate more uniformly hot and moist than almost any other part of the globe, and teems with natural productions which are elsewhere unknown. The richest of fruits and the most precious of spices are here indigenous. It produces the giant flowers of the Rafflesia, the great green-winged Ornithoptera (princes among the butterfly tribes), the man-like Orang-Utan, and the gorgeous Birds of Paradise.

Alfred Russel Wallace, *The Malay Archipelago*, 1868

We poled our way through the forest gloom, with trees to right of us, trees to left of us, trees before us, trees behind us, trees above us, and, I may write, trees beneath us, so innumerable were the snags and tree trunks in the river.

Isabella Bird, *The Golden Chersonese*, 1883

Not so long ago, the entire landmass of Borneo and the Malay Peninsula was a carpet of trees stretching from coast to coast. Today, just over fifty per cent of that forest remains standing, though that figure gets chipped away at with every passing year. Fortunately, the Malaysian government has seen fit to protect some of the more important patches of rainforest by establishing dozens of national parks. Together, these provide one of the most compelling reasons for visiting Malaysia, holding within their boundaries a wide range of ecosystems and a staggering biodiversity.

Almost twenty per cent of world's animal species can be found in Malaysia. This might not sound out of the ordinary until you consider that Malaysia represents just 0.002% of the world's landmass (a little smaller in size than Germany). The range of plant life in Malaysia is even greater. Claims are frequently made, for instance, that the Gunung Kinabalu National Park in Sabah is the most biodiverse patch of land on the planet. In neighbouring Sarawak, meanwhile, a single hectare of rainforest alongside the Rejang River was found to contain 711 separate species of tree (there are only 171 indigenous trees in the whole of North America).

The key to this great biodiversity is the age of Malaysia's rainforests. The plant and animal species that live here have had 130 million years to establish themselves. That makes the rainforests of Malaysia and neighbouring Indonesia the oldest in the world. During the last Ice Age (which ended around 10,000 years ago), Peninsular Malaysia, Borneo, Java and Sumatra were joined together in one landmass known as Sundaland. This temporary land bridge to the Asian mainland allowed animals to wander freely and establish themselves in areas that were later cut off by rising sea levels. Naturalist Alfred Russel Wallace (*see* p.312), author of *The Malay Archipelago* (1868), was the first to establish this fact, discovering through his research a transitional boundary which runs between Bali and Lombok, and over which very few animals have crossed. Species to the east of the 'Wallace Line' – formed by a deep water channel – evolved independently of those to the west, where contact with the Asian mainland allowed for greater biodiversity.

Malaysia's varied ecosystems range from lowland dipterocarp rainforest, mangrove swamp and heath forest to montane oak forest, mossy cloud forest and alpine forests, each spawning their own peculiar life forms. Delicate necklace orchids cling to the rock face of Mount Kinabalu. Carnivorous pitcher plants hang from the shrubby trees of Bako National Park. The rare Rafflesia, the world's largest flower, spreads its fleshy petals at Gunung Gading National Park. The greatest variety of life is spawned in Malaysia's lowland rainforest, where dipterocarp trees balance on giant buttresses, their smooth bare trunks reaching as high as 50 metres (165ft) into the jungle canopy. The fight for light high up in the canopy means that few plants are able to survive on the shady floor of the rainforest, which makes moving around relatively easy; the stereotypical tangle of foliage often associated with the word 'jungle' is only found in secondary forest, where the removal of the largest hardwood trees has allowed sunlight to penetrate to the forest floor.

The largest and most visited national park on Peninisula Malaysia is the Taman Negara (Malay for 'national park'), which has plenty of well-marked trails, a canopy walkway and several hides. The best places for spotting wildlife, particularly large mammals, are in Malaysian Borneo. Sarawak's Bako National Park provides excellent opportunities for spotting the unusual proboscis monkey, while the Kinabatangan Wetlands and the Danum Valley offer the best chances for seeing elephants and orang-utans. In Brunei, the Ulu Temburong National Park is a beautiful and little-visited wilderness. All of the region's national parks are covered in detail within the regional chapters.

Mammals

The largest mammal inhabiting Malaysia's rainforests is the **Asian elephant**, which weighs up to four tonnes. Despite its size, it is rarely seen. The biggest populations are found in the Taman Negara on Peninsular Malaysia, and the Danum Valley and Kinabatangan Wetlands in Sabah. Elephants occasionally wreak havoc in rural villages, where they have been known to knock down houses in search of salt.

The rarest of the large mammals is the **Sumatran rhinoceros**, which has been hunted almost to extinction (on the Chinese market, their horns are worth more than their weight in gold). These small, hairy rhinos were once so common that British colonials complained of them trampling their back gardens. Today only a few dozen survive in isolated pockets of rainforest, including the Taman Negara, Endau Rompin National Park, Tabin Wildlife Reserve and the Danum Valley.

Other large mammals that are more frequently sighted include the wild **seladang** (largest of the world's cattle species) and the unusual **Malayan tapir**, which has a curled snout, black and white markings, and often weighs in at 450 kg (1,000 lbs). The **wild boar** is common on Peninsular Malaysia, as is the huge **bearded pig** in Malaysian Borneo. Several species of deer inhabit the rainforests too, from the domestic-cat-sized **lesser mouse deer** to the **barking deer** and the **sambar deer**, which weighs up to 250 kg (550 lbs).

Despite centuries of hunting, the **tiger** still survives in the interior rainforests of Peninsular Malaysia, feeding mainly on wild pig, deer and tapir. A population of around 100 tigers survive in the Taman Negara. There are also relatively frequent sightings around Tasek Bera (Malaysia's largest freshwater lake) and in the Cameron Highlands. Other wild cats found in Malaysia are the **panther**, the **clouded leopard**, the smaller **leopard cat**, the **marbled cat**, the **flat-headed cat** and the **golden cat**. The largest of the omnivores is the **Malayan sun bear**, which has a predilection for honey.

Of the smaller mammals there are numerous species of **civet cat**, **mongoose** and **squirrel**. The long-tailed **giant rat** measures up to 70cm from nose to tail, while the **colugo** – often wrongly identified as the flying lemur – is able to glide up to 100 metres between trees.

Visitors to East Malaysia often have one thing in mind: an encounter with an **orang-utan** (*see* 'Man of the Forest', pp.382–3). These large apes, which are endemic to the jungles of Borneo and Sumatra, have suffered the effects of logging and are now the subject of major conservation efforts. Most tourists encounter orang-utans at wildlife rehabilitation centres in Sarawak and Sabah, where semi-wild apes return to be fed. With perseverance, it is also possible to spot fully wild orang-utans in both the Kinabatangan Wetlands and the Danum Valley.

The acrobatic **white-handed gibbon** and **siameng** complete Malaysia's population of apes. The latter is identifiable by its beautiful, melancholy song produced with the aid of an inflatable laryngeal sack. Malaysia is also home to several species of monkey, including the omnipresent **crab-eating macaque**, the larger **pig-tailed macaque** and various species of gentle **leaf monkey** (or langur). The rare and peculiar **proboscis monkey** (*see* 'The Proboscis Monkey', p.387), largest monkey in the world, was once known to the Malays as *orang belanda* ('Dutchman') because of its pot belly and pendulous nose. These can be observed at the Bako National Park in Sarawak,the Kinabatangan Wetlands in Sabah and just upriver from the capital in Brunei.

Malaysia also has a healthy population of **bats**. At the Mulu National Park in Sarawak, a metropolis-sized population (which includes 27 separate species) make their homes among the caves (*see* 'Bat Facts', p.349).

Birds

The region is well-known for its varied birdlife; so far, more than 620 species have been recorded on the peninsula alone. Among the myriad forest birds, whose songs form the soundtrack of the jungle canopy, there are hornbills, orioles, racket-tailed drongos, sunbirds, humming birds, birds of paradise, bulbuls, barbets, argus pheasants, kingfishers, woodpeckers and weaverbirds – to mention just a few. The most characterful of them all is the **hornbill** (*see* 'The Secret Lives of Langkawi's Birds', p.216), of which there are nine different species in Malaysia. The most common is the black-and-white pied hornbill, and the largest, the great hornbill, which measures 1.5 metres (5ft) from head to tail. Fractionally smaller is the rhinoceros hornbill of Borneo, attributed mythological status by the tribespeople of Sarawak.

Of the region's birds of prey, the fish eagle and the Brahminy kite are most common. Migratory water birds flock to several wetland areas in Malaysia, including the Kuala Selangor Nature Park, where there are boardwalks and bird-watching hides for visitors. The Kinabatangan Wetlands, home to the extremely rare **Storm's stork** and the sinuous oriental darter (or snakebird) is one of Malaysia's most exciting birding destinations.

Reptiles

Scientists are forever discovering species of reptile and amphibian new to science in Malaysia's rainforests. Getting on for 300 different species of reptile have so far been identified. The largest of them are the giant leatherback turtle (*see* 'Seas and Lakes' below) and **estuarine crocodile**, which has been known to reach seven or eight metres in length. Much rarer is the threatened **Malayan false gharial**, an odd-looking snout-nosed crocodile. Lizards are everywhere. **Geckos** (the commonest of which are known locally as 'chit-chats') hunt mosquitoes around artificial lights, **flying lizards** glide between trees, while **monitor lizards** slouch about after scraps in coastal areas. The largest of the monitor lizards can reach 8 ft (2.5m) in length.

Malaysia has 100 different species of land snake, as well as 20 sea snakes. Of the land snakes only 16 are venomous. The most lethal is the **king cobra**, though it is rarely encountered (the cobra feeds on other snakes and avoids humans). The **python** is more common, as is the beautiful **paradise tree snake** and the green-and-yellow striped **Wagler's pit viper** (whose bite is venomous but not fatal).

Insects

The number of insect species present in Malaysia is monumental, with new species emerging with every passing year. Among the butterflies, the **Rajah Brooke birdwing** is perhaps the most spectacular, with its slender wings and iridescent, zigzag markings. One of Malaysia's largest insects is the huge **Atlas moth**, while the largest beetle is the glossy-black **rhinoceros beetle**, with its outlandish horns. The **giant stick insect** can grow as long as a man's forearm, the **empress cicada** has a wingspan of 30cm and the **giant ant** grows to 4cm. The **praying mantis** (so-called because of the pose it adopts before striking out at its prey) is fairly common too.

Insects to avoid include the **banded hornet** and the **giant honey bee**, both aggressive if provoked and deadly when they attack in numbers. The **fire ant** and **weaver ant** both give painful bites at the least provocation. **Scorpions** are common: their sting, though painful, is not dangerous to humans.

Seas and Lakes

Malaysia's offshore islands are ringed by coral reefs and abundant marine life. With the growth in the tourist industry, these reefs are now coming under threat, but many of them remain among the world's richest; the waters around tiny Pulau Sipadan off Sabah are home to more marine life than any other spot known to man.

Marine turtles are plentiful in the seas around Malaysia. Islands off the east coast of Malaysia and off Sabah form important nesting grounds for **green turtles** and **hawksbill turtles**, which come ashore to lay their eggs in the sand under cover of darkness. The beaches of Rantau Abang, on Peninsular Malaysia's east coast, once drew tourists in their thousands to witness the spectacle of **giant leatherback turtles** heaving themselves ashore to lay their eggs. These mysterious animals, which can grow to three metres in length and weigh a metric tonne, are now critically endangered (*see* 'Decline of the Warm-Blooded Reptile, p.247).

The full quota of reef fish are present around Malaysia's tropical islands, from **reef sharks** and **barracuda** and **garupas**, to **bump-head parrotfish**, **big-eye trevally** and

scorpion fish. Twenty species of **sea snake** live off Malaysia's coastline, each of them hugely venomous (though it is virtually unheard of for humans to be bitten).

A number of Malaysia's islands attract pelagic species, like **whale sharks**, **manta rays** and **hammerhead sharks**. The open waters, meanwhile, provide prime game-fishing territory, with **blue marlin** and **tuna** in abundance. For freshwater fishing, Malaysia's rivers and shallow freshwater lakes provide habitats for highly prized catches such as **tiger barbs**, **harlequins**, **marbled goby** and the rare **Asian arawana**.

Bioprospectors and the Bintangor Tree

Like striking oil or sourcing gold, the lucky bioprospector can unearth a commodity worth millions. Of the world's top-selling pharmaceuticals, nearly half were sourced from animals, plants or micro-organisms. Malaysia's wide-ranging topography combines with a life-spawning climate to create one of the world's most precious regions of biodiversity. Factor in the age-old knowledge possessed by the region's tribal communities – experts in jungle resources – and you have prime bioprospecting ground.

Use of indigenous knowledge by pharmaceutical companies, as a precursor to screening, often takes place with little regard for intellectual property. Potential profits are huge but the original owners of this property often see none of it – a fact that is being viewed by more and more people as an infringement of biological copyright.

In the 1980s an American scientist began investigating the latex of the Bintangor tree, common in the swamp forests of Sarawak. He managed to isolate Calanolide, a compound now undergoing clinical trials for the treatment of HIV AIDS. Sarawak's indigenous people have long used the Bintangor tree for its medicinal properties: a poultice made from its bark is said to cure headaches or skin rashes. Such knowledge is a signboard for bioprospectors. Those holding the signboard have habitually been consulted, then cast aside, seeing none of the long-term profit.

It was with this in mind that the Convention on Biological Diversity (CBD) was set up in 1992, an international agreement signed by 179 nations, with the exception of the USA. The convention recognises the sovereign right of every nation to regulate the use of its own biological resources. Bioprospecting in Sarawak is now illegal without a licence from the state government. And Sarawak has successfully laid claim to 50% of all future profits gained by the American pharmaceutical company presently testing Calanolide.

However, there is little doubt that clandestine sample-taking still goes on in the hunt for 21st-century treasure (compounds that can be used to treat big-money diseases like AIDS and cancer). And even if Sarawak succeeds in pocketing some of the returns, few have confidence that local people – original owners of the intellectual property – will receive financial reward. It is all too easy to draw comparisons with logging: politicians and businessmen benefit handsomely from

Sarawak's hardwood resources, while those at the bottom of the pile suffer all the disadvantages, losing their homelands, their traditions and their right to live the lives they desire.

Kampung Games

Did football originate in the Malay world? Probably not: there are distant stories of Roman legionaries using bulls' bladders for a kick-around. However, 'keepy-uppy', as we know it today, certainly did originate in Southeast Asia. Among the Malays, it has been a favourite kampung (village) game for centuries. The principle of ***sepak takraw***, as the game is known, is simple: to stand in a circle and keep aloft a grapefruit-sized ball made from strips of rattan with the use of any part of the body except the arms and hands. *Sepak takraw* is mentioned in the Malaysia's greatest historical document, the *Sejarah Melayu* (Malay Annals), which records the game being played in 15th-century Melaka.

During the 1930s, the game underwent a strange mutation. By this time, badminton had become a popular sport on the Malay Peninsula, and some bright spark decided to exchange racket and shuttlecock for legs and rattan ball. The result was ***sepak raga***, an acrobatic game that was soon all the rage in Malayan schools. In 1960 the Malayan Sepak Raga Federation was born. When Malaysia played host to the Southeast Asian Games in 1965, *sepak raga* was among the events.

Possibly the most popular kampung game, however, is the flying of *layang-layang* (**kites**). It is a common sight in Malaysia for the skyline to be dotted with kites of all shapes and sizes. Kites were traditionally flown at the end of the rice harvest to celebrate the fact that all the hard work was over and done with. On the east coast, kites are known as *wau*. Today kite-flying (and making) remains popular with children and adults alike. Kite-flying competitions take place throughout the year, with judges awarding points for craftmanship (*wau* are beautiful, colourful objects set on bamboo frames); sound (all Malay kites are designed to create a specific sound as they are buffetted about in the wind); and altitude (kites are sometimes flown to heights of 500 metres – that's higher than KL's Petronas Towers). The *wau kuching*, or cat kite (it makes a mewing sound), of Terengganu has been adopted as the logo for Malaysia Airlines. The most photographed style of kite is the Kelantanese moon kite, which is crescent-shaped and measures 3m by 3m. Scaled-down versions are made for sale to tourists.

On Peninsular Malaysia, another popular east-coast pastime is **top-spinning**. Like kite-making, careful craftmanship is required to create the most competitive spinning tops (*gasing*), some of which spin for two hours at a time. Though top-spinning is popular among children, it is really a man's game, requiring a great deal of strength and skill. Coils of rope are wound around the top, which is carefully carved from *afzelia*, a dense and heavy hardwood. To set the top in motion, the rope is yanked hard as the top itself is flung to the ground. *Gasing* are beautiful objects in themselves, often crafted and bought purely for aesthetic reasons.

The board game ***congkak*** is popular among Malay women and children on Peninsular Malaysia. Stones, marbles, beads or shells are moved around a wooden board consisting of twelve or more holes. *Congkak* (or *mancala*, as it is sometimes known) is acknowledged as the oldest game in the world. Its origins can be traced back thousands of years to Ancient Egyptian times. The earliest known *congkak* board was found carved into the roof tiles of a 3,400-year-old temple in Karnak, Egypt. For all we know, with its African origins, *congkak* may well have been a primeval game that helped sharpen the analytical skills of our distant ancestors. *Congkak* boards themselves were not always necessary: a makeshift board could be made by digging small holes into the soil.

However old the game may be, it was Egytian traders on the seafaring route to China who brought *congkak* to the Malay peninsula many centuries ago – in fact, they dispersed the game around the globe; it is played today across Africa, Asia and the Americas. Each culture has invented its own variations on the game, some of which are said to have as much mathematical scope as chess.

Cockfights and Thunder Teeth

Amateur ethnologist Ivor H. N. Evans took up his post as a junior civil servant of the British North Borneo Company in 1910. This was his chance to study 'savage' culture at first hand. He noted with interest that archaeologists in neighbouring Sarawak had already unearthed ancient stone implements, and he hoped to pioneer the discovery of such treasures in British North Borneo.

Armed with the trusty catalogue of the Scottish Museum of Antiquities, Evans set off to make enquiries among the local villagers. To his surprise, he found that they recognised some of the illustrations in his catalogue, stabbing excited fingers at the smooth, palm-sized stones labelled as adze-heads. These, the villagers informed him with straight-faced authority, were not adze-heads at all, but *gigi guntor*, or 'thunder teeth'. To be precise, they were thunderbolts, charmed objects that could be found among the roots of coconut palms which had been struck by lightning. Evans – who was not about to go digging for thunderbolts beneath coconut trees – set off to get a second opinion.

In the next village, the illustrations were recognised once again as *gigi guntor*. Evans found that the stones – generally pieces of jade, smoothed after centuries of handling – were highly prized as charms. Water in which they had been soaked was given as a cure-all to sick people; the blades of parangs and spears were stroked with them to ensure their deadliness; and they were left secretly among padi stores to keep the rice in top condition. Unfortunately, no one had a *gigi guntor* to hand, and Evans left once more disappointed.

After lunch on the following Sunday, Evans joined the crowds outside the Chinese shophouses of Kota Belud to watch the weekly cockfight. Cockfighting was one of the primary sources of entertainment for peoples of the Malay world. In Kota Belud, the

Bajaus, the Dusuns, the Malays and Chinese all gathered to place bets on well-hyped fights. It was a similar story on the Malay peninsula. British Resident of Pahang Sir Hugh Clifford (1896–1901) enjoyed attending cockfights near his residency. He admired what he saw as the dignity of the sport – the fact that it was the birds themselves who declared the outcome of the bout by the raising of tail feathers (a submissive gesture).

At every contest an umpire was present. Only he and the owner-trainers were allowed inside the cockpit, which was constructed of bamboo fencing. As the owners appeared on the scene, cocks tucked carefully beneath their arms, the crowd would erupt with jeers and cheers. Both the ringside preparations of a cockfight, and the bout itself, have direct parallels with the paraphernalia of modern boxing.

Each owner takes to his corner of the cockpit. He squats with his bird, massaging legs and wings so as to loosen muscles. On the umpire's command, the birds are set against one another. They peck and dart and jab with their claws (traditionally no artificial spurs are used). Sometimes, a bird runs its neck beneath the shoulder of the other bird and the two are locked in a momentary embrace – until the umpire stands in to part them once more. A round is declared over on the temporary defeat of one of the birds, signalled by the turning of its back and raising of its tail feathers. Alternatively, a timer is used: a section of coconut in which a hole has been bored is set floating in a bowl of water. At the bell, the birds are led back to their corners and the careful attentions of their trainers, who douse them in water, comb their head and plumage, and swab the beak and throat with a damp feather. Sometimes, charms are applied with stroking movements to the beak and feet.

In Kota Belud, it was this part of the fight which most roused Ivor Evans' attentions. In the far corner, the Bajau owner had removed from his pocket a beautiful stone implement, with which he stroked the feet of his bird, all the while muttering incantations. Evans went straight to the local Bajau leader, who was among the crowd, and asked him to get hold of the cockfighter so that he could take a look at his charm.

When later the man was taken to one side, he very reluctantly removed his charm for inspection. It was a beautiful little adze-head of smoothed jade. Evans at once offered a handsome sum for the implement, but the Bajau would not part with it for any amount of money; neither would he allow Evans to handle the implement for fear that this would diminish its potency as a charm. As far as the Bajau was concerned, the *gigi guntor* was the secret of his success.

The use of *gigi guntor* was just one of many tactics employed by cockfighters to give their birds the winning edge. In fact, one popular legend relates the Malay conversion to Islam with charms and cockfighting. Many centuries ago an Arab missionary is said to have landed on the shores of Sumatra, hoping to bring the Malay peoples into the fold. He met with little hostility but little enthusiasm either; the Malays were indifferent to his teachings – teachings for which he had been touted in other parts of the world as a living saint. In Sumatra he found a people whose passions were roused only when discussing the relative merits of fighting cocks.

One day a local Malay arrived on the wise man's doorstep to ask if (on the off chance) he might have a charm for his fighting cock, which was soon to be pitted against a champion bird from across the valley. It dawned on the Arab that he had found his vessel for conversion. As a charm, he taught the unknowing Malay the Muslim Confession of Faith, and sent him on his way.

To the Malay's delight, his cock prevailed. He was quick to attribute his success to the wise man's charm, and soon the Arab was overwhelmed with similar requests. To every cockfighter who arrived on his doorstep, he taught the Muslim Confession of Faith. It wasn't long before the first Malay returned, complaining that his personal charm was now public property and that his bird no longer had the edge over opponents. The Arab smiled inwardly and, as a replacement charm, offered the man the Five Daily Prayers (Salat). In this manner, the Arab missionary managed to teach the Malay people all the doctrines of the Islamic faith.

Luckily for Ivor Evans, stone implements remained high on the list of favourable charms among cockfighters, even after conversion to Islam. Though the Bajau at Kota Belud was not forthcoming, word soon spread that Evans was offering a bounty for *gigi guntor*. Before long, he had to his name a handsome collection of hand-polished thunder teeth. Evans went on to become the official ethnographer of Museums of the Federated Malay States.

Food and Drink

05

On the streets of Malaysia, Singapore and Brunei, the greatest hubbub always surrounds the making and the eating of food. 'Have you eaten yet?' is akin to saying 'hello' in this part of the world. In short, Malaysians, Singaporeans and Bruneians are obsessive about their food, which makes visiting these countries all the more pleasurable.

One thing is for certain: you will never go hungry. Even in the remotest of locations, there will be someone on hand to cater for your cravings. And if you are open to new tastes, the variety of available dishes will seem almost infinite.

Historically, Malaysia's towns and ports catered for hungry merchants on the trade route between India and China. Hawkers wheeled their little stalls about the streets and marketplaces, luring traders with their signature dishes – often a local variation on a regional classic. The centuries passed, and the plural society of the Malay world took root, its doors wide open to cuisines from around the world. Chinese, Indian and Malay cooking dominated, but these cuisines took on influences from Thailand, Java, the Arab world, Portugal, even Britain. Other culinary combinations were inspired closer to home: the rich, spicy, coconutty cuisine of the Straits Chinese – which evolved behind the scenes in domestic kitchens – took Chinese classics and reinvented them with the aid of typically Malay flavours.

Whether you eat at a simple roadside stall or in a formal restaurant, standards of cooking are extremely high in each country. Unlike in the West, poor standards of cooking are not easily tolerated; to turn out a shoddy plate of food for public consumption is seen as something of a disgrace. For those unfamiliar with Asian cooking practices, heading out into the streets for dinner can seem a little daunting. But if you take a little time to learn about the most popular dishes (and where they are served), you will be rewarded. When it comes to eating out in Malaysia and Singapore, it pays to be adventurous.

Cuisines and Specialities

Rice and noodles are the staples in Malaysia,Singapore and Brunei. Both are cooked, flavoured and shaped in dozens of different ways, from savoury rice-flour porridge and fried biryani to sweet glutinous rice cakes and the coconut-soaked rice of *nasi lemak*. Of course, rice is often served plain, and there is a strict hierarchy of quality, with connoisseurs rating Bario rice for its delicate aroma. Noodles, too, are flung together in myriad ways. There are thread noodles and flat noodles, rice noodles and wheat noodles, round noodles and yellow noodles, egg noodles and bean noodles, fried noodles and boiled noodles. Every meal in Malaysia, Singapore and Brunei is based on either rice or noodles or – more often than not – both.

Unlike your typical Westerner, Malaysians, Singaporeans and Bruneians are not finicky about fish. An all-time favourite dish in Singapore, for example, is fish-head curry, for which aficionados will pay good money. For first-timers, however, the sight of a snapper's eye peering up from the bowl can be a little off-putting, especially when you find out that it is the fleshy muscle around the eye that is the dish's *raison d'être*. But don't let the likes of fish-head curry (or *perut ikan* – fish stomach curry) put you off; other fish dishes won't test your squeamishness in quite this way, and the variety on offer is staggering. Fish is a common ingredient in *laksa*, one of Malaysia's most delicious offerings, with different variations cooked up in Penang, Melaka and Sarawak. *Ikan bakar* (barbecued fish) is another Malaysian favourite: a whole fish marinated in spices and grilled over hot coals. The Malays serve fish balls with satay sauce and the Chinese steam fish for many of their dishes. *Ikan bilis*, or deep-fried anchovies, are commonly served with rice and sambal in Malaysia. Chilli crab is a much-loved dish in all three destinations, while squid and prawns appear in a wide range of dishes. Lobster, meanwhile, is incredibly cheap by Western standards.

Chicken, which is equally common as fish, is served across the board in Malay, Indian and Chinese dishes. Beef in this part of the world tends to be a little tougher than in the West, though it forms the base for some delicious dishes like beef *rendang*. Mutton is also common, served mainly in Malay and Indian dishes. Pork, forbidden to Muslims, is the most common meat used by the Chinese. Tofu and fermented soya beans feature widely in Chinese cooking, and provide a tasty alternative to meat. Indian cooking in Malaysia, Singapore and Brunei makes good use of pulses, with dhal forming a mainstay.

Fruits

Many visitors will find their intake of fruit rise dramatically when they visit Malaysia, Singapore and Brunei. The variety of fruits on offer is staggering, and you can be sure to come across plenty of fruits you have never heard of (let alone tasted) before. The most common fruits are bananas, coconuts, watermelons, pineapples and mangos.

King of Fruits

Despite being crowned the 'King of Fruits' in Malaysia and Thailand, the durian has divided opinion for centuries. Indifference is unheard of. You either love the durian or you hate it. Its pungent aroma is the stumbling block for many people. For this reason, top-end hotels do not allow it through their doors, while in Singapore, durians are banned from public places. But this doesn't stop locals hankering after the fruit when it comes into season, paying handsomely for the freshest specimens. Orang-utans, incidentally, go wild for durians.

In Anthony Burgess's trilogy of novels *The Malayan Trilogy* (see 'Further Reading'), the durian experience is likened to 'eating a sweet raspberry blancmange in a lavatory'. For those who can bear the smell (some find it inoffensive), this is a unique and delicious fruit, high in protein, vitamins, fibre and calories. The Chinese categorise it as a 'heaty' food that should be counterbalanced with something 'cooly', such as a banana. Combining durian and alcohol is thought to be a bad idea.

There are two durian seasons each year, with seasons differing depending on geographical location. Durians are large, heavy fruit with thick, sharp spikes. The large seeds inside are surrounded by smooth creamy flesh. To find a durian stall, follow your nose.

Other common fruits that are less well known in the West include **durian** (*see* 'King of Fruits', p.57); **jackfruit** (huge pear-shaped fruit – some in excess of 50cm across – with a rough green exterior and sweet yellow flesh); **mangosteen** (thick, round, purplish rind, with delicious nodes of white flesh inside; sweet, with a touch of sharpness); **longan** (sweet white flesh around a large stone; similar to the lychee); **pomelo** (largest of the world's citrus fruits, about the size of a football, and similar in appearance to grapefruit, though with a less acidic taste); **rambutan** (bright red exterior with soft spines; similar to lychees and longans but with a more perfumed taste); **papaya** (smooth thin skin similar to a mango's, with slightly creamy orange flesh, commonly served in fruit salads; very high in vitamin C and A); **star-fruit** (pale, yellow-green fruit with thin waxy skin and star-shaped cross-section; pale juicy flesh with only a faint flavour; star-fruit juice is delicious); and **salak** (small fruit easily identified by its skin, which is like a snake's or an armadillo's; flesh has a sharp taste).

Malay Cuisine

Many people find it hard to pin down exactly what differentiates many elements of Malay food from its Indian and Chinese counterparts. Malay cuisine has evolved in the home, and this is where it has tended to remain, with relatively few exclusively Malay restaurants and food stalls. Though Malay food has borrowed from Indian, Thai and Chinese cooking, it is certainly worthy of being called a separate cuisine in itself – despite the fact that it is the 'Nyonya' fusion of Malay food with Chinese food which sometimes steals the limelight.

Malay cuisine makes good use of coconut milk, and it is this that gives many Malay dishes their rich, creamy character. The other foundation of Malay cooking is *belacan* (shrimp paste), which is used as a base for *sambal*, a rich sauce or condiment made from *belacan*, chillies, onions and garlic. Malay cooking also makes plentiful use of lemon grass and galangal.

If you want to sample a range of Malay curries, look out for *nasi campur,* which is served at Malay *kedai kopi* (coffee shops). *Nasi campur* comprises a buffet of vegetable and meat curries served with steamed rice. The best-known Malay dish is the universally popular satay (skewers of barbecued chicken or beef served with a sweet spicy peanut sauce), while the most widespread dish is *nasi lemak* (coconut

Origins of Ketchup

It may be the definitive condiment of the West, but ketchup has its origins in the East. The word was acquired by the traders of the British East India Company when they visited the Malay peninsula back in the 17th century. There they found a tasty Chinese condiment known as *kicap* (pronounced *kee-chap*), a Malay variation on *ke-tsiap*, a pickled fish sauce from southeastern China. The British brought the sauce home with them, calling it 'catsup', or 'catchup'. As the centuries passed, the recipe mutated. By the 19th century, tomatoes had been added; the sauce was widely known at this time as 'tomato soy'. In 1876, the F & J Heinz Company began selling 'tomato ketchup'. Today, ketchup can be found in 98 per cent of American kitchens.

rice with deep-fried anchovies, *sambal*, peanuts, egg and cucumber), a traditional breakfast. Beef *rendang* is common too, as is nasi goreng, a standard fried-rice dish with available chicken, meat, prawns and vegetables.

Nyonya cuisine is the food of the Peranakan (or Straits-born) Chinese, a people with mixed Malay-Chinese blood. They took to spicing up Chinese dishes with typically Malay ingredients, such as *sambal* and coconut milk. Nyonya cuisine can be found in Singapore, Melaka and Penang. For more on Nyonya food, *see* 'Peranakan Cuisine', p.425.

Chinese Cuisine

Chinese cuisine is dominant across Malaysia, Singapore and Brunei, with an almost limitless variety of dishes available in the urban centres – Cantonese, Hokkien, Teochew, Hainanese, Foochow, Hakka and Szechuan cuisine have all stamped their mark upon this part of the world, brought south by a constant trickle of Chinese immigrants from China's southern provinces.

Cantonese cuisine, usually a hit with the Western palate, is widespread across Malaysia and Singapore. Dim sum (steamed and deep-fried stuffed dumplings served in little bamboo steaming baskets) is one of the most popular Cantonese offerings, usually served for breakfast and/or lunch. *Wantan mee* (*see* 'Food Glossary') is a popular variation on Cantonese cuisine, while shark's fin soup and birds' nest soup are traditional delicacies. The relatively simple cooking of Hainan Province has provided one or two staples in Malaysia and Singapore, notably Hainanese chicken rice, which can be found everywhere. Hakka dishes are popular particularly in Sarawak, where Hakka gold-miners settled in the 19th century. Hakka food makes good use of glutinous rice, and staples include pig's trotter and *yong tau foo* (stuffed tofu). Preserved salty vegetables are a common ingredient (the salt was said to help rehydrate workers after a hard day of manual labour).

Hokkien cuisine has had a big influence on the region, particularly in Singapore, where the Hokkien form one of the biggest dialect groups. Widespread dishes include *Hokkien mee* (fried yellow noodles with prawns), the ubiquitous *char kuay teow* (a flat rice-noodle dish) and the spring roll.

Szechuan cuisine is common, particularly at smarter restaurants; it is considered among the most sophisticated of Chinese cuisines, with abundant use of spices and chillies. Teochew cooking is known for its rice 'porridges' and clear soups. Other Chinese cuisine worth looking out for include 'claypot' dishes (cooked in earthenware over a fire) and the steamboat, a delicious Chinese take on the fondue.

Indian Cuisine

The very different styles and flavours of North Indian and South Indian cooking are both present across Malaysia and Singapore. Cuisine from the North makes plentiful use of breads (naan, chapati, roti) and is less reliant on rice, unlike the South, where rice is served with every meal, often with a spread of vegetable curries.

Classic North Indian cuisine includes tandoori chicken (marinated in spices and yoghurt, then cooked in a special tandoori oven). Indian Muslim, or *mamak* cooking of the North has been adopted almost as a national cuisine in Malaysia. From dusk till dawn, *mamak* stalls turn out the country's favourite snack food, *roti canai* (pancake made from ghee-rich dough served with a saucer of curry sauce or dhal). This is usually accompanied by a glass of *teh tarik* (frothy sweet milky tea). *Murtabak* is a delicious and filling elaboration on *roti canai*, with a stuffing of egg, onions and/or meat. *Mamak* stalls are easily identified by the dexterity of their chefs, who fling dough above their heads to shape *roti canai*, and pour tea between beakers with out-stretched arms to create the frothy head on *teh tarik*.

Though South Indian cuisine relies more heavily on rice, one of its staples is *dosai*, Tamil-style pancakes made from rice and ground lentils, and served with a range of curries. One of the cheapest and most satisfying meals in Malaysia is the banana-leaf curry, known in Malay as *daun pisang*. A range of vegetable curries and condiments are served alongside a pile of rice on a washed section of banana leaf. This is another Indian dish which has taken on a life of its own in Malaysia, available wherever there is a Tamil presence.

Drinks

On the whole, **tap water** is safe to drink in Singapore, Malaysia and Brunei. However, most visitors play safe and stick to bottled water, which is widely available. When travelling in remote areas, however, be sure to avoid the tap water.

Fresh juices are widely available across the region, making use of an almost limitless supply of fruits. Star-fruit juice is particularly refreshing. Indian stalls and restaurants often mix fruits with yoghurt to form fruit *lassi*, a delicious, reviving drink. The usual soft drinks are widespread, as is soya milk, usually sold in little cartons.

Tea and **coffee** are drunk as obsessively here as they are in the West. Every street has its *kedai kopi* (traditional coffee shop), where the rich local *kopi* (coffee) is served in little cups and saucers. For black coffee, ask for *kopi-o*. You will otherwise be served *kopi susu*, sweet milky coffee, which seems particularly suited to the climate. It is the same with *teh* (tea): unless you specify otherwise, *teh susu* will be served (black tea with sweet condensed milk). For tea without milk or sugar, ask for *teh kosong*. Meanwhile, *teh tarik* (literally 'pulled tea') is an elaborated version of *teh susu*, only the tea is sloshed rapidly between beakers to create a frothy head. Chinese coffee shops serve the full range of green teas. The local tea is Boh tea, grown on the beautiful Boh Tea Estates of the Cameron Highlands (*see* p.288). Strangely, coffee shops all seem to serve hot Milo as an alternative to tea or coffee.

Lager is widely available in Chinese restaurants and coffee shops. Obviously, Muslim establishments don't serve alcohol. The most common brands are Tiger beer and Anchor, both refreshing local lagers. Guinness by the bottle is also strangely popular among the Chinese, who have taken to its 'health-giving' properties. Wine is only available in top restaurants or from specialist wine merchants in Singapore and Kuala Lumpur. In East Malaysia, **rice wine** is the staple tipple. Known in the Iban dialect as *tuak*, it is often served as a welcome drink in longhouses. At festival time, tribespeople drink it by the barrel-load (most rice wine is about the strength of beer). Alcohol is prohibited in Brunei

Dining Practicalities

Across Malaysia, Singapore and Brunei, food is served in three types of establishment: the hawker stall, the *kedai kopi* (coffee shop) and the more formal restaurant. **Hawker stalls** are often the best places to eat, with each stall specializing in a single, well-honed dish. Traditionally, 'hawkers' wheeled their tiny stalls about the streets, announcing their wares in coded cries. Today, most hawkers congregate in food courts (often found inside shopping centres) or line up in permanent stalls on the streetside. Hawker stalls can also be found at markets, particularly the regular *pasar malam* (night markets). Despite appearances, standards of hygiene are high; ingredients are fresh and dishes are cooked over a high heat right in front of you. Hawker stalls never have menus, only large placards advertising each stall's speciality (rarely in English). In food courts, tables are not specific to individual stalls: once you have ordered your food, sit anywhere and wait for your meal to be brought to your table. It is normal practice to pay when the food arrives. Hawker stalls generally open from around 10am, though those catering for breakfast are open from dawn.

A ***kedai kopi*** – sometimes called *kopi tiam* – is a coffee shop that serves food. In Malaysia, 'kedai kopi' is often used as a general term for an informal restaurant or café. In towns, virtually every street will have one or more *kedai kopis*. Chinese *kedai kopi* often specialize in dim sum (delicious steamed or fried dumplings with fillings) and are good places to track down a cold beer; Malay *kedai kopi* tend to serve *nasi campur* (a buffet of Malay dishes served with rice); and Indian *kedai kopi* serve a range of curries. Muslim Indian *kedai kopi* specialize in *mamak* cuisine, with *roti canai* (a type of pancake served with curry sauce) and *teh tarik* (a frothy, milky glass of tea – 'tea cappuccino', if you like).

The bigger cities, particularly KL and Singapore, have growing numbers of up market **restaurants** serving the full range of cuisines. East-West 'fusion' food is particularly common. Meanwhile, a growing number of cafés lure homesick backpackers through their doors with smoothies, banana pancakes and fried breakfasts.

More often than not, Malaysians and Singaporeans eat out for **breakfast**, stopping by at a roadside stall on the way to work. Many food stalls and restaurants cater for this by opening their doors at dawn. Indian Muslim 'mamak' food has in many ways been adopted as 'Malaysian' cuisine: one of the most popular breakfasts is a glass of sweet *teh tarik* served with *roti canai*. Other traditional breakfasts include *nasi lemak* (rice cooked in coconut milk and served with a range of condiments) and dim sum (steamed and deep-fried stuffed dumplings). On Peninsular Malaysia's east coast, *nasi dagang* (a variation on *nasi lemak*) is a popular breakfast. Though most Malaysians eat first thing, breakfast is served throughout the morning. In fact, 'breakfast' can refer to any meal or snack taken before midday. Most towns and cities

Food Glossary

Ais kacang
A popular dessert comprising a bowl piled high with shaved ice soaked in rose syrup, condensed milk and topped with strips of jelly and a medley of other ingredients, which can include sweetcorn, red beans and small pieces of fruit.

Banana-leaf curry
'*Daun pisang*' in Malay, this South Indian staple meal consists of a mound of rice served with chutneys, curries and poppadums – with a washed section of banana leaf for a plate.

Bee hoon
Thread noodles fried with a range of ingredients, which might include prawn, chicken, egg, beansprouts. One of the most common dishes in Malaysia. *Bee hoon* refers specifically to the thread noodles.

Belacan
A common ingredient in Malay dishes, *belacan* (pronounced *bla-chan*) is made from tiny shrimp crushed into a paste and fermented.

Biryani
Saffron rice cooked with fried chicken, beef or fish. A speciality of North India.

Chai kueh
Chinese steamed dumplings filled with strips of root vegetables such as turnip and carrot.

Chapatti
Unleavened Punjabi bread.

Char koay teow
Flat rice noodles (similar to tagliatelle) fried with prawns, egg, beansprouts, chilli and a type of sausagemeat. One of the most popular Chinese dishes.

Char siew
Marinated barbecued pork served in a variety of ways – either with rice, or as a dim sum item in a *char siew* bun, or sliced finely to be served as *wantan mee*.

Chendol
A dessert made from pandan-flavoured noodles, served in a sweet coconut sauce often with shavings of ice. A speciality of Penang.

Claypot
Dishes cooked in an earthenware pot over a fire to create a slightly smoky taste. Claypot chicken is common, served with rice.

Congee
Often listed as 'porridge' on signs and menus, *congee* is a kind of savoury rice pudding served with slices of meat or fish.

Dhal
Common Indian dish made from lentils, onions, ghee and spices.

Dim sum
A delicious assortment of steamed and deep-fried dumplings with fillings of prawn, pork and fish. Served in little steaming baskets and usually pushed round on a trolley. A traditional Cantonese breakfast staple (though it is sometimes served for lunch and dinner too).

Dosai
Tamil-style pancakes made from rice and ground lentils, served with a range of curries and dips.

Fish-head curry
Hugely popular dish, particularly in Singapore. The head of a snapper served with a tomato curry with okra.

have **bakeries**, all of which open in the mornings and sell a wide range of breads and pastries, many of them stuffed with sweet and savoury goodies. The larger hotels, and cafés in the tourist resorts, serve Western-style breakfasts.

Despite the Malaysian/Singaporean love of a hearty breakfast, **lunch** tends to be a substantial affair too. And Malaysians will never skimp on dinner. In fact, any time of

Gado gado
Vegetable salad mixed with beansprouts, bean curd, potatoes, egg and spicy-rich satay sauce. A Malay-Indonesian speciality.

Goreng pisang
Battered, deep-fried banana wedges, often served at the roadside.

Hainanese chicken rice
A very popular, simple dish. Chicken breast served with cucumber and stock-flavoured rice with a ginger-garlic chilli sauce and a dash of light soy sauce.

Hokkien char
Fried egg noodles with prawns and pork, served with *sambal* and soy sauce.

Hokkien mee
Yellow noodles served in a hot prawn stock, with chilli, beansprouts, egg, *kankong* (see below), prawns and pork ribs.

Ikan bilis
Deep-fried anchovies, served sprinkled over a number of Malay dishes, including the breakfast staple *nasi lemak* (see below).

Kankong
A tasty dark-green leaf vegetable served fried in a *belacan* sauce, often with shrimps.

Koay teow th'ng
A popular dish of flat rice noodles with fish balls, shredded duck, and fish cakes either in a clear soup or fried in soy sauce.

Kuih muih
The umbrella term for the vast range of Malay sweets made from glutinous rice flour.

Laksa
There are three main types of *laksa* found in the region – Penang *laksa*, Sarawak *laksa* and Singapore *laksa*, each of them noodle dishes with a different soup base. Penang *laksa* is served in a distinctive, slightly sour, fish stock, with fish, prawns, cucumber, onions and pineapple. Sarawak *laksa* is served in a rich creamy soup, which combines coconut cream with lemon grass, tamarind, garlic and chilli. Chicken, prawns, omelette strips and *bee hoon* noodles are served in the soup. Singapore *laksa* is somewhere between the two.

Lemang
Glutinous rice cooked in a section of bamboo over an open fire. An Iban speciality.

Lok lok
A kind of Chinese steamboat, sometimes known as *satay celup*. Choose from a huge array of skewered raw delicacies, then sit round a pot of boiling broth in which the skewers are dunked. Delicious and fun.

Lorbak
A delicious deep-fried hawker dish, comprising pork wrapped in a skin of bean curd.

Mee goreng
Literally 'fried noodles', this standard dish is served in virtually every Malay or Indian food stall. Usually comprises yellow noodles fried with beansprouts, bean curd, chicken, prawns, chilli – and whatever else comes to hand.

Mee jawa
A yellow noodle dish smothered in a distinctively rich meat gravy, with lime juice.

Mee rebus
Yellow noodles, boiled and topped with a rich sauce made from tomatoes and meat stock, usually served with bean curd and beansprouts.

day is a good time to eat. It must be something to do with the climate: Malaysians on the whole are a lean people. Lunch is usually limited to a single – albeit hearty – main course, commonly taken at makeshift tables outside food stalls.

Dinner is the biggest meal of the day, often eaten straight after work, with a big spread of dishes rounded off with a local dessert. It is not uncommon, later in the

Murtabak
A meal-in-one Indian pancake stuffed with egg, onion and chicken or mutton. In many ways, an elaborate serving of *roti canai* (see below).

Nasi campur
This is the cuisine on offer at your typical Malay food stall; a buffet of meat and vegetable dishes and curries served with steamed rice.

Nasi goreng
Like *mee goreng*, this is another universal dish (*nasi goreng* translates as 'fried rice'). Rice is fried up with vegetables, chicken, egg, meat or seafood.

Nasi kandar
A *mamak* (Indian Muslim) version of *nasi campur* (see above). A buffet of curries served with rice. Traditionally hawker food.

Nasi lemak
The classic Malaysian breakfast. Basmati rice is cooked in coconut milk and herbs and served with hard-boiled egg, fried peanuts, cucumber, *ikan bilis* (deep-fried anchovies) and a *sambal* condiment. Often served (and stored) wrapped in a banana leaf and shaped into a little pyramid.

Otak-otak
These Nyonya fish cakes consist of fish mashed together with coconut and chilli paste and steamed in a banana leaf.

Pansoh manok
A speciality of the Iban tribe of Sarawak, this is a tasty chicken dish cooked over an open fire in a section of bamboo, along with herbs, gentle spices and garlic.

Peking duck
Well-known duck dish achieved with the aid of a rich marinade, which includes wine, soy sauce, spring onions, ginger and star anise.

Popiah
A delicious Nyonya-style roll stuffed with grated turnip, lettuce, prawns, peanuts, egg and bean curd. Served with a sweet sauce.

Pulot serikaya
Sweet glutinous rice cakes made with pandan and coconut, often bright green in colour.

Rendang
Spicy coconut-based dish, usually served with beef. A classic Malay dish.

Rojak
A bizarre sounding, but strangely moreish Malay speciality consisting of freshly diced tropical fruit, served with sesame seeds and nuts in a dark, sour-sweet hoisin sauce with *belacan* paste.

Roti canai
A popular Indian pancake made with ghee-rich dough that is flung into shape. Usually served with a curry dip, and sometimes stuffed with egg, meat or banana.

Sago pudding
A pudding made from sago starch, coconut, egg and palm sugar.

Sambal
Rich, spicy Malay condiment served with many dishes. The usual base for *sambal* is *belacan* paste mixed with garlic and chilli.

Samosa
Deep-fried parcels of curried potatoes or meat. A staple Indian snack food.

evening, for Malaysians to head back out to the streets for a small snack before bedtime. Hawker centres are often open until the small hours.

Malays traditionally eat using the fingers of their right hand. The left hand, which is considered unclean, is never used for handling food (or, for that matter, for shaking

Sar hor fun
Flat rice noodles fried with pork, liver, green chilli and vegetables, then topped with a rich gravy.

Satay
Delicious skewers of marinated chicken or beef, barbecued and served with a sweet, peanut-based dip, also called satay.

Steamboat
Chinese version of a fondue. Raw ingredients are dunked into a boiling broth which sits in the middle of the table.

Umai
Served in Sarawak, this is the Melanau equivalent of *ceviche* – a salad of raw fish and shallots doused in lime juice and chilli.

Wantan mee
Egg noodles served with shredded chicken, green vegetables and steamed prawn parcels (*wantan*). Can be served dry with soy sauce, or in a clear soup.

Basic Food and Drink Vocabulary

makan food
minum drink
ayam chicken
babi pork
daging beef
biri-biri mutton
kambing goat
ikan fish
sotong squid
udang prawn
udang karang lobster
ketam crab
telur egg
kacang beans (also nuts)
sayur vegetable
sayur saja vegetables only
tahu bean curd
nasi rice
mee noodles
roti bread
pisang banana
kelapa coconut
garam salt
gula sugar
goreng fried
bakar grilled/barbecued
rebus boiled
kukus steamed
air minum drinking water
teh tea
teh tarik sweet, milky cappuccino-style tea
teh susu tea with milk (usually condensed milk)
teh kosong tea served without milk or sugar
kopi-o black coffee
kopi susu white coffee (usually with condensed milk)
bir beer
tuak Iban rice wine
todi palm-tree spirit
jus fruit juice
lassi Indian yoghurt drink, often with added fruit
kelapa muda young coconut (served with a straw)
ais ice
makan pagi breakfast
makan tengahari lunch
makan malam dinner
restoran restaurant
gerai food stall
pasar malam night market
bil bill
menu menu
garfu fork
pisau knife
sudu spoon

hands or passing objects to another person). Always try to avoid using your left hand whenever you eat in a Muslim restaurant.

Perversely, the Muslim fasting month of Ramadan is one of the best times of year for food in Malaysia; after dark, the streets come alive with food stalls to cater for those who have been fasting during daylight hours. The down side, of course, is that

Malay and Indian Muslim restaurants and food stalls will be closed during the day (during Ramadan, Chinese and non-Muslim Indian restaurants do a roaring trade).

Vegetarians can have a hard time in many places, where it seems the term 'vegetarian' does not preclude a little white meat or fish. However, there are a few pleasant surprises for the vegetarian in both Malaysia and Singapore, starting with the south Indian 'banana-leaf' restaurant, where a delicious assortment of mild vegetable curries are served up on a section of (washed) banana leaf. Other places to look out for include vegetarian Chinese restaurants (strict Buddhists are vegetarian), which work wonders with soya and beancurd as meat substitutes. Don't be put off by the menu, which will whet the appetite of the most ardent of carnivores; all the 'chicken' and 'pork' is replaced with convincing soya and bean-curd substitutes. Elsewhere, the safest way to ensure you get a vegetarian meal is ask for '*sayur saja*' (vegetables only). Confusingly, the Malay word *daging* often doubles up as both 'beef' and 'meat' – so if you ask for a dish '*tanpa daging*' (without meat), you may well be served pork.

For prices and tipping etiquette, *see* 'Eating Out' in the Practical A–Z chapter, pp.79–80.

Travel

06

Getting There

By Air from UK & Ireland

There are plenty of nonstop flights from **London** to KLIA (12–13hrs), **Kuala Lumpur**'s slick new airport, with Malaysia Airlines (MAS), British Airways, Royal Brunei Airlines and Qantas offering the most regular services. Fares cost in the region of £500 return, though promotional deals can bring prices down to £400 or less. Malaysia Airlines also run direct services from **Manchester** to Kuala Lumpur, and from London to **Penang** and **Langkawi**. For a cheaper option it might be worth looking into indirect flights (*see* 'Airline Carriers', below) via places like Dubai (Emirates) or Amsterdam (KLM). Alternatively, you could consider flying to Bangkok or Phuket in Thailand, then travelling on to Malaysia overland. There are no direct flights from **Ireland** to Malaysia or Singapore. Passengers will need to transfer in London or elsewhere in Europe.

Getting to **East Malaysia** requires passengers to connect with an internal flight from KL to **Kuching** (around £50 return) or **Kota Kinabalu** (around £100 return). An alternative is to fly direct from London to **Brunei** (with Royal Brunei Airlines) and cross into Sabah or Sarawak from Brunei.

Singapore Airlines, British Airways, Royal Brunei Airlines and Qantas fly regular direct services from London to Changi International Airport in **Singapore**, while dozens of other airlines offer indirect routes to Singapore. Fares cost around £500, though again, promotional deals can bring prices down to £400 or less. Remember that Singapore is connected to West Malaysia by road, rail and air.

By Air from USA & Canada

Malaysia Airlines operates regular services between **New York** and **Kuala Lumpur** via Dubai (around 20hrs total travel time, fares from US$900), and from **Los Angeles** to **Kuala Lumpur** via Tokyo (around 19hrs total, fares

Airline Carriers

UK & Ireland:

British Airways, UK **t** 0870 850 9850, Ireland **t** 1 890 626 747, *www.ba.com.*
Cathay Pacific Airlines, UK **t** (020) 8834 8888, *www.cathaypacific.com.*
Emirates, UK **t** 0870 243 2222, *www.emirates.com.*
Finnair, UK **t** 0870 241 4411, Ireland **t** 1 844 6565, *www.finnair.com.*
Gulf Air, UK **t** 0870 777 1717, *www.gulfairco.com.*
Air India, UK **t** (020) 8560 9996, *www.airindia.com.*
KLM, UK **t** 0870 507 4074, *www.klm.com.*
Malaysia Airlines, UK **t** 0870 607 9090, Ireland **t** 1 676 1561, *www.malaysiaairlines.com.my.*
Qantas, UK **t** 0845 774 7767, Ireland **t** 1 407 3278, *www.qantas.co.uk.*
Royal Brunei Airlines, UK **t** (020) 7584 6660, *www.bruneiair.com.*
Singapore Airlines, UK **t** 0844 800 2380, Ireland 1 671 0722, *www.singaporeair.com.*
Thai Airways, UK **t** 0870 606 0911, *www.thaiair.com.*

USA & Canada:

Asiana Airlines, **t** 1 800 227 4262, *www.flyasiana.com.*
British Airways, **t** 1 800 AIRWAYS, *www.ba.com.*
Air Canada, **t** 1 888 247 2262, *www.aircanada.com.*
Cathay Pacific, **t** 1 800 233 2742, *www.cathay-usa.com.*
Air France, USA **t** 1 800 237 2747, Canada **t** 1 800 667 2747, *www.airfrance.com.*
Japan Airlines, **t** 1 800 525 3663, *www.japanair.com.*
Korean Airlines, **t** 1 800 438 5000, *www.koreanair.com.*
Malaysia Airlines, **t** 1 800 552 9264, *www.malaysiaairlines.com.my.*
Northwest Airlines, **t** 1 800 225 2525, *www.nwa.com.*

from US$800). Singapore Airlines fly regularly from New York to **Singapore** via Frankfurt and from **Los Angeles** and **San Francisco** via Asian cities such as Hong Kong, Tokyo and Seoul. Travel times and prices are similar to Malaysia Airlines' fares to KL.

If you don't mind extending the length of the journey, there are dozens of alternative (and sometimes cheaper) routes via cities around the world. Seoul is the most common transfer hub. Try Korean Airlines and Asiana Airlines. Booking through agents (*see* 'Tour Operators', pp.72–3) is often a way to save a little money on fares. Because Malaysia and Singapore lie on the other side of the world from the US and Canada, many people choose to buy combination (round-the-world) tickets, which allow for stopoffs along the way.

From **Canada**, passengers will need to take connecting flights from places like Taipei, Tokyo and Seoul. Canada Airlines flies daily from Toronto, Montréal and Vancouver to these destinations, while Singapore Airlines flies from three times a week from Vancouver to Singapore via Seoul. Fares start from around CA$2,000.

By Rail

An alternative way of getting to Malaysia (or Singapore) is to fly to Thailand, then cross the border by train. There is a daily 'International Express' service between **Bangkok** and **Butterworth**, with onward connections to **Kuala Lumpur** and **Singapore**. See the official website of the Malaysian Railway (*www.ktmb.com.my*) for up-to-date timetables and fares. It's also possible to cross into Malaysia at the east-coast border town of Rantau Panjang (just north of Kota Bharu): catch the train from Bangkok to Sungai Golok, via Hat Yai.

For a truly memorable experience, travellers with pennies to spare can take the **Eastern & Oriental Express** (UK **t** 0845 077 2222, USA **t** 1 800 674 3689, *www.orient-express.com*) from Bangkok to Singapore. The luxurious journey is stretched over three days, with stops along the way.

Singapore Airlines, USA **t** 1 800 742 3333, Canada **t** 1 800 387 0038, *www.singaporeair.com.*
Thai Airways, **t** 1 800 426 5204, *www.thaiair.com.*
United Airlines, **t** 1 800 538 2929, *www.ual.com.*

Charters & Discounts

UK & Ireland:

Apex Travel, Ireland **t** 1 241 8000, *www.apextravel.ie.*
Ebookers, UK **t** 0800 082 3000, *www.ebookers.co.uk.*
Joe Walsh Tours, Ireland **t** 1 241 0888, *www.joewalshtours.ie.*
Lee's Travel, UK **t** 0870 273 388, *www.leestravel.com.*
STA Travel, UK **t** 08701 630 026, *www.statravel.co.uk.*
Trailfinders, UK **t** 0845 058 5858, *www.trailfinders.com.*
Travel Bag, UK **t** 0800 082 5000, *www.travelbag.co.uk.*

USA & Canada:

Flight Centre, Canada, t 1 888 967 5355, *www.flightcentre.ca.*
High Adventure Travel, USA t 1 877 247 8735, *www.airtreks.com.*
STA Travel, USA t 1 800 781 4040, *www.statravel.com.*
Travel Cuts, Canada t 1 866 246 9762, *www.travelcuts.com.*

Websites

www.bargainholidays.com
www.cheapflights.co.uk
www.cheapflights.com
www.ebookers.com
www.expedia.co.uk
www.expedia.com
www.flightsdirect.com
www.lastminute.com
www.priceline.com
www.responsibletravel.com
www.skydeals.co.uk
www.travelocity.com

By Road

There are various border crossings between **Thailand** and Malaysia, though by far the easiest route is to catch a bus from Hat Yai to Georgetown via the border crossing at Bukit Kayu Hitam. If you want to head straight to Malaysia's east coast, then cross the border on foot at Sungai Golok (accessible by bus or train) and catch a bus or taxi from the Malaysian border town of Rantau Panjang to Kota Bharu.

In effect, **Singapore** is part of the Malaysian bus network, so arrival in Singapore from Malaysia is a straightforward procedure by road. With the recent opening of the 'Second Link', Singapore now has two land-bridge connections with Malaysia. Most people still cross into Singapore on the Causeway, which links the Malaysian city of Johor Bahru with the north end of Singapore. The longer 'Second Link' connects the west side of Singapore with Geylang Patah, a route which saves time if you're heading up the west coast of Malaysia.

The most straightforward entry point from **Indonesia** is via the daily bus service from Pontianak (in Kalimantan) to Kuching (capital of Sarawak in Malaysian Borneo).

There are daily buses between Bandar Seri Begawan, in **Brunei**, and Miri, in Sarawak.

By Sea

A number of daily ferry services connect Satun in southern **Thailand** with the north Malaysian town of Kuala Perlis and the Langkawi archipelago. In peak season, and at a price, Langkawi is also accessible from Phuket.

The most plied sea route between **Indonesia** and Malaysia links Medan (north Sumatra) with Penang; there are daily services. There is also a ferry connection between Dumai (Sumatra) and Melaka. In East Malaysia, meanwhile, the most popular entry point from Indonesia is the hour-long ferry service from Nunakan to Tawau in Sabah.

Meanwhile, speed ferries ply the short hop between Bandar Seri Begawan, in Brunei, and Limbang, in Sarawak.

Entry Formalities

Citizens of the UK, Ireland, USA, Canada, Australia and New Zealand do not need a visa to enter Malaysia or Singapore. In Peninsular Malaysia, new arrivals have their passports stamped, entitling them to a three-month stay. If you want to stay on longer than three months, simply stop by at one of the Immigration Department offices situated in all major towns (contact the local tourist information centre for addresses and opening times). Depending on queues, this can involve a lot of waiting around, in which case it might be simpler to pop across the border to Singapore: on re-entering Malaysia, you'll be entitled to three more months.

Annoyingly, the East Malaysian states of Sarawak and Sabah have their own separate immigration procedures, with passport stamps allowing for a 30-day visit. Again, visit any Immigration Department office in either state if you want to extend your stay for a further 30 days. Remember that, in Sarawak, permits are required to visit certain parts of the state (see relevant text for details).

New arrivals to Singapore are granted a month's stay (some people, strangely, are given two weeks, though this can usually be extended to a month if you ask). For extensions beyond a month, apply to the Immigration Department. Again, it is probably easier to hop across the causeway to Johor Bahru and get a fresh stamp in your passport when you return later in the day.

Visitors to Brunei from the UK and New Zealand are granted 30 days without a visa. Australians are issued visas on arrival for visits not exceeding 14 days. US citizens are allowed three months. Citizens of Ireland and Canada must apply for a visa before arrival.

For more information contact the relevant embassy/consulate:

Malaysian Embassies & Consulates

Australia: 7 Perth Avenue, Yarralumla, Canberra, ACT 2600, **t** 02 6273 1543.

Canada: 60 Boteler Street, Ottawa ON K1N 8YZ, **t** 613 241 5182.

Ireland: Level 3A-5A, Shelbourne House, Shelbourne Road, Ballsbridge, Dublin 4, **t** 01 667 7280.

New Zealand: 10 Washington Avenue, Brooklyn, Wellington, **t** 644 385 2439.

UK: 45-46 Belgrave Square, London SW1X 8QT, **t** (020) 7235 8033.

USA: 3516 International Court NW, Washington DC 20008, **t** 202 572 9700.

Singaporean Embassies & Consulates

Australia: 17 Forster Crescent, Yarralumla, Canberra ACT 2600, **t** 02 6273 3944.

Canada: Mission of Singapore to the UN, 231 East 51st Street, New York, NY 10022, **t** 1 212 826 0840 (accredited to Canada).

Ireland: 9 Wilton Crescent, Belgravia, London SW1X 8SP, **t** (020) 7235 8315 (accredited to Ireland).

New Zealand: 17 Kabul Street, Khandallah, Wellington, **t** 04 470 0850.

UK: 9 Wilton Crescent, Belgravia, London SW1X 8SP, **t** 020 7235 8315.

USA: 3501 International Place NW, Washington DC 20008, **t** 202 537 3100.

Bruneian Embassies & Consulates

Australia: 10 Beale Crescent, Deakin, Canberra, ACT 2606, **t** 02 6285 4500

Canada: High Commission of Brunei Darussalam, 395 Laurier Avenue East, Ottawa, ON K1N 6R4, **t** 613 234 5656.

UK: High Commission of Brunei Darussalam, 19-20 Belgrave Square, London SW1X 8PG, **t** (020) 7581 0521.

USA: Permanent Representative of Brunei Darussalam to the United Nations, 771 United Nations Plaza, New York, NY 10017, **t** 212 697 3465.

Getting Around

By Air

Malaysia has a well-developed domestic air network, with cheap connections between all the major towns (and a number of the minor ones too). The main hub, of course, is Kuala Lumpur, and most services are routed via the capital. **Malaysia Airlines** (MAS; *www.malaysia airlines.com.my*) offers the most services, though Air Asia (*see* below) is fast catching up. As well as all the major towns, MAS flies 18-seater Twin Otters to remote destinations in East Malaysia, including Bario, Kapit and Mulu.

The low-cost carrier **Air Asia** (*www.airasia.com*) has expanded its network to link most major Malaysian towns with Kuala Lumpur. In West Malaysia, there are services from KL to Penang, Langkawi, Alor Setar, Kota Bharu, Kuala Terengganu, Johor Bahru and Singapore. Air Asia also flies from KL to Kuching, Sibu, Bintulu, Miri, Pulau Labuan, Kota Kinabalu, Sandakan and Tawau (all in East Malaysia), and from Johor Bahru to Kota Bharu and Kota Kinabalu.

The get-away islands of Pulau Tioman, Pulau Redang and Pulau Pangkor are accessible with **Berjaya Air** (*www.berjaya-air.com*), a tiny carrier which flies 50-seater Dash 7 aircraft out of Kuala Lumpur and Singapore.

At the time of writing, fares for one-way flights start from a remarkable RM40 (KL to Penang with Air Asia) and rise to around RM450 (KL to Kota Kinabalu with MAS). Competition from Air Asia is helping to bring down prices across the board. Families, and those travelling in groups of three or more, are entitled to discounts on all MAS flights: one fare is paid in full and the rest are eligible for a 25% discount.

By Rail

Malaysia's first railway sleepers were laid back in 1884, and the rail system has been an important form of public transport ever since (though cheap flights are now making many of the longer routes redundant). In West Malaysia, the peninsula is dissected by two lines, one running up the west coast from its starting point in Singapore to the Malaysia border town of Padang Besar, another cutting north across the interior towards Kota Bharu.

Trains are operated by Keretapi Tanah Melayu (KTMB; enquiries **t** 03 2267 1200, Singapore **t** 02 6222 5165, *www.ktmb.com.my*). Free timetables are available at every station, and online. The trains are generally very comfortable, with tickets divided into three classes (at the time of writing a ticket from Kuala Lumpur to Singapore costs RM19 for 3rd class, RM34 for 2nd class and RM68 for 1st class). Express trains, which run only on the west-coast line and avoid many of the smaller

Tour Operators

(For local tour operators, see individual chapters.)

UK & Ireland:

The Adventure Company, 15 Turk Street, Alton, Hampshire GU34 1AG, **t** 0870 794 1009, *www.adventurecompany.co.uk*. Offers a two-week guided tour of Sarawak and Sabah, with a trek up Mount Kinabalu.

Asiaworld, Forrester House, St Peters Street, St Albans AL1 3LW, **t** 0870 78 77 78 77, *www.jetlife.co.uk*. Package tours and tailor-made trips.

Bales Tours, Bales House, Junction Road, Dorking, Surrey RH4 3HL, **t** 0870 752 0780, *www.balesworldwide.com*. Guided tours of Sarawak and Sabah, with trips into the interior and an emphasis on responsible tourism.

Discovery Initiatives, The Travel House, 51 Castle Street, Cirencester, Gloucestershire GL7 1QD, **t** (01285) 643 333, *www.discoveryinitiatives.com*. Organizes orang-utan conservation holidays in Borneo.

Exodus Travels, Grange Mills, Weir Road, London SW12 0NE, **t** 0870 240 5550, *www.exodus.co.uk*. Leads the way with responsible tourism (winner of 2004 Responsible Tourism Awards), with a focus on adventure holidays and interaction with host communities.

Explore Worldwide, 1 Frederick Street, Aldershot, Hants GU11 1LQ, **t** 0870 333 4001, *www.exploreworldwide.co.uk*. Specializes is small-group guided tours with general themes (on foot, by bike, family tours etc.).

Gecko Travel, 94 Old Manor Way, Portsmouth PO6 2NL, **t** (023) 9225 8859, *www.geckotravel.com*. Southeast Asia specialists, with an overland Bangkok to Kuala Lumpur tour and a coast-to-coast tour in Malaysia, taking in Penang, interior rainforests, tribal peoples and the Perhentian islands.

Golden Days in Malaysia, 10 Barley Mow Passage, London W4 4PH, **t** 0800 783 7321, *www.goldendays.co.uk*. Specialist tour operator with a dozen separate packages to Malaysia.

The Imaginative Traveller, 1 Betts Avenue, Martlesham Heath, Suffolk, IP5 7RH, **t** 0800 316 2717, *www.imaginative-traveller.com*. Tour-led holidays with a focus on interaction with local cultures.

Intrepid Travel UK, Unit 202, Buspace Studios, Conlan Street, London W10 5AP, **t** (020) 8960 6333, *www.intrepidtravel.com*. Run dozens of themed tours covering most corners of Peninsular Malaysia, Singapore and East Malaysia.

stations, are considerably faster than the local trains which stop at every station.

The interior line, known commonly as the 'Jungle Railway' (*see* p.280), provides passengers with a glimpse of some of West Malaysia's more remote regions. The single line from Singapore splits at Gemas, from where the jungle railway cuts north into the mountainous interior, skirting the Taman Negara (National Park) via Kuala Lipis and winding down towards Tumpat, near Kota Bharu.

At the other end of the scale is the service run by the Eastern & Oriental Express (Singapore **t** (65) 6392 3500, UK **t** 0845 077 2222, USA **t** 1 800 674 3689, *www.orient-express.com*), which runs along the west-coast line between Singapore and Bangkok. The journey is spread over three days with stops along the way and costs in the region of RM7,000 (£1,000/US$1,800).

In East Malaysia, the rail system is limited to a single narrow-gauge line in Sabah, which runs the 50km between Tanjung Aru (just south of Kota Kinabalu) and Tenom in the interior. It chugs along at jogging pace and cuts through the Padas Gorge. Despite the slow pace, the line remains a vital mode of transport for the few inhabitants of the region (and for tourists on whitewater-rafting trips down the Sungai Padas).

By Road

Peninsular Malaysia's road network is excellent, by Asian standards, and it is improving as every year goes by. The six-lane **North-South Highway** (also known as the

Kuoni, Kuoni House, Dorking, Surrey RH5 4AZ, **t** (01306) 740 5000, *www.kuoni.co.uk*. This major operator offers a range of different tours taking in Peninsular Malaysia, Singapore and East Malaysia.

Magic of the Orient, 14 Frederick Place, Clifton, Bristol BS8 1AS, **t** (0117) 311 6050, *www.magicoftheorient.com*. Far East specialists, with some off-the-beaten-track destinations and a good range of prices.

Peregrine Adventures UK, First Floor, 8 Clerewater Place, Lower Way, Thatcham, Berkshire RG19 3RF, **t** (01635) 872 300, *www.peregrineadventures.co.uk*. Wildlife tours of Sabah and Sarawak. Also runs a subsidiary called Gecko's Grassroots Adventures for the budget/backpacker market.

USA & Canada:

Abercrombie & Kent, 1520 Kensington Road, Suite 212, Oak Brook, Illinois 60523-2156, **t** 1 800 554 7016, *www.abercrombiekent.com*. Luxury tour operator who run occasional trips to Malaysia.

Asian Affair Holidays, 360 North Sepulveda Blvd, Suite 3008, El Segundo, CA 90245, **t** 1 800 742 3133, *www.asianaffairholidays.com*. Offer packages which combine Singapore with other destinations in Asia. In association with Singapore Airlines.

Asian Pacific Adventures, 6065 Calvin Avenue, Tarzana, CA 91356, **t** 1 800 825 1680, *www.asianpacificadventures.com*. Offer adventure and wildlife tours of Sarawak, Sabah and the Taman Negara in Peninsular Malaysia.

Earthwatch, 3 Clock Tower Place, Suite 100, Box 75, Maynard, MA 01754, **t** (USA/Canada) 1 800 776 0188, *www.earthwatch.org*. Run conservation 'expeditions' around the world. In Malaysia, projects include the conservation of green turtles off the east coast of the peninsula, and the conservation of bats in the interior.

iExplore, 954 W. Washington Blvd, Suite 3W, Chicago, IL 60607, **t** 1 800 4397 5673, *www.iexplore.com*. In association with National Geographic, and with a focus on adventure travel.

Malaysia Travel, P.O. Box 3427, Carbondale, IL 62902-3427, **t** 618 529 8033, *www.emalaysia travel.com*. In association with Malaysia Airlines (MAS), with a City-Jungle-Beach package, among others.

Pacific Holidays, 12 West 32nd Street, 6th Floor, New York, NY 10001, **t** 212 629 3888, *www.pacificholidaysinc.com*. Run a wide range of tours, including river safaris in Sarawak and two-week tours of the Peninsular Malaysia.

Lebuhraya) runs the length of the country along the west coast, from Johor Bahru as far as Bukit Kayu Hitam on the Thai border. Because of toll charges the highway is generally free of traffic. The **East-West Highway**, meanwhile, cuts across the mountainous north section of the peninsula, linking the two coasts. A decent single-lane coastal road (**Route 3**) runs the length of the east coast, while there is an ever-expanding network of roads into the interior.

In **Malaysian Borneo**, the main mode of transport remains riverboat; the road network is yet to penetrate the interior to any great extent, though there is a servicable coastal road in Sarawak, Sabah and Brunei. As one would expect, **Singapore**'s roads are impeccable, though the comprehensive public transport system makes driving completely unnecessary.

The simplest way to get about Peninsular Malaysia is **by bus**. Every town has a bustling bus station, where dozens of private coach companies vie for customers. **Transnasional** (*www.nadi.com.my*) has the largest fleet of express coaches, with more than 1500 vehicles on the go at a time. Simply shop around at the ticket booths for the route/price that suits you best. Prices are very reasonable, with no journey costing more than a few dozen ringgit. Bear in mind, though, that there are often ludicrously cheap domestic flights on offer (*see* above).

In Sarawak,Sabah and Brunei, coaches ply the coastal highways, though minibuses are equally popular (and faster). Many of East Malaysia's remote destinations are only accessible by riverboat or by 4WDs which navigate the maze of logging tracks.

In most Malaysian towns, bus stations also serve as **long-distance taxi** ranks, where it is possible to negotiate reasonable fares to virtually any destination.

Car hire is an attractive option on Peninsular Malaysia; rates start at around RM60/day, cars on offer are reliable and roads are good. Petrol prices hover around the RM1.80/litre mark. Remember to drive on the left-hand side of the road. All the main international car rental agencies operate in Malaysia (*see* below for contact information). There are also a number of reputable local agencies, including Hawk Rent-a-Car (**t** 03 2164 6488/03 2164 6455, *www.hawkrentacar.com.my*). In certain towns and cities, it is also possible to hire **motorbikes**. Georgetown (Penang) and Langkawi have plenty of informal agencies aimed at tourists.

Major car-hire agencies:

Avis, UK **t** 08700 100 287, *www.avis.co.uk*; Ireland **t** 01 605 7500, *www.avis.ie*; USA **t** 1 800 230 4898, *www.avis.com*; Canada, **t** 1 800 272 5871, *www.avis.com*.

Hertz, UK **t** 0870 844 8844, *www.hertz.co.uk*; Ireland, **t** 01 676 7476, *www.hertz.ie*; USA **t** 1 800 654 3001, *www.hertz.com*; Canada, **t** 1 800 263 0600, *www.hertz.com*.

Local Transport

Local transport varies in standard from place to place; details are given in the respective chapters. With the exception of Singapore and Kuala Lumpur – both of which have sophisticated public transport systems, combining state-of-the-art light rail services with efficient bus services – local transport is limited to local buses, minibuses, taxis and, in some places, trishaws.

Practical A–Z

07

Calendar of Events

January–February

Chinese New Year: Massive festivities, with parades, lion dances, floats, firecrackers and street food. Families hold open house, *ang pao* (red envelopes containing money) are given as gifts to children, and businesses traditionally settle their debts. Everywhere, people wish one another '*Gong Xi Fa Cai!*'. The celebrations last two weeks and finish with Chap Goh Meh.

Thaipusam: The biggest festival on the Hindu calendar, Thaipusam celebrates the birthday of Lord Subramanian and takes place in late January or early February. *Kavadi*-carriers, their skin pierced through with hooks and spikes, parade through the streets before statues of Lord Subramanian. The biggest celebrations take place at the Batu Caves, where a million devotees gather (*see* p.115).

Hari Raya Aidiladha: This celebration, which takes place in the 12th month of the Muslim calendar, marks the end of the annual pilgrimage to Mecca. Goats and cattle are slaughtered for distribution to the needy.

Pongal: The Tamil harvest festival, with food offerings at temples across Malaysia and Singapore. Marks the beginning of the Hindu month of Thai (mid-January).

Federal Territory Day: Celebration for Malaysia's three independent federal territories – Kuala Lumpur, Putrajaya and Labuan – with fireworks, cultural shows and base jumps from the Menara Tower in KL.

Le Tour de Langkawi: This cycle race takes place each year, beginning in Langkawi and weaving a route across the peninsula to finish in Kuala Lumpur (2 weeks in February).

Johor International Kite Festival: On Bukit Layang-Layang (Kite Hill), 30km from Johor Bahru, kite enthusiasts showcase their skills and craftmanship and compete for various prizes. Kite-making is an ancient craft of the Malays, who traditionally flew their kites after the harvest. Mid-February.

National Day Celebrations: Brunei's celebration of independence at the Hassanal Bolkiah National Stadium (23 February).

March–May

Malaysian Grand Prix: Second race of the Formula One season, held in March on the steaming tarmac of Sepang, near Kuala Lumpur.

Easter: Celebrated by Christian communities across Malaysia and Singapore, with the biggest ceremonies taking place in Melaka and predominantly Christian East Malaysia.

Chaitra Vishu: Hindu New Year (mid-April), with festivities and cash gifts given to children.

Wesak Day: Celebration of the Buddha's birthday on the May full moon. This is the major event of the Buddhist calendar.

Children

Singapore (and to a lesser extent Malaysia and Brunei) is a great destination if you have kids in tow. And not least because of differing cultural attitudes towards children. At food stalls, even late in the evening, families often come out en masse for a meal or a snack. Tolerance is the norm, and there are few places in either country where the presence of a child warrants a frown. Singapore is packed full of kids' attractions, the transport system is flawless, and children's facilities are excellent. Though kids' attractions in Malaysia are less widespread, and the facilities less developed, Malaysia remains one of the better-equipped Asian countries for a family holiday. Brunei is similarly well-equipped, and there's even a theme park complete with roller coasters.

Be prepared, however, for plenty of friendly attention, particularly if you are travelling with younger children. Bear in mind, too, that only the top-end hotels are likely to provide cots as standard. Other places will probably be able to find a cot for you with a bit of notice. All restaurants and coffee shops generally provide highchairs. Fresh cow's milk is hard to come by in Malaysia. Supermarkets in the bigger cities usually sell it, but milk elsewhere will be UHT. Nappies and formula milk are widely available.

Prayers, the exchanging of gifts and the symbolic release of captive animals (birds and turtles mainly) take place on this day.

Colours of Malaysia: A recently conceived, month-long celebration of Malaysia's blend of cultures; exhibitions, performing arts, crafts and food stalls involving participants from each of the nation's 13 states.

Penang International Floral Festival: Large flower festival held in May (sometimes June) at Penang's Botanical Gardens, which were first established by the British back in 1884.

Sabah Fest: A celebration of Sabah's cultural diversity, with cultural shows, handicrafts and musical performances in Kota Kinabalu. End of May.

Royal Brunei Armed Forces Day: Celebrates the formation of the Royal Brunei Armed Forces, with military parades and displays. 31st May.

June–August

Gawai Dayak: The biggest festival across Sarawak, when the indigenous population traditionally celebrate the end of the rice harvest. City dwellers head upriver to the ancestral longhouses for days of partying fuelled by rice wine. A great time to visit a longhouse (you'll be swept along in the festivities). 1st and 2nd June.

Penang International Dragon Boat Festival: A popular spectacle with tourists, the June festival involves races between local teams in beautifully carved traditional boats. Dragon boat races have their origins centuries ago in China. The first Penang Dragon Boat Festival was held in 1979.

Festa de San Pedro: This festival, held in late June, honours the patron saint of the fishing community. It centres on the Portuguese-Eurasian community of the Pasir Ujong area of Melaka. Fishing boats are decorated for the occasion, songs are sung in the local dialect and fiery street food is dished up to allcomers.

Rainforest World Music Festival: Held each year in the Sarawak Cultural Village near Kuching (early June most years), combining workshops, talks and evening performances of 'ethnic' music by indigenous peoples from round the world.

His Majesty the Sultan's Birthday: The Sultan of Brunei honours his birthday with a national holiday, a royal address, an investiture ceremony and public festivities. 15th July.

Hungry Ghost Festival: The Chinese community across Malaysia celebrate the Hungry Ghost Festival during the August full moon, when the hungry spirits of dead ancestors are said to return to earth to feast on offerings (cakes, noodles, sweetmeats) which are left about the streets. Chinese operas and puppet shows are also performed. Penang and Singapore are the best places to watch the festivities.

Climate and When to Go

The climate in Malaysia, Brunei and Singapore is hot and humid year-round (Singapore sits just above the equator). Lowland daytime temperatures hover around the 30°C (86°F) mark, while night-time temperatures rarely drop below 22°C (70°F). Seasonal variations are dictated by the pattern of the monsoon rains.

Generally speaking, the rains are too erratic to rule out any particular time of year (with the exception of the east-coast islands; *see* below). On the west coast of Peninsular Malaysia, there are two supposed monsoon seasons – March to April and October to November – though the levels of rainfall are only marginally higher during these months than at other times of year (so there's no need to avoid the west coast during these periods). Even during the monsoon, the rains tend to come in sharp bursts, almost invariably during the afternoon, with sunshine for the rest of the day. The rains bring temporary relief from the heat and for this reason are the favoured seasons among locals.

On the east coast and in the interior of Peninsular Malaysia, it is a different story. The monsoon hits hard from November to mid-February, churning up the seas and making many of the island destinations inaccessible (most of the hotels and ferry services close down for these months). Similarly, inland destinations such as the Taman Negara, close to the public for the worst of the monsoon. If you don't have plans to head out to the

Singapore National Day: Celebration of Singapore's independence with a big show at the National Stadium. 9th August.

Malaysia National Day: Parades in Malaysia's major cities mark the anniversary of the nation's independence. 31st August.

September–December

Kelantan Cultural Festival: This week-long festival in September serves as a showcase for Malay culture (95 per cent of Kelantan's population is Malay). Included are performances of *wayang kulit* (shadow-puppet plays) and *silat* (the Malay martial art), along with top-spinning, kite-flying and musical contests. A wide variety of craftspeople display their skills too.

Mount Kinabalu International Climbathon: One of the world's most arduous races, with athletes scrambling to the summit of Mount Kinabalu (4100m) in Sabah, then down again, in just three hours (mere mortals need two full days for the ascent and descent). Early October.

Navaratri: Festival of 'Nine Nights' dedicated to, among others, the universal mother Durga, with rituals, fasting and dance.

Ramadan: The ninth month of the Muslim calendar, during which Muslims fast through the daylight hours. Ironically, this is often the best time of year to sample Malay food – after sundown, the faithful flock to food stalls to break their fast. Ramadan starts around early September (though it follows the Islamic calendar, and so moves back a little each year).

Hari Raya Puasa: This festival marks the end of Ramadan, with families getting together to celebrate with a feast. Many return to their kampungs and take a week or so off work.

Deepavali: A major Hindu festival, commonly called the Festival of Lights, which celebrates the victory of light over dark (Rama's victory over the demon king Ravana). Oil lamps are lit and placed outside homes which are scrubbed clean for the occasion, while temples are decorated with garlands and offerings of fruit and coconut milk. October.

Kusu Island Pilgrimage: Tens of thousands catch boats across to Kusu Island, off Singapore, to pray for prosperity and fertility at the Tua Pekong Temple. Late October/ early November.

Zoukout: Southeast Asia's biggest dance-music festival, held outdoors and attended by tens of thousands, with big-name DJs. (Early December.)

Christmas in the Tropics: Singapore has latched on to the Christmas-time commercial bandwagon with a Christmas shopping extravaganza which begins in mid-November. Major cities in Malaysia also decorate their shopping streets for Christmas.

islands, however, this can still be a pleasant time to visit the east-coast mainland; you'll probably be the only tourists around and, though the thunderstorms may be frequent, there will be plenty of sunshine too.

Rainfall in Borneo is higher than on the peninsula. The wettest season falls between October and March, particularly in Sarawak, which receives more rainfall than any other state. Places that are only accessible by sea (such as the Tanjung Datu National Park) are closed during the rainy season.

Crime and the Police

Levels of recorded crime in Malaysia compare favourably with other Asian countries. Theft and violent crime, though present, are relatively rare. Statistically, you're safer in Kuala Lumpur than in London, for example. That said, as a tourist you remain vulnerable and it is always a good idea to take the necessary precautions to look after your valuables.

Police stations are marked on all maps of cities and towns in Malaysia. If you do need to report a crime, don't expect too much sympathy. The police tend to be fairly laid-back and aloof when it comes to dealing with crime against tourists. Remember that drugs charges carry high penalties in Malaysia and Singapore; in worst-case-scenarios, convictions carry the death penalty.

Singapore is famous for its long list of finable public offences. Smoking in public places, eating on the MRT, and littering (anywhere) all carry heavy fines. However, it is a popular misconception that chewing gum is illegal in Singapore. It is *selling* gum which has long been outlawed. And in 2004 even that ban was lifted – though vendors (exclusively pharmacists selling it under the umbrella of dental hygiene) can only sell gum to registered chewers.

Disabled Travellers

Malaysia is not very well equipped for disabled travellers. None of the public transport is adapted to accommodate wheelchairs, and pavements are either uneven or non-existent. Even cutting-edge Kuala Lumpur, which likes to see itself as a progressive city, has a long way to go when it comes to accessibility. Most of the top-end hotels in the tourist resorts and big cities do have good access (though this is not the case with mid-range and budget hotels). The major carriers that fly to Malaysia (British Airways, KLM, Qantas, Malaysia Airlines) all provide aisle wheelchairs and adapted toilets.

Though not up to the standards of major Western cities, **Singapore** is leaps and bounds better than Malaysia in terms of accessibility. Most hotels make provision for disabled guests, pedestrian crossings bleep, and there are specialist taxi cabs for accommodating wheelchairs (contact TIBS Cabs, **t** +65 6555 8888, plus internet booking service *www.etaxis.com.sg*). The free publication *Access Singapore* provides detailed information about amenities for the disabled across the city (published by the National Council of Social Service, 01-02 NCSS Centre, 170 Ghim Moh Road, Singapore 279621, **t** +65 6210 2500, *www.ncss.org.sg*).

Specialist Organizations:

UK & Ireland:

RADAR (Royal Association for Disability and Rehabilitation), 12 City Forum, 250 City Road, London EC1V 8AF, **t** (020) 7250 3222, *www.radar.org.uk*. A good range of information about travelling abroad. RADAR have also launched a website for holiday accommodation : *www.radarsearch.org*.

Holiday Care Service, 7th Floor, Sunley House, 4 Bedford Park, Croydon, Surrey CR0 2AP, **t** 0845 124 9971, *www.holidaycare.org.uk*. Dedicated to all aspects of travel for disabled people, with a long list of publications available.

Irish Wheelchair Association, Aras Chuchulainn, Blackheath Drive, Contarf, Dublin 3, **t** (01) 818 6400, *www.iwa.ie*. Ireland's national organization for those with limited mobility.

USA & Canada

Alternative Leisure Company, 165 Middlesex Turnpike, Suite 206, Bedford, MA 01730, **t** 718 275 0023, *www.alctrips.com*. Organizes vacations abroad for disabled people.

Mobility International USA (MIUSA), PO Box 10767, Eugene, OR 97440, **t** 541 343 1284, *www.miusa.org*. Information about international exchange and development schemes overseas for disabled people.

SATH (Society for Accessible Travel & Hospitality), 347 Fifth Ave, Suite 610, New York, NY 10016, **t** 212 447 7284, *www.sath.org*. Provides travel and access information, plus links to other resources.

Websites

Access Able, *www.access-able.com*. Worldwide access resource, with destination information.

Disability Online, *www.disabilityonline.com*. An information directory with thousands of links (though not all are up-to-date).

Disability World Web-Zine, *www.disabilityworld.com*. Bi-monthy 'web-zine' for international disability news and views.

Emerging Horizons, *www.emerginghorizons.com*. Online travel newsletter for people with disabilities.

Global Access, *www.geocities.com*.

Wheels Up!, *www.wheelsup.com*. Wheelchair travel specialists, with discount air fares and specialist tours.

Eating Out

Eating out is one of the great pleasures of visiting Malaysia, Singapore and Brunei, both of which offer up an enormous variety of cuisines at cheap prices. Chinese, Malay and

Restaurant Price Categories

Malaysia

Price categories for a full meal for one (excluding alcohol):

Expensive	RM50+
Moderate	RM12–50
Inexpensive	under RM12

Brunei

Price categories for a full meal for one (excluding alcohol):

Expensive	B$25+
Moderate	B$12–25
Inexpensive	under B$12

Singapore

Price categories for a full meal for one (excluding alcohol):

Expensive	S$50+
Moderate	S$20–50
Inexpensive	under S$20

Indian food is available just about everywhere, while the bigger towns and cities have plenty of international options, from European and Middle Eastern to Japanese and Indochinese.

In Malaysia a simple meal at a food stall or *kedai kopi* (coffee shop) can be bought for little more than the equivalent of GB£1 or US$2. In Singapore and Brunei it will cost about double this. Be sure to have small change if you are eating a cheap meal; it will not go down well if you pay for your RM5 noodle dish with a RM100 note.

Tipping is not expected at informal restaurants and food stalls. Staff at top-end restaurants in the bigger cities might be hoping for a tip, but even here, tipping is not common practice; all bills include service charges and government taxes.

See the 'Food and Drink' chapter for an in-depth look at eating out in Malaysia and Singapore, including a food glossary.

Embassies and Consulates

Malaysia

British High Commission, 185 Jalan Ampang, 50450 Kuala Lumpur, **t** 03 2170 2345, *www.britain.org.my*. Open Mon–Fri 8.30–12.30 (phone line open Mon–Fri 8.30–4.30).

Embassy of Ireland, The Amp Walk, 218 Jalan Ampang, 50450 Kuala Lumour, **t** 03 2161 2963, *ireland@po.jaing.my*.

American Embassy, 376 Jalan Tun Razak, Kuala Lumpur, **t** 03 2168 5000, *http://malaysia.usembassy.gov*. Open Mon–Fri 7.45–4.30.

Canadian High Commission, 17th Floor, Menara Tan & Tan, 207 Jalan Tun Razak, 50400 Kuala Lumpur, **t** 03 2718 3333, *klmpr-td@dfait-maeci.gc.ca*.

Brunei:

Australian High Commission, 4th Floor, Teck Guan Plaza, Jalan Sultan, **t** 222 9435.

British High Commission, Level 2, Block D, Yayasan Complex, **t** 222 2231, *brithc@brunet.bn*.

Canadian High Commission, 5th Floor, 1 Jalan McArthur, **t** 222 0043.

US Embassy, 3rd Floor, Teck Guan Plaza, Jalan Sultan, **t** 222 9670.

Singapore:

Australian High Commission, 25 Napier Road, **t** 6836 4100.

British High Commission, 100 Tanglin Road, **t** 6424 4270.

Canadian High Commission, 1400 Fuji Xerox Towers, 80 Anson Road, **t** 6325 3200.

US Embassy, 27 Napier Road, **t** 6476 9100.

Festivals and Events

With such a broad ethnic mix, Malaysia has no less than 16 public holidays each year, and many more holidays particular to each individual state. All the major Muslim, Buddhist and Hindu religious festivals are observed, so that it is rare for a month to go by without festivities of some sort taking place. The religious festivals all follow their respective lunar calendars, so each year their dates shift backwards a little.

The biggest festivals are Chinese New Year (which stretches over a two week period); Deepavali and Thaipusam (celebrated by Hindus, the latter in spectacular fashion); and the collective events surrounding Ramadan, a month when Muslims fast during daylight hours. Many of these festivals and celebrations make for wonderful spectacles, though bear in mind that accommodation may get fully booked on these dates. Access roads, too, are often gridlocked prior to major events.

Cultural performances (music, dance, handicraft demonstrations) are the mainstay of those holidays conceived since independence, many of which celebrate the plurality of Malaysian and Singaporean society.

For a detailed list of major events, and their approximate dates, *see* 'Calendar of Events', pp.76–8. For exact dates for any given year, contact the tourist board, or visit the Tourism Malaysia website (*www.tourism.gov.my*).

Health and Emergencies

Officially, no **inoculations** are required for visiting Malaysia, Singapore or Brunei, though it is wise to update your tetanus, hepatitis A, polio and typhoid inoculations before travelling. If you have recently visited South America or Africa, you should bring proof of yellow fever vaccination (the authorities reserve the right to ask for this). If you want to be extra cautious (and can afford to spend the extra money), you may want to look into vaccinations for rabies and Japanese B encephalitis. **Health insurance**, of course, is vital in case of emergency.

The major towns and cities are well developed, with good medical facilities and low risk of contracting disease. Private clinics with English-speaking doctors are widespread. Visitors spending long periods of time in Malaysia, and those who visit remote areas off the tourist trail, will find themselves more at risk. Though protection against disease in the tropics is not something to be taken lightly, it is worth bearing in mind that illnesses among travellers (though relatively common) are rarely serious or life-threatening.

For up-to-date information about health hazards, visit your GP or book an appointment at a specialist travel clinic (the latter can provide on-the-spot inoculations too). In the UK, the British Airways Travel Clinic provides a speedy and thorough service (213 Piccadilly, London W1J 9HQ, **t** 0845 600 2236, walk-in service Mon–Fri 9.30–5.30, Sat 10–4). The World Health Organisation (WHO) website, *www.who.int*, is an excellent resource, with up-to the-minute information on travel health and disease outbreaks such as SARS.

It is important that visitors to Malaysia seek advice about precautions against **malaria**. Most people will find that there is little or no threat: malaria has been wiped out in developed parts of the country. However, in some remote areas, and in parts of East Malaysia, malaria is still present. This should by no means put people off visiting these areas (the risks of contracting the disease remain low) but be sure to take medical advice. For those visiting East Malaysia, doctors are likely to advise malaria tablets, though these are never one hundred per cent effective and, over periods of time, can carry side effects. The most reliable way to protect yourself is by deterring the mosquitos from biting you in the first place: bring plenty of repellent, use mosquito nets and smoke rings (the latter are widely available in Malaysia). Such precautions are are also preventative measures against dengue fever and other rarer mosquito-borne diseases.

The strength of the tropical sun can pose problems to those arriving from temperate climates. Allow a day or so to adjust and do as the locals do: avoid the **heat** of the midday sun. You will (and should) find yourself drinking large volumes of liquid to replace lost fluids and keep yourself hydrated. Hats, sunglasses and sunscreen are essential items.

Take precautions against **stomach complaints** by eating only freshly cooked food (to be safe, avoid raw vegetables and salads). Stick to unpeeled fruit and avoid tap water in rural areas (tap water in the cities meets international standards). Contrary to popular belief, hawker stalls are among the safest places to eat; ingredients are fresh and cooked on the spot.

In the rare event of a poisonous **snakebite**, apply a tourniquet to the affected limb and remain calm and immobile (rushing off in search of help will only pump the venom round the blood stream). Try to identify the snake, so that doctors can administer the correct antidote. Remember that the vast proportion of snakes are not venomous.

Jellyfish stings are more common; applying vinegar to the rash will ease the pain and counteract the poison. Avoid walking on the sea bed to prevent wounds from sharp coral and sea urchins, both of which are liable to cause infection.

Emergency telephone numbers:

Malaysia

Ambulance and Police: **t** 999
Fire: **t** 994

Brunei

Ambulance: **t** 991
Police: **t** 993
Fire: **t** 995

Singapore

Ambulance and Fire: **t** 995
Police: **t** 999

Maps and Publications

Whether you are looking for a decent road map, a city map or a topographical map of the country, there are plenty available in Kuala Lumpur and Singapore. (Try the excellent Kinokuniya bookstore, which has branches in both cities: at the foot of KL's Petronas Towers, Level 4, Suria KLCC, **t** 03 2164 8133; on Singapore's Orchard Road, Takashimaya Shopping Centre, 391 Orchard Road, **t** 6737 5021, *www.kinokuniya.com.sg*.)

In Kuala Lumpur there are a variety of free city maps on offer, few of which are very detailed. You can pick up the perfectly adequate Official Map of Singapore from tourist offices and hotels. The best map of Singapore is the spiral-bound *Street Directory* (Mighty Minds Publishing, available in bookstores and at newspaper stalls), which has every building marked and labelled, and even comes with its own magnifying strip.

For 'security' reasons, the Brunei government keeps a close eye on the publication of maps. As a result, decent maps of Brunei, even road atlases, are more or less impossible to obtain.

If you want to pick up a few maps before you travel, try the following bookshops:

Stanford's (UK), 12–14 Long Acre, London WC2E 9LP, **t** (020) 7836 1321, *www.stanfords.co.uk*.
The Travel Bookshop (UK), 13–15 Blenheim Crescent, London W11 2EE, **t** (020) 7229 5260, *www.thetravelbookshop.co.uk*.
National Map Centre (UK), 22–24 Caxton Street, London SW1H 0QU, **t** (020) 7222 2466, *www.mapsnmc.co.uk*.
Eason's Bookshop (IRE), 40 O'Connell Street, Dublin 1, **t** 01 873 3811, *www.eason.ie*.
The Complete Traveller (USA), 199 Madison Ave, New York, NY 10016, **t** 212 685 9007, *www.completetravellerbooks.com*.
World of Maps (CAN), 1235 Wellington Street, Ottawa, Ontario K1Y 3A3, **t** 1 800 214 8524, *www.worldofmaps.com*.

Money and Banks

The safest way to carry your money around is as **traveller's cheques**. These can be cashed by any bank, by licenced moneychangers and by top-end hotels. However, it is perfectly possible to survive in both countries with only your debit/credit cards; **ATMs** are widespread across Malaysia, Singapore and Brunei and all of them accept major credit cards (Visa, Mastercard, American Express). Many ATMs accept Maestro too, so debit cards can be used to withdraw money. If you find yourself somewhere without an ATM, banks are usually happy to advance cash against credit cards. Remember to bring along the international phone number for lost/stolen cards.

The major banks in Malaysia and Singapore include HSBC, Citibank, Maybank and Standard Chartered Bank. Banking hours are generally Mon–Fri 9.30–3.30 and Sat 9.30–11.30.

The Malaysian currency is the **ringgit** (RM; pronounced *ring-git*). At the time of writing, the exchange rates were as follows: GB£1=RM6.75 and US$1=RM3.70. For live exchange rates visit *www.xe.com/ucc*. The old Malaysian currency was the dollar, and you may still here the term used in place of ringgit. In Singapore, the currency is the **dollar**. Exchange rates at the time of writing were as follows: GB£1=S$2.90 and US$=S$1.60

The Brunei dollar is pegged to the Singapore dollar, and the two currencies are interchangeable.

Everything, from accommodation to food and transport, is more expensive in Singapore and Brunei than in Malaysia, though Singapore is still cheap by western European standards. That said, when it comes to shopping, there is little difference in the price of many of the goods (particularly cameras and electrical items, which sell for approximately the same amount in either country). As a tourist, visiting Peninsular Malaysia is generally cheaper than visiting East Malaysia; the infrastructure in the latter is not so well developed, and visitors are forced to rely more on tour companies and private means of transport.

Places of Worship

At various times of day (outside prayer times) non-Muslims are welcome at **mosques**. Check about times before waltzing in, and make sure that you are appropriately dressed (for men, shirt and trousers; for women, long dress or skirt, sleeves and headscarf). Shoes must be left at the entrance. Those mosques most frequented by tourists often have someone on hand to provide cloaks and headscarves. In every mosque, the main prayer hall is out-of-bounds to non-Muslims.

Visitors are welcome in **Hindu temples** and **Buddhist temples** across Malaysia and Singapore. Remember to remove your shoes before entering a Hindu temple. Christian churches, too, are open to allcomers (though in Sabah where they predominate, a church is often no more than a shack). For more about mosques and temples *see* 'Art and Architecture' chapter).

Post Offices

In Malaysia, post offices are usually open Mon–Sat 8.30–4.30. In the predominantly Muslim east-coast states of Kelantan and Terengganu, post offices are closed on Fridays rather than Sundays. In Singapore, post offices are open Mon–Fri 8–6 and Sat 8–2. In Brunei, post offices are open Mon–Thurs and Sat 7.45–4.30, Fri 8–11 and 2–4. The postal service in both countries is very efficient.

Shopping

Everyone knows that Singapore and shopping go hand-in-hand (*see* p.450 for information about shopping in Singapore), but Malaysia is not a bad place to part with your money either. With the fast pace of change in Malaysia, the variety of goods on offer expands with every year, and yet prices seem to remain competitive.

Be prepared to bargain wherever you shop (unless you are inside a department store, where prices are fixed). Haggling isn't such a frenetic pastime as it is in the Middle East, but with a little polite haggling, you are likely to knock a third off the quoted price. Prices vary widely, depending on where you shop. You will pay the highest prices inside Kuala Lumpur's glitzy new shopping centres, though by Western standards you will still make substantial savings (even on designer goods).

For international labels, Kuala Lumpur and – to a lesser extent – Penang are the places to head for. Elsewhere you tend to find only local goods. The Malaysian tourist board makes a big deal of the duty-free shopping on the islands of Langkawi and Labuan, but the shops here are disappointing, and it's not worth going out of your way for.

Malaysia's major commercial centres tend to be split down ethnic lines, which makes orientation for shoppers a little easier. In Chinatown, you will find the usual Chinese shophouses, some of them convenience stores crammed full of jumbled goods, others traditional medicine halls with herbs and dried animal parts stored in glass jars on shelves. In places like Melaka, there are dozens of traditional Chinese antiques shops, where you will find furniture, porcelain, jade, jewellery, musical instruments and textiles.

The Indian quarter is the place to visit for colourful imported textiles. Finding traditional Malay goods in Peninsular Malaysia is often a little harder. Government craft centres are good for Malay handicrafts, though goods can be a little overpriced in these. To get real value for money, you need to buy at markets (or *pasar malam*), which are held at set times of the week (a few of the major *pasar malam* are held every afternoon). The east-coast states of Kelantan and Terengganu form the heartland of traditional Malay culture, and these are the best places to buy Malay handicrafts, such as shadow puppets, kites, spinning tops, woodcarvings, batik and *songket* textiles. Selangor is famous for its pewterware, and Kelantan for its intricately worked silver.

Tribal handicrafts are easy to come by in East Malaysia. The state capitals of Kuching and Kota Kinabalu have plenty of craft shops and antiques shops selling ceramic vases, woodcarvings, *parangs* (jungle knives), rattan basketry, mats, beadwork and tribal textiles. If you head upriver and buy direct from the longhouses where these items are crafted, you will pay a fraction of the cost.

Sports and Activities

With its expanses of virgin rainforest, its mountains and cave systems, and its coral-fringed islands, Malaysia makes an excellent destination for an 'adventure' holiday.

Diving and **snorkelling** are among the more popular activities on offer in Malaysia. The best dive sites are found off the east coast peninsula and off Sabah (Malaysian Borneo), where Pulau Sipadan and Pulau Layang-Layang rank among the world's best dive sites. By comparison, the dive sites off the west coast of the peninsula are poor, though easily accessible.

Peninsular Malaysia is a great place to take PADI-registered (Professional Association of Diving Instructors) courses, with islands like the Perhentians geared up almost exclusively for just this. Rates are cheap too, by international standards: the five-day Open Water course for beginners costs from as little as RM750. Dive sites off the west coast of the peninsula include Pulau Pangkor and Pulau Paya, though you're better off crossing to the east coast, where Pulau Tioman, Pulau Perhentian and Pulau Redang offer much better visibility. Even snorkelling, you are sure to see marine turtles (beautiful, effortless swimmers), reef sharks and other large fish, such as barracuda and bump-head parrotfish. Green turtles and hawksbill turtles breed off many east-coast islands, dragging themselves ashore to lay their eggs in the sand.

Dive fanatics are in for a treat at Pulau Sipadan, a tiny oceanic island off Sabah's east coast. According to the WWF, it is home to more marine life than any other spot known to man. The prime attraction here is a stunning wall dive: just metres from the main beach, the sea bed plunges a vertical 680m to the ocean floor. Schooling barracuda and big-eye trevally provide one of the highlights, but pelagic species such as manta rays, hammer-head sharks and whale sharks are often sighted too. Dive contacts are listed in the relevant chapters.

The shallow bay at Cherating on the east coast of Peninsular Malaysia provides the ideal conditions for surfing and **windsurfing**: international events are staged here every now and then.

Angling too is a popular activity among visitors; the country's rivers are home to more than 300 species of fish, while deep-sea fishing provides the opportunity for catching tuna, grouper, shark, barracuda and blue marlin. For further information contact the Malaysian Anglers Association (*No.99 Jalan 15/4C, Subang Jaya, 47500 Petaling Jaya,* ***t*** *03 738 8864,* ***f*** *03 733 8213*).

Malaysia is home to the world's oldest rainforest, so it comes as little surprise that **jungle trekking** is the most popular outdoor activity with tourists. Among the remaining stands of primary forest, there are dozens of national parks, each laced with hiking trails. The Taman Negara, in Peninsular Malaysia, has the most extensive network of trails and, as such, is the most popular and accessible national park. It also has a canopy walkway and a number of hides for spotting wildlife. The nearby Kenong Rimba National Park has a lower profile and (as a result of this) a higher density of wildlife. A visit to the less accessible Endau Rompin National Park, which straddles the Johor/Pahang border, requires greater planning and expense, though you're unlikely to bump into anyone else along the trail. The cooler climate of the Cameron Highlands on the Perak/Pahang border makes it a popular trekking destination. All of Malaysia's national parks are covered in detail in the regional chapters. For further information you can try contacting the Wildlife and National Parks

Department (*Km10 Jalan Cheras, 56100 Kuala Lumpur*, **t** *03 632 9422*, **f** *03 635 8773*).

Despite logging and development, much of East Malaysia remains cloaked in rainforest, and tour operators all offer jungle trekking packages in both East Malaysia and Brunei. In many places, such as the Kinabatangan Wetlands in Sabah, jungle trekking can be combined with river safaris, which provide the best chance of spotting Bornean wildlife such as orang-utans, elephants and proboscis monkeys. In Sarawak, the best trekking territory can be found at Bako National Park, just north of Kuching, and at the stunning Gunung Mulu National Park, where there are numerous peaks to conquer and one of the world's great cave systems to explore. In fact, the variety of **caving** opportunities at Gunung Mulu is virtually unprecendented; the mountainous terrain here is threaded with between 600km and 800km of cave passages. Serious cavers often come to the park to visit the Sarawak Chamber, the world's largest known cave chamber. For further information contact the Malaysian Nature Society Caving Group (17 Jalan Tanjung SD 13/2, Bandar Sri Damansara, 52200 Kuala Lumpur, **t** 03 632 9422, **f** 03 635 8773).

Malaysia also presents a number of **climbing** opportunities. The major climb is Mount Kinabalu in Sabah, which, at 4,101m (13,500ft), is the tallest mountain between New Guinea and the Himalayas. The climb to the summit and down again takes mere mortals two days, with a night at the base camp below the summit. The main route to the summit requires no technical climbing and is one of the most popular reasons for visiting Sabah. Athletes are drawn to the mountain every October for the Mount Kinabalu International Climbathon, one of the world's most arduous races (the best of them make it up and down in less than three hours).

Golf courses are spreading like wildfire across Malaysia, with many of them linked to top-end hotels. There are now more than 200 courses across the country. Some of the best of them can be found on Langkawi.

Telephones and Internet

Public **telephone** booths are widespread in **Malaysia**. They accept 10sen (RM0.10) and 20sen (0.20) coins, though if you are calling abroad it makes sense to buy a phonecard (at least half of the phone booths accept cards). Phonecards can be bought from newsagents, service stations and some general stores. The most widespread phones are those of government-run Telekom, though there are two or three private companies with phone booths too. If you want to make an international call, look out for phone booths which carry the international logo. Alternatively, visit a Telekom office (located in every town and some villages too).

Most phone booths in **Singapore** take phonecards nowadays; all of these can be used to make international calls. Like Malaysia, phonecards are available from newsagents, service stations and some convenience stores. In **Brunei**, 'Hallo Kad' phonecards can be used to make international calls from any phone. You can also make international calls from your room in many of the hotels. Coin phones take 10 and 20 cent pieces.

Internet cafés are widespread in Malaysia, Singapore and Brunei. Having planted itself firmly in the new media age, Malaysia has a greater density of internet cafés than most industrialized nations. Every town and village is online (even remote Bario in the interior of Sarawak has its own internet café). In Malaysia internet access costs RM2.50–6 per hour. In Singapore and Brunei it costs around S$3 per hour.

The **international access code** for Malaysia is +60; for Singapore it is +65; for Brunei it is +673. To make an international call from Malaysia or Brunei, dial 00 followed by the country code. From Singapore dial 001 followed by the country code.

Time

Malaysia, Brunei and Singapore are eight hours ahead of Greenwich Mean Time (GMT), 13 hours ahead of Eastern Standard Time and 16 hours ahead of US Pacific Standard Time.

Tourist Information

Malaysia

Malaysia's tourist board is known as Tourism Malaysia (*www.tourism.gov.my*), with offices throughout the country (*see* listings within the regional chapters). Standards vary widely, as do opening times, though visitor centres are most commonly open Mon–Fri 8.30–4.30 and Sat 8.30–11.30, with a long lunch break on Fridays. Tourist offices abroad have provide plenty of general information:

Canada: 830 Burrard Street, Vancouver, British Columbia V6Z 1X9, **t** 1 888 689 6872, *www.tourism-malaysia.ca*.

UK: 57 Trafalgar Square, London WC2N 5DU, **t** (020) 7930 7932, *www.malaysia trulyasia.co.uk*.

USA: 120 East 56th Street, Suite 810, New York, NY 10022, **t** 212 754 1113, *www.visit malaysia.com*.

Brunei

Brunei Tourism (*www.tourismbrunei.com*) offers limited information. On arrival in Brunei, visit the main tourist office in Bandar Seri Begawan and pick up a copy of the useful *Explore Brunei* visitor's guide. For information before you travel, contact the Brunei High Commission in your home country.

Singapore

The Singapore Tourist Board (STB; *www.visitsingapore.com*) is an excellent source of information, with well-stocked offices and helpful staff (*see* Singapore listings for details). The free maps of downtown Singapore are excellent, as are the free listings magazines, such as *I-S Magazine*, *Juice* and *Where Magazine*. For information closer to home, visit:

UK: 1st Floor, Carrington House, 126–130 Regent Street, London W1B 5JX, **t** (020) 7437 0033, *www.visitsingapore.com*.

USA: 1156 Avenue of the Americas, Suite 702, New York, NY 10036, **t** 212 302 4861, *www.visitsingapore.com*; 4929 Wilshire Boulevard, Suite 510, Los Angeles, CA 90010, **t** 323 677 0808, *www.visitsingapore.com*.

Websites

Malaysia:

http://allmalaysia.info
http://star-ecentral.com
www.borneotravel.com
www.ecoborneo.com
www.emedia.com.my
www.infosabah.com.my
www.journeymalaysia.com
www.klue.com.my
www.malaysia-by-malaysian.com
www.malaysiakini.com
www.mytravelguide.com
www.sarawakalive.com.my
www.sarawaktourism.com
www.sabahtravelguide.com
www.thingsasian.com
www.tourism.go.my
www.visionkl.com

Brunei:

www.brunei.gov.bn
www.empire.com.bn
www.jungle-drum.com
www.tourismbrunei.com

Singapore:

www.visitsingapore.com
www.getforme.com
www.makantime.com
www.nac.gov.sg
www.nparks.gov.sg
www.singaporeartsnculture.com
http://singaporeeverything.com
www.straitstimes.com.sg
www.theexpat.com
www.thingstodo-singapore.com
www.tourismsingapore.com
www.tws.com.sg

Where to Stay

In both Malaysia and Singapore, there is a wide choice of accommodation at the **top end** of the market, including a handful of gems. Hotels like The Datai (p.210), the Pangkor Laut Resort (p.194), and the Tanjong Jara Resort (p.248), have all won international awards, while others like Singapore's Raffles Hotel and Penang's E&O Hotel need little introduction.

In Malaysia, resort hotels are also leading the way in the evolution of certain types of contemporary 'tropical' architecture, where climatic elements and regional motifs are taken into consideration. Some architects have taken the kampung setting as a template, injecting the necessary luxury as discreetly as possible. Others have incorporated elements of indigenous design into the architecture.

The presence of upmarket hotels exceeds demand in Malaysia, with a glut of hotels built during the pre-1997 boom years. In the wake of the Asian Economic Crisis, room prices at these hotels plummeted. In many cases, their rates have remained low. As a rule of thumb, always ask about promotions when booking a room in the more expensive hotels. More often than not, they offer promotional rates (the best of these can half the price), but if you don't ask, you may well be charged the published rack rate for your room. Of course, those hotels with international reputations can get away with charging the full whack throughout the year.

Accommodation in Brunei is somewhat lacking. Still, few tourists stop by, so there are always plenty of rooms to spare. Moderate and budget options are few and far between, though the top-end hotels in Brunei are often a bargain; even the uber-luxurious 6-star Empire Hotel offers great deals when occupancy is low.

The **mid-range hotels** in Malaysia are a bit hit-and-miss (in Singapore, the standard of accommodation is high across the board). If you are unlucky with your choice of mid-range hotel, you'll be getting the same facilities as someone in a budget hotel, but at double the price. If you're lucky, you might find a spotless room with en-suite bathroom for as little as RM70–80 (approximately UK£10 or US$20). But many of Malaysia's mid-range hotels are functional, tatty, unwelcoming places. Always take a look at the upmarket options first. With promotions, you may find a comfortable room for just a small jump in price. Hotels that fall into the 'moderate' category are common in Malaysia, but this guide places more emphasis on the top-end hotels and the better 'inexpensive' and 'budget' options (where the best deals can be found). The exceptions to the rule for the moderate category are the **government resthouses**, often set in old colonial-style villas. Resthouses originated in colonial days as accommodation for visiting officials. As such, they had standards to maintain, and in the most part this has carried through to the modern day. Rooms are often enormous, if a little mildewed, and it isn't hard to cast your mind back to the 'good old days'.

Hotels at the **lower end** of the market tend to be simple Chinese-run places, with precarious-looking ceiling fans and communal bathrooms. In Malaysia, these can be very cheap (as little as RM25 per night), but they are rarely pleasant places to stay. At best, they are functional; at worst, noisy and seedy. The cheap hotels usually have a few rooms on the side with air conditioning. **Guesthouses** tend to provide the best options in the 'inexpensive and 'budget' categories. Standards vary widely, but the best of them are warm, friendly environments with helpful staff and a good range of extra facilities. Most guesthouses are geared up specifically for Western travellers and backpackers. Many now provide internet access, laundry services, book exchange, Western-style breakfasts and tours of local sights. Just about every guesthouse provides dormitory beds, which is the cheapest form of accommodation (around RM10 in Malaysia and S$10 in Singapore). In a few of Malaysia's towns and tourist hotspots there are **homestay programmes**, which provide a good

Price Categories

Malaysia

Price for a double room (excluding taxes):

Luxury	RM500+
Expensive	RM200–500
Moderate	RM80–200
Inexpensive	RM40–80
Budget	under RM40

Brunei and Singapore

Price for a double room (excluding taxes):

Luxury	S$350+
Expensive	S$200–350
Moderate	S$100–200
Inexpensive	S$50–100
Budget	under S$50

way of sampling local life and trying out some home-cooked cuisine. Tourist offices provide information about homestays, many of which are only available seasonally.

The most rewarding homestays are those found in Sarawak and Sabah, where tourists can stay in indigenous **longhouses**. The indigenous peoples of Borneo are a proudly hospitable people, and it is not uncommon for tourists to receive informal invites to stay at a local longhouse. Any invitation is likely to be completely genuine, and you can be assured that you will be treated well by your hosts – hospitality is a matter of pride in Borneo. If you do receive an informal invite to a longhouse, you will not be expected to pay for the accommodation (more often than not, a mat on the floor), but it is customary to bring along a gift. Today, however, the most common means of visiting longhouses is as part of an organized tour. In these cases, mattresses and mosquito nets are provided. If you visit at the time of the harvest festival (known as Gawai Dayak, *see* 'Calendar of Events', pp.76–8), you are in for one of the parties of your life.

The only time when accommodation may be in short supply is during major festivals, such as Hari Raya and Chinese New Year. If your visit coincides with these dates (*see* 'Calendar of Events') it is best to play safe and book in advance. 'Double room' in Malaysia is sometimes interpreted as 'twin room', so it is best to be clear about the sort of room you want. All hotels add **services charges** and **government taxes** to the room bill. These extras are denoted by '++' on the list of rates, and are rarely included in the quoted rate. Service charge is ten per cent, government tax is five per cent.

Women Travellers

Singapore is a cosmopolitan, multicultural city and women travellers should have no particular problems. Malaysia and Brunei are predominantly Muslim countries, and as such, it is sensible for women to pay some attention to their dress. At beach resorts with an international clientele, or in places used to Western holiday-makers, swimming in a bikini is unlikely to raise eyebrows – but skip into the sea scantily clad anywhere else, and it most certainly will.

In Brunei, and on the east coast of Peninsular Malaysia, women travellers should make the effort to cover their legs and arms. There's no real need for non-Muslims to wear a headscarf, unless visiting a mosque. Still, if you prefer to feel inconspicuous (and especially if you're fair-haired), a headscarf can be a good thing when visiting rural Muslim areas. In the major towns and cities, dress conventions are not so important. Take the Chinese women and the expatriate population as an example; as non-Muslims, many of them are happy to wear shorts and T-shirts out-and-about.

Women travelling on their own can expect a bit of attention beyond the main towns and cities, but sexual harrassment is minimal in Malaysia. A wedding ring is always a good decoy, and women who travel with men are unlikely to receive any unwarranted attention. Couples should bear in mind that physical contact between men and women in public (even holding hands) is frowned upon in Muslim areas.

Kuala Lumpur and Around

08

Highlights

1 The myriad pleasures of the Lake Gardens

2 The sounds and smells of Chow Kit market and Little India

3 The mighty Petronas Towers

4 The cool heights of Fraser's Hill (*see* p.117)

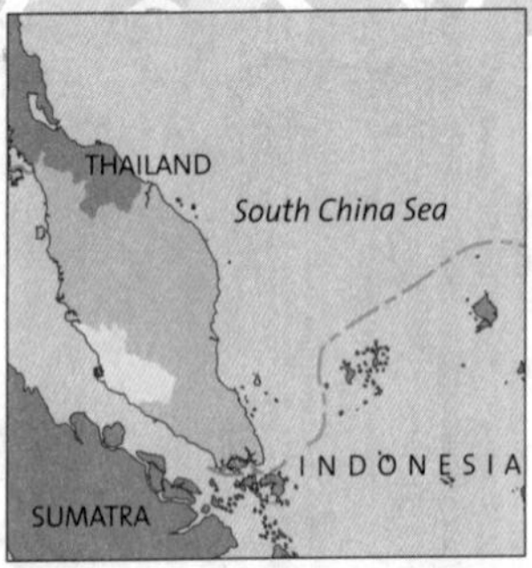

Kuala Lumpur, Malaysia's capital, has cleaned up its act since André Gide called it 'Kuala l'Impure'. It is no longer the unsightly traffic-choked sprawl that visitors skirt on their way in and out of the country: today's tourists tend to come away pleasantly surprised. Granted, traffic is still a problem, as is the shortage of pavements and the ongoing threat of 'The Haze' (smog caused by forest fires in Sumatra and Kalimantan), but it would be a mistake to visit Malaysia and leave the capital unexplored.

Strictly speaking, Kuala Lumpur is no longer the administrative capital of Malaysia; that honour has passed to nearby Putrajaya, the brand-new paperless city which was named seat of government in 1999. But it is Kuala Lumpur, or KL as it is more commonly known, that sets the pulse of the nation. It is the Big City (ten per cent of the population lives here), the place invested with the hopes and the aspirations of a rapidly developing nation. After decades of enterprise and development, KL has earned its stripes as a new Asian tiger – second city to Singapore in Southeast Asian economic prowess.

Everywhere in KL are the juxtapositions of East and West, a characteristic expressed most boldly in the new architecture of the city: the towering Dayubumi complex with its filigree grilling; the modernist-Islamic National Mosque; the National Museum and Putra World Trade Centre with their massive Minangkabau-style roofs. Then of course there are the mighty Petronas Towers, design hybrids and symbol of a nation.

Despite the fast pace of change, Kuala Lumpur retains much of its traditional character. Turn a few street corners and you soon stumble across the old KL. Hawkers of every description continue to ply their trades outside crumbling shophouses. At food stalls, men in songkoks knead, toss and fold dough to make *roti canai*, Malaysia's favourite snack food. Streetside medicine men can still be found crouched among herbs and oils and dried animal parts. Fake Rolexes are sold alongside prayer beads, while on billboards Hollywood fights Bollywood for big-screen presence.

If you come away from Kuala Lumpur with only one thing, it should be a heavy gut. At every corner the city bombards you with opportunities to fill your belly. Malay, Chinese and Indian restaurants are in plentiful supply, of course, but there are also a growing number of top-quality international restaurants serving European, Middle Eastern, Japanese, Indo-Chinese and fusion cuisine.

Surrounding the federal territory of Kuala Lumpur is Selangor, an ancient state dominated today by the industrial sweep of the Klang Valley. The coastal village of Kuala Selangor draws tourists for the nightly firefly spectacle which takes place on the banks of its river, while inland the old colonial hill stations of Fraser's Hill and the Genting Highlands provide easy city breaks. To the south, the small state of Negeri Sembilan offers a taste of the unique Minangkabau culture.

History

As capital cities go, KL's history is a fairly short one. By the 1820s there is thought to have been a small Malay settlement at the confluence of the Klang and Gombak rivers – site of present-day Kuala Lumpur and origin of the name (which translates as

Founding Father

Yap Ah Loy is the man usually credited as the founding father of KL. Which is a contentious issue, because he arrived on the scene many years after a settlement first took root at the confluence of the Klang and Gombak rivers. Malay interests like to name Rajah Abdullah (*see* below) as founder. Whichever way you look at it, it is was under Yap Ah Loy's influence that the settlement matured from a tiny trading post into a state capital.

Born into poverty in China in 1837, Yap Ah Loy sailed from Macau to Melaka at the age of 17, wooed by tales of easy fortunes in Malaya. He spent his early years as a coolie and, later, as a pig dealer – he lingered about the Ampang mines exchanging pork for tin, which he sold on at a profit further downstream. It was in these dealings that he came across Liu Ngim Kong, the man who was to become Kapitan China of the small settlement known as Kuala Lumpur. This was a time of inter-clan warfare, and Ngim Kong took on Yap Ah Loy as his assistant, impressed by the young man's strength and his fearlessness (despite his short stature, it was said that he had 'the strength of an elephant').

Yap soon developed a reputation as someone who could command both fear and respect. On his boss's death in 1868, he took the reins as Kapitan China of Kuala Lumpur. He ruled by terror. The following decade was dominated by the attempts of various factions to control the growing tin trade. For Yap, it was all-out war; he offered handsome rewards for anyone who presented him with the head of an enemy. The gory trophy would then be paraded around the marketplace before being left to fester forbodingly atop a stake. As effective warlord of KL, Yap Ah Loy ploughed his growing fortune into the development of the settlement, building roads out to the tin mines and claiming monopolies over opium dens, brothels, gambling dens and drinking halls – big business in an exclusively male world of mining, manual labour and constant danger.

Despite his tough-man image, Yap Ah Loy was a shrewd diplomat, able to leave heavy-handedness to one side when circumstances called for charm or subordination. Victorian travel writer Isabella Bird, who visited Kuala Lumpur in 1879, described him as 'a man of large aims and enlightened public spirit', a man who had the 'implicit confidence' of his countrymen and who was always 'loyal to British interests'. By the time of Yap Ah Loy's death in March 1885, Kuala Lumpur had superceded Klang as state capital of Selangor.

'muddy confluence'). There were certainly settlements at the nearby Batu Caves by that time. But it wasn't until the 1860s that Kuala Lumpur developed into a place of any note. And even then it was little more than a rough-edged trading post serving the tin mines of Ampang.

Malay historians credit Rajah Abdullah with founding the first trading post. He turned up in 1857 with a team of 87 Chinese labourers under his wing, landing on the site of Masjid Jamek and settling nearby. Of these workers, only 18 survived the ravages of malaria. But the lure of tin and the thirst for an easy fortune kept them coming, and the settlement grew in spurts in line with the growing European demand for tin.

Hiu Siew was Kuala Lumpur's first (though often unacknowledged) Kapitan China, or headman. It was he who encouraged *towkays* to erect sundry stores to serve the needs of passing miners and merchants. However, Yap Ah Loy (*see* 'Founding Father', opposite) is the name most often associated with early Kuala Lumpur. He became Kapitan China in 1868, and it was under his iron command that the settlement began to flourish. In those early days KL was a rough and functional place, full of opium dens, gambling halls and brothels. Secret society feuds were a constant threat to peace, and the settlement was burned to the ground on more than one occasion. But as the price of tin rose to meet demand (in 1878 alone the price doubled), so the boundaries of KL extended. By the time of the Pangkor Treaty (1874), by which the British laid administrative claim to the region, KL had become a sizable trading post.

In 1880 Kuala Lumpur superceded Klang as the state capital of Selangor. Frank Swettenham was appointed Resident of Selangor in 1882, and he set about transforming KL into an administrative centre worthy of the British Empire. Bricks and tiles replaced hardwoods and *attap*, and a railway line was constructed between KL and the port at Klang. The population increased tenfold during the 1880s and the settlement began to take on a semblance of grandeur and civility. Each day on the padang there were parades, with cricket matches at weekends and evening drinks at the clubhouse.

On the founding of the Federated Malay States (FMS) in 1896, Kuala Lumpur was chosen as federal capital (largely for its central position). Frank Swettenham was appointed Resident-General, and he set about centralizing and streamlining the administration of the federation, with KL at the heart of it all. British architects were shipped in to design a collection of monumental public buildings, including the Sultan Abdul Samad building, the Railway Station and Masjid Jamek. A Sanitary Board was established to regulate new development and maintain roads. Dust tracks were replaced by laterite gravel, and 'offensive trades' such as tin smelters and abattoirs were moved away from the centre of town. British love of open green spaces saw the appearance of the Lake Gardens to the west of town, while to the east, a racecourse was built.

Development continued at a fast pace into the 20th century. Successful Chinese towkays, tin merchants and rubber planters built their mansions along Jalan Ampang, one of many roads in early KL that led out to tin mines. The banks of the Klang and Gombak rivers were raised to prevent the monsoon flooding that had so regularly devastated the settlement – in such years sampans and dugouts replaced buffalo carts, and the padang became a lake. Residential districts were established beyond the limits of the town centre. There was concern that the resident Malays were being swamped by immigrant Chinese and Tamils: an early experiment in town planning saw the development of Kampung Bahru to the north of town. The development was billed as an 'agricultural scheme' and it was hoped that the kampung would become a centre for Malay cottage industries. But not all of KL's expansion was well planned and very early on traffic became a daily concern – a dilemma that remains unsolved today.

Between the wars, low-maintenance shophouses and office blocks began to spring up, often in Art Deco style. By now, the character of KL was defined largely by its scrappy mix of architectural styles. In late 1941 the Japanese overran British defences and took control of the city, shattering the inhabitants' unquestioning faith in British protection. Though KL suffered only minor structural damage during the war, the Chinese population faced cruel repression at the hands of the Japanese.

After the Japanese surrender in 1945, the British were looked upon with wariness and the push for independence began to gather steam. Sympathy with Mao's communist revolution in 1949 led to a period of unrest in the build-up to Independence – a conflict known as the Emergency (*see* p.20), during which the tension in KL was palpable. At midnight on 31st August 1957 the Union Jack was finally lowered from the flagpole on the padang. Kuala Lumpur became capital of the independent Federation of Malaya and the padang was renamed Merdeka Square ('Freedom Square'). In 1963 Kuala Lumpur became a federal territory and capital of newly formed Malaysia.

Independence was followed by a period of fast-paced development and racial tensions, which peaked in the bloody race riots of 1969. These tensions played a major role in the politics of independent Malaysia, though they began to take a back seat to the nation's almighty push towards economic progress. Cheap modern developments of the 1970s and 1980s gave way to the mega-projects of the 1990s. The Petronas Towers, at the heart of the KLCC complex, shot skywards at a rate of one floor every four days, with more than 2,000 workers on site 24hrs a day. Meanwhile the finishing touches were being made to Putrajaya, the government's new administrative centre and part of the ambitious Multimedia Super Corridor (MSC), which runs west of KL through the Klang Valley. Such projects, it was hoped, would ease the pressure of development on KL, though the Asian economic crisis of 1997 almost stopped them in their tracks. In June 1999 Putrajaya was named the federal administrative capital in place of Kuala Lumpur, which remains the nation's commercial and financial capital.

Today, Kuala Lumpur can be divided roughly into four zones, with Chinatown and the colonial quarter at the core, Little India and Chow Kit to the north, the Golden Triangle to the east and the Lake Gardens to the west.

The Colonial Core

Merdeka Square

The heart of the old colonial quarter is marked by **Merdeka Square** ('Freedom Square'), a rectangle of grass, fountains and flowerbeds flanked by the Royal Selangor Club, the ornate Sultan Abdul Samad building and the Old Post Office. Before independence, the site was known as the Selangor Padang, a turfed field used by British administrators for games and as a parade ground. An 1893 entry in the

Getting There

By Air

KL's flash new airport is situated 72km south of the city at Sepang. As well as being the major international point of entry to Malaysia, it is the hub of the domestic air network with flights to all destinations across the country. For further information and flight details check *www.klia.com.my*. The KLIA Ekspres train has made taxis and airport coach services redundant. The service links the city directly with the airport and takes just 28 minutes. Trains leave every 15mins.

By Train

Sentral Station, part of a large new business and commercial development in the Brickfields district, is set to become the new transport hub of KL. It is situated a few hundred yards south of the old Moorish station (*see* p.106). KL is on the west-coast railway line, which links Singapore with Bangkok, via Butterworth.

By Bus

The **Puduraya Terminal** on Jalan Pudu is KL's principle bus station. Ticket offices are located on the floor above the terminal, along with food stalls, an information booth and a left-luggage office. It is usually packed solid. Buses leave for all major destinations across the peninsula; some carry on into Singapore and Thailand. To the north of town, off Jalan Tun Razak, is the **Pekeliling Bus Terminal**, with bus services to interior destinations, such as the Taman Negara and Genting Highlands.

Getting Around

KL's **Light Transit Rail** (LRT) is the principle means of transport about the city. In 2003 this service was bolstered by the **KL Monorail**. The latter links 11 stations between the Pekelilling Bus Terminal to the north with Sentral Station to the south, passing through the Golden Triangle. Travel on both transport systems is slick and cheap, though there are perhaps not as many stops as one might expect of a city this size. Still, public transport in KL has improved dramatically over the last decade, easing congestion and making the city more pedestrian-friendly. Maps of the KL Transit System are available from tourist information centres (and LRT and Monorail stations).

At the time of writing, **taxis** in KL cost RM2 for the first kilometre, then a further 10 sen for every subsequent 45 seconds, which works out pretty cheaply. There are taxis stands all over town (taxis will not generally stop if you try to flag them down).

Car hire is easily arranged either in town or at the airport, where most of the international and local firms have offices. The tried and tested firms include Hawk Rent-a-Car (Ground Floor, UOA Centre, Jalan Pinang, **t** 03 2164 6455); Hertz (Ground Floor, Kompleks Antarabangsa, Jalan Sultan Ismail, **t** 03 2148 6433); Avis (Ground Floor, Menara Maa, **t** 03 9222 2087).

Tourist Information

The Malaysia Tourism Centre (109 Jalan Ampang, **t** 03 2164 3929) is the biggest of the tourist offices in KL. Computers are available for use; all have a special portal of information about Malaysia and the capital. The centre also hosts regular cultural performances. Other tourist information centres can be found at the new Kuala Lumpur Railway Station (Steysen KL Sentral, **t** 03 2274 3125); Putra World Trade Centre (Level 2, 45 Jalan Tun Ismail, **t** 03 4041 1295); KLIA (KL International Airport, Sepang, **t** 03 8776 5647).

Where to Stay

KL has a glut of hotels in the luxury category: the market is saturated, which means that most of the top-end hotels run year-round promotions offering excellent value (it is not unusual for a rate of RM600 to drop as low as RM250). Mid-range and budget hotels are poorly represented in KL.

Golden Triangle

Luxury

Mandarin Oriental, KLCC, **t** 03 2380 8888, **f** 03 2380 8833, *www.mandarinoriental.com*. KL's premier hotel (with the exception of the

Carcosa Seri Negara), nestled up against the Petronas Towers. Elite but not too stuffy. Service is immaculate, as are the bright, airy rooms, which are scattered with Malaccan furniture and fabrics with 'Malaysian' motifs. Book into one of the executive floors to enjoy full use of the club lounge, including limitless food and drink – all of it delicious. The hotel's six cafés and restaurants are fast gaining a name for themselves.

JW Marriott Hotel, 183 Jalan Bukit Bintang, **t** 03 2715 9000, **f** 03 2715 7010, *www.marriott.com*. This extravagant 5-star hotel is the top choice in the Bukit Bintang area. Attached to the Star Hill Shopping Centre and with good views across to the Petronas Towers. Recreation facilities include spa, gym, pool, tennis court and jogging track.

Ritz-Carlton Hotel, 168 Jalan Imbi, **t** 03 2142 8000, **f** 03 2143 8080, *www.ritzcarlton.com*. Calls itself a 'luxury boutique hotel', though with 250 rooms the tag doesn't really fit. Still, the service here is a little more personable than in some of the other top-end hotels. 5-star facilities.

Hotel Istana, 73 Jalan Raja Chulan, **t** 03 2141 9988, **f** 03 2144 0111, *istana.hik@meritus-hotels.com*, *www.hotelistana.com.my*. One of KL's top choices for the business traveller covering every conceivable need, including limousine transfers. Rooms are huge and there's a large and stylish fitness centre and a 'Greek-Roman' swimming pool complete with pillars and poolside gazebos.

The Regent, 160 Jalan Bukit Bintang, **t** 03 2117 4888, **f** 03 2142 1441, *www.fourseasons.com*. Competing with the Mandarin Oriental for pole position of KL's luxury business hotels. An extensive health centre, squash courts and a pool compliment the lavishly appointed rooms and 24-hour butler service.

The Renaissance, cr. Jalan Ampang and Jalan Sultan Ismail, **t** 03 2162 2233, **f** 03 2163 1122, *www.renaissancehotels.com*. Split into two over-opulent wings, each containing high ceilings, crystal chandeliers and a mine's worth of marble. Rooms are spacious, there are all-weather tennis courts and the gym is open 24hrs a day. The highlight, though, is the enormous Olympic-size free-form pool.

Expensive

Crowne Plaza Mutiara Hotel, Jalan Sultan Ismail, **t** 03 2148 2322, **f** 03 2144 2157, *www.crowneplaza.com*. A complete refit in 2003 has made this hotel one of the better top-end options in KL. Rooms are elegant and contemporary, with fresh orchids and locally inspired fabrics. Facilities include a gym, pool and five bars and restaurants.

Hotel Equatorial, Jalan Sultan Ismail, **t** 03 2161 7777, **f** 03 2161 9020, *www.equatorial.com*. Down pillows and duvets are two things to lure you to the Equatorial, one of KL's long-serving business hotels. 5-star facilities at excellent value, though there's nothing to make it stand above its competitors.

Radius International, 51A Changkat Bukit Bintang, **t** 03 2715 3888, **f** 03 2715 1888, *www.radius-international.com*. Good value and well placed for shopping along Bukit Bintang or eating out along Changkat Bukit Bintang. Rooms are adequate but nothing special. Promotions sometimes bring the price of a standard room down to RM150.

Hotel Maya, 138 Jalan Ampang, **t** 03 2711 8866, **f** 03 2711 9966, *www.hotelmaya.com.my*. Once the Park Plaza Hotel, the building was redesigned as a 'boutique urban resort', according to the literature. Rooms enjoy bamboo panelling and bronze fittings. On the northern border of the Golden Triangle.

Moderate

Concorde, 2 Jalan Sultan Ismail, **t** 03 2144 2200, **f** 03 2144 1628, *kl@concorde.net*, *www.concorde.net*. A great choice for business-class facilities at tourist-class prices. There's a cigar divan in the lobby, and next door is the Hard Rock Cafe. Rooms are smart enough, though not huge. Facilities include a gym and a small pool.

KL Lodge Hotel, 2 Jalan Tengah (off Jalan Sultan Ismail), **t** 03 2142 0122, **f** 03 2141 6819, *kllodge@tm.net.my*. One of the few mid-range hotels in this area. Rooms are a touch fusty, but likeable (with air-con, TV, decent bathrooms and hot water). The small outdoor pool makes this place good value.

Inexpensive–Budget

Pondok Lodge, 20–22C Changkat Bukit Bintang, **t** 03 2142 8449, *pondok@tm.net.my*, *www.pondoklodge.com*. Possibly KL's best budget choice, the friendly staff and clean surroundings mean that it is often fully booked. Simple, fan-only rooms or dorms and larger rooms with air-con. There are also sitting areas and a rooftop terrace. Great location among the bars and in-vogue restaurants of Changkat Bukit Bintang.

Historic Centre

Expensive

Swiss Garden Hotel, 117 Jalan Pudu, **t** 03 2141 3333, **f** 03 2141 5555, *www.swissgarden.com*. Well placed on the edge of the Golden Triangle and east of Chinatown. This hotel offers good value (often with promotions) for 4-star facilities, and attracts as many tourists as business travellers. There is a good spa, too, offering Balinese massage.

Moderate

Ancasa Hotel, Jalan Cheng Lock, **t** 03 2026 6060, **f** 03 2026 8322, *www.ancasa-hotel.com*. The rooms in this newish high-rise hotel are still in excellent condition. Facilities include 24-hour room service, mini-bar, satellite TV and bathroom with hot water. Good value.

Hotel Malaya, Jalan Hang Lekir, **t** 03 2072 7722, **f** 03 2070 0980, *www.hotelmalaya.com.my*. In the thick of things in Chinatown, with acceptable air-conditioned rooms – though they are on the small side and a little worn. If you want space, pick one of the suites, which go for as little as RM150.

Swiss Inn, 62 Jalan Sultan, **t** 03 2072 3333, **f** 03 2031 6699, *www.swissgarden.com*. Downmarket sister to the Swiss Garden Hotel (*see* above), set in the heart of Chinatown. Facilities are limited to en-suite bathroom, air-con, TV, fridge and kettle, though the rooms aren't bad for the price, and larger than most in Chinatown. Some rooms are windowless, so check first. There's a pleasant bistro downstairs.

Inexpensive

Heritage Station Hotel, Jalan Sultan Hishamuddin, **t** 03 2273 5588, **f** 03 2273 2842. This is KL's oldest hotel, set in the magnificent colonial-Moorish railway station. It is not as grand as it was, and few people seem aware that it still exists. There is lots of polished wood, along with broad corridors and large rooms, but there's an abandoned feel to the place despite refurbishment. Rooms range from dorms and standard rooms, with plain modern décor, to the huge Colonial Suite decked out with antiques and a bargain at RM200.

Hotel China Town Inn, 52-54 Jalan Petaling, **t** 03 2070 4008, **f** 03 2078 4033, *www.chinatowninn.com*. Simple spotless rooms with bathrooms and hot water make this a contender for the best of KL's cheap, central options. Helpful staff, too.

Budget

Golden Plaza Hostel, 106 Jalan Petaling, **t** 03 2026 8559, *goldenplazakl@hotmail.com*. Operates a '100% no bed bugs policy', which is saying something for budget digs in KL. Don't expect much ambience though. Accommodation includes 'aromatherapy infused dorms', singles and doubles, with full backpacker facilities and no curfew. In the heart of noisy Chinatown.

Backpackers Travellers Inn, 60 Jalan Sultan, **t** 03 2078 2473. One of the better run and more popular backpacker haunts. Plenty of information and facilities such as laundry, book exchange, lockers and left luggage.

YWCA (Young Women's Christian Association) If you're on a budget and the other options seem intimidating, this is a good bet. For women, married couples and families only. Rooms are plain, with fans and attached bathrooms. East of Chinatown.

Chow Kit and Little India

Luxury

Pan Pacific, Jalan Putra, **t** 03 4042 5555, **f** 03 4041 7236, *resv.kul@panpacific.com*, *www.panpacific.com*. A solid business option beside the Putra World Trade Centre. Rooms are large, well-kept and decorated in neutral colours. The best rooms are on the Pacific floors, where there is a butler service and club lounge with excellent breakfasts and daytime nibbles. Spa, gym, swimming pool, tennis and squash courts.

Expensive

The Legend, 100 Jalan Putra, **t** 03 4042 9888, **f** 03 4043 0700, *www.legendhotelkl.com*. Luxury guestrooms and serviced apartments inside what must be KL's largest building in terms of square metreage. The 620 rooms are plain with marble bathrooms and enjoy all the amenities of a 5-star hotel.

Moderate

Stanford Hotel, 449 Jalan Tuanku Abdul Rahman, **t/f** 03 2691 3103. A modest option in the heart of Chow Kit with newly refurbished rooms, all of which have air-con, TV, fridge and tea/coffee-making facilities. Backs onto the lively Chow Kit Market.

Palace Hotel, 40-46 Jalan Masjid India, **t** 03 2698 6122, **f** 03 2693 7528, *palacekl@tm.net.my*. The best of several mid-range options in Little India. The plain rooms all have TV, minibar and hot water.

Inexpensive

Coliseum Hotel & Cafe, 98-100 Jalan Tuanku Abdul Rahman, **t** 03 2692 6270. Established in 1921, this is one of KL's oldest guesthouses – and it looks it. Still, the downstairs café manages to retain its legendary status for steaks and British pies (*see* 'Eating Out'). Upstairs, the good-sized rooms are cast in perpetual twilight by a sea of stained wood – in varying states of petrification.

Budget

Ben Soo Homestay, 61B 2nd Floor, Jalan Tiong Nam, **t** 03 2691 8096/019 332 7013, *bensoohome@yahoo.com*. Offers both air-conditioned and fan-only rooms in a residential block. Included in the price is a breakfast of toast and hot drinks. Slightly irritating handwritten notes and warnings adorn every door and appliance.

Elsewhere

Luxury

Carcosa Seri Negara, Taman Tasik Perdana, Persiaran Mahameru, **t** 03 2282 1888, **f** 03 2282 7888, *www.carcosa.com.my*. This beautiful colonial mansion set amongst trees above the Lake Gardens is the former residence of the British High Commissioner. The upstairs rooms have been converted into 13 regency-style suites in which visiting dignitaries are pampered (Queen Elizabeth II is the most cherished of their past guests). There are two restaurants, the Mahsuri Dining Hall and Gulai House (*see* 'Eating Out'), and a colonial-style bar. English cream teas are served daily, while on Sundays there's curry tiffin. Other facilities include a swimming pool, gym, tennis courts and croquet. Book well in advance.

Eating Out

Eating out is the greatest pleasure of a visit to Kuala Lumpur. At every corner, Malay, Chinese and Indian specialities change hands, while in the better hotels and the latest chi-chi enclaves, international restaurants serve European, Middle Eastern, Japanese, Indo-Chinese and experimental 'fusion' cuisine. You can eat perfectly well without ever stepping inside a restaurant (and at a fraction of the cost). Traditional hawker stalls line the streets, while inside virtually every shopping centre is a food court – basically an air-conditioned version of the hawker experience. Hawkers are the guardians of local cuisine. In their hands traditional dishes have evolved and flourished and because of the competition, only those stallholders that turn out quality food can be sure of a livelihood. A useful rule of thumb is to eat at stalls with the longest queues. See 'Hawker Centres' below to locate the best, and flick through the glossary in the food chapter to familiarize yourself with local specialities. Restaurants are listed by cuisine.

Hawker Centres

Outdoor hawker stalls can be found in each of KL's central enclaves. In Chinatown, head for **Jalan Petaling** for delicious steamed dumplings, fish ball noodles, waxed duck or roast chicken. During the day **Jalan Masjid India**, the heart of Little India, is lined with stalls selling Indian snacks or *cincau* (grass jelly drink). Behind these makeshift stalls, permanent stalls sell *roti canai*, biryani, *murtabak* and curries. Within the Golden Triangle, parallel to Jalan Bukit Bintang, is **Jalan Alor**, which comes alive each evening with hawkers selling everything from satay, *nasi lemak* and fresh durian to Cantonese and Peranakan specialities. **Chow Kit Market** is a great place to sample Malay hawker fare.

There are dozens of indoor hawker centres, or food courts, across KL. All of them turn out excellent food though they charge slightly more than the traditional outdoor stalls. Even so, sitting down to a cheap meal inside one of KL's top-end malls will transform your idea of the shopping experience. The hugely popular food court inside **Suria KLCC**, at the foot of the Petronas Towers, offers a comprehensive pick of the local cuisine alongside international alternatives. Other popular food courts include those inside the shopping malls off Jalan Bukit Bintang. Two favourites are probably the food courts of **Lot 10** (bottom floor) and **BB Plaza** (top floor), both of which offer wide choice and excellent value. **Central Market** also contains some great indoor food stalls, mainly Malay.

Malay and Nyonya

Expensive

Restoran Berputar Seri Angkasa, Menara Kuala Lumpur, **t** 03 208 5055. Admire KL from all angles at this revolving restaurant perched at the top of the Menara Kuala Lumpur (the telecom tower which actually stands taller than the Petronas Towers because it rests on a small hill). A buffet of Malay food is served up daily for lunch and dinner. There's also afternoon tea (3.30–5.30pm). The food does not really live up to the price tag, but there is plenty of it – oysters, fish, lobster, curries by the dozen, and even roast beef.

Bon Ton Restaurant, 6 Jalan Stonor, **t** 03 2144 3848. Bon Ton has one of the finest settings of any of KL's restaurants, located in a restored colonial bungalow east of the KLCC gardens. The large menu features local, Western and fusion dishes. Many will be familiar, but a lot of effort is put into the visual effect – the cuisine here has been described as 'artistic comfort food'. One of the highlights is the list of set meals, including the Nyonya special, with chicken *kapitan* and mango *kerabu*.

Gulai House, Carcosa Seri Negara, Taman Tasik Perdana, **t** 03 2282 1888. Malay cuisine is not known for its pretensions, but at Gulai House you can combine fine dining with classic Malay dishes. Set in the Victorian splendour of the Carcosa Seri Negara, with piped gamelan music. Dishes include satay, *otak-otak*, beef *rendang* and a range of fish and seafood options. For dessert, try honeyed jackfruit stuffed with glutinous rice, coconut cream and caramel.

Moderate

Kafe Old China, 11 Jalan Balai Polis (off Jalan Petaling), **t** 03 2072 5915. In a wonderful setting surrounded by antiques: crossing the threshold is like stepping back into pre-war Chinatown (*see* p.109). Traditional Nyonya (Malay-Chinese) food is served.

The Kapitan's Club, 35 Jalan Ampang, **t** 03 2201 0242. Named after the man some consider to be the founder of Kuala Lumpur, and housed in an old clan association mansion. The food is Straits Chinese (Nyonya curries, kapitan chicken), along with local hawker favourites. The interior is decked out like a traditional Chinese coffee shop, with tiled floors and old ceiling fans.

Inexpensive

Restoran Ahmad Buhari, corner of Jalan Nagasari and Changkat Bukit Bintang. This permanent *mamak* stall opposite the Radius International Hotel serves delicious *roti canai*, *nasi lemak* and *nasi campur* – a simple antidote to the gentrified restaurants round the corner on Changkat Bukit Bintang.

Chinese

Expensive

Eden Seafood Village, 7 Jalan Kia Peng, **t** 03 2141 3611. One of KL's best-known seafood restaurants. Though many of the dishes are Chinese in origin (it is well known for its shark's fin soup) the restaurant is a bit of a hybrid of Mediterranean influences in a Malay-style house.

Shang Palace, Shangri-La Hotel, 11 Jalan Sultan Ismail, **t** 03 2074 3904. One of the better hotel restaurants, noted for its dim sum. There's a big menu of mainstay Chinese specialities. Try the delicious, but fearsome-sounding, wanton soup with hairy crab claw.

Shanghai Restaurant, JW Marriott Hotel, 183 Jalan Bukit Bintang, **t** 03 2716 8288. This restaurant specializes in the cuisine of Shanghai, which is where the chef himself hails from. The setting is traditional, with brush paintings on the walls, Chinese lanterns and lacquered screens. There's a heavy reliance on ginger, while dumplings replace rice at the table. Simple offerings such as the signature dish 'Imperial Jewels' (eggs cooked carefully in stock) contrast with crisp fried eel in aromatic black sauce, Shanghai dumplings or freshwater shrimp.

Lai Po Heen Restaurant, Mandarin Oriental Hotel, KLCC, **t** 03 2179 8885. Classic Cantonese cuisine (plenty of seafood and dim sum) in a grand setting modelled after the 'ancestral homes of Chinese tycoons'.

Moderate

Bangsar Seafood Village, Jalan Telawi 4, **t** 03 2282 2555. Popular destination for fresh seafood in all its guises. There's an indoor restaurant, a large outdoor section and a 'claypot corner' for noodle-based dishes.

Eatsun Hong Kong Restaurant, 59 Jalan Walter Grenier (off Jalan Imbi), **t** 03 2148 9771. Chinese coffee shop decor and delicious dim sum served in bamboo steaming baskets, with an open roast stall in the corner for duck, goose, chicken and pork.

Restoran Oversea, Central Market, Jalan Hang Kasturi, **t** 03 2274 6470. One of a chain of good-quality restaurants serving a range of Chinese cuisines (with a leaning towards Cantonese). The *pau* (stuffed steamed buns) and dim sum come highly recommended.

Inexpensive

Cameleon Vegetarian Restaurant, 1 Jalan Thamboosamy (faces onto Jalan Putra). A decent and inexpensive vegetarian choice situated near the PWTC stop on the LRT. There is a large range of mock meat and bean-curd-based dishes to choose from.

Indian

Expensive–Moderate

Bombay Palace, 215 Jalan Tun Razak (beside US embassy), **t** 03 2145 4241. A well-respected North Indian restaurant on the eastern edge of town. Specialities include biryani, chicken and prawn tandoori and a range of kebabs. Save a little room for the desserts.

Moghul House, 34 Changkat Bukit Bintang, **t** 03 2142 1455. Has a huge menu of North Indian classics, with lots of offerings from the tandoor oven. The *paneer* is delicious, as are the fruit *lassies*.

The Taj, Crown Princess Kuala Lumpur, City Square Centre, Jalan Tun Razak, **t** 03 2162 5522, ext. 5680. Fine dining on the 11th floor of the Crown Princess hotel, with great views of the KL skyline. Raj-style décor, live Indian music and top-rate North Indian cuisine make this a memorable dinner destination. If you've spared any room, try the home-made pistachio ice cream.

Inexpensive

Iskcon Govinda's Vegetarian Restaurant, 1st Floor, 19 Jalan Bunus 6. Just north of Jalan Masjid India, this is a popular lunch destination for the local community. Set lunch from the buffet costs a few ringgits.

Lakshmi Villas, Lebuh Ampang. A good choice for a South Indian banana-leaf lunch, located on the street which runs on from Medan Pasar, north of Chinatown.

Japanese

Expensive

Wasabi Bistro, Mandarin Oriental Hotel, KLCC, **t** 03 2380 8888. The cuisine here is rather ambitiously described as 'a modern take on traditional Japanese fare, with Californian influences'. The 'bistro' setting allows for soft lighting and wicker chairs. Known for its sushi, and extravagant mains such as Alaskan black cod. Set within the Mandarin Oriental Hotel, though independent.

Moderate

Hoshigaoka, 4th Floor, The Mall, Jalan Putra, **t** 03 4142 7561. In the mall beside the Putra World Trade Centre. Good-value alternative to expensive hotel restaurants in the area.

Inexpensive

Sushi King, Suria KLCC Food Court. Cheap sushi on a conveyor belt. There are a number of other branches dotted about town.

Thai

Expensive

Chakri Palace, 4th Floor, Suria KLCC, **t** 03 2382 7788. Stately restaurant with carved teak decor serving up 'Royal Thai' cooking. A vast array of authentic Thai cuisine.

Moderate

Rain Nudle House, Level 4, Suria KLCC, **t** 03 2382 0669. Closeby to Chakri Palace in the Suria KLCC shopping mall, but less formal. The sort of place you might drift into mid-shop. All the Thai staples are represented: *tom yam*, red curry, green curry and plenty of 'nudle' dishes.

The Red Chamber, 33 Telawi Tiga, Bangsar, **t** 03 2283 1898. Lushly decorated in boudoir style with healthy portions of Japanese and Thai food. Noodle dishes are recommended.

Middle Eastern

Expensive

Islamic Arts Museum Restaurant, Jalan Lembah Perdana, **t** 03 2274 6273. Popular Middle Eastern restaurant serving Lebanese pizza, tabbouleh, and shish kebab, with aubergine, lamb and lentils. In a tranquil setting, with Persian wall hangings, Iranian brass lamps and Islamic motifs on the wall panels. It is worth combining a visit to the museum with the buffet lunch. Closed Mon.

Moderate

The Terrace, 23 Jalan Sultan Ismail, **t** 03 2148 5860. An Arabic and Mediterranean café which serves a range of tasty Middle Eastern food – mainly snacks. There's a hookah for each table and a menu of easy-smoking fruit- flavoured tobaccos.

Indonesian

House of Sundanese, Level 4, Suria KLCC, **t** 03 2166 2272. Traditional food from the Indonesian province of Sunda. Sundanese *sambal* paste (a rich and spicy chilli and prawn mixture) is one of the primary ingredients. Try the *cumi-cumi bakar*, squid with sweet *sambal* grilled over charcoal.

International and Fusion

Expensive

Mahsuri Dining Hall, Carcosa Seri Negara, Taman Tasik Perdana, Persiaran Mahameru, **t** 03 2282 1888, **f** 03 2282 7888, *carcosa@mol.net.my*, *www.carcosa.com.my*. The Mahsuri has been named in the past as one of the best restaurants in Malaysia. It's probably the most expensive in the country too. The cuisine is 'contemporary European with a touch of Asian' and the setting, traditional but classy. Offerings may include squid stuffed with black ink risotto, foie gras, oysters, Szechuan-style goose liver or plain old veal tenderloin. A curry tiffin lunch is served on Sundays 12–2.30.

Frangipani Restaurant, 25 Changkat Bukit Bintang, **t** 03 2144 3001. Leave plenty of time to read the menu, a long and eloquent commentary by the Luxembourger chef on his varied European offerings ('Forget the sedentary, flabby Norwegian salmon; the sprightly Scottish variety is leaner and meaner and that is why we cook it rare. It is just too beautiful to cook to death'). Other items include duck, foie gras, fried oysters and fish in a variety of guises. The setting is stylish, crisp and trendy with tables set around a rectangular water feature.

Scalini's, 19 Jalan Sultan Ismail, **t** 03 2145 3211. The Milanese chef at Scalini's conjures up some of KL's best Italian cuisine. The extensive menu features classic dishes from both north and south and the atmosphere is subdued – conducive to a long staggered evening of eating and wine quaffing.

Aero Restaurant & Lounge, 2 Jalan Tengah, **t** 03 2141 7871. Mainly known as a place to stop at for a cocktail, with stylish décor, comfy sofas and floor-to-ceiling windows. However, the food is gaining a name for itself as well. A range of interesting entrées from salad-based concoctions to sesame scallops on black pasta cakes are followed by the likes of rack of lamb, seafood on spaghetti or fillet of beef with eggplant. Plenty of devilish desserts, too.

Le Bouchon, 14–16 Changkat Bukit Bintang, **t** 03 2142 7633. An old-world wine list complements classical French cuisine served up by a chef from Brittany. Fresh fillets of fish, cuts of meat in robust sauces, Burgundy snails and rabbit all feature on the menu.

Pacifica Bar & Grill, Mandarin Oriental Hotel, KLCC, **t** 03 2380 8888. Signature restaurant of the Mandarin Oriental Hotel, in a slick stylish setting with an open kitchen. The young Aussie chef serves up trans-ethnic cuisine with an Asian bent, such as lemongrass skewered scallops, seared liver with *balsamico* or quesadillas with lobster.

Moderate

Coliseum Hotel & Cafe, 98–100 Jalan Tuanku Abdul Rahman, **t** 03 2692 6270. The legendary downstairs cafe (*see* p.103) turns out steaks and British-style pies, which have drawn a faithful following since the hotel and cafe opened in 1921.

Ciccio Pasticcio, 15 Changkat Bukit Bintang, **t** 03 2141 8605. Serves KL's best wood-fired pizzas along with a glut of pasta dishes and home-made gnocchi. Doubles up as a bar which can get crowded at weekends.

The Artscafe, National Art Gallery, 2 Jalan Temerloh (off Jalan Tun Razak), **t** 03 4025 2315. This place outshines the National Art Gallery itself. The inventive offerings include triple-decker sandwiches stuffed with red snapper *sambal*, marinara (seafood stew) or fried *koay teow*. Each meal comes with a glass of Ice Flower Lemon Tea. The setting is bright and open-plan, and up-and-coming artists exhibit their works here.

Entertainment & Nightlife

Though it still has a long way to go, KL's nightlife gathers momentum year by year, and there are bars and clubs to suit most tastes. The suburb of Bangsar is KL's prime nightlife spot, though there are plenty of options in the Golden Triangle, particularly around Jalan Bukit Bintang. The best place to look for listings are monthly magazines such as *Juice*, *KLue* and *KL Vision*, available in bookshops.

Cultural entertainment in KL is limited, as far as capital cities go. The spacious and modern **National Theatre** (**t** 03 4025 2525), just south of Titiwangsa Lake, is home to the National Theatre Company and National Symphony Orchestra. Check listings in daily papers for performance schedules. The impressive Petronas Concert Hall (**t** 03 2207 7007), inside the Petronas Towers, is home to the Malaysian Philharmonic Orchestra.

There are regular 'cultural' performances at the Malaysia Tourism Centre (109 Jalan Ampang, **t** 03 2164 3929) and at Central Market.

Bars & Clubs

Coliseum Hotel & Cafe, 98-100 Jalan Tuanku Abdul Rahman. The scruffy bar downstairs is full of character and was a favourite drinking haunt of Somerset Maugham. The walls are hung with the work of Lat, a famous local cartoonist.

Bull's Head, Central Market, Jalan Hang Kasturi. Large and popular pub-style bar.

Frangipani, 25 Changkat Bukit Bintang. Sophisticated bar above the restaurant, with chill-out tunes.

Aero, 2 Jalan Tengah. Flash futuristic bar with floor-to-ceiling windows and a good menu of cocktails.

Ozeki, Menara TA One, 22 Jalan P. Ramlee. This bar has a crisp, Japanese interior and a huge variety of sakes to try out.

Hard Rock Café, Wisma Concorde 2, Jalan Sultan Ismail. The usual: rock memorabilia, American food and happy hours.

Alexis the Bar Upstairs, 29A Jalan Telawi 3, Bangsar. Sophisticated cocktail lounge with acid-jazz sounds.

Bar Zar, Jalan Telawi 3, Bangsar. Full of pillows and the smoke of hubble-bubbles. Cocktails and food available.

Finnegan's, 6 Jalan Telawi 5, Bangsar. Irish-theme pub and restaurant where Premiership matches are screened. Surprisingly smart clientele.

La Bodega, 16 Jalan Telawi 2, Bangsar. Big selection of wines and tapas.

Bliss, 12 Jalan Sultan Ismail. Hugely popular venue with a house trio of DJs and a great people-watching balcony.

O*Range, 1 Jalan Kia Peng. R&B inside an old colonial building with retro decor. *Open Wed–Sat.*

The Back Room, Menara Pan Global, 8 Loroong P. Ramlee. Harder beats alongside hip hop and R&B. Popular as an after-party spot.

The Disco, Central Market Annexe, Jalan Hang Kasturi. Techno, trance, soul and disco in a warehouse-style club. There's a pleasant outdoor terrace overlooking the river.

Liquid, Central Market Annexe, Jalan Hang Kasturi. Probably KL's best-known club, with a predominantly gay clientele. Loungey with house and chill-out music.

Nuovo, corner of Jalan Sultan Ismail and Jalan P. Ramlee. Fashionable club playing Latin, disco and house tunes. Numerous bars and a large mezzanine area with chill-out room.

Bilique, 34–36 Jalan Telawi, Bangsar. Likes to set itself apart from other clubs in Bangsar by playing a wide range of music. Pool tables and food available too.

Echo, Jalan Telawi 3, Bangsar. The longest-standing club in Bangsar, still popular, with a crew of house DJs.

Salsabar, Jalan Telawi 5, Bangsar. Salsa in a comfortable loungey atmosphere.

Shopping

KL likes to vie with Singapore as a great shopping emporium. In one sense it has the upper hand: prices are lower here – and with the ongoing development of the capital, the upmarket selection is growing too. There are in excess of 20 shopping malls dotted about the city, most inside the Golden Triangle. The most interesting places to delve about are the markets and the various weekly *pasar malam* (night markets).

Look out for Selangor pewter, batik, *songket* (Malay textile hand-woven with silver or gold thread), Kelantan silverwork, *mengkuang* basketry, woodcarvings and brassware from Terengganu. The fake designer watch selection isn't bad either.

Shopping Malls

Top of the list of shopping malls is **Suria KLCC**, situated at the foot of the Petronas Towers. This multilevel mall contains hundreds of designer boutiques, international brand names, bookshops, craft shops, upmarket restaurants and fast-food outlets. **Lot 10**, **KL Plaza** and **Star Hill**, provide further up market options in the Bukit Bintang area. Nearby, **Sungei Wang Plaza** and **BB Plaza** form the biggest mall along Jalan Bukit Bintang – a good spot to track down bargains.

Jalan Tuanku Abdul Rahman (Jalan TAR) is the other place to find goods at local prices. Jalan TAR was KL's original shopping street, and some of the old malls remain, namely **Globe Silk Store**, **Pertama Shopping Complex** and **Sogo Kuala Lumpur**. Further north, **The Mall**, beside the Putra World Trade Centre, is good for clothes, jewellery and luggage. If you're looking for American-style shopping try out-of-town **Mid-Valley Megamall**, complete with large cineplex and Carrefour.

Markets

The daily **Chow Kit Market** is KL's largest outdoor market and a great place to soak up the local atmosphere. Medicine men crouch among herbs, oils and dried animal parts. At food stalls, men in songkoks knead and toss *roti* into shape (*roti canai* is Malaysia's favourite snack food). Clothes, household goods, meat, fruit and vegetables abound.

Central Market is the first port of call for many visitors. The tourist board bills it as KL's Covent Garden (clearly a stretch of the imagination). Two floors of stalls and boutiques sell a wide range of antiques, handicrafts and souvenirs, from batik, silk and spices to pewter, woodcarvings and kites. Bargaining is essential.

The daily *pasar malam* (night market) on Chinatown's revamped **Petaling Street** is the other major draw for tourists. Fake watches, pirated CDs and DVDs are popular goods, though there's plenty of other stuff on sale, from fruit, flowers and herbal remedies to handicrafts and ethnic jewellery from India and Burma.

There's a weekly *pasar malam* at **Kampung Baru**, a Malay enclave on the north side of town. Sarongs, batik, *songket* and other Malay goods are sold alongside handicrafts and Malay snack food. The market begins on Saturday afternoon and is finished by lunchtime on Sunday.

For Indian goodies try the *pasar malam* in Little India (around **Jalan Masjid India**) or the sari stalls and Indian food stalls of **Lebuh Ampang**, just to the north of Chinatown.

Selangor Journal gives a sneering account of a Malay football match held on the padang. 'The players make apologetic charges and stand around in picturesque attitudes. The full back may be seen stretched at full length smoking a cigarette whilst a mildly fierce battle is being waged near the opponents' goal.' The wry contributor goes on to compare the game to a ladies' football match back in England.

Modern Merdeka Square is no longer used as a sports pitch, though football matches can sometimes be viewed on the giant screen (the World Cup sees Merdeka Square at its busiest). On 31st August each year Independence Day celebrations draw the crowds too. The spot where the Malayan flag was hoisted for the first time in 1957 is marked today in typical Malaysian manner: with the world's tallest flag pole.

Back in colonial days the padang would become a lake each time the River Gombak burst its banks – though that didn't stop hardened planters and administrators from wading across to the clubhouse for an evening at the bar. After the flood of 1926, the worst in KL's history, tens of thousands of banknotes were laid out to dry on the padang, under the watchful eye of the police – floodwater had breached the vaults of the Standard Chartered Bank, in the building which now serves as the **National History Museum** (Muzium Sejarah Nasional; *29 Jalan Raja,* **t** *03 2694 4590; open daily 9–6; free*). The museum broadly traces the region's timeline from the prehistoric (there's a 40,000-year-old skull on display) to the modern (the rose-tinted story of Malaysia's fast-track industrialization).

The Royal Selangor Club on the western edge of Merdeka Square was first built in 1884 as a social and cricket club. A fire destroyed part of the original clubhouse and most of the present mock-Tudor building was erected in 1978. The club was frequented by influential locals as well as planters, civil servants and lawyers. It was known to all as 'The Spotted Dog' (some say in reference to two dalmatians, pets of the Chief of Police's wife, that were often to be found mooching about the verandah; others pointed to the club's mixed-race membership).

Before the Petronas Towers stole the limelight, the copper-domed **Sultan Abdul Samad Building** was the symbol of Kuala Lumpur. Completed in 1897, it stands across the square from the 'Spotted Dog'. It now houses the High Court, though it was built as the Selangor Secretariat offices. Its eclectic style was the result of a collaboration of designs, though the building is generally credited to government architect AC Norman. The defining features are the clock tower and the two flanking circular towers with spiral colonnades, all topped with copper cupolas. Verandahs with arched colonnades surround the building on both floors. It is said that the Moorish influences were the inspiration of State Engineer Charles Spooner, who had served previously in India and Ceylon. He believed that a building of such importance should reflect local sensibilities; hence the 'Mohametan' (Spooner's own description) touches. Ideas were drawn from the British Raj-style architecture of India, and despite Spooner's best intentions, the result is as far-flung from traditional Malay architecture as it could be. On the grand opening, many were critical that such a fine-looking building should grace a frontier town with an uncertain future. Perhaps KL has the Samad building to thank for its pre-eminent status today.

Close by are a series of Moorish-styled buildings, including the Old Post Office, the Old City Hall and the Textile Museum (Jalan Sultan Hishamuddin; *open Sat–Thurs 9–5; free*). All date from around the turn of the 20th century and were designed to complement the Samad building. One exception is the Memorial Library, facing the southern end of Merdeka Square, with its Flemish gables, bay windows and brick pilasters. This was originally built as the government printing office and it seems likely that it was based on Norman's initial design for the Samad building.

Just south of Merdeka Square, across the river from Central Market (*see* p.103), is the **Dayabumi Complex**, a modern interpretation of Moorish architecture and one of the city's most striking buildings. From the base of the many-sided tower, which is formed of pointed Islamic-style arches, the building rises 35 storeys high. The entire body of the building is covered in a white grill of geometric motifs, which functions on a practical level as a shading device.

A Mosque and a Cathedral

Some would say that the impressive **Masjid Jamek** marks the true heart of KL; the mosque sits at the very spot where it all began – the *kuala lumpur*, or 'muddy confluence', of the two rivers Gombak and Klang. This is the city's oldest surviving mosque, a low-lying oasis of Mogul arches and palm trees ringed by modern-day tower blocks. Oddly, it was designed by an Englishman. Arthur Benson Hubback, who was government architect when the mosque was completed in 1909, took his influences from the mogul mosques of northern India. Before modern buildings crowded the skyline, the muezzin's voice was able to sail unimpeded across the settlement from two 90ft minarets. A pretty, arched colonnade marks the boundary of the mosque. Masjid Jamek served as the city's primary Muslim place of worship until the larger National Mosque (*see* p.108) was built in 1965 on the edge of the Lake Gardens.

The modest **Cathedral of St Mary the Virgin** stands just to the north of Merdeka Square. Originally St Mary's Church (it was raised to cathedral status in 1983), St Mary's was once the fulcrum of the Selangor's colonial community, its pews packed each week with worshippers sweating in their Sunday best. Outside in the tropical sun, Tamil *punkah wallahs* tugged on ropes so that the congregation could be cooled by great sheets of fabric swaying back and forth among the rafters. The church dates from 1894 and its structure incorporates buttresses in early Gothic style.

Grandest Station in Asia

Paul Theroux likened it to the North-Indian-inspired Brighton Pavilion, and he is not far off the mark. KL's famous railway station is a fantasy of the Orient, a cluster of domes, keyhole arches, colonnades, cupolas and minarets designed in 1900 by government architect A. B. Hubback, but not completed until 1911. It replaced the attap-roofed shed which had served as the railway terminal since 1886, when the first railway line was completed. Despite outward appearances, the building was constructed according to official specifications for railway terminals across the British

Empire – right down to the iron roof, which is sturdy enough to withstand up to a metre of snow. One wing of the building was set aside to function as Kuala Lumpur's first hotel, which served for years as the most luxurious accommodation on offer to visitors. The hotel was reopened in 1996, a cheaper and more jaded embodiment of its former self. The hotel is under the same management as the newly reopened Majestic Station Hotel in Ipoh (Ipoh's station was also designed by A. B. Hubback).

The old Railway Station no longer functions as KL's primary terminal. Modern Sentral Station, a few hundred yards to the south, serves that purpose today. The surrounding area is an enclave known as **Brickfields**, after the brickyards which once lined the tracks. Tamil railway workers settled the area back in the late 19th century, and Brickfields remains a distinctly Indian enclave – though it has lost much of its old character since the new station opened in 2002.

Lake Gardens

The Lake Gardens (Taman Tasik Perdana) have been around almost as long as Kuala Lumpur itself. Back in 1888 Sir Alfred Venning, chairman of the Sanitary Board, deemed a landscaped garden necessary to preserve the health of colonial officials. A large area of swampland and forest was drained and cleared to allow for a series of trails and grassy knolls. The gardens proved an immediate hit with the colonial community, who enjoyed the shaded walkways and the chatter of wildlife (in those days the gardens were backed by rainforest, providing frequent sightings of leopards, sun bears, monkeys and deer). Today the gardens are one of the highlights of a visit to KL, not least because they provide a refuge from the shadeless, traffic-choked streets. But there are many attractions here too, from the world's largest covered bird park (yes, another first for KL) to a boating lake, an orchid garden, a deer park, a planetarium and a couple of museums. At the northern reaches of the Lake Gardens is the **ASEAN Sculpture Park**, with a collection of abstract works from the leading artists of the ASEAN nations.

Presiding over the Lake Gardens, from a hill to the west, is the **Carcosa Seri Negara** (*see* 'Where to Stay', p.95), built in 1896 for Frank Swettenham, the first Resident-General of the Federated Malay States. Keen to ensure that the mansion coincided with his own ideals of a dream home, Swettenham was said to have played a large part in the design of the building, with its high ceilings and breezy wraparound verandahs. Space to entertain guests was an important consideration; he had complained that his previous residence was unbefitting a man of his station – it was too cramped and the roof leaked after heavy bouts of rain. When Malaya gained independence in 1957, Tunku Abdul Rahman (Malaya's first prime minister) presented the building to the British High Commissioner, who managed to hang onto it until 1989, by which time those in power were wondering why on earth the city's most impressive residence was being wasted on a Brit. It was promptly converted into a boutique hotel designed to transport guests back to the good old days of British patronage. Queen Elizabeth and Prince Philip are the most illustrious guests to have graced the visitors' book. Incidentally, they took separate suites.

K.L. Bird Park

Open daily 9–6.30; adm RM25/18.

The most popular of the attractions on offer at the Lake Gardens is the **K.L. Bird Park**. Nets stretch across a verdant 20-acre site, above the treeline, to create the world's largest walk-in free-flight aviary. The strange mass of netting is clearly visible from KL's two lookout points: the Menara Tower and the Skybridge on the Petronas Towers. Birds from across the world's warmer climes are represented. However, not all of the 3,000-plus birds are compatible and many pass their lives in traditional fashion, hopping unhappily about enclosed cages. North of the Bird Park is the less impressive **Butterfly Park** (*open daily 9–6; adm RM6/2*), the **Orchid Garden** (*open daily 9–6; adm free*) and, in honour of Malaysia's national flower, the **Hibiscus Garden** (*open daily 9–6; adm free*).

Deer Park

Open daily 9–6; adm free.

Right in the centre of the Lake Gardens is the **Deer Park**, a small enclosure full of spotted deer from the Netherlands. Look out too for mouse deer, tiny delicate creatures the size of domestic cats but with the twitching helplessness of mice, hence the name.

Planetarium

Open Sat–Thurs 10–4; adm RM3/2.

At the southern limits of the gardens is the **Planetarium**, where children will enjoy the small display of interactive games and exhibits (including a shuttle spaceball which, for a charge of RM1, will spin you in such a way that you experience zero gravity). Shows on the IMAX screen in the Space Theatre are held at 11am, 2pm and 4pm.

Muzium Negara

Jalan Damansara; open daily 9–6; adm RM2.

From the Planetarium a footbridge leads across to the **Muzium Negara** (National Museum), which stands on the other side of the new expressway. Though exhibits have been expanded upon in recent years, this is not the flagship museum the authorities once dreamed it would be. Its predecessor, the old Selangor Museum, was obliterated by bombs during the war, and things have never been the same since. Galleries cover Malay ceremonies, textiles, traditional music, pastimes (shadow plays, top-spinning), ceramics and natural history.

Masjid Negara

On the edge of the Lake Gardens, opposite the old Railway Station, stands the **Masjid Negara** (National Mosque), an unusual piece of Modernist-Islamic architecture from 1965. The main aluminium-plated 'dome' sits above the prayer hall like a giant bright-blue cocktail umbrella. The prayer hall itself is vast, with a capacity of up to 10,000, making it the largest in Southeast Asia. A single 75m-tall minaret rises like a sharpened pencil above the low-lying dome.

Islamic Arts Museum

Jalan Lembah Perdana; open Tues–Sun 10–6; adm RM12/6.

Just beyond the mosque is the excellent **Islamic Arts Museum**, housed in an extravagant open-plan structure with marble floors and an inverted dome, its interior surface finished by craftsmen from Iran and Uzbekistan (the latter being home to the legendary architecture of Samarkand and Bukhara). The museum is laid out on four levels. Level 3, bizarrely, is the place to start. Here you will find the Architecture Gallery with a reconstruction of the interior of an 18th-century Ottoman Syrian house, and scale models of some of the great monuments of Islam, from the Taj Mahal to the magnificent mosques of Medina and Mecca. Separate galleries on this level are dedicated in turn to the Islamic arts of India, China and the Malay archipelago. The galleries on Level 4 cover ceramics, textiles, metalwork and arms, while a large outdoor terrace provides views across the city. Temporary exhibitions, which occasionally outshine the permanent exhibits, are held in the 'special galleries' on Levels 1 and 2. The restaurant (*see* 'Eating Out', p.98) serves excellent Middle Eastern food, while the museum shop – stacked with superior souvenirs and antiques – is worth a browse even if you don't make it round the museum itself.

Chinatown

In Kuala Lumpur's days as a rough frontier town, the centre of action was Market Square (Medan Pasar), an area now dominated by banks. About the makeshift market stalls of the old Medan Pasar, Chinese headman Yap Ah Loy (*see* 'Founding Father', p.92) built a fine square of shophouses, which he let out as sundry stores, gambling dens and brothels – his workers needed something to spend their wages on, after all. The settlement soon expanded south along the east bank of the River Klang, into the heart of present-day Chinatown.

American zoologist William Hornaday, who visited Kuala Lumpur back in 1878, described Market Square as 'a place where fruits, vegetables, meats and various abominations of Chinese cookery are sold'. He went home a happy man, however, when he came across a shop selling champagne 'at sixty cents a quart... It was the proudest moment of my life'. His only regret was not filling a tub and taking a champagne bath.

Jalan Petaling

When people think of Chinatown today, they think of **Jalan Petaling** (or Petaling Street) and its daily market. In fact, 'Jalan Petaling' and 'Chinatown' have become interchangeable terms. Tourists home in on the street market for local snacks, cheap clothes and the irresistible spread of contraband goods, from pirated software and DVDs to quality fake watches, some of which sell for thousands of ringgits (and not just to mugs). In 2003 the face of Petaling Street changed for good after a process of 'beautification'. The mass of colourful umbrellas long associated with the street were made redundant by a transparent roof, which now runs above part of the street, while the market stalls were replaced with scrubbed-up kiosks. Reactions to the new look have been mixed; the façades of the heritage shophouses are now partly obscured and the roof is prone to leaks. Despite teething problems, tourists still come in their droves. Set back in old shophouses along Jalan Petaling are cafés, massage parlours, medicine shops and a couple of Taoist funerary shops selling elaborate paper offerings (paper mobile phones sell particularly well).

For a taste of Chinatown in the 1930s, veer west off Jalan Petaling into Jalan Balai Polis and step through the old saloon doors of **Kafe Old China** (*see* also 'Eating Out', p.99). The building is owned by the Selangor Laundry Association, whose founder members line the walls in portraits. The café doubles up as an antiques shop too. Name the right price, and the proprietor will sell you the chair you're sitting on.

Right at the southern end of Jalan Petaling is the temple of the **Chan See Shu Yuen Association**, one of the city's finer examples of temple architecture, completed in 1906. Inside, gilded wooden panels frame ancestral shrines, while outside, mythological figures in terracotta crowd the spine of the roof. The unusual gables, rimmed by glazed tiles in the undulating form of waves, are a feature borrowed from temple design in southern China.

Central Market and Medan Pasar

At the northern end of Chinatown, across the river from Merdeka Square, is the traditional commercial heart of KL, an area centred on Medan Pasar (Market Square) and, close by, the impressive Art Deco **Central Market**. The latter was built in 1936 as a means of containing the unsavoury sprawl of market stalls which had overrun the district. According to historian Ng Seo Buck, 'delapidated, filthy, vermin-stricken cow sheds stood on the site before this modern, imposing structure was built'. The new building served as KL's wet market up until the 1980s, when plans were unveiled to demolish the structure. However, local organizations campaigned for its conservation, and the building was reinvented as an arts and crafts centre. A mezzanine level was added and the market was divided into a series of tourist-oriented craft boutiques selling everything from Malay silverware, *songket* and batik to Chinese brush paintings and Balinese carvings. Today, Central Market likes to see itself as KL's Covent Garden; it hosts regular exhibitions and cultural performances, and is a popular browsing ground for tourists.

The Letter

After dark on 23rd April 1911, William Steward, former manager of the Salak tin mine, entered the grounds of the Victoria Institution by rickshaw and paid a visit to Ethel Proudlock, the headmaster's wife. He asked the rickshaw boy to wait outside the gate. A short while later the boy heard two gunshots. He then watched as William Steward stumbled across the verandah and fell down the steps onto the driveway. Ethel Proudlock followed and emptied the remaining four rounds at close range.

The event caused a sensation across Malaya and made headlines back in England. This was a killing within the British colonial community. A sordid relationship that had ended in murder – or so people began to believe. And the perpetrator was a woman – a wife and a mother. In court Ethel Proudlock claimed that Steward had attempted to rape her. Her hand 'came into contact with a revolver', she said, and she had fired in self-defence. The judge found her guilty of murder. She was locked up in Pudu Jail for five months, until a wave of petitions to the Sultan of Selangor finally secured her release. She set off back for England alone.

On a visit to Malaya in 1921, William Somerset Maugham stumbled across the defence lawyer from the Proudlock case. Here were rich pickings for a writer. The result was 'The Letter', a short story subsequently adapted into a Hollywood film starring Bette Davis. Maugham took the facts and twisted them into fiction. Ethel Proudlock becomes Leslie Crosbie, wife of a rubber planter, and she is acquitted, despite the existence of a letter that would have convicted her – the letter she wrote to her lover to lure him to the house on that fateful evening. The story revolves around the letter and the attempts to destroy it by those who know of its existence, particularly Leslie's husband, who ruins himself in the process.

Kuala Lumpur's first market was situated a little to the north, at present-day Medan Pasar. This is where the traders and tin miners of the early settlement would come to do business and spend wages. Yap Ah Loy, the influential Kapitan China who many people credit as the city's founder (*see* p.92), built his house on an adjacent street. On the square itself he set up gambling dens and brothels to occupy his workers. Today, Medan Pesar is lined with banks. Indian moneylenders, known as Chettiars, set up shop along Lebuh Ampang, which runs north from Medan Pasar.

Old High Street

Though Jalan Petaling is the modern heart of Chinatown, parallel **Jalan Tun H. S. Lee** can lay claim to being the district's historic artery. In the early days, it was called High Street because of its elevated position; it was the most sought-after street among immigrant Chinese because it avoided the annual monsoon floods. If they had the means, newcomers would rent out rooms above the shophouses; others became bed tenants, renting collapsible canvas beds and a few square feet of space along a crowded corridor.

Right at the northern end of this street stands the city's oldest row of shophouses, a crumbling, plain-looking terrace (Nos. 34–40) which no one seems to take much notice of. Equally discreet, filling little more than a crack between two later buildings close to Central Market, is the **Sze Si Ya Temple**, an old Taoist temple founded by Yap Ah Loy. It is dedicated to the patron deity of pioneers (Sze Si Ya), though Yap Ah Loy himself nestles in among the deities in the form of a black and white photograph, to the left of the main shrine. Much more prominent is the **Sri Maha Mariamman Temple**, with its towering multi-coloured *gopuram* (gate tower) sculpted with Hindu gods. The temple, which claims to be Malaysia's wealthiest, was founded in 1873 by Thamboosamay Pillai, an Indian tin and coffee tycoon, though the present building dates from the 1960s. The temple's main claim to fame is its extravagant silver chariot (constructed with 350 kilos of silver), which is pulled by white bullocks to the Batu Caves during the spectacular Thaipusam festival (*see* p.115).

Towards the southern end of Jalan Tun H.S. Lee is the old **Victoria Institution**, a place that has gone down in legend as the site of a colonial murder and the inspiration of a Hollywood classic (*see* 'The Letter', opposite). It was built in 1893 by colonial architect A. C. Norman in the style of an English cottage and served as KL's top English-language school. In the early days, the building sat within a bend of the River Klang and schoolboys had to take care to avoid the crocodiles which lurked in the shallows. The old Victoria Institution is now an arts centre. The school is still going strong, but in different premises.

Little India and Chow Kit

Jalan Tuanku Abdul Rahman (or Jalan TAR – pronounced 'tar'– as it is also thankfully known) stretches north from Merdeka Square past Little India and as far as Chow Kit. It originated as Batu Road, a muddy track that led through coconut plantations and secondary jungle to nearby tin mines. Its southern boundary was marked by a Malay kampung in the area of present-day Jalan Melayu. Indian settlers soon joined the Malays; funded by *chettiars* (Indian moneylenders), they took advantage of the constant flow of traffic along Batu Road by opening market stalls and warehouses. Shophouses followed, many of them Art Deco in style. Traders, shoppers and traffic have gridlocked the road ever since.

Only Jalan TAR's extremities – namely Little India to the south and Chow Kit 2km to the north – are worth exploring today. Little India confines itself to **Jalan Masjid India**, a short stretch of road that briefly runs parallel with Jalan TAR. As befitting the Indian enclave of any city, Jalan Masjid India is a burst of colour and spicy aromas, though it is much smaller than people expect. Silk by the yard, saris, scarves, *songkets*, and samosas are in steady supply. There is a definite Malay presence too; if you are a fan of *mamak* cuisine (Indian-Muslim food) or Malay staples such as *nasi lemak* and satay, then be sure to pay Little India and its surrounding streets a visit. And drop by for the Saturday *pasar malam* (night market).

Across Jalan TAR from Little India is the **Coliseum Café and Hotel**, a strange and eclectic place, to say the least. It was opened by three Hainanese friends in 1921. They named it after a legendary amphitheatre in Rome and decided to specialize in that best-loved of world cuisines – British. Expanses of wood and swinging saloon doors give it the feel of a frontier-town watering hole. Whatever you make of the place, Somerset Maugham found it to his taste. And little has changed since his day.

KL's biggest daily street market can be found at the north end of Jalan TAR, behind the Stanford Hotel. **Chow Kit Market** is up and running by dawn, and still going strong after dark. Every conceivable item passes hands here, from shellfish, seasonal fruit and crockery to cheap jeans, mobile phones, Malay textiles and dubious-looking medicinal remedies. To local ears, the words 'Chow Kit' have other associations beyond market produce. This enclave is seen as the traditional haunt of the destitute – the drug pushers, streetwalkers and *pondans* (transvestites), who parade their own clandestine goods in back lanes and double-dealing 'coffee shops'. By day, Chow Kit is a workaday place full of local shoppers and office workers from the nearby Putra World Trade Centre (PWTC). After nightfall, Chow Kit's other face rears into view, though the authorities have taken measures to clean up the streets in recent years.

East of Chow Kit is **Kampung Bahru**, a grid of streets rarely visited by tourists. This is the one area within city confines where you will find clusters of traditional Malay houses on stilts – modest wooden homes that are completely at odds with the mansions and five-star hotels across the river on Jalan Ampang.

The Golden Triangle

The Golden Triangle is where modern KL stamps its mark. Clean and uncluttered in contrast to the old centre, this is the new cityscape in which the fast-developing nation invests its pride and flexes its muscles. Bordered to the north by Jalan Ampang, to the east by Jalan Tun Razak and to the south by Jalan Pudu and Jalan Impi, it is both the workplace and the playground of KL's growing middle classes. There are bars, international restaurants, green spaces and glittering shopping complexes to rival those in Singapore. The jewels in the crown, of course, are the Petronas Towers, tallest buildings in the world until Taiwan's 'Taipei 101' clinched the record in late 2003.

Bukit Bintang

The area around Bukit Bintang is Kuala Lumpur's primary shopping and entertainment hub. Jalan Bukit Bintang itself, and its delta of surrounding streets, is lined with upmarket shopping malls, hotels, bars and restaurants. The epicentre of it all is **Bintang Walk**, a neon-lit promenade of streetside bars and cafés which stretches from Lot 10 shopping mall as far as the JW Marriott Hotel. The ambience is international and generic. Locals and tourists alike come here to people-watch, window-shop, nibble French pastries or sip on Starbucks coffee. At weekends live jazz bands strike up on the street. Nearby Changkat Bukit Bintang (which runs perpendicular to its namesake) has mutated into a gentrified row of stylish bars and restaurants.

Despite the changes, it's easy enough to find a piece of the old KL, even in the midst of the new. Jalan Alor, which peels off from Changkat Bukit Bintang, is lined each day with the collapsible tables and chairs of hawker stalls. At the intersection of the two streets a handful of stalls are responsible for the perpetual reek of durian: connoisseurs of the 'king of fruits' come here each day to gorge themselves, thus balancing their yin and yang (durian is acknowledged as a 'heaty' food as opposed to, say, pineapple, which is cooling).

Off Jalan Conlay, just east of Bukit Bintang, is the **Kompleks Budaya Kraf** (*63 Jalan Conlay, **t** 03 2162 7533; open daily 10–6*), probably the best place in KL for buying local handicrafts, from batik, *songket* weavings and basketwork to silverwork, pewter and pottery. The complex houses shops, stalls, a craft museum and workshops, where visitors can either watch craftsmen at work or try their own hand.

North of Bukit Bintang stands the **Menara Kuala Lumpur** (Kuala Lumpur Tower; *Jalan Punchak, **t** 03 208 5448; open daily 10–10; adm RM15/8*) one of KL's major landmarks. Elements of Iranian design were incorporated into the structure of the tower, which stands 421m tall. From its position atop Bukit Nanas, the telecommunications tower rises above even the Petronas Towers. Visitors can take a lift up to the observation deck, which provides wonderful views over the city. An audio-tour, included in the price, helps identify KL's various quarters and landmarks. A bar and a revolving restaurant (*see* 'Eating Out', p.98) occupy floors above the observation deck. At the foot of the tower is a tiny patch of jungle, all that remains of Malaysia's oldest gazetted forest reserve. Now known as the **Bukit Nanas Recreational Park**, it is ringed with 'jogging' trails.

KLCC

Race day was a big event for the residents of colonial Kuala Lumpur, who would tramp out in numbers to the Selangor Turf Club racecourse, east of town. This old racecourse, built in 1896, was a recent victim of progress. An oval of level ground just 2km from the city centre, it represented prime real estate – the perfect spot for a new statement of nationhood. After all, any city aspiring to the status of Asian tiger needs its skyline of skyscrapers. As if to shift the focus of attention from old to new, the 40-hectare precinct was promptly named 'Kuala Lumpur City Centre' (or KLCC to acronym-mad Malaysians).

At the heart of the KLCC development are the **Petronas Towers**, which stand almost half a kilometre tall and dominate the skyline for miles around. Designed by Cesar Pelli, and completed in 1998, the towers gained instant iconic status as a symbol for the new Malaysia – or at least, as a symbol for the aspirations of a nation on the fast track to developed status. Controversially, it was the stainless-steel spires atop the towers that sent the buildings briefly into the record books. With their record snatched by the Taiwanese, Malaysians now make do with the description 'tallest twin towers in the world'. Wranglings aside, the buildings are an impressive spectacle. Clad in 40,000 tonnes of glinting steel, and linked by a precarious 'skybridge', the towers wouldn't look out of place in Gotham City. Much of the design is based on Islamic geometric motifs:

the floor plate superimposes two squares with circular infills, and many of the interior walls feature motifs inspired by *songket* weaving patterns.

The towers house the offices of the national petroleum company, among other multinational companies, while its lower floors contain the impressive Suria KLCC shopping complex. Beneath this is the new **Aquaria KLCC** (*open daily 11–8; last admission 7pm; adm RM38/22*), a large aquarium housing 5,000 varieties of tropical fish, complete with underwater walk-through tunnel. Visitors are not allowed access to the upper floors, though they can visit the **Skybridge**, which links the two towers at the midway point. Visit in the afternoon, and there's every chance you'll witness a dramatic thunderstorm rolling into town. Tickets are free, but there are strict daily limits on visitor numbers. Tickets are distributed on the concourse level from 9am. Typically, visitors will need to arrive before 9am to have any chance of getting hold of a ticket (which will be for an allocated time later in the day). The top-end hotels are often happy to get hold of Skybridge tickets on behalf of their guests.

At the foot of the towers is a 20-hectare landscaped park with fountains and a giant freeform paddling pool. Just beyond the park at No.2 Jalan Stonor – a tranquil spot beyond the mayhem of the city – is a mock-Tudor house from 1925, home to the **Badan Warisan**, Malaysia's Heritage Trust (*open Mon–Sat 10–4*). The building houses regular art and photography exhibitions and provides information about conservation projects across the country. Antiques, gifts and books are sold in a small shop. The Badan Warisan also publish excellent heritage-trail pamphlets. Within the grounds is **Rumah Penghulu** (*open Mon–Sat, tours at 11am and 3pm; adm RM5*), a beautifully restored, traditional Malay house, its cool airy rooms perfectly designed for the tropical climate. The house was originally built in the 1920s for the headman of a rural kampung in Kedah. It was dismantled in 1996 and relocated to its present position. Also within the grounds is a bamboo hut built by Orang Asli (aborigines) of the Temiar tribe.

Jalan Ampang

Jalan Ampang emerges out of the top end of Chinatown and meanders along the northern boundary of the Golden Triangle, mimicking the course of the Klang River. The road began life as a stately avenue lined with the riverside mansions of KL's early tin moguls. Today it serves mainly as the diplomatic enclave – many of the old mansions survive in the form of embassies – though high-rise hotels have muscled in on the scene too. The most evocative of the old mansions is Bok House, home to Le Coq d'Or restaurant until 2001, though presently empty and forlorn. The mansion was built in 1929 in Palladian style by entrepreneur Chua Cheng Bok, who cornered the car trade after humble beginnings selling bicycles. While the restaurant flourished it was the favoured hang-out of the colonial élite, who would hobnob in the wood-panelled dining room beneath Art Nouveau chandeliers. The Malaysia Tourism Centre is housed in one of Jalan Ampang's best-preserved mansions, built in 1935 by a wealthy rubber planter and tin miner. Regular cultural performances (*open Tues, Thurs, Sat, Sun 3.30–4.15; adm RM2*) are held in the building too.

Outside the Centre

Batu Caves and Thaipusam

It was the keen sense of smell of American naturalist William Hornaday that led to the official discovery of the Batu Caves back in 1878. The waft of bat guano led his hunting party through thick jungle to the cave opening. They promptly set fire to bamboo torches and ventured inside. 'We found ourselves in a grand cathedral', writes Hornaday in his account. 'At the far end, the roof rose in a great round dome... perfectly resembling St Peter's in Rome.'

The caves, which sit halfway up the face of a huge limestone outcrop 13km north of Kuala Lumpur, had in fact been known for centuries to local Malays and Jakuns, semi-nomadic Orang Asli who visited the caves to hunt for bats. But the Batu Caves really owe their fame to Thamboosamay Pillai, the Indian tin and coffee tycoon who founded KL's Sri Maha Mariamman Temple back in 1873 (*see* p.111). For years, he scouted for a suitable location for a new temple to be dedicated to Lord Murugan (also known as Subramanian). In Hindu mythology the deity Murugan spends much of his life in self-imposed isolation on a hill top: when Pillai came across the precipitous Batu Caves in 1891, he judged them to be the ideal location for a shrine to this god.

Ever since then, the Batu Caves have served as the focal point of the **Thaipusam** festival (held January/February), when many thousand Malaysian Hindus walk in procession from the Sri Maha Mariamman Temple to the Sri Subramanian Temple (the Murugan shrine). En route, devotees parade the streets of KL smashing coconuts in the path of a silver chariot pulled by two white bullocks. By the time they reach the foot of the caves, a crowd of up to a million devotees and onlookers have gathered. It is one of Southeast Asia's greatest spectacles.

The festival is an orgy of penitence, the culmination of a month of preparations whereby devotees abstain from worldly pleasures and comforts (no meat, no sex and only the floor for a bed). *Kavadi* carriers (literally, 'burden carriers') gather on the banks of the nearby Batu River, where they work themselves into a trance with the aid of drum beats. Hindu priests then adorn the hardiest *kavadi* carriers in gruesome manner – by pushing hooks through their flesh and skewers through their cheeks. It may seem a macabre spectacle, but the wounds are superficial and the devotees feel no pain in their trance-like state. Offerings are hung from the hooks before the devotees proceed up the 272 steps to the main shrine inside the cave. Separate offerings of milk, flowers, rock salt and fruit are also made.

Visiting the Caves

The Batu Caves are open to visitors daily from 7am to 6pm. Numerous buses make the journey from Medan Pasar, near the padang in KL. Beside the huge staircase which leads up to the main cave is a path leading to the 'art gallery cave', whose walls are splashed with murals depicting scenes from Hindu mythology. At the top of the 272 steps (patrolled by a macho troop of macaques) is the entrance to the main cave, which stretches 100m in length and the same distance in height. Hindu statues line the walls and the cave is lit by shafts of light which penetrate the cave roof.

Bangsar

The affluent suburb of Bangsar is where residents and expats head to let off steam. It is Kuala Lumpur's prime night spot, a grid of streets situated 5km southwest of the centre, with bars, coffee shops, stylish restaurants and nightclubs. Bangsar is so popular with expats that it has earned the nickname Kweiloh Lumpur ('kweiloh' is Mandarin for foreigner). The only sensible way of getting there is by taxi.

The suburb began life back in the 19th century as a kampung founded by a Sumatran immigrant. Later, it was the site of a rubber plantation owned by a man called Bunge (Bungsar Road was named after him). Bangsar first evolved into an entertainment district when night owls began frequenting Bangsar's late-night hawker stalls. With the emergence of Petaling Jaya, otherwise known as PJ (the industrial satellite 15km southwest of KL), property prices in well-placed Bangsar boomed. Though today most people visit Bangsar for something a little stronger than *teh tarik*, the hawker stalls are still very much up and running, providing a welcome (and cheap) alternative to the rash of Continental-style cafés.

Lake Titiwangsa

The recreational lake gardens of Titiwangsa lie just 3km north of the city centre. At weekends the gardens are packed with locals, who come here to entertain their children and eat at the many hawker stalls. There are rowing boats and kayaks for hire, tennis courts, squash courts and horse-riding facilities.

South of the lake, close to the national theatre, is the **National Art Gallery** (*2 Jalan Temerloh, off Jalan Tun Razak,* **t** *03 4025 4990, www.artgallery.org.my; open daily 10–6; adm free*), which traces the course of Malayasian art – its Western influences and its more recent attempts to capture something of Malaysia's modern identity. The permanent collection is somewhat limited, with little by way of commentary.

Selangor

Surrounding the Federal Territory of Kuala Lumpur is Selangor, the ancient state from which Kuala Lumpur emerged. Modern Selangor is dominated by the industrial sweep of the Klang Valley. In recent decades the area has been transformed by the emergence of Malaysia's Multimedia Super Corridor. The new development is characterized by a string of modern blueprint cities, which include the new administrative capital Putrajaya. Few of these 'cities' are properly inhabited yet. The valley runs southwest from KL past the state capital Shah Alam as far as Klang itself, once Malaysia's busiest port and seat of the old sultanate.

For young Malaysians, the Klang Valley is 'where it's at', though visitors will find little that appeals until they venture beyond the urban sprawl. On the coast, the only real

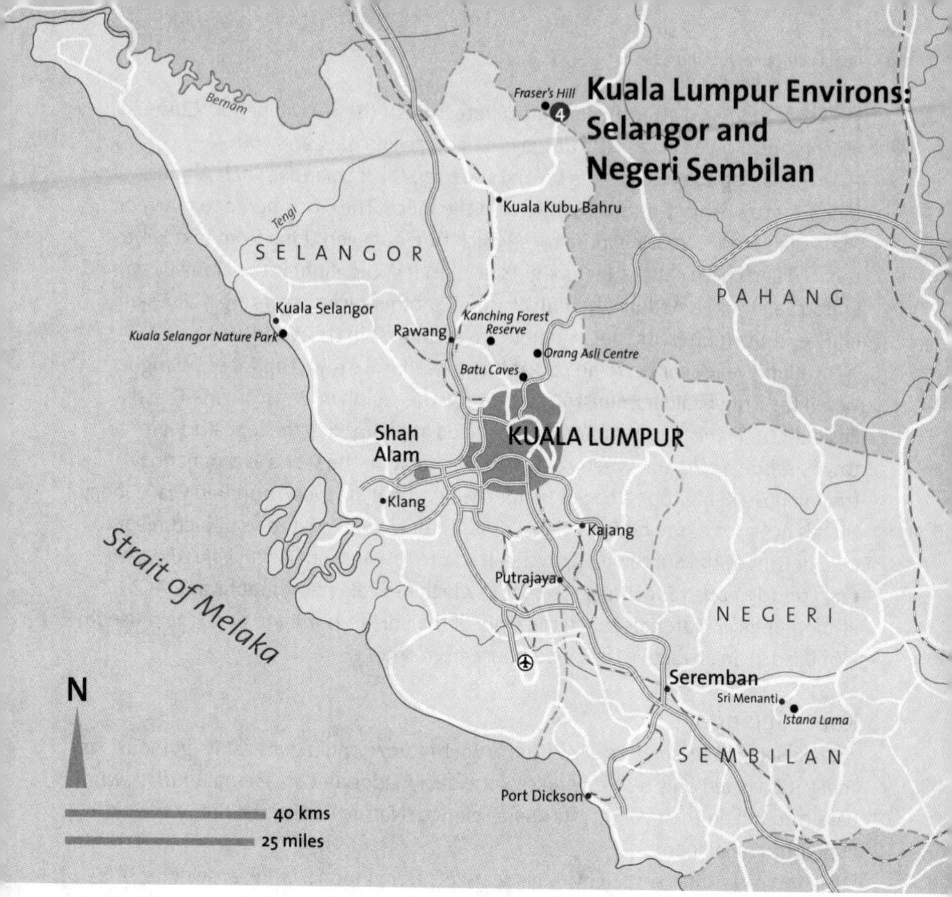

attraction is laid-back Kuala Selangor, with its little-visited nature park and nightly firefly spectacle, while inland two colonial hill stations provide respite from the heat.

Klang Valley

Over the course of Mahathir's premiership, one planned city after another sprouted along the course of the Klang Valley, a zone often referred to as the nation's new Multimedia Super Corridor. Built from scratch upon the guidelines of government blueprints, these developments are seen as the vision of 21st-century Malaysia. Rhetoric aside, this new administrative and industrial zone is still in its infancy: many of the new urban spaces remain underpopulated and, as one might expect, rather soulless. There is little of interest here for the visitor, beyond a couple of mega mosques.

In 1999 **Putrajaya** was named administrative capital of Malaysia. The new 'city' is home to the Prime Minister's Department and the Prime Minister's Official Residence. Along with its new twin township, Cyberjaya, Putrajaya has been billed a paperless city, complete with a fully digital telecommunications infrastructure. A 650-hectare lake snakes through the city, designed to act as a natural cooling system. Putrajaya's most dominant feature is the Putra Mosque, a monumental blue-domed structure modelled after the Persian architecture of the Safavid period. Curious visitors are allowed access to Putrajaya daily between 9am and 5pm.

Further along the valley is the official state capital of Selangor, **Shah Alam**, another blueprint township, this one built back in the 1960s. The city is home to many of Malaysia's manufacturing industries, which turn out everything from textiles, to tobacco and chemicals. As far as sights go, the city's highlight is the clumsily named Sultan Salahuddin Abdul Aziz Shah Mosque, another record-breaking Malaysian edifice: at 142 metres, its four minarets are the tallest in the world.

The Klang Valley comes to an end at **Klang** itself, once royal capital of Selangor. When the British laid administrative claim to the region in 1874, the first British Resident, Sir Frank Swettenham, was installed at Klang. Rich tin deposits were the town's *raison d'être*, and when Kuala Lumpur burst on the scene as a major new trading post, Klang took a back seat for the first time in several hundred years. Today there's not a lot to see or do in Klang, other than wander past rows of picturesque shophouses in the old town or pay a visit to the Tin Museum (*Jalan Raja Abdullah,* ***t*** *03 559 0050, open Sat–Thurs 10–6; free*), which uses old photographs and ethnographical materials to tell the story of the port's tin-mining past. The museum is housed in an attractive tiled warehouse from 1856.

Kuala Selangor

Kuala Selangor is such a sleepy little town that few would guess at its glorious past. Today it is visited only by bingeing seafood aficionados and occasional tourists, who pass through on their way to the Kuala Selangor Nature Park or the firefly spectacle at nearby Kuala Kuantan.

The town was first settled by Bugis seafarers from Indonesia. Because of its strategic location at the mouth of the Sungei Selangor, the settlement flourished, and by the 14th century, it was one of the peninsula's major ports. A series of forts were established atop Bukit Melawati, a small hill which overlooks the town. The latest of these, a fort built by the Dutch in their attempts to control the tin trade, was destroyed during the Selangor Civil War (1867–73). All that remains are foundation stones and a few cannons. These guns would once have looked out across the Straits of Melaka. But the river delta has since expanded and much land has been reclaimed. Still, it is worth climbing the hill for the view alone, which takes in the whole delta with its wooden fishing trawlers, stilted kampungs and fringes of mangrove swamp. Much of the delta falls inside the bounds of the **Kuala Selangor Nature Park** – which provides the main reason for visiting the town.

The nature park is a haven for birds and wildlife, with in excess of 100,000 migratory species congregating here at peak times of year. Rare sightings include the milky stork, Norman greenshank and mangrove pitta. Otters, silver leaf monkeys and leopard cats also make the park their home. Secondary forest accounts for the larger part of the nature park: after land reclamation the mangroves, which once covered the whole area, were unable to sustain themselves. Protecting what few mangroves do remain (around 100 acres of the 500-acre park) is one of the park's primary functions. Numerous trails and boardwalks lead through the secondary forest, the mangroves and around a series of brackish man-made lakes which contain water diverted from the estuary. Year-round, the lakes are alive with water birds and waders, which are best viewed from the hides which are dotted about the main lake. Bring plenty of mosquito repellent. The excellent visitor centre is open daily 8am-6pm and chalets are provided for accommodation (A-frames RM25, chalets RM45).

Ten kilometres upriver is **Kuala Kuantan**, home to one of the world's largest colonies of **fireflies**. Fireflies, or *kelip-kelip* in Malay, are not flies at all but tiny beetles which emit a cool green glow in bursts from their lower abdomen. What is unusual about the fireflies of Sungei Selangor is the synchronization of their flashes. At dusk, millions of the little beetles gather in the branches of *berembang* trees (a type of mangrove) on the banks of the river. As night settles, they begin to flash their abdominal beacons at a rate of three times a second, and in complete synchrony, so that it appears the whole bank is laced with fairy lights. The nightly spectacle is an act of communal courtship; by midnight the lovestruck beetles have paired off for the night and the light show fades into the darkness.

Fraser's Hill

Fraser's Hill is not strictly in Selangor: it straddles state borders, with its summit falling inside Pahang. However, access is only possible from Selangor, and most visitors make the journey straight from Kuala Lumpur. Along with the Cameron Highlands, Maxwell Hill and the Genting Highlands, Fraser's Hill was developed by the British as a Raj-style 'hill station' – somewhere homesick colonials could go to escape the oppressive heat of the lowlands, tend gardens, grow strawberries and play golf.

Fraser's Hill – which actually comprises seven small hills – forms part of the Titiwangsa range and rises to an elevation of 5,000ft (1,500m). It was named after Scotsman Louis James Fraser, a shady entrepreneur who built a bungalow here back in the 1890s. Tin was mined up on the hills and Fraser established a mule service to

Getting There

Fraser's Hill is 100km northeast of KL and is accessible by taxi or by bus from the Pudu Raya bus terminal. Passengers will need to change at Kuala Kubu Bharu, where two buses daily (8am and 2pm) complete the journey up Fraser's Hill. The buses descend again at 10am and 4pm. The last stretch of road is known as the Gap – a twisting road so narrow that vehicles ascend and descend on alternate hours.

Tourist Information

For information about bird-watching tours or accommodation contact the **Fraser's Hill Development Corporation**, **t** 09 362 2044.

Where to Stay

There are places to stay on Fraser's Hill to suit most budgets. Accommodation tends to be a little overpriced and standards are not particularly high – with the notable exception of Ye Olde Smokehouse:

Expensive

Ye Olde Smokehouse, Jalan Jeriau, **t** 09 362 2226, **f** 09 362 2035, *www.thesmokehouse.com.my*. Designed to resemble an English mock-Tudor country house, with rustic dining room, conservatory and bar with open fire. Rooms are huge and some have four-poster beds. Full English breakfasts are served. The best place to stay on Fraser's Hill.

transport the extracted metal down to level ground. He later ran a notorious opium and gambling den at the foot of the hill, popular among planters and miners.

It wasn't long before a permanent access road was hacked through the forest, and by 1922, Fraser's Hill had become a hill station proper. English-style cottages and bungalows sprang up across the hill and work began on a golf course right away. In 1951, the road from Kuala Bubu Bharu to Fraser's Hill was the scene of an assassination: British High Commissioner Sir Henry Gurney was ambushed on the road and shot dead by communist insurgents during the conflict known as the Emergency (*see* p.20).

Many of the hill station's original bungalows survive today – timber-framed and built with local limestone blocks, with trim little gardens full of roses and chrysanthemums. Devonshire tea is still served at The Tavern and Ye Olde Smokehouse, two mock-Tudor lodges that are straight out of rural England.

Eight well-marked jungle trails provide the best reason for visiting Fraser's Hill, which is a haven for birdlife: more than 270 species have been recorded here over the years. Every June, birders congregate on Fraser's Hill to participate in the annual International Bird Race (a race against the clock to see who can tot up the most species). Most of the jungle trails can be tackled without guides. Horse riding is a popular activity on Fraser's Hill, where there's a paddock for Bajau ponies and larger 'polo horses'.

Genting Highlands

The Genting Highlands hold little in common with Malaysia's other hill stations: where the others are places of escape, the Genting Highlands have been transformed into a 24-hour entertainment resort. Brash, over-developed and with little historical appeal, Malaysians nevertheless flock here at weekends to visit the amusement park and the nation's only casino (which, in fact, is one of the largest in the world). Situated 50km from KL, and at an altitude of 2,000m, the Genting Highlands provide a climatic escape from the city – if nothing else. A twice-hourly air-conditioned bus service operates between KL's Pudu Raya bus station and the Genting Highlands. The final stage of the journey is completed by cable car. There is plenty of resort-style accommodation on offer, should visitors want to stay over, though it is easy enough to visit on a day trip from KL.

Kanching Recreational Forest

A small section of the Kanching Forest Reserve, 20km northwest of Kuala Lumpur, has been set aside for picnic trails and jungle trekking. Little visited by tourists, it is nonetheless a popular weekend getaway for inhabitants of the capital. The main attraction is a series of multitiered waterfalls, some of which collect in pools deep enough for bathing. Trails lead up to different levels; the further you climb, the more likely you are to have the trail to yourself. Lata Bayas is the highest waterfall, at an altitude of 1,030m.

A taxi ride to the entrance to the reserve takes about 30 minutes. Regular buses (Nos. 66, 72 and 83) leave from KL's Pudu Raya bus terminal for the Kanching Recreational Forest each day.

Orang Asli Museum

2 Jalan Pahang, Gombak (off old Gombak Road), **t** *03 6189 2122; open Sat–Thurs 9–5. The easiest way to get there is by taxi, though bus No. 174 makes the journey every hour from Lebuh Ampang.*

This museum, 25km northeast of Kuala Lumpur, records the culture of Peninsular Malaysia's indigenous inhabitants: *orang asli* is Malay for 'aborigine'. There are two dozen or so different tribes of Orang Asli, each with a separate ancestral heritage, inhabiting different parts of the peninsula. Though a good deal of Malaysia's Orang Asli have been absorbed into the cultural mainstream, a number of tribes still live the hunter-gatherer lifestyle. As the rainforests recede, so does a way of life that has remained practically unchanged for millennia.

The museum plots the wide distribution of Orang Asli across the peninsula, detailing the differences between various groups and exhibiting artefacts from fishing traps and musical instruments to spirit masks and blowpipes. For more on the Orang Asli *see* 'Indigenous Tribes of Malaysia', p.40.

Negeri Sembilan

Negeri Sembilan is one of Malaysia's smallest and least prominent states, and yet, as the home of Malaysia's Minangkabau culture, it has one of the most interesting heritages. The workaday town of **Seremban** is state capital, centred round a noisy grid of old shophouses and modern malls. **Sri Menanti**, the old royal capital inland from Seremban, provides the best reason for visiting Negeri Sembilan, with its magnificent wooden palace. Down on the coast, **Port Dickson** is hugely popular as a weekend seaside resort, particularly among the city dwellers of KL – though the beach here is nothing special, and there is little of interest to detain the foreign visitor. The few sights that Negeri Sembilan has to offer are best visited on day trips from either KL or Melaka, where there is a much wider range of accommodation.

Drawn by the remarkable early success of Melaka, a group of Malays from Sumatra settled the hills behind the thriving port sometime in the 15th century. The nine principalities founded by the original settlers later joined together to form Negeri Sembilan, or 'Land of the Nine Territories', ruled not by a sultan but by a Yang di Pertuan Besar, literally 'He Who is Greatest'. Over the centuries, the people of Negeri Sembilan clung fiercely to their cultural heritage, which is remarkable for two things: its distinctive architecture and its matrilineal society, which is governed by a code of behaviour known as *adat pepatih*. On marriage, the husband takes the wife's name, while inheritance of property passes down the female line, from mother to daughter. Minangkabau *nagari*, or villages, each consisted of a number of matrilineal clans named after the female line. To keep their men sweet, Minangkabau women left political power in the hands of their menfolk.

Today, the Minangkabau are a forward-looking people; the state is a stone's throw from the hi-tech Klang Valley, while the ultramodern international airport sits on the state border with Selangor. By now, the people of Negeri Sembilan are thoroughly integrated with the rest of the nation's Malay population. Their enduring legacy is Minangkabau architecture, whose distinguishing feature is the sweeping and ornate 'buffalo-horn' roof.

The buffalo plays an integral role in Minangkabau folklore, and it is this that is represented in their architecture. The central legend is a Minangkabau version of David and Goliath: after decades of war with the Javanese, the two factions decided that enough blood had been shed, and that they would settle their differences once and for all with a buffalo duel. On the day of the duel, the Javanese presented a prize specimen with a barrel chest and sharp, sweeping horns. The Minangkabau, on the other hand, turned up with a scrawny buffalo calf; the war had been a costly process and all their prize buffaloes were sold. Or so they told the Javanese. To even up the contest a little, the Minangkabau were permitted to tie knives to the head of the calf, which, still of suckling age, rushed straight beneath the buffalo to feed, fatally wounding it in the process. *Minang* translates as 'victorious', *kabau* as 'water buffalo'.

Traditionally, the curved buffalo-horn roofs of the Minangkabau were thatched in *attap*, though more modern versions have a covering of wood shingles. The magnificent **Istana Lama Sri Menanti**, the old palace at the royal capital Sri Menanti, is the crowning glory of Negeri Sembilan's Minangkabau heritage. Raised from the ground on 99 hardwood piles, the four-storey palace was pieced together in 1908 without a single nail. The building served as the official royal residence of Negeri Sembilan until 1932. In 1992 the building was opened to the public as the Royal Museum (*open Sat–Thurs 10–6*), with displays of regalia.

For a more in-depth understanding of Minangkabau culture and architecture, head for the **Teman Seni Budaya** (Cultural Park), on the outskirts of Seremban. This is the site of the Muzium Negara (*State Museum; open daily 10–6, closed Fri 12.15–2.45; free*), with a mediocre display of historical artefacts and local handicrafts. Of more interest are the relocated Minangkabau houses set in the grounds: the elaborately carved Istana Ampang Tinggi, originally built in 1860 near the site of the Sri Menanti palace, and two examples of Minangkabau homes, modest in comparison to the old palace.

Melaka

09

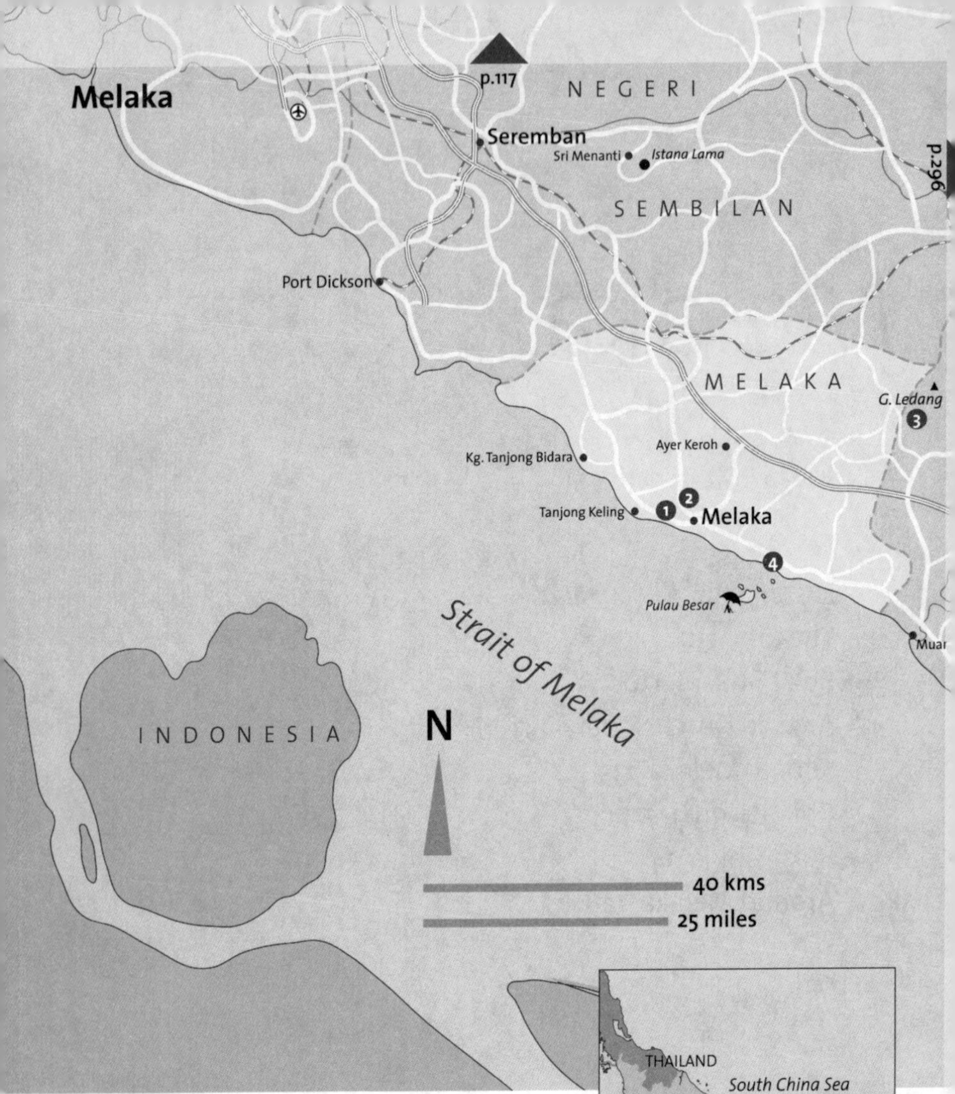

Highlights

1 The colonial sights of Bukit St Paul and Dutch Square in the city of Melaka

2 Peranakan architecture along Jalan Tun Tan Cheng Lock, in Melaka's Chinatown

3 Puteri Falls – escape the city for these dramatic cascades with pools suitable for swimming

4 Try *ikan bakar* (barbecued fish) served up at beachside stalls

The visitor will first be struck by the curious spectacle of a town with its legs in the sea.
Frank Swettenham

In Melaka's heyday, stilted godowns and shophouses lined the estuary, their back ends flung out towards the hubbub of commercial activity in the harbour. The city rang with the cries of 100,000 people speaking dozens of languages, all vying for deals in what was then the marketplace of the East. The sultanate's sphere of influence extended across the entire Malay Peninsula, as well as the eastern slice of Sumatra. It was the powerhouse of the East, its rulers claiming direct descent from Alexander the Great.

By the turn of the 20th century, after nearly four centuries of colonial rule, Melaka had acquired a laid-back air, though it remained an important port of sorts: 'one foot on land, one in the sea', according to the British Resident-General Frank Swettenham. One fact holds true to this day: look for the origins of all things Malay and you wind up, inevitably, in this, Malaysia's oldest city.

Today Melaka's glories have slipped off the streets and into the museums, leaving the ruins of successive colonial administrations alongside the rich heritage of the Straits Chinese, commonly known as Babas and Nyonyas (*see* below). The town is split roughly in two by its narrow river, with Chinatown on the north bank and the colonial centre on the south, beside Little India. Its compact centre is run through with narrow streets that limit the weight of traffic, with some of the overspill plying the busy highway on land reclaimed from the sea. In fact, so much land has been reclaimed that modern Melaka can no longer be called a town with its legs in the sea. Nor is the prospect from St Paul's Hill quite what it was, with the construction of a manmade island – Pulau Melaka (*see* p.136) – dragging the waterline still further from the old centre of town.

The clash between conservation and 'progress' in this rapidly developing nation is nowhere more in evidence than here in Melaka. Restoration of historic buildings and conservation of mangrove swamps inevitably comes second to the construction of shopping malls, apartment blocks and bypasses. But as standards of living improve and the middle class expands, so does an awareness of the importance of Melaka's heritage – after all, tourism is the state's biggest money-spinner (over two million visitors were recorded in 2000).

For newcomers Melaka may seem a sketchy mix of old and new, a place not quite sure where it's at. Postcards and tourist brochures highlight the 17th-century Dutch complex, painted a uniform clay red as if to mark it out as the city's architectural centrepiece. For most visitors, though, the Peranakan shophouses and terraced mansions along Jalan Tun Tan Cheng Lock (Heeren Street) are of greater interest. Then there's the string of museums and the upmarket *pasar malam* on Jonker's Walk, stuffed with antiques, trinkets and food stalls.

Most of all, though, Melaka is a great Malaysian example of racial unity, a weaving together of Islamic, Chinese and European cultures. On aptly named Harmony Street, Malaysia's oldest Chinese temple stands just down from the Moorish minaret of

Kampung Kling mosque, which lies, in turn, within shouting distance of Melaka's earliest Hindu temple. In Christ Church, Church of England services are conducted in English, Mandarin and Tamil, while in St Peter's Church, Mass is attended by a congregation of Portuguese Eurasians. Year-round the streets are alive with evidence of this cultural diversity in the form of Chinese dragon dances, open-house Sikh feasts, Portuguese folk music, the rituals of Thaipusam devotees run through with hooks and, of course, the ever present wail of the muezzin.

History

Beginnings

Melaka was founded on a whim in 1400 (*see* 'The Founding of Melaka', opposite). And yet, within a matter of years, the new settlement had matured into a sophisticated trading port. It was perfectly placed, which helped. With a prominent hill that overlooked every approach, Melaka sat in the bottleneck of the straits and on the estuary of a river which snaked a path inland through rich jungle towards gold mines. Soon local sampans were converging on Melaka with jungle exotica, while larger vessels from the Arab world, India and China anchored outside the estuary. But it was not until the emperors of the Ming Dynasty took an interest in Melaka that the settlement truly flourished. Parameswara readily accepted China's protection and his title was officially recognised. Avoiding the middlemen, a succession of Chinese trade missions arrived in Melaka, and it wasn't long before the bustling port matured into an international marketplace.

Success was boosted by the establishment of the Melaka Laws and a formalized trading system. Port charges were standardized and four *syahbandars* (harbour masters) of different nationalities were appointed to deal with incoming trade from their respective ethnic groups. Coins were minted from tin and inscribed with the name of the reigning sultan, who found himself stockpiling the gold and silver that flooded in as royal taxes.

Cocooned in splendour and pampered by dignitaries, the sultans took on airs befitting their increasing fortune. They claimed direct descent from Iskandar Zulkarnain, or Alexander the Great, and set themselves up as demigods at the head of the state, instigating a bemusing set of privileges: only the sultan was allowed to wear gold or yellow, for example, unless he bestowed the privilege on a worthy subject, who then must wear the item till his death; white parasols and summerhouses were also the preserve of the lucky sultan. Bound by the constraints of ceremony, much of the day-to-day administration was left to the *bendahara*, or chief minister, who increasingly came to wield much power. For important decisions, he met in council with three other ministers and a number of titled nobility, with decisions agreed by *muafakat* (consensus). It was a setup inherited from Melaka's predecessor, the kingdom of Srivijaya.

Crucible for Malay Culture

As is the nature of entrepôts, the Melakan community was a gathering of races, each with a fair degree of autonomy over its own affairs. From India were the

Bengalis, the Tamils, the Klings and the Gujaratis; from China the Hokkien, the Cantonese, the Hakkas, the Hainanese. All the races of Southeast Asia had representatives in Melaka, as did the Arabs, Jews and Japanese. Despite this maelstrom of creeds and customs, Melaka was the crucible out of which the Malay language and culture emerged – as the tourist board today is at pains to emphasize.

By the time the European colonists appeared on the scene in the early 1500s, Malay was the lingua franca of the trading world in the East. 'Their language is in vogue through the Indies as French is here,' noted Dutchman Linschoten, whose *Itinerario* (1594) received a wide European audience. Nor was Malay just the language of trade;

The Founding of Melaka

Prince-consort Parameswara of Palembang, a murky character only half-drawn by the various accounts, is the common starting point for Malay histories. Hot-headed and ambitious, he married a Javanese Princess, had his fill of her, then renounced relations with the powerful state that was once her home. This rash move soon had Parameswara on the run from his homeland in Sumatra. Some time around 1390 he fetched up on the forested island of Singapore, or Temasek as it was then known, where he befriended the chief, had him killed, then set up home. His stay was short-lived: Temasek had close relations with Patani, a vassal state of Siam, and news that the Siamese battle fleet was mobile sent Parameswara on his way once more.

Muar, up the west coast of the Peninsula, was Parameswara's next base. It is thought he stayed for six years, raiding passing junks and fishing the estuary. But the settlement never came to much and we get the impression that Parameswara had a higher calling. An empire-builder at heart, he was also a studied vagrant and was soon on his princely wanderings once more, setting up a temporary base at Bertram, before heading north towards the Melaka estuary.

According to the *Sejarah Melayu* (the 'Malay Annals', elaborated for dramatic effect in the tradition of oral histories), the episodes above stretch over a number of generations, with the occupation of Singapore lasting for a century rather than four or five years. And it's not just the Siamese and Javanese that pose a threat to the forefathers of Melaka: according to the *Sejarah Melayu*, the move from Singapore to Muar is precipitated by an attack from a shoal of swordfish, while the arrival in Muar is hampered by a pack of ferocious monitor lizards.

On one score, however, the *Sejarah Melayu* and the European accounts more or less concur – the legend of the founding of Melaka. One day, Parameswara and his son Iskandar were out hunting near present-day Melaka Hill, hot on the pursuit of a mouse deer (a timid animal the size of a domestic cat). On reaching the coastline the mouse deer suddenly turned on the hunting group and kicked one of the dogs into the sea. This was taken as a propitious sign by young Iskandar (or at least a ready excuse): he promptly suggested that his father build him a palace on top of the hill. Parameswara agreed, and the two of them puzzled over a name for the new settlement. They were standing beneath a melaka tree. The year was 1400 and the seed of the Melakan empire was sown.

Islam was on the march across Southeast Asia and Malay, with its Arabic script, became its vessel of conversion.

When the ruling family converted to Islam and mosques began popping up around town, a whole new wave of arrivals boosted Melaka's reputation, as prosperous Indian Muslims found the port more conducive to good business. A booming religious and trading centre, Melaka's fast-developing culture and style of government became fashionable. Malay customs today hark back to these glory days, while Malaysia's modern states remember the Melaka of old as the archetypal sultanate.

The Portuguese Take Note

It wasn't long before the Europeans got wind of a good thing. Early wanderers came home with tales of extravagance. Tomé Pires, a Portuguese diplomat, marvelled at the sight of kids on the street playing with gold. He had recognised, like others before him, that Melaka was the key to control of the spice trade, famously declaring, 'whosoever is lord of Malacca has his hands on the throat of Venice' (Venice dominated supply of eastern goods at a time when a single peppercorn was worth its weight in gold, literally).

In 1511, after a protracted squabble with the sultan over the release of Portuguese hostages, a heavily armed force under Albuquerque laid waste to the city. It was cannonballs against bows and poison arrows. The *Sejarah Melayu* records the bewilderment of the Melakan defenders: 'What may be this round weapon that is sharp enough to kill us'.

Before long the Portuguese, or the 'white Bengalis' as they were known to the local Malays, had begun work on a fortress. They flattened the old mosque and laboured on a series of walls several metres thick. Within these walls rose a medieval town of stone, with five churches, a prison, a 120ft keep tower, the governor's palace and a neighbourhood of houses for Portuguese administrators. The fortress became known as 'A Famosa' (the famous). Beyond the walls many of the visiting merchants continued their lives of old, bartering goods and residing in Malay village communities. Only at times of threat would they retreat inside the city walls, where the Portuguese were rumoured to live in great luxury (Melaka was talked of in European circles as 'Babylon of the Orient'). The colonials excused their excesses as reward for a dangerous lifestyle: malaria was a big killer in 16th-century Melaka, as were resurgent attacks by supporters of the old sultanate.

Corruption soon began to undermine the smooth running of the trading port and the undermanned Portuguese watched control of the waterways slip from their grasp. Muslim traders, persecuted by the Portuguese, looked elsewhere for business and, by the time of Portugal's union with Spain in 1580, their eastern empire was a fragile possession. Of the world-famous fortress only the Porta de Santiago has survived to this day, though a more potent reminder of Melaka's Portuguese past lives on in a small Eurasian settlement to the east of town. Its inhabitants – practising Roman Catholics who speak a Creole combining archaic Portuguese and Malay – are the distant children of liaisons between the Portuguese and local Malays.

Tigers and the Bishop

At the time of the founding of Melaka, tigers were a common sighting and a constant hazard. They struck fear among the populace and were both loathed and revered. Myths and folk tales abounded. Early Chinese traders who visited Melaka brought home tales of tigers that snooped about town in human form, until it was opportune to reveal their true and fearful symmetry. If found out in time (the storytellers didn't tell how), the feline intruders were promptly executed by the authorities. Manuel Godhino Eredia, a Portuguese historian who visited Melaka, tells of wild men from the deep jungle – shamans of untold powers – who could turn themselves at will into tigers. Often these tiger-men would stalk quietly into Melaka by night and drag a victim away into the trees. When Melaka fell under Portuguese rule, the first Bishop of the city decided to deal with the killers once and for all. One High Mass, in front of a full congregation, the prelate solemnly excommunicated all tigers from the Church. From that moment on, not a tiger entered Melaka.

The Dutch try their Hand

The Dutch presence in Melaka coincided roughly with the founding of the Dutch East Indies Company (VOC) in 1602. Dutch naval supremacy was consolidated under the monopoly of this all-powerful company. In many ways the VOC was a mini-state in itself, with the power to wage war, sign treaties and appoint governors. Based in Batavia (Jakarta), the company's early years were spent wooing Melaka's rivals in Johor and Acheh. By the time the Dutch took control of Melaka in 1641, the port had resigned itself to its new role as an outpost rather than a leading entrepôt. The Dutch siege of Melaka didn't help matters, stretching over five or six months and wiping out around 90% of the population. Now part of a vast commercial network, Melaka became something of a backwater, with ships pulling into the harbour to pay dues rather than offload their cargoes. The northern Sumatran state of Acheh had by now inherited Melaka's role as centre of the Malay world and trade from China and India was gradually dispersed among other Southeast Asian ports.

After the destructive siege of Melaka, the Dutch rebuilt the town in their own style, with the imposing Stadhuys complex as the centrepiece. Alongside this they built Christ Church, which stands today as the city's symbol of its colonial days. Despite hostilities between Catholics and Protestants in Europe, the Dutch tolerated Catholic descendants of the Portuguese and proclaimed religious freedom in Melaka in 1702. Given Dutch tolerance in spiritual matters it was hardly surprising that they adopted a neutral position in local conflicts. Their Malay allies, however, upheld a different logic: you're either friend or enemy. And so, like the Portuguese before them, the Dutch soon lost the faith of the Malays.

The British Breeze In

Meanwhile, British interests in Southeast Asia – in the form of the British East India Company – were chipping away at Dutch control of the region. Power finally slipped from Dutch hands in 1795, when a force of 2,000 British soldiers breezed into Melaka without firing a shot: William of Orange, on the run from Napoleon, had ordered Dutch colonies to open their doors to British troops as protection against the French.

For a decade the future of Melaka hung in the balance. The British East India Company, based in Penang, was unhappy with the cost of maintaining the garrison at Melaka. Lengthy discussions ensued over how best to prevent Melaka draining further funds. The fortress, it was decided, would be destroyed. Governor Farquhar prepared the scene, burying gunpowder deep beneath the walls. He struck the match himself, lit the fuse and watched as hunks of stone – some 'as large as elephants', according to one witness – were sent tumbling into the sea.

This done, the authorities in Penang began arrangements for dismantling the rest of Melaka and resettling its inhabitants in Penang. The historic city was saved from this further humiliation at the hands of its ruthless caretakers by the written report of an ambitious 26-year-old called Thomas Stamford Raffles. He proved that the city had the means to be self-sufficient and reminded the authorities of the huge prestige Melaka carried among the Malays. This seemed to do the trick and talk of abandonment petered out.

Melaka officially fell into British hands in 1825, when it was lumped together with Penang and Singapore in an administrative entity known as the Straits Settlements. While Penang and Singapore bloomed, Melaka looked more and more the sluggish backwater by comparison. Swathes of land around town were cleared for rice and tapioca, but returns were poor and Melaka remained a financial liability for the British. Then, in 1895, the first rubber tree was planted by Tan Chay Yan, a local tapioca planter, and the automotive industry boomed across Europe and the USA, bringing wealth once again to Melaka. But Melaka was never destined to become a boom town in the manner of Singapore or Penang and it soon mellowed into the harmonious and laid back sort of place its inhabitants have long been accustomed to. The British established a solid infrastructure, with a sturdy network of roads, a railroad link and a telephone network, which went some way towards preparing the state for independence in 1957.

Melaka's primary significance today is that it remains the one place in Malaysia where it is possible to trace the entire thread of the nation's history.

The City

Bukit St Paul

The old centre of Melaka sits on and around Bukit St Paul, which was nothing but a jungled mound before Parameswara, legendary founder of Melaka, built a palace on its summit in the early 1400s. When the Portuguese captured the city a century later they set about constructing a defensive fort, ringing the hill with a 3m-thick stone wall. Hundreds of men laboured in the tropical heat, dismantling mosques and plundering Malay graveyards for stone. In place of the city's great mosque and the sultan's elaborate wooden palace, the Portuguese built sturdy stone churches, a neighbourhood of houses, hospitals, a prison and a school. The crowning glory was a 100ft keep tower. It was like something straight out of medieval Europe, and the fort was named '**A Famosa**' (the famous). The fortress stood for almost three centuries until the British came along and vandalized the place. The bosses of the British East India Company decided that Melaka should be dismantled and its inhabitants relocated to Penang, the Company's base. A team of convicts with pickaxes and sledgehammers set to work on the fort, but did little more than chip the masonry. So, in an extravagant display of pyrotechnics, huge quantities of dynamite were buried beneath the walls and detonated with devastating effect. Melaka was never quite the same again, its confidence dented. 'Like a woman bereaved of her husband, the lustre gone from her face', wrote Raffles' Malay scribe Munshi Abdullah. When the fort was all but gone, Raffles himself intervened to prevent resettlement of Melaka's inhabitants.

Today Jalan Kota marks the old boundary of A Famosa's walls. Its southern stretch is the domain of Melaka's colourful, chrome-encrusted trishaws, which swing between the sights, music pumping from built-in sound systems. Most of them begin or end their journeys on the south side of St Paul's Hill, beside the **Porta de Santiago**. This crumbling arched gateway is the one remaining fragment of Melaka's great fortress. Two very Dutch-looking figures are carved above the inscription 'Anno 1670'. These were added by the mighty Dutch East India Company after they crushed the Portuguese.

Behind the Porta de Santiago a stairway climbs the hill to the picturesque ruins of **St Paul's Church**. At one time the hillside here slipped straight down to a wide estuary busy with Chinese junks, Malay *perahus* and other trading vessels. Today's views are not so evocative. The river has silted up, denying access to larger boats, and a great slab of land has been reclaimed from the sea. This has pushed Bukit St Paul further inland, with views over the the gargantuan Century Makhota Hotel to man-made Pulau Melaka (*see* p.136).

The hill-top church was built by the Portuguese in 1521 and named 'Our Lady on the Hill'. It once stood proud above the fortress and was a favourite preaching ground of the Jesuit missionary St Francis Xavier. He was said to have performed one of his greatest miracles here, raising a young girl from her grave behind the church three days after her death. When St Francis himself died on the small island of Sancian in 1553, his remains were shipped to Melaka and buried at St Paul's Church for nine months, before being transferred to Goa. A marble statue in front of the church commemorates the saint, while a plaque marks the spot where he so briefly lay. Soon after the statue was erected in 1953 – so the story goes – a storm brewed, felling a casuarina tree and snapping the saint's right arm from his marbled torso. Nothing out of the ordinary in itself. But 400 years back, when the flesh-and-blood remains of St Francis were doing the rounds of Asia, it was noticed that he seemed to have escaped the usual processes of decomposition. In the hope that proof of this might speed through an application for canonization, his right arm was severed and packed off directly to the Pope. No doubt the poor old man had the shock of his life (not a pretty parcel to open) and gave his blessing on the spot.

The Dutch East India Company reconsecrated the church into the Protestant fold in 1641, renaming it St Paul's Church. A century later, work began on Christ Church (see opposite) at the foot of the hill, and St Paul's Church fell into disrepair. By the time the British entered Melaka, St Paul's Church had lost its roof, serving from then on as a defensive post. Inside the ruins, 8ft-tall granite tombstones lean up against the walls. Most of these mark the graves of Dutch officials who died young, of malaria and other tropical illnesses. On the east side of Bukit St Paul stands an ornate replica of the Malacca Sultanate Palace. The airy wooden building houses the **Muzium Budaya** *(Cultural Museum; open Wed–Mon 9–6; closed Fri 12.15–2.45; adm RM2)*. The Malacca Sultanate Palace is deemed to be one of the most spectacular pieces of Malay architecture of all time. The Sejarah Melayu, which offers a detailed description of the original istana, was used as a manual for the modern reconstruction (though one suspects the latter lacks something of the original craftmanship and grandeur). Made entirely without the use of nails, with an elaborate set of roofs and sweeping verandahs, this impressive structure was originally built during the 15th century, at the height of Melaka's powers. The palace was stuffed full of those much-coveted treasures plundered by Albuquerque then loaded onto his flagship, the *Flor de la Mar*, and lost in a storm off the Sumatran coast. Sotheby's valued the haul at over $9 billion (*see* pp.134–5). Inside the replica palace are a series of displays evoking the forms and functions of the Malay court and the cultural history of Melaka as a trading post. Strange-featured mannikins, dressed up in antique finery, strike poses at every turn, while miniature replicas of other great istanas chart the geographical spread of Malay architecture. Opposite the museum is a well-kept formal garden. In the centre, an odd-looking monument topped with a royal headdress commemorates the declaration of Melaka as a 'Historic City'.

Between the Muzium Budaya and the Porta de Santiago stands a squat stuccoed mansion in the colonial style, with a dash of the East in its two miniature golden domes. To most it is known as the Malacca Club, built by the British in 1912 and used as a meeting place and drinking den. William Somerset Maugham usually features in any mention of the building. It was here that he was told the true story of a planter murdered by his wife and her lover, which he duly spun into the short story, 'Footprints in the Jungle'. Ironically the building is now called the **Proclamation of Independence Memorial** (*open Tues–Sun 9–6; closed Fri 12.15–2.45; adm free)* and it houses a flash new exhibition charting the nation's struggle towards independence. It's upbeat, heavily sponsored and not worth much more than a quick browse. Across the road is the Padang Pahlawan, or Warrior's Field, where the nation's first Prime Minister declared the Independence of Malaya in 1957. The very spot is marked by the Independence Obelisk, a strange little granite pyramid, each side graced with a red 'M' on a yellow star (where M = Merdeka). The towering grandstand at the edge of Warrior's Field serves as seating for the Sound and Light Show *(daily 8.30pm; adm RM10)*, an hour-long one-sided history of Melaka, with the help of music and lights.

Recent plans to expand the 'historical complex' around Bukit St Paul have resulted in the new **Islamic Museum** (*open Tues–Sun 9–5.30; closed Fri 12.15–2.45; adm RM2*). The intriguing Museum of Enduring Beauty, next door, failed to endure the ravages of a fire in 2002 and the new museum isn't what it was.

Around Dutch Square

Everything in Melaka, including the traffic, seems to gravitate towards Dutch Square (or Town Square, as it is also known). Small and rather cluttered, the square is flanked on one side by colonial Dutch buildings, and on the other by the murky Sungai Melaka. Most of the original square has been claimed by the roundabout and main road. What space is left is occupied by a fountain, clock tower, miniature windmill and tourist office. Old paintings of the square capture the picturesque languor of the town as it was under colonial control – sturdy Dutch architecture presiding over a scene of tropical ease. Ox-carts rest in the dirt, smoke hangs above a solitary hawker's wok, a rain tree shades a pair of traders happy to wait for business to come their way. Until very recently, public scribes sat under the same trees with their portable typewriters, ready to tap out a letter or contract. Now it's all traffic (navigating the one-way system) and tourists (shopping at souvenir stalls and passing between Christ Church, the Stadhuys and the tourist office).

The **Stadhuys** was constructed between 1641 and 1660 as a town hall and as a home for the Dutch governors of Melaka. One myth holds that the Dutch buildings acquired their red coat when locals began spitting betel juice at the walls as an expression of their distaste of Dutch rule. The more likely explanation is that, like Christ Church, the Stadhuys was constructed from the laterite stone found all over the district. The fiery paint that today blankets the building picks up on the stone's original red tinge. Multiple windows and airy verandahs were a concession to the heat. Otherwise the construction is typical of Dutch municipal buildings of the era. Today the Stadhuys houses the **Museum of History and Ethnography** (*open daily 9–5.30; closed Fri 12.15–2.45; adm RM5*). The large meandering exhibition is full of well-labelled artefacts and paintings tracing the history and traditions of Melaka. There's enough to keep the attentive visitor occupied for hours. For those left hanging about, there's a pleasant whitewashed courtyard and a series of shaded benches on an enclosed lawn alongside the verandah. An attached building on the hillside houses the **Literature Museum**, a limited display of Islamic writings and fables. The old Dutch building to the left of Christ Church, which is part of the original Stadhuys complex, has been given over to the **Youth Museum** (*open Wed–Mon 9–5.30; closed Fri 12.15–2.45; adm RM2*), a strange collection of photos, documents and handicrafts from Malaysian youth groups – specialist interest only.

It is easy to assume that **Christ Church** is part of the Stadhuys complex. In fact, it was built a century later on the centenary of the Dutch conquest of Melaka. Its plain façade, viewed across the Queen Victoria Fountain (erected to commemorate her Diamond Jubilee), is probably the most photographed feature of Melaka. The

Flor de la Mar

The sultan's throne; a set of four gold lions with precious stones for eyes, teeth and claws; a further sixty tons of gold in the form of tigers, monkeys, elephants and bullion; hundreds of chests stuffed with gems – the stuff of treasure hunters' dreams. All this and more went down with the *Flor de la Mar*, flagship of the Portuguese fleet, when a storm smashed it against a reef after the sacking of Melaka in 1511. Alfonso de Albuquerque, Admiral of the fleet, had hurriedly loaded his flagship and was determined to present his loot to the king of Portugal; and some loot it was. 'The richest treasure on earth that I have ever seen', was Alfonso's opinion in the aftermath of the wreck. From documentary evidence, it's an opinion that still rings true today. Sotheby's estimated the treasures on board to be worth a minimum of $9 billion, which makes the languishing *Flor de la Mar* the richest wreck in the world. Quite some scoop for an enterprising salvager. One problem though: no one knows exactly where the wreck lies.

Jumping the gun, the governments of Malaysia, Indonesia and Portugal are debating ownership of the treasures, should they be dredged from the ocean bed. The wreck is thought to lie just off the Sumatran coast at the northern entrance to the Straits. 'Our territory, our possession', runs the Indonesian argument. (The government is still smarting after British 'salvager' Michael Hatcher recovered gold ingots and Chinese porcelain from a 17th-century Dutch wreck in similar waters, auctioning the haul for $15 million in Amsterdam in 1986.) The Malaysian authorities point out – with undertones of long-suffering bitterness – that the treasures amount to stolen goods which should be returned to their rightful owner, the Sultanate of Melaka (never mind that Melaka is a sultanate no more). The Portuguese argument is

structure comprises bricks shipped from Holland then faced with laterite stone. The little bell tower and weather vane were added by the British, and the building was reconsecrated into the Church of England in 1838. To this day, C of E services are conducted in English, Mandarin and Tamil.

Inside Christ Church is a simple rectangular space with no division between nave and chancel – as one would expect of a Dutch Reformed church. The aisle stretches 80ft and is lined with the original pews, hand-carved locally from teak. The altar was added by the British and is inlaid with a marble frieze of the Last Supper. Forty feet up are a series of great ceiling beams, each 48ft long and hewn from a single tropical hardwood tree. A number of tombstones are laid in the floor. Oddly, most of them are Portuguese and were probably displaced from St Paul's Church by Dutch burials. One tombstone commemorates an Armenian trader born in Persia. The inscription (in Armenian) asks the reader to bring news of the 'freedom of my countrymen'. Elsewhere in the flooring are granite blocks inscribed with marks and letters. These are thought to have found their way to Melaka as ships' ballast, which would explain the lettering as storage instructions. The carved fanlight above the heavy timber door at the entrance is a Dutch feature widely adopted on later Melakan houses.

a touch opportune, but equally serious: when the ship went down ownership was in their hands – the spoils of war, and all that.

Then there are the salvagers, the treasure hunters, the ones who dedicate their time, money and equipment to recovering ancient treasures. They see themselves as modern-day adventurers, sailing the seas, studying ancient charts and raising dripping treasures from the deep for posterity (and for a small personal fortune). Others see them, at best, as glorified beachcombers profiting from the misfortune of others; at worst as thieves.

One thing is certain: there are dozens, possibly hundreds, of treasure-laden wrecks in the waters around Malaysia, and modern technology means finding them is no longer the stab in the dark it once was. Some of the toys that modern salvagers have at their disposal enable them to pinpoint wrecks deep beneath the sediment of the ocean bed – which, incidentally, is where most wrecks end up after centuries of alluvial deposits and oceanic currents.

In the early 1990s there were rumours that the great *Flor de la Mar* had been located beneath a concrete-like layer of sediment somewhere off the Sumatran coast. A salvage team was contracted by the Indonesian government to investigate, with words of reassurance sent out to Melaka and Portugal that any claims they may have would be taken seriously, particularly if they helped out with salvage costs. Location of the wreck was, of course, top secret, with the authorities desperate to avoid the hit-and-run tactics of troublesome treasure hunters. For years it was hush-hush. Now, a decade on, doubts are beginning to surface. It looks like another false call. Still the world waits to set eyes on 'the richest treasure on Earth'.

Behind Christ Church, off Jalan Laksamana, are the whitewashed towers of **St Francis Xavier's Church**, built by Frenchman Reverend Farve in 1849. The Gothic design is thought to be based on the Cathedral of St Peter in Montpelier, southern France. The true centre of the Catholic Church in Malaysia lies further east, at **St Peter's Church**. Built in 1710 on land donated by the Dutch, this is the oldest church in Malaysia. Good Friday, Easter Sunday and the San Pedro festival (an all-night fiesta held in June in honour of the patron saint of fishing) draw crowds of Catholics to St Peter's from all round the country. With its large arched windows full of stained glass, its exaggerated gables, and its interior wood panelling, the design is closely related to Portuguese architecture in Goa. The huge bell, visible high up in the tower, was itself cast in Goa long before the church was built. To get there, walk east down Jalan Bendahara, along the edge of Little India (which is, in effect, no more than a few sari shops and the odd banana-leaf restaurant).

Sungai Melaka

Today Sungai Melaka is little more than a stream stretching its muddy limb into the Strait. Over recent centuries, silt deposits have raised the riverbed, allowing access only to small vessels. River-tour boats weave their daily path between colourful fishing sampans moored according to the race of their owners. Delicate schooners from Sumatra sometimes stop by to offload charcoal or timber. Otherwise the river is somewhat redundant – a murky stream populated by a growing dynasty of monitor lizards, which bask on the banks like watchful crocodiles (they're harmless, actually). In Melaka's prime, dozens of ships dropped anchor in the deep harbour each day, while merchants rushed from their stilted godowns to barter the riches of the East. The prominent **Maritime Museum** on Jalan Quayside (*open Wed–Mon 9–6, closed Fri 12.15–2.45; adm RM2*), housed in a replica of the Portuguese galleon *Flor de la Mar* (*see* 'Flor de la Mar', pp.134–5), charts this maritime history with old paintings and plenty of models.

For a closer look at Sungai Melaka, **river tours** leave from behind the tourist office (*daily 10–2, one or two boats an hour; 45mins; adm RM8*). These head upstream past old wharves, ramshackle houses on stilts and fishing boats (which remain moored to the river bank until late afternoon, when they return to open waters). Take no notice of epithets such as 'Little Amsterdam' or 'Little Venice' – it's not the prettiest of journeys and there's not much to look at. (As a way of filling in the gaps, the guides have allocated names to every resident monitor lizard.) The furthest point on the river tour is **Kampung Morten**, a Malay village purpose-built in the 1920s on land acquired by two wealthy Melakans. JF Morten, the British District Officer at the time, donated funds. The main attraction here is **Villa Sentosa** (*open daily 9–1 and 2–5; donation expected*), a private Malay bungalow that has opened its doors to the public. Inside is some family memorabilia (including an old Malay-English dictionary presented to the late Hj. Hashim by Queen Victoria), but little else of interest. Elsewhere in the kampung are examples of the Melakan courtyard house. This hybrid style is characterized by a raised courtyard linking two traditional Malay bungalows. The bungalows are made of teakwood, the courtyard of masonry with airbricks for ventilation – a feature borrowed from the Chinese. Ornamental tiles from China typically grace the stairways of these types of houses.

The modern mouth of Sungai Melaka is man-made. The river now cuts through almost a kilometre of reclaimed land before depositing its load in the sea. Right by the river mouth a new island has popped onto the map. **Pulau Melaka** was dreamed up with Manhattan Island and Australia's Gold Coast in mind: condominiums, shopping arcades, a marine tourism theme park and a yacht club are planned. The construction of the island has been controversial. It is thought that between Pulau Upeh and Pulau Jawa – the very site of Pulau Melaka – lie numerous ancient shipwrecks. Pulau Jawa was known to the Portuguese as 'Island of Ships', as it was such a popular place to drop anchor, while Pulau Upeh (Malay for 'Island of Stones') provided laterite for the construction of A Famosa fort. One local historian has evidence that at least six Portuguese ships sank here during the Dutch blockade of 1610. Any artefacts are now buried beyond reach.

Another addition, **Melaka Pier**, now reaches out towards the northern tip of the island from in front of the Century Mahkota Hotel. A seafood restaurant, an

Babas and Nyonyas

One of Melaka's richest cultural legacies is that of the Straits Chinese, also known as Peranakans, or more commonly Babas (for men) and Nyonyas (for women). Their hybrid culture – a set of customs and beliefs that is ostensibly Chinese and yet infused with Malay touches – has come to be a defining feature of Melakan heritage.

Some time in the 1450s Princess Hang Li Poh set sail from China with 500 handmaidens and presented herself to Sultan Mansur Shah of Melaka as a sign of goodwill from the Chinese emperor. The sultan married her and dispersed her handmaidens among his court officials. This event is often taken as the genesis of Peranakan culture, though the truth is that most Babas and Nyonyas are the descendants of Chinese traders and Malay women (women very rarely made the journey from China). This growing community took on and adapted a number of Malay customs, while maintaining Chinese religious beliefs. Ancestor worship, for example, remains an integral ritual among Straits Chinese. (At the annual Hungry Ghosts festival, which falls in the 7th lunar month, gluttonous quantities of food are offered to the hungry departed whose spirits still walk the Earth.) Nyonyas took to wearing sarongs and spicing up Chinese dishes with typically Malay ingredients such as *sambal* (chilli shrimp paste) and coconut milk. In fact Nyonya cuisine is reason enough in itself for visiting Melaka – rich flavours, generous use of spices and beautiful presentation are all integral to a Nyonya spread.

A growing community of Straits Chinese bloomed in Penang and Singapore, as well as Melaka, and Baba Malay evolved into a language in its own right: although based loosely on Malay, the patois is speared with a rich vein of Hokkien vocabulary as well as a sprinkling of English, Dutch, Portuguese and Tamil words. By the 19th century, Peranakan culture had entered its golden age. The Babas, long known for their trading acumen, rose to prominence under the British administration and were soon

amusement park and craft shops on two storeys are accessible on foot or on a light rail transit system, which runs the quarter-mile length of the pier.

Conceived during the wave of optimism prior to the 1997 Asian financial crisis, this new swathe of land was built to allow a growing population to stretch its limbs. Unfortunately 'For Rent' signs have become a common sight among these flat featureless suburbs. Office space, apartments and shops remain vacant as they wait for a new wave of optimism to hit town. Recently the **Taman Melaka Raya** area has shown the way forward with a new batch of restaurants and bars.

Chinatown

Though there has always been an influential Chinese presence in Melaka, it wasn't until British colonial rule that numbers boomed. 'Melaka is to most intents and purposes a Chinese city', noted Isabella Bird after a visit in 1879. The British, who looked favourably on the Chinese work ethic, encouraged immigration, and new

known in colonial circles as 'the Queen's Chinese'. The British valued the Babas for their wealth and as intermediaries between the races. In turn, the Babas were seduced by a British sense of decorum, adopting numerous British traits. Members-only clubs were set up and games such as billiards and tennis became popular. The Nyonyas stayed home, honing their culinary skills and grooming themselves – Nyonyas were known for their elegance. Rice grains were crushed to a powder and applied to the face, while hair was swept up and painstakingly styled each day. Younger girls typically wore their hair 'telephone style', with buns on each side of the head. Many of the women had bound feet and wore embroidered shoes only three or four inches in length. Others wore Peranakan beaded slippers, or *kasut manek*, which were all the rage in the 19th century (and still are with tourists today).

Houses of wealthy Straits Chinese in Melaka were stuffed with furniture combining Victorian tastes with intricate Chinese ornament. Furniture, staircases, screens and walls were coated with mother-of-pearl, gold leaf and delicately carved hardwood. Tea was served up in custom-made china sets, known today as Nyonyaware and distinguished by its vibrant use of colour. Such pieces are now sought after by antiques hunters, as is Peranakan furniture.

The days of the Babas and Nyonyas have long passed their prime. While younger generations see themselves as new Malaysians, many of the old Peranakan shophouses have been destroyed – conservation is a sour point in Melaka. Still, a few remain, particularly on Jalan Tun Tan Cheng Lock. A number of these have been restored to their former elegance, most notably the privately owned Baba Nyonya Heritage Museum (*see* opposite). Tourism is now the last repository of Baba Nyonya culture. Yeo Sing Guat, the owner of Wa Aik Shoemaker, prides himself on being the very last shoemaker for bound feet. At the latest count he had one surviving customer – and she can no longer walk. His new breed of customer, the large-footed souvenir hunter, has proved less elusive; business is booming.

generations of Melakan Chinese rose to prominence in the city. Tan Chey Yan planted the first rubber tree in Melaka state in 1895. Meanwhile other wealthy Chinese ploughed capital into tin mining. By the early 20th century, Malaya was the world's biggest producer of rubber and tin, thanks largely to Chinese efforts. The wholesale and retail sectors were also dominated by the Chinese, with the shophouse and Peranakan townhouse becoming some of Melaka's dominant architectural features. Until recently such buildings were not valued as important pieces of heritage, and many have been bulldozed or left to rot. Still, Melaka's Chinatown is an area dense with attractions, from ancient temples and clan halls to boutique hotels and antiques.

Jalan Tun Tan Cheng Lock

Jalan Tun Tan Cheng Lock remains the best-preserved enclave. This street (formerly Heeren Street) once backed onto the sea and was the preserve of Melaka's wealthiest Chinese. Known in the 19th century as Millionaire's Row, it was lined with extravagant townhouses, many of which have been renovated to reap the rewards of increasing tourist figures. The street itself was built with ox-carts in mind and is narrow. Likewise the house fronts are narrow (Melaka inherited the Dutch system of paying rent according to the width of a property). However, some of the houses stretch to 70m in length, packing in a series of high-ceilinged rooms and courtyards. **The Baba Nyonya Heritage Museum** (*open 10–12.30 and 2–4.30; adm RM8*), at No. 50, offers a glimpse inside a lavish Peranakan mansion. Built in 1896 by planter Chan Cheng Siew, this private residence has been lavishly renovated and opened to the public. Both the structure of the house and the contents are an amalgam of Chinese and European styles, often referred to as Chinese Palladian. It was typical for the wealthy Baba to boost the status of his traditional Chinese shophouse with neoclassical columns and pilasters decorated with elaborate stucco work. Louvred windows were borrowed from the Portuguese, wood-carved half-doors (known as *pintu pagar*) from the Malays, while glazed tiles were imported from Europe or China to decorate the façade or the courtyards. Step inside the Baba Nyonya museum and the immediate sensation is one of sensory overload – Victorian clutter meets Oriental ornament. Everything is painstakingly detailed, from the Chinese/Victorian blackwood furniture, which glistens with Dutch mother-of-pearl and delicate gold leaf, to silk-embroidered lanterns, beaded slippers and lurid Nyonyaware ceramics.

Some of the renovated houses along Jalan Tun Tan Cheng Lock serve as art studios and galleries, including No.70 with its Dutch-style frontage. Others are boutique hotels, notably Heeren House and Puri Hotel. The latter's narrow entranceway opens out into an elegant courtyard shaded by Japanese frangipani. In an adjoining room, the owners allow swiftlets to nest, harvesting the nests each year for soup. A small 'History Room' exhibits well-labelled engravings and antiques. The most ostentatious address along here is the pale green and pink **Chee Mansion**, built in 1919 in an eccentric mix of Chinese and European styles. Set back from the street behind a gate, the original Dutch building was renovated with the addition of a small golden dome, Chinese decorations and a few Art Nouveau touches. The Chee family made its fortune in rubber and tapioca.

Jalan Hang Kasturi to Jalan Hang Jebat

Jalan Hang Kasturi (Second Cross Steet) cuts east from Heeren Street towards the river. This once-important street originally stretched from the seafront to the river. A number of artisans still ply their trades along here: silver, clogs, rattan furniture, traditional lacquer signboards and batiks. The eastern stretch has been dubbed 'Tofu Lane' after the bean-curd hawkers who set up stall each weekend. Beyond here, at the junction with Jalan Kampung Pantai stands the **Tomb of Hang Jebat**, the tiny mausoleum of one of Melaka's legendary warriors, after whom the old Jonker Street was named. Third Cross Street (or Jalan Hang Lekir), which links Heeren Street with Jonkers Walk, was once the realm of the dead: a series of funeral parlours churned out ornate teakwood coffins, which would be conveyed with their occupants to Bukit Cina for burial. Today it is one of Melaka's liveliest spots, with a couple of late-opening bars. There is also one of Melaka's original junk shops along here – worth a stop for the serious antique hunter.

Jalan Hang Jebat, or Jonker Street, is the busiest stretch of Chinatown, home to antiques shops, clan houses, art galleries and cafes. The street is known primarily as Melaka's (and indeed Malaysia's) antiques centre. In recent years it has been jumped on by the tourist board, who have erected signs advertising the street as 'Jonker Walk'. This refers to the weekend market, for which the street is pedestrianized and lined with stalls selling food, crafts and gadgets. Most of the old shophouses have been stuffed with desirable but overpriced antiques and crafts for tourists, though there are further examples of renovated Peranakan houses along the way, such as the Jonkers Melaka restaurant (*see* 'Eating Out', p.144). The main Chinese clan houses of the Hokkien, Teochew and Hainanese Associations are found along this street; poke your head through the entranceways at weekends and you're likely to catch a formation of sweaty clan members working through an aerobics session. Also keep an eye out for the nostalgic Atlas Ice Company, about halfway down. The entranceway opens out into a courtyard where horsecarts once pulled up to be loaded with coffin-sized slabs of ice.

Harmony Street and Around

Running parallel to Jonkers Walk are a series of streets known collectively as Harmony Street. As the individual street names imply, this was once the territory of Melaka's blacksmiths and goldsmiths, though trade has long since fizzled out. However, the key attractions are three places of worship that have stood side by side since the period of Dutch rule: a Chinese temple, a mosque and a Hindu temple. Harmony indeed. **Cheng Hoon Teng Temple** (Temple of the Green Clouds) on Jalan Tokong is the oldest Chinese temple in Malaysia. First built in the early 17th century, the present temple hall was constructed in 1704. It has since served the religious and social needs of the southern Chinese clans, acting at one time as official headquarters of the Kapitan China. The whole complex has been painstakingly restored over recent years. Timber beams from the main hall were replaced, while paintings on the gable walls and figurines on the roof ridges were restored by a team of craftsmen from China. This form of decorative work, originating in southern China and known as Chien Nien, involves cutting and pasting shards of custom-made porcelain to create mythological scenes. The temple itself is dedicated to Kwang Ying, the Goddess of Mercy. Her image, cast in solid bronze, sits at the main altar. Outbuildings surrounding the main hall house a range of deities strewn daily with offerings. Across the road is the traditional 'theatre building', used solely for administrative purposes today. Towards the end of the street is Melaka's most famous little shop. Wah Aik Shoemaker (*see* p.138) is one of the last makers of shoes for bound feet – or 'three-and-a-half-inch golden lotus feet', as they are known – a custom outlawed in China in 1912.

A little south of the temple, past colourful stalls selling joss sticks, candles, little plastic buddhas and papier-mâché dragons – the latter sent up in smoke at funerals to ensure safe passage into the next life – is the pagoda-like minaret of **Kampung**

Kling Mosque. Kampung Kling was the village inhabited by Indian Muslim traders at the time of the Sultanate of Melaka. The unusual free-standing minaret is clearly a result of Chinese influence, though one senses an element of competition in the design, built so close as it is to the Buddhist temple. The Peninsula's earliest mosques were built here in Melaka, acquiring a peculiar style of their own. As with all things Melakan, this style became a synthesis of numerous influences. The prayer hall of this mosque built in 1748 is held aloft by Corinthian columns, the lampposts and ablution pools display Arabic touches, and the floor tiles are from England and Portugal. The basic shape of the tiered roof is similar to that of the Southeast Asian Great Mosque (*see* p.36), very few of which survive because traditionally they were made of timber.

A few strides away stands the **Sri Poyyatha Vinayagar Temple**, the Indian Hindu offering to Harmony Street. Inside, the black-stone head of an elephant represents the deity Vinayagar (more commonly known as Ganesh) to whom the temple is dedicated. The three-tiered *gopuram*, or entrance tower, is strikingly unadorned compared with other South Indian temples found in Malaysia. That said, three Hindu gods strike poses on different tiers of the tower, and a line of bright yellow cows adorn the eaves. The temple was built on land provided by the Dutch in 1781 and is said to be the oldest (Hindu temple) in the country. Its relative simplicity is a characteristic temple design of the Chitty Indians, who worship here along with other Hindu communities. The Chitties are Straits-born Indians who, like the Babas and Nyonyas, have adopted many elements of Malay culture while retaining their original faith.

North of Harmony Street, on Jalan Masjid, is **Kampung Hulu Mosque**, built a little earlier than Kampung Kling Mosque and of a similar style. Chinese influence is again evident in the free-standing minaret and the roof tiles, while the roof structure is related to that of mosques built long ago in parts of Indonesia. Across the river from the mosque is the site of the old Central Market. In the 1930s the swampy mangrove-strewn bank east of the river was developed into a new commercial zone, with a covered market at its centre. The surrounding area became known as New Chinatown. In the 1980s the Central Market was demolished, but the area remains a lively extension of Chinatown. Hawker fare is widely available at the daily *pasar malam* (6pm–10pm) on Jalan Kee Ann.

Bukit China

Within walking distance of the centre, Bukit China rises steeply on the eastern fringe of Melaka, offering a panorama of the city and beyond. Chinese graves, some dating back to the 15th century, blanket the rounded undulations of this historic plot, now popular as a place to escape from the city.

The hill was placed in Chinese hands way back in *c*.1450, when Sultan Mansur Shah married Princess Hang Li Poh of China. Prior to the marriage – so the story goes – the Ming emperor had sent a magnificent ship to Melaka, the great curve of its hull pierced with innumerable gold needles. The accompanying message read, 'For every

Getting There

By Air

Melaka's airport is situated 10km away at Batu Berendam. Only Pelangi Air fly there (airport office **t** 06 385 1175). They also operate services to and from Singapore, Ipoh and the Sumatran airports of Medan and Pekan Baru. The big hotels offer shuttle taxi services from the airport. Bus no. 65 will also get you into town.

By Sea

High-speed ferries operate between Melaka and Dumai in Sumatra. The journey takes about 2hrs and costs around RM100. Three companies operate ferries: Madai Shipping, **t** 06 284 0671; Tunas Rupat Utama, **t** 06 283 2506; Masamas, **t** 06 281 8200.

By Rail and Bus

Melaka has no railway station. The nearest is at Tampin, 38km away. By bus, Melaka is 2hrs away from KL, 90mins from KLIA and 4hrs from Singapore. There are two bus stations off Jalan Hang Tuah, within walking distance of the town centre. The long-distance bus terminal is crushed up against a bend in the river and is not the most picturesque welcome to the city you might hope for. Taxis from here to any of the hotels should not cost more than a few ringgits. Tickets to all major Peninsula destinations are available at a cluster of ticket booths surrounding the long-distance station.

By Taxi

The long-distance taxi stand is opposite the local bus station. Drivers are willing to head to most destinations in the southern portion of the Peninsula. A taxi to or from KL should cost around RM100. For more information call **t** 06 282 3630.

Getting Around

Melaka is a compact place, smaller than most people imagine. Even in the tropical heat, it's possible to tramp around the whole town on foot. As ever, traffic is a bit of a problem, with a series of one-way systems snaking their way through the centre. A number of shops and guesthouses rent out bicycles. Otherwise you could ride about in one of the colourful, bopping trishaws – though expect to pay tourist prices; the locals wouldn't go near them. As usual, there are reasonably priced, metered taxis everywhere if you're feeling hot and bothered. Car rental: Hawk Rent-a-Car, 126 Jalan Bendahara (opposite Renaissance Melaka), **t 06** 283 7878, **f** 281 8788, *www.hawkrentacar.com*.

Tourist Information

The helpful tourist office, **Jalan Kota**, **t** 06 281 4803 (*open daily 9–5, closed Fri 12.15–2.45*) is on Dutch Square, by the roundabout. They have lots of brochures, including a good guide to Chinatown and a booklet of discount vouchers. Internet cafés, dotted all about town, come and go with frequency. Ask at the tourist office.

Where to Stay

Luxury

Renaissance Melaka, Jalan Bendahara, **t** 06 284 8888, **f** 284 9269, *info@mkzpo.jaring.my*, *www.renaissancehotels.com/mkzrn*. Melaka's

gold needle, I have a subject; if you can count their number, then you will know my power!' Bullish talk. But the Sultan felt up to it and reciprocated with his own huge ship stuffed full of sago grain. This he sent on its way to Imperial China with a corresponding message. Evidently the emperor was pleased with the response. For his next move, he shipped off his daughter and 500 specially chosen handmaidens. The sultan married the princess and offered her and her maids Bukit China as a private residence, promising never to reclaim the land. It seems in his happiness he top hotel, with facilities that include tennis, squash and an outdoor pool. Opulence is the order of the day: crystal chandeliers and marble in the lobby, conservative décor in the rooms. Frequent promotions take it down a price category.

Expensive

Hotel Equatorial, Jalan Bandar Hilir, **t** 06 282 8333, **f** 06 282 9333, *info@equatorial.com*, *www.equatorial.com*. After a recent renovation the Equatorial is vying for Melaka's business-hotel top spot. 5-star facilities and situation (a few hundred yards from Bukit St Paul) make this a good stopover option. Reasonable prices too.

Century Mahkota Hotel, Jalan Merdeka, **t** 06 281 2828, **f** 06 281 2323, *cmh@tm.net.my*, *www.centuryhotels.com.my*. This monster hotel beside Melaka Pier has over 600 rooms, many with attached kitchen. Big range of facilities available, including two pools and mini golf, but rather impersonal and lacking in atmosphere.

City Bayview Hotel, Jalan Bendahara, **t** 06 283 9888, **f** 06 283 6699, *cbviewmk@tm.net.my*. A reasonable business-oriented hotel with swimming pool and 4-star facilities. Centrally located in 'new Chinatown'.

Moderate

Heeren House, 1 Jalan Tun Tan Cheng Lock, **t** 06 281 4241, **f** 06 281 4239, *www.melaka.net/heerenhouse*. The most characterful place to stay in Melaka. Six rooms with four-poster beds and antique furniture on the first floor of an old godown overlooking the river. Downstairs in the café is a little exhibition of maps and engravings from the 16th–18th centuries. Set tea is served 12–3. Book well ahead for a room. Air-con.

Hotel Puri, 118 Jalan Tun Tan Cheng Lock, **t** 06 282 5588, **f** 06 281 5588, *enquiries@hotelpuri.com*, *www.hotelpuri.com*. A boutique hotel in a stunning restored Peranakan town house. The lobby, with its covered courtyard, is tastefully decorated with antique furniture and modern paintings for sale. A small 'History Room' provides a great introduction to Melaka, while the hotel café is set in a secluded courtyard beneath Japanese frangipani. Lower-priced rooms are plain.

The Baba House, 125–7 Jalan Tun Tan Cheng Lock, **t** 06 281 1216, **f** 06 281 1217, *thebabahouse@pd.jaring.my*, *www.melaka.net/babahouse*. Another renovated Peranakan mansion with beautiful furniture and a decorative screen in the lobby. Rooms are spartan in comparison, but good value nevertheless.

Hallmark Hotel, 68 Jalan Portugis, **t** 06 281 2888, **f** 06 281 3409. Excellent value hotel – sanitized, modern and clean, though makes no attempt at character. A 15-minute walk from the centre of things.

Inexpensive

Kancil Guesthouse, 177 Jalan Parameswara, Bandar Hilir, **t** 06 281 4044, *kancil@machinta.com.sg*, *www.machinta.com.sg/kancil*. Though situated on a busy narrow road with no pavement, this is the best inexpensive choice in Melaka. Upstairs are several beautifully decorated doubles. The big room at the back, with its own balcony overlooking the garden, is worth booking in advance. Downstairs are a row of basic, budget rooms. There's a little library, as well as internet facilities and bike rental. 20-minute walk to the centre (or bus no.17).

never got round to returning the favour (no doubt the disappointed Ming emperor had boasted to his friends that a Malay harem was on its way).

For centuries now the hill has belonged to the Chinese community, who have used it as their sacred burial ground. Confucius taught the importance of duty to the dead: the worship of parents' spirits and the maintenance of their graves. Elevated above the city, Bukit China's harmony with the elements was seen to provide ideal roaming ground for ancestral spirits. Now the graves sprawl over 42 hectares, making it the largest – and oldest – Chinese graveyard outside China. Some of the huge horseshoe-shaped tombs

Hinly Hotel, 150 Jalan Parameswara, **t** 06 283 6554, **f** 06 283 9537. An unusual house set back from a busy, narrow road, with 20 clean and basic rooms. All rooms have attached bathroom with hot water, air-con and TV. Good value.

Sunny's Inn, 270A/B Taman Melaka Raya 3, **t** 06 226 5446, *sunnyinn@hotmail.com*. Primarily a hostel serving backpackers, though there are a few bargain air-con rooms with attached showers. There's a big communal lounge with games and a roof terrace. Situated on the unappealing swathe of reclaimed land south of the town centre.

Budget

Eastern Heritage Guesthouse, 8 Jalan Bukit China, **t** 06 283 3026, *www.eastern-heritage.com*. An elegant Chinese house near Bukit China with lots of tilework and gold leaf downstairs. The fan-only rooms are basic, with huge landscape scenes painted on the walls and shared toilets and showers. The highlight is a dipping pool at the foot of the stairs. There's also a batik workshop out back. Midnight curfew.

Malacca Town Holiday Lodge 2, 52 Kampung Empat, **t** 06 284 6905. A budget option on a quiet residential street. Peranakan antiques lining the corridors add character. A number of rooms have attached bathroom. Decent value in a quiet spot. Not to be confused with the affiliated Lodge 1.

Malacca Hotel, 27A Jalan Munshi Abdullah, **t** 06 282 2252. Though not inviting at first sight, the clean, spacious rooms are perfectly acceptable for the price. It's only yards from the long-distance bus station (use the little walkway over the river) and will do as a temporary or last-minute option.

Eating Out

Unlike elsewhere in Malaysia, Melaka does not burst at the seams with food. Finding the culinary highs – and there are lots – requires a little delving about. What the city lacks in quantity is made up for in variety: the usual Malay, Chinese and Indian cuisines are lined up alongside wonderfully rich Nyonya cuisine and fiery Portuguese Eurasian food. Nyonya food, which features on many Melakan menus, combines a Malay predeliction for spices with a Chinese cooking style. Exquisite cakes are also in abundance. Portuguese cuisine is harder to come by and often disappointing. The handful of restaurants in the little Portuguese settlement are clearly geared towards tourists and, as such, are overpriced. Another Melakan speciality is Hainanese chicken rice. The women of Hainan (in southern China) once rolled rice into balls for their husbands to eat out in the fields. Nowadays the rice balls are enriched with chicken fat and served with a perky chilli-ginger sauce.

Melaka has a handful of food courts, listed below, as well as two night markets: the weekend *pasar malam* on Jonker Walk (Jalan Hang Jebat), with a wide range of snack stalls, and the daily *pasar malam* on Jalan Kee Ann, in 'new' Chinatown across the river. Vegetarians especially will delight in the foodstalls of 'Tofu Lane', which line up on Friday and Saturday evening towards the east end of Jalan Hang Kasturi.

Expensive

Harpers, 2–4 Lorong Hang Jebat, **t** 06 282 8800. An upmarket riverfront restaurant in a prime position. There's a mixed

belong to the Kapitan Chinas of the colonial era, while a few weather-beaten graves date right back to the Ming dynasty. These facts were of no concern to the state government of the early 1980s, who demanded RM10 million in rent arrears going back half a millennium – knowing it could never be paid. They were then planning the seafront reclamation project, and had turned their beady eyes on the great mound of earth that was Bukit China. Naturally, the Chinese community was disgusted at this demand for money, and at the implication that their burial grounds might be forked into the sea and laid over with shopping malls. They won their case and, in doing so,

Mediterranean menu and a long bar. Lots of fish options, oysters, spaghetti vongole, rack of lamb.

Long Feng, Renaissance Melaka Hotel, Jalan Bendahara. The signature restaurant of the Renaissance Melaka, serving beautifully presented Cantonese and Szechuan cuisine in an opulent setting (rosewood furniture, Chinese watercolours on the walls).

Kampachi, Hotel Equatorial, Jalan Bandar Hilir. A Japanese restaurant inside the Equatorial Hotel, with crisp pine furnishings and a large menu of top-class Japanese cuisine.

Moderate

Coconut House, 128 Jalan Tun Tan Cheng Lock, **t** 06 282 9128. An upbeat restaurant in a restored Peranakan town house. Pizzas with a local influence are the mainstay (toppings include satay sauce, yam and white nuts). The desserts are wonderfully rich, and the setting is fashionable – modern art for sale all over the place, jazz on the stereo and a young crowd. *Open 11am–midnight*.

Jonkers Melaka, 17 Jalan Hang Jebat, **t** 06 283 5578. One of Melaka's best-known Peranakan houses, full of art and antiques. The best reason to come, though, is for the Nyonya set lunch. A platter of Nyonya specialities (vegetarian available) is followed by green-tea ice cream with ginger and lime or cheesecakes. *Open daily 10–5*.

Heeren House, 1 Jalan Tun Tan Cheng Lock, **t** 06 281 4241. Open daily from 12–3 for Nyonya and Portuguese lunches, or just tea and cakes. Western breakfasts are available earlier in the morning. It's set in a lovingly restored godown which once backed onto the sea.

Ole Sayang Restaurant, 199 Taman Melaka Raya. Probably the best-known Nyonya restaurant, and very touristy as a result. Nevertheless, the Nyonya food is authentic and the décor – marble-top tables and cane furniture – is appealing. Try prawns and pineapple in a rich coconut-milk sauce, or *kangkong belacan* (a type of green vegetable fried in shrimp paste).

Geographer Café, 83 Jalan Hang Jebat, **t** 06 281 6813. Airy and tastefully decorated café in the heart of Chinatown. Very popular with tourists. A range of snacks and salads are available, including *nasi lemak* and *manis melaka* (ice cream with a nutty topping). There's a substantial wine list, as well as fruit juices and coffees. Open late.

Ringo Classics & Antiques, Jalan Hang Jebat. Opposite the Geographer Café, and in the same vein. The attraction here is the wood-fire-oven pizzas. Open late; live music at weekends.

Restoran de Lisbon, Medan Portugis. Set in the heart of the Portuguese settlement, this is the best of several restaurants aimed specifically at tourists. Typical dishes include devil curry, chilli seafood and baked fish. Malay influence predominates over Portuguese.

Inexpensive

Restoran Veni, Jalan Temenggong. A fabulous south Indian banana-leaf-curry restaurant in Little India. The servings are huge and the mutton curry is particularly tasty. Though an unassuming place (and probably the best-value restaurant in Melaka), it's popular with a string of local dignitaries.

Café Madras, Jalan Temenggong. One of the most popular breakfast choices for

renewed interest in Bukit China, which had been waist-high in *lalang* grass for years. Trees have been planted and a network of paths have been laid, to the delight of the many locals (mainly joggers), who have adopted the hill as their city park.

At the foot of Bukit China sits the **Hang Li Poh Well**, dug on the orders of Sultan Mansur Shah for his new wife. The waters have never once run dry, though they were poisoned on several occasions with devastating effect. In 1551 a band of indignant Malays contaminated the water killing 200 Portuguese. It is said that anyone who

Melakans on their way to work. Great *roti canai* and speedy service are the main draw.

Capitol Satay, 41 Lorong Bukit China, **t** 06 283 5508. A popular satay restaurant (known as *satay celup*). Similar in concept to the Chinese steamboat: choose from a huge array of skewered raw delicacies, then sit round a pot of boiling broth in which the skewers are dunked. The record, in one sitting, is 169 skewers (though most will be pushed to eat more than 10!). Extremely cheap and very tasty.

U.E. Teahouse, 20 Lorong Bukit China. An old Chinese teahouse with a daily display of steamed dumplings. The dumplings – some stuffed with pork or fish, others sweet – make an unusual snack alongside Chinese tea or Melakan coffee.

Nancy's Kitchen, 15 Jalan Hang Lekir. An attractive little place serving well-priced Nyonya food. Stop off here for one of the best Nyonya cendols in Melaka.

Riverside Kopitian, 17 Jalan Laksamana, **t** 06 283 9854. An attractive spot just up from the Stadhuys, with tables overlooking the river. Serves a range of cheap local specialities and the usual Western offerings. *Open daily 9am–11pm.*

Restaurant Famosa Chicken Rice, Jalan Hang Jebat. A good place to sample Hainanese chicken rice (*see* p.144), about halfway down Jonker Walk.

Kafe Loony Planet, 40 Jalan Laksamana. Open daily 10am–midnight. If the name doesn't put you off, you'll find a decent range of imported beers here and large servings of local and western food. Popular with budget travellers and expats. A battered old Melakan sings karaoke most nights.

Tart & Tart (T&T) Bakery, 45 Lorong Hang Jebat, **t** 06 282 1181. This little bakery is great for snacks. The *nasi lemak* here is renowned, while the Portuguese tarts are worth every ringgit.

Tian Tai, 3 Jalan Hang Lekir. A great example of a Melakan *kedai kopi*, with tiled floor and Straits marble-top tables.

Food courts: Bunga Raya Food Court, an attractive paved spot with palms and potted plants, is tucked away between Jalan Bendahara and Jalan Bunga Raya. A ring of Chinese stalls (one vegetarian), a wood-fire pizza stall and a bar surround the tables. East of here is **Centrepoint Stalls**, Melaka's largest hawker centre, while in front of the Mahkota shopping mall (on Jalan Taman Merdeka) is **Glutton's Corner**, a string of permanent stalls. At the east end of Jalan Temenggong are some **Chinese noodle stalls**, in front of which local Chinese barter for durians in season. Between the Equatorial Hotel and Bukit St Paul are the **Padang Pahlawan Malay Hawker Stalls**, with the usual array of dirt-cheap Malay dishes and drinks.

Nightlife

Melaka doesn't have much of a nightlife. Those out to socialize tend to head for restaurants serving alcohol. A few imitation pubs have appeared in Taman Melak Raya in recent years, but most visitors spend their evenings around Melaka's Chinatown. Jalan Hang Lekir is a popular spot for an evening drink (mainly with tourists). Tables spill out onto the road from the **Geographer Café**, which has a large wine list, and from **Ringo Classics & Antiques**, which also has a well-

drinks from the well will return to Melaka some day. (Judging by the colour of the water, you'd be lucky to make it out of the city in the first place.)

Right next to the well is the **Sam Poh Kong Temple**, built in 1795 in honour of Cheng Ho, a Chinese eunuch from the court of the third Ming Emperor. Admiral Cheng Ho was the first ambassador from China to cement relations with Melaka (*c.*1405). For two decades he sailed round the known world, establishing trading links and a reputation for bravery. The title 'Sam Poh' ('Three Jewels') was conferred on him in 1431, and he has since been deified by overseas Chinese. One bizarre tale tells of a fish stocked bar. At **Coconut House** (128 Jalan Tun Tan Cheng Lock; *see* p.145) you can take a seat round a 200-year-old well, or admire artwork in the adjoining gallery. This tasteful bar-restaurant is open late at weekends. Next door the **Galleri Café** (part of Hotel Puri) is a good place for a drink. Wines and beers are on offer alongside a Nyonya-based menu.

Taman Melaka Raya is now the liveliest area after dark. A number of pubs with pool tables and piped-in music serve the young executive crowd and a smaller number tourists. One such is **Jessie's Florist and Café** (341 Taman Melaka Raya), which is popular with expats and has a token flower stall. The only real club in Melaka is **Downtown Exclusive Dance Club** (9 Bangunan Draland, Jalan Merdeka), where techno beats attract a young crowd.

The Traders Lounge, in the lobby of the Equatorial Hotel, is a nice spot for a cocktail. Comfortable leather sofas, occasional live jazz and soft lighting help things on their way (though it's hard to forget you're in a hotel lobby). Another upmarket place is **Harpers** (2–4 Lorong Hang Jebat; *see* p.144 with its long bar and river views. **The Bulldog Café** (145 Jalan Bendahara) is a more laid-back spot, with bright orange walls and a little pond full of carp. Western and local snacks are served, as well as imported beer and cocktails. For an alfresco drink try the **Bunga Raya Food Court** (between Jalan Bunga Raya and Jalan Bendahara), where there's a curved bar on an elevated patio. **Bunga Raya Café** (155 Jalan Bunga Raya) has beer and wine on tap.

Shopping

Melaka is definitely the place to buy gifts and souvenirs. Crafts and trinkets are available in abundance on Dutch Square and along Jalan Laksamana. The streets of Chinatown are lined with antiques, art galleries and more craft shops. **Jalan Hang Jebat** is seen as Malaysia's primary antiques centre, though many of the shops sell imitation pieces. Prints of old maps, specialist books, Bornean woodwork, model boats, old coins, and batik are also in abundance. The greatest demand is for Nyonyaware and Peranakan furniture – Victorian-style items often inlaid with ornate mother-of-pearl and gold leaf in Chinese motifs. The serious antiques hunter would do well to pore through the traditional 'junk' shops dotted about Chinatown. Upmarket galleries and antiques shops line Jalan Tun Tan Cheng Lock. Prices are inflated, so bargain hard (ignore claims that prices are fixed).

One of Melaka's best-known shops is **Wah Aik Shoemaker**, Jalan Tokong. For over a century this family business has hand crafted Peranakan slippers and tiny shoes for Chinese women with bound feet. Today most of the shoes are sold as souvenirs. Head south to the junction with Lorong Hang Jebat for the **Orang Utan House**, 59 Lorong Hang Jebat, where local artist Charles Cham sells his bold paintings, as well as printed T-shirts. For unusual homemade chutneys, a Portuguese Eurasian family (the Theseiras) have opened a tiny stall in front of their bungalow (which sits next to the Assumption Church off Jalan Melaka Raya 14). Their mango pickle is particularly delicious. The huge **Mahkota Parade** shopping mall south of the river is the best spot for general shopping. Otherwise try **Madam King's** department store on Jalan Bunga Raya.

– known locally as *ikan talang* – which saved Cheng Ho's life by wedging itself into a hole that had appeared in the side of the admiral's ship.

Medan Portugis

The presence in Melaka of Luso-Malays, or Portuguese Eurasians as they are more commonly known today, is a remarkable story of survival. Descendants of 16th-century marriages between Portuguese colonists and Malays, these people have retained a stubborn sense of community for almost five centuries. They speak a Portuguese-Malay creole known as Cristao, they are devout Catholics (they call themselves *Kristang*), they bake their fish like the Portuguese, and they dance to the beat of Latin rhythms. In a broader sense, their ethnicity today can barely be distinguished from the Malays – any Portuguese blood in the community is nearly 500 years old, and heavily diluted. Despite this it is only recently that the community has gained a political voice: for many years UMNO would not accept Portuguese Eurasians into the party. (The link between being Malay and being Muslim remains steadfast.) While the tourist board encourages the community to exhibit the Portuguese aspect of their traditions, members of the younger generation are keener to cover up their distant origins so that they can integrate and get on in life.

The Portuguese settlement is situated 3km east of town centre (get onto Jalan Parameswara and look out for Jalan D'Albuquerque, a small turning on the right; bus 17 from local bus station). The settlement was opened in 1930 by the British Resident Commissioner after an appeal from French missionary Pierre François. The original state-built houses were wooden with *attap* roofs and earthen floors. Few members of the community were inclined to move in, until the government replaced the old huts with modern housing laid out on a grid. Today barely a thousand Luso-Malays inhabit the settlement – it is eerily quiet most of the time and of limited appeal to the visitor. **Medan Portugis** (Portuguese Square), at the end of Jalan D'Albuquerque, is the centre. The sturdy whitewashed archway was added in 1985. Through here are a couple of 'Portuguese' restaurants and a souvenir shop masquerading as a small exhibition. Once a year, on 29 June, the square comes alive for the Feast of St Pedro, with Portuguese folk music, dancing and lots of food and wine.

Just beyond the Portuguese settlement is Kampung Hilir, an area traditionally linked with the Portuguese. In 1760 the Dutch demolished a Catholic chapel on a nearby hill and built **St John's Fort** – both to protect Melaka from inland attack (notice how the cannon embrasures face inland), and to keep an eye on the remaining Portuguese. Today the fort lies on the edge of a busy road and access is difficult without a car. Only a few walls of the original fort remain.

Around Melaka

Other than the old city itself, tourist attractions are thin on the ground in the little state of Melaka. That said, a mountain, an island, a coastal village (or two) and a recreational park all vie for the attentions of those with a little time on their hands. Gunung Ledang (most of which lies in Johor state) rises out of nowhere from the Melakan plain, its flanks blessed with a spectacular series of waterfalls; Pulau Besar offers a touch of beach-lazing, as do the villages of Tanjung Kling and Tanjung Bidara; meanwhile the museums and recreational forest of Ayer Keroh serve as the city's playground.

Ayer Keroh

Ayer Keroh is a recreational complex with a cluster of low-key and frequently deserted attractions lined up along the main road 12km inland from Melaka. Bus 19 from the local bus station will get you there for a ringgit. An easy stroll can be had at the **Hutan Rekreasi** (recreational park), where a series of paved trails cut through patches of secondary forest around a man-made lake. Just off the main road **Mini Malaysia** (*open Mon–Fri 9–5, Sat, Sun and hols 9–5.30; adm RM5*) exhibits a range of traditional Malay architecture, with 13 timber houses representing each of Malaysia's 13 states and furnished accordingly. Though the exhibits inside are lacklustre, you get a real sense of how well these houses are adapted to a tropical climate. Next door, **Mini Asean** (*same opening times and adm*) works on the same principal, with traditional houses representing each of the member states of ASEAN (excluding Malaysia): Thailand, Philippines, Indonesia, Singapore and Brunei. Further along the road is **Malacca Zoo** (*open daily 9–6; adm RM5*), one of the nation's largest, with over 200 species, including tigers, rhinos and orang-utans.

Directly opposite the zoo is the Crocodile Farm and the **Orang Asli Museum** (*open daily 9–6; closed Fri 12.15–2.45; adm RM1*). This tiny museum set on wooden piles, on two levels, is packed with information about the eighteen or so tribes that comprise the Orang Asli ('original men', or aborigines, of Peninsular Malaysia). Their beliefs and customs are showcased alongside well-written labels. Outside the Orang Asli Museum stand a few colourful bullock carts, saddled up and ready to go (for a small fee). Ornate carts with peaked roofs such as these were once used to ferry the rich about the narrow lanes of Melaka.

Gunung Ledang

Gunung Ledang (1276m), or Mount Ophir (as it was called by the British), rises abruptly beyond the eastern edge of Melaka state, its peak standing in Johor. The mountain is perhaps linked with the Ophir of the Old Testament, the legendary land from which King Solomon acquired his gold. In ancient times gold, sandalwood, ivory and monkeys were thought to have been procured from the site. The Malays named the mountain after Puteri (Princess) Ledang. This legendary princess (of great beauty, needless to say) was reported to have killed her husband in a fit of passion. She then retired to Mount Ophir, vowing never to set eyes on another man. Subsequently, Sultan Mansur Shah of Melaka was said to have been besotted by her, but she repelled even his lusty advances with a string of requirements worthy of a Homeric epic: seven trays of mosquito hearts, seven jugs of areca-nut water, a cup of his son's blood, and a vat of his own tears.

Today the mountain is a popular spot, with weekenders flocking to the **Puteri Falls**, a series of dramatic cascades with pools suitable for swimming. Souvenir stalls, picnic clearings and a simple resort hotel have gathered near the foot of the falls. Various trails lead to the summit of the mountain, one from near Sagil in Johor, the other from Asahan in Melaka. The falls are accessible only from Sagil. Scaling the peak is not possible in one day, but it is worth following the steep tracks some of the way. The primary forest that blankets the mountain is especially rich in flora. The turning for the waterfall is signposted 3km beyond Sagil on Route 23.

Islands and Coastal Villages

Pulau Besar ('Big Island') is not very big. Only a few kilometres in length, it is possible to cover the island in a day on foot. Pulau Besar was a popular jumping-off point for traders and missionaries during the glory days of the Melaka sultanate. A shrine to a 15th-century Muslim trader and missionary, and a few bunkers from the Japanese occupation, are the limit of the island's historical interest. Like many spots on the west coast, the sea is a little murky (though it beats the waters off the mainland). Regular ferries leave from Anjung Batu, a jetty near the village of Umbai 12km southeast of Melaka. This stretch of coastline is famous for its *ikan bakar* (grilled fish) served up at beachside stalls.

Pulau Upeh (Island of Stones), just west of Melaka, is even smaller and not quite as attractive. During the construction of A Famosa, the Portuguese plundered Pulau Upeh for its laterite rock (hence the name). Despite the environmental damage caused by land reclamation around Melaka, the island remains a sanctuary for hawksbill turtles, which drag themselves onto the beaches to lay eggs by night.

West of Melaka the coast is dotted with new resort hotels, which clammer up against a long but dismal beach. Most of them congregate around the village of **Tanjung Kling**, where the mausoleum of legendary warrior Hang Tuah can be found. Further up the coastline are the beaches of **Tanjung Bidara**, the state's best, if only for their tranquility. Access to this stretch of coastline is by rural roads that cut through small farms, paddy fields and plots of stout oil palms.

Another possible day trip from Melaka is a visit to the old estuarine town of Muar (*see* p.303), across the border in Johor. En route, take a few minutes to stop off at the ornate **Rumah Penghulu Abdul Ghani**, a traditional Malay house situated 2km east of Merlimau. Built in 1894, the house is a beautiful example of the fusion of Malay and Chinese styles so common in Melakan architecture.

Penang

10

Penang

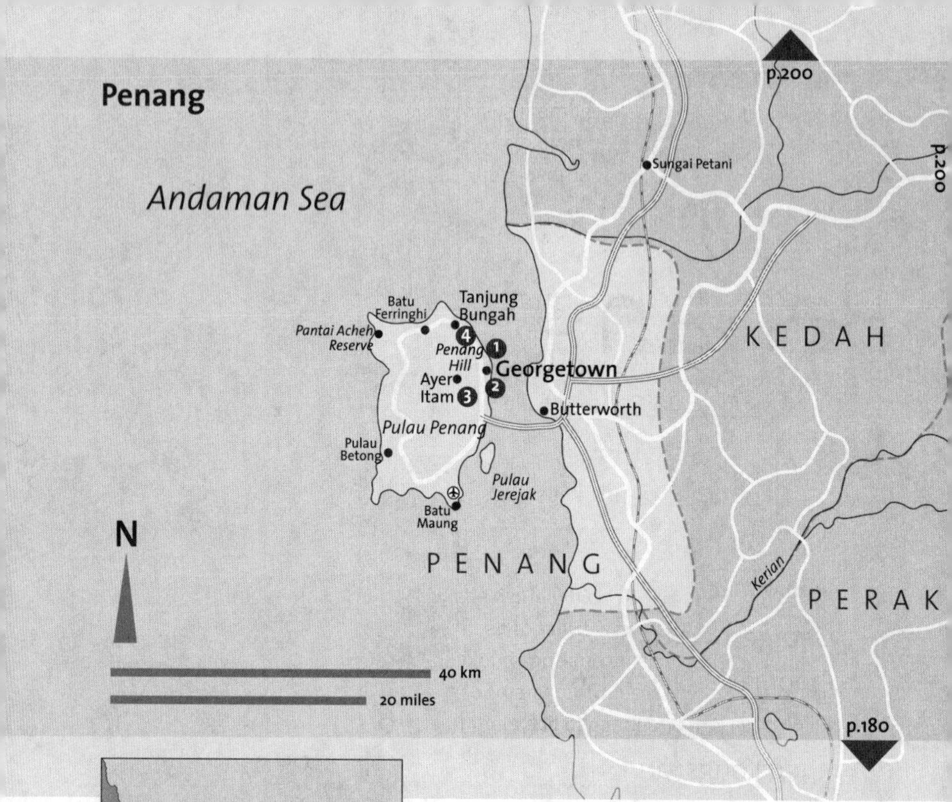

Highlights

1 Cheong Fatt Tze Mansion – Penang's heritage showpiece

2 The Kek Lok Si temple complex outside Georgetown – the largest of its kind in Malaysia

3 Penang cusine – a combination of Chinese, Malay, Indian, Thai, Indonesian and European influences

4 The Botanical Gardens – a 72-acre escape from the hubbub of Georgetown

The state of Penang comprises the large island of the same name and Seberang Prai, a slice of mainland centred round Butterworth. Known by the British as Province Wellesley, the level plains of Seberang Prai were once dominated by rubber and sugar-cane plantations. Today industrial estates and housing developments are encroaching on that open space. Somehow the name Butterworth, with its colonial connotations, does not tally with the modern industrial township across the strait from Pulau Penang. For the purposes of the visitor, Butterworth is little more than a transport hub; most hop straight across to Georgetown, drawn by its long heritage

and delectable range of cuisines. Georgetown is Malaysia's second city and one of its leading tourist destinations. The 15km stretch of sand along Pulau Penang's northern coast has drawn package tourists since the 1970s, while the hilly interior of the island – punctuated by isolated kampungs and spice plantations – remains largely unspoilt.

History

Until Pulau Penang came under British control in 1786, the island fell under the dominion of the Sultan of Kedah. Its shores were lined with areca palms, which produced *pinang* (betel nut), hence the island's name. A scattering of Malay fishermen were the only inhabitants, despite the island's strategic position. The Siamese threat to Kedah from the north left the sultan vulnerable towards the end of the 1700s. War stories trickled south: in Patani (just over today's border with Thailand) towns and villages were razed, their inhabitants bound and trampled to death by elephants. To make matters worse, the Bugis of Selangor attacked from the south, forcing the sultan to flee his capital.

The sultan's plight was a happy coincidence for Francis Light and the British East India Company, who were looking for a base in the region. Trade in opium and tea was booming and a port midway between India and China would help refit laden cargo ships, while a navy presence would protect the eastern approach to the Bay of Bengal. Francis Light was the young trader who made it all happen. He spent his early twenties as an officer in the navy, before taking up service as ship's captain for various European firms working out of Madras. He taught himself Malay and began negotiating trade deals in and around Sumatra and the Malay peninsula. In 1771 he met with the Sultan of Kedah, who offered him trading privileges in return for military protection. Light had already taken note of Pulau Penang, with its sheltered bay and deep channel, and he recommended the island as a base for the East India Company.

Fifteen years later, after the American War of Independence had come and gone, the plan was revived and negotiations began. On 11 August 1786 Light formally took possession of Pulau Penang, renaming it Prince of Wales Island, after the eldest son of King George III.

When Light landed on the island's northeastern cape with three ships and a small garrison, he found the surrounding land dense with ironwood trees. 'In cutting the trees our axes suffer much; the wood is so exceeding hard that the tools double up like a piece of lead,' he complained in his diary. To speed things up, it is said, Light gathered as many locals as he could find and equipped them with axes. He then filled a cannon with silver coins and blasted them into the foliage. In no time a camp was cleared, and a new colonial presence had stamped its mark on the Malay world.

A wooden fort was constructed and named after Marquis Cornwallis, the Governor-General of India. The settlement itself was named after King George. Francis Light declared the fledgling Georgetown a free port in a bid to attract settlers and divert trade away from Dutch bases. Within only a few years the population boomed and the settlement developed in the cosmopolitan tradition of Malay trading ports: Chinese, Indians, Malays, Burmese, Sumatrans all homed in on this new tariff-free trading zone. Opium, tea, porcelain, pepper, textiles and local spices such as cloves and nutmeg were among the goods that changed hands in a flurry of trading.

But not everyone was happy. Malaria was on the rampage – its little carriers droning into town from the mangrove swaps – and the island soon gained the unenviable epithet 'White Man's Grave'. Meanwhile, on the mainland, a disgruntled sultan was still waiting for his promised military support to arrive. To make matters worse, the money he received as rent for Penang was less than he had been promised. As the years progressed it became clear that the East India Company had no intention of protecting anything more than 'Prince of Wales Island' itself. The sultan assembled a force at Prai and made ready to attack. Light caught wind of developments and crushed the insurgents in hours, claiming a small strip of the mainland, later named Province Wellesley. A formal treaty was signed in 1791 ceding Penang to the East India Company in return for an annual rent of 6,000 Spanish dollars.

Francis Light himself fell prey to malaria in 1794 and died soon afterwards. In a single decade, and with meagre funds, he had turned Penang into a thriving settlement. By 1805 the East India Company recognised the importance of Penang and endowed the fledgling port with the status of 'Presidency', alongside Bombay, Calcutta and Madras in India. British law was introduced and fifty new officials appointed – among them the 24-year-old Stamford Raffles. He learned his trade in Penang, before going on to found Singapore, which soon outstripped Penang as a trading post and strategic port. Though Penang's importance was in decline, it became nominal capital of the Straits Settlements (1826), which united Penang, Singapore and Melaka as a single administrative entity. Singapore soon replaced Penang as the capital, much to the resentment of Penangites (years later they unsuccessfully petitioned the British government for separation from Singapore). While Singapore boomed, Penang settled back into its unpropitious role as a staging post on the trade route to China.

Georgetown soon became famous as a centre of vice. As opium traders channelled their activities through the port, a swelling contingent of addicts loitered at the edges. Dockyard workers, rickshaw drivers and – at the bottom of the pile – manual 'coolies' of the new urban centre all provided a growing market for traders. Gambling dens and prostitution were also big business: a disproportionate section of the immigrant population was male. Chinese women rarely emigrated, while the unsavoury climate of the tropics was generally deemed unsuitable for the sensibilities of white women.

Chinese settlers arriving in Georgetown aligned themselves with their respective *kongsi*, or clan, whose leaders came to wield much power. Triad, or secret society, activities easily infiltrated clan-based rivalries. Georgetown, after all, was a free port left largely to its own devices under the laissez-faire administration of the East India Company.

It was not only the Chinese who sought protection within community organizations. The Red and the White Flag Societies were founded in the 1830s by the Indian Muslim community. By the 1860s many of the island's Malays had become members. Disputes over territorial control of Georgetown pitted the White Flags against the Red Flags, who both made alliances with powerful Chinese clan houses. Full-scale riots broke out in 1867 after a member of the White Flag Society reportedly flung a rambutan skin at one of his rivals. Fighting escalated, knives replaced fruit peel, and hundreds were killed.

The Penang Riots proved to be an eye-opener for the British Government, who promptly transferred administration of the Straits Settlements from the East India Company to the Colonial Office in London. The British negotiated a peace agreement and persuaded Islamic leaders to issue a fatwa preventing Muslims from joining secret societies. Then, in the insidious advance of Empire, the British set about dismantling the powerful multi-ethnic alliances that competed over tin mines on the mainland. Each race found itself slotted into a specific administrative role within British Malaya. Meanwhile, leaders of the Chinese clan houses were vilified as gangsters by the colonials. Many reinvented themselves as Anglophile Straits Chinese, absorbing Victorian trends and easing into a life of British patronage where business dealings came second to tiffin at the clubhouse.

With a growing international market for tin, and, later, rubber, Penang emerged from the doldrums to became an important port and distribution centre. The population boomed, fortunes were made and elaborate mansions popped up around town – many of which have survived to this day. Penang's Golden Age preceded the rubber crash of the late 1920s. By then the island was known as 'Pearl of the Orient' and was visited by the wealthy and famous from Europe and America. New arrivals stepped from the luxury of their P&O cruise liners to the equal indulgence afforded by the Penang society lifestyle: endless cocktail parties, motorcar excursions round the island, games of cricket or banquets at the famous Eastern & Oriental Hotel (E&O). In the nickname of this old hotel – the 'Eat & Owe' – was a sign of the carefree decadence of the times.

Economic depression was followed by Japanese occupation during the Second World War. That Georgetown survived virtually unscathed is apparent in the predominance of pre-war architecture still standing. After the war, the municipality continued to grow until Georgetown was awarded city status in 1957. When Kuala Lumpur became capital of the new Malaysia, Georgetown began to stagnate. Its duty-free status was removed in 1974 and much of the old architecture was neglected. During the 1980s Penang was singled out as an industrial-free zone and has been on the up ever since – though at the expense of some of its heritage.

Today Georgetown is Malaysia's second city, and also the one with the highest proportion of Chinese residents (more than half the population is of Chinese origin). Much of the interior remains surprisingly rural, with clove and nutmeg plantations among the jungle-clad hills, and fishing kampungs along the shores.

Georgetown

Georgetown is a fascinating place, home to more than a million people and Malaysia's second city. Crossing the water from Butterworth to Georgetown, with its skyline of high-rises and frenetic vibe, is like approaching Hong Kong's smaller, scruffier sibling. There is an intense energy about the place which some people love, and which puts others right off. Cars, rickshaws and scooters dash about the streets; mahjong tiles clatter inside open doorways; joss smoke wafts through the moist air to mingle with the smell of food and drains and refuse.

Georgetown, as the most Chinese of Malaysia's cities, has more than 40 *kongsis* (Chinese clan associations), though the Indian enclave is substantial enough to provide a good deal of variety. There is still the whiff of the British about Georgetown too; the city retains much of its colonial architecture, from the Eastern & Oriental Hotel and the remains of Fort Cornwallis, to a clutch of churches and the extravagant, neoclassical offices of the old colonial administration. Penangites are also proud of their cuisine, which has evolved its own unique tastes, providing dishes which have made names for themselves across Asia, such as Penang *laksa* and *char koay teow*.

Colonial Quarter

Georgetown's surviving colonial architecture is concentrated round the northeast tip of the city, sometimes known as Penaga Point. Fort Cornwallis marks the very spot where Francis Light landed in 1786 (*see* p.153). Next to the fort lies the padang, centre point of colonial Malaya, with Lebuh Light running parallel to the northern shore. Beyond here is the Protestant Cemetery and what remains of 'Millionaire's Row', now the busy Jalan Sultan Ahmad Shah. To the south of the fort, Pengkalan Weld and Lebuh Pantai (Beach Street) are studded with the mouldering offices of the colonial administration.

Around the Padang

On taking control of Penang, Francis Light at once set about clearing the tangle of ironwood trees that hugged the cape, before building a temporary defensive stockade made of *nibong* palm. Within this wooden enclosure he threw up a series of office buildings and a stately bungalow for his own residence. With the help of convict labour from India, the stockade was reconstructed in stone and brick in 1810 and named **Fort Cornwallis** (*open daily 8.30am–6.30pm; adm RM3*) after the Governor-General of India, Marquis Cornwallis. Though it was ringed by an 8m-wide moat, with a swamp off its south wall and an emblasure of cannons off its north and east walls, the star-shaped fort was more a show of strength than a bastion of defence. It was perhaps lucky then that the fort never once saw action. Instead it developed into an administrative complex, with a series of offices and a chapel for the use of employees of the East India Company. A flagstaff was raised to fly the Union Jack, and a primitive lighthouse was constructed to announce the docking of mail ships, or the arrival of dignitaries who deigned to descend from the cool heights of Penang Hill on sedan chairs.

By way of a fort, there's not much to look at today. Wander alongside the padang, then round the corner onto Lebuh Pantai, and you might not notice the fort at all. Its brick walls are slung low between the ramparts, while a line of trees both outside and within the walls conceal its shape (usually referred to as a star). Still, Fort Cornwallis is said to be one of the best-preserved colonial forts in Southeast Asia. Restoration work is underway to rebuild the west wall and protect the remaining structure. At present the fort houses a small amphitheatre and an insignificant 'history gallery'. On the north-facing ramparts a Dutch cannon known as Seri Rambai stands erect. The cannon was forged in Holland 400 years ago, offered as a gift to the Sultan of Johor, stolen away to Sumatra by Acehnese raiders, presented to the Sultan of Selangor and finally smuggled to Penang by the Madras Native Infantry. For Penangites the worldly-wize cannon has become a symbol of fertility: local women are sometimes seen slinging wreaths over the barrel in return for the blessing of offspring.

On the roundabout just south of the fort is the **Victoria Memorial Clocktower**, built 60ft tall to mark the Queen's Diamond Jubilee (one foot for each year). The monument was funded by Cheah Chen Eok, a third-generation Fukien community leader. He was a devoted Anglophile known for throwing lavish cocktail parties at

The *POW Island Gazette*

The first newspaper to appear in the Malay peninsula – the *Prince of Wales Island Gazette* – was pioneered under the instruction of the new British administration in 1806. As well as keeping inhabitants abreast of events in India and Europe, the weekly rag also proclaimed public notices on behalf of the government and spun out local stories of murder and intrigue for the pleasure of its readers. One smear campaign in the paper's first year of publication was levelled at colonial administrator Francis Simon, who had been granted a piece of land along Penang Road in 1794. Foolishly, he had allowed his plot to become 'a noisome and pestilential swamp, the exhalations from which are highly prejudicial to the health of the inhabitants'.

In 1827 the paper reports the murder of a milk seller called Kairasob, who claimed to hold the secrets of alchemy. He was killed by one of his students, who could not contain his disappointment when his own lump of tin would not reinvent itself as gold. As way of explanation, the student penned a lengthy account of his discontent and pinned it to the corpse.

The paper also ran book reviews, listed prize kills (a 15ft 'alligator' at Tanjung Tokong; a man-eating tiger in Province Wellesley), and advertised revenue farms, or monopolies, that were up for auction (a monopoly to deal opium was one of the items). Proof of the existence of mermaids was reported to Penangites in 1822.

By 1930 the *Singapore Chronicle* and the *Malacca Observer* presented stifling competition to the *POW Island Gazette* and, as Penang began to slip into the backwaters, the paper quickly went out of print.

his stately homes, where his band, the Penang Chinese Jazz Lads, would serenade the guests.

To the west of Fort Cornwallis is Georgetown's **Padang Kota Lama**, an open lawn or field common to most of the nation's colonial towns and cities. Presiding over the grassy space is the grand **City Hall**, built in 1903 by the British in Palladian style, with Corinthian pillars and lofty gables. Next door is the neoclassical **Town Hall**, similar in style but built a couple of decades earlier. The building became known to local Chinese as Ang Mo Kong Kuan (the European Club): the first-floor balconies were a favourite spot with the local élite, who would gather to watch cricket matches down on the padang. Today the buildings seem somewhat out of place. Late in the afternoon hawkers set up shop beneath the flaking whitewash of these colonial monoliths and local families stretch out on the grass to eat their sticks of satay or fly their kites.

Until relatively recently, Nyonya maidens would walk in procession along the **Esplanade** during the annual orange-throwing festival, one of the rituals of the Straits Chinese community. The girls famously cast oranges into the sea for good luck, before strutting their stuff under the eager gaze of eligible Peranakan bachelors. Today families and couples flock to the esplanade and waterfront each evening for the daily *passeggiata*, Penang-style.

Lebuh Farquhar and Millionaire's Row

Head west along Lebuh Light and you pass the Supreme Court building. In the grounds stands a memorial to James Richardson Logan, editor of the *Prince of Wales Island Gazette*, the first newspaper to appear in the Malay Peninsula (*see* p.157). South of the court, on Lebuh Farquhar, is the **Penang Museum and Art Gallery** (*open Sat–Thurs 9–5, adm RM1*), an excellent introduction to the island's past. In the forecourt, an old Penang Hill funicular carriage serves as the museum shop. Parked alongside the carriage is the very car in which British High Commissioner Sir Henry Gurney was murdered by communist guerillas in 1951. Thirty-five bullet holes riddle the frame. The ground floor of the museum is packed with well-labelled artefacts, documents, costumes and furniture outlining the customs of Penang's constituent ethnic groups. Upstairs is a gallery of photos and paintings by colonials, arranged to form a pictoral history of the island. The elegant old building was once the Penang Free School, where Malaysia's first Prime Minister Tunku Abdul Rahman was educated.

Next door to the museum is the **Cathedral of the Assumption**, built in 1860 for the Eurasian community – Catholic descendants of European settlers who intermarried with local Siamese. Inside is an old pipe organ and a series of beautiful stained-glass windows with swirling Art Nouveau flourishes. Opposite the cathedral, near the junction of Lebuh Light and Lebuh Farquhar, is the famous **Convent Light Street**. Outside school hours, visitors are free to wander among the courtyards and cool arcaded verandahs of this historic plot: Francis Light's bungalow, built during the 1790s, still stands in the grounds. The site was redeveloped as an orphanage and convent in the mid-19th century, with outbuildings for student boarders. Students still rise at dawn for prayers before classes. Later in the day, duties at the St Xavier Institution include clearing up swift droppings and replacing tiles flipped off by crows in their attempts to catch lizards.

Further west along Lebuh Farquhar stands the **Eastern & Oriental Hotel**, once known as 'the premier hotel east of the Suez'. In 1884 Tigran Sarkies, an Armenian newcomer to Penang, opened the Eastern Hotel on Light Street. It was a roaring success with colonial visitors and rubber planters, and Tigran's brother Martin joined him to open another hotel close by – this one called the Oriental. In 1889, with younger brother Aviet in on the act as well, the two hotels were joined to become the E&O on Farquhar Street. The youngest Sarkie brother, Arshad, was installed as manager. He initiated wide-ranging extensions and innovations. Each of the hundred rooms was furnished with a telephone and a bath tub with running hot water (a novelty at the time), while the stretch of grass at the back was acknowledged as the longest seafront lawn in the world. The literati of the Golden Era were drawn to this gem of Eastern luxury, among them Noel Coward, Rudyard Kipling, Herman Hesse and, of course, beady-eyed Somerset Maugham. Recent renovations have returned the E&O to its former glory, and it is worth stopping by for a drink on the lawn and a stroll through the elegant domed lobby. The bulbous Art Deco building opposite the E&O was once a showroom for luxury automobiles from Britain. The building now house the upmarket Garage shopping mall (*see* p.169).

At the junction with Lebuh Farquhar and Jalan Sultan Ahmad Shah is the tranquil **Protestant cemetery**, bright with the bloom of frangipani trees. This is the resting place of some of Penang's early Governors, including Francis Light himself. Another grave belongs to young colonial officer Thomas Leonowens, whose widow Anna was immortalized in the Broadway musical 'The King and I' – rehashed more recently in the film 'Anna and the King'. After the death of her husband, Anna settled in Siam (Thailand), where she became a schoolteacher. She left diaries of dubious authenticity which describe her liaisons with King Rama IV, the then Thai king.

Opposite the entrance to the Protestant cemetery is the beautiful restored mansion known as Number Thirty-Two, now home to a bar and restaurant (*see* 'Eating Out', p.165). Inspired by a tour of European cities, Chinese businessman Leong Yin Kean commissioned a Scottish architect to design the original building with a layout that mimicked the style of a European club. Number Thirty-Two marks the beginning of 'Millionaire's Row', or **Northam Road** (now Jalan Sultan Ahmad Shah), a length of seafront adopted by wealthy colonial planters and administrators as the site for their dream homes. Towards the end of the 19th century many of the Europeans moved out of Northam Road to be nearer their clubs in Georgetown's southern suburbs. Wealthy Chinese took their places along Millionaire's Row, though with the collapse of fortunes in later generations, many of the houses have since crumbled. One mansion – commonly known as Homestead – which still stands was designed with the Palladian splendour of Holkham Hall, Norfolk, in mind. The dual worlds through which the Chinese owner moved were reflected in its two separate wings, each kitted out with two sets of furniture – one European, the other Chinese.

The Eastern Seaboard

South of Cornwallis Fort, Lebuh Pantai and Pengkalan Weld also reflect Georgetown's colonial legacy. **Lebuh Pantai** (Beach Street) was one of the first streets laid out by Francis Light. It is now the heart of Georgetown's financial district, with banks lined up inside colonial-style civic buildings. In the late 19th century a massive land reclamation project established a new eastern seaboard at **Pengkalan Weld** (Weld Quay). Swettenham Pier, north of where the passenger ferries berth, was completed in 1904. South of here (opposite the end of Gat Lebuh Armenia) are the **Clan Jetties** – tiny villages on stilts which extend into the strait. Each of the original seven jetties is inhabited by members of a distinct Hokkien clan, whose ancestors found manual work at the port. Some of the village elders recall arriving in Penang from southern China as teenagers. To earn a living they lugged sacks of rice, rubber and tin about the port, or ferried passengers to and from steamships docked in the strait. Some 3,500 descendants live on in their stilted homes. The Penang state government has acknowledged the 'heritage value' of these ramshackle jetties and plans to inject money into their conservation.

Harmony Street and Little India

Like Melaka, Georgetown has its own Harmony Street. Along its length stand a Taoist temple, a Hindu temple, a *kongsi*, a church and a couple of mosques – all within striking distance of one another. For centuries the street's official name was Pitt Street (after William Pitt the Younger), though recent maps – ignoring the harmonious spirit of things – have it marked down as Jalan Masjid Kapitan Keling, after the mosque. Cannon Street, which extends south of Jalan Masjid Kapitan Keling to Lebuh Acheh, is also included under the umbrella of 'Harmony Street'. Houses of worship have been sited along this stretch of road since the early 1800s, when the East India Company allotted space here for the purpose. To the east of Harmony Street lies the heart of Little India.

A Church, a Temple and a Mosque

St George's Church stands at the northern end of the Jalan Masjid Kapitan Keling. The hulking neoclassical edifice was designed by Captain Robert Smith, whose famous oil paintings of Georgetown hang in the Penang Museum. The façade, with its Doric pillars, lends it the appearance of a Greek temple. In fact, it is Malaysia's oldest Anglican church, dating from 1818. In the grounds stands a classical-style rotunda erected as a memorial to Penang's founder, Francis Light.

A little way down, on the corner of Lorong Stewart, the **Goddess of Mercy Temple** (Kuan Yin Teng) is a hive of activity at most times of the day. Come here during Chinese New Year, or for the birthday celebrations of the Goddess of Mercy herself (she has three per year), and the smoky clamour of devotees bowing their heads and waving offerings of incense is overwhelming. Inside one of the temple's inner chambers, an 18-armed statue of Kuan Yin sits within a perpetual mist of sandalwood smoke. The temple forecourt is a sociable spot at any time, with hawkers peddling joss sticks and nibbles. On festival dates the open space serves as a stage for Chinese operas and traditional puppet shows. The temple was founded by Taoist members of Penang's immigrant Hokkien and Cantonese communities around 1800, and is thought to be Penang's oldest Chinese temple.

Keep walking south along Jalan Masjid Kapitan Keling and you come to the mosque of the same name. The Kelings, or Klings, were Muslim immigrants from southern India, and their community leaders were known as *kapitans*. The first **Masjid Kapitan Keling** was built on this site during the early years of the 1800s with funds raised by the *kapitan* himself. Workmen were shipped over from India for the job. The mosque was rebuilt under the influence of British architects, who added Indian Mogul touches, such as crenellated archways, a large onion dome and a spray of miniature domes. The minarets too were an Indian import: early Malay mosques were equipped instead with a large drum, which was struck as a call to prayer.

Little India

Across the road from Masjid Kapitan Keling, a little way down Gat Lebuh Chulia, stands the **Mahamariamman Temple**, its *gopuram* (entrance tower) cluttered with a mass of sculptures in cake-icing pastels. This small Hindu temple is Georgetown's oldest, and perhaps its most significant. Inside is a priceless and much-revered statue of Lord Subramanian encrusted with diamonds, emeralds, gold and silver. During the Thaipusam festival, Hindu devotees carry the statue through town at the head of a chariot procession.

The tight network of streets around the Mahamariamman Temple (east of Harmony Street) forms the heart of Georgetown's **Little India**. This is the commercial and social hub of Penang's Indian community, dense with *mamak* stalls, South Indian 'banana leaf' restaurants, Hindi music shops, Ayurvedic centres, spices, saris and pottery – all packed inside neat rows of pre-war shophouses. Under colonial rule Lebuh Pasar (then Market Street) was known as Little Madras. To local Tamils, nearby Lebuh King was Padavukara Tharuva, or 'Street of Boatmen'. Throughout the 19th century, Indian migrants arrived in Penang to work in the dockyards or out in the spice plantations. Later, another wave arrived to build railroads on the mainland. A number of them settled for good in Penang. When Victorian travel writer Isabella Bird stopped by in 1879, it was the streets of Little India that provided her with her most vivid impressions of the Penang's polyglot population. She was particularly endeared to the 'handsome, brightly dressed Klings surrounded by their bright-hued goods', who she found 'much pleasanter to buy from than the Chinese'.

Getting There and Away

By Air

Penang's busy international airport is near Bayan Lepas at the southern end of the island. Regular domestic flights service KL, Langkawi, Kota Bharu and Johor Bahru. There are also international services to Singapore, Phuket, Bangkok, Hong Kong and Medan in Sumatra. Indirect flights – often very good value – arrive from London, Los Angeles and Sydney.

By Sea

Despite the bridge linking Penang with the mainland, passenger ferries still ply back and forth between Georgetown and Butterworth. They operate round the clock from the jetty on Pengkalan Weld, arriving next to the main bus terminal in Butterworth. The fare is 60 sen. Ferries also run to and from Medan and Langkawi: ticket offices for these destinations are situated beside the tourist offices on Jalan Tun Syed Sheh Barakbah.

By Bus and Train

The 13km bridge linking Butterworth with Penang means that some buses depart from (and arrive in) Georgetown itself. The main terminal is in the basement of the Komtar Centre. However, many more services operate from Butterworth. Nip across to Butterworth by ferry and you can usually get straight on a long-distance bus to virtually all mainland destinations without reserving a seat in advance. Butterworth also has a train station with not-so-frequent services to KL, Singapore and Bangkok.

By Taxi

Long-distance taxis operate from beside the jetty on Pengkalan Weld. The journey to KL takes at least 4hrs. Fares are cheaper if you depart from Butterworth.

Getting Around

A free bus shuttle weaves round the main roads of Georgetown. The *Penang Tourist Newspaper* contains a map of all the stops. The service operates every 12mins 7am–7pm on weekdays and 7am–2pm on Saturdays. Taxis slope about the streets day and night. Arrange a fare before the journey. Any destination within the city should not exceed RM6. Taxis to the airport cost RM20. Bicycle rickshaws operate (mainly for tourists) round the backstreets of Georgetown. Bicycles (RM10/day) and motorbikes (RM20–40/day) can be hired from many places, particularly along Lebuh Chulia. There are a number of car rental companies based in Penang. Of the reputable firms the best deals can be had from Hawk Rent a Car, S-1-23 Mutiara Arcade, t 04 881 3886, f 04 881 1315.

Tourist Information

The best tourist office in Georgetown (though it's not the main one) is the Tourist

Khoo Kongsi and Around

At the southern end of Jalan Masjid Kapitan Keling the road narrows into Lebuh Cannon. Along here on the right is a beautifully kept terrace of 1930s 'Straits Eclectic' houses. Opposite these, a narrow passageway leads into the open courtyard of the **Khoo Kongsi**, Malaysia's finest example of clan-house architecture. The original *kongsi* temple was built between 1894 and 1902, but was gutted by a mysterious fire – later attributed to angry gods provoked by the extravagance of the craftmanship. The new temple, though regarded today as a masterpiece of its kind, was built with a touch more modesty. Still, the elaborately curved Fujian-style roof, said to weigh more than 25 tonnes, is caked in porcelain shard work depicting flora, figurines and

Information Centre on the 3rd floor of the Komtar building (**t** 04 261 4461; open Mon–Fri 8–5, Sat 8–1). It is a little tricky to find: look out for the sign opposite one end of McDonalds then follow the corridor round. It is managed by the Penang Tourist Guides Association, with staff who are knowledgeable and willing to give you their time. Guides, maps, brochures and free copies of the *Penang Tourist Newspaper* are available from here. Two less helpful offices can be found in front of Cornwallis Fort on Jalan Tun Syed Sheh Barakbah (Tourism Malaysia, **t** 04 262 0066 and Tourist Promotion Board, **t** 04 261 9067).

Where to Stay

With one or two distinct exceptions, Georgetown lacks high quality hotels in the expensive and moderate categories, though there are lots of mediocre options about. New budget hotels emerge every year in and around Lebuh Chulia. Because of the competition, you can bargain for very low rates. Many of the budget hotels are uninviting or run down, so stick to the listed places.

Luxury

Eastern & Oriental Hotel, 10 Lebuh Farquhar, **t** 04 222 2000, **f** 04 261 6333, *reservations@e-o-hotel.com*, *www.e-o-hotel.com*. Massive refurbishment in 2001 has restored this elegant old hotel to something of its former grandeur. First opened by the famous Sarkies Brothers in 1885 (*see* p.159), the 101 suites – butler included – still hark back to their Victorian origins: expansive timber floors, Persian rugs, bone-china tea sets and old English bathrooms and toiletries all help to set the scene. The E&O's presidential suite, which sprawls over an excessive 600 square metres, can be yours for RM12,000 a night. A long list of wealthy return-customers – many elderly by now – keep the place alive. Many celebrity guests, including Noel Coward and Somerset Maugham, can be found in the visitors' book. Guests (and walk-in visitors) can take afternoon tea in the conservatory or sit down to a sumptuous dinner in The 1885 restaurant. The outdoor pool is set in gardens on the seafront.

Shangri-La Hotel, Jalan Magazine, **t** 04 262 2622, **f** 04 262 6526, *slp@shangri-la.com*, *www.shangri-la.com*. Penang's premier business hotel with the complete range of 5-star facilities, including pool, health centre and a huge conference hall. Situated next to the Komtar centre. Look out for promotions which bring rates down by 40%.

Expensive

Cheong Fatt Tze Mansion Homestay, 14 Lebuh Leith, **t** 04 262 0006, **f** 04 262 5289, *cftm@tm.net.my*, *www.cheongfatttze mansion.com*. Sixteen themed rooms are now available as part of a homestay at this stunning mansion – one of Penang's premier tourist sights in its own right (*see* p.169). The en suite courtyard bedrooms are spacious

mythological beasts, while much of the interior woodwork is hidden beneath a spread of gold leaf.

Kongsis, or clan associations (literally 'partnership' or 'shared company'), served a variety of purposes for the Chinese community of the Straits Settlement. Nineteenth-century immigrants from southern China were drawn towards fellow clan members who had arrived before them. *Kongsis* became the support groups of their respective communities. They preserved the social welfare of their members, controlled employment, offered accommodation, promoted education and served as banks. More than anything though, they were a repository of customs and values, helping to preserve tightly-knit Chinese communities intact in a foreign land. The most powerful clans set out to build *kongsis* that reflected their standing. They became power bases thrust into direct competition with one another – a fact reflected in the and full of period furnishings. Facilities include air-con, tea/coffee and kettles, and a personal valet service. Alfresco breakfast is served each morning in the courtyard. Rates are near the bottom end of this price category. Highly recommended.

Cititel, 66 Jalan Penang, **t** 04 370 1188, **f** 04 370 2288, *resvnpen@cititelhotel.com*, *www.cititelhotel.com*. A large corporate-style hotel with a gargantuan ice-cold lobby, a pool, gym, health spa and more. Great views over town from higher up the tower. Often has good promotional rates, bringing prices well down into the moderate category.

Moderate

City Bayview Hotel, 25 Lebuh Farquhar, **t** 04 263 3161, **f** 04 263 4124, *cbvpg@tm.net.my*. A high-rise business hotel with views over the straits. 4-star facilities including a swimming pool and a revolving bar and restaurant on the top floor. Good value, though the rooms are nothing special.

Hotel Malaysia, 7 Penang Road, **t** 04 263 3311, **f** 04 263 1621, *hotelmal@tm.net.my*, *www.hotelmalaysia.com.my*. A tower-block business hotel at the end of Jalan Penang. No style but all the usual facilities. Frequent promotions make this a good deal.

Hotel Continental, 5 Penang Road, **t** 04 263 6388, **f** 04 263 8718, *hotelconti@po.jaring.my*. Next door to Hotel Malaysia and very similar, though there's a pool here and more up-to-date décor. Again, promotions make this a viable option.

Inexpensive

Paramount Hotel, 48 Jalan Sultan Ahmad Shah, **t** 04 227 3649, **f** 04 228 1597. Characterful rooms in a run-down old colonial-style mansion on 'Millionaire's Row'. Behind the hotel, moored fishing boats bob on the waves, and there's even a patch of white-sand beach. The attached seafood restaurant (Ocean Green, *see* p.166) draws devotees on most nights. Situated 2km from the centre of Georgetown.

Cathay Hotel, 15 Lebuh Leith, **t** 04 262 6140, **f** 04 263 7906, *waldorf@pc.jaring.my*. A grand old mansion in the colonial style right opposite the Cheong Fatt Tze house, complete with airy atrium and big bright rooms. Hints of tattiness reflected in the competitive rates.

The Merchant Hotel, 55 Jalan Penang, **t** 04 263 2828, **f** 04 262 5511. A plain tower block opposite the Cititel with a marbled lobby and excellent value rooms for what you get (air-con, TV, tea/coffee facilities, mini-bar).

Budget

Oasis Hotel, 23 Love Lane, **t** 04 261 6778. One of Georgetown's most popular budget hotels, and rightly so. This old Chinese house with courtyards and carp-filled ponds is situated in a quiet enclave just off Chulia Street. Beware though, the rooms are rather dilapidated.

Wan Hai Hotel, 35 Love Lane, **t** 04 261 6853. This simple, well-ventilated place is one of the cheapest deals in town, with some

design of the Khoo Kongsi, with its narrow approaches and guarded gateways. Key members lived within the complex, which included administrative buildings and a theatre for staging Chinese opera. The temple itself was the key feature, with its all-important prayer hall for housing ancestral tablets.

All of Penang's guilds and *kongsis* – there are more than 40 of them – are still very much active in providing for the welfare of their members. However, many of the Khoos find it hard to identify with their *kongsi*, now that it has become one of Penang's must-see tourist sights. Private association and tourist attraction: the two roles hardly go hand-in-hand. There was even talk a few years ago of turning the Khoo Kongsi, with its nicely proportioned square, into a 'tourist village'.

A second passageway leads out of the Khoo Kongsi onto Lebuh Armenia, one of Georgetown's most charming streets. The Penang Heritage Centre is found here at the end of this street, housed in the airy **Syed Alatas Mansion**. Architectural plans line doubles as low as RM15 and a basic breakfast included. Upstairs is a little roof terrace with a pergola.

Love Lane Inn, 54 Love Lane, **t** 04 016 412 9002. Ten squeaky-clean rooms and a dorm, with a library of books, ticketing services and a laundry. A popular place, though the rooms suffer from a lack of windows.

75 Travellers' Lodge, 75 Lebuh Muntri, **t** 04 262 3378, **f** 04 263 3378. A clean friendly place on a quiet street with all the usual backpacker facilities and an open-air terrace. Air-con rooms available.

SD Motel, 24 Lebuh Muntri, **t** 04 264 3743. Twenty-one well maintained rooms with and without air-con; a reading room with a spread of daily newspapers; good information about Penang; and a quiet location make this a solid option.

Stardust, 370 Lebuh Chulia, **t** 04 263 5723. This family-run guesthouse has seven plain but clean rooms, some with air-con. The café downstairs serves well-priced Western food and Penang staples.

Blue Diamond Hotel, 422 Lebuh Chulia, **t** 04 261 1089. Looks a bit garish from the outside, but this airy old Chinese house with an attractive atrium and cheap rooms is a notch up from some of the alternatives on Chulia Street.

Eating Out

Eating out is one of the great pleasures of visiting Penang, which likes to see itself as the matriarch of Malaysian cuisine. Chinese, Malay, Indian, Thai, Indonesian and European cuisines have all been thrown into the Penangite pot and stirred up into something special. Nyonya food has a unique twang in Georgetown: Chinese standards are spiced up Thai-style, while Malay curries are made extra creamy with coconut milk and a general excess of spices. *Mamak* (Indian Muslim) cuisine is also big in Penang, with *murtabak* and *roti canai* stalls elbowing for space among Georgetown's predominantly Chinese eateries. Penang *laksa* has become a national favourite: hollow rice noodles are served in a distinctive sour soup with fish, shrimp paste, pineapple, onions and cucumber – unlikely combinations for a Western palate, but it works a treat. *Char koay teow* (fried flat noodles with prawns, egg, beansprouts and chilli) and Hokkien chicken or noodle dishes are also Penang specialities.

There are countless good restaurants right across Georgetown, while the city's famous hawker food should be missed on no account. In the past hawkers would wheel their stalls about the streets, announcing their offerings in coded cries. Today they tend to huddle together in hawker centres. The best of them are often sweaty, scruffy-looking places that can be intimidating. Dishes are advertised only in Chinese or Malay, so it's sometimes hard to know what you're getting. For a much-enhanced experience read through the glossary in the Food chapter of this book before venturing out. A selection of the hawker centres are listed below under

the walls, illustrating the evolution of the Penang shophouse, from the simple Early style to Straits Eclectic and Art Deco. Syed Alatas, a powerful Achehnese merchant, lived here in the 1870s with his wife, a Malay girl of royal descent.

The Syed Alatas Mansion stands at the junction with Lebuh Acheh, site of the **Acheen Street Mosque**. This is Penang's earliest mosque, founded by an merchant-prince from Acheh, who settled in Georgetown in 1792, while Francis Light himself was still around. An elegant minaret forms the centrepiece, surrounded by a Moorish-style arcade added in the early 20th century. The tiny circular window in the minaret is said to have been created when a cannonball blasted through the masonry during the Penang Riots of 1867 – a more likely story than that of the origins of Cannon Street, which was purportedly bombarded into existence by cannon shot during the same riots. The unlucky minaret was struck by lightning in 1997, and has since been

'Hawker Food'. Many of Georgetown's bars also serve food (*see* Nightlife).

Expensive

Forum, Level 3 Island Plaza, Jalan Tanjung Tokong, **t** 04 899 0088. A boutique Chinese restaurant inside the Island Plaza shopping mall. Stylish décor and exquisite dim sum – many say the best in Penang. Fish straight from the tank is delicately steamed, while vegetarians have an unusually wide choice.

Thirty-Two, 32 Jalan Sultan Ahmad Shah, **t/f** 04 262 2232. A restaurant and bar with a growing reputation, set in a stunning renovated mansion on the seafront. They specialize in 'Straits Cuisine', a modern fusion of Asian influences, though there are quite a few Mediterranean dishes too. The wine list is extensive.

Kirishima, Cititel Hotel, Jalan Penang, **t** 04 370 1188. Excellent traditional Japanese cuisine cooked and styled by a long-established chef. Comes recommended by Penangite dining connoisseurs.

The Brasserie, Shangri-La Hotel, Jalan Magazine, **t** 04 262 2622. A local take on Continental cuisine and 5-star service make this restaurant perennially popular, particularly its buffet lunch (where oysters, sushimi and other tender delicacies are likely to feature).

Moderate

Jaipur Court, 11 Lebuh Leith. Artfully created classic dishes from north India served in an airy, renovated building that was once the servants' quarters of the Cheong Fatt Tze Mansion. The atmosphere is classy but subdued and the prices mid-range rather than high. Attentive service and a real treat for the price.

Old China Café, 11 Jalan Balai Polis. This high-ceilinged building was unveiled more than 160 years ago as a Dutch bank. Today it is a good place to splash out a little on an evening meal or to stop by for a daytime drink after a visit to nearby Cornwallis Fort. Adventurous Chinese and Nyonya set dinners are offset with a menu of Western favourites. After 10pm the space is turned into a club playing 1940s tunes.

Ocean Green, 48 Jalan Sultan Ahmad Shah. Set right on the sea behind the Paramount Hotel, this restaurant is one of Georgetown's most popular seafood outlets. Catches of the day are steamed, fried or grilled and combined with Chinese sauces. Lobster, when available, is the speciality. Best to get a taxi here.

Coca, Level 3 Island Plaza, Jalan Tanjung Tokong. This Thai restaurant is famous for its piquant steamboats served with a secret Thai sauce. Top-quality fresh ingredients are provided for dunking into the steamboat, while staple dishes like pad thai are also served.

Ching Lotus Humanist Space, 83 Lebuh China (*closed Mon*). Above the photography and art gallery in this restored Chinese shophouse is a restaurant with a small

renovated. Within the mosque compound are houses that once belonged to wealthy members of the community.

Lebuh Chulia to Jalan Penang

Lebuh Chulia is Penang's answer to Khao San Road in Bangkok. Backpackers haggle over a handful of ringgit for a bed, then spend three times as much on imported beer in the reggae-themed bars which line the street. Craft shops, ticketing agencies, internet cafés, bike rental shops, bookshops and breakfast booths fight for the attentions of travellers, who have been stopping off here since the 1960s, when the overland route through Southeast Asia was first popularized. Many of the budget hotels are converted brothels; before the 1960s Lebuh Chulia was the centre of menu of carefully chosen Chinese dishes. Lengthy descriptions in English help whet the appetite.

Soho Free House, 50 Jalan Penang. An English-style pub right down to the dim lighting, wood-chip wallpaper and clutter of collectables. Fish and chips, steak and chips, sausage and chips, and shepherd's pie can all be had here.

Inexpensive

Tai Tong Restoran, 45 Lebuh Cintra. This large open-faced restaurant serves exquisite dim sum and is seriously popular with the local Chinese. Mouthwatering morsels of prawn or pork or pumpkin (or any number of things) are freshly steamed or fried in the industrious kitchen, then wrapped in pastry or rice paper or fresh leaves. Meanwhile you can sit back in your plastic chair and sip your way through unlimited pots of Chinese tea while plucking dishes from the dim sum trolleys, which are wheeled round and round till you're fit to burst. What's more, it's absurdly cheap.

Hameedijah, 164 Lebuh Campbell. Serves cheap North and South Indian food. The speciality is *murtabah* – a kind of omelette heavily stocked with curried vegetables or meat and wrapped in a thin pancake. There is seating upstairs, but it is hectic and not a little sweaty. Takeaway is an option.

Green Planet Restaurant, Lebuh Cintra. An atmospheric traveller-friendly restaurant with Western food (apple crumble and ice cream, falafel, baked potatoes) and some local dishes including Nyonya specialities and their signature dish Curry Davil – Malay-style beef curry with big chunks of potato.

Restoran Poshni, 3/5 Lebuh Light. The menu here has a full range of cheap and tasty Thai dishes, along with a few Malay favourites. Prepare to squint: the tables are pink and the walls rapeseed yellow. Situated opposite the padang.

Luk Yea Yan Vegetarian Restaurant, 148 Jalan Macalister (*closed Wed*). A popular Chinese vegetarian restaurant which serves up hearty helpings of tasty meat-substitute dishes. Even hardened meat eaters won't be complaining.

Western Oriental Café, 81 Lebuh Muntri. An attractive café with marble-top tables and wicker furniture. Serves Western food and Nyonya specialities for both lunch and dinner.

E.T. Komtar Steamboat Restaurant, opposite tourist information in KOMTAR Centre. Perversely, they don't make steamboats here, but the noodle soups are wonderful – very large servings full of juicy mushrooms and Chinese greens. This is one of several E.T. Restaurants about town (the others serve steamboats).

Hawker Food

Hawker stalls can be found dotted all over town either in small roadside clusters or within large food courts. **Jalan Macalister** is the site of some of the city's best stalls: the junction with **New Lane**, not far from the

Penang's red-light district, popular with sailors and itinerant traders. The street earned its name in the 19th century when it was composed entirely of Indian bazaars, from where the immigrant Chulia and Kling communities traded their colourful textiles.

If it was possible to pin down one area of Georgetown and call it **Chinatown** (in effect Georgetown is one large Chinatown with a scattering of Indian and Malay enclaves), then you would look to the network of streets to the east of Jalan Penang and south of Lebuh Chulia. A high concentration of Chinese outlets – coffee shops, medicine halls, steamboat restaurants and dumpling stalls – make this an interesting stomping ground for visitors. Lebuh Campbell, once Penang's shopping high street, now has the luxury of Western-style pavements with wrought-iron lampposts in addition to the usual five-foot ways.

KOMTAR Centre, is overrun with mobile hawkers each night. Further up Jalan Macalister is **Hong Kong Tea Garden**, one of three spaces packed tight with stalls. **Lorong Selamat**, which runs north off Jalan Macalister, is often named as a favourite picking ground by locals. All of Penang's specialities can be found here after 5pm.

Another sociable spot is the seafront at **Padang Kota Lama**, beside Cornwallis Fort. Families and friends browse the food stalls that appear here each night, then sit in groups on the padang. Head west along the seafront towards Pulau Tikus and you reach Pesiaran Gurney (Gurney Drive), a waterside esplanade with a huge and popular hawker centre at its western end. Not far south of Cornwallis Fort back in town is the **Sri Weld Food Court** (on Lebuh Pantai, opposite Lebuh Bishop), a large covered food court with a big range of hawker staples.

For indoor food courts you could try the building adjoining the Eastern & Oriental Hotel, which offers a sanitized version of the hawker experience, with a series of permanent stalls serving specialities at slightly elevated prices. Inside the **KOMTAR** building is a huge food court – not the most atmospheric of places but with a good spread of Penang favourites.

The heart of Chinatown, round Lebuh Cintra and Lebuh Kimberley, is dotted with little restaurants and food stalls, while Little India (bound by Lebuh Bishop, Lebuh Pasar and Lebuh King) offers the full range of Indian cuisine, from *mamak* (Indian Muslim) to South Indian banana-leaf eateries. Every two weeks a *pasar malam* (night market) is held in a different part of Georgetown – further excuse for a feeding frenzy.

Nightlife

In the centre of Georgetown **Lebuh Chulia** is dotted with cafes aimed at the traveller scene. Most of them serve beer and are open beyond midnight. There are a cluster of popular places near the junction with Love Lane (Lorong Cinta), including the little **Betelnut Café**, the **Hard Life Café** (reggae theme) and the long-serving **Hong Kong Bar**, popular with the expat armed forces. Opposite the Cheong Fatt Tze Mansion is one of Georgetown's more fashionable bars, **20 Leith Street**. This restored house is painted brilliant blue and furnished with antiques. Beer, wine and finger snacks are served. The outdoor terrace is an 'in' spot to drink and relax. If you're peckish there's a Japanese bistro attached. At 50 Jalan Penang is the **Soho Free House**, a spookily authentic, dimly lit pub with a 'happy hour' from 5–9pm. Staple English pub food is also served.

More formal bars can be found in all the top hotels. **Thirty-Two** (32 Jalan Sultan Ahmad Shah; *see* restaurant above) has an elegant bar on the waterfront with a wide range of wines and spirits, while the **Old China Café** gets more popular by the day. The vaults of this old Dutch bank are now used as a wine cellar.

Lorong Love, which cuts north from Lebuh Chulia, speaks for itself: in the past, needy sailors would make their way here after months at sea. Today it is the site of a few of Penang's better-run budget hotels.

Also along here is the temple of the **Carpenters' Guild**, dedicated to Lo Pan, patron deity of carpenters. Lo Pan was a contemporary of Confucius and is credited with the invention of a number of basic tools – plumb line, right-angled rule and extendable ladder. Some also say he invented the umbrella (but then orang-utans too are known to fashion umbrellas out of forest leaves). In the 19th century the Carpenters' Guild was known as the Mother of Kongsis. All Chinese craftsmen arriving in the Malay world would first call in here before seeking employment. Inside, the scene conjures images of a medieval banqueting hall, though the clatter of mahjong pieces places

After 10pm the restaurant closes and the café turns into a club playing 'good old tunes'.

There are no clubs or discos in the centre of Georgetown that lend themselves to recommendation, though predictable karaoke bars can easily be tracked down. The new scene has moved several kilometres west of the centre to **Pulau Tikus** (literally 'Isle of Rats'). The suburb has tidied its act of late and is now the stomping ground of expats and young, moneyed Penangites. Trendy bars and clubs are becoming commonplace around here. One such place is **Orange Café & Bar** (Jalan Burmah), with its blue and orange walls and retro style. After 11pm the dance floor upstairs fills out to the tunes of drum 'n' bass.

Shopping

Georgetown has most things for most shoppers – a throwback to Penang's days as a duty-free island. The towering concrete **Komtar** building in the centre of town houses a huge shopping centre in its lower floors, with department stores, a wide range of smaller shops, a food court and a cinema. High-street clothes and shoes are particularly good value here. **The Garage** (2 Jalan Penang) is an interesting upmarket shopping centre situated opposite the Eastern & Oriental Hotel. The curvy Art Deco building originated as a showroom for British cars (Austin, Morris, Triumph, Rolls Royce, Jaguar and Daimler). Boutique shops now line the interior complete with 5-foot walkways and mock louvred windows in 'old Georgetown' style. Gifts, antiques, designer fashion and accessories are all on offer. One place to look out for is **Purser's Choice**, which sells furniture crafted from teak and embued with the colonial influences of the British, Dutch and Portuguese. Ikat textiles from Borneo are on display here, as are designer household accessories.

For more antiques head for the **100 Cintra Street Bazaar**, a restored 19th-century space where twenty or so traders sell artefacts, furniture, paintings, stamps, old photographs and other curios. Jalan Pintal Tali (Rope Walk) has a string of shops selling antiques from all round Southeast Asia, while the constant presence of tourists on Lebuh Chulia has attracted a handful more craft shops. While you are there, pop your head into **Eu Yan Sang** (156 Lebuh Chulia), an archetypal Chinese medicine shop housed in a four-storey Art Deco block. Any ailment you can think of, and a whole lot more, can be dealt with here. 'Essence of chicken' is one of the common cure-alls on offer.

For more shopping centres head out to the suburb of Pulau Tikus: **Island Plaza** is an upmarket mall on Jalan Tanjung Tokong, while the **Midland Centre** houses a bowling alley, hawker stalls and a large collection of smaller shops. A walk around the suburb reveals other curiosities, such as **Clay Craft** (24 Jalan Moulmein) with lamps, vases, murals, teapots, giant water jars (for feng shui) and other local and ASEAN-made ceramics.

you firmly in the East. Members of this guild, past and present, are responsible for building and restoring much of Penang's heritage architecture. Along nearby Lebuh Muntri is the gilded hall of the Goldsmith's Guild, founded in 1832 and, at No.59, the Restaurants and Teashops Association (look out for the teapots and vegetables wrought into the gate).

On Lebuh Leith is Penang's heritage showpiece, the **Cheong Fatt Tze Mansion** (*entry by tour only, Mon–Fri 11am and 3pm, Sat–Sun 11am; 1hr; adm RM10*). This 38-roomed perfection of feng shui was lovingly restored in recent years, with some of the bedrooms converted for B&B use (*see* 'Where to Stay', p.163). The floor plan is traditional Chinese-style, though there are Peranakan and colonial influences, such as English floor tiles and Art Nouveau stained glass.

Cheong Fatt Tze himself arrived in Southeast Asia penniless. He ran steamships between Medan and Penang before building a vast business empire and becoming the Qinq government's Consul-General in Singapore. After a visit to the US in 1916 he was dubbed 'China's Rockefeller'.

His mansion is the most extravagant of its kind outside China. Throughout the house delicately carved timber furnishings are inlaid with ebony and gold leaf, while the setup aims to maximize 'chi' (inner energy). The building faces the sea and has a number of courtyards with open skylights, so that the elements of wind and water are ever-present. Beneath the flooring of the entire house is an intricate system of piping, so that rainwater collected in the courtyards can be transported through all the rooms. This also has a cooling effect. In the central courtyard are two heavy stone monuments, placed there to prevent the house from flying away.

Behind the Cheong Fatt Tze Mansion is **Jalan Penang**, a busy shopping thoroughfare that marks the western border of the old town centre. The road runs south from the E&O Hotel to the 65-storey **KOMTAR** centre, Penang's commercial and transport hub. The upper storeys are reserved for the use of government officials, though it is possible to catch a lift up to the viewing gallery on the 58th floor (*open Sat–Thurs 10–10; adm RM5*). South of KOMTAR is a residential grid known as the **Seven Streets Precinct**, an area earmarked for conservation. This inner suburb is home to the Penang Hokkien community, who live in neat rows of terraced houses in the Straits Eclectic style (moulded columns and louvred windows), similar to those on Lebuh Cannon.

Around Georgetown

Botanical Gardens

One of the easiest escapes from the city is the **Botanical Gardens** (*open daily 5am–8pm; Bus 7 from Lebuh Chulia*), near the affluent suburb of Pulau Tikus. Landscaped by the British in 1884, the 72 acres shelter a stunning variety of plant life, some of it shipped in from London's Kew Gardens. The primary attraction here was once the 400ft waterfall, but this came to be an important water supply and a reservoir was established at its foot. The waterfall is presently being 'renovated', though it is possible to visit with the permission of the Penang Water Authority. Paths loop through landscaped lawns past ponds, ornamental gardens, orchid houses and a fern house. A further series of paths snake up into the surrounding jungle, where you're likely to see a profusion of hanging lianas, dusky leaf monkeys and tree nymph butterflies gliding about on great elegant wings. Steer clear of the macaques, however, who are likely to rob you of any visible food you carry. Try and visit during the week when the gardens are not so crowded.

On the main road a few hundred yards from the entrance to the Botanical Gardens is a circular gateway known as Moon Gate. This marks the start of a trail to the summit of Penang Hill (*see* below) – an alternative to joining the crowds on the funicular railway. The trail winds through primary forest with views of Georgetown along the way (allow up to 2hrs for the ascent and 45mins for the descent). Nearby **Pulau Tikus** ('Isle of Rats') is where moneyed Penangites and expats are increasingly choosing to live. Once very run-down (and infested with rats), the suburb was named after the small island off Penang's north coast.

Ayer Itam and Penang Hill

On a hill top above Ayer Itam is Malaysia's largest temple complex, the **Kek Lok Si Temple** (*open daily 9–6; regular buses from KOMTAR or Lebuh Chulia*). The original temple was built between 1893 and 1905 with the funding of the Straits Chinese élite. It has since turned into a bit of a Buddhist theme park, a proliferation of gilded buddhas and hanging lanterns, with a steady stream of visitors filing through the shrines. At peak times crowds of tourists, as well as devotees, edge up the steep covered approach to the temple, which is lined with souvenir stalls. Near the top, a mass of turtles fight for survival in 'Liberation Pond', a grimy concrete pool. The turtles, a symbol of eternity, are deposited here for good luck. The temple itself is composed of three ornate halls and a seven-tiered pagoda, visible from several miles away. The Pagoda of a Thousand Buddhas was built in three stages by workmen from China, Thailand and Burma respectively. It is possible to climb the 193 steps of the pagoda for RM2. The views are well worth the effort.

Ayer Itam is situated along the fertile valley of the same name. Now a prime spot for housing developments, the valley was once a string of villages and market gardens. The stalls that line the road at the foot of the temple form the island's main market for fresh fruit and vegetables. Until the 1980s, hundreds of Indian dhobi (or laundrymen) lined the banks of the river near here. A few relics of the trade live on, beating clothes in the shallows and smoothing items with charcoal-heated irons. Also in this area is **Suffolk House**, a colonial mansion thought to have been built as the residence of Francis Light. Surrounded by fruit and pepper plantations, Light called it his 'garden house'. For a century after his death the mansion served as the governor's residence. Unfortunately, the building lies in ruins, though the Penang Heritage Trust is raising funds for its restoration.

Other than hiking up one of the steep trails that lead to the summit, the only way of getting up **Penang Hill** is by the old funicular railway (*RM4 return*), which climbs in two stages from near the market in Ayer Itam (the station is a 20min walk from the market, or a 5min ride on Transit bus 8 from the T-junction). Rising 830m above Georgetown, Penang Hill became the first 'hill station' of the British Empire. Temperatures at the summit are a good five degrees cooler than in Georgetown and it is notably less humid – conditions that attracted the first colonials to build second homes here. In the early days, the only way to reach cooler climes was on foot – or if you were lucky, on the legs of Indian coolies, hired to lug privileged individuals up the jungled slopes on sedan chairs. Francis Light's longing for a home from home led him to clear land for the cultivation of strawberries (in the early days the hill station was known as Strawberry Hill). Another name still in use is Bukit Bendera (Flagstaff Hill) after the flagstaff on the summit, used to send signals down to Cornwallis Fort.

Views aside (on a clear day you can see right across the plains of Kedah to the Titi Wangsa mountains), the summit itself is a bit of a disappointment. It is an overcrowded spot with a plain little hotel, some concrete-paved gardens, a small mosque and a Hindu shrine. However, you don't have to walk far to find peace; the hill is crisscrossed with walkways lined with orchids, birds of paradise and rare plants such as the monkey cup. A few colonial bungalows remain, including the **Convalescent Bungalow**, built by the East India Company in 1818 for the recuperation of invalids. During the 1850s several victims of the Crimean War are said to have been transported here by steamship. Trails lead off in all directions to different parts of the island (ask at the Bellevue Hotel for maps and directions). One well-marked 45min trail leads down to the Botanical Gardens.

Where to Stay

Batu Ferringhi

Though most of the resort hotels in Batu Ferringhi fall into the top price categories, there are usually some excellent promotional offers available, which pull rates down into the moderate category. The budget guesthouses (there are seven or eight of them) are all much of a muchness. The best of them are listed below.

Luxury–Expensive

Rasa Sayang Resort, **t** 04 881 1811, **f** 04 881 1984, *www.shangri-la.com*. One of the long-established hotels on Batu Ferringhi and the most attractive by far (the priciest too). Minangkabau architecture throughout (elegant curving roofs) and giant rain trees within the gardens set this hotel apart in terms of atmosphere. Breakfast and dinner included in the price. 5-star facilities. Recent redevelopment has added a major new spa complex.

Golden Sands Resort, **t** 04 881 1911, **f** 04 881 1880, *gsh@shangri-la.com, www.shangri-la.com*. Centrally positioned on the beach with a large complex of pools. All sorts of arranged activities on offer. Like the Rasa Sayang, this hotel is under Shangri-la management and guests are free to use facilities at both hotels. Perks include free non-motorized watersports, 'free' breakfast and dinner and 6pm checkout.

Holiday Inn, **t** 04 881 1601, **f** 04 881 1389, *reservation@holidayinnpenang.com, www.penang.holiday-inn.com*. Another huge hotel, with two wings – one on the beachfront, the other set back from the road. There is a new sparkle to the rooms, all of which have undergone recent refurbishment. The facilities are excellent (they even offer 'kidsuites' in jungle, treasure island or out of space themes, play station included). However the tropical feel and Malay architecture of some of the other hotels give them more appeal.

Lone Pine Hotel, **t** 04 881 1511, **f** 04 881 1282, *info@lonepinehotel.com, www.lonepinehotel.com*. Established in 1948, this was the first hotel to appear on Batu Ferringhi beach. There are only 50 rooms here, set within four acres of garden. There is a stylish L-shaped pool, though the plain functional architecture is a little dour.

Bayview Beach Resort, **t** 04 881 2123, **f** 04 881 2140, *bbrrsvn@po.jaring.my, www.bayviewbeach.com*. The bigger the better: everything at this hotel is on a huge scale. In the enormous lobby cavity two glass-fronted lifts slide up and down the ten floors. There are seven bars and restaurants, extensive services and facilities. The overall feel is a little impersonal.

Grand Plaza Park Royal Resort, **t** 04 881 1133, **f** 04 881 2233, *www.parkroyalhotels.com*. With 5-star facilities and spacious rooms, this is one of the better choices along the beach. There's an attractive garden and comprehensive facilities for kids.

Budget

Ah Beng, 54C B. Ferringhi, **t** 04 881 1036. Offers a few simple, decent-sized rooms with a

The Northern Coast

The beaches of Penang's northern seaboard were once regarded as a tropical idyll, a dream getaway destination: fifteen kilometres of golden sand backed by palms and casuarinas and populated only by fishermen. During the 1960s and 70s **Batu Ferringhi** became widely known as a hippy hangout, with long-termers tending fruit gardens and living the 'kampung' lifestyle. One of the first upmarket hotels to cash in on the setting was the Rasa Sayang Resort in the late 1970s. Since then the entire length of **Tanjung Bungah** and Batu Ferringhi has become the domain of the package tourist, with self-sufficient resort hotels dominating the scenery. A little further west, Teluk Bahang has hung on to its roots as a fishing kampung.

pleasant communal verandah on the first floor. A quiet spot. Airc-on available for RM40.

Ali's Guesthouse, 53&54B B. Ferringhi, **t** 04 881 1316, **f** 04 881 2703, *alisgues@tm.net.my*. Designed specifically with the western traveller scene in mind, with a shady little front courtyard and bar. The grotto-like interior is dotted with unusual works of art and sculpture. There's a restaurant, with tables under the palms.

Baba Guesthouse, 52 B. Ferringhi, **t** 04 881 1686. Set back from the road, this is a clean, friendly place with a talkative owner who once rented rooms to travellers for RM2/night. Prices have risen tenfold, but then the house has been rebuilt, and air-con rooms are now available.

Teluk Bahang

Luxury

Mutiara Beach Resort, 1 Jalan Teluk Bahang, **t** 04 886 8888, **f** 04 885 2829, *www.mutiarahotels.com*, *salpg@mutiarahotels.com*. Set completely on its own on the beach at Teluk Bahang, this is probably the best choice among the resort hotels of Penang's northern coast. All rooms have sea-facing balconies, and the facilities are extensive. Two award-winning restaurants, House of Four Seasons and La Farfalla, provide Asian fusion and Italian cuisine respectively.

(At the time of going to press, the Mutiara was being rebranded to become the InterContinental Beach Resort.)

Budget

Fisherman Village, **t** 04 885 2936. A neat and friendly little family home with a little aviary out front and tidy rooms for less than RM20/night. To get here head straight over the roundabout and turn right when you reach the cluster of hawker stalls (there's a small sign for the guesthouse).

Miss Loh's, 159 Main road, **t** 04 885 1227. Set inland a little in a sprawling, dusty garden full of fruit trees (rambutan, mango, jackfruit, star-fruit). It has been running since the Seventies and is still popular with long-term travellers. There is a fully equipped kitchen and a locker room. Miss Loh lives off-site, so travellers have the place to themselves most of the time. Clean, very simple rooms. (It is unsigned and a little hard to find: turn left at the roundabout, carry on past the mosque and take the next main right turn. It's 200m down on the left.)

Pulau Jerejak

Expensive

Jerejak Resort & Spa, Zone 4, Pulau Jerejak, **t** 04 658 7111, **f** 04 659 7700, *www.jerejakresort.com*. A strange new 'eco-tourism' resort on Jererak Island (an ex-leper and penal colony) with an 'adventure village' of dormitories and, up on the hill, a 'spa village' comprising up-market chalets and an open-air spa with views across the sea.

One of the main disappointments today is the seawater, which more often than not is murky and thick with jellyfish. Some say the murkiness is the result of over-development; others, that a slight rise in sea levels is drawing silt from the mangrove swamps along the east coast. Either way, it is an embarrassment to the tourist authorities, who persist in adding aquamarine tints to their promotional photos and eulogizing about 'deep blue waters'. Nevertheless, the water problem is seen as a serious matter – Penang relies on its image as a leading holiday destination and plans are underway to protect the mangrove swamps with sea groynes.

Heading west from Georgetown, Tanjung Tokong and Tanjung Bungah are the first places you pass. These are soulless spots consisting of towering hotel blocks and little else. Visitors will do better to move further west to Batu Ferringhi. The beach here is

Eating Out

Batu Ferringhi

Expensive

Akebono, Jalan Batu Ferringhi. An excellent Japanese restaurant with almost painfully attentive service and a huge menu covering most staples. The speciality is grilled belly of salmon. The set lunch menu is very good value.

Ferringhi Grill, Rasa Sayang Resort. An old favourite decorated in the style of an English country manor, with roast beef and Yorkshire pudding as its speciality. Chinese influence fused into some of the European dishes.

Tiffins, Park Royal Resort. The colonial theme to the décor is extended to the menu – a feast of Dutch *rijsttafel*, for instance, is served by a procession of waiters. But it is the Asian fusion dishes which are the focus of this restaurant. A succession of top chefs have left their marks on the menu.

Moderate

Eden Seafood Village, Jalan Batu Ferringhi. Packed with large groups of tourists on most nights, with 'cultural' shows to accompany the seafood. Not the most relaxing of places, yet the fish and seafood is excellent. Fresh lobster straight from the tank, grouper, eels, *soo mei* are some of the offerings.

Jasmine's Kitchen, Jalan Batu Ferringhi. A popular little spot near the western end of Batu Ferringhi, with a range of cuisines. The best options are the North Indian dishes (this was once an exclusively Indian restaurant). Good-value food bordering on the inexpensive.

Inexpensive

Guan Guan Café, Jalan Batu Ferringhi (next to Park Royal Resort). One of the best cheap eateries on the tourist strip. Serves familiar Chinese dishes and Western alternatives like steak and chips.

Bayu Senja Food Court, on the beach next to the budget guesthouses. This is the place to come for an informal selection of different cuisines. A succession of stalls churn out good quality dishes at cheap prices.

Teluk Bahang

Moderate

End of the World, at the far end of Teluk Bahang. This local restaurant is well known for turning out beautifully cooked seafood dishes. Depending on the market price, it can be unexpectedly expensive (little effort is made with the décor), but the servings are large and staple dishes are cheap.

Inexpensive

Dali's Café, opposite the Mutiara. An informal roadside restaurant offering a delicious range of homemade Malay curries. Excellent value for money.

Seafood and Tomyam, signed off the main road in Teluk Bahang. Always crowded with villagers, this is a cheaper alternative to End of the World.

clean and golden, and though little more than a tourist village, Batu Ferringhi can at least claim a buzzing atmosphere and very competitive rates for upmarket rooms. A series of huge resort hotels dominate the beach, though there is also a huddle of budget options beneath the palms west of the beachfront food court. Jalan Batu Ferringhi, set well back from the beach, is lined with restaurants, bars and souvenir stalls. At No. 58 is the Yahong Art Gallery, an arts-and-crafts showroom with work by famous batik artists on display alongside the usual souvenir pieces.

Four kilometres round the headland is the tranquil fishing village of Teluk Bahang. As yet, the only resort here is the glass-faced Mutiara Hotel (*see* 'Where to Stay', p.173), which claims the eastern flank of the bay. Opposite the hotel is the **Pinang Cultural Centre** (*open Sat–Thurs, 3 tours daily*), set in a grand Malay *balai* (meeting house). A tour of the handicraft exhibition, followed by a buffet meal and a contrived 'cultural' performance, comes at a hefty RM130. Teluk Bahang proper, with its Malay bungalows and fish restaurants, begins just beyond the roundabout. In the bay a long rickety jetty reaches out between the fishing *sampans* which putt-putt about the calm waters.

West of Teluk Bahang is the **Pantai Acheh Reserve**, along whose fringes a series of secluded coves and beaches go largely unnoticed. A number of trails lead into the reserve from behind the End of the World Restaurant (*see* 'Eating Out', p.174). One trail climbs to the lighthouse at Muka Head, built at the turn of the 20th century by a firm from Birmingham, UK. Some of the beaches are accessible only by boat (local fishermen and resort hotels are happy to arrange trips). West-facing **Pantai Kerachut**, a 3.5hr hike, is a nesting site for green, and olive-ridley, turtles. Further access to the Pantai Acheh Reserve from the south is under development.

A Loop of the Island

Along with Georgetown itself, the resorts along the north coast are the only places in Penang that offer accommodation to visitors. Other parts of the island can only be visited on a day trip from either Georgetown or Batu Ferringhi (where it is possible to jump on a tour bus or hire cars, motorbikes and bicycles).

On the main road 3km south of Teluk Bahang is the **Penang Butterfly Farm** (*Mon–Fri 9–5, Sat–Sun 9–6;* **t** *04 885 1253; adm adults RM12.50, kids RM6.25*). Thousands of butterflies (from among 120 species) fly free within a network of walk-through cages, among myriad flowering plants and sealed tanks housing less benign creatures – snakes, scorpions, iguanas and 'six-legged' tortoises (I could count only four legs). In the adjoining rooms are a large collection of insect specimens, a batik gallery and stacks of antique buddhas and artefacts for sale.

From here the road climbs south past a dam and reservoir before twisting away into the hills. The **Tropical Fruit Farm** (*open daily 9–6; tours every half-hour; RM20*) is well signed off the main road. This small 25-acre farm cultivates over 200 varieties of tropical and subtropical fruits. Nowadays it is more of a tourist enterprise than a farm, with a conveyor belt of coaches from the resort hotels offloading their guests for educational tours. However, it is well worth stopping off to sample some of those

Island of Outcasts

Other than the rotting timbers of a hospital ward, a few decrepit bungalows and a pack of feral dogs who survive by scavenging for crabs, nothing much remains of Pulau Jerejak's days as a leper colony. From the arrival of the first Europeans, this tiny island off Penang's eastern shoreline has been home to social outcasts of one sort or another. When the British shipped labourers from India to help construct the new settlement of Georgetown, Pulau Jerejak was used as a quarantine station. A century later and it was patients of a new leprosarium that were held in confinement on the island. Patients were segregated according to their race, with respective places of worship constructed, while couples were provided with beachside bungalows in which to live out their days.

The only Europeans to have any contact with the lepers were a woman from Lancashire and her Australian husband, who lived in their own bungalow in the heart of the colony. Hemmed in by thick rainforest, the only space to stretch their legs was on the beach in front of their house. Passing ships noted the island's paradisical aspects – its coral-white beaches, its swaying coconut palms and chattering jungle – but none stopped. There were no roads or permanent tracks through the jungle, and transport between settlements was by sampan. It was an isolated existence.

During World War Two, German forces took advantage of the island's isolation and established a base for their deadly U-boats, wreaking havoc on Allied vessels that attempted to pass through the Straits. After the war, with the emergence of tuberculosis as the poor man's disease in place of leprosy, the sanitorium took on a new breed of patient. When the TB epidemic ebbed, the settlement was converted into a penal colony for hardcore criminals. It became known as the Alcatraz of Malaysia, developing a reputation as somewhere prisoners went to die. During the 1960s and 70s prisoners were forced to grow their own food in an attempt to stave off hunger.

In a strange irony, this idyllic island might well have had a more auspicious history. Colonel Arthur Wellesley (who became Duke of Wellington and defeated Napolean at the Battle of Waterloo) stopped off at Penang in 1797 en route to the Philippines. A malaria epidemic was then decimating the white population of Georgetown (Francis Light had himself died of the disease three years previously) and Wellesley proposed that the British naval base be moved from Georgetown to Pulau Jerejak. Opposite the new base, on the eastern shore of Penang island, Wellesley proposed a new settlement, to be called Jamestown. But it all came to nothing.

In the eyes of many Penangites, Jerejak's future looks a little brighter. Plans are afoot to fling the island into the modern mainstream. The penal colony is no more – the last inmates were shipped back to the mainland in 1991 – and a new 'eco-tourism' resort has opened its doors to visitors. Much of the pristine jungle that covers the island has been gazetted as a forest reserve. One of the prison blocks will be transformed into a museum and, where the watchtower once stood, another will be built in its place for the purpose of offering tourists views across Penang. Meanwhile the dogs of Jerejak can look forward to a bit of company and – with a bit of luck – a more extensive diet.

fruits you're always meant to try. Tables are laid out on a terrace set on a steep hillside with far-reaching views through interlocking valleys towards the sea. Try the *rojak* fruit salad, an exotic combination of local fruits steeped in a rich spicy sauce with sesame seeds.

As the road descends towards the west coast, it passes the **Titi Kerawang** waterfall (just off the road up a track), a popular bathing spot, though the fall is no more than a trickle for most of the year. Along the southbound road, several isolated kampungs lie hidden deep within palm oil plantations. Paddy fields stretch west towards the coast, and there are two organic farms that welcome visitors.

Inland a little, and back up in the hills past clove, nutmeg and fruit plantations, is the small market town of **Balik Pulau**. Arrive in season and the high street is thick with the stench of durian. There are few diversions here other than a good selection of local restaurants and food stalls.

The southwest foot of Penang is the place to look for secluded beaches. At the small village of **Pulau Betong,** take the left fork in the road (signed 'Kem Bina Negara'); this leads past a lagoon to a long windswept beach, where you'll be alone with local Malay children playing in the waves or fishing from rocks.

Batu Maung, a Chinese fishing village in the southeast corner of Penang, is home to a strange shrine on the water's edge. Set into a smooth rock is a huge footprint said to belong to the legendary Admiral Cheng Ho (*see* 'Bigfoot and the Eunuch', p.178). On the evidence of his shoe size, he must have stood 20ft tall.

A small island northeast of Batu Maung, known as **Pulau Jerejak** (*see* 'Island of Outcasts', p.176) has recently been opened to visitors. For centuries it served as an island of outcasts: a quarantine station, then a leper colony, then a top-security penal colony. Its cover of rainforest has been gazetted as a forest reserve, and work on an eco-tourism resort has recently been completed (*see* 'Jerejak Resort & Spa', p.171). The island is accessible via a seven-minute ferry ride from the Jerejak jetty, which is close to the Marine Police jetty in Batu Uban.

The final well-touted sight of Penang is the **Snake Temple** at Sungai Kluang, just north of the airport. Built in 1850 and otherwise known as Temple of the Azure Cloud, this Buddhist shrine was once surrounded by rainforest. For reasons unknown, the temple became a refuge of wild snakes, particularly the beautiful green-and-yellow striped Wagler's pit viper. Some say the snakes were attracted by the incense. Others that it was the steady supply of rodents within the temple walls. Either way the incense had a sedative effect on the creatures: harmless in their lethargy, they were left in peace by worshippers. When Noel Coward visited the temple in 1930, he was shocked to find dozens of snakes coiled around pillars, deities, candlesticks and furniture. Today, overdevelopment and floods of tourists mean that the vipers are no longer wrapped randomly about pillars, but placed strategically on pot plants in the annex. A temple photographer will encourage you to handle the snakes, then persuade you to hand over RM30 for a photo of your bravery (bear in mind that today's poor snakes have had their fangs removed). Having conjured the image of the temple as it was, a visit today is always going to be a disappointment.

Bigfoot and the Eunuch

Malay elders credit a legendary giant known as Gedembai with the 85cm footprint stamped into a rock at the Batu Maung shrine. Mistaking a jumble of bamboo stalks for another giant, Gedembai bolted in terror and leapt towards the sea, leaving the thunderous impression of his left sole for posterity... so the story goes. Local Indians have a different explanation: it is the work of Hanuman, the great monkey god who stars in the Ramayana epic. He left his mark after leaping across the Indian Ocean to seek a herbal cure for a dying soldier friend.

Local Chinese are more numerous in Batu Maung than Malays or Indians, and it is their version of events which has stuck fast. So then, this is the footprint of great Chinese Admiral Cheng Ho, who stepped ashore en route to India in the 15th century.

Cheng Ho was born in 1371 in the province of Yunan, China. At the age of 13 he was taken prisoner by the Imperial army, who were carrying out a routine subjugation of their territories. He was delivered into the hands of one of the Emperor's 26 sons, who had him castrated before taking him on as a servant to the royal household. Cheng Ho excelled in his tasks, becoming a favourite of the prince, who appointed him admiral of the navy when he himself became Emperor. Decades before Columbus, Cheng Ho set sail on seven famous voyages to explore the oceans of the East. On his maiden voyage, he embarked with some 30,000 men aboard a fleet of 62 ships – the biggest of which were a colossal 125m in length and 50m wide.

It was on this maiden voyage that the imperial eunuch first set foot on the Malay peninsula. Though lacking in some departments, Cheng Ho was a giant in others, if that footprint in Batu Maung is anything to go by.

Cynics among you may say that the 'footprint' is no more than a depression scooped into being by the action of ancient waves. But this does not explain the footprint of similar dimensions found in a slab of granite on the hillside not far from Batu Maung – a complementary right sole, no less. So what's the answer? A clumsy giant? A simian deity? A 20ft-tall eunuch? Or perhaps a local version of the Yeti: a Malayan Bigfoot. Take your pick.

Perak

11

Highlights

1 Taiping, for its gracious, wide streets and a peaceful hill station
2 Kellie's Castle – an unlikely ruin nestling on the jungle's edge
3 The sleepy royal town of Kuala Kangsar for a vision of old Malaya
4 The small tropical island of Pulau Pangkor

Perak is full of colonial echoes. It was on Pulau Pangkor – today one of the west coast's most appealing island destinations – that the 1874 Pangkor Treaty was signed, by which the British consolidated their influence over the region. 'Perak' is Malay for silver, clearly a euphemism for the vast tin deposits that, in its heyday, were to make Perak the wealthiest state in the region. When the tin-hungry British moved in, top colonial architects were shipped across from India to ensure that the pioneer settlements became towns worthy of the British Empire. Much of this architecture still stands in places like Ipoh, Taiping and Kuala Kangsar. Perak also gave birth to Malaysia's rubber industry, prompting a boom which lasted well into the 20th century. Kellie's Castle, the unfinished dream home of an eccentric Scottish planter, is a fascinating testament to those years of plenty.

The landscape in Perak is dominated by peculiar limestone massifs and outcrops, particularly in the Kinta Valley. These outcrops are pitted with caves, many of which have been adopted as Buddhist and Hindu cave temples. Cave paintings on the outskirts of Ipoh suggest that the area has been inhabited since 8000 BC.

Today, visitors tend to associate Perak with the Cameron Highlands (Perak is the entry point to the highlands, though they lie just across the border in Pahang; *see* p.286). But Perak does have Maxwell Hill to its name, Malaysia's best-preserved colonial hill station. It also has the beaches and resorts of Pulau Pangkor, and the sleepy charm of Kuala Kangsar, seat of the sultanate and a vision of old Malaya.

Ipoh

Ipoh is a noisy metropolis with neither the glitter of KL nor the character of Georgetown. As a workaday place centred around commerce, there's a sense of introspection about Ipoh that makes it somewhere tourists don't easily warm to. But the city has an important place in history due largely to its location at the highest navigable point on the Sungai Kinta. Most visitors will pass through on their way to the popular **Cameron Highlands** (*see* p.286), just over the border in Pahang.

Late in the 19th century the Kinta Valley became the world's largest tin field, and it was Ipoh – at the expense of Taiping – that became the tin capital of the Federated Malay States. Sungai Kinta, the river which cuts straight through Ipoh, became the main communication channel of the tin trade. Tin ore was stockpiled here, before being ferried to the port of Kampung Paloh and exported to the rest of the world.

The name Ipoh was established sometime in the 1880s, though there was a Malay village on the site as long as anyone can remember. The settlement was named after the *ipoh* tree (then frequent in these parts), the sap of which is used by the Orang Asli to make poison darts for their blowpipes.

Ipoh took shape under the influence of Chinese immigrants who came to mine the tin fields. By 1890 the population had reached more than 40,000, and the town developed in the manner of all Victorian boom towns: the fortunate built mansions and grew fat on their wealth; the rest worked themselves to an early grave. Despite the later decline in demand for tin, Ipoh remained a major player in the trade, and in

Getting There

The Sultan Azlan Shah airport is located 15km south of Ipoh. There are frequent connections with all the major towns and cities in the country. Malaysia Airlines, Pelangi Air and Air Asia all offer a schedule of flights. Airport Taxis, **t** 05 312 6897. The west-coast train line runs through Ipoh. The magnificent Moorish-inspired train station in the centre of town was built by the same man who designed the station in KL. Ipoh is also a main transport hub for long-distance buses. The inter-state terminal is just south of town, off Jalan Tun Abdul Razak.

Getting Around

The easiest way to get around Ipoh is on foot, though Ipoh is a compact and congested city. To call out a taxi try BK Taxi, **t 05** 253 4188. The following car rental companies have an office in Ipoh: Friends Rent-a-Car, **t** 05 255 2939; Avis **t** 05 312 6586; Hertz **t 05** 312 7109.

Tourist Information

Perak Tourist Information Centre, Jalan Tun Sambanthan, **t** 05 241 2959, **f** 05 241 2958; open Mon–Fri 8–1 and 2–4.30, Sat 8–12.50, closed 1st and 3rd Sat of the month.

Where to Stay

Expensive

Hotel Syuen, 88 Jalan Sultan Abdul Jalil, **t** 05 253 8889, **f** 05 253 3335, *syuenht@tm.net.my*, *www.syuenhotel.com.my*. Ipoh's largest and plushest central hotel. Business-oriented with 4-star facilities and a neoclassical theme in the lobby. There is a pool, squash courts, sauna and gym, as well as six food and drink outlets. Good value at not much more than RM200.

Casuarina Parkroyal, 18 Jalan Gopeng, **t** 05 255 5555, **f** 05 255 8177. If you're willing to stay out of town, this is probably the best hotel on offer. Rooms, on ten floors, have king-size beds and views of the surrounding limestone hills. There is a good outdoor pool and a range of other facilities.

Heritage Hotel, Jalan Raja Di Hilir, **t** 05 242 8888, **f** 05 242 4959, *sales@heritage.com*, *www.heritage.com.my*. Another four-star place a touch closer in to town. This hotel has four dining outlets and a health club, but no pool. Rooms are spacious and elegantly finished in wood panelling.

Moderate

Majestic Station Hotel, Bangunan Stesen Keretapi, **t** 05 255 5605/255 4217, **f** 05 255 3393, *www.majesticstationhotel.com*. Inside part of the old colonial railway station, this hotel is by far the most characterful place to stay in Ipoh. There is a faded grandeur to the great high-ceilinged rooms, which open onto a long verandah overlooking some gardens. All 100 rooms have air-con, phone and TV. There are often crazy deals on offer.

Eastern Hotel, 118 Jalan Sultan Idris Shah, **t** 05 254 3936, **f** 05 255 1468, *hoteast@po.jaring.my*. A faded mid-range hotel near the central market. Rooms have air-con, TV, mini-bar and phone. This was probably one of the top hotels back in the 1970s.

1937 took over from Taiping as state capital of Perak. Today Ipoh is Malaysia's fourth largest city with a population of half a million.

The City

The Sungai Perak splits Ipoh neatly in half, leaving all the historic sights in the old town west of the river. The new town is where most of Ipoh's hawker stalls and hotels are found, but the city is compact and crossing between the two sides is easily possible on foot. Though Ipoh is Perak's principal town – and has been for over a

Inexpensive

New Caspian Hotel, 6–10 Jalan Jubilee, **t** 05 242 3327, **f** 05 243 3329. Decent, clean, functional rooms in a safe-feeling environment. With TV, phone and air-con in all rooms, this is a reasonable deal.

Robin and Merloon Hotel, 100–110 Jalan Mustapha Al-Bakri, **t** 05 242 1888, **f** 05 242 5881. Two hotels next door to one another that have merged under the same management. The rooms are dated, but all have bathroom, air-con, phone and TV.

Budget

Shanghai Hotel, 85 Jalan Mustapha Al-Bakri, **t** 05 241 2070. This small Chinese-run hotel with only nine rooms is probably the best budget option in town. The rooms are spotless and have an attached bathroom. However, the walls are built partly with air bricks, so you hear all the noise from down on the street. Still, it is a better place than any of the seedy budget hotels in the southeast of town.

Eating Out

The best thing going for Ipoh is its cuisine. There are hawker stalls set up all about town, and they offer the full range of Malaysian food. Specialities include Ipoh *char kuay teow* (flat noodles fried in a rich sauce); *rojak* (a salad of fruit, veg, nuts and spices in a sweet, dark sauce of hoisin and *belacan* paste); *sar hor fun* (a soup of flat rice noodles with prawns or pork, shallots and bean sprouts); and Ipoh *popiah* (a delicious type of pancake stuffed with minced prawns, beansprouts, shredded turnip, onion and a sweet chilli sauce). All about town the fruit stalls sell locally grown pomelos – a seedless citrus fruit the size of a football, with flesh that is a subtle version of grapefruit.

In the evenings most people eat at hawker stalls. One of the most popular **hawker centres** is found at the end of Jalan Mustapha Al-Bakri. Stalls here stay open into the early hours each night. For lunch there are dozens of **kedai kopi** serving the range of Chinese food. For good cheap *laksa* try **Chuan Fong**, 175 Jalan Sultan Iskandar. For decent slap-up Indian cuisine (also dirt-cheap) try **Restoran Darul Ridzuan**, 72 Persiaran Greenhill.

One oddity is a restaurant called **Beacon Point**, 41 Lintasan Perajurit 6, **t** 05 546 9916, which is out in the suburbs (catch a taxi). This is a civilized little neighbourhood restaurant serving – a rarity in Malaysia – beautifully cooked Western food, such as chicken pie or beef stew with an array of roasted vegetables. The cook trained under a Swiss chef and has worked in Canada and the US. The food is served as a buffet, with soup as a starter and a big display of cakes (such a blueberry cheesecake) for dessert. For RM16 you can eat all you can. Back in town, **Coffee Craft**, 81 Jalan Sultan Abdul Jalil (opposite Syuen Hotel), is a place that is popular with expats. They offer a range of freshly brewed coffees, teas and cakes, plus things like pasta and pizza.

Ipoh's most historic eatery is the **FMS Bar & Restaurant**, set inside a 19th-century Chinese shophouse across the road from the *padang*. Frequented largely by European miners and planters, the bar was founded by a Hainanese immigrant in 1906, when Ipoh was part of the Federated Malay States (hence FMS).

century – there is not much by way of tourist sights: only some colonial architecture and a few 19th-century shophouses, in the old town. Eating seems to be one of the main concerns in Ipoh, and this alone could be reason enough for a visit; the hawker centres here have an unusually wide variety of offerings (*see* 'Eating Out', above).

The centrepiece of Ipoh's colonial architecture is the **Railway Station**. Though not as grand as locals would have you believe – they call it the Taj Mahal – it is an impressive piece of Moorish-Victorian architecture; a bit showy perhaps, but redolent of gin and tonic, wicker furniture and bellboys in Bombay bowlers. Rooms at the Majestic Station Hotel (*see* 'Where to Stay', opposite) open out onto the first-floor verandah, surely one of the world's longest at nearly 200m. The building was completed in 1917 and was designed by A.B. Hubback, who also turned out the railway station in KL and the beautiful Ubadiah mosque in Kuala Kangsar. A symbolic 'ipoh' tree has pride of place in the well-kept gardens that front the railway station. Across the gardens is the **City Hall**, a neoclassical structure and one of Ipoh's oldest buildings (built 1881).

Back towards the river along Jalan Dato Sagor, a series of 40m-tall minarets rise above the mosaic-tiled dome of **Masjid Negeri**, a modern, massive and rather unattractive mosque. Opposite this is the **Birch Memorial Clocktower**, erected in 1909 in memory of the first British Resident of Perak, who was shot dead in Kuala Kangsar in 1875 (*see* 'Bath-House Assasination', opposite). By the turn of the century Birch was regarded as a bit of a hero by the British – a martyr to the noble cause of colonial expansion. In reality he brought about his own assassination: with little knowledge of Malay traditions, and less concern, he blundered forward in an attempt to gain control of Perak at the expense of the Sultan – paying almost inevitably with his life.

Ipoh has a couple of minor museums, the **Darul Ridzuan Museum** (*open daily 9.30–5; free*) and the **Geology Museum** (*open Mon–Fri 8-4.30, Sat 8–12.45; free*). The former is housed in an attractive mansion complete with porte-cochere and Palladian dimensions. The mansion was built in 1926 by a Chinese tin mogul. It was later acquired by the British administration as office space. Inside is a simple history of Ipoh. The Geology Museum tackles the very limited subject of tin ore and exhibits the many fossils found during mining.

Around Ipoh

For many visitors, Ipoh is used simply as a springboard to other more interesting attractions in Perak and Pahang. The unusual landscape around the city is pitted with cave temples, and there are a few unusual pieces of architecture that are worth visiting. Ipoh is also the access city to the **Cameron Highlands** (*see* p.286). A newly constructed road between Ipoh and the Cameron Highlands has cut the journey time down to less than an hour (the old route takes up to four hours).

Kellie's Castle

South of Ipoh, between the villages of Batu Gajah and Gopeng, stands an unlikely thing: the ruin of a Scottish castle – or, to be exact, the folly of a Scotsman, in both senses of the word. In 1890 William Kellie Smith, aged 20, set sail for Malaya from his village in the north of Scotland. For a number of years he worked on the construction of roads in Perak. Then he bought a small plot of land in the Kinta district, which he cleared to plant rubber. Within a decade Kellie Smith had made his fortune.

He began work on his folly in the early 1920s. It was to be one of the grandest homes in colonial Malaya, complete with Moorish arches, battlements, a roof terrace and a six-storey tower – the perfect place to host parties for the wealthy planters and administrators of the district. But on a trip to Europe to purchase an elevator for his folly, Smith caught pneumonia and died. Work on the castle halted and the building was claimed once more by the jungle.

Today it stands as a symbol of the colonial dream, out of time, out of place and unfinished. Walking round the abandoned rooms today, and peering across the river from between the battlements, it is not hard to sense Kellie Smith's dream. Just down the road from Kellie's Castle is the **Sri Maha Mariamman Temple**. The Scotsman funded construction of the temple for the Tamil builders who were working on his folly. Locals insist it was built to appease the gods after a few of his workers died of influenza. He no doubt infuriated the gods further by placing himself among their ranks: look carefully among the statuettes of Hindu deities that line the roof and you will notice a European in pith helmet and billowing shorts.

Access to Kellie's Castle costs RM3 for adults and RM1 for children. It is situated on the roadside midway between Batu Gajah and Gopeng and is open daily 8.30am–7pm.

Not far from Gopeng is **Gua Tempurung**, an impressive 2km cave system within one of the region's many limestone massifs. A series of walkways lead through an ancient gallery of stalactites and stalagmites.

Tambun Hot Springs

Tambun Hot Springs (*open daily 8am–10.30pm; adm RM5; catch a taxi towards Tanjung Rambutan*) comprises a series of looping ponds and a large rectangular bath set in an arena of vertical limestone crags. Though the semiderelict building at the entrance spoils things a little, it is nevertheless a spectacular setting. The water in the main bath is piping hot, though just bearable, and the waters of the natural ponds, which are even hotter, are said to have healing properties. Amazingly, several species of fish have adapted to the 45 celsius heat. Walls have been built around the source of the spring to create a natural steam bath. A small bar near the entrance serves drinks and baskets of fresh eggs, which can be soft-boiled in the hottest pool.

It is likely that people have bathed in the waters of this hot spring as far back as 8,000 BC; on a nearby outcrop of rocks, prehistoric wall paintings provide evidence of an ancient civilization in the Kinta Valley. The paintings include an unambiguous representation of a dugong (otherwise known as a manatee or sea cow).

Cave Temples

Ipoh is surrounded by craggy limestone outcrops, most of which are pitted with caves. Early Chinese immigrants were drawn to these caves, which they soon came to value as sacred (the striking similarity between this scenery and the landscape of Chinese brush painting must have been reassuring to settlers from China). The first cave temple was founded by a Buddhist monk late in the 19th century. He used it as a meditation grotto, but it soon grew to the proportions of a temple. Now known as the **Sam Poh Tong** temple complex, it is set among pomelo stalls off the main road 4km south of Ipoh, and draws worshippers in their thousands at the time of Chinese festivals. Several huge caverns house buddha statues and an order of monks.

North of Ipoh, is the **Perak Tong** temple, Perak's largest cave temple. Inside the main chamber is a 40ft golden buddha; dotted about the adjoining caves are another 40 or

Bath-House Assassination

When J W W Birch was appointed Resident of Perak in 1874, he had little knowledge of Malay customs, and less concern for the pride and dignity of the Malay chiefs. Birch was an ambitious man, high-handed in his actions; after all, he had served nearly 30 years in the colonial service in Ceylon and four years as Colonial Secretary to the Straits Settlements. He believed that firmness and speed were essential qualities in dealing with 'natives', be they deck hands or chiefs. Inevitably, he caused offence wherever he stepped foot.

One of Birch's first actions was to try and stamp out 'illegal' toll stations for the collection of taxes. Standard practice for sultans of this time was to farm out tax collection to the local chiefs, in exchange for ready money. These chiefs then taxed within their boundaries and in their own names. Birch did his popularity no good when he ordered that the chiefs of Perak – many of whom did not recognize his authority in the first place – could no longer levy taxes in their own names. And he backed his word with military force whenever he came across such tolling stations on his river trips.

The Resident's dealings with Sultan Abdullah of Perak began to sour as the sultan saw his power gradually chiselled away: on signing the Pangkor Treaty, the sultan had assumed that the British Resident would act as an advisory official within the framework of his own jurisdiction. It didn't help matters that interactions between the two were carried out through an interpreter: being able to speak Malay engendered respect among local rulers and was a primary requirement for colonial administrators in this part of the world (Frank Swettenham and Hugh Low being good examples).

Birch was not unaware of the threat to his person and began building a stockade about his Residency. Meanwhile Sultan Abdullah called a secret meeting of the Perak chiefs and sparked a movement for the removal of the British Resident. One of the chiefs, Maharajah Lela, went so far as to offer to do the dirty work himself. The sultan, who had been told by a magician-priest that Birch's death was imminent, approved the maharajah's offer and sent him a sharpened kris for the purpose.

On 1st November 1875, during a routine tour of the district, Birch visited Maharaja Lela at his home in the village of Pasir Senak. His purpose was to distribute copies of new proclamations and instructions from the British administration. Confronted with an unambiguous scene of armed hostility, Birch was undeterred: he posted the proclamations on the walls of Chinese shophouses all about town. This action proved the final straw. The proclamations were torn down and Birch was stabbed to death through the *attap* walls of the riverside bathhouse near which his boat was moored.

The death of James Birch sparked what later became known as the Perak War, which amounted to the British consolidation of power in Perak through military force. Sultan Abdullah claimed the assassination was nothing to do with him. The other chief perpetrators (including Maharajah Lela) were rounded up and sent to the gallows. The whereabouts of Maharajah Lela's grave has since been a mystery. Local legend has it that the British, fearing the mystical powers of the maharajah, dissected the corpse into three parts before disposing of the remains.

so statues. In the back chamber – the walls of which are decorated with Chinese calligraphy and paintings – is a stairway up to the 125m limestone pinnacle.

Pasir Salak

Pasir Salak is a small Malay village 70km downriver from Ipoh on the Sungai Perak. Its main claim to fame – other than its durians – is that J W W Birch, first British Resident of Perak, was stabbed to death here while bathing on the river bank (*see* opposite). A small stone memorial to the event leaves little doubt that this is something the village should be proud of.

Pasir Salak also serves as a showpiece for traditional Perak architecture, every wooden *rumah* intricately decorated with traditional designs and motifs from the natural world. The **Pasir Salak Historical Complex** (*open Mon–Fri 10–5, Sat–Sun 10–6; adm RM5 adults, RM3 children*) traces the history of the Malay Peninsula and showcases two Perak-style *kutai* houses, containing various local artefacts. The houses are constructed entirely of wood, without the use of nails.

South of Pasir Salak is another of Perak's architectural oddities, known as the **Leaning Tower of Teluk Intan**. This 25m pagoda-like structure with a leftward slant has been adopted by the authorities as a tourist sight. From the outside, the tower appears to have eight storeys, but inside, there are only three; the tower was erected in 1885 by a Chinese tycoon to serve as a water tank for the village of Teluk Intan.

Elsewhere in Perak

Taiping

Taiping lays claim to one of Malaysia's grandest collections of colonial architecture, its wide streets laid by the British in the 1870s. To this day giant, century-old rain trees (*angsana*) scatter their seasonal blossom across the roads, and provide welcome shade to pedestrians – as was the intention of the original town planners.

Oddly, the town of 'everlasting peace' (as Taiping translates from the Chinese) was born out of war. Taiping stands on the site of the old coal fields of Larut, which drew thousands of Chinese settlers during the mid-19th century. Tin was a valuable commodity back then and the stakes were high: tension peaked and a bloody feud erupted between rival Chinese factions. On one day alone it was recorded that more than 3,000 miners were slaughtered, and before long Larut was no more than a pile of cinders. That was 1873, and the following year the British thought it timely to take control of Perak's precious tin mines themselves. They signed the Pangkor Treaty, renamed Larut 'Taiping', and employed a mercenary band of Sikh soldiers – who became known as the Perak Armed Police – to keep the peace. These policemen obviously tickled the fancy of Victorian traveller Isabella Bird, who writes: 'They are splendid looking men, with long moustaches and whiskers... When off duty they wear turbans and robes nearly as white as snow, and look both classical and colossal.'

The streets of Taiping were re-layed and widened to 70ft to help accommodate the fast-expanding town. In true horticultural spirit, the British transformed some of the

Getting There

The nearest **airport** to Taiping is the Sultan Azlan Shah airport 15km south of Ipoh. The **train station** is just west of the centre of town on Jalan Steysen, and the express bus terminal is a further 7km away. The foot of Maxwell Hill is a few kilometres east of town. **Buses** or **taxis** head to the office at the foot of the hill, from where government-run Land Rovers ferry visitors to the summit.

Tourist Information

Tourist Visitor Centre, 355 Menara Jam, Jalan Kota, **t** 05 805 3245, open Mon–Fri 8.30–5.30, Sat 8.30–3. Unusually helpful tourist office, with excellent brochures on Taiping and Perak.

Where to Stay

Taiping

Moderate

Legend Inn, 2 Jalan Long Jaafar, **t** 05 806 0000, **f** 05 806 6666, *www.legendinn.com*. The most comfortable hotel in Taiping, with all the standard facilities including room service. Very good value.

Hotel Seri Malaysia, 4 Jalan Sultan Mansor, **t** 05 806 9502, **f** 05 806 9495, *central@serimalaysia.com.my*, *www.serimalaysia.com.my*. Right beside the Taiping Gaol, overlooking the lake gardens. Handy too for the Perak Museum and Maxwell Hill. Nicely laid out, but a bit bland. Small outdoor pool and a cheap restaurant.

Hotel Fuliyean, 14 Jalan Barrack, **t** 05 806 8648, **f** 05 807 0648, *hf@cyberoffice.com.my*. Clean spacious rooms, relatively modern, with air-con, TV, phone and attached bathroom. Promotions bring price down to inexpensive category.

Casuarina Inn, 1 Jalan Kota, **t** 05 804 1339, **f** 05 804 1337. Set on its own in the Lake Gardens on the site of the old Residency. The drive leading up to the hotel passes through the stone pillars that are all that remain of the the first Resident of Perak's house. Rooms are enormous and have great views over the gardens towards Maxwell Hill. It's all a bit dilapidated, though.

Inexpensive

Peking Hotel, 2 Jalan Idris, **t** 05 807 2975. A beautiful old Chinese house, built in 1929 and which served as headquarters for the

redundant mining pits into lake gardens on the edge of town, while nearby Maxwell Hill (Bukit Larut) was billed as the Malay States' first hill resort for British officers suffering from the heat. And the hill resort was not Taiping's only 'first': the town also became the site of the first British Residency; the first printing press for newspapers; the first museum; the first English-language school; the first prison; and the first railway line (linking Taiping's tin mines with the coastal port of Fort Weld).

Taiping continued to prosper until Ipoh took over as tin capital of Perak, and eventually as administrative capital too. The population peaked, the pace of life slowed and Taiping settled into the laid-back rhythm that is characteristic of the town today.

The Town

Taiping has a sleepiness and faded grandeur about it that confirms its modern status as a bit of a backwater. Built on industry, the town is now looking to tourism to provide an income. There are historic buildings dotted about town, though many of them are crumbling. Nevertheless the tourist office does an excellent job at sparking

Japanese military police during the occupation. Lots of character, but the rooms are in need of a scrub. Air-con throughout.

Panorama Hotel, 61–69 Jalan Kota, **t** 05 808 4111, **f** 05 808 4129. In the centre of things, with 80 air-con rooms, attached bathrooms, TV, phone, kettle. Decent enough and good value, but no character.

Budget

Hotel Malaya, 52 Market Square, **t** 05 807 3733, **f** 05 807 3755. Right in the centre beside the covered market. Neat, clean, fan-only rooms in good nick. This is the best of the budget options in town.

Maxwell Hill (Bukit Larut)

There are facilities on Maxwell Hill to sleep around 50 people. Four **bungalows** with beds for eight are available for the public to rent out. They go for between RM100-200/night and come with kitchen facilities. There are also two VIP bungalows for RM200-300/night. Near the Land Rover drop-off point is the **Bukit Larut Resthouse**, which offers simple double rooms for a bargain RM20. There is an attached café here with good views over the forest. Higher up, near the VIP bungalows is the **Gunung Hijau Resthouse**, with similar-priced rooms to the Bukit Larut Resthouse, and a campsite. All accommodation on Maxwell Hill must be booked in advance. The office at the foot of the hill, where the Land Rovers depart, is the place to make bookings. Call in advance on **t** 05 807 7241.

Eating Out

Taiping is crowded with food stalls, and these are often the best places to eat. There is a wide range of options inside the covered market. Otherwise try the **Friendly Food Court**, opposite the Peking Hotel. **Restoran Bumi**, on Jalan Kota, is a decent little Malay place serving lunchtime *nasi campur* (a wide range of rice and curries). **Sayuran Su Hean Vegetarian Restaurant**, at 25 Jalan Kota, is a delicious Chinese vegetarian place that does wonders with soya and bean curd. Non-veggies will enjoy the food too. The extensive menu includes the likes of butter chicken and mutton curry (all meat-free of course). Just up the road (45 Jalan Kota) is **Kum Loong**, which serves delectable dim sum and is packed every morning until 10. **Lao Di Fang Café**, on Jalan Taming Sari, is a stylish café with young management. It's lovingly decorated and serves a delicious selection of coffees, teas, fruit juices, ice creams, cocktails, sandwiches, sushi, pasta and baked potatoes.

interest and flagging all the historic sights. The office itself is situated in a quaint, fortified clock tower known as the **Police Station**. The building was originally constructed of wood in 1881, and served for many years as the police and fire station.

As a whole the town centre consists of a grid of low-rise shophouses set on broad streets and centred round the old **Taiping Market**, which, for well over a hundred years now, has been housed in two colossal Victorian structures. The grandest colonial pile is the **District Office**, situated at the top of Jalan Kota. This whitewashed neoclassical building with towering gables – uncannily similar to Georgetown's City Hall – was opened in 1898 to house the offices of the colonial administration. Behind the District Office is the **Public Library**, formerly the Recreation Room for officers of the government, who would have met here after a game of cricket on the Esplanade across the road. Another piece of architecture to look out for is the **King Edward VII School** on Jalan Stesen, its long colonnade shaded by century-old rain trees. Built in 1883 by the British, this was the first English-language school to appear in the Malay world. Some of its classrooms served as torture chambers for the Japanese during the Occupation.

Continue past the public library and the road opens out into the **Lake Gardens**, an immaculate expanse of lawns, lakes, bridges and gardens, with the forested flanks of

Maxwell Hill (Bukit Larut) as a backdrop. This area was once swampland dotted with the stagnant pits of abandoned tin mines. The site was drained and landscaped by the British in 1884. Nowadays, the gracious canopies of Taiping's famous rain trees provide the lasting impression. Blended carefully into the Lake Gardens is **Taiping Zoo** (*t 05 808 0777, www.zootaiping.gov.m;, open daily 8.30–6.30; adm RM4 adults, RM2 children*). This is large and well-maintained with the full range of animals from tigers and tapirs to giraffes, hippos and orang-utans. There are also birds, reptiles and fish such as the giant Amazonian arawana, which is known to leap out of the water to catch birds and small mammals. Keep an eye on the orang-utans, who have been known to throw stones over the walls of their enclosure.

At the edge of the Lake Gardens lie the remains of **The Residency**, an extravagant house built for the first Assistant Resident of Perak, George Maxwell. All that remain are the 16ft stone pillars on which the house stood. Fortunately for us, Isabella Bird stayed with the Assistant Resident during the 1880s, and described the house in her book *The Golden Chersonese*: 'The Residency is large and lofty, and thoroughly draughty, a high commendation so near the Equator. It consists of a room about thirty feet wide by sixty long, and about twenty feet high at its highest part, open at both ends, the front end a great bow window without glass opening on an immense verandah. This room and the verandah are like the fore cabin of a great Clyde steamer.'

Taiping's modern District Officer lives nearby in the old **Secretary to the Resident's House**, a beautiful two-storey building from the 1890s, with louvred windows and a room extending over a porte-cochere. North of here are the towering walls of **Taiping Gaol**, first opened in 1879 to house the large number of Chinese who continued to break the 'eternal peace'. Today Taiping can be grateful to these former prisoners, whose labour was employed to rebuild much of the town. They also supplied the town with bread and ran a laundry.

Opposite the gaol is the **Perak Museum** (*open daily 9–5; adm free*), a stunning colonial building with hundreds of tiny latticed windows climbing the towers on either side of tall gables. The museum is Malaysia's oldest: the idea was Sir Hugh Low's when he was Resident of Perak, and the collection took shape from 1883. What remains of the collection today is nothing special – stuffed animals and poorly labelled ethnographical artefacts, Orang Asli handicrafts and a weapons gallery.

A few hundred yards from the country's oldest museum stands **All Saints Church**, one of the country's oldest Anglican Churches (the tourist board claim it as the oldest, but St George's Church in Penang beats it by 68 years). It is a plain, ramshackle wooden building. In its cemetery lie many of Taiping's first colonial administrators, who fell prey to tropical diseases such as beriberi and malaria.

Around Taiping

Maxwell Hill

The main reason many people pass through Taiping is to visit **Maxwell Hill** (Bukit Larut), which lays claim to being Malaysia's first hill resort. It was named after George

Maxwell, first Assistant Resident of Perak, and was established with the colonial hill stations of India in mind. Tea was planted and a bridlepath was hacked into the 1,035m hillside, so that colonial administrators could escape the heat (temperatures never exceed 25 celsius).

In the early days the ascent was made on the backs of ponies or on sedan chairs lugged uphill by coolies. The same path is used to this day, though it is now tarred. It is so steep and narrow that only government Land Rovers have access. They make the journey hourly from 8am to dusk and can carry up to eight passengers at a time (*RM3*). Alternatively, it is possible to hike to the top in around four hours.

Though this is the smallest and least known of Malaysia's hill stations, it is the best preserved and, in many ways, the most rewarding for the visitor. The rainforest which shrouds these hills is full of life. In fact, this is one of the best places to spot the siamang, largest of Malaysia's gibbons. These furry black primates spend most of their time foraging at the top of the jungle canopy. If you don't spot them on a visit to Maxwell Hill, you will certainly hear them if you are around early or late in the day. Adult siamangs have an inflatable laryngeal sacks which helps them propel their song from one valley to the next. It is a sound both haunting and beautiful. A whooping call builds in speed and pitch until the finale, which is a single, plaintive note that falls then rises once more – something like the song of a humpback whale.

Because of the restricted access, Maxwell Hill is a peaceful retreat, with a handful of faintly trodden trails and numerous bungalows for rent (*see* 'Where to Stay', p.189). The most adventurous trail leads to the summit of Gunung Hijau (1,449m) where, on a clear day, there are views as far as Penang and Pulau Pangkor. The path is often overgrown, so ask before heading out without a guide.

Matang Forest Reserve

The enormous Matang Forest Reserve, west of Taiping, stretches along 50km of Perak's coastline and consists of 43,000 hectares of mangrove forest and tidal flats. At the northern end of the reserve is the **Kuala Gula Bird Sanctuary**, which supports large colonies of local and migratory birds. It is the breeding ground for the endangered milky stork (only around 100 birds left worldwide at the time of writing), and is also a good place to spot otters and ridge-back dolphins. The best time to visit is between September and December, when thousands of migrating birds flock the tidal flats. For information contact the Wildlife Department and National Parks' Interpretive Centre (***t*** *05 527 3411*) or ask at the visitor centre inTaiping.

Further south at **Kuala Sepatang** it is possible to watch the traditional processing of charcoal. Only mangrove trees older than 30 years are allowed to be felled. These are then processed by licensed kiln owners, of which there are 600 around Kuala Sepatang. The mangrove trunks are transformed slowly into charcoal inside the enormous kilns. Most of the kilns have been up and running since the 1930s.

Kuala Kangsar

Kuala Kangsar comes as close as you get to a vision of old Malaya. Seat of the Sultanate of Perak, this sleepy royal town is a small architectural showpiece, with Malaysia's most photographed mosque, two palaces and a school known as 'Eton of the East' all lined up along a lazy bend of the Sungai Perak. A small cluster of shophouses forms the centre of activities, while across the copper waters of the river is a traditional Malay kampung.

In landscaped grounds on the hill top overlooking town is the extravagant **Istana Iskandariak**, home to the present sultan. There is no access to the public, of course, but you get views of the voluminous building from various points along the road (and visions of the sultan twiddling his thumbs in a small room at the top of one of the many domed towers). The palace was built in 1926 in Indian Islamic style, with Art Deco influences.

Behind the palace is the **Royal Museum** (*open daily 9.30–5; adm free*), housed in the small Istana Kenangan, which was the temporary home of Sultan Iskandar Shah in 1931–33 while the larger palace was being built. This fine example of Perak architecture is crafted with exquisite detail. It is made entirely of timber, with no nails. The wall panels, constructed of bamboo and bertam palm, are woven into intricate floral and symmetrical designs that are painted black, white and gold. Inside this airy, stilted building is a large collection of royal memorabilia, with endless photos, including some beautiful century-old shots of Kuala Kangsar – and others of the present-day sultan practising his golf swing. Also on show are a few pieces of early correspondence from colonial officials. Look out for one from the Resident to the High Commissioner, signed off, 'I enjoy the great honour of being, sir, your humble servant'.

The **Ubadiah Mosque** is one of the nation's finest-looking, with its tight mass of minarets and huge golden dome. It was designed by A. B. Hubback, an Englishman who served as Chief Architect of Malaya. Hubback also designed the railway stations in KL and Ipoh, and the combination of Moorish and classical influences is evident throughout. Work on the mosque began in 1912, but progress was hampered when two of the Sultan's elephants trampled the Italian marble which had been imported specially. The building was finally completed in 1917.

Getting There

The main west-coast train line passes through Kuala Kangsar: the station is off Jalan Sultan Idris. Buses for all the main regional destinations leave from the central bus station on Jalan Raja Bendahara.

Where to Stay and Eat

Most people will visit Kuala Kangsar as a day trip, but there are two places to stay. The first is the **Seri Temenggong Resthouse** (*moderate*), Jalan Istana, **t** 05 777 3705, **f** 05 777 3872. This is set in a colonial building overlooking the river and offers enormous musty rooms with air-con. For RM100 you get a huge suite to yourself. The other option is the **Double Lion Hotel** (*budget*), Jalan Kangsar, **t** 05 776 1010, which has a few decent-sized rooms with fan and attached bathroom. Eating is limited to the food stalls in the centre of town.

A few hundred yards inland is the exclusive **Malay College Kuala Kangsar** (MCKK), established in 1905 to educate the sons of the Malay élite. The college has turned out a long list of distinguished politicians and scholars. During school hours pupils in immaculate white uniforms can be seen passing through the colonnaded portico of this grandiose, neoclassical building, which is fronted by an immaculate strip of playing fields. Novelist Anthony Burgess taught at the school from 1954-59, during which time he wrote his hilarious *Malayan Trilogy* (1956). In 1959 he collapsed in one of the classrooms and was given 12 months to live after being diagnosed with a brain tumour. The diagnosis turned out to be false, but it sparked the prolific writing habits which stayed with the author till his death in 1993.

Kuala Kangsar's final claim to fame is an old **rubber tree** which stands beside the District Office on the corner of Jalan Raja Chulan and Jalan Tun Abdul Razak. It is the only remaining tree from the pioneer batch of seedlings sent to Malaya from Brazil in the 1870s. Within years the nation was the world's top producer of rubber – thanks largely to 'Mad Ridley' (*see* 'Singapore Botanic Gardens', p.431), who pioneered the idea (he was known to carry seeds in his pocket at all times, with a view to handing them out to any farmer he happened to stumble upon).

Pulau Pangkor

When it comes to idyllic tropical islands, the west coast of Peninsular Malaysia suffers in comparison to the east. Pulau Pangkor is perhaps the exception. Come mid-week and you'll have a string of pristine beaches to yourself. Weekends and public holidays bring a rush of mainlanders after some sea air, but there's enough space to accommodate everyone. Not that Pangkor is a big island: hire a bicycle and you can complete a loop of the coast in less than a day, with stops. Hotels and beachside accommodation are limited to the more picturesque west coast of the island. The east coast is another place altogether, with a series of industrious fishing villages hard at work transforming the daily catch into dried products for the Chinese market. The rocky interior is cloaked in virgin rainforest, with several trails offering steep treks.

In the 17th century Pulau Pangkor was an important base for the Dutch, who were keen to monopolize the Perak tin trade. The ruins of a Dutch fort still stand south of Pangkor Town. Early in the 19th century Pulau Pangkor, along with the coastal strip known as the Dindings, was ceded to the British as a base for the suppression of pirates. Later in the century the island had its name stamped indelibly on history with the signing of the Pangkor Treaty (1874). This agreement between the Perak Chiefs and the British signalled the beginning of British rule in Malaya – which got off to a shaky start with the assassination of Perak Resident J W W Birch (*see* p.186).

During the 1980s the western shores of the island were developed for tourism. Pangkor Laut, an islet just off the southwest shore, is now home to one of Malaysia's most exclusive resorts. The beautiful Belanga Bay to the north is the site of another resort, while Teluk Nipah is the destination of western tourists on a budget. The long stretch of tranquil beach fronting Pasir Bogak is more popular with Malaysian visitors.

Getting There

By Air

Pangkor's tiny airstrip runs behind Teluk Dalam on the north side of the island. Berjaya Air (**t** 03 7846 8228, **f** 03 7846 5637, *reserve@berjaya-air.com*, *www.berjaya-air.com*) fly once daily from KL Subang airport (except Tues and Thurs). Their banged-up old propellor planes do the journey in 40mins.

By Sea

Ferries depart daily from Lumut to Pangkor every half-hour from 6.30am–9pm (RM4 return). All ferries dock at the jetty in Pangkor Town, where there is a ticket office. Boat transfers for guests of the Pangkor Laut Resort and the Pankor Island Beach Resort head straight to their own jetties.

Getting Around

One circular road runs round the island, with two spokes heading off north and south. The circuit is 27km in length. Minibus taxis are readily available at reasonable prices if you bargain.

Many of the guesthouses rent out bicycles, which is an excellent way of exploring the island if you are vaguely fit. Motorbikes are also available for hire in Pangkor Town, Teluk Nipah and Pasir Bogak. Bikes should cost around RM15/day, motorbikes RM30/day, with helmets.

Tourist Information

There is no tourist office on Pulau Pangkor. The Lumut office distributes information about the island. Right at the start of Main Road in Pangkor Town is a Maybank with an ATM (*open Mon–Fri 9.30–4, Sat 9.30–11.30*). There are a number of internet cafés along this road, notably Fisherman's Café, which has the cheapest access on the island at RM3/half-hour. A little further down is Farmasi JH, a large modern pharmacy.

Where to Stay

Pulau Pangkor has three international-class resorts. The rest of the accommodation consists mainly of chalet complexes at Teluk Nipah and Pasir Bogak on the west coast, which tend to come and go quite frequently. There are a few hotels in Pangkor Town, but there's little point in staying here, with the best beaches and clearest waters just 2km away on the other side of the island. Western travellers tend to congregate at Teluk Nipah, while Asian tourists head for Pasir Bogak.

Pangkor Laut

Luxury

Pangkor Laut Resort, **t** 05 699 1100, **f** 05 699 1200, *plr@po.jaring.my*, *www.pangkorlautresort.com*. One of Malaysia's top resort hotels, set on its own island. Even at 80% capacity it often seems that you've got the

Pangkor's East Coast

All ferries dock at the jetty in **Pangkor Town**, the island's main settlement. The town is centred round its harbour, where the daily catch of *ikan bilis* (anchovy) is sorted and packed off to the mainland to be devoured over breakfast tables as *nasi lemak*. Main Road, the town's high street, is lined with traditional *kedai kopis*, simple Chinese restaurants and stalls selling dried fish produce. There is not much worth stopping for here, other than amenities such as a bank, a chemist, a few internet cafés and a hairdresser (which offers a mean head massage for RM10).

Cross the bridge at the south end of Main Road and you soon pass beneath the welcoming arch of **Teluk Gedung**, Pangkor's prettiest kampung, its sandy streets and tidy Malay houses bordered with flowers. On the right beyond the village are the ruins island to yourself. A jungle trail leads across the hill to beautiful Emerald Bay, though there is also a road with a steady supply of 4X4s to ferry guests back and forth. Luxury villas stretch out on stilts over the east-facing bay, or perch high on the hillside. All buildings are Malay-style, with rich timberwork and woven bamboo. Many villas have private courtyards with sunken baths open to the sky. 'Estates' are also available: luxury houses set in private grounds with their own pool, jacuzzi, dining pavilion and chef. There are eight restaurants and bars to choose from, including an old Chinese junk which floats out into into Emerald Bay at sunset (weather permitting). Among the facilities are three swimming pools, a spa centre and tennis and squash courts.

Teluk Belanga

Luxury–Expensive

Pankor Island Beach Resort, **t** 05 685 1091, **f** 05 685 1852, *www.pangkorislandbeachresort.com*. The resort's main attraction is its idyllic 1.2km beach sheltered within Belanga Bay. Only guests and fee-paying visitors have access. A wide variety of rooms are available in several blocks. At the north end of the bay are the 'Houses on the Rocks', free-standing chalets on stilts by the water. Behind these are a range of bungalows. A number of restaurants provide excellent cuisine from round the world. Facilities include two pools, tennis courts, a small golf course and watersports. In terms of service and exclusivity, this place does not compare to Pangkor Laut, but then neither does the price, with frequent promotions offering good value.

Teluk Dalam

Expensive

Teluk Dalam Resort, **t** 05 685 5000, **f** 05 685 4000, *www.pangkorresorts.com*. A 4r-star resort designed in the style of a Malay kampung (loosely speaking). Chalets behind the beach are set in 40 acres of gardens. There is not much shade and the layout is a little regimented. The beach itself is nice enough, but doesn't match some of those on the west coast. There's a landscaped pool with a slide and a couple of decent restaurants.

Teluk Nipah

Moderate

Hornbill Resort, **t** 05 685 2005, **f** 05 685 2006. This little hotel is as sophisticated as Teluk Nipah gets. The attractive wood-panelled rooms with air-con, TV, balconies and attached hot showers are all sea-facing. Breakfast included.

Horizon Inn, **t** 05 685 3398, **f** 05 685 3339. A Chinese-run guesthouse on the seafront with sturdy sea-facing rooms and tiny balconies. Rooms have air-con and TV but are otherwise overpriced.

Nipah Bay Villa, **t** 05 685 2198, **f** 05 685 2386. Offers a row of comfortable chalets with tinted windows, air-con and attached hot showers. Not bursting with character.

of **Kota Belanda**. This old Dutch fort was first built in 1670 for the protection of tin deposits, which were floated down the Sungai Perak from mines in the Kinta Valley. The fort was destroyed by local Malays in 1690 and later rebuilt. It is not much to look at – just a small ruin of bricks – though the authorities have tried to make the most of it with a new landscaped approach. A few hundred metres past the fort stands an unlikely structure: a huge rounded boulder sheltered beneath a roof. Walk round the side of the rock and you'll see the emblem of the Dutch East India Company alongside the faded depiction of a tiger attacking a child. Locals say the drawing recounts the grisly end of a Dutch child who disappeared on the island (though some think the child was kidnapped by indignant Malays). Just how such a large stone arrived at this spot by the beach, no one is sure. Some say it fell from the heavens to crush the offending tiger.

Motorbikes are available for hire (*RM30/day*).

Suria Beach Resort, **t** 05 685 3922, **f** 05 685 3921. Substantial rooms with balcony, TV, air-con and room service in a distinctive white-pillared building.

Inexpensive

Ombak Inn Resort, **t** 05 685 5223, *http://ombakinn.tripod.com*. One of the more attractive places in this category, with a range of options from A-frames to air-con units or attractive wooden huts with verandahs.

Palma Beach Resort, **t** 05 685 3693, **f** 05 685 4431. A line of 14 wood-panelled chalets with attached bathrooms. Included in the price is breakfast, dinner and the use of a rowing boat, bicycle or motorbike. Mainly attracts Malaysians.

Purnama Beach Resort, **t** 05 685 3530, **f** 05 685 3539, *pbr2000@tm.net.my*, *www.purnama.com.my*. A well-ordered simple chalet complex with a decent restaurant attached (*see* opposite).

Budget

Nazri Nipah Camp, **t** 05 685 2014. Very relaxed travellers' camp with A-frames and scruffy huts with attached showers. An informal restaurant serves basic food throughout the day, though if you want breakfast before 9.30 you have to make it yourself. Hammocks are slung between the trees and there is a small library of dog-eared novels.

Joe Fisherman Village, **t** 019 562 3941. Directly opposite Nazri Nipah and even more laid-back, if that's possible. This was the first travellers' accommodation to appear at Teluk Nipah. Bicycles are available for hire here (RM15/day). Fishing trips and treks into the interior are also organised.

O Lala Chalet, **t** 05 685 5112. The best value accommodation in Teluk Nipah. Nine immaculate chalets with tea/coffee-making facilities and attached bathrooms. Set back from it all at the end of the road.

Mizram Resort, **t** 05 685 3359. Next door to O Lala Chalet and also good value. There are many more rooms to choose from here and it rarely fills up.

Senang Hati Camp, **t** 012 517 9591. The cheapest accommodation on Pangkor. Fifteen basic chalets are set close together on an incline. Walk to the end of the track behind the Senang Hati restaurant at the north end of Teluk Nipah.

Pasir Bogak

Expensive

Puteri Bayu Beach Resort, **t** 05 685 1929, **f** 05 685 1050, *www.puteribayu.com*. A well-equipped resort hotel, probably the most attractive of its kind on Pangkor – but at a price. Well-appointed chalets are set in a carefully landcaped garden. Caters mainly for the Asian market.

Moderate

Pangkor Village Beach Resort, **t** 05 685 2227, **f** 05 685 3787. The only place towards the northern end of Pasir Bogak that is actually set on the beach. A range of

North of Pangkor Town a string of coastal villages extend their reach into the Straits with the aid of stilted platforms. With little flat land on Pangkor, these platforms serve as drying yards for fish – mainly anchovies and cuttlefish, which turn crisp in a matter of minutes beneath the tropical sun. Kampung **Sungai Pinang Besar**, just north of Pangkor Town, merges with Kampung **Sungai Pinang Kecil** in a cacophony of two-wheeler traffic. Chinese coffee shops and dried-fish warehouses predominate. In between the two kampungs a lane leads off west towards the **Foo Lin Kong Temple**, an ornate Buddhist temple encircled by a diminutive Great Wall of China. The wall forms the perimeter of the temple's garden, which contains ponds full of carp and terrapins. There's also a peacock cage and a sorry family of macaques caged up next to a couple of sluggish pythons. Visible from the main road a little further north is the garish roof of the little Hindu **Sri Pathirakaliaman Temple**. From here a series of accommodation, from tiny basic huts to spacious air-con chalets, are set out under the shade of trees. Slightly overpriced.

Sea View Hotel, t 05 685 1605. A pristine Chinese-run place with views across to Pangkor Laut. Rooms in the main block and chalets with sea views are available. Boat trips can be organized from here.

Inexpensive

Chandek Kura Hotel, t 05 685 2163, f 05 685 1164. At first sight this concrete block behind the road at the north end of the bay looks fairly unappealing, but the rooms are clean and well-ordered. Further up the hill is a complex of wooden chalets with great views over the bay. Good value.

Beach Hut Resort, t/f 05 685 1159. A fan of chalets just back from the beach. This well-established place is decent value, though a little worn out and noisy due to the proximity of a school.

Pangkor Paradise Village, t 05 685 5303. A beautiful secluded spot away from the main village with a little restaurant, a few small chalets, coconut palms and a soft-sand beach. The chalets are basic and can be overpriced. To get here follow the path round the side of the school, then cross the little footbridge over the stream.

Budget

Standard Camp Pangkor, t 05 685 1878. A variety of good-value A-frames and chalets packed tight like a barracks. Bicycles available for rent.

Eating Out

In Teluk Nipah by far the most popular place to eat is **TJ's Restoran**, an Indonesian place serving excellent spicy dishes and a nightly fish and seafood barbecue. It gets packed and the food is notoriously slow in coming. If you get fed up waiting, the restaurant at the **Purnama Beach Resort**, opposite, serves a fantastic squid sambal, along with a good range of other cheap Malay dishes. Other than this there is the friendly family-run **Gerai A'n'Z Restaurant** on the main road, with an open kitchen and a limited Malay menu, or the **Fisherman Seafood Village**, a Chinese place serving well presented seafood at higher prices. All of the chalet operations serve food – most of it cheap and reliable. Beer is widely available, but is left off menus, so ask. On the beach are a string of **snack stalls** selling fried fish and banana fritters.

A few basic **Chinese food stalls** line the road at the northern end of Pasir Bogak, while on the road that leads down to the sea are some **Indian stalls**. Behind these is **Restoran Pasir Bogak**, a Chinese place very popular with the locals. For even better Chinese food, head east along the main road towards Pankgor Town and look out for **Ye Lin Restaurant**, on the right. Again, all the hotels and chalet operations have attached kitchens.

Pangkor Town is lined with *kedai kopis* and food stalls. Opposite the Maybank is **Fook Heng Seafood Restoran**, where you can devour mountains of cheap Chinese-style seafood and learn about 'Molluscs of Malaysia' from wall posters. Pulau Pangkor has no nightlife to speak of.

fishing kampungs stretch northwards as far as Teluk Chempedek, where a boatyard services fishing fleets that anchor in these waters. The jetties and platforms along this stretch are strewn with timber and the skeletal frames of new fishing boats.

A sign off the main road north of the boatyard signals a jungle trail to the summit of **Bukit Pangkor** (371m). Note that it is a very steep 1.8km trek to the top. On the whole, the interior of Pulau Pangkor is untouched rainforest. Both the world's largest and smallest species of orchid have been found here, as have carnivorous pitcher plants. Ever-present macaques, monitor lizards, snakes of varying shapes and sizes and pangolins (scaly anteaters) have all been sighted. Down on the shores, sea otters are not uncommon, while the skies are full of sea eagles, Brahminy kites and, to a lesser extent, hornbills.

Pangkor's West Coast

Most visitors head for the quiet coves and beaches of the west coast, particularly **Teluk Nipah** with its double crescent of sand backed by palms and rising hills. The shallow bay here is excellent for swimming. At low tide during a full moon (otherwise known as 'spring tide', when the gravitational pull is at its greatest) it is possible to walk out to Pulau Giam, a tiny island about 200m offshore. At such times stranded sea cucumbers and clams languish in the sun – easy pickings for villagers, who spread themselves across the sand flats to pick through the bleached coral for edibles. In 1990 this idyllic stretch of beach was backed by little more than jungle, but now, chalet complexes line up along two roads that reach back into the trees. Most of them are low-key and are not visible from the sea. Kayaks and snorkelling gear are available for rent on the beach. For the most part Teluk Nipah is quiet, laid-back and popular with budget travellers – many of the chalets lie empty during the week.

At the end of Teluk Nipah's northern beach is the little Lin Je Kong Temple, perched on the rocks. It is little more than a Buddhist shrine, with an incongruous model of Daffy Duck to welcome you through the arch. Round the side is a fantasy world of mysterious doorways, giant mushrooms and frogs. Follow the path round, cross the little bridge, and it is possible to clamber over the rocks to **Coral Bay**. This uninhabited spot with emerald waters is the best place for snorkelling. Beyond here the towering headland prevents access to **Teluk Belanga**. The only way to get there is by road, and you'll have to pay a fee at the resort hotel, who lay claim to the pristine bay. East of here is **Teluk Dalam**, where there's a little kampung, a resort hotel and an airstrip.

Just south of Teluk Nipah is **Teluk Ketapang**, a deserted lip of sand famous as a landing beach for turtles. Until recently giant leatherback turtles could be seen dragging themselves onto the beach by night to bury their eggs deep in the sand. Now these incredible creatures – as old as the dinosaurs – face the real prospect of extinction (*see* p.247).

Next along is **Pasir Bogak**, the largest settlement on the west coast, with a school, a cluster of foodstalls and a jungle information centre (which was closed indefinitely at the time of writing). A string of upmarket hotels along the main road cater mainly for the Malaysian market. The beach here is long and sandy, though very narrow at high tide. Off season and on weekdays Pasir Bogak turns into a bit of a ghost town. Schoolkids take advantage by racing their scooters in the streets. About halfway along the coastal road a track leads up into the rainforest, providing an alternative trail to the summit of Bukit Pangkor. At the southern end of Pasir Bogak, a wide 2km stretch of road cuts across the island to Pangkor Town.

The island of **Pangkor Laut**, which sits in rich emerald waters off Pasir Bogak, is the exclusive reserve of the Pangkor Laut Resort (*see* 'Where to Stay', p.194). On its west side is a sock-shaped cove known as Emerald Bay. In his book *The Jungle is Neutral*, Spencer Chapman describes the true story of his escape from Japanese-occupied Malaya. He swam out to sea from this very bay and was rescued by submarine. Today lucky guests luxuriate on the beach here – acknowledged as one of Malaysia's best – while immaculately dressed waiters stand surreptitiously beneath the shade of leaning casuarinas.

Kedah and Perlis

12

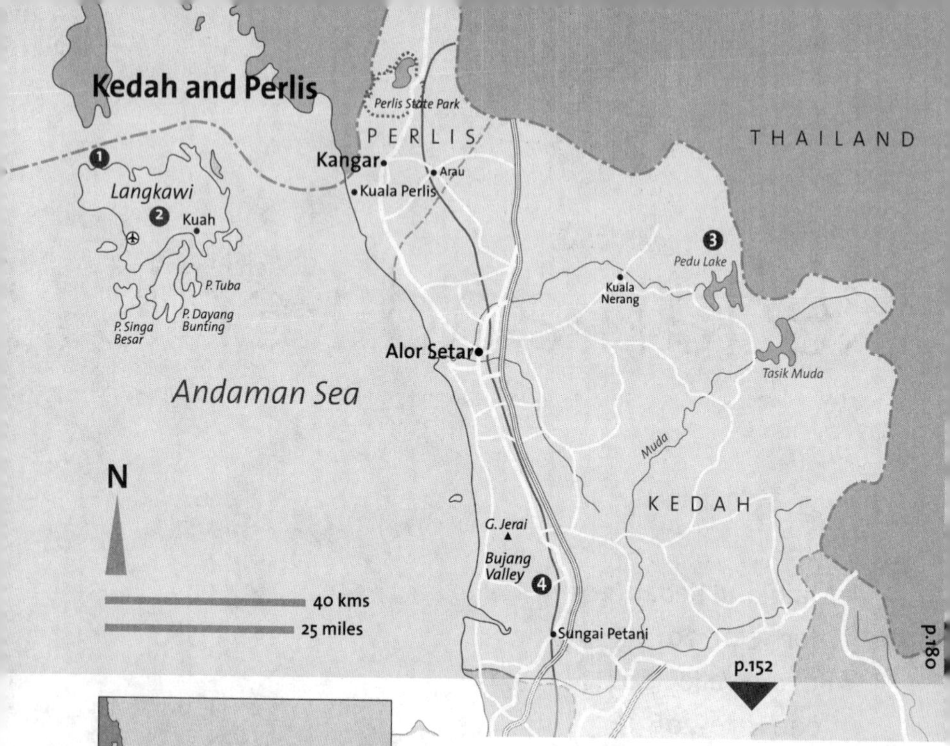

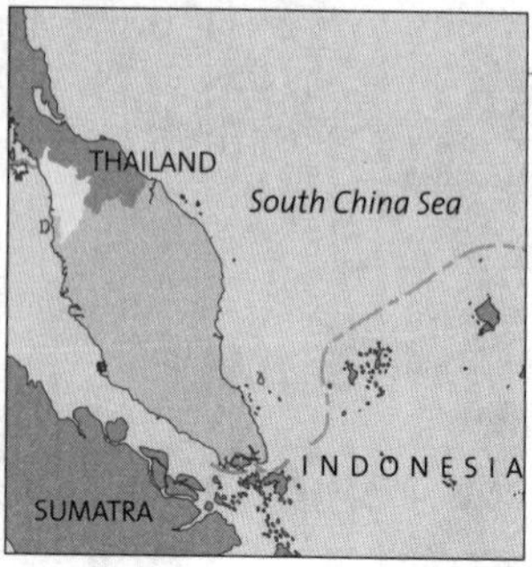

Highlights

1 Datai Bay – a pristine patch of beach-fringed rainforest on the edge of the Machinchang Reserve in Langkawi

2 Langkawi's stunning birdlife, especially the Great Hornbill, measuring 1.5m from head to tail

3 Pedu Lake – surrounded by 50-million-year-old rainforest, and great for kayaking

4 The Bujang Valley, archaeological hot spot and a trading kingdom as early as the 4th century AD

Until colonial times Perlis was part of Kedah. Today, as in the past, the two states band together to form the rice bowl of Malaysia; the landscape of both states is dominated by wet paddy, with unusual nodes of limestone rising randomly from the level ground. Historically the states have close associations with Thailand, but they remain typically Malay in character. In fact, when Islam found its way across the Indian Ocean early in the 11th century, it was the ruler of Kedah who was the first to name himself Sultan. Today's royal family can be traced back further still, to a time when Bujang Valley was the site of one of Southest Asia's most powerful trading kingdoms.

For centuries Kedah and Perlis were passed back and forth between the dominant regional powers. When the British first arrived with their imperial aspirations, it was the Sultan of Kedah who made first contact. He was tricked into handing Penang

(then part of Kedah) to the British. Without the military support that was promised in return, Kedah and Perlis fell under the control of Thailand, before passing, finally, to the colonial power. Throughout all this upheaval, the Malays of Kedah and Perlis retained a strong sense of their own identity, and their traditional agricultural lifestyles remain largely unchanged to this day.

All this history translates into very little when it comes to tourist sights. The main attraction lies 30km off the coast of Perlis: the archipelago of Langkawi, with its miles of white-sand beaches, is West Malaysia's premier tourist destination. On the mainland, the worthwhile sights are limited to a few architectural landmarks in state capital Alor Setar, some remote caves in Perlis, an even more remote lake up in the Kedah hills near Thailand, and the ruins of an ancient Hindu-Buddhist kingdom in the Bujang Valley.

Mainland Kedah

Alor Setar

Alor Setar (pronounced 'star') is the state capital of Kedah, the seat of Malaysia's oldest sultanate and the birthplace of ex-Prime Minister Mahathir. Knowing this, the town itself is bound to come as a bit of a disappointment. It is the sort of place most people will want to pass straight through – small, rough round the edges and with an air of insignificance. However, Alor Setar's long history has left it with some important architectural landmarks, most of which are on display beside the padang in the centre of town.

The bulk of the town – a workaday block of streets north of the river and centred around the Pekan Rabu market – falls to the east of the padang. Though there is a notable Thai influence in Alor Setar, this town is about as Malay as you get, by west-coast standards. It is the site of one of Malaysia's best-loved mosques, while the Pekan Rabu market is well-known for its *songkok* stalls and Malay delicacies, such as *durian dodol* (a pungent equivalent of Turkish delight).

For most visitors, Alor Setar is no more than a springboard to other destinations within Kedah. Several kilometres west of the centre, in Kuala Kedah, is the main jetty for ferries to and from Langkawi. To the south, near Sungai Petani, is the archaeological zone of Bujang Valley, littered with ancient Hindu temples and the trade wares of pre-Islamic merchants. The final attraction, in the hills to the east of town, is Pedu Lake, a remote reservoir in the midst of the rainforest.

Around the Padang

The **Balai Besar**, an ornate wooden structure that sits on the *padang*, was originally built by Sultan Mohamed Jiwa in 1735. He was the first of Kedah's sultans to make Alor Setar his capital. Balai Besar means 'Great Hall' and, like the great hall of 'Beowulf', it is used as a venue for royal audiences and functions. The carvings above the pillars and the design of the roof denote a strong Thai influence: for much of the

Getting There

By Air

The Sultan Abdul Halim Airport is 10km north of town, off Lebuhraya Darul Aman. MAS offer flights from here to KL and Kota Bharu.

By Train

The railway line between KL and Bangkok runs through Alor Setar. Many of the trains do not stop here, so check. The station is set on a dusty road (Jalan Steysen) lined with traditional Malay houses on stilts. The station-master is clearly conscientious: the platforms overflow with flowers and potted plants.

By Bus

The main bus station is 5km outside town. Taxi fares from here to the centre should cost RM6. Otherwise you can catch one of the many local buses for a few sen.

Tourist Information

State Tourist Office, En. Rosli Bin Abu Bakar, Aras 3, Blok B, Wisma Darul Aman, Leburaya Darul Aman (phew!), **t** 04 730 1957. The office is located just north of the hospital in Wisma Darul Aman, an attractive state building 3km north of Masjid Zahir.

OHB Computer Centre, 3rd floor, City Plaza. Internet connection for RM2/hour.

Where to Stay

Alor Setar

Accommodation in Alor Setar is of the practical sort. There is nowhere outstanding to stay, but everywhere offers good value. It is best to steer clear of the many dirty budget options.

Expensive

Holiday Villa, 162 Jalan Tunku Ibrahim, **t** 04 734 9999, **f** 04 734 1199, *hvas@pd.jaring.my*, *www.holidayvilla.com.my*. This 4-star hotel is the plushest place in town, with 160 spacious modern rooms, a pool and a gym with steam bath and sauna. The restaurant downstairs is great for steamboats.

Expensive–Moderate

Hotel Grand Continental, **t** 04 733 5917, **f** 04 733 5161, *kedah@grandcontinental.com.my*, *www.grandcontinental.com.my*. A good-value hotel with the full range of facilities from 24-hour room service to a health club. Perhaps a little sterile. Frequent promotions keep prices low.

last millennium Kedah fell under the control of the Siamese. The present structure was rebuilt in 1904, at great expense, to host the marriages of Sultan Abdul Hamid's five children. The event went on for 60 days and became known as the 'three million dollar wedding', leaving the state virtually destitute.

Behind the Balai Besar is the newly renovated **Muzium di Raja** (*Royal Museum; open daily 10–6; free*), housed on the site of the former Istana Kota Setar, a palace built around the same time as the Balai Besar. The present building dates from 1851, though it was spruced up for the great wedding of 1904. The modest collection traces the long lineage of the sultanate of Kedah. Although the Siamese influence in Kedah has always been strong, Islam gained its first proper foothold on the Malay Peninsula with the conversion in 1136 of the Al-Muzaffar Shah, who became the first sultan.

At the north end of the *padang* is the **Balai Nobat**. Like the Balai Besar, this pagoda-like tower topped by an onion dome is also tied up with the ceremony of the sultanate. Its function is virtually unique: to house the instruments of the *nobat*, or royal orchestra. No royal ceremony is complete without the haunting strains of the *nobat*, which consists of three drums (reputedly a 15th-century gift from the Sultan of Melaka), a gong and a reed flute.

Moderate

Grand Crystal, 40 Jalan Kampung Perak, **t** 04 731 3333, **f** 04 731 6368, *crystal@grandcontinental.com.my, www.grandcontinental.com.my*. Under the same management as the Grand Continental. Not as central as its sister hotel, but with the extra luxury of a swimming pool and cheaper rates. Good deal.

Moderate–Inexpensive

Hotel Regent, 1536-G Jalan Sultan Badlishah, **t** 04 731 1900, **f** 04 731 1291. A good-value mid-range choice. A lot of effort has gone into decorating what is a plain building: bold colours upstairs, and an attractive lobby below. All rooms come with bathroom, air-con, TV and phone.

Hotel Samila, 27 Lebuhraya Darul Aman, **t** 04 733 8888, **f** 04 733 9934. Another reasonable mid-range choice, not so high on character, but with a decent restaurant serving Western and local specialities.

Budget

Hotel Lim Kung, 36 Jalan Langgar, **t** 04 732 8353. Very basic accommodation in a characterful tumbledown house, entirely of wood. The owner is knowledgeable, friendly and very fond of the UK. Rooms from as low as RM15.

Hotel Miramar, 246 Jalan Putra, **t** 04 733 8144, **f** 04 731 1668. A step up from the other plentiful budget options – a clean straightforward Chinese-run place with plain rooms.

Flora Inn, 8 Compleks Medan Raja, Jalan Pengkalan Kapal (on the riverfront), **t** 04 732 2375, **f** 04 730 8058. Very basic apartment-style accommodation, with some of the rooms overlooking the river.

Pedu Lake

Expensive

Mutiara Pedu Lake, **t** 04 730 4888, **f** 04 730 4488, *sales@mutiarahotels.com, www.mutiarahotels.com*. Around 100 wooden chalets on a man-made islet 50 yards off the east side of the lake. Each chalet has a large balcony with glorious views. There is a pool, tennis court, gym, watersports facilities and an 18-hole golf course which tries hard to blend into the trees. (It's a tricky course with lots of water obstacles and the odd trench in the middle of a fairway: the groundsmen fight a long-running battle with wild boars who dig up the fairways each night in search of worms and grubs.) On the west side of

Across the road from the Balai Nobat is the majestic **Masjid Zahir**, with its huge black dome and candy-white minarets. This is a fine example of a Moorish-style mosque, and visitors are allowed to walk through the long arcades (non-Muslims are not allowed inside the central prayer hall). Sign in at the north entrance and don a long gown before entering the mosque.

The small **State Art Gallery** (*open daily 10–6; free*), which exhibits modest works by local artists, is set inside the stuccoed colonial building on the southern flank of the *padang*. South of the river is the wooden kampung house that was the childhood home of Dr Mahathir. It is know as **Rumah Kelahiran Mahathir Mohamad** (*18 Lorong Kinang; open daily 10–5; free*). Inside is a small museum detailing the life history of Malaysia's longest-standing Prime Minister.

Further afield is the '19th tallest telecom tower in the world', Alor Setar's modern landmark. The **Menara Telecom Tower** stands 165m from top to bottom, with a viewing station 88m up. On a clear day you can see over the paddy fields and limestone outcrops to the Langkawi archipelago. Gunung Keriang, a spitting image of Ayers Rock (minus the red-tinted sandstone) is plainly visible among the level rice fields. The sheer walls on this limestone outcrop are popular with climbers.

the lake is a fishing camp owned by the hotel, with basic facilities for an overnight stay. The resort is used mostly by Malaysians and Japanese, though is often virtually empty. Not the most attentive service.

Expensive–Moderate

Desa Utara Resort, **t** 04 732 8888, **f** 04 732 4999, *desautara@maju.com.my*, *www.desautara.com*. Kampung-style chalets of wood, with rattan-woven walls, scattered about 400 acres of grounds beside the lake. Like the Mutiara, the Desa Utara's occupancy figures are woeful – which makes for some excellent deals. In hard times, the management have been known to offer the chalets for budget prices. Watersports facilities, swimming pool and jungle trekking are all on offer.

Gunung Jerai

Peranginan Gunung Jerai, Jalan Kaki Bukit, **t** 04 422 3345, **f** 04 729 788. Spacious family chalets are available for moderate prices, though there are several dingy standard rooms available for less and a some camping plots. The restaurant serves the usual Malay fare.

Eating Out

Alor Setar

There are dozens of Malay stalls and cafés dotted about Alor Setar, as well as a handful of Thai places. The **Pekan Rabu** market at the south end of Jalan Tunku Ibrahim is dominated by stalls stacked high with Malay snacks such as *kuih muih* (sweet cakes made from glutinous rice flour). The best Chinese restaurant in town is the **Szechuan Garden Restaurant** inside the Holiday Villa hotel (*see* p.202). The speciality here is steamboats. An excellent little family-run Chinese can be found in an open courtyard beneath the Flora Inn (*see* p.203). It's called **Cheow Kee** (in Chinese characters), and serves a large selection of dishes. **Restoran Rose**, on Jalan Sultan Badlishah serves excellent value Malay food with an Indian twist, with the likes of *murtabah*, biryani and great fresh fruit juices. **Hajjah**, on Jalan Tunku Ibrahim (opp. City Plaza), serves basic Thai cuisine, with some seafood specialities. Nearby at No. 33 is **Queen's Cake and Ice Cream**, which sells apple pie, banana cake, cheesecake and savoury pastries. **Bamboo Restoran**, south of the market on Jalan Tunku Ibrahim, is one of several stalls that serve the usual Malay rice and noodle dishes. Next door is a popular fruit juice stall done-out in Rasta colours.

Bujang Valley

Between the lone peak of Gunung Jerai to the north and the narrow estuary of Sungai Muda to the south is a fertile delta punctuated by paddy fields and chilli plantations. This is the Bujang Valley (Lempah Bujang), where dozens of excavated *candi* (a form of Hindu-Buddhist architecture; *see* opposite) point to the existence of a powerful trading kingdom from as early as the 4th century AD. It is Peninsular Malaysia's archaeological hotspot, and the probable site of Kataha, an influential kingdom recorded in early Indian literature.

There are a number of reasons why the Bujang Valley was the perfect site for a trade-based kingdom. Its location at the entrance to the Strait of Melaka, on a latitude similar to that of the southern tip of India, meant that ships could sail due east or due west without fear of getting lost. The lone 1,217m peak of Gunung Jerai also served as the perfect shipping beacon for vessels approaching from India and the Arab world. And for those wishing to avoid the pirate-infested waters further south, there was the network of rivers in south Kedah that stretch deep into the peninsula, allowing access to the east coast and a short cut to China.

Among the finds in the Bujang Valley was a stone stele from around AD 500 inscribed with prayers for safe passage to India. It is thought to have been erected by a Buddhist sea captain from Kelantan before he set out on the hazardous journey across the Bay of Bengal. Perhaps the most important single find, however, is that of a little bronze buddha, unearthed by British archaeologist Quaritch Wales in 1941. This has been dated to the 5th century and is the earliest surviving Buddhist image to be found in Malaysia.

All in all, the archaeological finds provide insight into the extent of early Indian influence on the Malay Peninsula. Unfortunately there is not all that much to see today. The little **Bujang Valley Archaeological Museum** (*open daily 9–4, Fri 9–12 and 2.45–5; adm RM2*) is the only focal point for visitors. Without use of a car or taxi, the museum can be accessed from Sungai Petani, an unappealing and rapidly growing town to the south, by catching a bus to the small village of Merbok (*RM2*). From here, it is a pleasant walk uphill through chilli plantations to the museum, which charts the excavation process and provides a brief history of the valley. The area around the museum is dotted with the ruins of Hindu temples (*see* 'Candi Architecture', below) and is the site of ongoing excavation work. The bases of some of the temples have been reconstructed; others have been left as they were found. The best-preserved is Candi Bukit Batu Pahat, which was originally situated a good 10km north of the museum site, before being reconstructed here. The temples are not much to look at –

Candi Architecture

In Southeast Asia the word *candi* (pronounced 'chandi') is the general term used to describe architecture dating from before the coming of Islam. More specifically it is refers to a Hindu or a Buddhist religious shrine: *candi* derives from Chandika, the name of Lord Siva's wife. She was also known as the deity of death and this points to the *candi*'s function as a place in which to honour ancestors and consecrate dead kings. The temple would also have been a focal point for all other religious rites. In Kedah, *candi* architecture from before the 10th century AD is usually associated with Buddhism, while later sites are Hindu (by the 11th century Kedah was dominated by the Cola kingdom of South India). Unfortunately only the bases of these temples have survived – the pillars were wooden and the roofing *attap*.

The Hindu temples consist of two sections: the *vimana*, an enclosed sanctuary where the main icon was kept (usually a lingam, or phallus), and the *mandapa*, an open-sided hall. Seated among the wooden pillars of the hall was the statue of a bull. A special drain was employed to catch the sacred water, which was used to bathe the icon, while a spout outside the *vimana* enabled worshippers to collect the waters. Above the *vimana* a wooden framework supported a multitiered roof, which narrowed to a point. In symbolic terms, the roof of such temples was conceived as a representation of the legendary Mount Meru, which in Hindu-Buddhist mythology is identified as the abode of the gods.

the ruins are no more than a series of low-lying laterite blocks minus their wooden pillars and *attap* roofs – but it is an attractive spot with a waterfall cascading close by.

This particular part of the Bujang Valley had come to prominence by the end of the 10th century and many of the artefacts found here are associated with Hinduism. The original 5th-century capital was further west on the banks of Sungai Mas, and there the artefacts point to Buddhism as the main influence.

One of the Bujang Valley's primary functions was as a major bead-making centre: together, the various excavations have unearthed many thousands of beads. Besides their association with prayer (the English word 'bead' derives from the Saxon *biddan*, meaning 'to pray'), beads functioned as trade items, ornaments and currency. The earliest beads were fashioned from seeds, teeth, claws, shells and ivory. Later, metals, stones and glass were used. It is thought that beads have been in use on the Malay Peninsula since as early as 30,000 BC.

The whole valley sits in the gentle shadow of **Gunung Jerai** (1,217m), which rises slowly from the the level plains of Kedah. In the 1920s archaeologists discovered the remains of an ancient Hindu temple on its summit: the sanctity of high places is a common belief among many Asian cultures. As well as the remains of a central temple, which contains a bathing shrine and dates form the 7th century, nine square stone foundations were found near the summit. These may have been connected with the Navagrahas, or nine sacred planets of Hinduism.

Ten years ago the foot of this mountain was set to become an oversize theme park in the vein of Disney World. However, massive protests by paddy farmers stopped the project in its tracks. Today a road winds up to the summit, though the archaeological zone is not usually accessible to the public. It might be worth the trip for the views alone: on a clear day Sumatra can be made out across the Strait of Melaka. Mid-range chalet accommodation is available on the mountain (*see* 'Where to Stay', p.204).

Pedu Lake

Pedu Lake (Tasek Pedu) is entirely man-made. But it still makes for a serene escape: deep blue water surrounded by 50 million-year-old rainforest, with the nearest habitation at least 50km away. From the water, the horizon is a ragged line of limestone peaks that mark the border with Thailand. And the lake itself is huge: you could fit Penang more or less exactly inside its banks.

The journey to Pedu Lake is pleasant too; the road inland from Alor Setar cuts through the kampungs and paddy fields of rural Kedah as far as Kuala Nerung, before climbing into primary jungle for the last stint of the journey. (There are regular buses to Kuala Nerung. Taxis charge RM50 to cover the final stretch.) At the moment Pedu Lake is a bit of a secret. However, the authorities are searching for a site to build an airstrip. Before long the lake is sure to bear the burden of development; if you can catch it before then, it is a rare hideaway treat.

Before the dam appeared, the site was a forested valley with two small villages. The inhabitants were relocated when the dam was completed in the mid-1960s, and it

Monsoon Squabble

Pedu Lake made prime-time news in the late 1990s when an argument between the dam authority and one of the lakeside resorts blew out of hand.

In a typical year, the lake's water level rises and falls up to 12ft as the lake fills during the monsoon then subsides when water is released for irrigation during the dry season. The hotel had made preparations for this, but in 1998 the monsoon dragged on longer than usual and the water levels rose alarmingly, submerging the resort's beloved golf course and threatening to put much of the hotel itself below the waterline.

The management demanded that the dam authority release some water to save the hotel. But their wishes were declined: the dam authority pointed out that releasing the water would damage the state's already-saturated rice crop.

Luckily for the resort, Pedu Lake had been earmarked by the government as a new tourism hotspot, and a compromise was reached: the dam authority was instructed to release water gradually and divert it elsewhere, thereby saving the hotel as well as the all-important rice crop.

took a further five years for the lake to reach its full depth (98m at its deepest). As well as supplying water to Alor Setar, it irrigates the paddy fields of Kedah and Perlis. The area was once a stronghold for communist guerillas and the dam itself is still carefully guarded by the Malaysian army. It lies near the Thai border, and if the dam walls were to be breached, the impending torrent would wash Alor Setar into the sea.

The jungle canopy that fringes the lake is a wonderful place for spotting wildlife – particularly if you approach quietly in a canoe (which can be hired from either of the resorts). This is an eerie world in which to paddle about: little channels lead off into the undergrowth, and all round the edges of the lake the sun-bleached tops of trees – submerged nearly 30 years ago – break the surface of the water.

Wild boar, sun bears, elephants, leopards and deer have all been sighted in the surrounding rainforest; but it is the giant honey bee that gets most of the attention. Its honey is particularly prized, though harvesting it – or 'swarm hunting' – is a dangerous pursuit, with many recorded deaths. The bees nest exclusively in the smooth-barked *tualang* tree, a giant dipterocarp that can support up to 100 hives.

Honey gathering from these trees is an ancient pursuit rich in ritual. Before ascending the tree on makeshift ladders, the gatherers – who show great respect to the ferocious bees – chant incantations and leave offerings near the trunk. In the dead of a moonless night, one of them ascends the ladder in total darkness. Once up in the canopy he lights a torch of liana to flush out the bees, who swarm in pursuit of the torrent of sparks that fall to the ground. With the sharpened shoulder bone of a cow, he extracts sections of honeycomb from the hive, which are lowered to the ground in buckets of hide. This liquid gold – the world's most sought-after honey – commands high prices at local markets for its purity and medicinal properties.

Between December and May, when the bees are nesting, arrangements can be made with either of the resorts to accompany a crew of swarm hunters on their night's work.

Langkawi

Langkawi is an archipelago of 99 islands bordering Thai waters. Two decades ago it was an Eden of easy subsistence, its main island cloaked in virgin jungle and run through with limestone spines that rise to a plateau of paddy fields, its coastal lowlands lapped by emerald waters and dotted with fishing kampungs and coconut plantations. Then in 1987 Langkawi was declared a duty-free zone. It has since reinvented itself as Malaysia's 'Tourism Island of Culture', with ex-Prime Minister Mahathir at the forefront of the island's new image: he practised as a doctor in Langkawi before entering politics.

With almost two million visitors annually, the race is on to overtake Indonesia's Bali and Thailand's Phuket in the revenue stakes. What Langkawi lacks in history (there is no architecture to speak of), it makes up for in legends of dubious authority. Every rock, it seems, has been allocated its place in Langkawi's mythical past. Rainforest reserves, waterfalls, caves, museums, even the Kedah cement factory – all are marketed aggressively as tourist attractions. Meanwhile new restaurants and resort hotels fight over the best sweeps of sand.

Though much of the rainforest has disappeared, the brakes are being grudgingly applied on further development. The downturn in the Asian economy is largely the cause of this, but there is also the realization that the outstanding diversity and beauty of Langkawi's natural habitat is the key to the island's long-term future as a tourist destination. At more than 500 sq km, not all of Langkawi has succumbed to the tourism push. Pockets of rainforest, such as the Machinchang Reserve, are alive with fauna and diverse plant life, while the rugged coastline and pristine beaches will prove an enduring attraction if some of them can remain that way. Fishermen still bring in their staple catch of *ikan bilis* (anchovies), plantation workers still tap rubber and, in the interior, buffalo still work the paddy fields.

The Coast

Kuah

Malay speakers must laugh whenever they hear the name of Langkawi's main town. Kuah, or 'Gravy', earned its fine name from one of Langkawi's many legends – this one involving two giants and a pot of curry.

Kuah is the archipelago's transport hub and its main settlement, with around 15,000 inhabitants. The main jetty is situated here, as are the shops. Considering what the rest of the island has to offer, there is not much in Kuah to detain the visitor. The one attraction – if indeed it can be called an attraction – is **Legend Park** (*open daily 9–7; adm free*), 50 acres of reclaimed land with walkways and covered terraces alongside ex-Prime Minister Mahathir's brainchild: a monstrous statue of a brown eagle standing 12m tall on the water's edge. Strangely, Langkawi's trademark symbol (*lang* means 'bird' and *kawi* means 'brown') bears more resemblance to the bald eagle (national bird of the USA) than to any of the eagles that haunt Langkawi. A

Getting There

By Air

Langkawi has an international airport at Padang Matsirat, which serves a number of chartered flights from Europe. MAS operate daily between Langkawi, Penang, KL and Singapore. The MAS office is in the Langkawi Fair building on Jalan Pesiaran Putra (**t** 04 966 6622). Air Asia (**t** 04 955 5688) offer the cheapest flights between KL and Langkawi.

By Sea

There are daily ferry services from Kuala Kedah (1hr) to Kuah (Langkawi) between the hours of 8.30–6.30. Services between Kuala Perlis and Langkawi (45mins) operate from 9–4.30. There are daily ferries to and from Georgetown (3 hours) and other services to Satun and Phuket in Thailand. Ferry companies include Langkawi Ferry Service (**t** 04 966 9439), LADA Holdings (**t** 04 966 8823), Nautica Ferries (**t** 04 762 1201), Bahagia Ekspress (**t** 04 966 5784).

Getting Around

There is no public transport on offer for tourists, so taxi drivers have the monopoly. Fares from Kuah to Pantai Cenang/Tengah cost RM15. To get round to the north side of the island costs significantly more. If you want to explore Langkawi, it works out cheaper to hire a car or motorbike. There are many agents at the Kuah jetty who will bombard you with offers for tours and car hire. If you barter you can get a car for RM70/day or less. Try Langkawi Nature Beauty Tours (*see* Tour Operators below). You can hire low-performance motorbikes all over the island. At Pantai Cenang, A & A Motorbike (next to Grand Beach Motel) are the cheapest, with motorbikes for RM25–30/day. Otherwise try The Shop, Pantai Cenang (RM35–50). Although the roads on Langkawi are pretty traffic-free, look out for jaywalking buffalo.

Tourist Information

Langkawi Tourist Information Centre, Jalan Persiaran Putra (about 1km from the Kuah jetty), **t** 04 966 7789, **f** 04 966 7889. There is also an information centre at the airport.

Tour Operators

Langkawi Canopy Adventures, Bukit Morang, Kedawang, **t** 04 955 4744/012 484 8744, *www.emmes.net/langkawi-natur*. An adventurous way of seeing the jungle canopy known as 'air trekking', under the tutelage of an experienced and very well-informed German naturalist.

Crystal Yacht Holidays, Porto Malai, **t/f** 04 955 6544, *www.infocrystalyacht.com*. Upmarket yacht cruises around Langkawi. One-day 'eco adventure cruise' offered, with a complimentary on-board bar open all day.

Coral Island, Jetty Point Complex, Kuah, **t** 04 966 1368. One of many agents offering day trips to Pulau Payar. The company will ferry you to the marine park, where you will be left to snorkel and sunbathe for 4–5 hours. Packed lunch and snorkelling equipment included. Price RM130/person.

Langkawi Nature Beauty Tours, Jetty Point Complex, **t** 04 966 2661, **f** 04 966 3637. Offers competitively priced tours to all of Langkawi's main sites. Also has cars for hire at reasonable prices.

Langkawi Coral, Jetty Point Complex, Kuah, **t** 04 966 7318. The upmarket way to visit Pulau Payar. On arriving at the marine park, the speed boat attaches itself to a reef-viewing platform, well away from the crowds. Price RM220/person (diving extra).

Where to Stay

Luxury

The Andaman, Datai Bay, **t** 04 959 1088, **f** 04 959 1168, *andaman@ghmhotels.com*, *www.ghmhotels.com*. Sister hotel to the more famous Datai resort, just along the bay. All the rooms are in the main block, set back from the beach within the canopy of the rainforest. The lobby, with a traditional Malay *balai nobat* as the centrepiece, is unusually impressive, while the rooms are spacious and stylish. The focus of the hotel is the pristine habitat within which it is set: in the welcome pack there is a beautifully illustrated guide to the birds of the island. In the grounds, a swimming pool meanders between *tualang* trees, while at the back, there is an open butterfly garden. Set into the steep eastern flank of the bay is the luxurious Jamu Nature Spa, which looks down onto the turquoise waters of the bay. There are also three award-winning restaurants serving Mediterranean, Malaysian and Japanese cuisine (*see* Eating Out, p.213). Back inland is an immaculate 18-hole golf course, shared with the Datai.

The Datai, Datai Bay, **t** 04 959 2500, **f** 04 959 2600, *datai@ghmhotels.com*, *www.ghmhotels.com*. Built on the same eco-sensitive principles as its sister hotel next door, The Datai has received much acclaim for its sympathetic architectural design and beautiful setting (*see* Datai Bay p.217), and it has less of an 'international' feel than the Andaman, which gives it the edge. Trained elephants, rather than clumsy bulldozers, were used to fell trees during construction. There are 35 private villas dotted about the rainforest, as well as 54 rooms in the main block. It is probably safe to say that the Datai is Malaysia's most outstanding resort hotel. The rooms are luxurious, spacious and painstakingly furnished. A variety of restaurants serve top-notch dishes from Thailand, Malaysia and the Mediterranean. Room service is equally impressive. Facilities include two pools, a spa, a health club, a watersports pavilion and guided jungle trekking. The free dusk and dawn nature walks, under the tutelage of naturalist Irshad Mobarak, are excellent.

Tanjung Rhu Resort, Mukim Ayer Hangat, **t** 04 959 1033, **f** 04 959 1899, *resort@tanjungrhu.com.lmy*, *www.tanjungrhu.com.my*. Set in 1000 acres of grounds among the casuarinas of Tanjung Rhu bay, a secluded spot with a 2.5km beach and a peppering of limestone islets. Langkawi's main river flows into the bay, clouding the water at one end. Along the estuary are a mangrove park and a few fish farms with dozens of fish eagles soaring overhead. The resort has three restaurants, non-motorized watersports, tennis courts and two pools – one beautifully landscaped, the other with a little man-made beach. Not nearly as chic or exclusive as the Datai and Andaman, but more family oriented. The rooms are all in blocks.

Four Seasons Langkawi, Jalan Tanjung Rhu, **t** 04 950 8888, **f** 04 950 8899, *www.fourseasons.com*. At this resort (opened 2005), golf carts navigate the grounds, where Mogul and Moorish elements are blended in the architecture. Most of the rooms are situated in a series of pavilions, all of them spacious and fully equipped. Away from the main buildings, a collection of luxurious stone villas are set around an infinity pool. Three expensive restaurants serve seafood, Mediterranean and Asian fusion cuisine.

Casa del Mar, Pantai Cenang, **t** 04 955 2388, **f** 04 955 2228, *info@casadelmar-langkawi.com*, *www.casadelmar-langkawi.com*. A low-rise Spanish-style building in terracotta, with 29 elegant rooms (with balconies), a pool, spa and immaculate service. This is the top spot along Pantai Cenang. The elegant restaurant serves an unusual fusion of Mediterranean and Japanese cuisines (*see* Eating Out, p.213). It's sophisticated and intimate, but you pay for it.

Pelangi Beach Resort, Pantai Cenang, **t** 04 952 8888, **f** 04 952 8899, *pelangi.pbl@meritus-hotels.com*, *www.pelangibeachresort.com*. A 5-star resort set on a quiet stretch of sand, north of the main section of Pantai Cenang. Attractive Malay-style architecture predominates, with rooms set around a pond or on the beach. It has a pool, gardens, restaurants, tennis and squash.

Sheraton Perdana, Jalan Pantai Dato Syed Omar (near Kuah), **t** 04 966 2020, **f** 04 966 6414, *www.sheraton.com/perdana*. An enormous place set on its own beyond the jetty in Kuah. A fully self-sufficient resort with a series of pools and a great view over the bay towards some of Langkawi's smaller islands. Full 5-star facilities with large rooms. However, the beach here isn't one of Langkawi's best.

Sheraton Langkawi Beach Resort, Teluk Nibong, **t** 04 955 1901, **f** 04 955 1968, *www.starwoodhotels.com/sheraton*. A large resort in typically unsubtle Sheraton style, but the peaceful forest setting makes up for it. Rooms are all very large with balconies and full-length French windows. There is a pool, a spa and watersports facilities. Six food outlets provide plenty of dining options. It beats the Sheraton Perdana for atmosphere.

Luxury–Expensive

Berjaya Langkawi Beach & Spa Resort, Burau Bay, **t** 04 959 1888, **f** 04 959 1886, *resvn@b-langawi.com*, *www.berjayaresorts.com*. A huge resort with over 400 rooms, some on stilts over the water. All accommodation is in Malay-style chalets set either among the trees or over the water. An attractive spot, though the beach here is sometimes non-existent. All sorts of indoor and outdoor recreational options. There is also a luxurious Japanese-concept spa.

Mutiara Burau Bay, Teluk Burau, **t** 04 959 1061, **f** 04 959 1172, *adminbb@mutiarahotels.com*, *www.mutiarahotels.com*. Accommodation in 150 'cabanas', which are dotted around the resort. Full range of facilities, including a pool, tennis courts, a gym and three restaurants. Pleasant setting but not up to the standard of some of the others.

Expensive

Rebak Marina Resort, Pulau Rebak, **t** 04 966 5566, **f** 04 966 9973, *www.rebakmarina.com*. The only accommodation off the main island of the Langkawi archipelago. Situated offshore on Pulau Rebak, and aimed at passing yachties, with its substantial marina and boatyard. This is a kampung-style setup with electric buggies to wheel you about the resort. The newly renovated rooms are all comfortable enough and most have four-poster beds. There's a pool, a narrow stretch of beach, a mangrove swamp with boardwalk and (oddly) a crystal showroom. A bird park is planned for the centre of the island. The facilities are good for the money, but it's a 45min ferry ride back to the main island, which can be isolating, and it's not far from the airstrip so jets fly low overhead. Ferries for the island leave every hour from behind the ruins of the old water park.

Kampung Tok Senik, Mukim Ulu Melaka, **t** 04 955 7288, **f** 04 955 7257, *toksenik@maju.com.my*, *www.toksenik.com*. Comfortable accommodation in a longhouse and a group of bungalows arranged kampung-style. Beautiful hilly setting among the trees, inland between Kuah and Pantai Cenang. A peaceful retreat – if that's possible in Langkawi – with authentic rooms adorned with local woodcarvings and woven *attap* roofing. Facilities include a pool, a gym and a spa. It is often pretty empty and is good value.

Tanjung Sanctuary Langkawi, Jalan Pantai Kok, Tanjung Belikit, **t** 04 955 2977, **f** 04 955 3978, *sanctuary@tm.net.my*, *www.langkawihotel.com*. One of the best settings of all Langkawi's hotels, with a glorious sweep of secluded beach backed by rainforest. Thirty-two suites, with wooden floors and wicker furniture, are set in 67 acres of forest. There's a small pool, watersports facilities and a restaurant on stilts over the water.

Holiday Villa, Pantai Tengah, **t** 04 955 1701, **f** 04 955 1504, *lhvreservation@po.jaring.my*, *www.holidayvilla.com.my*. A sprawling resort hotel, with most of the 260 rooms in an uninspiring U-shaped block. It sits on a good stretch of beach and has a very large swimming pool with open-air jacuzzi. Chinese, Japanese and Italian cuisine is served at the hotel's various restaurants.

Langkawi Village Resort, Pantai Tengah, **t** 04 955 1511, **f** 04 955 1531, *lvr@pd.jaring.my*, *www.langkawi-villageresort*. Probably the best place to stay on Pantai Tengah: two-storey chalets set on the beach among the palms of an old coconut grove, with a decent pool and tennis courts. Rooms are all kitted out with air-con, minibar and TV, and have either a private terrace or a balcony.

The Gates, Jalan Persiaran Putra, Kuah, **t** 04 966 8466, **f** 04 966 8443. A large hotel in Kuah, with good-sized rooms and the usual range of facilities. Nothing special (and there's really no reason why anyone should stay in Kuah), but the promotional discounts here are often staggering (with rates in the 'Inexpensive' category).

Expensive–Moderate

Bon Ton Resort, 1047 Pantai Cenang, **t** 04 955 6787, **f** 04 955 6790, *www.bontonresort.com*. A handful of 100-year-old restored Malay *rumahs* set among the leaning palms of a quiet coconut grove. Each house is individually designed; the oldest has a four-poster bed, dressing room, bathroom and antique furniture, with kettle, fridge and toaster provided. The other houses have air-con. There are two gazebos for private dining, an elegant little pool and a couple of timber yachts that can be chartered. A small cooking school is housed on site in an 80-year-old Malay house and the elegant alfresco restaurant serves Asian fusion delights (*see* 'Eating Out', p.213). Highly recommended.

Awana, Porto Malai (south of Pantai Tengah), **t** 04 955 5111, **f** 04 955 5222, *www.awana.com.my*. A big hotel on the southern tip of Langkawi at Porto Malai (where the cruise ships dock). There's no beach here; instead a long boardwalk lining the hotel overlooks yachts in the marina. Though not unattractive, the whole setup is eerily reminiscent of Port Solent in Portsmouth, UK. Rooms here, with full facilities, are good value – though probably not what you'd expect on a tropical island.

Moderate

Sunset Beach Resort, Pantai Tengah, **t** 04 955 1751, *sunvil@tm.net.my*. Cramped but carefully-laid-out chalets set among flowers and a koi pond. Rooms come with air-con, TV, hot shower and fridge.

The Paloma, Pantai Cenang, **t** 04 955 9006, **f** 04 955 9066. A nondescript block set on the other side of the road from the beach, with a pool and spacious rooms with all the trimmings. Lacks character, but is a good deal if comforts are a priority.

Beach Garden Resort, Pantai Cenang, **t** 04 955 1363, **f** 04 955 1221, *combeer@pd.jaring.my*. A quadrangle of attractive rooms set around a tiny pool, lost in a tangle of tropical plants. The twelve rooms are all en suite with fridge and air-con. The attached beachside restaurant is popular in the evenings. Intimate and good value.

Semarak Beach Resort, Pantai Cenang, **t** 04 955 1159. Attractive well-spaced chalets set among palms and flowers beside the beach. Fairly basic rooms, but clean and with air-con. Along the main drag of Pantai Cenang.

Sandy Beach Resort, Pantai Cenang, **t** 04 955 1308. A range of chalets on the beach, from simple A-frames (*inexpensive*) to more upmarket refurbished chalets that are definitely worth a look. There are air-con hotel rooms across the road too. The chalets are a little too tightly packed.

Beringin Beach Resort, Jalan Pantai Dato Syed Omar (near Kuah), **t** 04 966 6966, **f** 04 966 7970. Set in a secluded bay, round the corner from Sheraton Perdana, with its own small beach and mangroves. Very unpretentious, with acceptable cabin accommodation complete with air-con, TV and kettle. Plans are afoot to build a pool and a jetty.

Inexpensive

Beachview Chalets, Pantai Cenang, **t** 04 955 8513, *beachvu@hotmail.com*. A friendly and popular backpackers' spot, with a great breakfast bar (try the mango *lassis*). The rooms are small and simple, though most have air-con and splashy murals. Prices have risen – so it is no longer one of the better deals along this stretch – but it can't be beaten for atmosphere. Beachview Chalets by name only (there is no beach view).

Grand Beach Motel, Pantai Cenang, **t** 04 955 1457, **f** 04 955 3846. One of a handful of clean and simple chalet complexes on the beach. This place has friendly management and a few wooden shelters with deckchairs set up on the beach. No frills, but cheap, particularly off season when rates can drop into the 'Budget' category.

Cenang Resthouse, Pantai Cenang, **t** 04 955 9928, **f** 04 955 9921. Simple beachside accommodation, clean rooms with air-con and TV, but a little low on atmosphere. Very keen management.

AB Motel, Pantai Cenang, **t** 04 955 1300. Beachside chalets among the palms. One of the older setups, with organized tours of Langkawi on offer. Fan-only and air-con chalets available.

Charlie Motel, Pantai Tengah, **t** 04 955 1200, **f** 04 955 1316. Right on the large southern sweep of Tengah beach, where the development has more or less stopped. Fan-only and air-con rooms, with a simple covered restaurant. A little worn.

Eating Out

On any circuit of the island, you can't miss the roadside stalls which sell market produce and food such as banana fritters, sweet potato pastries, noodles and *nasi lemak* wrapped in a banana leaf. There are also makeshift restaurants and food courts dotted about. Notable ones include the huddle of Thai seafood restaurants at the end of the road behind the Tanjung Rhu Resort. This is where you will find the cheapest seafood on the island (though the land is now owned by the resort, who are stuffy about the presence of down-market outlets. Whether the restaurants are allowed to stay remains to be seen). Most of Langkawi's tourist-orientated restaurants are concentrated along Pantai Cenang and Pantai Tengah. There are decent restaurants in most of the big hotels. Only the best of those have been listed here.

Expensive

The Gulai House, The Andaman, Datai Bay, **t** 04 959 1088, **f** 04 959 1168, *www.ghmhotels.com*. Last order 10.30pm. Set back from the beach in an open-sided Malay house with attap roofing. Access is either by a 300m nature trail through the rainforest (lit by gas lamps), or by the stunning beach on Datai Bay. Eating here is quite an experience: low tables with cushions, and the tinkle of traditional music set the scene. A comprehensive menu of Malay and Indian delicacies is offered alongside a well-priced wine list. Many of the spices come fresh from a spice garden round the side. North Indian cuisine is available from the tandoori counter.

Kamogawa, The Andaman, Datai Bay, **t** 04 959 1088, **f** 04 959 1168, *www.ghmhotels.com*. Last order 10.30pm. Top-class Japanese cuisine in authentic setting. As well as an à la carte dining area, there are two *tatami* rooms (with a seating capacity for either six or fourteen guests), and two *teppanyaki* counters (with seating for eight in each). The restaurant has received many awards.

Bon Ton Restaurant, Pantai Cenang, **t** 04 955 6787, *www.bontonresort.com*. A fusion of Mediterranean and Asian cuisine, with dishes such as coriander and lemongrass pesto with cashew nuts and penne, or rock lobster tails with satay suace and guava salad. Nyonya specialities are also on offer. Tranquil setting in an old coconut plantation, with open-sided restaurant and lots of plush fabrics.

The Lighthouse, Pantai Tengah, **t** 04 955 2586, **f** 04 955 2633. Sat on its own at the quiet end of Pantai Tengah, with glorious views over the bay (west-facing for the perfect sunset drink). Alfresco dining on the sand in front of the bar, or fine dining upstairs. Serves Mediterranean and Malay cuisine. Chef Shukri Shafri, who holds cookery classes in his own traditional Malay *rumah*, is fast developing a reputation as an authority on Malay cuisine. Lots of seafood, Malay classics, and a daily promotional meal for two that offers great value for money.

Barn Thai, Kampung Belanga Pecah, **t** 04 966 6699, **f** 04 966 6669. A unique restaurant set in a mangrove swamp at the end of a 450m walkway. Classic Thai dishes are served to the sounds of jazz and blues. Even if you don't eat (the food is decent but over-priced), it's worth a visit for the walkway alone: the mangroves are swarming with kingfishers, crabs and monkeys.

Casa del Mar, Pantai Cenang, **t** 04 955 2388, *www.casadelmar-langawi.com*. Al fresco hotel restaurant with an unusual fusion of Mediterranean and Japanese cuisines. This is a popular place, partly because there is access from the main Pantai Cenang beach.

Moderate

Champor Champor, Pantai Cenang. A cosy place done out in African décor, with Moroccan, Mediterranean and Asian fusion cuisine. Good value and understandably very popular.

Hot Wok, Pantai Cenang. Lashings of fresh fish and seafood, Chinese-style. This has the best prices of the many seafood restaurants along this stretch.

Fat Mum's, Pantai Tengah. Popular alfresco Thai restaurant with little gazebos for privacy. Serves the usual Thai fare, including delicious *tom yam* soup, plus its signature dish 'flaming noodles', fiery-hot in both senses.

Jezabel's Italian Bistro & Pizzeria, Pantai Cenang. Attached to Beachview Chalets, and mainly alfresco. The pizzas here are surprisingly good.

The Bird Cage, Pantai Cenang. Mexican cuisine, with fajitas and the like in pleasant surrounds. Around RM30/head.

Little India Cuisine, Pantai Tengah. A tiny restaurant next to Sunset Beach Resort, attractively done out for a tête-á-tête dinner. Classic North Indian fare.

Tang Lung Seafood Restaurant, Pantai Tengah. An attractive alfresco Chinese restaurant beneath *attap*-roof shelters hung with myriad lanterns (*tang lung* means lantern). All the familiar dishes plus more exotic fare like ostrich meat and venison.

Inexpensive

Maharajah's, Pantai Cenang (on site with Beachview Chalets). Set vegetarian dinner: for just a few ringgit, choose from either lamb or chicken, or *thalai* (an Indian pancake with various fillings). Tasty South Indian cuisine and you won't find a cheaper meal.

Beachview Chalets Breakfast Bar, Pantai Cenang. Comprehensive Western breakfast, with eggs, pancakes, muesli, yoghurt and fresh fruit juices. The mango *lassi* is divine, as is the banana pancake with cinnamon.

The Breakfast Bar, Pantai Cenang. Another place for Western breakfasts; German-owned, this one is set round a bar and serves up similar offerings to Beachview, but the standards are not quite up to it.

Ros Tea, Pantai Cenang. A simple, lovingly designed Thai restaurant with a large menu of good-value classics. The green curry is delicious.

Aliah Restoran, Pantai Cenang. A cheap Malay restaurant beneath a tarpaulin on the sand. Satay, seafood, rice and noodle dishes – all in large helpings. There is a bring-your-own-beer policy.

Jammin, Panti Cenang. Bar and restaurant with tables stretching onto the beach. Lots of candles, reggae music and some reasonable Indian cuisine and seafood barbecues.

Jaja's Fruit Juice & Café, Pantai Cenang. Smoothies and fruit juice combinations of every conceivable kind. For food, there is a menu of basic Malay food with a Thai twist.

Boom Boom Corner, Pantai Tengah. A fast-moving Pakistani restaurant, with great-value food – lamb masala, *murtabah*, dhals, a range of naan breads and delicious mixes of fresh fruit juice.

Water Garden Hawker Centre, Jalan Pandak Mayah, Kuah. A string of stalls very popular with locals. Great *nasi lemak*.

Nightlife

Langkawi has no nightlife to speak of, beyond hotel bars and karaoke (though being a duty-free island, alcohol is cheaper here than on the mainland). A few of the restaurants listed above are good spots for an evening drink: The Lighthouse has an attractive alfresco bar with beautiful sunset views, while there are a number of other outlets on Pantai Cenang that make most of their money serving alcohol.

Shopping

Langkawi is billed as a duty-free shopping paradise, but don't take too much notice. The souvenir stalls and shopping malls are uninspiring and, in terms of the quantity or range of goods, bear no comparison to those on offer in Penang or KL. Prices are no better here either.

The largest shopping complex is **Langkawi Fair**, along the main road from the jetty and next door to the LADA (Langkawi Development Authority) office. Near Pantai Kok is another complex called **Oriental Village** (*open daily 10–10*), with the full range of duty-free goods. The shops – which are designed in the style of a theme park – are set around a pond at the foot of Gunung Machinchang. Next to Pantir Pasir Hitam is the Komplex **Budaya Kraf** (Craft and Cultural Complex, *open daily 10–6*), which is a good place to buy pottery, batik, pewter and the like. Langkawi crystal (elaborate, hand-crafted pieces in many colours) can be bought direct from the various production sites dotted about the island.

series of tableaux are dotted about the park to provide a comprehensive tour of Langkawi's legends.

Away from the reclaimed land, Kuah retains a hint of its old character, with a string of shophouses and market stalls. Not far from the waterfront rise the domes and minarets of the Al-Hana mosque, built in 1961 when Kuah was no more than a small fishing village. Nearby is a popular hawker centre that comes to life at night, while to the east of town is a fish farm which opened its boardwalks to the public in 2002. Kuah's *pasar malam* (night market) is held every Saturday and Wednesday.

Pantai Cenang and Pantai Tengah

A new road hugs the limestone hills along the coastline between Kuah and the west beaches. The road bypasses an isolated Thai fishing village known as Bukit Malut, which offers a taste of old Langkawi. An elaborate series of wooden jetties reach far out to sea; this is where the main *ikan bilis* catch is hauled ashore to be dried in the sun. From here the road rises high, then drops towards the west coast and Pantai Cenang, which is lined with restaurants, chalet complexes and low-rise hotels. It is Langkawi's liveliest spot, and the place to come for watersports. The sands of Pantai Cenang and Pantai Tengah converge on a small rocky headland to form Langkawi's longest stretch of beach. For the most part the accommodation on Pantai Cenang is mid-range or budget. Pantai Tengah is a little quieter and a touch more upmarket. The beaches here are west-facing, and every night the sun sets into a scattering of small islands. After dark the horizon twinkles with the lights of fishermen, who use powerful torches to lure squid up from the deep.

To the north of Pantai Cenang, water buffalo graze in the level fields. Since tourism took off in Langkawi many of the island's old paddy fields have gone to seed, leaving herds of redundant buffalo: it is a common sight on the roads after dark to see buffalo warming their bellies on the tarmac. **The Rice Museum** (Laman Padi; *open daily 9–6; adm free*), at the northern end of Pantai Cenang, traces the history of Malaysia's oldest industry. This attractive museum is surrounded by paddy fields, where you can see workers and their buffalo in action. The museum showcases the traditional practices and artefacts of *padi* farming, and offers visitors the chance to walk the fields and plant some paddy themselves (depending on the time of year).

Just up the road from here is Bon Ton Resort (*see* 'Where to Stay', p.211, and 'Eating Out', p.213), an old coconut plantation where you can take a close look at a few traditional Malay *rumahs* (houses). The houses – one of which is more than 100 years old – were relocated here from elsewhere on Langkawi, then renovated to serve as guest rooms. Further north towards the airstrip is the **Morac Karting Circuit** (***t** 04 955 5827; www.morac.com; open daily 10–7; RM35/10mins*), a large go-cart track offering cheap rates by Western standards.

At the other end of Pantai Cenang, on the way to Pantai Tengah, is **Underwater World Langkawi** (***t** 04 955 6100, open daily 10–6; RM28 adults, RM18 under-12s*). This is Malaysia's largest aquarium, with over 500 species of marine life on display and a 15m walk-through tunnel tank containing giant groupers, sharks, green turtles, stingrays and more. At 3pm each day, a brave member of staff enters the tank in scuba gear to feed the fish. There is an interesting section on feng shui, with warnings against placing an aquarium in the bedroom or above head height (which forebodes drowning).

Pantai Kok

One of Langkawi's most attractive beaches, Pantai Kok was the site of ongoing land reclamation at the time of writing. Before the dredgers set to work, 20th Century Fox chose the site to build a Thai-style **Summer Palace** (*open daily 9am–10pm; adm RM3.50*) for the filming of *Anna and the King* in 1999. The palace stands on stilts over the water and contains props from the film set, a restaurant and a souvenir shop.

Just inland from Pantai Kok on the flanks of Gunung Machinchang is **Telaga Tujuh** (Seven Wells Waterfall), a spectacular series of falls and natural pools. Centuries of

The Secret Lives of Langkawi's Birds

Langkawi is one of the few places in the world where the Great Hornbill can be seen. Measuring up to 1.5 metres from head to tail, it is the largest of the ten species of hornbill found in Malaysia. At the top of its outlandish beak it sports a huge chunk of 'ivory' the shape of a mortar board. (For many centuries the birds were hunted for their ivory, which was carved into ornaments and dagger handles.) Considering its size, it is a wonder the Great Hornbill gets airborne at all, though the racket it makes as it flaps between trees reflects something of its proportions: imagine the sound of a pterodactyl beating its wings, and you get some idea of the noise.

Hornbills mate for life. A group of young males will compete for the attention of an eligible female, offering her nuts and berries. Eventually she will make her choice and accept food from only one of the males. The frisky pair then practise passing fruit back and forth between their beaks, before finding or excavating a hole in a tree trunk. After mating, the female seals herself inside the hole with a mix of her own droppings and bark chippings. Once the work is complete, only her beak protrudes. Safe from predators, she will remain cocooned in her own dung for 8-10 weeks until her solitary egg has hatched and her fledgling grown. Meanwhile the male ferries food to her, using the technique practised during courtship.

Langkawi's white-bellied sea eagles also practice monogamy. Once a pair are committed, they consummate their lifelong union by locking talons mid-flight and tumbling in spirals towards the waves. Swiftlets, on the other hand, do not mate for life. But they have mastered another feat of endurance: many of their kind spend up to four years on the wing, without rest. The swiftlet skull has evolved so that one half the brain is able to sleep while the other works overtime.

The brain of the Langkawi's great slaty woodpecker is also something of a wonder. It slams its beak into tree trunks with such ferocity that scientists long wondered how its brain was not shaken to pieces. So they delved inside and found that the skull and brain were floating free in kind of gel. This piece of natural engineering was the inspiration for the technology behind Formula One racing helmets.

rainfall have worn the rocks smooth and, when the water is at the right level, it is possible to slide from pool to pool. It is best not to carry food up the steep ascent: macaques (who have developed a taste for snack food) lie in wait like highway robbers. The alpha males are particularly aggressive and will intimidate tourists until they hand over their food. Carry a stick if you can find one and carry your possessions in a backpack. As well as monkeys, the area around the falls is an excellent place to spot the spectacular Great Hornbill (*see* opposite).

Not far from the start of the trail to Telaga Tujuh is the lower station of the new **Langkawi Cable Car** (*runs Thurs–Mon 10–8, Tues–Wed 11–8; adm RM15 adults, RM10 children*). The lower station is next door to Oriental Village, a themed shopping complex with four restaurants (*see* Shopping, p.214).The cable car climbs via a middle station to the peak of Gunung Machinchang (708m), where there are observation towers and nature trails. The stone formations of this mountain are the oldest in Southeast Asia; scientists recently found fossils in the siltstone bed that date back some 500 million years.

Datai Bay

In the northwest corner of Langkawi is Datai Bay, a pristine patch of beach-fringed rainforest that goes largely unnoticed by tourists – unless, that is, they are lucky enough to be staying at the Datai or the Andaman (*see* 'Where to Stay', pp.229–10). The towering *tualang* trees of the Machinchang Reserve climb the surrounding hills and run down to a barren beach backed by mangrove swamps. The bay's perfect crescent of sand – coral-white and soft underfoot – is Langkawi's best endowed. Unfortunately, it is only possible to access the beach from the two hotels, which blend inconspicuously into the rainforest.

The forest surrounding Datai Bay is packed with wildlife, among them the colugo, one of Langkawi's more unusual residents. Sir David Attenborough himself came here to film this doleful mammal with its large round eyes and thick pelt of fur. During daylight hours the colugo – which is often wrongly identified as a flying lemur – clings motionless to the trunk of a tree. Come dusk it edges skywards, scaling the tree with the shuffling technique of a coconut collector, before hopping into the air and gliding up to 100m on extendible flaps. Sea otters, dusky leaf monkeys, slow loris and a profusion of birdlife from hornbills and eagles, to woodpeckers and racket-tailed drongos are regularly spotted here.

On the way to Datai Bay the road passes **Pasir Tengorak**, another secluded beach popular among locals for swimming. The name translates as 'beach of skulls': convicts of an ancient penitentiary across the bay are said to have been buried here. High up on the hillside, in the shade of giant-buttressed dipterocarp trees, sits the **Ibrahim Hussein Museum and Cultural Foundation** (IHMCF) (***t*** *04 959 4669, www.ihmcf.org; open daily; adm RM12*). This extraordinary building – all right angles and whitewashed cuboids that glow bright in the tropical sun – is the home and gallery complex of Ibrahim Hussein, a one-eyed Malay from the paddy fields of Kedah who transformed himself into Malaysia's foremost artist.

From inside, tall slim windows offer views over the rainforest to the blue and emerald palette of the Andaman Sea. Two floors exhibit local artists alongside Hussein's work – mainly abstract canvases and cartoon-like storyboards tackling key events in recent history. The handover of Hong Kong, for instance, is recorded in a collage of words and images. As well as providing gallery space for Malaysia's leading artists, the IHMCF hosts the annual Langkawi International Festival of Arts (LIFA), which attracts fellow artists, musicians, poets and dancers from round the globe.

The IHMCF also places the Machinchang Reserve in the spotlight. With the fast-track development of its coastline, the outstanding diversity and natural beauty of this reserve is one of the keys to Langkawi's long-term future as a tourist destination. Irshad Mobarak, naturalist and friend of Ibrahim Hussein, is a regular feature at the IHMCF, where he gives talks and guides visitors round 'Ib's Nature Trail'. The trail takes in lowland and mangrove rainforest and offers the chance of seeing flying foxes, dolphins swimming in the bay, and plenty of fireflies. For information on the trail ask at the IHMCF, or call Irhad Mobarak direct on ***t*** *04 959 4772/012 584 6184*.

Just off the road nearby is the **Temurun Waterfall**, dramatic in the rainy season but not much more than a trickle when it is dry. Still, the plunge pool is deep enough to swim in year-round.

Back towards the main road along Jalan Datai is **Crocodile Adventureland** (***t*** *04 959 2559; open daily 9–6; adm RM15 adults, RM10 under-12s*). Inside the compound are more then 3,000 live crocs, a breeding pond, a 13ft crocodile with no teeth and a 25ft python. Once you have seen these prehistoric beasts in the flesh, you can take something of them away with you in the form of a wallet or handbag. This seems horribly callous, but it's licensed and is seen as a way of protecting wild crocodiles which are illegal to hunt.

Tanjung Rhu

The road between Pantai Kok and Tanjung Rhu, Langkawi's northernmost point, passes Malay kampungs, rubber plantations and an unsightly cement factory (which actually lays on tours for visitors). Just east of here is the incongruous **Pantir Pasir Hitam**, or 'Black Sand Beach'. For years it has been said that volcanic ash in the sand gives the beach its colour. But there has been no recent volcanic activity in the area; the real cause is the heavy concentration of minerals, such as tourmaline and zircon, in the granite bedrock. Across the road from the beach stands the Kompleks Budaya Kraf (*see* 'Shopping', p.214).

The scenery at Tanjung Rhu contrasts with the dense foliage found elsewhere on Langkawi; the cape gets its name from a delicate forest of casuarina trees that line the 2.5km beach. More than a thousand acres of land here is owned by the Tanjung Rhu Resort (*see* 'Where to Stay', p.210), though the beach is still accessible to the public. A peppering of small islands is visible from the bay, while round to the east a small river feeds into a large lagoon, which sustains an extensive mangrove forest. Spirals of watchful sea eagles circle the fish farms that take advantage of the calm waters of the lagoon. Dolphins have also been spotted in the brackish water. The cape itself, which points out from the mainland like a crooked finger, rises almost vertically from the sea. At its tip is **Gua Cerita** (Cave of Legends), accessible only by boat. Koranic verse is inscribed onto the walls of the cave, which is believed to have served as a sanctuary for Arab missionaries on their voyages between Sumatra and the Malay Peninsula. Tour companies offer trips to the cave, the fish farms and an old-fashioned charcoal factory deep inside the mangrove forest. You can save money by chartering a small boat from the Thai fishermen who have set up stalls at the east end of the beach.

The Interior

The interior of Langkawi is punctuated by beautiful expanses of paddy ringed by forested mountains. The state of Kedah, after all, is the rice bowl of Malaysia and Langkawi follows suit. **Padang Matsirat**, inland from the airport, is one area dominated by rice plains and wallowing buffalo. This is the old site of Kampung Raja, the ancient capital of Langkawi. Every Sunday, Langkawi's *pasar malam* (night market) is held here, drawing thousands of locals to barter their wares.

Nearby is the **Field of Burnt Rice** (Beras Terbakar), one of many sites on Langkawi steeped in dubious legend. Several centuries back the Siamese took control of mainland Kedah and began an attack on Langkawi. The island's inhabitants set fire to their entire crop of rice in an attempt to starve out their invaders. Even today charred grains of rice can be found mixed in with the soil (that much is true).

Further into the interior, past a series of laid-back kampungs and fruit plantations, is **Makam Mahsuri** (Mahsuri Tomb) (*open daily 7.30–6; adm RM2 adults, RM1 children*), a shrine erected in honour of Langkawi's favourite legend. The little complex is set inside landscaped gardens that overlook a wide stretch of paddy fields cradled by hills. The legend goes like so: some two hundred years ago a young Siamese settler called Mahsuri was wrongly accused of adultery and sentenced to death by stabbing. With her dying words she placed a curse on her adopted homeland: she decreed that for seven generations Langkawi would fail to prosper. As luck would have it, by 1987 Langkawi was emerging from the clutches of Mahsuri's curse, just in time for duty-free shopping.

Visitors to the shrine can walk through a traditional Malay house which has been erected on site. Inside, musicians play a selection of traditional Malaysian instruments such as the reed flute and gongs in various shapes and sizes. Beside the house is a stall selling tasty old-style Malay sweets made from brown sugar and coconut milk, while outside the entrance are stalls selling a range of drinking coconuts.

A few kilometres from Makam Mahsuri is the **Snake Sanctuary** (*open daily 10–6, snake show 11.30 and 2.45; adm RM12 adults, RM6 children*). Most of the snakes lie about in motionless coils during the daylight hours. Still, it's good to see at close quarters what you might bump into out in the forest. One display helps you identify the most venomous species found in Malaysia, with tips on how to survive a bite.

Kampung Buku (Book Village) (*open daily 9.30–5.30; free*) is situated at the foot of Gunung Raya. A series of Malay-style bungalows, which sell books, are set beside a stream on a landscaped hillside. The whole setup is meant to be conducive to reading – though, as Manager Ahmad Zaki Ahmad will readily admit, Malays don't read much. So Kampung Buku is usually deadly quiet. Strangely, the book village was modelled on Hay-on-Wye in Wales. One of the bungalows is even named after 'King' Richard Booth, founder of Hay-on-Wye's book village. Though the collection is modest, the village is home to more than 500 rare books, some of them centuries old.

Looming over Kampung Buku is **Gunung Raya**, Langkawi's tallest peak at 900m above sea level. A road winds its way right to the top (*by car the journey takes 20mins and a toll of 50 sen is charged; road closed after dark and during bad weather*). On the peak is the Measat Satellite Control System and a police watchtower, but it's all out of bounds. A little further down is a teahouse with a viewing platform – a great place to take in the stunning geology of Langkawi's 99 islands. Not far from here a staircase plunges down into the rainforest. 4,287 steps lead at a steep incline to the foot of the mountain. The descent takes 2–2.5 hours. The flanks of Gunung Raya are one of the best places to spot the Great Hornbill. Look out for these unwieldly birds flapping from tree to tree around a third of the way up. For the best chance of spotting them visit between four and six in the evening.

On the northern flank of the mountain are the hot springs of **Air Hangat Village** (*open daily 9–6; adm RM4 adults, RM2 children*). The complex is advertised as a 'cultural village', but there's not much here other than a storyboard recounting yet more legends, a few souvenir stalls and some slimy green pools with water drawn from the spring. Nearby is the **Durian Perangin Waterfall**, another good place for bird-watching. A 3km trail leads up from the main road to the fall, which has a plunge pool that remains deep enough year-round for bathing.

To the east of Gunung Raya the main road passes through teak plantations and the island's only Indian village, with its own Hindu temple. The original inhabitants emigrated from India to tap rubber on Langkawi's plantations. Towering crags of limestone provide a backdrop to this stretch of road. There is also a good vein of marble that runs through the rock on this side of the island. The Kedah Marble Factory, which is situated on the approach to Kuah, has a showroom where visitors can buy a range of marble products from ashtrays and vases to chess sets and table tops.

The coast on this side of the island is dominated by mangrove forest. One good way to explore this eerily beautiful habitat is by visiting the Barn Thai Restaurant (*see* 'Eating Out', p.213), which is set on stilts deep inside the mangroves. A 450m raised walkway leads safely through the muddy netherworld (visitors using the walkway are not obliged to eat). Mudskippers sloop about in the sludge and chattering kingfishers zip from tree to tree in flashes of colour. Meanwhile a mass of little crabs harvest the ground for detritus, the bright red of their shells contrasting with the gloomy mud. Troops of macaques also patrol the mangroves, as do dusky leaf monkeys.

Galeria Perdana (*open daily 8.30–5.30; adm RM5 adults, RM2 children*) is also situated off the main road to the east of Gunung Raya. This museum is the offering of ex-Prime Minister Mahathir. It contains a staggering collection of state gifts from round the world – all housed in an extravagant building on two levels. It's worth a look, if only out of curiosity. Inside you'll find everything from cars and armoured vehicles to priceless ceramics, silverware and tacky portraits of the premier himself.

Other Islands

Although Langkawi is an archipelago of 99 islands, only two of these have any accommodation: the main island and tiny Pulau Rebak. One look at Langkawi from the air will reveal the dramatic topography of its islets, most of which are no more than the jagged limestone peaks of underwater mountains.

The second largest of Langkawi's islands, **Pulau Dayang Bunting**, is a popular day trip. A freshwater lake known as **Lake of the Pregnant Maiden** (Tasik Dayang Bunting) is the usual destination. A fairy princess is said to have committed her dead child to the waters of this lake, which now hold miraculous powers to help barren women conceive. The setting is dramatic, with rocky outcrops bearing down on the lake. Swimming, boating and fishing are possible.

Another outing, this one popular for its wildlife, is **Pulau Singa Besar**. The island provides sanctuary to mouse deer, monkeys, eagles, hornbills and the ubiquitous monitor lizard. Trails have been cut into the forest and wooden bridges erected, so trekking is an option. A circuit of the island would take around eight hours. Other things to look out for include the cycas plant, which has been around since the time of the dinosaurs, and the *kelubi* tree, a giant from the dipterocarp family.

The best coral gardens off the west coast of Malaysia are found around **Pulau Payar**, an hour's boat ride south of Langkawi. Many tour operators in Langkawi offer day trips here, lunch and snorkelling/scuba equipment included (*see* 'Tour Operators, p.209). The reef supports a great variety of marine life, including black-tipped reef sharks, moray eels, barracuda, giant groupers and myriad coral fish – all of which can be viewed from an underwater observatory or while snorkelling in the shallows. However, visibility is not great and the marine park is usually overcrowded. Dive sites off Malaysia's east coast are far superior.

Perlis

Kangar

Back on the mainland, Kangar (not to be confused with Kuala Kangsar in Perak) is the main town in Perlis, Malaysia's smallest state and largest producer of sugar cane and mango. Wedged between Kedah and Thailand, much of Perlis is an extension of Kedah's paddy plains, though striking limestone outcrops – most of them cave-ridden – are a key feature. The state experiences Thailand's marked dry season between November and April, when a dry 'winter wind' can turn foliage an autumnal brown.

Though state capital, Kangar is really no more than a small rural town, with a few blocks of dreary modern shophouses. However, the place is not completely without appeal; a clear sense of civic pride is evident in the clean streets, newly planted flower

Where to Stay

Expensive–Moderate

Kangar Travelodge, 135 Persiaran Jubli Emas, t 04 976 7755, f 04 976 1049. The only upmarket place to stay in Kangar, with 4-star facilities and an outdoor pool.

Inexpensive

Malaysia Hotel, 63–67 Jalan Jubli Perak, t 04 976 1366. A small hotel with good-sized clean rooms (fan or air-con), with wardrobe, writing desk and attached bathroom.

borders and flashing neon palms. The population is a mix of Malays, Thais, Indians and Chinese, and the cuisine reflects this: try the *laksa Perlis*, a rich and fiery noodle soup with a splash of Thai influence.

At a stretch for things to do, the visitor could pop into the **Muzium Negeri Perlis** (*Jalan Kolam,* **t** *04 977 1366; open Sun–Fri 9–4, Sat 9–12.45; free*). This stately building was residence of the British administration until 1941. After independence it served as the chief minister's office. Inside are the royal collections, mostly household objects handed down by the rajahs who ruled Perlis under Thai suzerainty.

There is a lively *pasar malam* in town every Wednesday and another one on Fridays in **Arau**, the royal town of Perlis. Several kilometres from Kangar is the tiny coastal town of **Kuala Perlis**, where ferries leave for Langkawi and Satun in Thailand.

Perlis State Park

The Perlis State Park, in the far northwest of the state, is rich in rare species of ginger, fern and the cycad (a primitive seed plant similar to a palm in appearance). Black panthers have been sighted, as well as the rare stump-tailed macaque and six species of hornbill. The park, which opened in 2000, comprises 5,000 hectares within the Matu Ayer Forest set in the midst of the Nakawan Range, a long stretch of limestone hills that straddle the border with Thailand.

At the edge of the park is a visitor centre (**t** *04 945 7879*) with a small exhibition and basic accommodation. Before entering the park you must obtain a permit form and hire a guide. Contact the park in advance to make arrangements (*Perlis State Park Project, c/o Jabatan Perhutanan Negeri Perlis, Km2 Jalan Kaki Bukit, Kangar,* **t** *04 976 5966*).

Recent exploration in the area has uncovered a network of deep caves to rival the great cave chambers in Sarawak. While Perlis was under British occupation, a number of the caves were mined for tin, and a few of these are now open to visitors. Gua Kelam is the main show cave, with a suspension bridge leading over Sungai Pelarit, a subterranean river. Nearby, another cave leads almost 4km into the rock. Numerous trails lead to other caves, waterfalls and a couple of scenic lakes. You can also scale Gunung Perlis (allow 3–5 hours). The 'Heritage Trail' follows an old footpath that was once the only access to Wang Kelian, an isolated community famous for its Sunday market (which attracts traders from both sides of the border with Thailand).

Kelantan

13

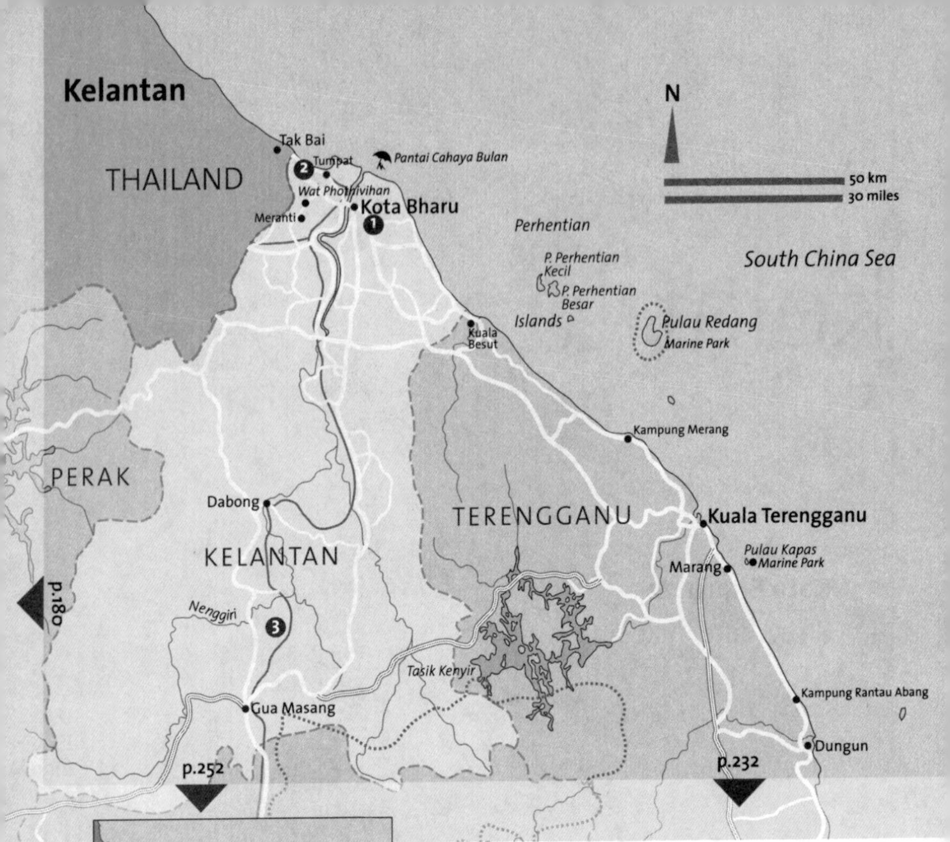

Highlights

1 The daily *pasar malam* in Kota Bharu, its stalls dedicated solely to food

2 The beautiful Thai temples on the border, across the river from Kota Bharu

3 A taste of rural Kelantan from the window of a carriage on the old Jungle Railway – running from Tumpat to Gemas in Negeri Sembilan

Kelantan has spent much of its history as a vassal state. This has helped foster a strong sense of identity among its inhabitants, who have kept themselves to themselves over the years and clung to many of their age-old traditions. Local customs and pastimes still serve their social function to this day – unlike elsewhere in Malaysia, where they sometimes linger on only as cultural displays for tourists.

Mountainous rainforests to the south and west have sheltered the state from immigration, resulting in a very different ethnic mix from the rest of the country: 95% of the Kelantan population is Malay. Mining for tin and gold never really kicked off here, and the influx of prospectors and workers passed Kelantan by. Even in urban areas, such as state capital Kota Bharu, the Chinese population is insignificant (elsewhere in Malaysia, the towns are dominated by Chinese).

All this has left Kelantan as a modern repository of the Malay arts. *Wayang kulit* (shadow-puppet plays) and *silat* (the Malay martial art), along with top-spinning, kite-flying and musical contests traditionally accompany local festivals such as the rice harvest (rice and tobacco are Kelantan's economic mainstay), while *songket* weavers, silversmiths, woodcarvers and batik artists keep the Kelantanese cottage industries alive and flourishing. Historians trace the original source of some of these traditions back to the legendary kingdom of Langkasuka, a powerful sovereign state which is thought to have dominated the northern slice of the peninsula nearly 2,000 years ago (*see* p.7). Archaeological discoveries of prehistoric earthenware in the caves of Gua Musang and Gua Chua in the interior of Kelantan point to the existence of human settlements from as long ago as 3,000 BC.

For much of its history, however, Kelantan has succumbed to the power of neighbouring states – the mighty kingdom of Srivijaya in Sumatra, the Melaka sultanate, the Siamese, and finally, the British. Through all of this domination, Islam has retained its ideological hold. Today the ruling political party in Kelantan is the PAS (Pan-Malayan Islamic Party), whose long-term aim is to impose syariah (Islamic law) on the state. Every so often the state makes the Western press for its authoritarian ambitions. In 2003, a 17-year-old with a mohican was detained by Kota Bharu's Islamic Development Unit and given a forced haircut and a lecture against emulating 'destructive culture'. Media coverage of this sort may be turning the political tide in Kelantan; in 2005 PAS lost an important by-election, leaving them in control of the state by only a single seat.

Though conservative, the people of Kelantan are generally tolerant and hospitable, while the authorities – ever aware of the growing gap in wealth between the east and west coast – are looking to tourism to help fill their coffers.

Kota Bharu

In the northeast corner of Peninsular Malaysia is Kelantan's state capital Kota Bharu, complete with palace complex and state mosque. It is a rare example of a major Malay town (Kuala Terengganu is the only other one). Kelantanese women, shielded from the sun by colourful sarongs and headdresses, appear to run the show here – if not politically, then at least in terms of commerce. Stallholders at Kota Bharu's nightly *pasar malam* and photogenic central market are almost exclusively female.

Though the local ruling party is the PAS (the ultra conservative Pan-Malayan Islamic Party), there is a congenial atmosphere to Kota Bharu; in fact tourists are welcomed with open arms, both because of the money they bring in and because of Kelantanese pride in their traditions, which are showcased all over town. Female visitors who are worried about covering up will take heart from the sight of local Chinese, who dress as scantily as they wish.

Getting There

There are direct internal **flights** from KL, Penang and Alor Setar to Kota Bharu's airport, which is about 10km out of town. Wakaf Bharu, 5km from the centre of Kota Bharu, is the last stop on the jungle **railway** line (*see www.ktmb.com.my* for timetable). The three **bus** terminals in Kota Bharu serve all main destinations on the peninsula. Most buses leave from the central station off Jalan Padang Garong. The **East–West Highway**, Malaysia's greatest feat of roadway engineering, now links Kota Bharu with the west coast, crossing the mountainous interior. The scenery along the route is unrivalled – no palm-oil plantations, just jungle, for the time being.

Getting Around

As well as the multitude of **taxis** that cruise about town, the traditional **trishaw** is still a means of getting from A to B in Kota Bharu. Trishaw drivers usually charge only two or three ringgit per kilometre. Kota Bharu is not a large place and most people opt to move around on foot.

Tourist Information

Kelantan Tourist Information Centre, Jalan Sultan Ibrahim, **t** 09 748 5534, **f** 09 748 6652, open Sun–Thurs 8–1 and 2–4.45 (closes 4.30 on Thurs). All of the budget guesthouses in Kota Bharu provide a wealth of information on the sights of Kelantan and the Perhentian Islands. KB Backpackers Lodge (*see* opposite) are happy to offer information and advice, whether you are staying there or not.

Where to Stay

Kota Bharu has a decent range of hotels in the town centre, as well as a number of themed homestays around town (contact the Tourist Information Centre for details). Hosts include a farmer, a fisherman, a kite-maker, a silversmith, a top-maker and a batik manufacturer. There is quite a large backpacker scene, perhaps because many people use the town as a springboard to the beautiful Perhentian Islands. As a result, the budget guesthouses are well-maintained and great places for information and bookings.

Expensive

Renaissance Kota Bharu, Kota Sri Mutiara, Jalan Yahya Petra, **t** 09 746 2233, **f** 09 746 1122, *www.renaissancehotels.com*. Situated on the southern edge of town, and part of the international Renaissance chain, this is Kota Bharu's top business-class hotel. There are twenty floors and a range of facilities, from tennis and squash to gym, sauna and 24-hour room service.

Diamond Puteri Hotel, Jalan Post Office, **t** 09 743 9988, **f** 09 743 8388, *dph@ktm.net.my*. A smart business hotel with glorious views over the broad Kelantan River. Over 300 rooms and suites with the usual range of facilities and a central location. There are also three good restaurants serving Chinese, Malay, Thai and Western dishes.

Moderate

Mawar Hotel, Jalan Dato Perdana, **t** 09 744 8888, **f** 09 747 6666. Perfectly situated next to the night market, and the best choice in town for the money. The rooms, though not large, are tastefully decorated. In lean times, room prices come right down.

On the surface Kota Bharu is not all that attractive; it has a history that goes back many centuries, but most of the architecture has not survived (traditional Malay buildings were constructed entirely of wood). Even late in the 19th century, the sight of masonry in Kota Bharu was a rare one, as noted by a visiting British official: 'The only brick house in Kota Bharu is owned by a well-to-do Chinese, called the Interpreter. All the other buildings are of planks or bamboo partition and the Sultan's palace is built entirely of wood...'

As was the case with all Malay centres, the town evolved around the sultan's palace and the mosque. These form the centre of Kota Bharu's historical district today, with

Hotel Perdana, Jalan Mahmud, **t** 09 748 5000, **f** 09 744 7621. A subdued top-end option on the south side of town. The spacious rooms are often on promotion and facilities include a pool, tennis, squash and gym. Silverware and batiks are on sale in the lobby.

Crystal Lodge, 124 Jalan Che Su, **t** 09 747 0888, **f** 09 747 0088, *www.crystal-lodge.com.my*. A squeaky-clean hotel offering carpeted, air-conditioned rooms with satellite TV. Breakfast and newspaper also included.

Safar Inn, Jalan Hilir Kota, **t** 09 747 8000, **f** 09 747 9000. Set on its own in the historical district between the Cultural Village and Customs Museum. The simple air-con rooms all have TV, mini-bar and coffee-maker.

Budget

KB Backpackers Homestead (KB3), Taman Sri Laksamana, Jalan Mahmood, **t** 09 773 7077, *info@kb-backpackers.com.my*, *www.kb-backpackers.com.my*. This place feels like a proper homestay, with bright, basic rooms and batiks on the walls. No air conditioning, but the best budget option – it outdoes some of the mid-range hotels too. The house is a bit of a sanctuary for orphaned animals. *Note that the phone number is the same as for KB Backpackers Lodge, below.*

KB Backpackers Lodge, 2nd Floor, Jalan Padang Garong, **t** 09 773 7077, *info@kb-backpackers.com.my*, *www.kb-backpackers.com.my*. A friendly place with doubles, singles, a dorm, a communal lounge and kitchen. The staff are a fountain of knowledge about Kelantan and the Perhentians, and you don't have to stay here to pop in for a bit of advice.

Zeck's Travellers Inn, Jalan Cemerlang, **t** 09 743 1613, **f** 09 743 9785, *ztraveller@hotmail.com*. Another popular backpacker option. Facilities are basic, but the location is quiet.

Eating Out

The highlight of Kota Bharu's culinary offerings is the daily ***pasar malam*** in the centre of town. Unlike most Malaysian night markets, this one is almost exclusively dedicated to food, and Malay food at that. Hundreds of hawkers peddle their wares, which can be eaten at the many tables and chairs laid out round the edge of the square. Kelantan specialities all share one key ingredient: coconut. They include *nasi percik* (pronounced pear-chick), pieces of barbecued chicken on wooden skewers marinated in a rich and spicy coconut-based gravy; *nasi kerabu*, a rice dish with local fish, spices and coconut; and a delicious array of coconut-based sweets and cakes. The market really goes to town at the weekends.

Most visitors spending a day or two in Kota Bharu will have no inclination to go elsewhere to eat. But for a change of atmosphere, you could head for **Restoran Terapong Tambatan Diraja**, a floating restaurant on the Kelantan River (down from the padang on the waterfront), which offers a simple menu of Malay dishes. Even if you don't eat, it's a pleasant place for a drink (soft, of course). Next door is **Restoran Mestika**, a popular place that specializes in *ikan bakar* (chargrilled fish) and the traditional Malay breakfast dish, *nasi lemak*. Two popular places for the *mamak* classic, *roti canai*, are **Restoran Lah** (Jalan Padang Garong), and an unnamed stall beneath the old school (**Sekolah Kadir Adabi**) in the centre of town. This place is well known among locals; the stallholder begins flinging his dough first thing in the morning and serves up more than 400 *roti canai* each day. **Restoran Meena**, on Jalan Gajah Mati, serves quality South Indian banana-leaf curries.

the *padang* running down to the riverfront. Fierce monsoon rains mean that the Sungai Kelantan frequently floods its banks – a major inconvenience for town-dwellers, but a blessing for rural Malays whose fields are left with a rich layer of alluvial deposits. Road traffic is kept to a minimum by the multicoloured trishaws, which are used to this day by locals.

The Sights

Kota Bharu's 'historical zone' is centred around the fenced-off **Istana Balai Besar**. This is the old palace of Kelantan's sultans, built in 1844 and now used only as an audience hall for state functions. Across the road from the palace is the **Istana Jahar**, an elaborate piece of Malay architecture set in manicured gardens. Construction of this smaller palace, with its attractive portico and decorative panelling, was initiated by Sultan Mohammed in 1847 and completed forty years later by Sultan Ahmed, who gave it to his son. Today it serves as the Royal Customs Museum (*open Sat–Thurs 8.30–4.45; adm RM3*), with a mediocre display of textiles (mainly *songket*-weaving), weapons and reconstructions of royal ceremonies.

Next door to the Royal Customs Museum is the **Istana Batu**, a single-storey, pastel-blue villa built by Sultan Ismail in 1939 as a house for guests. This too has been converted into a museum (*Kelantan Royal Museum, open Sat–Thurs 8.30–4.45; adm RM3*), or what is in effect a storeroom for regalia and royal hand-me-downs.

Visible across the street from here is the **Kampung Kraftangan** (*Handicraft Village, open Sat–Thurs 8–4.45*), an attractive compound of reconstructed Malay *rumahs* housing gift shops and a café.

Back towards the waterfront, you pass through a flimsy-looking wooden archway (built to mark the historical zone) and onto **Padang Merdeka**. This strip of lawn, laid after World War I, is the signature of the British – most important colonial towns in the East were graced with one. Around its edges are a number of important buildings, including **Masjid Negeri**, the state mosque and Islamic centre. Though relatively modern (1926), this is the original site of Kota Bharu's earlier mosques and therefore the epicentre of town: the boundaries of Malay towns were usually determined by the distance up to which the call-to-prayer could be heard (towns must necessarily have been small in the days before voice amplification).

Set on the fringes of the *padang* are two more museums. Kelantan was once dubbed 'Annex to Mecca', and the **Islamic Museum** (*open Sat–Thurs 8.30–4.45; free*) helps put this in context, with a collection of Islamic artefacts and a record of the parts played by the various sultans of Kelantan in the spread of Islam. Next door, the **World War II Memorial Museum** (*open Sat–Thurs 8.30–4.45; adm RM3*) tells the story of the brutal Japanese occupation during World War II (Kelantan was where the Japanese first landed in 1941).

The best place to get acquainted with the history and culture of Kelantan is the **State Museum** (*open Sat–Thurs 8.30–4.45; adm RM3*), beside the roundabout towards the south end of town. Paintings, photographs, musical instruments, kites and ceramics tell the piecemeal story of the state and its heritage. One wing of the museum is reserved for temporary exhibitions.

If you only do one thing in Kota Bharu then visit the **Gelanggang Seni** (*open Mon 3.30–5.30, Wed and Sat 3.30–5.30 and 9pm–12 midnight*), a cultural centre on Jalan Mahmud which showcases a range of traditional Kelantanese pastimes. It is not the usual hammy cultural display, but rather a relaxed series of demonstrations. The atmosphere is congenial and visitors can either get involved themselves or just stand by and watch. Demonstrations – most of which overlap – include *pencak silat* (the Malay art of self defence, usually performed by two boys – with drums, gongs and Indian oboes setting the tempo, the performance is more of a dance routine than combat); *wayang* *kulit* (shadow puppet plays); *sepak raga* (Malay football: a version of keepy-uppy with a rattan ball; *see* 'Kampung Games', p.51); kite-flying; top-spinning; traditional music and board games such as *congkak*.

Aside from taking a dose of Malay culture, the other major attractions in Kota Bharu are the two markets. During the day, **Central Market** is the hub of activities: housed in a three-storey octagonal building are a wet market, a fruit and vegetable market, a clothes and crafts market and a hawker centre. Climb to the second or third storey of the building and look over the balcony into the central well, where Kelantanese women sit among their radiant displays of fruit and vegetables. It's a godsend for photographers: a skylight in the roof sends a diffuse yellow light over the scene below, enriching all the colours.

Late in the afternoon, attention moves from Central Market to the large car park opposite the bus station on Jalan Padang Garong. Within half an hour the space is transformed into Kota Bharu's nightly *pasar malam*. This night market is dominated by food stalls (*see* 'Eating Out', p.227) and is as hugely popular with local families: feasting at the stalls is cheap and tables are laid out for those who want to linger over dinner.

Elsewhere in Kelantan

Kelantan emerged out of relative isolation when the East-West Highway was completed in the 1990s. This road cuts across the peninsula's mountainous spine, linking Kota Bharu with the west coast and bypassing the attractive Temengor Lake, a huge reservoir which spreads its fingers deep into the surrounding rainforest. Many visitors pass through Kelantan with other destinations in mind, namely Thailand and the Perhentian Islands (*see* p.237): the Thai border town of Tak Bai is just a taxi- or bus-ride from Kota Bharu, while Kelantan's state capital is also the best place to book a trip to the Perhentians (Kota Bharu is the nearest major town to Kuala Besut, departure point for ferries to the islands). However, the state has several other diversions to offer visitors with time on their hands.

Thai Temples

Hop across the river from Kota Bharu, and you know the border with Thailand cannot be far away: *wats*, or Thai temples, punctuate the roadside, as do packs of mangy dogs – a common sight in Thailand, not so in Malaysia. In the compound of **Wat Phothivihan** is a reclining buddha which locals claim to be the largest in Southeast Asia. The monstrous 41-metre statue, sheltered by a makeshift hangar, draws thousands of Thai pilgrims each year, particularly during festivals such as the Day of Vesak (held on the full moon in May). Other festivals fall in November and April.

Several kilometres away at **Wat Phikulthong** is another impressive buddha, this one 15 metres high and decorated with tiny mosaic tiles. Next door at **Wat Cheng Buddhavas** are seven little shrines, one for every day of the week, each with a buddha striking a different pose. In the centre of this peaceful compound, among the chickens and wandering dogs, is a beautiful temple from the 1940s shaded by trees and climbing plants. All can be reached by taxi from Kota Bharu for no more than RM10.

Beaches

On the coastline north of Kota Bharu are a string of sandy beaches backed by windswept coconut groves (in fact, one long beach extends virtually unbroken along the length of Malaysia's east coast). Fisherman in these parts take great pride in their brightly coloured *perahu* (small high-prowed fishing boats), which they paint with mythological figures, geometric or floral designs. On **Pantai Dasar Sabak** fleets of *perahu* can be seen beached high on the sand once the catch has been landed in the late afternoon. Pantai Dasar Sabak was where the invading Japanese forces first set foot in Malaya during World War II.

North of here is a beach popular with weekenders from Kota Bharu. It was known for years as Pantai Cinta Berahi (Beach of Passionate Love) until the ruling PAS found a less titillating alternative that would fit the same acronym: they came up with **Pantai Cahaya Bulan**, or Moonlight Beach.

The Interior

One foolproof way to get a taste of rural Kelantan is from the windows of an air-conditioned carriage: the old Jungle Railway (*see* p.280) runs from Tumpat, just outside Kota Bharu, to Gemas in Negeri Sembilan, a mammoth cross-country route that serves as the transport artery for the interior. It is a fascinating journey, though most tourists only make stops at Kuala Lipis and Jerantut (gateway to the Taman Negara).

One of the stops on the Kelantan stretch of the line is **Gua Musang**, a boom town full of Chinese merchants cutting deals on timber – not exactly characteristic of Kelantan, 'cradle of Malay culture'. The key interest here is the cave of Gua Musang itself, inside which archaeologists discovered evidence of human habitation as far back as 5,000 years ago. The train line passes within a few hundred metres of the precipitous cave opening. Keen cavers will have no problems hiring a guide in town for a tour of the main cavern.

Another possible stop along the train line is Dabong, gateway to the **Jelawang Forest Reserve**. This little-known patch of primary forest, limestone caves, hills and waterfalls nestles up against the northwest corner of the Taman Negara. Wild boar and elephant trails provide routes for trekking or climbing a seven-tier waterfall (tallest in Southeast Asia, so they say). There is also a Rafflesia and orchid flower trail. Activities include bamboo rafting and a canopy walkway. Tours of the Jelawang Reserve are generally arranged by agents in Kota Bharu; KB Backpackers Lodge (*see* 'Where to Stay', p.227) organize extensive three-day packages.

Terengganu

14

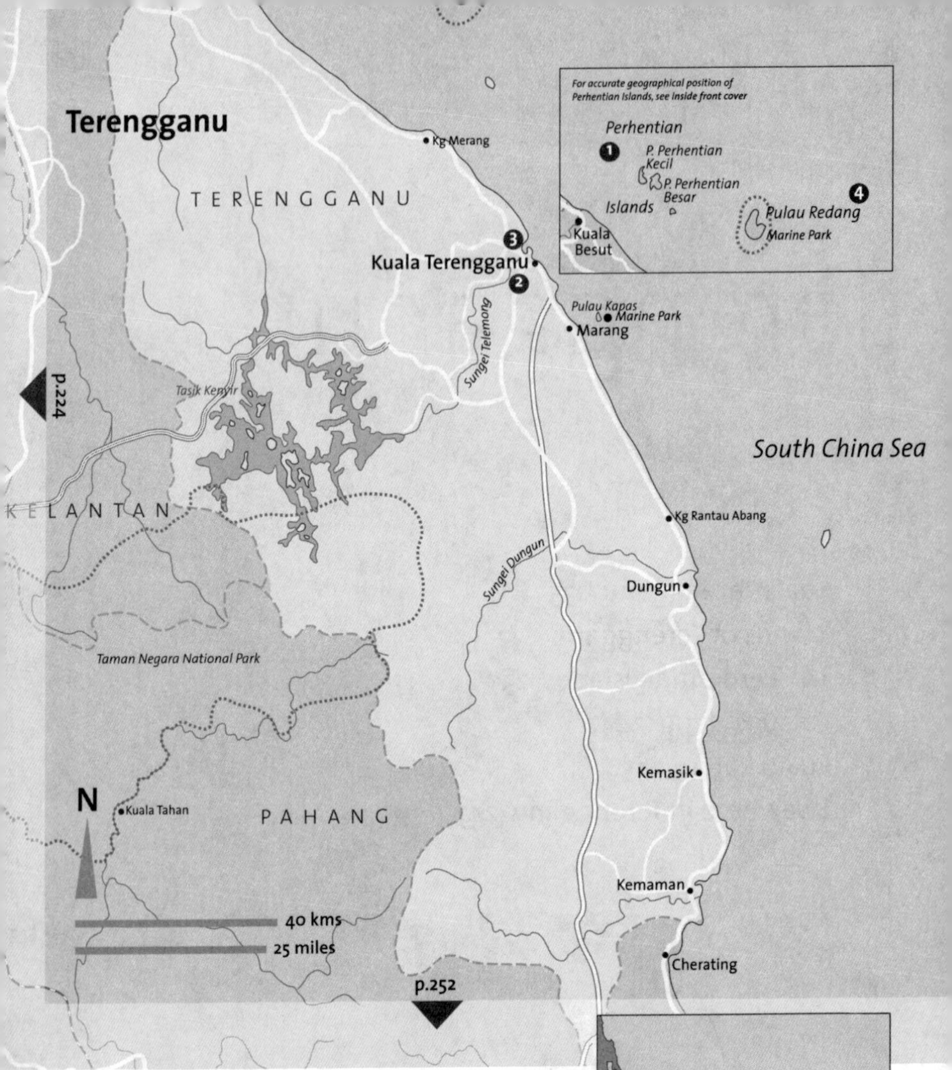

Highlights

1 Picture-postcard beaches and fantastic snorkelling on the Perhentian Islands

2 Kuala Terengganu – home to a thriving cottage industry in Malay crafts

3 Muzium Terengganu – one of Malaysia's best museum complexes, in a tranquil riverside setting

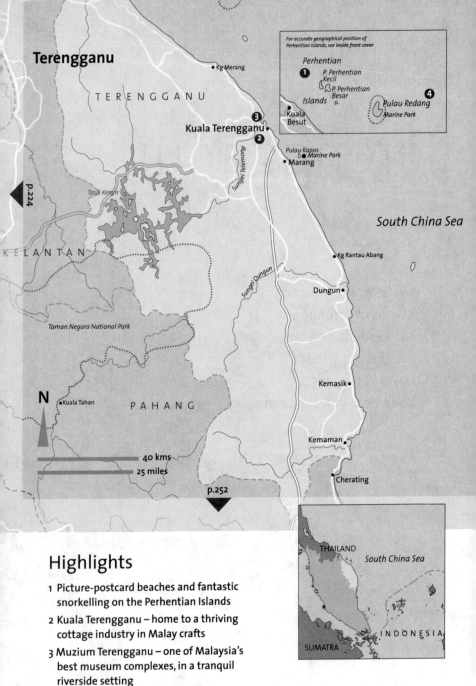

4 Pulau Redang, for dazzling marine life away from the backpacker trail

Terengganu prides itself on being the place where Islam first touched Malay shores. And they have an inscribed stone to prove it: even before Melaka had established itself as the peninsula's first Malay kingdom, the Terengganu Stone (*see* 'Muzium Terengganu') was spelling out the tenets of *syariah* (Islamic law) to the people of the east coast. *Terenggani* is a Tamil word meaning 'hilly country': the region was named many centuries ago by Indian traders, though the Malays have any number of dubious legends which claim Malay origins for the name.

Like Kelantan, the vast majority of Terengganu's modern-day population is Malay, and like Kelantan, Terengganu is a state full of artisans: among the sleepy coastal kampungs that are Terengganu's enduring image, can be found *songket* and *mengkuang* weavers, batik painters, white-brass beaters, *keris*-makers, boat-builders and woodcarvers, each plying their ancient trades.

The discovery of oil in the 1970s, 200km off Terengganu's shore, wooed some of the state's workforce with the promise of a quick fortune. To some degree, this changed the face of Terengganu (wealth is visible in the main towns, while a string of refineries blights the southern stretch of Terengganu's coastline), but with most of the new revenue contributing to the federal pot, the old ways of life have lived on. Fishing remains the state's primary earner and beautiful little fishing *perahus* with their brightly painted woodwork can be seen beached and moored along the full 200km length of Terengganu's coastline – which, incidentally, is one long sandy beach.

For most visitors, however, the lure of Terengganu are its islands. The Perhentians and Pulau Redang are two of Malaysia's most beautiful island getaways, each sporting talcum-powder beaches and coral-rich waters.

Kuala Terengganu

You would be forgiven for not knowing it today, but Kuala Terengganu was once one of the great trading ports of the Malay Peninsula. The riverine town made its first appearance on a 2nd-century map penned by Greek geographer and astronomer Ptolemy, and is known to have served as a minor entrepôt for many centuries since.

When 'black gold' was found off the state's coastline in the 1970s, Kuala Terengganu was little more than a glorifed fishing village and market town. As is the case with all Malay towns, Kuala Terengganu developed as a collection of close-knit kampungs: 'Malay town' is really a kind of oxymoron. Despite its new-found wealth, there is an air of affluence to modern-day Kuala Terengganu that comes as some surpise; high-rise buildings dominate the commercial quarter, while flash 4X4s roll about well-kept streets lined with flowers (some of them potted in the hulls of miniature fishing boats).

Despite the oil wealth, the old town feels as traditional as ever, with the stilted back ends of shophouses extending over the slow-flowing waters of the estuary, and stallholders cluttering the narrow streets around the central market. Like Kota Bharu, the vast majority of inhabitants are Malay, though an attractive Chinatown, aptly known as Kampung Cina, is one of the features of the waterfront.

Getting There

MAS run **flights** from all major Peninsular cities to the Sultan Mahmud airport 15km north of town. The long-distance **bus** station is at Medan Selera on the northern outskirts of town. The central bus station on Jalan Masjid Abidin serves destinations within Terengganu. The primary **taxi** stand is next to the central bus station; long-distance rates are competitive.

Information

Tourist Information Centre, Jalan Sultan Zainal Abidin, **t** 09 622 1553. Open Sat–Thurs 8–5. The Ping Anchorage Travellers' Homestay (*see* Where to Stay) has an attached travel agent with lots of good no-obligation information about the state.

Where to Stay

Expensive–Moderate

Primula Park Royal, Jalan Persinggahan, **t** 09 622 2100, **f** 09 623 3360, *primula@tm.net.my*, *www.primulaparkroyal.com*. This is Kuala Terengganu's top spot, situated on a blustery beach about a kilometre south of town. There are all the usual 4-star facilities, including a decent outdoor pool set among casuarinas, and three restaurants. Look out for promotional rates – sometimes below RM100.

Hotel Grand Continental, Jalan Sultan Zainal Abidin, **t** 09 625 1888, **f** 09 625 1999, *hgckt@pd.jaring.my*, *www.grandcontinental.com.my*. The cheaper of two international-class hotels in Kuala Terengganu. Grand lobby, spacious rooms, a range of food outlets and an outdoor pool.

Moderate

Hotel YT Midtown, Jalan Tok Lam, **t** 09 623 5288, **f** 09 623 4399, *ythotel@po.jaring.my*. Probably Kuala Terengganu's best mid-range choice, situated in the centre of town with a good range of facilities, including cable TV, safe and 24-hour room service.

Hotel Seri Malaysia, Jalan Hiliran, **t** 09 623 6454, **f** 09 623 8344, *www.serimalaysia.com.my*. Well placed on the river, and central, but a little stark in feel, as is the case with all the hotels in this chain. Rooms are comfortable with the full range of facilities. Frequent promotions make this hotel good value.

Seri Indah Resort, 898 Jalan Haji Busu, Batu Burok, **t** 09 622 2633, **f** 09 624 8548. An incongruous little hotel on Burok beach a few kilometres south of town. The style is Mediterranean and there's a curvy pool among palms. Rooms are all en suite, with fridge, TV, phone and kettle.

Inexpensive

Hotel Seri Hoover, 49 Jalan Sultan Ismail, **t** 09 623 3833, **f** 09 622 5975. Reasonable value hotel block with functional rooms, some of which have tiled bathrooms with hot showers and large baths. Rooms all have air conditioning, TV, phone, fridge and kettle.

Traditional craftmanship is still very much a way of life here. If they are not fishermen, locals are likely to be skilled craftsmen of one sort or another. One of the city's best-known products is white brass, a combination of yellow brass and zinc that is unique to Terengganu. The outskirts of town, particularly around Kampung Ladang, are dotted with brassware, batik and *mengkuang*-weaving workshops, while Pulau Duyong, an island in the estuary, is well known as a traditional boat-builders' yard.

Running south from Kuala Terengganu is Pantai Batu Buruk, a coconut- and casuarina-fringed beach popular with locals at weekends. Colourful kite stalls and food stalls line the beach at intervals.

Seaview Hotel, 18 Jalan Masjid Abidin, **t** 09 63322 1911, **f** 09 622 3048. This hotel overlooks Istana Maziah and the lighthouse on Bukit Puteri. Rooms are plain, but in good nick with air conditioning and attached bathrooms.

Budget

Awi's Yellow House, Pulau Duyong, **t** 09 624 5046. A unique guesthouse in the heart of the boat-building village on Pulau Duyong. Boat-builder Awi has put his carpentry skills to use on six or seven *attap*-thatched huts linked by walkways on stilts over the river. It is a cool, airy setup with pot plants and flowers draped all over the place. Amenities are basic (none of the huts have fans and the attached toilet consists of a hole in the floor above the river) but nights are wonderfully cool, with a gentle breeze generated by the flowing river. A functional kitchen, with gas supply and wok is available for use. Popular with writers, artists and long-termers.

Ping Anchorage Travellers' Homestay, 77A Jalan Dato Saacs, **t** 09 626 2020, **f** 09 622 8093. A crisp, clean, unadorned place with a roof terrace. Rooms are fan only. The attached travel agent provides lots of good information on Terengganu (no obligaton).

Eating Out

The best places to eat in Kuala Terengganu are the **food stalls**, which can be found all about town. As elsewhere along Malaysia's east coast, *ikan bakar* (barbecued fish, literally 'burnt fish') is something that every visitor should try; after all, Kuala Terengganu was little more than a large fishing village until oil was found off its shores in recent decades. Another local favourite is *keropok lekor*, strips of deep-fried strips of sago mixed with minced fish and served with a sweet-chilli dip, which locals devour as snack food at any time of day. The local breakfast speciality is *nasi dagang*, glutinous rice served with tuna fish curry in a coconut sauce. Local desserts are tasty too. *Buah gomok* are sweet balls of dough made from glutinous rice flour, coconut shavings and a sweet syrup derived from the flowering stalks of the coconut palm, while *bronok*, made from sago and a sugar solution, has the appearance and consistency of Turkish delight.

The best **hawker centre** can be found in Chinatown, on Jalan Kampung Tiong behind Jalan Bandar, with stalls arranged by cuisine. Nearby, the **Golden Dragon** (Jalan Bandar) serves excellent Chinese food at around RM6/dish. South of here, on Jalan Kuala Hiliran, is a good South Indian banana-leaf restaurant, known as **Restoran Kari Asha**, while the **kedai kopi** next to the Seaview Hotel is one of the town's most popular spots for *roti canai* and other Malay staples. Every Friday the **night market** on Pulau Duyong, beside the road bridge, is a good place to sample local specialities. For Western food try **Chef's Steakhouse**, 28 Jalan Tok Lam, a themed place that often has good promotions. If you pass by the Hotel Grand Continental, stop by at the **Jala Mas Coffee House** for jackfruit pie and fruit punch (*RM6*).

The Old Town

Kampung Cina is the heart of the old town and the architectural highlight: a great fire in 1880 levelled the *attap*-roofed houses of the Malays, and in their place the small Chinese community built the elegant banana-bend of 19th-century shophouses that line Jalan Bandar. These heritage shophouses – complete with hand-painted chick blinds, louvred windows and original tilework – are under constant threat from contractors (though having survived the initial spree of oil-injected development, the street's chances don't look too bad). The rear ends of these shophouses extend on stilts over the river: traditionally, goods would have been delivered by boat.

At the northern end of Jalan Bandar is the **Pasar Besar** (Big Market), the soul of Kuala Terengganu. This two-storey building comes alive at dawn when local fishing boats deliver their catch (most of which is beached a few kilometres south at Chendering). Fruit stalls cluster around the base of the market building, while the first floor is packed with local handicraft stalls: batik, *songket*, brassware and *pandan*-woven mats and bags predominate.

Behind the market is one of the town's few historical sights, the ruins of an old fort on **Bukit Puteri** (Hill of the Princess). Ignore the plaque at the base of the hill – and all the tourist literature – which claims the little hillock stands 200m tall: it's barely 20m. The fort was built in the early 19th century using bricks, honey, lime mortar and eggs (which sounds more like a recipe for the Gingerbread House). Near the ruins is the Big Bell of Bukit Puteri, which for centuries was used to rally locals around the Sultan's palace at times of crisis; the present 175kg bell was installed in 1908. Istana Maziah, the official residence of the present Sultan, sits at the foot of the hill.

Pulau Duyong

One place unscathed by recent development is Pulau Duyong, an islet in the estuary directly opposite the old town. Traditional Malay houses are scattered among coconut and banana palms and boat-builders' yards. Over the years the island has supplied whole fleets of fishing boats for communities along the east coast. Boats are crafted from a local ironwood. The methods, though painstaking, have won some of the craftsmen wide renown: commissions come in from round the world. The boats are built without the use of plans and without nails, which are associated with coffins and death. Ironwood pegs are used instead. It takes a team of six approximately one year to craft a 40ft deep-sea fishing boat.

The best way to reach the island is by ferry (*10mins/50 sen*) from the jetty near the Pasar Besar, or from the jetty further south next to Hotel Seri Malaysia. Since the road bridge was completed in 1990, it is also possible to catch a bus (No. 16 or 20) to Pulau Duyong. Every Friday night there's an excellent little *pasar malam* near the road bridge on Pulau Duyong, where you can try all the local specialities. Large quantities of fruit, clothing and sundry items also change hands. One of the island's draws is the delightful flower-decked guesthouse known as Awi's Yellow House (*see* p.235), where many guests become long-termers. Next to the guesthouse, Awi's brother (a boat-builder) runs a little craftshop full of miniature yachts and fishing boats – all exact replicas, down to the wooden pegs that replace nails. He has built a number of models for visiting dignitaries.

Muzium Terengganu

Visitors to Kuala Terengganu should not miss the **Muzium Terengganu** (*Bukit Losong,* ***t*** *09 622 1444; open Sat–Thurs 9–5; adm adults RM5, children RM2*), which claims to be Malaysia's largest museum, sprawling over some 27 hectares and with buildings of awesome size. The complex, which took ten years to complete (1984–94), is situated on the river at Kampung Losong, a few kilometres west of town. The architecture is based on the traditional Terengganu *rumah,* with sloping three-tiered roofs and intricate carvings on the eaves and fascias inspired by local flora and Islamic motifs. The sheer scale of the main building means that much of it is constructed from modern-day building materials rather than timber (the 'carved' panels are made from glass-reinforced concrete, as are the 16 'stilts' which support the building), but the effect is nonetheless impressive. The connecting buildings follow the metaphor of the extended family (when the son marries, he builds a house for his new family nextdoor to his parents' home). The museum and grounds are eerily quiet most of the time: although foreign visitors will certainly be impressed, locals keep away, believing the museum to be another case of showy oil money ill-advisedly spent by the state government.

In the first room is the famous Batu Bersurat (Inscribed Stone, otherwise known as Terengganu Stone), found at Kuala Berang in 1887 and dated to 702 Hijrah (1303 CE). This is the earliest confirmed evidence of Islam in Malaysia. The inscription on the stone proclaims Islam as the state religion of Terengganu and lists some of the dire consequences of straying from the path. Take adultery as an extreme example: offenders were buried to their waists and stoned to death.

The most comprehensive collection is found in the Textile Gallery, with exhibits on the process and development of weaving. *Songket*, *limar*, *pelangi*, *cindai*, *gerus* and *telepuk* fabrics are all featured, as is batik. The work that goes into weaving these pieces is painstaking. *Telepuk* fabrics are polished with cowrie shells before being stamped with gold dust, while *cindai*, used in traditional medicine (the fabric was often used to dress wounds), has for centuries been the most sought-after fabric in these parts – the process of tying and dying one piece takes almost a year.

The Craft Gallery is also worth some time, particularly for its woodwork displays. Beautiful boat-shaped *congkak* boards (*see* 'Kampung Games', p.51), coconut scrapers carved into the form of dragons or tigers, Koran lecterns, and a range of spinning tops, showcase the ancient skills of the East Coast woodcarvers.

Elsewhere there's a not-so-appealing Royal Gallery, a Natural History Gallery (full of grimacing, poorly stuffed birds and animals), a Contemporary Arts Gallery and the inevitable Pertroleum Gallery. Outside, attractive landscaped gardens border a gentle stretch of the Sungai Terengganu, with a couple of small fishing and seafaring galleries and a collection of traditional fishing boats, their bowsprits beautifully decorated in vivid floral motifs. The wonderfully preserved **Istana Tengku Nik** has also been resited to these gardens.

Islands of Terengganu

The Perhentian Islands

The Perhentians' growing reputation as an unspoilt island paradise is beginning to take its toll. Stretch out in the shade of a coconut palm for an afternoon nap, and your slumbers will likely be disturbed by hammering workmen. Every year more chalets are thrown up to meet demand, and every year, in peak season, the islands reach their

Getting There

Most people set off for the Perhentians from Kota Bharu in Kelantan. Others start from Kuala Terengganu. Either way, you need to get to Kuala Besut, a tiny village on the coast in between the two state capitals. It is possible to get to Kuala Besut by bus, but most hire a taxi to save time (from Kota Bharu the taxi – approximately RM25 split between the passengers – takes one hour, the bus two and a half). It is a lovely journey through idyllic kampungs, orchards and coconut plantations. A number of ferry companies operate from Kuala Besut, and bookings can be made either in Kota Bharu or Kuala Terengganu. The slow boat (an old fishing boat) chugs out to the islands in one and a half hours (RM20), while the speed boat (RM30) does the journey in 45mins. Ferries will drop passengers at whichever beach they choose. KBB Holidays (Jalan Padang Garong, Kota Bharu, **t** 09 743 2125, **f** 09 743 0887, *www.kb-backpackers.com.my*) are reputable agents.

Getting Around

For those who don't mind trekking through the jungle, trails lead between most of the bays. Otherwise, taxi-boats are the way to get around. Canoes can also be hired from a number of the resorts and chalet operations.

Dive Operations

Diving is cheap and popular on the Perhentians. There are dozens of dive schools on both islands. All of them offer a range of diving options, including the 4–5 day PADI Open-Water course, which is usually on offer for RM750. **Steffen Sea Sports Malaysia**, Flora Bay (next to Everfresh Chalets), **t** 019 213 8350, *enquiry@steffenseasports.com*, claims to be the first dive operation on the Perhentians and offers the cheapest rates (RM600 for the open-water course; RM110 for two dives inclusive of all the gear). **Flora Bay Divers**, **t** 09 697 7266, **f** 09 697 7267, *www.florabaydivers.com*, is the biggest dive operation on Flora Bay. On Perhentian Besar's main beach, **Seahorse Dive School**, **t** 019 962 4017, comes recommended as a great place to learn. Further up the beach is a more upmarket option, **Watercolours Dive Centre**, **t** 019 981 1852, **f** 09 691 0019, *www.watercoloursworld.com*. Another good bet is **Turtle Bay Divers**, which has a school on Perhentian Besar (**t** 019 913 6647), or on Long Beach, Perhentian Kecil (**t** 019 333 6647), *www.turtlebaydivers.com*). As well as dive sites around the Perhentians, this oufit also offers trips to even better dive sites at Pulau Redang and Lang Tengah.

Where to Stay

Note that most chalet operations close for the monsoon (approximately Nov–March); contact the individual resorts for exact dates.

Perhentian Besar

Expensive

Perhentian Island Resort, Teluk Pauh, **t** 09 697 7775, **f** 09 697 7199, *pir@po.jaring.my*,

capacity, leaving late-comers no option but a night beneath the stars. Those who visited Perhentian Besar or Perhentian Kecil (as the two islands are known) in the early 1990s, will have a very different experience if they visit again today, with the high turnover of backpackers and the constant whir of outboards.

Even so, with no infrastructure to talk of, and with only one tiny village of permanent inhabitants, these islands are not far off the mark of the tropical idyll. Only the main beaches – soft, coral-white stretches of sand – are backed by chalet operations, leaving much of the Perhentians in their untouched state, while the coral gardens which fringe the shores are among the world's richest.

Ten thousand years ago, at the end of the last Ice Age, the Perhentians were part of the Southeast Asian landmass (with so much water locked up in glaciers, sea levels *www.perhentianresort.com.my*. This is the Perhentians' top resort, and the only place with a swimming pool – though the crystal-clear waters of Teluk Pauh make the pool seem a little redundant. The resort sits on a long and immaculate curve of beach, with traditional-style timber chalets set back among lawns and paved footpaths. There are the expected diving facilities and tennis courts too.

Expensive–Moderate

Coral View Island Resort, Main Beach, **t/f** 09 697 4943. Situated next door to the Perhentian Island Resort, on either side of the rocky headland at the northwest tip of Pulau Besar, with plenty of beach and nearby coral. A popular resort-style hotel, with upmarket chalets ranging from RM100-500. There is a laid-back family atmosphere to the place. It offers the usual diving and snorkelling options, plus fishing, canoeing, turtle-watching and jungle trekking.

Moderate–Inexpensive

Mama's Chalets, Main Beach, **t** 010 984 0232. Solid chalets beneath coconut palms on the main stretch of beach (at this point the beach is a beautiful, though narrow, strip of sand in the shade of leaning palms). Chalets are roomy and all have en suite facilities.

Paradise Resort, Main Beach, **t** 010 981 0930. Chalets beneath the palms, along the same lines of Mama's next door. Eight of the chalets have sea views; the remaining 25 are set back in the main garden compound.

Flora Bay Resort, Flora Bay, **t** 09 697 7266, **f** 09 697 7267, *www.florabayresort.com*. Quite a smart chalet complex with a range of accommodation from large family bungalows to basic chalets. It is a slick operation with friendly staff and the usual diving activities on offer. The management have a second (budget) complex further along the bay, known as **Flora II**.

Inexpensive

Abdul's Chalets, Main Beach, **t** 09 697 7058/ 010 983 7303. Simple, solid chalets in great condition – the best-value accommodation of Pulau Besar. All chalets have en suite showers and a balcony. The chalets are a little tightly packed, but they overlook a nice spot right at the southern end of the main beach. More popular with families and couples than backpackers.

Everfresh Beach Resort, Flora Bay, **t/f** 09 697 7620. Tranquil chalet complex at the western end of Flora Bay, with hammocks slung between casuarina trees and a decent choice of food in the restaurant. Family and standard chalets, and A-frames available.

Fauna Beach Chalet, Flora Bay, **t** 09 985 6843, **f** 09 697 7507. Chalets in a garden setting midway along the bay. All rooms are fan-only and have an attached bathroom.

Samudra Beach Chalets, Flora Bay, **t** 010 983 4929. Decent chalets set right on the beach, with large balconies from which to enjoy the view. All have en suite bathrooms.

Budget

Seahorse Chalets, Main Beach, **t** 019 962 4017. The cheapest place to stay on Pulau Besar,

were then much lower). As the Perhentians made the transition from mainland to island, the rainforest which cloaked them evolved undisturbed, and many of the plant and animal species found on the peninsula live on in the Perhentians to this day. The belief that the islands support a diverse array of species – including more than 800 orchids and several hundred mammals – has prompted a joint British-Malaysian project to research this pristine habitat. With a little luck, the Perhentians and their reefs will be targeted as a site for high-grade conservation, and plans for large-scale development will be nipped in the bud.

People visit the Perhentians mainly to dive and to snorkel. The clear turquoise water, the density of marine life and the easily accessible coral gardens make this a great place to learn (diving here is cheap, too). Turtles cruise the reefs, as do large fish such with an encampment of A-frames in a compound behind the dive school. A good alternative to staying in budget accommodation on Long Beach.

Wanderer's Inn, Flora Bay (no phone). A simple compound of budget A-frames with communal facilities. Laid-back, friendly atmosphere.

Perhentian Kecil

Moderate

Impiani Tropical Resort, Pasir Petani, **t** 010 934 0500. The most upmarket place to stay on Perhentian Kecil, though if you want to spend the money, facilities are better at similar-priced resorts on Perhentian Besar. Chalets have air conditioning and attached bathrooms. The beach here is wonderful and secluded.

Moderate–Budget

D'Lagoon, Teluk Kerma, **t** 010 985 7089/012, *erine@tm.net.my*. The only place to stay at secluded Teluk Kerma bay on the northeast tip of Perhentian Kecil. It is an idyllic getaway with bungalows, A-frames, a tree house and a longhouse. One of the main attractions is the huge coral garden just off the beach in the tranquil waters of Teluk Kerma. The accommodation is fairly rustic, though it will suit a range of budgets: the longhouse serves as a dorm for backpackers, while two of the bungalows are air-conditioned and go for RM100. D'Lagoon offers packages inclusive of food and snorkelling trips.

Petani Beach Chalet, Pasir Petani, (no phone at time of writing: check with tourist board). The cheaper of two places on this idyllic beach at the southern end of Perhentian Kecil. Chalets are set on the beach and in gardens behind; there are two 'deluxe' chalets and ten standard chalets for RM80 and RM60 respectively. Facilities are basic; there is an artificial well for water and a generator for electricity. The downside of staying on this beach is a reliance on water taxis.

Inexpensive–Budget

Moonlight Chalets, Long Beach, **t** 09 697 7603. Wooden chalets and A-frames inclined on a steep hillside at the northern end of Long Beach. There is a sprawling café, active day and night, and a buzzing feel to the place, though most of the rooms have seen better days.

Panorama Chalets, Long Beach, **t** 010 912 2518. This operation is set well back from the beach, with chalets inclined on a hillside among trees. Offers a bit more peace and quiet than some of the Long Beach options and the chalets are reasonably well-kept.

Matahari Chalet, Long Beach, **t** 09 956 826/ 019 956 5756. Matahari's was once the only accommodation available on Long Beach and it remains popular today, with large and well-spaced chalets and a decent restaurant. The chalets are spartan and some of them seem a little overpriced.

Butterfly Resort, Coral Bay, **t** 09 697 7603. Among the rooms on offer are a couple of

as the colourful Napoleon wrasse, the harmless black-tip reef shark, rays, groupers, barracudas and the bump-head parrotfish, which bites off tennis-ball-sized lumps of coral with industrial-strength incisors. Unfortunately, the constant activity of motorboats and swimmers has laid waste to coral stands off the main beaches.

The monsoon hits these islands with ferocity between November and early February. Most of the ferry services and chalet operations close down during these months. The best time to visit is just after the monsoon, when water visibility is at its peak (the rough weather cleanses the seas).

brightly coloured chalets set on rocks above the sea at the southern end of Coral Bay. Good value if you can secure one of these.

Budget

Mira Chalets, Mira Beach, **t** 019 964 0582. This tiny operation has been going since 1984, when the islands were virtually untouched, and it hasn't changed a jot since: this is the place to come for the real Crusoe experience. It is set on its own on the west coast of Perhentian Kecil, half an hour south of Coral bay by foot (through virgin jungle). The 'Mira' sign is made out of driftwood, as are some of the chalets (there are five or six), none of which have electricity or running water; evenings are illuminated by candlelight, and bathing involves drawing water from a well. The setup is run by a warm-hearted family, who live on site. Mira's wife cooks for guests each evening.

Simfony Chalets, Long Beach, **t** 013 743 2691. Rustic A-frames packed in tight at angles around sandy pathways. There is a pleasant atmosphere to the place – if you don't mind being close to your neighbours. One of the few places where you can change money (thought at a poor rate).

RGR Guesthouse (no phone). Quaintly dilapidated chalets set on the rocky hillside at the southern end of the beach. Very cheap, and popular with hardened backpackers.

Aur Beach Resort, Coral Bay, **t** 019 963 0391. A mini-village of basic chalets stretching back from the beach. All chalets have en suite facilities and are better kept than those at DJ's next door.

Eating Out

Isolated as the Perhentians are, the only places to eat are generally the restaurants attached to chalet operations (it is perfectly acceptable to eat somewhere other than where you are staying). Most of them serve a limited menu of Malay rice and noodle favourites, though fresh seafood is often available.

On Perhentian Besar, **Coral View Island Resort** has the best choice of food. Several open-air restaurants here serve a mix of Malay, Thai and Western dishes to cater for a variety of budgets (the claypot dishes are very good value). **The Perhentian Café** (between Coral View and the Paradise Resort) is a popular Chinese restaurant, with delicious seafood dishes for RM15 and upwards. The restaurant attached to **Abdul's Chalets** is a good, cheap place to eat; the set barbecue each night, with fresh fish and seafood, sells for RM12. Tiny **Café Kita**, just up from Abdul's is a great place for breakfast; they serve drinks, pancakes and *roti cani*.

On Flora Bay, the **Everfresh Beach Resort** restaurant has a comparatively extensive menu of standard Malay and Chinese dishes, all at budget prices. The bar at **Moonlight Chalets** on Long Beach, Perhentian Kecil, is a popular spot for a drink or a snack. The other restaurants on Long Beach are all much of a muchness.

Perhentian Besar

The convex stretch of sand on the west side of Perhentian Besar, or Large Island, is where the the greatest concentration of accommodation is found. It is a pleasant spot, even by Perhentian standards, with coconut palms leaning over a narrow strip of sand (which widens as you move south). A small rocky headland separates this beach from **Teluk Pauh**, a north-facing curve of sand, immaculate in its formation. The waters around the headland are stacked with coral, while the bay of Teluk Pauh itself is known to divers as **Turtle Point** – both the hawksbill turtle and the larger green turtle (which can weigh as much as 400kg) are present in large numbers around both islands.

Tiga Ruang (Three Bays) is another good site for spotting turtles. It lies round a series of headlands to the east of Teluk Pauh and is in many ways the highlight of the Perhentians. In the shallow, sandy waters of these secluded bays are some beautiful coral formations, particularly on the east side. The larger pieces of table coral found here are thought to be over 1,000 years old. The best way to explore Tiga Ruang is to hire a canoe from one of the resorts and, weather permitting, set off round the headland with a mask and snorkel as ballast. Care should be taken on the beaches of Tiga Ruang between May and September, when turtles come ashore to lay their eggs.

Flora Bay is the only other stretch of sand on Perhentian Besar that is developed. This long, textbook beach, deep-set within its bay, is lined with well-spaced chalet operations and a handful of dive schools. Though the beach's seclusion is a definite attraction, water visibility is not so good in the bay itself, which is more open to the elements than other areas of the island. Most people arrive here by boat, but there is a jungle trail that links Flora Bay with Big Island's main beach: head south beyond Abdul's Chalets and past two jetties until you reach a little fishermen's café. The trail leads inland from the café and up a steep ridge; allow 30mins to reach Flora Bay from the café.

Near the tongue of rocky headland which separates Flora Bay from Perhentian Besar's main beach is **Shark Point**. This is one of the popular dive sites and, as the name would suggest, is a cruising ground for sharks (though don't take dive-site names too literally: given patience, you are likely to spot both turtles and sharks – of the harmless variety – wherever you dive or snorkel).

Perhentian Kecil

Perhentian Kecil (pronounced *kay-cheel*, meaning 'small') was once the quieter of the two islands, with just a few makeshift chalets serving the backpacker scene. In recent years this scene has grown, as the islands secure their place on the Singapore-Bangkok backpacker trail. In many ways, the Perhentians have evolved as an antidote to the Thai islands further north: there is no party scene here. After all, this is Muslim Terengganu. Alcohol is available, but you have to dig around for it and prices are comparatively high.

Most backpackers disembark at **Long Beach** – wide and picture-perfect if you ignore the peak-season crowds. Sunbathers, volleyball nets, cafés, dive schools and chalet operations line the beach. Behind all this, piles of refuse lie festering in the undergrowth: an indictment to over-hasty development. Giant monitor lizards – some in excess of two metres in length – pick at the rubbish, while overhead, huge spiders catch bluebottles in webs the size of bedsheets. Unfortunately for arachnophobes, the trail to **Coral Bay** passes right through this nightmarish feasting ground. A narrow neck of land separates the two bays.

South of Coral Bay, which is a smaller, west-facing version of Long Beach, a trail leads through the rainforest to **Mira Beach**, a tiny cove where, in 1984, the islands' first chalets were rented out to tourists. Mira Chalets (*see* Where to Stay) remains popular with those looking to fulfil their desert-island longings: there is no running water or electricity here, so guests must read by candlelight in the evenings, and draw water from a well before washing.

Another less well-beaten path leads from Mira Beach to beautiful, south-facing **Petani Beach**, where Small Island's only resort accommodation is found. The Perhentians' single **kampung**, a tiny, scruffy fishermen's village, is round the corner from Petani Beach on the southeast edge of Perhentian Kecil.

The best snorkelling off Perhentian Kecil is found in the 'lagoon' near the northeast tip of the island. The coral garden starts just off the beach and covers the entire bed of this sheltered bay.

Pulau Redang

The marine life around the shores of Pulau Redang is unrivalled among the accessible islands off Peninsular Malaysia. At 7km in length, Pulau Redang is the largest island in the Terengganu Marine Park, which includes Pulau Kapas, Lang Tengah and the Perhentian Islands 30km away. Redang's beaches are of fine, dazzling-white sand while the aquamarine shades of the South China Sea are equal to any vision of a tropical paradise, with water visibility frequently in excess of 30m.

Getting There

Berjaya Air (**t** 03 7846 8228, *www.berjaya-air.com*) have daily **flights** (45mins) to Pulau Redang from Kuala Lumpur and Singapore. Pulau Redang is also reached by high-speed motorboat from the small fishing village of Merang (45mins). All boats are operated by the resorts and charge RM80 return (the boat transfer is usually included in the package). The nearest airport is just outside Kuala Terengganu and the journey from here to Merang by taxi takes 35mins. Buses from major towns also service Merang.

Where to Stay & Eat

Virtually all accommodation on Redang is at resorts, most of which are geared up for Asian tourists – which means karaoke and en-masse arrivals. For the money you pay, rooms are pretty uninspiring, but the prices include transfers, snorkelling trips and all meals and non-alcoholic drinks. There are no restaurants on Redang other than those at the resorts; a full-board package is usually the only option.

Luxury–Expensive

Berjaya Redang Resort, **t** 09 697 3988, **f** 09 697 3899, *www.berjayaresorts.com*. This is by far the largest resort on Redang, with nearly 300 rooms and suites on offer. Most rooms are situated near the northern end of the island in blocks of double-decker chalets. Facilities include a large pool, a gym, non-motorized watersports and five bars and restaurants. There is a smaller offshoot of the Berjaya resort at Teluk Siang on the south side of the island, with 100 more chalets perched on a clifftop. The airstrip Berjaya recently built on the island caused uproar among conservationists and locals – environmentalists give this hotel a wide berth.

Coral Redang Island Resort, **t** 09 623 6200, **f** 09 623 6300, *www.coralredang.com.my*. Forty detached and semi-detached chalets, set among palms behind the beach. There is a restaurant, a beachside bar and a pool.

Laguna Redang Resort, **t** 09 631 0888, **f** 09 631 3322, *www.lagunaredang.com.my*. This resort opened in 2003 to compete with the Berjaya. There are over 200 rooms in oversize blocks described as a 'modern interpretation

In many ways this gives Pulau Redang the edge over the Perhentian Islands. However, the two destinations could hardly be more different. While the Perhentians are establishing their place on the backpacker trail, Pulau Redang is keeping visitor numbers down with high prices. This is a mixed blessing. Fewer visitors means less damage to the marine ecosystem, but exclusivity brings with it the damaging practices of resort hotels. In fact, the island is split down the middle both literally and ideologically: the resort hotels, which are popping up all along the island's east coast, are at odds with the conservationists, who have free rein of Redang's west coast.

The beaches on the northern and western flanks of Pulau Redang are important nesting grounds for marine turtles and are out-of-bounds to visitors. The Chagar Hutang Turtle Research Unit was established on one of the northern beaches in 1993 and conservation work is ongoing in partnership with charities such as Earthwatch. As research efforts gather momentum on the west coast, so does the spread of resort-style accommodation on the east: the Berjaya Resort recently built a 1.1km airstrip in the face of years of controversy.

Caught between the two factions are the islanders themselves, descendants of Bugis settlers who travelled here from Indonesian waters many centuries ago. They

of traditional Malay architecture'. The resort is big on karaoke.

Expensive

Redang Holiday Beach Villa, t 09 624 5500, **f** 09 624 5511, *www.redangholiday.com*. Situated at the northernmost end of Pasir Panjang, this is one of the best resort choices. The spacious chalets are built of local hardwoods and equipped with air con and hot water, with balconies and mezzanines complete with wicker furniture.

Redang Beach Resort, t 09 623 8188, **f** 09 623 0225, *www.redang.com.my*. Offers 120 rooms in newly built villa-style chalets just behind Pasir Panjang beach.

Redang Bay Resort, t 09 620 3200, **f** 09 624 2048, *sales@redangbay.com.my*, *www.redangbay.com.my*. More reasonable than some of the other resorts, though the economy block is stark. Facilities include canoes, karaoke and a smallish pool.

Redang Kalong Resort, t 09 622 3537, **f** 09 622 8186, *www.redangkalong.com*. The only resort-style accommodation on Teluk Kalong. Chalets are fairly basic for the price, though all have air conditioning.

Ayu Mayang Resort, t 09 622 0793, **f** 09 631 1370, *www.ayumayang.com*. This small resort has five family chalets and eight standards ones, all made from timber and designed to blend in with the surroundings (sand and lofty palms). The rates include full board and transfer to/from the airport.

Redang Lagoon Chalet, t 09 666 5020, **f** 09 666 5018, *www.redanglagoon.com*. Simple wooden chalet accommodation, most rooms with air conditioning and all with attached bathrooms. Set on a beautiful stretch of beach, with a volleyball net and dive shop. A more rustic experience.

Inexpensive

Redang Campsite, t 09 622 5552, **f** 09 622 0063, *redangcamp@yahoo.com*. Staying at the Redang Campsite on Teluk Kalong, south of Pasir Panjang, is the cheapest way of visiting Redang. You won't get the best night's sleep, but it is a secluded spot with some beautiful coral a little further up the bay.

In late March 2006 part of the campsite was demolished by the Land Office after wranglings over the licence. It remains to be seen whether or not the campsite will reopen.

settled first on Teluk Kalong on the east shore, then moved south to Pulau Pinang, one of the constellation of islets that forms the Redang archipelago. When the state government decided that the waters around Pulau Pinang would serve nicely as a marine park for snorkellers, the villagers were relocated to a stilt village on the main island's estuary. A decade or so later, the authorities decided to put the 2,000-strong community out of sight completely, relocating them into the interior of Pulau Redang – though the remnants of the stilt village remain.

The Marine Park is touted as the snorkelling highlight of a visit to Redang, though there are many finer spots off the main island. The Park is perpetually crowded with snorkellers, most of them thrashing about in livid red life jackets. Unfortunately the tour guides have a habit of feeding the fish; though this attracts shoals in large numbers it interferes with their natural feeding habits. One of the guides' favourite games is to make a show of feeding the baby sharks (for which the reef acts as a nursery), though teaching young sharks to associate humans with food can only be a bad thing.

The large reef off the main island, between Teluk Kalong and Pasir Panjang, is hugely superior as a place to snorkel. Enormous boulders of brain coral provide shelter for endless varieties of reef fish and soft corals, with cruising turtles in large supply. Some of the best dive sites are located around the islets off the east coast of Redang, each of which is surrounded by a pristine reef. Out here divers and snorkellers are more than likely to have the reef to themselves.

Pulau Kapas

Pulau Kapas is the most accessible island of the Terengganu Marine Park (which includes Redang and the Perhentians). Just 6km off the coast of Marang, there's little to do here but flap about in turquoise waters and walk the string of powdery beaches that line up along the 2km stretch of western shoreline. On the exposed east shore is nothing but crashing waves and a sea cave, which can be visited by chartering a boat.

Pulau Gemia is the tiny island across the channel of water to the north of Kapas. The island's beaches are nesting sites for green and olive ridley turtles. A shallow shelf of coral patrolled by giant bump-head parrotfish parrot fish and reef sharks stretches right across the channel, making it possible to swim between the islands. There are several other good snorkelling spots around Kapas and a couple of dive sites, including an offshore wreck, but visibility does not compare to Redang and the Perhentians.

Sometime in April or May the island hosts an annual squid fishing festival, during which representatives from each state set off for an evening of squid 'jiggling' (jiggle your rod up and down, so they say, and you catch more squid). At the end of the evening each catch is weighed and a winner is announced. Tourism Malaysia have pounced on the event, and it is now possible for tourists to join one of the crews for a small price.

Getting There

Marang is the jump-off point for Pulau Kapas. Any of the guesthouses in Marang will arrange boat transfers to the island, which should cost around RM30 return. A cluster of agents near Marang's main jetty also sell tickets throughout the day. There are no set timetables: boats leave when they have enough passengers.

Where to Stay

Expensive

Gem Island Resort, **t** 09 669 5910, **f** 09 669 5920, *enquiry@gemresorts.com*, *www.gemresorts.com*. The only resort on rocky Pulau Gemia, separated from Kapas by an 800m, coral-filled channel. Spacious wooden chalets, and larger double-storey villas, hug the rocks that fringe the island. All rooms feature hot-water showers, air-con, fridge and TV. The resort has its own restaurant and runs a turtle hatchery on one of the island's beaches (turtles hatch May–Oct).

Moderate

Tuty Puri Island Resort, **t** 09 624 6090, **f** 09 626 2106, *tutypuri@tancoresorts.com*. The classiest looking place on Pulau Kapas: attractive chalets are set in landscaped gardens, with an excellent open-sided restaurant (*see* Eating Out).

Kapas Island resort, **t** 09 631 6468, **f** 09 631 1469, *www.kapasislandresort.com*. The only place on Kapas with a (small) swimming pool. Malay-style chalets set in a grassy landscaped compound. Packages available (3 day/2 night) for RM299, including all food and snorkelling trips.

Moderate–Inexpensive

Beautisland Resort, **t** 09 624 5088. Set well back from the beach between Tuty Puri and the Kapas Island Resort. Plain chalets are set around a spacious compound, some with, some without air conditioning.

Inexpensive

Kapas Garden Resort, **t** 010 984 1686. The bar at this Dutch-run resort is the only place on the island that serves beer. Attractive chalets are set within a well-kept compound.

Budget

Lighthouse, **t** 09 626 5541. Set at the southern end of the main beach behind the widest stretch of sand. Accommodation is in an elevated wooden building with roomy doubles surrounding a long dorm. The rooms are quite decorative for the price, but can be noisy if there are lots of people in the dorm. There's a large verandah strewn with comfy chairs and a garden compound with hammocks slung between trees.

Zaki's Beach Chalet, **t** 09 613 1631/019 983 3435. Decent, though basic, chalets lined up on Kapas' most popular beach. Often full.

Mak Cik Gemuk, **t 09** 624 5120/012 928 3269. More simple chalets in a plain compound; less space than at Zaki's nextdoor.

D'Legend Campsite, **t** 019 947 3192. A small compound nextdoor to Lighthouse, with a handful of tents to rent, cooking facilities and kayaks for hire.

Harmoni Campsite, **t** 013 939 0616. This small campsite is set on its own on the northernmost beach – a neat curve of sand with some shallow coral in the bay.

Eating Out

Food on the island is limited more or less to the resorts, most of which have their own restaurants.

The only independent place is just by the end of the jetty, a small nameless café serving simple Malay dishes.

The other cheap option is **2BC Café**, attached to **Zaki's Beach Chalets**, which has a wider selection of good-value local dishes. Beautisland Resort has a reasonable menu and is the only place to serve *roti canai*, for those who have caught the bug.

The best place to eat by a long way is the **Tuty Puri Restaurant**. Dinner is served in an intricately carved, open-sided Malay pavilion, with *wayang kulit* shadow puppets hanging from the woodwork. The menu covers local, Western and Indonesian cuisines. The *gado-gado* is delicious.

Elsewhere in Terengganu

Rantau Abang

An air of despondency hovers over the Rantau Abang of today, a tiny kampung north of the fishing port of Dungun. A few roadside food stalls, a failing guesthouse or two and a complex of buildings attached to the Fisheries Department is all that remains of a kampung which once attracted tourists in their thousands. For Rantau Abang is (or was) one of the world's rare nesting sites of the giant leatherback turtle, the most elusive – and endangered – of the marine turtles. Adult turtles (wonderfully aqualined with rubber-like skin and fetching black and white markings) have been known to reach three metres in length and up to a tonne in weight (the heaviest recorded leatherback weighed in at 916kg).

During the April to August nesting seasons of the 1960s and 1970s, as many as 60 turtles a night landed on the beach at Rantau Abang to lay their eggs. In 2002

Decline of the Warm-Blooded Reptile

The failure of four decades of conservation work at Rantau Abang has served to highlight the risks of playing god – albeit a well-meaning, conservation-minded god. Back in the 1960s, despite some 10,000 landings at Rantau Abang each nesting season, it was becoming evident that the giant leatherback turtle population was suffering. So a hatchery was established to give the turtles a helping hand.

Back then, little was known about these sea-going reptiles other than their wide range; leatherbacks have been sighted right across the globe and are known to swim thousands of miles from their nesting grounds in search of food (a staple diet of jelly fish). The largest recorded turtle, a male weighing almost one metric tonne, was found beached on the coast of Wales in 1988. At the time it was thought that the turtle must have lost its way and died of cold. Only recently have scientists learned how leatherbacks survive in waters of such varying temperatures: they are warm-blooded. This makes them unique among reptiles and has led some scientists to believe they merit their own classification.

The decline in turtle numbers has long been linked to modern fishing practices and the illegal collection of eggs. But In 2001, when only 28 leatherbacks nested at Rantau Abang and none of the eggs hatched, it was suspected for the first time that the hatchery itself may have had something to do with the decline of this particular population. As it turned out, for decades the hatchery had produced only female hatchlings: by 2001 there were no males around to fertilise the eggs.

The sex of turtles – it is now known – is determined by temperature: cooler incubation conditions produce males, warmer conditions produce females. By leaving nesting sites exposed to the fierce tropical sun, the Rantau Abang hatchery had unknowingly engineered generation after generation of exclusively female turtles. Those turtles that survived to maturity had made the epic journey back to the place of their birth and laboured high onto the beach, only to unburden a sterile load.

Where to Stay and Eat

A few diehard guesthouses still offer rooms to passing tourists. Though the leatherbacks are no longer making an appearance, Rantau Abang can still offer a peaceful day or two by the sea. There are a couple of non-descript guesthouses set back from the beach near the Turtle Information Centre. The best places to stay lie outside the kampung (*see* below). For dinner there are several roadside food stalls in the village. The pick of the bunch is a simple Malay restaurant a few hundred yards south of the Turtle Information Centre.

Luxury

Tanjong Jara Resort, Batu 8 off Dungun, **t** 09 845 1100, **f** 09 845 1200, *travelcentre@ytlhotels.com.my*, *www.tanjongjararesort.com*. Malaysia's top East Coast resort hotel, situated 8km south of Rantau Abang, boasting an award-winning combination of Malay architectural styles, much of which is based on sultans' palaces from the 17th century. The beachside rooms come equipped with large, outdoor, sunken baths and their own private garden. The resort offers three food outlets, including The Nelayan ('The Fisherman') which cooks up the catch of the day from local fishermen. Stylish and costly (approaching RM1,000 per night for a standard room), with 5-star facilities.

Moderate–Budget

Dahimah's Guesthouse, t 09 845 2843, *dahimahsguesthouse@hotmail.com*. Situated 800m south of the village – walk there and back along the beach – and run by an English woman, this place offers a range of rooms and chalets, which are all in great nick.

there were only three unofficial landings throughout the whole season, and the eggs were poached before conservationists could get to them. Though hugely successful as a species – their ancestry goes back 150 million years – these lumbering giants are on the brink of extinction. Research suggests that between 1950 and 1998 we lost 99 per cent of the world's leatherback population. Fishing practices and illegal egg collecting (turtle eggs are a delicacy throughout Southeast Asia) are the main culprits, though failed conservation efforts have not helped either (*see* 'Decline of the Warm-Blooded Reptile', p.247).

The roadside Turtle Information Centre (*open Sat–Thurs 9–1 and 2–4.15*) contains a small but informative exhibition, with an out-of-date video shown on demand and a whiteboard recording turtle landings. A few hundred yards up the road are the offices and laboratories of TUMEC (Turtle and Marine Ecosystem Centre), where a new and larger exhibition is planned.

Marang

For several decades now, Marang has attracted travellers as an archetypal Malay fishing village; it also serves as the jump-off point for Pulau Kapas (*see* p.245). A narrow spit of land stretches in front of the village to create a beautiful lagoon, providing a calm channel for local fishing boats. Marang has expanded inland in recent years, and with the construction of a large new harbour, it is not the slow-paced kampung it once was. That said, the tiny fishing village across the lagoon has not changed at all; a couple of footbridges lead across the water to a cluster of Malay *rumahs* beneath the palms.

There are no real sights in Marang, other than the outdoor market near the jetty, but there are plenty of guesthouses for those with time on their hands.

Where to Stay

Moderate

Seri Malaysia, **t** 09 618 2889, **f** 09 618 1285, *central@serimalaysia.com*, *www.serimalaysia.com.my*. This well-priced business-oriented hotel with 50 rooms and a swimming pool is part of Malaysia's largest chain. Good sized, clinical rooms all have air-con, hot water, TV and coffee-making facilities.

Inexpensive–Budget

Marang Guesthouse, Bukit Batu Merah, **t** 09 618 1976, **f** 09 618 4386. Situated on the hillside above the main road, this is one of the better places to stay, with views across to Pulau Kapas. The chalets are large and clean, some with air conditioning, and the reception is a good source of information. Food here is not one of the plus points. Night fishing trips can be arranged, as can river trips that take in wildlife, traditional gold mines and local weaving.

Budget

Green Mango Inn, **t** 09 618 2040. A characterful spot amid abundant foliage up the hill from the jetty. A real travellers' haunt, with books, an excellent hand-drawn map of Marang for sale and a kitchen. There are rooms inside the main house and A-frames in the courtyard. To get here climb the steps just south of the jetty.

Island View Resort, **t** 09 618 2006. Small, mildly run-down rooms built round an attractive little garden courtyard. Rooms with air-con are great value at RM30. Situated opposite the lagoon.

Eating Out

Being a traditional Malay fishing village, the only places for a meal out are the open-air **food stalls** dotted about town. The obvious place to eat is the line of stalls beside the market square. All serve simple Malay food. **Pak Din**, a *roti canai* stall, is the most longstanding of them all, with review clippings from *The Star* proudly displayed. North of here, along the banks of the lagoon, are a couple more food stalls; every evening elderly villagers gather here to sip *teh* and play boardgames beneath the trees. Just south of the jetty is **Marang Seafood & Souvenir**, set in a modern interpretation of a Malay house. Local seafood is served from a counter overlooking the fishing boats in the harbour, with tables surrounding a fountain at the foot of the bell tower.

Merang

Confusingly Merang, like Marang, is both a Malay fishing village and the jump-off point for one of Terengganu's popular island getaways. Merang is the smaller of the two, its centre consisting of little more than a couple of shops and a coconut stall on the corner of the coastal road north of Kuala Terengganu. It is well worth timing a visit for Friday, when an interesting little **night market** is held. Piles of local fruit, including rambutans and durians, are interspersed with a wonderful spread of sweet and savoury food stalls. Avoid the things that look like dimpled ping-pong balls: they are turtles' eggs, a local delicacy more likely than not supplied by illegal collectors. Though the state government issues a limited number of licences for egg collecting, and prosecutes those caught collecting without a licence, it is proving difficult to wean Malaysia's East Coasters off a food source that has been an established part of the local diet for many centuries.

A side road leads down from the main road to the jetty, where the Merang of old coexists side by side with the modern trappings of the tourist industry. Traditional wooden fishing boats pass behind high-powered speedboats which line up to collect

Where to Stay

Luxury

The Aryani, **t** 09 653 2111, **f** 09 653 1007, *thearyani@thearyani.com, www.thearyani.com*. A boutique resort that plays on the theme of a Malay palace, with 20 villas set in 9 acres of gardens. Each villa has its own gateway and garden and sunken, outdoor bath. The two suites are stunning: the Heritage Suite is a reconstructed Malay *rumah* stuffed with antiques, while the Modern Suite is wonderfully spacious with pale woods and a bed large enough to sleep four. The resort offers spa treatments and has two restaurants.

Inexpensive–Budget

Kembara Resort, **t** 09 653 1770, **f** 09 653 1900, *kembararesort@hotmail.com*. This guesthouse is set on its own in a beautiful spot. To get there, head south from the site of the night market for about 1km, then turn left down a small lane. Pass through coconut groves towards the beach and Kembara Resort is on the right. Basic fan-only rooms line up in two perpendicular buildings, while a row of well-spaced, air-conditioned chalets with balconies stretch down towards the beach. It is a quiet, secluded spot with hammocks slung between trees, an equipped kitchen for the use of guests and internet access.

Stingray Beach Resort, **t** 09 653 2018. One of several mediocre guesthouses on the beach just round from the jetty. A row of 20 plain rooms line up in front of a fenced-off patch of beach. They offer a three-day package which includes a trip to Redang.

tourists on pre-arranged packages to Pulau Redang (*see* p.243). Walk a little inland from the tour agencies' stalls, and you bump into gangs of local fishermen sitting about mending nets and chatting above the deep purr of outboards, wondering, no doubt, what has happened to their little village.

From the jetty the road loops round north along the beach, where a few guesthouses have set up shop; most offer packages to Redang.

Pahang

15

Highlights

1. Taman Negara – more than 130 million years old and Malaysia's flagship national park
2. The Cameron Highlands, largest and most popular of Malaysia's colonial hill stations
3. Pulau Tioman, for white-sand beaches, diving, snorkelling, treks in virgin rainforest and climbing
4. Tasek Bera – Malaysia's largest freshwater lake system, home to the Semelai tribe

Pahang is Peninsular Malaysia's largest and most destination-packed state. Within its borders are some of the world's oldest rainforests, accessible to visitors via the Taman Negara and other state parks. Then there are the rolling tea plantations of the Cameron Highlands, the lotus-strewn wetlands of Tasek Bera, and the dramatic twin peaks of Pulau Tioman, which rise one kilometre above the coral-rich waters of the

South China Sea. There's even a tired old hippy hangout at Cherating, a coastal town that attracts backpackers on the route between Bangkok and Singapore.

Pahang once encompassed the whole southern portion of the peninsula. In fact, before the Sultanate of Melaka was established in 1400, the peninsula itself was known to many as Pahang. Pahang's first Sultan, Muhamad Shah, appeared on the scene in 1469, by which time Pahang had become a tributary sultanate under the control of Melaka. Muhamad Shah was the eldest son of the Sultan of Melaka and a convicted murderer (hence his father shipped him off to Pahang, denying him the sultanate he was heir to).

For several hundred years Pahang was passed back and forth between the dominant powers in the region, each eager to get their hands on the tin and the gold for which Pahang had long been famed. It was these mineral resources that led the British to establish a Resident of Pahang in 1888, and later, to undertake the massive project of building a 'Jungle Railway' (*see* p.280) through the peninsula's mountainous interior.

Pahang's population today is representative of the rest of Malaysia, with a mix of Malay, Chinese and Indians, though there are more Orang Asli here than in any other state. Modern Pahang combines the East Coast charm of Terengganu and Kelantan

Getting There

Kuantan's **airport** is about 20km out of town. MAS provide connections with KL, Kuala Terengganu and Kota Bharu. Hundreds of **buses** ply the East Coast highway and the cross-peninsula highway to KL.

Getting Around

Kuantan is a good place to hire a car: Hawk Rent-a-Car, 146 Jalan Telok Sisek, **t** 09 555 1055, *www.hawkrentacar.com*; Orix, Ground Floor, Hotel Grand Continental, Jalan Gambut, **t** 09 515 7488, *www.orixcarrentals.com.my*. The centre of town can be covered on foot.

Tourist Information

Tourist Information Centre, Jalan Mahkota, **t** 09 517 1007, open Mon–Thurs 9–1 and 2–4.30, Fri 9–12.15 and 2.45–4.30, Sat 9–1; closed 1st and 3rd Sat of the month.

Where to Stay

As well as the hotels listed below there are a number of places to stay at Teluk Chempedek and Beserah (*see* p.255).

Expensive–Moderate

M.S. Garden Hotel, Lorong Gambut, **t** 09 555 5899, **f** 09 552 2016, *hikua@tm.net.my*. The plushest hotel in town and Kuantan's most dominant modern building. All rooms have balconies and 4-star facilities, including movie channel. There's a large fitness centre and a pool with a fake 20ft waterfall. The Yuen-Yuen Restaurant serves great dim sum.

Moderate

Mega View Hotel, off Jalan Besar, **t** 09 517 1888, **f** 09 556 3999, *megaview@pd.jaring.my*, *www.megaviewhotel.com*. A high-rise hotel with great views over the river. Rooms are spacious and offer mini-bar, phone, TV and air-con. There's a coffee house and a restaurant which serves buffet meals.

Hotel Grand Continental, Jalan Gambut, **t** 09 515 8888, **f** 09 515 9999, *www.ghihotels.com*. Decent-value business hotel with ample, but characterless, rooms. Facilities include pool and room service.

Hotel Seri Malaysia, Jalan Telok Sisek, **t** 09 555 3688, **f** 09 555 3118, *www.serimalaysia.com.my*. The usual good value associated with this chain of business hotels. Frequent promotions mean rates often dip into the 'inexpensive' category.

with the colonial British influences that stamped their mark in places like Pekan and the Cameron Highlands. But it is the surviving tracts of wilderness for which the state is best known to modern visitors.

The old colonial hill station of Fraser's Hill is covered in the Selangor chapter (though it falls just inside Pahang's borders, access is from Selangor).

Pahang's Coast

Kuantan

Despite being capital of Peninsular Malaysia's largest state, Kuantan does not offer much of interest to the visitor. A busy place on the banks of the Sungai Kuantan, the city serves as the transport hub of the East Coast and is consequently choked with traffic during daylight hours.

That is not to say the city is without its modest charms. Hidden from view behind busy Jalan Besar is the riverfront, where colourful East Coast fishing boats chug back

Rooms have en suite, coffee-making facilities, TV and phone. There's also a pool.

Shahzan Inn, Jalan Masjid, **t** 09 513 6688, **f** 09 513 5588. Mid-range hotel in a central location, with a swimming pool. Rooms are well kept, with air-con, phone and TV.

Moderate–Inexpensive

Classic Hotel, 7 Jalan Besar, **t** 09 516 4599, **f** 09 513 4141, *chotel@tm.net.my*. The best-value option in town. Rooms are well decorated, with en suite bathroom, TV, phone and air-con. Some rooms have views over the river.

Inexpensive–Budget

Oriental Evergreen, 157 Jalan Haji Abdul Rahman, **t** 09 513 0168, **f** 09 513 0368. An uninspiring high-rise hotel with spacious rooms, all with air-con and en-suite bathrooms. Has seen better days.

Eating Out

There are numerous food courts along the waterfront serving the full range of Asian cuisines. The little open-air market on Jalan Mahkota (opposite the mosque) is a great place to stop at for fresh fruit. Otherwise there are several restaurants dotted about town:

Expensive

Le Parisien, Lorong Sekilau 22, Bukit Sekilau, **t** 09 14 8893/013 932 7972, closed Mon. A popular new restaurant that really is French: all foods are imported from Europe and the chef is French too.

Tjantek Art Bistro, 46 Jalan Besar, **t** 09 516 4144. A trendy design-oriented bistro, strangely out of place in Kuantan, serving steaks, a range of coffees and other drinks.

Inexpensive

The Cheese Cake Factory, 6 Lorong Tun Ismail. A modern place conceived in the style of a European café and serving 15 different types of cheesecake, as well as a menu of simple savoury dishes (local and Western).

Restoran House of India, 61 Jalan Teluk Sisek. A very clean and slick Indian restaurant with a range of north and south Indian dishes, from *roti canai* to *thosai* and biryani. Food is served at varnished wooden tables and the restaurant is air-conditioned.

Chilli Restoran, Jalan Besar. A big menu of Malay, Western and Chinese dishes, with excellent *nasi lemak* and Chinese noodle soups. You can order sirloin steak here for RM11.

and forth from the ocean. The riverfront is pedestrianized and lined with food stalls alongside a kilometre stretch of the lazy Kuantan River. On the opposite bank is nothing but dense mangrove forest.

The only real sight in Kuantan is the **State Mosque** (Masjid Negeri), a huge pastel confection built in 1991 and sporting four pencil-sharp minarets and a blue and mint-green dome. Appropriately dressed tourists, though not permitted to enter the prayer hall, are welcome to wander through the surrounding galleries, which link four attractive courtyards. Visit in the late afternoon and notice how the slanting sunlight illuminates the stained-glass windows.

Opposite the mosque is the city's obligatory *padang*, with a colonial-style courthouse on one side and a daily fruit market across the road on Jalan Mahkota, itself lined with 1920s shophouses.

Around Kuantan

Several kilometres east of town is **Teluk Chempedek**, Kuantan's modern beachfront. Though a little gaudy, it is pleasant enough and strangely reminiscent of a European beach resort. The seafront is lined with bars, hotels and seafood restaurants. In the evenings, particularly at weekends, Kuantan folk flood here for an *Italian-style passeggiata*, with couples and whole families dressed up for a stroll along the waterfront. You'd never guess this was East Coast Malaysia. Infrequent buses make the 3km journey from in front of the state mosque on Jalan Mahkota during daylight hours. After dark you have to rely on taxis to get back into town, and the drivers bump up the fares accordingly.

Where to Stay

Teluk Chempedek

Expensive

Hyatt Regency, t 09 566 1234, **f** 09 567 7577, *resvn@hrktn.com.my*, *www.hyatt.com*. This snooty resort hotel dominates Teluk Chempedek. It is nicely designed in 'kampung' style, and has two swimming pools and four restaurants.

Moderate

Hotel Kuantan, t/f 09 568 0026. A slightly peculiar Chinese-run hotel behind the Hyatt, with air-conditioned rooms at a good price.

Beserah

Budget

Beserah Beach Resthouse, t 09 544 6427/016 950 3179. This low-key resthouse with views over the coconut palms is the only place to stay in Beserah. Very simple (no air-con or hot water) but charming, especially if you get the big room with the huge verandah.

Eating Out

The seafront at Teluk Chempedek is lined with seafood restaurants all vying to draw in the evening crowds. The most popular of them is **Restoran Pattaya**, which has a huge menu and a good dessert section. The road leading back up from the beach is lined with bars, most of them a little seedy, though the **Mecinta Bistro** is nicely decorated with sofas.

Right on the beach at Beserah are two or three simple restaurants which offer up the catch of the day, still twitching. Low prices make this a great place to feast on fish.

A few kilometres north of Kuantan is an altogether different scene: **Beserah**, a peaceful Malay fishing kampung where local fishermen continue the ancient practice of employing water buffalo to haul the daily catch through the shallow surf and onto the beach. The best time to visit if you want to see the buffalo in action is between midday and 1pm (though the animals are only used for large catches). At other times of day the herds roam the beach, grazing at its fringes. Beserah is a wonderful place to come for fresh *ikan bakar* (barbecued fish) on the cheap, and for a stroll along a beautiful, wild stretch of beach. You should have the place virtually to yourself.

About 25km inland from Kuantan, along the Sungai Lembing is **Gua Charah**, a series of caves tucked high within a spectacular limestone outcrop, which towers over the surrounding sea of oil-palm plantations. Thai Buddhists have made the place their home, erecting a reclining buddha at the far end of the largest cave. For a small donation, visitors can climb the steep and rough path to the cave entrance. A guano-smeared track leads deep into the belly of the cave in the direction of the 9m-long buddha. Dim fluorescent lights illuminate your way, but a torch comes in handy. For a moment of revelation, arrive at the foot of the buddha for approximately 11am; at about this time every day the climbing sun sends a beam of light onto the buddha through a small crack in the roof of the cave.

Higher up the outcrop are further caves and views over the monotonous carpet of oil palms. To reach the caves by public transport, catch the bus that heads upriver along Sungai Lembing and get off at Panching. The caves are a 4km walk from here through the oil palms; locals will be happy to drive you there for a fee.

Pekan

The sleepy royal town of Pekan was state capital of Pahang until 1898. On the banks of the Sungai Pahang, just upstream from the estuary, Pekan was ideally situated for a sultan wishing to maintain contact with the outside world. Rather than face pirate raids in the lower reaches of the Strait of Melaka, maritime traders often crossed the peninsula by navigating the Penarikan Route (also known as Jalan Penarikan). From Melaka, traders would head up Sungai Muar, hauling their boats overland for a

Getting There

Pekan is a little over 30mins south of Kuantan by bus. The town sits just off the main coastal road, so there are frequent daily services. The last bus leaves Pekan at 8pm.

Where to Stay

Inexpensive

Chief's Rest House, Jalan Istana Permai, **t** 09 422 6941. This airy, stilted house built in 1929 was a gift from the Sultan. It is a wonderfully atmospheric place to stay, run by 'Daddy K'. The nine spacious rooms are lined up behind a wide verandah, each with an attractive timber bed, coffee-making facilities, TV and bathroom with hot water. In the breakfast room is a huge antique cabinet. There's a small dorm too, with two sets of bunk beds.

kilometre or so to reach the Sungai Serting, then link up with the Sungai Pahang, with Pekan as the last stop before the great expanse of the South China Sea.

A scattering of istana (Malay palaces) and colonial mansions are the only legacy of these days. The centre of town is an unappealing, somewhat desolate grid of low-lying houses. However, the town's sights are strung together on a loop of streets that make for an enjoyable walk. Head west along the river from the market and you reach the **Muzium Sultan Abu Bakar** (*open Tues–Sun 9.30–5, closed Fri lunch; adm RM1*), housed in a grand building constructed in 1929 for the British Resident. By provincial Malaysian standards, the museum holds a surprisingly large collection, with a royal gallery (where there's a real Cadillac on display), a pastimes gallery (shadow puppets and *congkak* boards), a textile and ceramics gallery and a natural history section, where there sits the largest skull you will ever have seen (it belongs to a whale). Across the road is the Watercraft Gallery, an outdoor space exhibiting full-scale traditional fishing boats (*perahu* and *kolek*) and old photographs.

Just west of the museum are two mosques, the squat Masjid Abdullah with a shallow dome in a pale sky blue and Art Deco flourishes, and the ornate Masjid Sultan Ahmad Shah, with its gold onion domes. Beyond these mosques, the road bends before passing through a strange archway of tusks towards the *istanas*. The attractive colonial bungalow beside the archway serves as a boys' school for Koranic studies. A little further down is the Chief's Rest House (*see* 'Where to Stay', opposite) and then the Istana Mangga Tunggul, a dilapidated bungalow covered in ornate woodwork and closed to the public. From here the well-tended road, which is lined with flowers and drooping lampposts, cuts down towards the polo field and skirts the grounds of the present sultan's *istana*, an enormous, extravagant mess of styles. Within the rolling grounds are stables, orchards and a football pitch. Access, of course, is restricted.

On reaching the huge polo field (the sultan and his sons are obsessed with the sport), bear left, then take the first left again onto a lane which leads through peaceful **Kampung Permatang Pauh** and back to the centre of town. The lane crosses Sungai Parit, a stream with water as opaque as local coffee, and weaves between the beautiful kampung houses, the palms and the fruit trees. It is like the Malay version of a Suffolk village.

Cherating

Cherating has undergone a series of transformations in recent times. The original fishing kampung was set upon by hippy travellers in the 1970s. They took root in homesteads among the coconut groves, setting the trend of things to come – until developers made an appearance in the 1990s and top-end resorts began popping up along the coast.

Today Cherating is a curious mix of mainstream package tourists and hardened travellers who stay for months, even years. Understandably, locals have turned their hand almost exclusively to providing for the visitors. Guesthouses, travel agencies, batik workshops and souvenir stalls stand where once were only coconut palms.

Getting There

Cherating is 47km north of Kuantan and regular buses run between the two. There are also buses north to Kuala Terengganu and Kota Bharu. Passengers are dropped on the main road, leaving a walk into the village itself.

Getting Around

Cherating can be explored on foot. For those wanting to go further afield, you can rent bicycles and motorbikes on the road that runs parallel to the beach. Transport to some sights can be arranged by guesthouses and agents.

Information

There is no tourist office in Cherating, but Pahang Tourism in Kuantan produce brochures on Cherating. The hotels and guesthouses are excellent sources of information. A recommended travel agent is Badgerlines Information Centre, who happily offer no-strings information.

Where to Stay

Luxury

Eastern Pavilion Cherating, **t** 09 581 9500, **f** 09 581 9178, *www.holidayvilla.com.my*. This is the pick of the bunch, comprising 12 villas, each with pool and butler service, and three restaurants. Pricey, but there are promotions.

Expensive

Club Med Cherating, **t** 09 581 9133, **f** 09 581 9172, *www.clubmed.com*. A huge tourist 'village' with well-equipped rooms, a range of sporting facilities and a lovely stretch of beach where green turtles come to nest.

Impiana Resort, **t** 09 581 9000, **f** 09 581 9090, *www.impiana.com*. An impressive resort on a pleasant stretch of beach with Malay-style buildings, a huge pool and a range of activities. All rooms have four-poster beds.

Legend Resort, **t** 09 581 9818, **f** 09 581 9400, *www.legendsgroup.com*. Rivals the Impiana Resort in grandeur and facilities, with two pools and plenty of sporting facilities. Rooms are bright and airy with huge beds. Promotions can bring rates right down.

Moderate–Inexpensive

Cherating Palm Resort, **t** 09 581 9378. The most pleasant of several downmarket resorts; air-con and mini-bar in rooms. Also has a pool.

Tanjung Inn, **t** 09 581 9081, *tanjunginn@jaring.my*. A range of chalets set among immaculate landscaped gardens; the centrepiece is an idyllic pond.

Budget

Coconut Inn, **t** 09 581 9299. Spacious rooms set around a tiny garden. Full of character but a bit run down – see a room first.

The Moon, **t** 09 581 9186. This travellers' hang-out is set inland from the beach on a hillside among trees. Large basic chalets are scattered across the hillside. Free laundry and lots of books and board games.

Matahari Chalets, **t** 09 581 9835. Budget chalets facing one another across a grassy compound. The big draws here are the batik workshop and the large fridge in each room.

Eating Out

Apart from a row of food stalls opposite the Badgerlines office – one of which serves the best *roti canai* on the east coast – there are also a handful of beachside restaurants.

Expensive

Mario's, at Eastern Pavilion, **t** 09 581 9500. Italian restaurant that's well worth a splurge and great value in Western terms.

Moderate–Inexpensive

Seaside Seafood Restaurant, right on the beach. Great Chinese specials, focusing on seafood. Worth it for the setting.

Tidak Lupa Seafood Restaurant. The 'Not Forget Restaurant', as the name translates, is a popular Chinese seafood restaurant on the road that runs parallel to the beach.

Payung Café. A handful of tables beneath an *attap* roof; pizza, pasta, salads and soups are served, along with beer.

Deadly Nightshade, at The Moon (*see* Where to Stay). Atmospheric, makeshift bar serving local and western food.

Despite the changes, Cherating remains a relaxing, low-key place to while away a few days, or weeks.

Cherating's beach is a long crescent of sand backed by casuarinas. At low tide the sea retreats to leave a shallow lagoon, a safe and natural swimming pool for kids – though swimming off the beach can be a frustrating business as the sea is shallow for hundreds of metres. Conditions, however, are ideal for windsurfers and Cherating plays host to regular international competitions.

Because of the constant presence of tourists, there is plenty to keep the visitor occupied, from snorkelling on **Pulau Ular** (Snake Island) and horse-riding along the sands (head for the stables at the north end of the beach) to canoeing, batik-painting and turtle-watching: each night scouts patrol **Chendor Beach** to the north in search of egg-laying turtles. Some of the travel agents have cottoned on to this and will ferry you to the beach at short ntice, should a turtle land (leave your name and room number at Badgerlines: *see* 'Information', opposite). During the day you can visit the **Sanctuari Penyu Cherating** (*open Tues–Sun 9–5.30, Fri 9–12 and 3–5.30*) on Chendor Beach, where there is a small exhibition and a hatchery. Two turtles, a green and a hawksbill, glide about in a pool round the back.

For a taste of authentic East Coast life head several kilometres north to **Kuala Kemaman**, a fishing village proper, lined with stalls selling *kerapok*, dried fish, *otak-otak* and exotic seashells. There are also a number of beautiful routes for bike rides; one heads inland past a sa mill and through watermelon, rambutan and durian plantations, before looping back to the main road.

Pulau Tioman

Pulau Tioman advertises itself across dozens of miles of emerald ocean, its majestic twin peaks jutting more than a kilometre from coral-ringed waters. Little wonder it was a popular berth for mariners as far back as the 9th century. In the 1950s the setting was chosen for the mythical paradise of Bali Hai in the Hollywood musical *South Pacific*. Ever since, tourists have enjoyed the white-sand beaches, the abundant coral and the slow pace of life.

For many centuries Tioman was a key port of call on the trade route between the Middle East and China. A 9th-century Arab account mentions the island as a source of 'sandalwood, rice, edible birds, coconuts and superior camphor'. Eight centuries later the Englishman William Dampier noted Tioman as 'a place often touched at for wood, water and other refreshments'. Pulau Tioman's spine of jagged mountains, thrown up from the sea by volcanic activity and cloaked in virgin rainforest, ensures a constant supply of fresh water and a unique biodiversity. Scientists are forever discovering new species of reptile and amphibian among the island's steamy recesses. A research team in 2002 revealed one frog, four lizards and three snakes – all new to science. One better-known reptile that never fails to go unnoticed on Tioman is the great lumbering water monitor. These giant lizards, which can reach 8ft in length and are a larger version of their mainland cousins, can be seen sliding in and out of freshwater streams all round the island.

Activities

Diving and Snorkelling

The waters around Tioman host an unusually wide variety of marine life. There are numerous dive schools at Salang, Air Batang, Tekek and Juara, all of which run a range of PADI courses at competitive prices. Many places also offer snorkelling and fishing trips. B&J Dive Centre (**t** 09 419 5555) is the most established place, with schools at Salang and Air Batang. They also offer an underwater photography course (of sorts). In Tekek, a good choice is Sudin Scuba (**t** 09 419 1843), attached to Swiss Cottage. Sign up for a course here and you get free accommodation.

Live coral is accessible directly from the main beaches, with the best spots clustered around the headlands. You are likely to see myriad coral fish, rays, and perhaps groupers, black-tip reef sharks and hawksbill turtles. To see the best of it, though, you need to head out to one of Tioman's sheltered islets. **Pulai Tulai**, northwest of Salang, is often the first port of call. Just off the island, boulders and underwater channels are coated with hard and soft corals. Angel and butterfly fish are common, as are jacks and turtles. This is a good spot for snorkelling as well as diving. East of here, **Magicienne Rock** is a popular dive site, submerged 8m below the surface at its highest point. Sharks, rays, yellow-fin snappers, groupers and large barracudas are usually sighted. **Pulau Sepoi**, **Pulau Labas** and **Tiger Reef**, just south of Tulai, are good places to spot white-tip and black-tip sharks, huge bump-head parrotfish, green and hawksbill turtles and, occasionally, manta rays. Of these three, only Pulau Labas is suitable for snorkelling. Southwest of Tioman are other sites, including **Bahara Rock**, which has colourful soft corals, bump-head parrotfish, black-tip sharks and the odd nurse shark. A number of wrecks from WWII have become established dive sites too.

Jungle Treks

Only coastal areas of Tioman are inhabited. The whole interior of the island is cloaked in virgin rainforest. There is a large native population of monkeys, porcupines

Tioman is hit hard by the east-west monsoon from November to February, when swimming can be dangerous and most places shut down. In a bid to fight the elements and turn the island into a year-round holiday destination, Tioman has been granted duty-free status and a new marina in Tekek is under construction. Many islanders have expressed concern over the effects of the ongoing development, though the extreme topography of the island strictly limits the damage that can be done (after one look at Tioman's steep flanks, surveyors deemed more than 80 per cent of the island unsuitable for development). Though Tioman is not quite the remote paradise it was once known to be, it has preserved many of its charms and remains surprisingly underdeveloped, considering all the hype. The entire interior is uninhabited, with the island's 3,000 locals living in a handful of coastal kampungs. Many islanders – who once lived in bamboo huts in the jungle and worked coconut plantations – have turned their hands to tourism, running chalets and dive centres or operating sea-taxis. But local fishermen still skirt Tioman's rich waters in their and mouse deer. Snakes and lizards slither about the jungle floor, while fruit bats, emerald kingfishers and golden orioles fly about the canopy. As usual in the jungle, you'll be lucky to see more than lizards and monkeys.

Because of Tioman's spine of jagged mountains, much of the interior is inaccessible. The main route through the jungle links Tekek on the west coast with Juara on the east. It starts north of the airstrip in Tekek: look out for the sign. For much of the way the route is paved, which takes away the sense of adventure, but you'll still be weaving between ancient *tualang* trees and strangling figs. The hike takes up to three hours and is very steep in parts.

Another trail leads between Air Batang and Salang, via beautifully secluded Monkey Bay. This trek is much more rewarding, even though it follows the coast. However, it is virtually unmarked and extremely hard to follow. Take plenty of water. If you get lost follow the power line slung on low branches between the two bays. Allow at least three hours.

South of Tekek, you can follow jungle trails that link kampungs as far as Genting.

Climbing

The vertical face of **Nenek Semukut** is a paradise for experienced climbers. This towering peak at the southern edge of the island – known locally as 'Dragon Horn' – offers up a slab of vertical rock in excess of 500m in height and lined with fissures and 'roofs'. This climb is not for novices – it was only in the year 2000 that the summit was conquered for the first time. In 2001 two Malaysians made it halfway, hauling their gear in self-made bags sewn from gunny sacks. At night they attached nylon hammocks to the vertical rockface. From these vertiginous beds they flashed their torches in the direction of Kampung Mukut – so they told a national newspaper on their descent. To their surprise, villagers replied by flashing back: 'Lights were flickering from jetty, kampung houses and fishing boats'. The Dragon Horn is accessible from Kampung Mukut.

colourful fishing *perahus*, while fishing crews from Terengganu come ashore each morning to do their washing in streams that trickle down from the mountains.

For many, Tioman's primary attraction is its rich marine life. The surrounding waters are littered with tiny islets and submerged rocks, which sustain coral reefs and attract pelagic species from the open waters. The lucky few may catch sight of manta rays and whale sharks basking at the surface, while a couple of hours snorkelling is usually rewarded with the sight of a harmless reef shark, or a turtle quietly nosing about in the coral. Climatic changes brought on by El Nino in 1998 bleached large areas of hard coral along the seashore, but the hardy polyps have since begun regenerating themselves. Water visibility is not as good as some of the other East Coast islands, though 10–20m is not unusual.

A number of tough trails strike out into the island's virgin jungle, presenting an alternative to beach-lazing. If Tioman can stave off the negative aspects of its new

Getting There

By Air

A tiny airstrip runs behind Tekek, allowing just enough space for a Dash 7 propellor plane to land. Berjaya Air (**t** 03 7846 8228, **f** 03 7846 5637, *reserve@berjaya-air.com, www.berjaya-air.com*) fly twice a day from KL Subang airport and once daily from Singapore.

By Sea

Most people get to Tioman by ferry from Mersing. The ferry terminal here is lined with ticket stands and touts, who will try to sell you their most expensive tickets. Prices vary from RM25-45 for a one-way ticket, depending on the speed of the boat. A return ticket saves no money. The fastest do the 59km journey in around 90mins, though it's a bumpy, claustrophobic ride. Larger ferries take 2hrs or longer. Departure times depend on the tide: most boats won't leave until mid-morning, while the last ferries depart around 4pm.

Getting Around

The only road on Tioman is the one that links the airstrip in Tekek with the Berjaya resort. North of Tekek, a narrow concrete path used by pedestrians and motorbikes runs the length of Air Batang. There are a number of arduous jungle trails linking some of Tioman's kampungs (*see* 'Activities', p.260). A daily sea-bus (an old fishing boat) chugs between Juara and the Berjaya resort, stopping off at Salang, Air Batang and Tekek en route. There is only one departure a day from Juara, at 3pm, and the journey takes 2hrs. Charges vary: Juara to Air Batang costs RM15. The boat then does the journey in reverse. Often, the only means of transport around Tioman is the sea-taxi (any old little boat with an outboard) – and operators know it. Fares are high, with a journey from Air Batang to Salang costing around RM20. Many of the chalet operations operate sea-taxis, advertising their fares on boards. Beware that after nightfall fares rise steeply: if you need to get back from Salang to Air Batang after 7pm, for example, you'll be charged in excess of RM60.

Tourist Information

There is no tourist office on Tioman. There is a bank opposite the airstrip, with an ATM that takes major credit cards and Maestro. The Berjaya resort and a few of the chalet operations will change travellers cheques, but at poor rates. The best time to visit Tioman is from March to October – during the Nov–Feb monsoon most of the ferry services and chalet operations shut down.

Where to Stay

Until development of Tioman really begins to kick in, the international-class Berjaya Resort south of Tekek remains the only standard hotel accommodation available. Chalets of varying degrees of comfort make up the rest of what's on offer. Most of the outfits – clusters of simple chalets with an

duty-free status, and if rumours about the construction of a new airport turn out to be false, then it will quietly remain one of Malaysia's top destinations.

Tekek

Kampung Tekek ('Village of Lizards') is a bit bleak. It is Tioman's largest settlement, situated in the armpit of the island's west coast. Development in the 1980s tailed off, leaving Tekek a bit derelict and dog-eared. It remains the island's administrative centre, with a large jetty and an airstrip. It is not an attractive place to stay. That said, the beach south of town is wide and quiet, and there are a number of good places to eat. Set back from the beach, next to the airstrip, is the **Pulau Tioman Muzium** (*open daily 9.30–5; adm RM1*), with a small display of archaeological finds and an outline of attached restaurant – are family-run and fall inside the 'inexpensive' or 'budget' categories. Many throw in a few smarter chalets with air-con for around RM100.

Tekek

Luxury-Expensive

Berjaya Tioman Beach Resort, **t** 09 419 1000, **f** 09 419 1718, *reserv@b-tioman.com*, *www.berjayaresorts.com*. The island's one international-class resort, on a good stretch of beach south of Tekek. Facilities include watersports, horse-riding, two swimming pools, tennis courts, a golf course, several bars and four restaurants. Accommodation is in oversize chalet blocks in Malay style. The facilities are great but, as with all Berjaya resorts, there are few concessions to environmental concerns. Frequent promotions bring the rates down, especially if you fly in with Berjaya Air.

Moderate

Persona Island Resort, **t** 09 419 1213. Twenty-five rooms with air-con, hot water and verandahs in a single double-storey building 200m from the beach. There's a large patch of lawn with a children's play area. Somewhat lacking in character. Prices start at RM120.

Babura Seaview Resort, **t** 09 419 1346, **f** 09 419 1139. Clean chalets and further rooms, all with air-con, in a double-storey house on a wide stretch of beach south of Tekek. The rooms are well-kept, but cramped.

Inexpensive

Swiss Cottage, **t** 09 419 1642, *www.samudra-swiss-cottage.com*. The only recommendable cheap accommodation in and around Tekek (though a few of the chalets fall in the moderate category). Attractive timber and bamboo chalets are set beneath palms and casuarinas in an attractive shady compound. The beach at this point is wide, and far enough from Tekek to be peaceful. The operation doubles as a dive school: if you sign up for one of their dive courses, they offer free accommodation. No air-con.

Air Batang (also known as ABC)

Moderate–Inexpensive

Bamboo Hill, **t** 09 419 1339, **f** 09 419 1326, *bamboosu@tm.net.my*, *www.geocities.com/bamboosu*. The most tasteful accommodation on Tioman. Six timber chalets – each with balconies and views – perch among flowers on rocks at the end of the bay. Though there's no air-con, it's a breezy spot and there are nice touches in each chalet, such as gas lamps, fridges, tea/coffee-making facilities and a WWF guide to coral reefs. They also provide filtered water, internet access and a great little library. Book in advance online.

ABC Beach Chalets, **t** 09 419 1154. Next door to Bamboo Hill and benefitting from the curve of sand at this end of the bay. This is one of the original operations along Air Batang (hence the name), with a well-established restaurant on the beach and a series of chalets of varying prices set round a garden.

the island's long history. Further north is the Tioman Marine Park Information Centre (*open daily 9.30–4.30*), which concentrates mainly on the protection of coral reefs. Tioman's only road leads from the airstrip to the Berjaya resort, while a concrete path climbs rocks at the north end of the bay in the direction of Air Batang. Another path cuts east through steep rainforest to Juara (*see* 'Activities', pp.260–1).

Air Batang

Air Batang is a peaceful 2km stretch of coastline lined with well-spaced chalet operations. All buildings are single-storey and fairly discreet. At low tide, rocks are exposed and swimmers are forced to head for the crescents of sand at either end of the bay to access the sea. Pockets of live table coral can be found close to these

The new air-con chalets just off the sand are the best, though a little overpriced.

Johan's Resort, **t** 09 419 1359. Sturdy chalets inclined on a hill in a pleasant garden setting. Prices range from RM25 to RM120 with a number of air-con chalets available. The attached restaurant offers a big range of fresh seafood.

Nazri II, **t** 09 419 1375. Most of the accommodation comprises spacious air-con units, though round the back are a few tumbledown fan-only chalets. The attached **Hijan Restaurant**, elevated on a slope, is one of the better places to eat along Air Batang. Well-prepared fish and seafood are a little more expensive here but worth it. Canoes are available for hire (non-guests welcome).

Nazri's Place, **t** 09 419 1329/013 933 4010. The most southerly spot on Air Batang, with the best patch of beach. A handful of air-con chalets sit next to the beach, while simpler fan-only units nestle against the jungle. The attached restaurant is very popular. Reflexology and body massages available.

Budget

South Pacific Chalets (SPC), **t** 09 419 1176. The first place you come to north of the jetty. Basic chalets set round a little garden. Good value, though there's no beach to speak of at this point.

Mawar Beach Chalet, **t** 09 419 1153/013 702 1332. This line of simple sea-facing chalets on the beach is the first accommodation you come to south of the Air Batang jetty. Basic but good value. The beach here is very narrow. The odd hammock slung between palm trees adds to the appeal.

My Friend's Place, **t** 09 419 1150. A small simple operation south of the jetty (just down from the batik workshop). Basic chalets, a few equipped with air-con.

Panuba Bay

Moderate–Inexpensive

Panuba Inn Resort, **t** 09 419 1184/019 777 9865. Just round the headland from Air Batang, this is a quieter option, with a lovely beach and good snorkelling. There are four grades of chalet available, from fan-only to chalets with air-con, hot water, TV and fridge. All are sea-facing with bathroom and balcony and most have excellent views. Because it's the only place in the bay, guests are forced to eat here each night (or pay RM10 per person for a one-way sea-taxi to Air Batang). PADI diving courses can be taken here.

Salang Bay

Moderate

Salang Sayang Resort (or **Zaid's Place**), **t** 09 419 5019, *www.salangsayangtioman.com*. Rows of chalets, some with sea views, others facing a small garden. Right at the southern end of the bay and in front of the best bit of beach. On the hillside are a few larger air-con chalets for four, which go for RM200. This is the most popular spot with Western travellers.

beaches. At high tide, waves lap a narrow beach lined with palms and casuarinas. A few trees play host to flocks of 'flying foxes' – large fruit bats that hang chattering from the branches as they wait restlessly for sundown. At seven sharp the bats flap away into the jungle for a night of foraging. A narrow path runs the length of the bay and south over the headland to Tekek.

To the north, a steep track leads across the rocks from Bamboo Hill (*see* 'Where to Stay', p.263) to tiny **Panuba Bay**, which has its own jetty and two little secluded beaches. There is a decent patch of coral in the waters of Panuba Bay, with a couple of resident hawksbill turtles. A poorly marked jungle trail heads north from here towards **Monkey Bay**, a deserted cove with shallow turquoise waters and a stretch of beach backed by nothing but the chattering jungle: the stuff of desert island fantasy (*see* Activities, pp.260–1).

Moderate–Inexpensive

Salang Indah Resort, **t** 09 419 5015, **f** 09 419 5024. The biggest resort on Salang Bay with a range of accommodation, from rooms in an unappealing block behind the mini-market, to family chalets with air-con right on the water. Some of the chalets are good value, but they vary in quality.

Salang Beach Resort, **t** 07 799 2337, *www.tioman-salang.com*. A Chinese-run place just north of the Salang Indah Resort, with tight-packed chalets curled round a restaurant.

Inexpensive

Pak Long Chalet, **t** 09 419 5000. A group of large chalets behind the freshwater lagoon. Very simple but clean. Some have air-con.

Salang Pusaka Resort (or **Khalid's Place**), **t** 09 419 5317. Also behind the lagoon in a landscaped garden. The layout is smarter than Pak Long's, but the chalets are not quite so good. The attached restaurant specializes in Thai-style seafood.

Juara

Inexpensive

Juara Saujana Resort, **t** 414 5349. Located across the rocks at the southernmost point of the bay. This is a peaceful spot, about 45min by foot from the jetty. A dozen or so colourful chalets sit on a beautiful stretch of beach among small palms. Rooms in the longhouse are less appealing.

Juara Mutiara, **t** 07 799 4833, *www.thejuaraway.com*. The rambling complex of chalets just south of the jetty, which come at a range of prices. Large rooms are available for up to six people.

Budget

There are a handful of budget chalets along the bay, many rundown and out of action. Several, though, are worth mentioning. Riverview Place offers six basic beach huts right at the northern end of the bay, beside the mouth of a little river (the clean cool water flows straight down from the peaks). There's an attached restaurant, a small library and a volleyball net. Paradise Point, a little further south, is similar, but a little more rundown. Rainbow Chalet, down near the rocks south of the jetty, offers a handful of very basic little chalets with hammocks slung between nearby palms. In a secluded spot south of the rocks (on the way to Juara Saujana Resort) is Mizani's Place, a U-shaped formation of basic chalets among flowers and young palms.

South of Tekek

Moderate

Melina Beach Resort, **t** 09 419 7080, *www.tioman-melinabeach.com* A secluded spot between Kampung Paya and Kampung Genting on a 300m stretch of palm-fringed sand. This German-run place offers seven rooms in tasteful semi-detached chalets. The rooms are wood-panelled, with air-con,

Salang

The smaller bay of Salang on the northwest coast lacks the peace and simplicity of Air Batang, conforming more readily to the idea of a beach-holiday destination. Salang is presently the island's liveliest spot, though that's not saying much: its offerings amount to a handful of beachside restaurants and two or three bars that stay open into the night. The bay, with its beautiful half-kilometre sweep of soft sand, is a little overcrowded with chalets, dive schools and monitor lizards (who haunt the freshwater lagoon behind the beach). A large concrete jetty and the outlet of the lagoon split the bay in two, with the best stretch of beach to the south. Some of Tioman's best dive spots are close at hand: west of Salang is uninhabited Pulau Tulai with its archipelago of tiny islets and submerged reefs. Getting elsewhere from Salang is a little difficult.

hot water and verandahs. The restaurant serves European, Malay and Chinese dishes.

Inexpensive

Nipah Resort, t 011 764 184. A handful of simple, clean, wooden chalets some hung with batiks and painted brightly. Set in the isolated Nipah Bay. Hammocks are slung about the place, and there is a small restaurant.

Eating Out

With the exception of a few places on Salang Bay, all restaurants are attached to hotels and chalet operations. Usually there is not much between them. Fresh grilled fish and seafood are the main items on all menus, along with Malay rice and noodle dishes. More often than not, the daily catch is displayed on ice tables. Barracuda, shark, yellow-fin tuna, stingray, kingfish, squid, lobster and giant prawns are commonly available. For breakfast, 'Western' offerings such as omelette are on offer.

At the Berjaya resort there are a number of upmarket restaurants. **Fortune Court** serves Cantonese delicacies, while the **Sri Nelayan** coffeeshop serves a range of Western and Malay dishes. In Tekek itself there are a few good **Malay food stalls**, particularly along the strip north of the jetty. **Liza**, a moderately priced restaurant at the southern end of the bay, serves Malay and Western food and comes recommended.

On Air Batang, the **Hijau Restaurant** at Nazri II stands out above the others. The beachside restaurants at ABC Beach Chalets and Nazri's Place are also popular. Otherwise, stroll along the bay and choose from the displays of fresh fish and seafood.

Salang Bay has a few independent cafés and restaurants catering largely for the traveller scene. **Salang Dream** restaurant, near the end of the jetty, is the most popular spot for seafood. Also near the jetty is the tiny **Amin Café**, serving satay and other Malay favourites. For an attempt at self-catering, head for the mini-market attached to Salang Indah Resort.

At Juara there is a large menu of local and Western dishes at the informal **Beach Café**, near the end of the jetty. Further south is **Bushman's**, a dive school that doubles up as a café and bar by night.

Nightlife

Tioman is a far cry from some of the Thai islands in the South China Sea: no one comes here for the nightlife. The Berjaya resort has the obligatory 'disco', but that's as far as it goes. For the most part, beer drinking is confined to chalet restaurants. However, Salang has two or three bars which play tunes into the early hours. **Ng Cafe**, north of the jetty is a popular bar with a reggae theme. Further along is **Four-S Café**, the most atmospheric place to drink and listen to music. At Juara the only place to buy beer is **Bushman's**.

The overland trip to Air Batang, for example, takes three long sweaty hours on foot through primary jungle. Expensive sea-taxis are the only alternative.

Juara

Across a spine of mountains on the east coast is Kampung Juara, one of Tioman's oldest settlements. Villagers of Juara are thought to be descendants of Bugis tribespeople who arrived from the Riau archipelago in Indonesia over 1,000 years ago. In 1976 locals unearthed ancient ceramics while levelling a small football field. Many of the finds – produced in China during the 12th–14th-century Song dynasty – sat around in villagers' huts before being sold to drooling antiques dealers and tourists. Those that survived are displayed in the museum at Tekek.

In terms of natural beauty, this side of the island is probably Tioman's highlight. Behind Juara a horseshoe of towering peaks mimic the curve of the bay, providing a stunning approach to the village. A wide windswept beach stretches several kilometres, split by the mouth of the Sungai Keliling. To the south of the river, the long stretch of beach is punctuated by just two small chalet operations, which provide some of the island's best getaway options. North of the river mouth are a few more places to stay and a couple of beachside cafes. Villagers live inland from the beach.

Because Juara is east-facing, it is open to the ravages of the South China Sea, making it inaccessible during the monsoon. When it comes to diving and snorkelling, the waters here do not compare with those off the west coast – even outside monsoon season the visibility is often poor. For these reasons, Juara remains very quiet and undeveloped. The most picturesque means of reaching Juara is by the sea-bus, an old fishing boat which labours slowly round the island each day. Otherwise a steep jungle trail links Juara with Tekek (*see* 'Activities', pp.260–1).

South of Tekek

South of Tekek on the west coast are a string of kampungs nestled into little coves, each accessible only by boat. Some are virtually uninhabited. Behind these coves volcanic rock rises steeply towards Tioman's tallest peaks, lending a vertical backdrop.

Just south of the Berjaya resort is **Kampung Paya**, a sandy half-kilometre bay very popular with Singaporean visitors. The beach is good for swimming and there's a little waterfall five minutes inland from the beach. Next along is **Kampung Genting**, a more substantial place with another lovely beach, though this one is packed tight with resorts catering mainly for local Chinese – expect lots of karaoke.

Tiny **Kampung Nipah** is probably Tioman's most isolated settlement. Sungai Nipah – more a trickling stream than a river – cascades from its source near the summit of Gunung Kajang (1,038m), the island's highest peak. Forty ceramic vessels from China's early Song dynasty were discovered in 1962 inside Gua Serau, a cave upstream from Nipah. Other finds within the village itself were identified as 10th-century ceramics from Guangdong Province in southern China, confirming Nipah to be Tioman's oldest settlement. The beach here is wonderful, as is the snorkelling.

At the southern point of Tioman is **Mukut**, a fishing kampung at the foot of towering Nenek Semukut. This vertical hunk of rock, also known as Dragon Horn, presents an extreme challenge to experienced climbers (*see* Activities, pp.260–1). East of here, near the deserted village of Asah, a trail leads to the famous 20m waterfall that featured in *South Pacific*.

Pahang's Interior

Taman Negara

The Taman Negara is Malaysia's flagship National Park (*taman negara* is Malay for 'national park'). First gazetted as the Tahan Mountain Game Reserve by the British in 1925, the Taman Negara now covers more than a million acres across mountains and lowlands in the three states of Pahang, Kelantan and Terengganu.

More species of tree can be found in a single hectare of the Taman Negara than in the entirety of North America. At least 300 species of bird, 200 different mammals and 15,000 species of plant have so far been identified within the park boundaries. Many more await discovery. The key to the great biodiversity of this swathe of primary rainforest is its age; with more than 130 million years under its belt, the rainforest of the Taman Negara is older than that of both the Amazon and the Congo.

Theodore Hubback was the British conservationist behind the original park, which was renamed King George V National Park in 1938, then Taman Negara on Independence in 1957. In those early days, being a conservationist didn't preclude a touch of hunting. In fact, big-game hunting was a keen pursuit of Hubback's, and he contributed to a number of books on the subject. Today, hunting is strictly controlled within park boundaries, with fines and jail sentences given to convicted poachers.

That is not to say that poaching has been wiped out; the pelts and organs of exotic creatures still fetch good money on the Chinese market; each year the park authority collects in excess of RM1 million in fines. Only the Batek tribespeople are given free rein to subsistence-hunt in the Taman Negara: the Batek are a subtribe of the Negritos, a group of Orang Asli whose lifestyle within these forests has remained virtually unchanged for 2,000 years. A handful of tribes still live out their hunter-gatherer lives within the park, collecting wild fruits and root vegetables, and using blowpipes to hunt game such as deer and monkey. (Strangely the prolific wild boar is not on their menu; ask them why they avoid hunting it and they shrug and say, 'We never tried it'. Perhaps they would rather not be in direct competition with the tiger, whose favourite prey is boar.)

Those who have never walked in primary rainforest before may be surprised at its accessibility. The real thing is a far cry from the impenetrable mesh of plant life that often springs to mind when the word 'jungle' is mentioned. The fight for light high up in the jungle canopy means that few plants can survive on the floor of the rainforest, unless they happen to be near the banks of rivers and streams, where lateral light can penetrate the foliage. Beneath the dense and lofty canopy is a microclimate of cool air saturated with moisture (the temperature rarely breaks 26 celsius though the humidity makes it feel hotter), where the predominant features are the twisted lianas and the giant trunks of the dipterocarp trees, their roots and buttresses splayed wide for stability.

Other people are disappointed by the scarcity of animal sightings. With well-tuned ears and careful observation, you are sure to spot many birds (exotic insects, of course, are everywhere). The other creatures of the rainforest tend to be masters of disguise and any sightings should be taken as a bonus. Even large mammals, such as the 1,000lb Malayan tapir, the *seladang* (largest of the cattle species) or the Asian elephant, tend to keep themselves to themselves, while the tiger and the endangered Sumatran rhino very rarely make appearances (recent research indicates that there are around 100 tigers and only a few dozen rhinos resident within the Taman Negara).

The 'dry' season falls between February and October and this is when most people visit the Taman Negara. In reality the rains fall year-round and the seasons are rather

Leeches

Leeches have a bad name. After all, they are parasites (and blood-sucking, slug-like hermaphrodite ones at that). First encounters with leeches are sometimes enough to make grown men shriek. But the fear soon wears off: a leech bite is painless and there is no risk of disease. After a few days in the jungle, you will have seen so many of them waving their suckers in your direction – they could have waited all year for such an opportunity – that you may even feel sorry for their limbless existence.

Leeches haven't always been unpopular. Their heyday came in the 19th century, when enthusiasts in Europe would collect them for the treatment of various ailments. In the case of a headache, the leech practitioner would attach one or two to each temple as a way of drawing out the 'bad blood'. Leeches are still used today to prevent clotting in certain surgical procedures.

Leeches are generally little more than an inch in length and are slimmer than a worm, unless bloated with blood. They breathe through their skin and have a sucker at either end of their bodies, which they use to move and to attach themselves to a host. Receptors on the leech's body enables it to detect the vibrations of passing animals. They also have primitive eyes, which can detect shadows and other abrupt changes in light.

Once a leech has attached itself to a host, and located a suitable patch of skin (which can take some time), it makes a tiny Y-shaped incision with three sets of teeth located at the thinner end of the body. An anti-coagulant in the saliva dilates the blood vessels and increases blood flow (this is why bites bleed slowly for a long time after the leech has been disposed of). It is also thought that the saliva has anaesthetic qualities (a leech can attach, feed and drop off without the host noticing).

So, what to do when you spot a leech attached to your leg? The first thing to realize is that leeches take their time before drawing blood; in most instances you can flick the leech away without too much trouble. If the leech is already bloated, then you need to be careful not to tear it off too vigorously, thereby leaving its mouth parts buried in your skin. If flicking doesn't work, then try Tiger Balm, DEET, salt or a naked flame. The tiny puncture will bleed for some time after the leech has dropped off.

There are numerous theories on how best to avoid leech bites. Some people clothe themselves from head to toe, or wear leech socks; others simply smear their skin with insect repellent. But leeches can squeeze between the fibres of clothing and climb round the edges of leech socks; and there is no evidence that repellent repels a leech that has waited up to a year between meals. Those in the know – take the Orang Asli as an example – venture into the forest in nothing more (and sometimes less) than shorts, shoes and T-shirt. That way it is easier to detect a leech on the skin and flick it away before it can bite: there are no folds of clothing in which they can bide their time unnoticed.

Know where the leeches lurk, and you have a better chance of avoiding them. Those in the leaf litter of the jungle trails are the easiest to spot – especially as they inch excitably towards you – but their favourite place of ambush is on the underside of a leaf, usually at ankle- or knee-height. As a final bit of advice, take no notice of the belief that leeches only come out after rain – or they'll catch you unawares.

unpredictable, so it is certainly worth risking a visit from October to January, especially if you want to avoid the crowds. Most visitors venture no more than a few hundred yards from their accommodation, so even in peak season the trails remain relatively undisturbed.

The Trails

Around park headquarters the rainforest is laced with trails that can be tackled in a single day. Though distances covered are small, some of these trails are both testing and rewarding, each offering their own unique slant on the rainforest habitat. A major attraction of the Taman Negara is that these trails can be tackled without a guide: the going is occasionally tough, but the paths are well marked. The excitement of venturing unaided into primary jungle, among the soothing chatter of birds and insects and running water, is something not easily forgotten.

For those who don't mind camping out in the jungle, there are many options for longer expeditions. Such trips offer much greater chances of spotting the larger mammals, and with careful planning, some of these trails can be attempted independently as well. However, for those unfamiliar with the rainforest, a knowledgeable guide will help bring the place alive: what appears to the untrained eye to be little more than a mass of oppressive foliage, is often seething with activity. As well as providing reassurance, a guide should be able to point out unusual plants, insects and animals. Some of the trails cross rivers and streams which, after heavy rains, may be impassable: check with park HQ before setting out on your own.

Around Kuala Tahan

The most well-trodden trail – and one not to be missed – is the **Canopy Walk**. A path leads from the resort along the bank of the Sungai Tembeling for about a mile, before arriving at the canopy walkway (*open Sat–Thurs 11–3, Fri 9–12; adm RM5*). Half a kilometre of wooden planks placed end to end and lined with wire cables are suspended between the giant trunks of *tualang* trees 150ft above the jungle floor. It is the longest canopy walkway in the world. From this vertiginous perspective it is easier to understand the three-dimensional nature of the jungle habitat. The canopy itself is the most active slice of this habitat; birds, squirrels, monkeys, gibbons, butterflies, snakes and lizards all live out their lives up here among the spray of leaves and flowers. Epiphytes, such as the exotic bird's-nest fern, cling to the boughs, and a myriad fungi feed off the bark. Unfortunately the walkway is open only during the sleepiest period of the day. First light and dusk see the greatest activity, and it may be worth making enquiries about visiting the walkway out of hours.

Inland from the canopy walkway, the terrain climbs up towards **Bukit Teresek** (334m), where there is a fabulous lookout point. The summit is only one mile from park HQ, but the trail follows a steep ridge and can take at least an hour to climb (one jungle mile is the equivalent of three or four miles on the flat). From park HQ, the trail follows the Sungai Tembeling for several hundred metres, before turning inland (follow the signs). There are two viewpoints on the hill top; the first, which is the

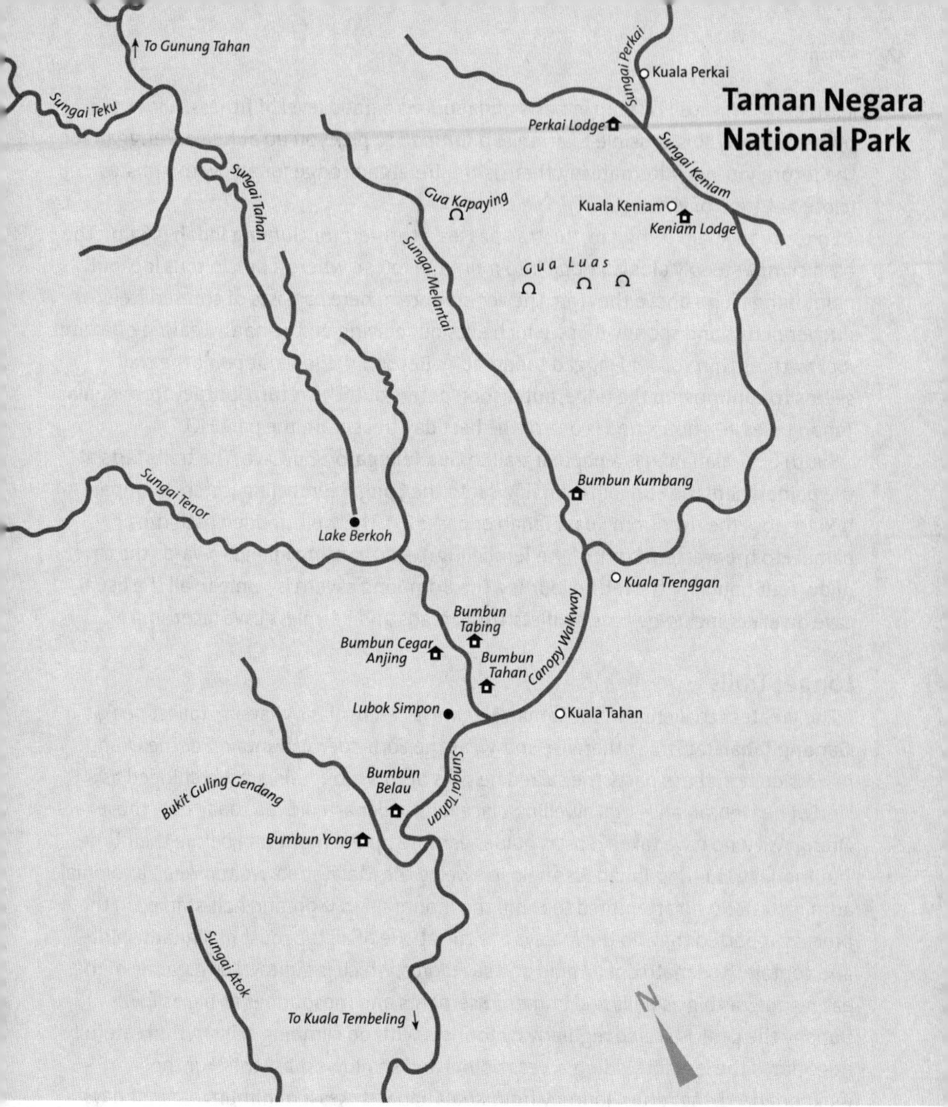

actual summit, looks down across the river to the forested hills outside the park boundary. But carry on a further 15mins to the second viewpoint, where 50km of the Taman Negara open out before you. The view takes in Bukit Tahan (tallest mountain in Peninsular Malaysia) and the jutting limestone peaks that conceal the caves of Gua Kepayang and Gua Luas. The Teresek trail then descends in a northwest direction towards Sungai Tahan, where it loops back along the river bank to Park HQ. Along the way, look out for **Lubok Simpon**, a 'water hole' along the Tahan that is known as a good spot for swimming. Allow at least three hours to complete the loop.

Kuala Trenggan is a 45-minute *sampan* ride north of Kuala Tahan (on the Sungai Tembeling), though it is possible to make the journey on foot: from the turn-off for the canopy walk,way a trail continues for six miles along a similar course to the

Tembeling. This trek is steep in parts and requires a good level of fitness. Allow 5–6 hours one-way. It is possible to arrange a *sampan* to pick you up at Kuala Trenggan for the return journey. Alternatively, there is the Trenggan Lodge for an overnight stay (closed at time of writing).

En route to Kuala Trenggan, the trail passes a turn-off for **Gunung Indah** (563m). The path climbs steeply along a ridge into montane forest, where a precipitous lookout point hangs high above the river. The vegetation up here consists of stunted trees, pitcher plants and spongy moss, which ekes out a living on the hard-wearing quarzite rock with its thin soil and jagged topography. Beyond the lookout point the trail seems to continue up the ridge, but it soon peters out. The return journey from Kuala Tahan takes 3–4 hours and is one of the best day treks from the park HQ.

South of Kuala Tahan is a popular trail to **Gua Telinga**, or 'Ear Cave'. The trail starts at the point where the Sungai Tahan flows into the Sungai Tembeling (catch a sampan taxi to cross the river from Kuala Tahan or park HQ). The well-trodden path runs parallel to the western bank of the Tembeling, before cutting inland towards the cave. Allow four hours for the return journey. The 80m-long cavern is home to all the usual cave dwellers, including bats, swiflets, frogs, toads and harmless cave racer snakes.

Longer Trails

The greatest challenge in the Taman Negara is Peninsular Malaysia's tallest peak, **Gunung Tahan** (2187m), otherwise known as the Forbidden Mountain. For the Orang Asli resident in these parts, the sacred heights of this mountain are worshipped as a kind of heaven, an ancestral dwelling place for the departed. Even today, only those Orang Asli who have taken jobs as guides venture up the mountain before their time. Traditionally, Gunung Tahan was held in awe by the Malays too. Walter Skeat, a colonial administrator who attempted to climb the mountain in 1899, and half-starved in the process, reported that, 'To the Malays it is the abode of all the most malignant spirits, and contains the matrix of all gold and silver ores, which is guarded by gigantic man-eating apes as big as bulls and immense serpents and mosquitoes as big as fowls'.

Today the peak is scaled regularly by tourists with no climbing skills. A trail carefully negotiates the less forbidding access points and shallowest ascents. For the inexperienced, the return journey from Kuala Tahan takes a minimum of eight days. At a more leisurely pace, or with diversions, the trek can take anything up to a fortnight (one popular diversion on the Gunung Tahan trail is a visit to the Four-Steps Waterfall, a beautiful 100ft cascade near the source of the Sungai Tahan).

A skilled guide is essential, as is thorough preparation and a good level of fitness. Night-time temperatures near the summit have been known to reach 4°C or below, so extra layers and a warm sleeping bag are required. Because food supplies need to be as light as possible, dried produce is ideal for the journey. All rubbish must be brought back to Kuala Tahan, so extra packaging should be dispensed with before setting out.

The trail meanders northwest from Kuala Tahan, crossing rivers, gullies and bare ridges. Heavy rains can make river crossings hazardous and raise the likelihood of

The Strangler Fig

The strangler fig is a common and vital player in the rainforest habitat of Southeast Asia. Its methods of survival and dominance are often misunderstood, deadly though they are. Figs are the favoured food of many birds and animals from hornbills to wild boar, and it is these that help propogate the species, dispersing seeds across wide areas of the forest. Though able to develop into trees from the ground, the strangler fig has a unique adaptation which has earned it its name.

Those seeds that are left in the boughs of trees by birds, bats, squirrels or monkeys become temporary epiphytes – plants that live and grow on a host. The young fig tree soon sends aerial roots alongside the trunk of the host and down to the jungle floor. These roots thicken and mould into a latticework that will eventually surround the entire trunk of the host.

Meanwhile the strangler fig sends leaf-laden branches skywards, often smothering the host's canopy and starving the tree of light. It is this – rather than the 'strangling' action of the roots – that will eventually kill the host. Even then, the host will survive in many cases, but being much older than the fig tree, will die first.

Once the host tree has rotted away, the hollows and crevices within the great cylindrical trunk of the strangler fig become the perfect refuge and nesting site for birds, mammals and reptiles alike. For visitors to the rainforest, the knarled and twisted trunk of the strangler fig – often many metres in diameter – will be an enduring memory.

flash floods, so the dry season is the recommended time to make the journey. Eight or so camps along the way provide space to pitch tents. As the trail rises out of the lowland dipterocarp forest, the vegetation changes dramatically and the scenery opens out. Oak trees and conifers make an appearance, before the weathered land gives way to the knarled and dwarfed tree species of the montane forest. On the Gunung Tahan plateau itself, the vegetation grows to only a few feet in height, stunted by poor soils. Scratchy shrubs, pitcher plants and orchids abound up here.

Kuala Tahan is not the only access point to Gunung Tahan. North of Jerantut on the jungle railway is the town of **Merapoh**. From here a road leads to the park ranger station at Sungai Relau. The return journey to Gunung Tahan from this point takes five days, with very steep climbs near the summit. The third and least used entry point to the park is **Kuala Koh** in Kelantan, from where a longer trail leads to the summit.

For those with less time on their hands there are trails in the vicinity of Kuala Tahan that can be completed in three days or less. The **Rentis Tenor** trail, which requires three days, leads into a remote part of the Taman Negara west of Kuala Tahan. The trail is very indistinct in parts and a guide is obligatory. Because this 35km trail is a loop, no backtracking is required for the return journey. Although difficult, the trail has its distinct attractions; the route bypasses Gua Talinga (*see* p.272) and several of the park's hides (which can be used as camps en route; *see* p.274), as well as taking in some great stands of lowland rainforest, a series of rapids on Sungai Tenor and the montane forest of Bukit Guling Gendang.

Getting There

Access to the Taman Negara requires a three-hour boat ride from Kuala Tembeling, near Jerantut in Pahang. Long, covered *sampans* leave at 9am and 2pm, cost RM19 one-way, and take around 3 hours (it is worth the money for the boat trip alone). There is one powerboat daily at 1pm (the journey takes just over an hour and costs RM30 one-way). It is a scenic journey past remote kampungs, paddy fields and small fruit plantations. Coach services direct from KL are timed to meet the boats, but many people stay in nearby Jerantut (*see* p.277) before making their way to the national park. Jerantut is one of the stops on the 'Jungle Railway' (*see* p.280). For treks up to the summit of Gunung Tahan, there are also access points from Merapoh (accessible as one of the stops on the jungle railway) and Kuala Koh in Kelantan, accessible by river.

Getting Around

Sampan taxis make the short hop across the river from Kuala Tahan to park headquarters between 7.30am and 11pm (50 sen). *Sampans* can also be chartered to visit the Lata Berkoh waterfall, or to travel upriver to Nusa Camp or the Trenggan or Keniam lodges.

Tourist Information

Before entering the Taman Negara, visitors must first register at the park office beside the jetty in Kuala Tembeling (if you are in a tour group the guide may do this for you). Before setting off on any of the trails, you must also register at park HQ (*open 8am–10pm*), situated behind the Mutiara Resort in Kuala Tahan. The park HQ is also the place to come to book a space at one of the hides. The staff provide superficial maps of the trails and general information. They also rent out equipment such as tents and flashlights. The Mutiara Resort has a small exhibition on the park and a nightly video showing (*see* opposite). The resort reception is another good information source, as are guesthouse receptions, such as the Teresek View Motel.

Tour agencies all over the country run trips into the Taman Negara. They are highly competitive and many of them are pushy about signing you up, particularly in Jerantut. Before signing up for something, bear in mind that many of your experiences will be enhanced if tackled independently. In any case, guides and tours can easily be arranged from Kuala Tahan itself, where you will have a better impression of the setup and your own requirements. Experiencing the Taman Negara needn't be an expensive business.

North of Kuala Trenggan (*see* p.272) are some excellent and little-visited trails, offering good chances of spotting wildlife. The lodge at **Kuala Keniam** is a leisurely two-day hike (20km) from Kuala Trenggan. The trail passes Bumbun Kumbang, the park's northernmost hide (*see* p.276), and a series of caves situated at the foot of several huge limestone outcrops. One of them, Batu Luas, offers some challenging ascents for climbers. From Kuala Keniam, another 5km hike through gibbon-rich forest leads to the Perkai Lodge, further up the pretty Sungai Keniam. At the time of writing, both the Keniam and Perkai lodges were closed due to disrepair.

The Hides

There are a number of hides within easy access of the park HQ. These offer the best chances of spotting wildlife. Each hide, a small wooden hut raised on stilts 20ft from the ground, is located on the edge of a small clearing or a salt lick. For mammals that inhabit the rainforest, salt licks are a vital source of minerals and, as such, make excellent sites for hides. The hides often get booked up well in advance: there are

Where to Stay

Most of the accommodation is found at Kuala Tahan, the hub of activities in the Taman Negara. At present there is just the one resort, as well as a handful of basic chalet complexes. A few miles upstream the Nusa Holiday Village offers a touch more seclusion, while further north still is the lodge at Kuala Trenggan. This was closed at the time of writing and is therefore not listed below, though there are tentative plans to reopen the lodge at some point. One experience that shouldn't be missed is a night in one of the park's hides (*see* p.274). These are all equipped with three or four bunk beds, so that you can catch some sleep if the animals don't perform.

Expensive–Inexpensive

Mutiara Taman Negara, t 09 266 3500, f 09 266 1500, *saltn@mutiarahotels.com*, *www.mutiarahotels.com*. An attractive luxury chalet complex set in 15 acres of grounds around the Park HQ. There are 70 chalets, a few double-storey suites and a handful of standard rooms (which go for around RM200). There is also an attached hostel, which costs RM60/person including a buffet breakfast, and a campsite (RM20 to rent a tent, plus RM3/person). The chalets are spacious, though low on facilities; there is no TV, phone, safe, tea/coffee maker or mini-bar (this *is* meant to be a jungle experience). The open-sided restaurant serves expensive buffet meals throughout the day and has an à la carte menu too. The quality of food is high considering the location. The Mutiara has a shop selling basic supplies for jungle trekking and an Interpretive Centre with a small exhibition on the park and a nightly video. Behind the reception is the Park Authority headquarters. They also rent out torches and provide information on the trails.

Moderate–Inexpensive

Ekoton Chalet, t/f 09 266 9897. A quiet spot above Tembeling Riverview, with eight comfortable air-conditioned chalets, and another eight fan-only rooms. There is also a nondescript dormitory, an attached laundry and a basic restaurant.

Nusa Holiday Village, t 09 266 2369, *www.tamannegara-nusaholiday.com.my*. Set on its own, 15 minutes upstream from Kuala Tahan by boat. Offers a range of accommodation from spacious and well-appointed 'Malay bungalows' to dorms and camping. This is a self-sufficient setup, with tour guides on hand, a basic restaurant and laundry. The Nusa Village is on the opposite bank of the river to the national park, so

three bunks in each, so numbers are limited to only six or seven people. Bookings must be made in person at the park HQ in Kuala Tahan. The cost is RM7/person.

There are certain factors vital to your chances of sightings. Most animals will only venture into a clearing under the cover of darkness, so you will need to spend a night in the hide. If an animal detects your presence, it will keep away. This means no cooking, no smoking and silence. Arrive at the hide well before sundown and preferably after eating (pack only dry food for snacks during the night). If you don't want to go without sleep, then stay up in shifts to watch for animals. Unless there is a full moon, you will need to sweep a torch beam across the clearing every few minutes.

Do not expect to experience anything along the lines of an African water hole: this is the jungle, where survival depends upon concealment rather than safety-in-numbers. Mammals that pay a regular visit to salt licks include tapir, deer, boar, elephants, *seladang*, civets and cats. If you are lucky, you may see a few of these (tapir, deer and boar are the most common). If not, your only encounter might be with rats after your biscuits.

guests here are dependent on boatmen to ferry them across.

Inexpensive

Tahan Guesthouse, **t** 09 266 7752, *jungletreker@yahoo.com* An attractive family-run hotel up the hill in Kuala Tahan (behind the police station). Rooms at the back of the house have little balconies with views over the jungle. All rooms have clean en suite bathrooms. There are framed illustrations of rare plants all over the walls.

Teresek View Motel, **t** 09 267 2243, **f** 09 266 9744. A few small fan-only chalets and some simple A-frames in the cente of Kuala Tahan. The reception doubles up as a small shop and internet café, and provides lots of information about the park.

Agoh Chalet, **t** 09 266 9570, **t** 09 296 6488, *www.agoh.com.my*. A rectangle of simple chalets set round a shady, dusty courtyard. All rooms are clean with attached bathrooms but no air-con.

Budget

Tembeling Riverview Chalet, **t** 09 266 6766, *rosnahtru@hotmail.com*. Clean, very basic rooms, with small bathrooms, overlooking the river. The restaurant, on the hillside above the river, serves tasty *roti canai* each morning. Internet access available.

Durian Chalet, **t** 09 266 8940, *aafzal@lycos.com*. In a beautiful spot beyond the police station: follow the lane through the little rubber plantation. A scattering of little chalets inclined on a hillside among flowers. There is also an attached camping plot among the trees. Renting a tent and equipment costs RM10.

Eating Out

The **Mutiara Resort** at Kuala Tahan has an attractive open-sided restaurant (near the park HQ), which serves expensive set meals for breakfast, lunch and dinner. There is also an à la carte menu with a good range of Asian and Western dishes on offer. Other than this, visitors are limited to eating at the other chalet complexes or at the floating restaurants on the Sungai Tembeling, most of which offer cheap Malay and Chinese staples: **Lia Restoran** serves good *roti canai* and delicious mango shakes, though the rice and noodle dishes aren't great. The best of the floating restaurants is **Rumbia Restaurant**, at the southern end of the stretch. It is wonderfully atmospheric, with an *attap* roof, beautiful hand-crafted menus and natural décor, including varnished leaves the size of baseball gloves. The food doesn't disappoint either; the rich fish curry is the speciality.

There are six hides in the park, though not all of them are likely to be open at the same time. The more distance you place between yourself and park HQ, the greater are your chances of animal sightings. The closest hide, **Bumbun Tahan**, is an artificial salt lick just 200m away.

Bumbun Tabing and **Bumbun Cegar Anjing** are about three hours north of park HQ (by foot) along Sungai Tahan. These are the most popular, as they offer fair chances of spotting wildlife, while being easily accessible (that said, reaching Bumbun Cegar Anjing involves fording the Tahan). The Tabing hide overlooks a natural salt lick, while the Cegar Anjing one overlooks an artificial lick in a clearing (once part of an airstrip).

About two hours' walk south of Kuala Tahan, past the turning for Gua Telinga, are **Bumbun Belau** and **Bumbun Yong**, though the latter is so close to the *sampan* traffic on the Tembeling that sightings here are reported to be rare.

Bumbun Kumbang is the most distant hide and the best for wildlife. The trail to the hide passes Bumbun Tabing then cuts north in the direction of Sungai Trenggan, which needs to be crossed before the hide is reached. Allow six hours for the walk. An alternative route is to hire a *sampan* to take you upriver to Kuala Trenggan, then walk the remaining 45mins to Bumbun Kumbang. Macaques, leaf monkeys and gibbons are common in these parts, while this hide probably offers your best chance of seeing elephants and *seladang* (remember, these animals roam widely over the Taman Negara so sightings still require luck).

Other Activities

Fishing is big sport in the Taman Negara. There are more than 200 species of fish in the rivers and tributaries of the park, and permits are easy to come by (from park HQ). Catfish, carp, snakeheads, jungle perch and the feisty mahseer (or *kelisa*, in Malay) are some of the prize catches. The lodges of Kuala Trenggan and Kuala Keniam are used largely as fishing lodges: the waters up here are said to be some of the best.

A straightforward **boat trip** is one of the most popular activities in the park. For those loathe to sweat it out on foot, a journey into the wilderness by sampan will be an experience in itself. The boatmen who hang around the floating jetty in Kuala Tahan will be only too happy to take you upriver, as long as water levels allow it. The commonest excursion is to **Lata Berkoh**, a beautiful waterfall at the highest navigable point on the Sungai Tahan. The waters here are clean and shallow and perfect for a paddle, while the banks provide a great site for a picnic.

Rubber-tubing down the Tembeling is another popular activity. The inner tubes of truck tyres provide buoyancy as you float down a few gentle rapids along the Sungai Tembeling, just upriver from Kuala Tahan. Ask at the floating jetties for details.

Jerantut

Otherwise a small and insignificant town, Jerantut has taken full advantage of its location on the doorstep of the Taman Negara. For tourists it is the traditional entry point to the national park. Many visitors, especially budget travellers, spend a night or two here before catching a *sampan* upriver from the jetty at nearby Kuala Tembeling.

A reception committee of touts haunt Jerantut's bus terminal, train station and taxi stand, waiting to greet new arrivals and compete for their custom. Extensive tour packages are thrust down your throat, and you will be left with the impression that you couldn't possibly venture into the Taman Negara independently. That is not the case, as will soon become apparent when you arrive inside park boundaries.

However, many people prefer to stop over in Jerantut to break the journey and stock up on provisions. The Jaya Emporium, a handy little supermarket, serves this purpose, while the daily open market near the bus terminal is great for local fruit and dried produce.

Getting There

Jerantut is one of the stops on the **jungle railway**; pick up a timetable or check the KTM website for details (*www.ktmb.com.my*). A large number of **bus** services run to Jerantut from all over Peninsular Malaysia. The bus depot and long-distance **taxi** stand are in the centre of town beside the market square.

Getting to Tembeling Jetty

Minibuses leave for Tembeling jetty each morning at 8.30 from most of the budget guesthouses. They are timed to meet departing river taxis at Kuala Tembeling. The minibus charge is RM5/person. Alternatively, a taxi to the jetty should cost only RM5-10.

Where to Stay

In terms of accommodation, Jerantut only really caters to the backpacker scene. A handful of guesthouses, each with affiliated tour agencies, compete fiercely for business – which can make arrival in Jerantut an unpleasant experience. The Sri Emas Guesthouse/NKS Travel is the most successful, but that is due solely to aggressive touting and the place is not to be recommended.

The **Jerantut Hill Resort**, Jalan Benta, **t** 09 267 2288, **f** 09 267 1188, *jhrsb@tm.net.my, http://jhresort.com.my* (*moderate-inexpensive*) provides the best accommodation, with plain standard rooms, family chalets, a sauna and a pool with a slide. Rates are good value and include breakfast. The hotel is on a hill just out of town. **The Jerantut Resthouse**, Jalan Benta (pass under the railway bridge heading out of town), **t** 09 266 3884, **f** 09 266 4884 offers a range of chalets from RM30-90 and a six-bed dorm. There is an attached restaurant, tour agency and internet café. The Resthouse is under the same management as the **Green Park Guesthouse**, Lot 34, Jalan Besar, same tel. This is a simple place with shared bathrooms, dorms, singles, doubles and triples, all for RM30 or less. The owner is an experienced jungle guide. An alternative budget choice is **Chong Heng Hotel**, 24 Jalan Besar, **t** 09 266 3693, situated above a characterful little *kedai kopi* with marble-top tables.

Eating Out

All of the guesthouses serve basic rice, noodle and egg-based dishes. By far the best place for a meal is the large hawker centre west of the market square.

Kuala Lipis

Slap bang in the centre of Peninsular Malaysia is Kuala Lipis, an unspoilt and little-visited riverine town that was state capital of Pahang until 1955. Situated at the confluence of Sungai Lipis and Sungai Jelai (which empties into the great Pahang River), Kuala Lipis has served for centuries as a major contact point between Chinese traders and tribespeople of the interior. Wild animals, aromatic woods, feathers, ivory, roots and herbs were brought here by the orang asli and traded for basic goods such as rice, salt and clothing – a way of life still in evidence to this day.

The British administration chose Kuala Lipis as the seat of the Pahang Residency in 1898. The only access in those days was by river boat, but the British were keen to open up the interior of Malaya in search of tin and gold. They immediately hacked an overland route through the jungle, linking Pahang's administrative centre with Kuala Lumpur. In the 1920s they improved access further by extending the railway line from Gemas to Kuala Lipis (*see* 'Jungle Railway' p.280). But by the 1950s the promise of gold and tin in the region had flagged. Power was transferred from Kuala Lipis to Kuantan, and the town reverted to its ancient role as a marketplace for jungle products. Of

Getting There

The railway line which cuts across the interior of the peninsula from Gemas to Kota Bharu passes straight through Kuala Lipis. The original wooden station is still in use behind Jalan Besar in the centre of town. Buses pull in to the stand at the west end of Jalan Besar.

Tourist Information

There is no official tourist office in Kuala Lipis, though a travel agent just opposite the train station advertises itself as such. They provide maps and (biased) information.

Where to Stay

Moderate

Lipis Centrepoint Hotel, **t** 09 312 2688, **f** 09 312 2699, *www.centrepointhotel.com.my*. This is the top place to stay in town (though it's far from being an upmarket hotel). Access is via a grubby lift to the 5th floor of the Centrepoint building. The hotel itself is surprisingly attractive, geared mainly to the local businessman. All rooms are in good nick with a good range of facilities.

Lipis Inn, **t** 09 312 4973, **f** 09 312 4975. The largest hotel in Kuala Lipis, of a similar standard to the Centrepoint, but with smaller rooms and higher rates.

Inexpensive

Kuala Lipis Resthouse, **t** 312 2599. The old British Residency on a small hill above town. Certainly the most atmospheric place to stay in Kuala Lipis, but the spacious rooms are fading fast, with peeling wallpaper and old, spartan furnishings.

Budget

Hotel Jelai, **t** 09 312 1182, **f** 09 312 1562. A Chinese-run hotel overlooking the Jelai river. Rooms all have air-con, but otherwise are simple. Ask for a river-view room with small balcony. The enthusiastic owner provides each guest with a hand-drawn map of town and some rubber seeds to plant back home.

Appu's Guesthouse/Hotel Lipis, **t** 09 312 3142, *jungleappu@yahoo.com*. A sociable little place on Jalan Besar geared to the backpacker scene, with dorms and a few very cheap doubles with fan. There is also one air-con double going for RM45. Appu has lots of information about the town and the Kenong Rimba park.

Hotel London, **t** 09 312 1618. A small hotel on Jalan Besar offering clean, simple rooms for RM20, or RM30-40 with air-con. Most rooms have no window.

Eating Out

On Friday evenings the best food in town can be found at the *pasar malam*, where hundreds of stallholders whip up their own particular speciality. The alleyway linking Jalan Besar and Jalan Jelai is lined with tiny food stalls, most of them serving just one or two dishes.

Restoran Sin Hoi Kee, Jalan Pekeliling. Very good Chinese dishes served just over the railway tracks. Wild boar is the favourite item on the menu.

Restoran Low Kuan, Jalan Besar. A Chinese restaurant specializing in river fish and freshwater prawns, which go for high prices. Simple staples are cheap.

Restoran Tai Choong, Jalan Besar/Main. Despite the name, this little place is a South Indian banana-leaf restaurant.

Lipis Tai Sok, just off the alleyway linking Jalan Besar with Jalan Jelai. This Chinese place lays tables out on the street in the evenings and is a favourite with locals. Great-value food and huge servings.

Mohamed Ali, Jalan Besar, at the top of the alleyway. A very popular little *mamak* stall, serving delicious *roti canai*.

course, the British had already stamped their mark on Kuala Lipis, leaving a colonial legacy in the form of austere, neoclassical architecture.

With only 7,000 inhabitants today, Kuala Lipis can barely be called a town. Movement on the streets is about as slow-paced as the copper waters of the Jelai river, which skirts the northern edge of town. Not so long ago, visitors would come to Kuala Lipis to see the *rakits*, or traditional house-rafts, which moored on the banks of the river: following a series of flash floods, the government relocated the boats one hour downriver. But some things in Kuala Lipis never change, and the Semai tribespeople still paddle in on their dugouts every Friday for the *pasar malam*, which overruns the bus stand at the west end of town.

The Sights

Most of the tourists that stop by at Kuala Lipis will be en route to the Kenong Rimba State Park (*see* opposite), but there are a handful of places in town worth making the effort to visit.

The centre of activity in Kuala Lipis is the small square of streets between the train station and the river. Packed in along these streets are pockets of tumbledown, Straits Eclectic-style shophouses from the late 19th century. Just east of here, past the little clock tower, is a footpath leading beneath the road bridge and onto the railway bridge, which crosses the mouth of little Sungai Lipis at the point where it meets Sungai Jelai. There's a rickety walkway on the bridge that runs alongside the railway track, from where there are great views downriver – particularly at sunset. At this time of day, local fishermen wade alongside the river banks, steadying their dugouts with one hand and using a paddle with the other to flush out fish from among the tangle of roots at the water's edge.

At the road junction south of the bridge is a turning which leads past the hospital to Kuala Lipis' oldest building, the **Pahang Club**. This worn wooden structure built by the British in 1867 is straight out of a Somerset Maugham story: wander about the great open verandahs, the billiards room, the bar, and it is not hard to populate the

Jungle Railway

During the 1920s Tamil workers under the instruction of the British hacked their way across the peninsula's mountainous interior to lay the 'Golden Blowpipe', as the jungle railway came to be known ('golden' after the failed glut of gold mining that took place early in the 20th century). In the early years the railway was used only for the transportation of tin and rubber, before opening to passengers in 1938.

The line is still open today. If you catch the slow train from Gemas the pace is a leisurely crawl (the journey to Kuala Lipis takes 7.5 hours), but the scenery is spectacular. Whereas the busy west-coast line (used by the famous Orient Express) passes through a monotonous landscape of palm-oil plantations, the jungle railway chugs across expanses of remote rainforest and through pretty Malay kampungs. Today, many brochure and guidebook descriptions of this line are outdated: the train may be full of villagers and their market produce – mainly Malays, orang asli and Tamil plantation workers – but the carriages are all air-conditioned and the seats comfortable. Four trains a day make the journey between Gemas and Kuala Lipis. There is one daily express train between Singapore and Tumpat on the northeast border with Thailand (13 hours).

space with gossiping planters' wives or gold prospectors sipping at stengahs. Even the stuffy club rules remain posted on the wall. Today the club has been adopted by locals and is still exclusive to members, though if you show even a hint of interest they will be delighted to serve you a drink at the bar – in exchange for a good bit of banter, of course.

From the club, the lane loops round towards **Clifford School**, the first multiracial school to appear on the peninsula. It started out in 1913 as an *attap*-roofed house in the centre of town, with only 12 pupils. The house was destroyed by floods in 1926 and the present stone building was commissioned by British Resident Sir Hugh Clifford in 1929. Like the college in Kuala Kangsar, the Clifford school has a reputation for turning out future statesmen. The neoclassical pile on the hill above the school – once the government offices of the British – now serves as the Lipis District Office. Notice how important buildings such as the District Office and the old Residency were built on high ground: in the floods of 1926 these were the only two structures left high and dry.

The Resthouse (the old Residency) sits at the end of a spiral drive on a knoll overlooking town. Between 1896 and 1903 it was home to Sir Hugh Clifford, British Resident of Pahang and later, Governor of the Straits Settlement. Today the building serves as a guesthouse, its crusty, spacious rooms in serious need of attention. A series of decrepit steps lead down from the Resthouse to the old golf course, long overgrown and now a haven for wildlife such as boar, birds and monkeys. The quiet road on the ridge above the golf course runs past a series of colonial bungalows and is a haven for the gentle dusky leaf monkey.

Kenong Rimba State Park

The Kenong Rimba is a little-known patch of lowland rainforest tacked on to the southwest corner of the Taman Negara (*see* p.267). All 130 sq km of the park, which is riddled with caves, streams and limestone escarpments, is open to the public – though registered guides are obligatory.

The Kenong Rimba is a raw experience in comparison with the Taman Negara setup, which offers all the usual tourist trappings; inside the park boundaries of the Kenong Rimba there is no accommodation to speak of, and access to the park involves a long boat journey and then an hour's trek through secondary forest. All this has its benefits. Some say that the constant presence of tourists in the Taman Negara has herded much of the wildlife into the Kenong Rimba. Though this is unlikely – the vast majority of visitors to the Taman Negara stray no further than a mile or two from park headquarters – the concentration of wildlife in the Kenong Rimba is known to be high. Several herds of elephant make seasonal visits to the park, while the nomadic orang asli have reported tiger sightings in recent years. The birdlife is also prolific; hornbills, flycatchers, drongos, *shammas*, bulbuls and kingfishers can all be seen.

Bateq hunter-gatherers, a subtribe of the Negritos, are indigenous to these forests. Though encouraged to settle and offered medical care by the government, they prefer to rely on the forest that has supported them and their ancestors for millennia.

The Bateq live in groups of 20–30 individuals who base themselves in temporary shelters for several months at a time before moving on. Visitors to the park may be lucky enough to pay the Bateq a visit if the tour guide knows where to look.

The Trails

Access to the park requires a two-hour boat ride from Kuala Lipis to a tiny jetty at Kampung Dusun. From here it is an hour's walk to the park base camp through secondary, then primary, jungle. En route, guides will often stop off at one of the houses in Kampung Dusun to demonstrate the process of rubber tapping and allow visitors to taste some of the fruits grown in the village. Once the trail enters the primary rainforest, there are diversions to three limestone caves, which are usually visited as part of the tour package.

The base camp is situated at the foot of a towering limestone overhang known as Gunung Kesong. There are four basic chalets and a 'longhouse' dormitory for up to 60 people. Otherwise the level slab of rock beneath the overhang serves as a place to sleep. Around the base camp are a number of caves with varying degrees of accessibility. The closest, Gua Hijau, is only five minutes away across a small bridge. Various species of bats are at the centre of the cave ecosystem. Mountains of guano mean that air in the caves is sharp with the breath of ammonia. Expect a guano shower too from the many bats fluttering about overhead. As well as bats, the caves are also home to porcupines, long-legged cave scorpions, cave racers (non-venomous snakes that feed on bats) and a plague of cockroaches which sift through the piles of guano. Elephants are also known to visit the caves in search of mineral salts: generations of these giant visitors have worn the rocks smooth in some of them.

At certain times of year, bees make a nuisance of themselves around the base camp, swarming about sweaty items of clothing from which they extract salt. Tapirs, porcupines and civet cats are occasionally seen around the base camp at night. Dusky leaf monkeys are also present, though they are favourite prey of the Bateq tribesmen, so are likely to keep out of sight.

From the base camp the main trail loops through the Kenong Rimba park via the Seven Steps Waterfall and Gunung Putih. It is possible to visit the waterfall as a day trip, though this requires up to eight hours walking and involves numerous stream crossings. Very few visitors complete the loop, a thoroughly rewarding experience which requires provisions for five days' camping.

Registered Guides

Access to the park is only possible in the company of a registered guide. As well as providing a measure of safety, this ensures controlled access and helps prevent littering and poaching. Unfortunately there are not many guides to choose from and some of them are reluctant to embark on the longer treks – they would rather earn their money pottering about the base camp. The most popular tour guide is Appu (*Appu's Guesthouse, Jalan Besar, Kuala Lipis,* **t** *09 312 3142, jungleappu@yahoo.com*), an Indian rubber tapper with years of experience as a registered guide. He charges

RM50/person/day and RM140 for the return boat fare (split between the group). This includes food cooked over a campfire and a groundsheet for sleeping on the rock beneath the overhang. Appu spends 200 nights of the year in the national park and will do everything in his power to argue against attempting the longer treks. For slightly more money, Pan Holiday Travel & Tours (*15 Tingkat Bawah, Medan Stesen,* **t** *09 312 5032, pantour@tm.net.my*) offer a number of packages from day trips to the five-day loop. Tourists are accommodated in chalets at the base camp. Encik Tuah (**t** 09 312 3277), whose travel agency is disguised as a tourist information centre opposite Kuala Lipis train station, also offers a number of packages.

Tasik Chini

Tasik Chini is a freshwater lake (or series of waterways) in the flood plain of Sungai Pahang, longest river on the peninula. During the dry season, the lake's waters recede, leaving swampland, only to be replenished when monsoon rains spill from the narrow Sungai Chini, a tributary of the Pahang River. For most of the year a maze of water channels weave their way through beautiful thickets of pandanus, and between May and September, the surface of the lake explodes in a pink bloom of lotus flowers.

Ecological disaster almost struck in 1995 after the state government built a dam at the point where the lake meets Sungai Chini. By keeping the water level topped up they had hoped to encourage year-round tourism. All they achieved were withering

Getting There

There are two access points to Tasik Chini. The first, and most interesting, is Kampung Gumum, via Felda Chini on the east side of the lake. There are regular buses between Felda Chini and Kuantan and one daily service to KL. From Felda Chini it is necessary take a taxi to Kampung Gumum, the lakeside Jakun settlement. The other access point is Kampung Belimbing on the Pahang River. Across the river from Kuala Belimbing is the Kuala Chini Tourist Complex, from where boats head up the Sungai Chini to the lake. It is possible to do the journey by bus, though it is considerably faster to drive.

Where to Stay and Eat

Moderate

Lake Chini Resort, t 09 477 8000, *tasikchini resort@hotmail.com*. Set on its own by the lake, with adequate rooms and a simple restaurant. The resort has its own jetty, canoes and boatmen for tours of the lake.

Budget

Kijang Mas Gumum Chalet, Kampung Gumum, **t** 09 422 1448. A very friendly family-run place owned by an Orang Asli cooperative; all profits go towards the development and education of the village. Simple chalet accommodation at low prices, plus a decent little restaurant. Jungle treks and boat tours can be arranged with Batin Awang bin Alok, guide and chief of the village.

Rajan Jones Guesthouse, Kampung Gumum, no phone, *jonesrajan@hotmail.com*. A no-frills ten-room guesthouse run by an eloquent Tamil Indian and his Orang Asli wife. Mattresses lie directly on floor mats, with mosquito nets hanging above. Rajan, who proudly offers any guest a cup of his own herbal tea made from jungle roots, offers educational jungle treks for very little cost. For accommodation and all meals he charges only RM18.

lotus plants and a plummeting fish stock (the lake acts as a nursery for fish, including rare freshwater species like the *kerisa* and giant snakehead). Luckily the error was acknowledged, and in 2000 the dam was redesigned to accommodate the seasonal rise and fall of the water level.

The tiny Jakun tribe are the Orang Asli indigenous to these parts. Most still earn a living collecting jungle produce such as rattan; others work as rubber tappers, and a few cater to the tourists as jungle guides. Many of the Jakun claim sightings of a legendary dragon – Tasik Chini's own Nessie – which they call Naga Seri Gumum. The beast is said to be like an oversized python and is thought to live in subterranean water channels. One certainty is the presence of the *kerisa* – or dragon fish – a freshwater species near extinction.

Another compelling legend tells of a sunken city beneath the lake. And there may be more to this than mere speculation: aerial photographs indicate what some claim to be the foundations of an ancient Khymer city beneath the waters. Malaysia's Angkor Wat? Or perhaps an ancient Thai kingdom: the forest surrounding the lake is full of gibbons, and 'chini' is Thai for gibbon.

Tours of the waterways by speedboat can be arranged, though the best way to explore the environment at close hand is by canoe, which can be hired from the resort (*see* p.283).

Tasek Bera

Tasek Bera is Malaysia's largest freshwater lake system, stretching 35km in length and 20km across. In 1994 it was declared a Wetland of International Importance and protected under the Ramsar Convention. Like Tasik Chini, the lake comprises a maze of water channels delineated by vast stands of pandanus. Islands of swamp forest hung with thorny rattans and pitcher plants rise from waters which, in season, are scattered with water lilies and lotus flowers.

This wetland wilderness, and its surrounding lowland rainforest, provides sanctuary for a huge variety of fish, birds and mammals. Highly prized catches like tiger barbs, harlequins, marbled goby and the rare Asian arawana draw sports fishermen to the shallow waters, while the presence of rare mammals – tigers, clouded leopards, elephants and the endangered Malayan false gharial (an odd-looking crocodile) have all been sighted in recent years – has attracted conservationists.

The lake is home to the Semelai, a tribe of Orang Asli who paddle the gentle waters in impossibly shallow dugouts, setting fish traps and hunting deer and wild boar. On the lake's fringes, they tap rubber and cultivate hill paddy. The largest settlement, at Pos Iskandar, welcomes tourists, though reaching this remote spot on the west bank of the lake involves a long, dusty drive along logging tracks.

With the help of Wetlands International, an organization called SABOT has been founded by the Semelai of Pos Iskandar in an attempt to manage tourism on the lake and ensure that any revenue generated is shared equally among the community.

Getting There

The only sensible way of getting to Tasek Bera independently is by hire car; the lake is remote and taxi fares high. To reach the tourism complex, approach the lake from the north. Head south from Temerloh towards Triang, and take the signed turning just before Kerayong. To reach Pos Iskandar where SABOT are based, approach the lake from the west and follow signs. This route follows dusty logging trails for miles. Bring a good road map.

Where to Stay

Moderate

Persona Lake Resort, signposted off Route 11, **t/f** 09 276 2505. Wooden cabins provide pretty basic accommodation at bumped-up prices. Still, it's a beautiful and remote setting right on the lake. There is a dormitory too, where a bed for the night goes for RM30. Various boats and kayaks are available for rent. Fishing and jungle-trekking packages available.

SABOT, Pos Iskandar, **t** 011 912 617 (or try Wetlands International Malaysia, **t** 03 7806 1944/03 7806 1942), *http://tasekbera.jones.dk*. The SABOT organization provides various accommodation options for those wishing to stay at the Semelai village of Pos Iskandar. A traditional Semelai house has been built for the use of visitors. The simple *attap*-roofed house sleeps 10; there is no electricity or running water, so guests have to make use of kerosene lamps and a well. SABOT also organize homestays (though do not expect your hosts to speak English) and have built sleeping pavilions at four camps in the rainforest. Call in advance.

SABOT offer homestays within the settlement, as well as jungle treks and river trips in Semelai dugouts. The river trips combine wildlife spotting with a visit to the tiny settlement of Jelawat, where a local family invite guests into their home and entertain them with traditional music, offering betel nut and home-rolled cigarettes.

Navigating in silence along the remote, calm waters of the lake is a serene and unforgettable experience, while the chances of spotting wildlife are better than in designated National Parks.

Kuala Gandah Elephant Conservation Centre

En route to Tasek Bera, from either Kuantan or KL, is the Kuala Gandah Elephant Conservation Centre (*ww.myelephants.org*), near the interior town of Temerloh. The centre was established in 1989 to complement the work of Malaysia's Elephant Relocation Team, and offers visitors a chance to learn about the plight of the Asian elephant, before getting up close and personal with the animals themselves.

Wild elephants, once abundant in the rainforests of Southeast Asia, are fast disappearing, with an estimated 1,000 left in Malaysia. With their habitat diminishing, elephant herds often encroach on farmland in search of food (they are particularly fond of the fresh roots of young palms). The elephants at the Conservation Centre have been trained to help round up their rogue cousins, prior to relocation to safer habitats such as the Taman Negara.

Visitors to the centre are shown a video and offered bareback rides on the trained elephants. For a real treat, you can jump into the nearby river and join in with the elephants' bathtime.

A Short History of Tea

Tea, the world's most popular drink, has been around for millennia. In about 2,750 BC the mythical Chinese emperor Shen Nung is said to have discovered tea in a moment of serendipity: he was sipping at his favoured drink of hot water, when a gust of wind blew some leaves into the mug. He liked the taste and later declared the brew 'helped kidney trouble, fever, chest infection and tumours that come about the head'.

Claims for the medicinal properties of tea run through its history. The first confirmed written records of the drink appear in the early centuries of the common era in China. Then in about AD 800, Lu Yu wrote the *Ch'a Ching*, the first text exclusively on the subject of tea. Around this time, tea cultivation – which is thought to have originated in the Szechuan province of China – had migrated down the length of the great Yangtze river, and crossed to Japan. Here Zen Buddhist monks revered the brew for its curative powers and its ability to help maintain concentration during meditation. By the 13th century, tea had become popular across the board in Japan: Shogun Monamoto Sanetomo was prescribed a regimen of tea and prayer after nearly killing himself from overfeasting. When the shogun recovered, his countrymen took up the habit with gusto. The tea ceremony of *chado*, or *sado* – meaning 'way of tea' and based around an aesthetic of hospitality and quietude – is practised to this day in Japan.

When tea was first brought to Europe in the 17th century by the Dutch, it had a mixed reception. The Dutch physician Nicolas Tulp declared that 'tea drinkers are exempt from all maladies and reach an extreme old age'. However, a German counterpart took a stand against the foreign brew by suggesting it 'hastened the

The Cameron Highlands

The Cameron Highlands are situated on a mountain plateau in the Main Range at an altitude of 1,500–1,800m. They form the largest and most popular of Malaysia's colonial hill stations, famous for their recuperative climate and scenery. Before dawn each day a mist rolls in from the forested peaks to settle in valleys of terraced vegetable farms, flower nurseries, fields of strawberries, dairy farms and tea plantations. As the sun climbs, the mists clear and the temperature rises to a pleasant 25 celsius (though the sun up here can be piercing). In recent years, a spate of unsympathetic development has changed the face of the Cameron Highlands – or the Camerons, as they are often known – but there remain vast tracts of jungle to explore and a colonial legacy to savour.

The region was first 'discovered' in 1885 by William Cameron, a British surveyor – though for centuries it had been a stronghold of the Semai, a tribe of Orang Asli indigenous to this patch of the Main Range. Though government initiatives now encourage the Orang Asli to settle permanently in purpose-built villages, many of the Semai still live as they always have done – in makeshift settlements whose

death of those over 40'. Even when tea was established as a popular drink across Europe, there was consternation: the physician to King George III of England warned that tea drove people crazy (no one's sure whether he expressed this view before or after the famous onset of his employer's insanity).

It was the British East India Company (which operated from 1600 to 1858) that helped popularize tea in the West. In the 1650s, tea was introduced to the coffee houses of London – this was a time when more coffee was drunk in England than anywhere else in the world. The elegant tea clippers of the East India Company – fastest ships in the world – transported hull-loads of tea leaves to Europe and America throughout the 18th century.

Then the Boston Tea Party put the worldly brew straight into the history books of the West. Heavy taxes were imposed on tea in 1773 by the British government in an attempt to perpetuate the monopoly held by the East India Company. In response protesters crept aboard British ships and dumped 342 chests of tea into the Boston harbour, sparking civil war and eventual American Independence.

In 1823 indigenous tea was discovered in Assam, northern India, and the British initiated a plan for tea cultivation in the colony. A whole century later, a British tea planter from Ceylon recognised the commercial potential for tea plantation in the Cameron Highlands, and hired a group of Orang Asli to clear the forest near Ringlet.

All tea is produced from the young leaves of one plant, *Camellia sinensis*, and its hybrids. There are three main types of tea: fermented, or black, tea; semi-fermented, or oolong, tea; and unfermented, or green, tea. Black tea is preferred in the West, green or oolong in the East. Today, more than half the world's population are tea drinkers. **(For a description of the production process *see* Sungei Palas Tea Estate, p.294.)**

whereabouts are determined by fruiting seasons and the movements of game: the fantastic diversity of flora and fauna is a characteristic of these parts.

As the first European to explore the region, Cameron described a 'fine mountain plateau with gentle slopes shut in by loftier mountains'. However, he failed to map his position accurately, and it is now thought that Cameron was describing a different place altogether. In any case, his reports sparked excitement among the homesick British, who were always on the lookout for a home from home, somewhere cool and misty to tend flower beds and grow strawberries. Sir Hugh Low, Resident of Perak, at once suggested it as a site for a health resort and hospital (the unsanitary conditions of Perak's mining settlements meant that colonial administrators were dropping like flies; unlike locals, they had little resistance to tropical diseases). However, building a road up into the highlands was a major task, and it was another forty years before the region was made properly accessible. Sir George Maxwell, founder of the hill resort at Maxwell Hill, initiated the final push in 1926. As soon as the road was complete, the Perak élite began building their weekend retreats. Farms appeared and a British army base was established.

A few years later, Malaysia's first tea plantation was cleared and planted by John Archibald Russell, a British tea planter from Ceylon. Today there are three estates, all of which work hard to produce some of the most prized tea in Southeast Asia. For most modern visitors, the enduring image of the Cameron Highlands will be the rolling network of manicured tea bushes, livid-green and soft-textured against the dark, unruly vegetation of the surrounding jungle.

Ringlet

At an altitude of 1,200m, Ringlet is the first town you come to in the Cameron Highlands (or the last, if you take the new road from Ipoh). All along the road between Tapah and Ringlet, stands of giant bamboo fight for canopy space with the other giants of the dipterocarp forest. The scenic 50km stretch of road winds through a series of Malay kampungs and Semai settlements. Many of the Semai live in simple *attap*-roofed dwellings on the roadside, where they set up stalls to sell blowpipes, hand-woven baskets and other souvenirs.

Ringlet was the first settlement to appear in the Cameron Highlands, though it was originally situated on the site of the Sultan Abu Bakar Lake, broadened in the 1960s by damming the River Bertram. Present-day Ringlet – a workaday, agricultural market town – is at a slightly lower altitude and of little interest to tourists.

On the banks of the lake it is hard to miss the mock-Tudor mansion known as The Lakehouse (*see* also 'Where to Stay', p.291). Black-beamed, with dormer windows, it was built in the 1970s by Stanley Foster, an ex-army British engineer who was based in the Camerons. He also built the more famous Smokehouse 35 years earlier.

Across the river, a small lane leads to the original **Boh Tea Plantation** (*open to visitors Sun–Tues 11–3*), which offers free guided tours of the production process (refer to the Sungai Palas Plantation on p.294 for a description of this process). In 1927 British planter John Russell hired a team of Orang Asli to clear the forest on this site. Two years later Malaysia's first tea plantation was up and running, tended by workers imported from the plantations of Madras in India. The descendants of these tea pickers form a major proportion of the Camerons' modern-day population – some of them still working the estates, others running guesthouses or restaurants in Tanah Rata and Brinchang.

Further north on the main road to Tanah Rata is the Bharat Tea Shop, which overlooks the steep manicured valley of the Bharat Tea Plantation.

Tanah Rata

Tanah Rata is the primary town of the Cameron Highlands and the hub of the backpacker scene. Most of the jungle trails begin in and around Tanah Rata, which makes it a good base from which to explore the hills (*see* 'Hiking in the Highlands', opposite). The town was developed in the 1930s when the British decided to establish an army base in the Cameron Highlands. A convent school was built on a small hill overlooking the south end of town; across the road on an adjacent rise stands the austere house built for the Catholic Fathers who ran the school. Today the building serves as a budget guesthouse (*see* 'Where to Stay', p.293). In its grounds stand a line of Nissen huts – tunnels of corrugated iron that were once soldiers' barracks and now serve as dormitories.

Hiking in the Highlands

There are many hiking trails that wind among the hills around Tanah Rata and Brinchang, most of them cleared by the British army for training purposes in the late 1930s. The Highlands provide the perfect climate for walking; cool air and lower humidity reduce stickiness, while the dense canopy of trees protects from the tropical sun.

A series of paths numbered one to twelve (with an additional Path 9A) are marked on any map of the Cameron Highlands. The maps are only approximate and are not much use while you are out on the trail. If you do not hire a guide, then get clear written directions for your chosen trail from your hotel or guesthouse. The short trails are very easy to follow on your own, but the longer ones are often ill-defined; without good instructions you may find yourself guessing which track to take. Make sure you know exactly which way you have come from and bring a compass as an added precaution. It is best to set off first thing in the morning – the rains fall like clockwork most afternoons. Take drinking water, a lighter, and make sure someone knows that you are gone.

The most commonly trodden paths lead east from Tanah Rata onto the flank of Gunung Berembun (1812m). There are two waterfalls in the vicinity: the Parit Falls and Robinson Waterfall, both a leisurely stroll away. Trails lead off from these falls either up towards the summit of Gunung Berembun, or down towards the Robinson power station. A longer trail leads north towards the Buddhist Sam Poh temple overlooking Brinchang.

West of Tanah Rata a path leads up towards the summit of Gunung Jasar (1670m) and along the spine of the mountain. This is a beautiful walk with numerous vantage points, but the trail is indistinct in parts. The path descends from Gunung Jasar into an Orang Asli village situated a kilometre or so west of the golf course. The village is like something out of a filmset; pretty huts are scattered across a hillside where children play among themselves. These Orang Asli were previously nomadic, but government incentives have encouraged them to settle. Rewards are given to the tidiest households (traditionally Orang Asli leave their rubbish where they've finished with it – in the past it was all biodegradable). The inhabitants seem to have taken to the challenge, and many of the new permanent settlements, including this one, are immaculate.

Just off the road north of Brinchang is the start of the Gunung Brinchang trail, which leads to the tallest summit of the Cameron Highlands, at 2,032m. There is a vast network of other trails, mainly used by the Orang Asli on their hunting expeditions, and longer overnight treks can be organized with guides.

At the north end of town are some pleasant gardens and a small Hindu temple serving Tanah Rata's large Indian community (descendants of the tea pickers brought over from India to work the first Boh tea estate). Despite being the centre of gravity in the Cameron Highlands, Tanah Rata is more of a village than a town – and a tourist village at that, its main road lined with overheating buses, souvenir stalls and

The Jim Thompson Mystery

On Easter Day, 1967, American 'Silk King' Jim Thompson set off on an afternoon stroll in the rainforest of the Cameron Highlands. He was never seen again. To this day, no one knows his true fate.

During the war Jim Thompson worked for the Office of Strategic Services, predecessor of the CIA. In preparation for a mission in Thailand, he was sent to Ceylon to train in jungle survival tactics. He returned home from the war enthusing about the East. Aged 40, he moved to Thailand and single-handedly transformed one of he country's cottage industries into a multi-million dollar business. He commissioned the design of hand-woven silk fabrics, gaining international acclaim for their shimmering colours and quality. His fabrics hit the catwalks and the US fashion magazines; some of his silk even found its way into Queen Elizabeth II's wardrobe.

So when Jim Thompson disappeared after lunch that day in 1967, it was big news. A massive search party was set in motion, involving Orang Asli trackers, the Malay police force, US Army helicopters and a detachment of British Gurkhas. But to no avail. Not a shred of evidence was unearthed.

Theories abound as to his fate. Some speculate that he was on a mission for the CIA that went wrong, or that he was captured by Communist guerillas operating in the area; others that he was the victim of rivalries within the silk industry, or that he was nailed after being associated with a planned coup in Thailand. A favourite theory is that he was killed and eaten by a tiger – tiger sightings were certainly more frequent back in the 1960s. Or was his disappearance nothing more than an innocuous accident: he suffered a heart attack and returned to the dust (or the jungle mulch) in an unexplored nook of the rainforest?

The friends Jim Thompson was staying with that day in the Cameron Highlands all agree on one thing: at the picnic lunch just prior to his disappearance, Thompson appeared nervous and anxious to return. Who knows, perhaps for once the conspiracy theorists are closest to the truth.

restaurants catering mainly to Western tastes. Though not unattractive in its own fashion, Tanah Rata is a far cry from what some visitors might be expecting – namely a twee colonial retreat. The crumbling concrete mess east of the main road was meant to be a flash new shopping complex; it stands today as a reminder of the development spree that was halted in its tracks by the Asian financial crisis of 1997.

North of Tanah Rata the road opens out into a mini-plateau surrounded by hills. The games-crazy British decided the space would be best employed as a golf course, and five holes were landscaped into the patch of ground. Today the **Cameron Highlands Golf Club** (weekday green fee RM40, weekend green fee RM63; green fee with clubs, balls and tees for RM95/RM115; green fee with half set RM85/RM105) has 18 holes squeezed into the plot. It is nevertheless a beautiful and well-maintained course.

On the edge of the golf course is **Ye Olde Smokehouse** (*see* 'Where to Stay', p.291), the Highlands' most photographed mock-Tudor building. Stand on the doorstep, look past the hanging flower baskets, the wrought-iron garden furniture, the stocks and

Getting There

Though the Cameron Highlands falls inside the state of Pahang, the only access is from Perak. Buses and taxis still ply the old route to the Cameron Highlands via the grotty little town of Tapah (a winding 3-4 hour ascent); today, most people understandably use the new road, which is accessible via Exit 137 on the North-South Expressway (at Simpang Pulai). The journey time from Simpang Pulai is less than an hour. There are direct buses from Kuala Lumpur with Kurnia Bistari Express (**t** 03 2031 8307) and Unititi Express (**t** 012 215 0044). Unititi Express also run a daily service from Singapore, which leaves at 10pm, arriving the next morning at 7am. The easiest route to the Cameron Highlands is via Ipoh, where Kurnia Bistari Express (**t** 05 491 1485) and Kinta Omnibus (**t** 05 491 1200) have numerous services each day.

Getting Around

To explore the Cameron Highlands thoroughly, it is best to hire a car (from Ipoh or KL). Taxis are available up in the Highlands, but fares are steeper than elsewhere in Malaysia. The Hillview Inn, in Tanah Rata, rents out 125cc motorbikes for around RM30/day. Buses to and from Tapah move up and down the main road in the Cameron Highlands, making it possible to move back and forth between Ringlet, Tanah Rata and Brinchang – if you are prepared to wait.

Information

There is no Tourist Office up in the Cameron Highlands. However, most of the hotels and guesthouses provide substantial information about the various sights and trails. Many of the shops in Tanah Rata and Brinchang sell useful maps too.

Where to Stay

The Cameron Highlands is a major stop on the backpacker trail and there are dozens of places competing for this market. Perhaps because of this, there are not many good places to stay in the moderate category. The remaining hotels fight for the upper end of the market.

Luxury

Ye Olde Smokehouse (next to the golf course between Tanah Rata and Brinchang), **t** 05 491 1215, **f** 05 491 1214, *cameron@thesmokehouse.com.my*, *www.thesmokehouse.com.my*. An uncannily authentic English-style country inn. There's even a red phone box on the roadside and some stocks in the garden. Built in 1937 in mock-Tudor style, this is one of the oldest buildings in the Cameron Highlands (*see* p.288). Inside, the hall and corridors are hung with brass and hunting scenes. The rooms – all of which are suites – are strewn with wooden antiques and each has its own four-poster bed. 'The Cottage' suite has an open fire, as does the bar downstairs. Rates are inclusive of a full traditional English breakfast served in the conservatory. Cream tea is available each afternoon and, weather permitting, is served at the wrought-iron furniture in the garden. The expensive restaurant serves the likes of beef Wellington (*see* 'Eating Out', p.293). Ye Olde Smokehouse is full of colonial charm – though if you are coming straight from England it won't seem like such a big deal.

Luxury–Expensive

The Lakehouse (north of Ringlet), **t** 05 495 6152, **f** 05 495 6213, *info@lakehouse-cameron.com*, *www.lakehouse-cameron.com*. Another Tudor-style mansion set on a hillside overlooking the Sultan Abu Bakar Lake, and designed by the same man who built Ye Olde Smokehouse. The theme is identical to that of the Smokehouse, though this is a much larger building. Eighteen rooms and suites are on offer; again all have four-poster beds, antiques and lots of space. The Lakehouse is near to one of the lower-altitude Boh Tea plantations; other than this the hotel is set rather on its own, making transport essential. The restaurant serves a mixture of traditional British offerings and spicier Asian dishes (*see* 'Eating Out', p.293).

Expensive

Strawberry Park (near Brinchang), **t** 05 491 1166, **f** 05 491 1949, *sprcmh@strawberryparkresorts.com*, *www.strawberryparkresorts.com*. Situated at the top of a hill north of the golf course, with excellent views over the rippling valleys of the Highlands. This is a huge complex, with a swimming pool, squash courts and tennis courts. The setting is great but the apartment-style buildings are oversize and a bit lacking in character. It is a 3km descent along a winding road to get back into the main valley. Along the way is a track leading off to Jim Thompson's bunglaow (*see* p.290).

Equatorial (Brinchang), **t** 05 496 1777, **f** 05 496 1333, *info@cam.equatorial.com*, *www.equatorial.com/cam*. The Highlands' most extensive resort with a high-rise tower block – mock-Tudor apparently – stuck on the top of a hill near Brinchang. If you want business-style luxury, that is what you will get at the Equatorial (there is even a heated indoor swimming pool), but it is hard to feel positive towards what is effectively the worst eyesore in the Cameron Highlands.

Merlin, **t** 491 1211, **f** 491 1178, *mirch@pd.jaring.my*. A smart hotel right on the golf course between Tanah Rata and Brinchang. Features of each room include private balcony, minibar, tea/coffee facilities and room service. The furnishings are floral and, overall, it is not the most inspiring of the Highlands' upper-end hotels (handy, though, if you're here for the golf).

Expensive–Moderate

Hotel Casa de la Rosa, **t** 05 491 1333, **f** 05 491 5500, *rosapsch@tm.net.my*, *www.hotelcasadelarosa.com.my*. A new top-end hotel on the edge of the golf course. There are 30-odd rooms and four penthouse suites with panoramic views. Probably not the most atmospheric of the available options, but promotional rates give very good value for money.

Heritage Hotel, **t** 05 491 3888, **f** 05 491 5666, *www.heritage.com.my*. A large high-rise hotel in familiar mock-Tudor style, on a hilltop overlooking Tanah Rata. There are 4-star facilities and the rooms are modern. Two restaurants serve Cantonese and Malaysian cuisine respectively. There is a bit of a dry feel to the place.

Moderate

Bala's Holiday Chalet, **t** 05 491 1660, **f** 05 491 4500, *balasch@hotmail.com*, *www.balaschalet.com*. A delightful place to stay, with rooms inside one of the Highlands' original 1930s mock-Tudor houses. The building was originally part of a boarding school for British expats – a branch of the famous Tanglin School in Singapore. There is a country-cottage feel to the place and the garden is beautifully maintained. As well as the standard en suite rooms, there are a few basic rooms on offer too, for around RM80. The cream teas here are vying for the top spot.

Cool Point Hotel, **t** 05 491 4914, **f** 05 491 1070. Set behind the main road in Tanah Rata, near the gardens. The rooms are en suite and spacious, with TV, tea/coffee facilities and phone. There's a funny feel to the place – perhaps because not a lot of imagination has gone into the décor. One of the few hotels in the moderate price category, though it would definitely be worth checking for promotions in the top-end hotels before checking in here.

Inexpensive

Cameronian Inn, 16 Jalan Mentigi, Tanah Rata, **t** 05 491 1327. Set in a small garden overlooking a field of vegetables, and tucked away a few hundred yards from the main road, this is one of the best places to stay in Tanah Rata. The more expensive doubles (RM55) offer great value; all are newly carpeted, with hot water, a bath, fresh flowers and pleasant views. The cheaper rooms are very spartan. The little restaurant offers *lassis* and traditional cream teas. 'Jungle George' offers guided trekking along some of the trails. Maps are provided for those who want to walk on their own.

Jurina Lodge, **t** 05 491 5522, **f** 05 491 5511, *www.jurina@tm.net.my*. Nestled up against a steep hill behind the Hillview Inn (*see* below), and very similar in appearance and setup. All rooms have TV, and there is a fully equipped kitchen for the use of guests. Again, pretty good value.

Inexpensive–Budget

Father's Guesthouse, **t** 05 491 2484, **f** 05 491 5484, *fathersonline@hotmail.com*, *www.fathersplace.cjb.net*. The most popular backpacker accommodation in Tanah Rata. The main building, set on top of a little hillock above town, was built in the 1930s as a retreat for Catholic clerics and teachers at the nearby convent school; and it has the feel of a monastery about it too. In the grounds are some Nissen huts used by British soldiers in colonial times. There are rooms in the main building and at the Nissen huts; all are clean but very simple. Facilities are all communal.

Daniel's Travellers' Lodge, **t** 05 491 5823, **f** 05 491 5828, *danielslodge@hotmail.com*. Set among the bungalows of a small Indian community, along a track that leads off the main Tanah Rata road. This lodge is clean, very basic and has a loyal following of backpackers. The full range of backpacker facilities are provided, along with lots of information about trekking in the Highlands.

Twin Pine Chalet, 2 Jalan Mentigi, **t** 05 491 2169, **f** 05 491 5007, *twinpinech@hotmail.com*. Another popular backpacker spot, with a permanent buzz of activity on the communal verandah. Rooms are clean and simple. The neglected building site on its doorstep has ruined the ambience somewhat.

Hillview Inn, **t** 05 491 2915, **f** 05 491 5212, *hillviewinn@hotmail.com*. Also overlooking the old building site, but offering great value if you want a touch more luxury. All the rooms are spacious, carpeted and have balconies. Each floor has its own lounge area. This is also one of the few places that rents out motorbikes.

Eating Out

Many of the best places to eat in the Cameron Highlands are attached to some of the hotels and guesthouses listed above. **Ye Olde Smokehouse** serves traditional British cuisine at steep prices (roast dinner with Yorkshire pudding, beef wellington and apple crumble all feature on the menu). **The Lakehouse** serves similar food alongside Asian fusion cuisine. Prices here are a little more reasonable and the food has the edge over that at the Smokehouse. **Bala's Holiday Chalet** offers a varied menu with a leaning towards Indian curries (one of which is a favourite with the local sultan). Cream teas are a bit of an institution up here, and all of the above guesthouses partake, as do the cafés at the the Boh Tea plantatations. The Cameronian Inn at Tanah Rata offers the cheapest cream teas in the Highlands. In Tanah Rata a number of places offer steamboats, a Chinese fondue-style dinner that is one of the Camerons' specialities. In true British tradition, fish and chips appear with strange regularity on some of the menus.

A few other independent restaurants worth trying out are listed below:

Moderate

Shal's Curry House, 25 Jalan Besar (Brinchang). This simple South Indian restaurant is run by an ex-manager of Ye Olde Smokehouse, so standards are high. Unfortunately, there are different prices for tourists and locals.

Restoran Hong Kong, main road, Tanah Rata. A very popular Chinese restaurant with delicious steamboat dinners for RM12 per person. Huge quantities are served.

Inexpensive

Kumar, main road, Tanah Rata. One of several Indian restaurants, specializing in *murtabak*, *roti canai* and curries. They also serve claypot rice and Western breakfasts (pancakes, eggs, *lassis*).

Bunga Suria, off Jalan Mentigi (Tanah Rata). A banana-leaf restaurant serving thalis and delicious South Indian set meals. Full most nights.

Nepenthes Monkey Cup Bistro, main road, Tanah Rata. A new place stylishly decorated with comfortable seating. Simple noodle dishes are served, as are cakes and fruit punch. The chocolate cake with strawberry ice cream is a favourite.

the authentic red phone box – a slight chill in the air – and you can well imagine that owner and architect Colonel Stanley Foster was pleased with himself. In the true tradition of colonial hill stations, this was indeed a home from home: the building and its environs are British down to the very last detail. Inside are low slung beams and roaring log fires, while the walls are cluttered with clocks, brass fittings, furnishings and paintings all imported from England at one stage or another. As well as being an example of the nostalgic tendencies of British eccentricity, Ye Olde Smokehouse is a reminder of the great sea journey British administrators had to undertake to return home: England was a long way away.

On the road back towards Tanah Rata is another of the Camerons' original 1930s buildings. Now operating as Bala's Holiday Chalet (*see* 'Where to Stay', p.292), the mock-Tudor building was originally the Tanglin Primary School, sister school to the famous Tanglin School in Singapore. Today it is a favourite place to stop in at for Devonshire cream tea.

Brinchang

Brinchang is the second town of the Cameron Highlands. As a place to stay, it has less appeal than Tanah Rata, with more high-rise development and less atmosphere. The small town is centred around a square where the Camerons' *pasar malam* (night market) is held every Saturday. For Highlanders this is the main event of the week.

North of Brinchang the road winds through a series of terraced valleys lined with vegetables and covered strawberry plots. There is a nursery to visit, a series of vegetable markets and a butterfly and honey-bee farm. Off to the left a steep lane leads up through the Sungai Palas tea estate to the summit of Gunung Brinchang (2,032m), the Camerons' tallest peak. If there is any cloud in the sky, you can be sure the summit will be shrouded. If the sky is clear, you can expect staggering views from the watchtower planted near the top. There is a noticeable chill in the air on the summit so bring an extra layer.

The **Sungei Palas Boh Tea Estate** (*open Tues–Sun 8.30–3; free tours thoughout the day*) is arguably the best plantation to visit; clinging precariously to the flanks of Gunung Brinchang, it is certainly the most picturesque. Next to the tea shop, there is a visitor centre with a small exhibition and video. Guided factory tours explain the production process first-hand. Out in the fields, Indian tea pickers meander through the lush maze of tea bushes, swiping with sheers and flinging leaf-tips into large hand-woven baskets strapped to their backs. Huge bundles of freshly cropped leaves are transported to a small factory, where the leaves are spread across troughs. Hot air is blown through perforations in the troughs to reduce moisture content by 50%. The partially withered leaves are then rolled and the fermentation process kicks in, turning the leaves from bright green to copper in colour. The leaves are then blasted with hot air once more until the remaining juices crystallize and the leaves take on their familiar, crisp, black form. The final process grades the leaves according to size and quality.

Johor

16

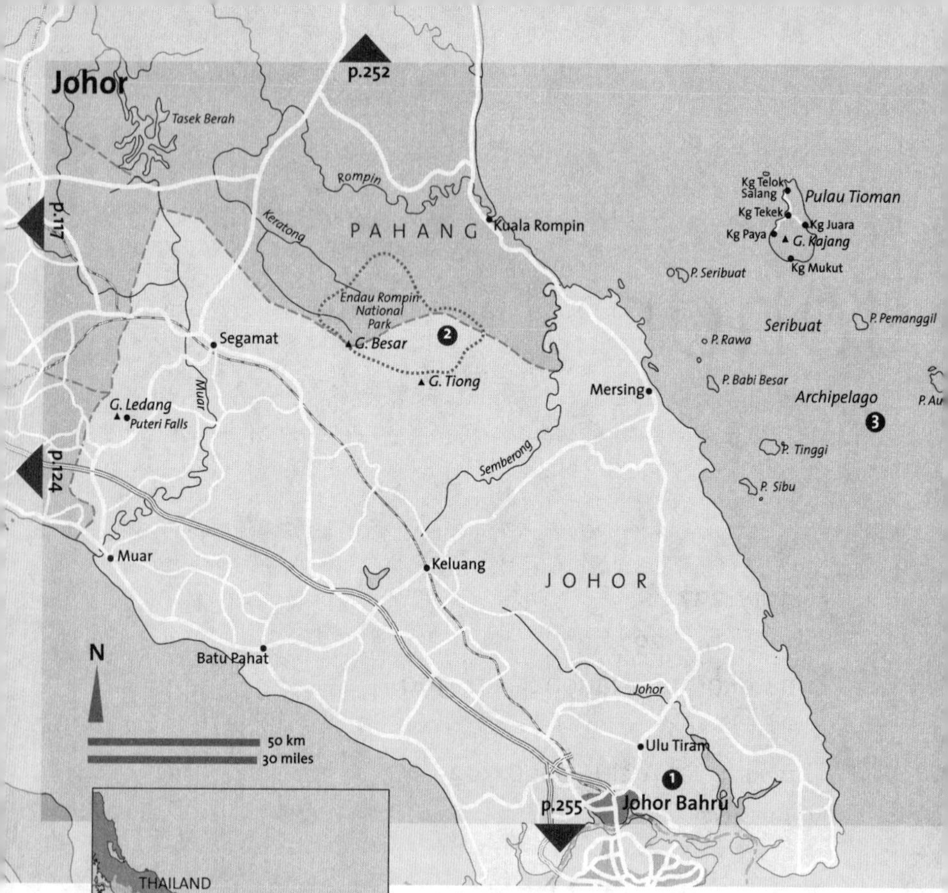

Highlights

1. Johor Bahru for the Royal Abu Bakar Museum and Malaysia's finest colonial-style mosque
2. Endau-Rompin National Park, one of the last remaining refuges for the Sumatran rhino
3. The Seribuat Archipelago, for lazy days of fishing, snorkelling and island-hopping

The state of Johor forms the southern tip of Peninsular Malaysia. It is the workhorse of the Malaysian economy, with a fast-expanding industrial base in IT and manufacturing. Its hinterland boasts oil-palm, rubber and pineapple plantations. State capital Johor Bahru is Malaysia's southern gateway, minutes from Singapore across the narrow Johor Straits. With a population approaching a million, Johor Bahru is one of Malaysia's largest, and least appealing cities, serving largely as Singapore's sordid playground).

Johor's greatest appeal lies at its fringes: the beautiful Seribuat Archipelago, and minor coastal settlements such as Muar and Kukup. Straddling the border with Pahang, meanwhile, is the virgin rainforest of the Endau-Rompin National Park, one of the last remaining refuges of the near-extinct Sumatran rhino.

History

Johor plays a prominent role in the evolution of the Malay Peninsula. After the Portuguese laid waste to the thriving port of Melaka in 1528, ousted Sultan Mahmud fled to Johor, where he re-established his court. A century of uncertainty followed, with the capital moving back and forth between Kota Tinggi, on the banks of the Johor River, and the Riau archipelago, south of modern-day Singapore. For much of this period, the fledgling kingdom was terrorized by the territory-hungry Acehnese of northern Sumatra. Stability for Johor was finally achieved by teaming up with the Dutch, who were looking to gain a trading foothold in the region. With the protection of their cannons, Johor soon emerged as a powerful trading entrepôt.

When the British muscled in on the scene in the early 19th century, the stability of Johor was ruffled once more, thanks in large part to the conniving diplomacy of the young Stamford Raffles, who was intent on establishing his own trading station for British interests. Determined to get his hands on the island of Temasek (soon to be Singapore), Raffles paid off would-be contenders to the Sultanate of Johor, before handing actual power to the *Temenggong* – the Malay minister whose traditional duties covered defence and justice.

When anglophile Abu Bakar became *Temenggong* in 1866, he moved his capital from the Johor River to Tanjong Putri, which he renamed Johor Bahru ('New Johor' in Malay). By ingratiating himself with the British – he was said be a personal friend of Queen Victoria – Abu Bakar earned himself the title of Sultan of Johor in 1877. Today, Abu Bakar is remembered fondly as the 'Father of Johor'. His son, Sultan Ibrahim, ruled right up until 1948, when Johor became part of the Federation of Malaya.

Johor Bahru

Johor Bahru, or JB as it is commonly known, is the southern gateway to Malaysia, with a history that dates back to the early 16th century (*see* 'History', above). Today it is a city defined largely by its proximity to Singapore, with only the narrow Johor Straits separating the two. As such, Johor Bahru has the feel and function of a large border town. During the week, workers from JB cross the causeway to earn Singapore dollars; come the weekend, the tide has turned as Singaporeans flock to JB to take advantage of favourable exchange rates or to prowl the thriving red-light district.

In recent decades, JB has grown in stature to become Malaysia's major manufacturing centre. A constellation of industrial estates encroach on the city, turning out goods for a wide international market. Meanwhile, in the town centre, high-rise office blocks, shopping malls and new hotels have sprung up to meet demand. Despite the emergence of a fresh new face to the central streets of Johor Bahru, tourists can be forgiven finding it a charmless place. Other than one exceptional museum (*see* below), an impressive old mosque and plenty of bargain-hunting opportunities, tourist attractions are decidedly thin on the ground – unless karaoke joints and hostess bars happen to be to your taste.

Getting There

Malaysia Airlines offers direct and very reasonably priced **flights** between JB and Kuala Lumpur, Kuching, Kota Kinabalu, and Langkawi. Air Asia (*www.airasia.com*) offer even cheaper flights to and from ten separate destinations in Malaysia. The Senai airport is located 25km north of JB. The main **bus station**, meanwhile, is situated 3km to the east of town on Jalan Geruda, with services to Singapore and most major towns on the peninsula. The Singapore-KL-Bangkok **railway** line runs through JB, with the station on Jalan Tun Abdul Razak.

Information

Johor Tourist Information Centre (JOTIC), Suite 5-2, 2 Jalan Air Molek, **t** 07 224 2000, *info@johortourism.com.my*, *www.johortourism.com.my*. Open Mon–Sat 9–5, Sun 10–4.

Where to Stay

Expensive

Hyatt Regency, Jalan Sungai Chat, **t** 07 222 1234, **f** 07 223 2718, *hyatt@hrjb.po.my*, *www.hyatt.com*. This is JB's top hotel, a kilometre or so west of the town centre, not far from the sultan's palace. The hotel sits on a rise, so most rooms have views across the large landscaped gardens to the straits. Full business-class facilities, including huge freeform pool and spa.

Puteri Pacific, Jalan Abdullah Ibrahim, **t** 07 223 3333, **f** 07 223 6622, *www.puteripacific.com*. The choice of JB's downtown hotels, if it's facilities you're looking for, though the colour schemes are a little nauseating. The fitness centre is the best equipped in town, while the restaurants (Chinese and Mediterranean) are among JB's most popular.

Mutiara Johor Bahru, Jalan Dato Sulaiman, **t** 07 332 3800, **f** 07 331 8884, *cro@mutiarahotels.com*, *www.mutiarahotels.com*. The Mutiara chain is one of Malaysia's best, for reliability at least. Rooms have full 4-star facilities and are regularly updated. Pay a little extra for a Junior Club Suite and you get a PlayStation with 50 games. Other facilities include a large outdoor swimming pool, squash court and health centre with sauna and steambath.

Moderate

Mercure Ace Hotel, 18 Jalan Wong Ah Fook, **t** 07 221 3000, **f** 07 221 4000, *mercure@po.jaring.my*. One of the town's newer hotels right in the centre. Each room has broadband internet connection, though there's no pool or fitness centre.

Seri Malaysia, Jalan Langkasuka, **t** 07 221 1002, **f** 07 221 3334, *johor@serimalaysia.com.my*,

Sights

If you have time on your hands in Johor Bahru, be sure to visit the **Royal Abu Bakar Museum** (*Jalan Sri Berlukar*, **t** *07 223 0555; adm*) set in the Istana Besar, a domineering whitewashed palace from 1866. The palace was home to Sultan Abu Bakar and remained in royal hands until 1991 when it was opened to the public as a museum. The building is stuffed full of treasures collected over the years by Abu Bakar and his son Ibrahim. There are golden thrones and crystal furniture from Europe, Japanese ceramics, and hunting trophies from the days of roaming rhinos and tigers. Outside, immaculately manicured gardens provide a welcome refuge from the baking streets.

On the hilltop west of the museum stands one of the country's finest colonial-style mosques, the **Masjid Abu Bakar**, completed in 1892. Like many of Malaysia's British-designed buildings, the Masjid Abu Bakar combines Moorish architectural styles with *www.serimalaysia.com.my*. Reliable choice offering good value, though it's 20 mins out of town near the Larkin bus terminal. TV, air-con and coffee/tea-making facilities.

Moderate–Inexpensive

Causeway Inn, 6A Jalan Meldrum, **t** 07 224 8811, **f** 07 224 8820. Situated at the quiet end of Jalan Meldrum, close to the causeway linking JB with Singapore. Clean and plain with 3-star facilities.

Budget

Footloose Homestay, 4H Jalan Ismail, **t** 07 224 2881. Twenty minutes' walk northwest of the town centre. Nevertheless, by far the most popular budget option for foreign travellers, with a clean dorm and one double room.

Eating Out

The best place to browse for a meal is the **pasar malam** (night market), situated between the train station and the Rajamariamman Hindu temple. Look out for local specialities such as *laksa Johor* (a spicy, coconutty, soup-based noodle dish very similar to Singapore *laksa*), *lontong* (cubes of rice cooked in a thick sauce) and *mee rebus* (a rich noodle dish introduced by immigrant Javanese). Seafood is also particularly good in JB. Head for the stalls on Lido Beach, or try the **Eden Floating Palace Restaurant**, anchored off the Johor Duty Free Complex. All of the major shopping centres have attached food courts, where hawker stalls offer a range of cuisines.

Many of JB's best restaurants are found within its top-end hotels. Sophisticated Hai Tien Lo (Puteri Pacific Hotel, *see* above) serves a wide range of Chinese food, from dim sum and abalone to shark's fin and roast poultry. The Paolo Restaurant (also in the Puteri Pacific) serves pretty decent Mediterranean cuisine. Within the Hyatt Regency is Piccolo (for Italian specialities and pizzas straight from a wood-fired oven) and Aska (contemporary Japanese cuisine with sushi bar, *teppanyaki* room and *tatami* room).

There are plenty of cheap South Indian restaurants within the vicinity of the Hindu temple. Try **Restoran Villa** (opposite the temple) for a traditional banana-leaf set meal.

Shopping

Shopping in JB is oriented specifically to suite the tastes of day-tripping Singaporeans, who hop across the Johor Straits in numbers, mainly to shop for groceries and household items. The main shopping centres, such as JB City Square, Plaza Kota Raya and the JB Duty Free Complex opposite the ferry terminal, sell a stripped down version of what Singapore's malls offer, only at marginally cheaper prices.

classical styles; there are four separate wings with minarets, domes and pinnacles, as well as classical columns, pilasters, pediments and turrets.

For a glimpse of old Johor Bahru, head for the weathered shophouses, Chinese-style coffee shops and traditional South Indian restaurants around **Jalan Ibrahim**, where day-to-day business runs along at its own age-old pace, despite rapid change elsewhere in the city.

Many Singaporean visitors strike out west from JB to the small fishing village of **Kukup**, near Peninsular Malaysia's southernmost point. Here, a collection of simple wooden restaurants stand on stilts above the water. The seafood here (chilli crab, squid *sambal*, garlic prawns, *ikan bakar* or barbecued fish) is acknowledged by many as the cheapest and best in Johor.

Endau-Rompin National Park

Endau-Rompin National Park straddles the ancient sandstone plateaus that provide a geological border between the states of Johor and Pahang. This beautiful park is one of the last remaining refuges for the Sumatran rhino, a smaller, hairier and more diffident version of its African cousin. In fact, some experts believe Endau-Rompin holds the world's largest concentration of these animals in the wild; that there are only an estimated 5–25 rhinos left in the park is an indication of just how endangered the species is.

It is perhaps a blessing then that Endau-Rompin receives only a tenth of the visitors that the Taman Negara does, and that much of the park is off limits to tourists. Authorities have divided Endau-Rompin into three, with a small zone for visitors, a larger one for scientists and researchers, with the remaining terrain – more than half the park – left as a sanctuary for wildlife. This latter zone recently became the site of an extraordinary 'scientific' expedition – to track down the legendary Hantu Jarang Gigi, Malaysia's version of Big Foot. The official expedition was launched by Johor's Chief Minister in early 2006, after Big Foot fever gripped the Malaysian press, with an escalation of unusual sightings on the fringes of the national park.

Administration of the park is split between Johor and Pahang, though the Pahang entry point has no visitor centre or accommodation (neither are there any entry fees). Pahang, after all, has the Taman Negara, and this is Johor's only jungle wilderness. Most visitors enter the park from **Kampung Peta**, a remote Orang Asli settlement in Johor, accessible only by red laterite tracks through palm-oil plantations. Kampung

Getting There

If you visit Endau-Rompin as part of a tour, getting to the park should be taken care of. Being the closest major town, Mersing is the best place to organise tours into the National Park, with many of the travel agencies here offering all-inclusive packages. Tours can also be arranged from travel agents in KL, Johor Bahru and Kuala Rompin in Pahang.

It is possible to visit the park independently, though this will involve a long drive through palm oil plantations and along logging tracks. Turn off the main road (Route 50) near the small town of Kahang. Endau-Rompin is signed. From here it is a two-hour drive along dirt tracks to the Orang Asli settlement of Kampung Peta, where the Visitor Centre is situated.

An alternative entry point is Pandang Endau, a small coastal town in Pahang. From here it is possible, for a high price, to hire a boat upriver along the remote waters of Sungai Endau, which hits Sungai Jasin near Kampung Peta.

Information

Tour operators in Mersing and Kuala Lumpur can provide plenty of advice about visiting Endau-Rompin. For further information, contact the Johor National Parks Corporation, Jalan Timbalan, Johor Bahru, **t** 07 223 7471, *www.johorparks.com*

Where to Stay

At Kampung Peta basic A-frame chalets are available. There are campsites along Sungai Jasin at the following points: Kuala Jasin, Kuala Marong, and Batu Hampar. Some of these have the odd A-frame or attap-roofed hut in varying states of disrepair.

Peta is where the Visitor Centre is now situated. Villagers, who are members of the Jakun tribe, have melded a subsistence lifestyle with tourism, many of them employed by the park authorities as guides.

The Trails

There are 25km of jungle trails within the park, mainly along the banks of Sungai Jasin and Sungai Marong. One of the most accessible trails leads inland from Sungai Jasin and onto the **Janing Barat** plateau, a strange world of waterlogged heath forest scattered with pitcher plants. The unusual terrain of Endau-Rompin – sharp escarpments and flat sandstone plateaus – was fashioned by powerful volcanic action more than 150 million years ago.

South of here another trail heads up the crystal-clear waters of Sungai Marong, deemed by the Malaysia Nature Society to be the cleanest riverine waters on the peninsula. Not far from the confluence of the Sungai Jasin and Sungai Marong is **Tasik Air Biru**, or 'Blue Lagoon'. It's not blue, or a lagoon, but the name gives the right impression; a neat bowl carved into the river bed provides an idyllic pool for bathing.

One of the toughest treks in the park leads to a spectacular waterfall at the headwaters of the Sungai Jasin, 300m above sea level. After rains, **Buaya Sangkit** is a wall of water 30m across and almost 50m in height. The trail to the waterfall is a gruelling 6–10 hour climb along the steep flanks of Bukit Segonggong.

The park is closed between December and February (inclusive) when monsoon rains make the access roads impassable.

Mersing

This bustling little fishing port near the border with Pahang attracts tourists as a springboard to the Seribuat Archipelago, Pulau Tioman and the Endau-Rompin National Park. There is not much to do in town, but a number of good guesthouses and restaurants help pass the time while you make plans for the onward journey.

Mersing's only architectural gem sits on the corner of Jalan Abu Bakar, beside the roundabout: one of Malaysia's prettiest shophouses, with multicoloured bas-reliefs on the walls and a little verandah above the doorway.

To escape the town, head along the pathway which runs north along the casuarina-lined seashore. Better still, jump in a car and head further north for the village of **Penyabong**, which has a sandy beach and calm sheltered waters that are good for swimming.

The most some visitors will see of Mersing will be its jetty, where boats, slow and fast, head out for the islands. Be prepared for the touts, who buzz about newcomers like hungry flies.

Where to Stay

Moderate

Hotel Timotel, 839 Jalan Endau, **t** 07 799 5888, **f** 07 799 5333, *www.timotel.com.my*. A small business hotel just out of town, with 44 rooms and a rooftop garden. Rooms are all air-conditioned and have mini-bar, safe, cable TV and hot water.

Seri Malaysia, 641 Jalan Ismail, **t** 07 799 1876, **f** 07 799 1886, *www.serimalaysia.com.my*. One hundred spacious rooms with the expected range of facilities, including a swimming pool. Good value for money.

Inexpensive–Budget

Kali's Guesthouse, t 07 799 3613. A beautifully decorated guesthouse on the coast 2km north of town. The chalets, some high on stilts, are set in a lush garden (Kali is obsessed with plants).

Mersing Inn, 38 Jalan Ismail, **t** 07 799 1919, **f** 07 799 2288. A plain hotel with acceptable en suite doubles with air-con and TV.

Budget

East Coast Hotel, 43 Jalan Abu Bakar, **t** 013 724 7081/012 762 4983, *salangrock@yahoo.com*. This little guesthouse will leave you feeling warm towards Mersing. It's very clean and simple, with tiled floors and unadorned walls. Guests have free use of the rooftop lounge and the kitchen, where tea and coffee is provided. Owner Rocky will go out of her way to help and provide information.

Omar's Hostel, Jalan Abu Bakar, **t** 07 799 5096, *o_bentris@hotmail.com*. A tiny place with a few simple rooms and a dorm run by man-about-town Omar, who offers tours of the area, including island-hopping in the Seribaut Archipelago aboard his converted fishing boat 'Black Sausage'.

Eating Out

Inexpensive

Kedai Kek Kilei, Jalan Abu Bakar. A bakery which also serves good coffees (cappuccino and espresso).

Restoran Ee Lo, on the roundabout in the centre of town. A small Chinese restaurant very popular with tourists, probably because of its offer on Tiger beer. The food's not bad too.

Restoran Halina, Jalan Abu Bakar. A local Malay restaurant serving delicious *roti canai*.

Loke Tien Yuen Restoran, Jalan Abu Bakar. This simple Chinese restaurant comes recommended by locals.

Restoran Laut Yung Chuan, Jalan Ismail. Large and popular Chinese restaurant with a huge menu. Good wild boar.

The Seribuat Archipelago

The sea around Mersing is studded with the volcanic islands that form the Seribuat Archipelago. The best known of them, and largest, is Pulau Tioman (*see* p.259), though this falls inside the state boundaries of Pahang. Many of the 60 or so islands are little more than rocky, coral-fringed outcrops, and only six offer accommodation for visitors. All have white-sand beaches and beautiful, clear waters, though diving visibility is much reduced around those islands closer to the mainland. The only permanent inhabitants are fishermen: look out for offshore fish traps (known as *kelong*) silhouetted against the horizon. These comprise stakes driven into the sea bed and are used to lure *ikan bilis* (anchovies), the Malay staple fish, which is dried under the sun and served up each morning as *nasi lemak*. The resorts on these islands have long been popular with Singaporean weekenders.

The nearest island to Mersing, and the most developed, is **Pulau Besar**, with resorts lining the sandy beaches, and trails leading through plantations to a small fishing village. North of here, tiny **Pulau Rawa** is one of Malaysia's longstanding island

Where to Stay

Below is a small selection of the accommodation available on the most accessible islands.

Expensive–Moderate

Rawa Safaris Island Resort, Pulau Rawa, **t** 07 799 1204, **f** 07 799 3848, *www.rawasfr.com*. Running more on reputation than quality of service, this once-exclusive resort has seen better days. Still, the facilities aren't bad and there is a good range of rooms, with lots of options for families, from stilted suites over the water to hillside chalets. The only accommodation on Rawa.

Aseania Resort (formerly Radin Island), Pulau Besar, **t** 07 799 4152. A fifty-chalet kampung-style resort with swimming pool. Each room has air-con, bathroom with hot water and mini-bar.

Hillside Beach Resort, **t** 07 799 4831, Pulau Besar. Well appointed chalets set on a hillside among palms and casuarinas, with magnificent views.

Nadia Inn, **t** 07 799 5582, Pulau Tinggi. A large resort with 3-star facilities and rather spartan rooms. There is a swimming pool, a kids' play area and a dive school.

Rimba Resort, **t** 07 223 1493, Pulau Sibu. A collection of twenty simple but attractive *attap*-roofed cottages with bathroom, dressing room and large verandah, but no air-con. The resort is set on its own on a secluded beach on the north side of the island.

getaways; the Johor royalty own the island and built their first resort here in 1971. The beach is idyllic, and though decades of visitors have decimated much of the coral, it is a good place to snorkel.

South of Pulau Besar there is more accommodation on **Pulau Tinggi**, at its centre a dramatic 650m cone of rock that was once an active volcano. Nearby **Pulau Sibu**, with yet more accommodation, is the site of one of the government's pilot projects: scattered among the traditional homes of the fishermen are dozens of solar panels, which generate all the power they need.

Speedboats for the islands set off from Mersing (*see* p.301), where travel agents book packages at the resorts or organize island-hopping trips. For a lazy day of fishing and island-hopping, it is possible to hire your own traditional boat, with captain and deckhand (enquire at East Coast Hotel, Mersing; *see* opposite). The most idyllic of the Seribuat islands require tourists to charter a boat to reach them. Pulau Pemanggil and Pulau Aur are two notable examples, 45km and 80km offshore respectively.

Muar

The attractive estuarine town of Muar, not far from the border with Melaka, is worth a stop for its avenue of colonial mansions set among peaceful gardens along the banks of a wide river. Old Portuguese maps show Muar to have had a significant population as far back as the 15th century. The *Sejarah Melayu* records how Parameswara fled Temesik (Singapore) and settled at Muar, where he built a wooden fort, before moving north to found Melaka. The key to Muar's long history is its river, Sungai Muar, which has long been an important trans-peninsular route, linking Pahang with the west coast. Local fishing boats and Sumatran schooners skirt the estuary, which is known for its oysters.

Muar is also acknowledged as the centre for an unusual Malay dance known as Kuda Kepang ('horse piece'). To the accompaniment of trance-inducing beats, nine

Getting There

Muar is not far off the North-South Expressway, near the northern border of Johor state. The long-distance bus station is just upriver from the main bridge. The journey from KL by bus takes 2.5hrs, from Johor Bahru 2hrs. Buses from Melaka (1hr) pull in at the local bus station, which is just downriver from the bridge. You can drive from Melaka in less than an hour.

Where to Stay

Moderate

Hotel Classic, 69 Jalan Ali, **t** 06 953 3888, **f** 06 953 6333. Muar's best hotel, with good-sized rooms, air-con, TV, mini-bar and en suite bathrooms. The Chinese restaurant here is a decent place to eat.

Riverview Hotel, 29 Jalan Bentayan, **t** 06 951 3313, **f** 06 951 8139. Another well-kept, though nondescript, modern hotel with spacious rooms, air-con, TV and bathroom.

Inexpensive

Rumah Persinggahan Tanjung Emas, 2222 Jalan Sultanah Fatimah, **t** 06 952 7755. This rambling old resthouse set in its own gardens was built in 1903. Its first guests were two Australian gold prospectors. The rooms are a little decrepit nowadays, but are very spacious, have air-con and look out over a large back garden. The hotel stands on its own: head past the mosque on Jalan Petri then turn left onto Jalan Sultanah Fatimah.

Eating Out

There are plenty of informal Chinese restaurants about town. Hotel Classic has a decent Chinese restaurant, while the Wetex Parade shopping centre has a large food court. There's also an outdoor food court off Jalan Petri at Tanjung Emas.

dancers sit astride a two-dimensional 'horse', made of hide or rattan, and render the exploits of nine Muslims spreading news of the prophet in Java.

Sultan Abu Bakar of Johor was instrumental in sparking Muar's prosperity at the end of the 19th century, naming the town Bandar Maharani (Queen's City) after his wife. He encouraged Javanese and Chinese immigrants to set up smallholdings, and Muar soon attracted greater numbers of traders to its estuary. Durian, mangosteen, betel nut, pepper and coffee were all produced and in durian season, according to records from 1911, every passing ship would load its hull with 25,000 of the spiky fruit. This prosperity encouraged development along **Jalan Petri**, where the Court House, Government Offices and Police Station, all elegant neoclassical colonial buildings, now stand. The most impressive structure is the **Masjid Jamek Sultan Ibrahim**, an elegant mosque built in 1925, combining Moorish and classical Baroque styles. The entranceways feature Doric pillars, while the minaret has been likened to a lighthouse. Directly across the river from here stands its 'mirror-image', **Masjid Jamek Kedua**, completed in 1999 – although the modern mosque was built to hold 5,000 for prayers and is constructed of modern materials so you'll do well to spot the link.

Beyond the old mosque a new waterfront walkway stretches the length of Tanjung Emas, a promontory lined with lawns and old rain trees. It's a peaceful spot, with boys fishing and old men lounging in the shade of trees. At the end is a small jetty. River cruises (*45 mins, RM10*), which do a loop of the estuary, leave from here. The rest of town is of little interest – Chinese shophouses and modern condominiums.

Sarawak

17

Sarawak

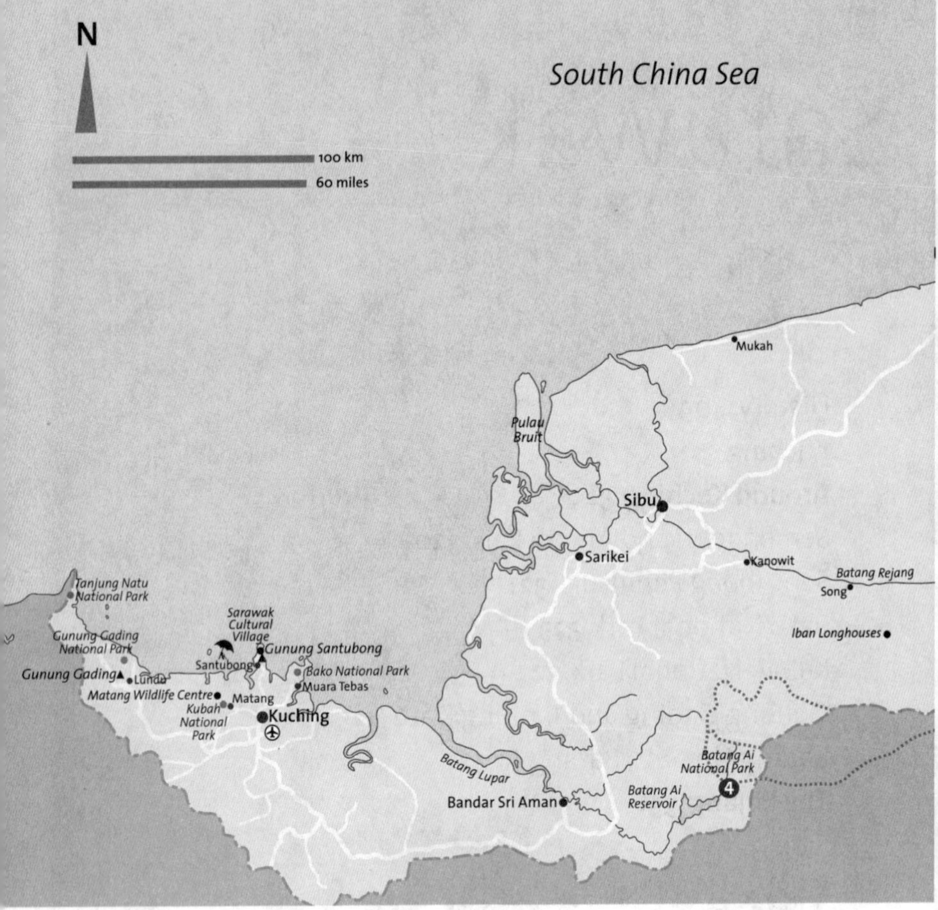

Borneo (of which Sarawak forms the northwestern part) has become a byword for the exotic, a template for jungle adventures and journeys into the unknown. It was during the autocratic dynasty of 'White Rajahs', who ruled Sarawak from 1841–1941, that stories of a primeval wilderness inhabited by head-hunters found their way back to Europe. In her autobiography, Sylvia Brooke, wife of the last rajah, describes her first impressions: 'There was something fearsome about the richness of this ancient foliage in a land of mysterious legends and beliefs; and yet, as I gazed at its luxuriant beauty... I knew that I was home'.

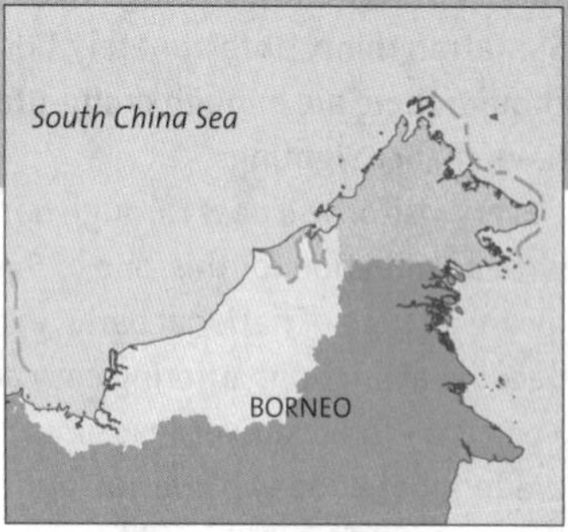

Highlights

1 The thunderous Batang Rejang river
2 Remote Bario, the highest settled community in Borneo, hidden in the Kelabit Highlands
3 Gunung Mulu National Park – a UNESCO World Heritage Site comprising more than 500 sq km of spectacular virgin rainforest
4 Nanga Sumpa, an example of a traditional Iban longhouse deep in the rainforest

At the centre of the mystique Sylvia Brooke talks of, and at the heart of Borneo's tribal culture, is the longhouse; an extended communal home where song, dance and rice wine are indulged to excess, and where smoke-dried human skulls, the grisly trophies of war, hang from the rafters.

Today Sarawak is the most accessible entry point to Borneo. It is Malaysia's largest state and its most ethnically diverse. Its unique history as the private kingdom of the White Rajahs has left its mark, and Sarawak bears little resemblance to other Malaysian states. One happy consequence of the Brooke era (for the modern tourist at any rate) is that the values and traditions of Sarawak's indigenous tribes have retained their integrity to this day. As such, the highlight of any trip to Sarawak is a longhouse visit. Tribal culture is renowned for its hospitality and there are longhouses to suit allcomers, from those close to Kuching, geared up specially for tourists, to remote Kenyah or Kelabit longhouses, where life goes on as it has done for centuries. For a closer look at Sarawak's principle tribes, *see* 'Indigenous Tribes of Malaysia', p.40.

Thanks in large part to oil reserves off the coast of Miri, Sarawak's main towns have a surprising feeling of affluence, and travel is not so cheap as it is in West Malaysia. Luxury 4X4s roll about the streets, and local travel agencies are slick operations, unlike their counterparts across the water. But there is still the feeling that geography dominates, that the natural world has not yet lost its grip on the state. Despite the slow devastation of logging and the march of the palm-oil plantations, much of Sarawak remains cloaked in some of the world's oldest virgin rainforest, which is in turn dissected by a network of rivers.

Though the road system has improved in recent years, river boats remain the primary mode of transport for most of the population. Mangroves dominate the swampy coastal plain, home to skilled Melanau fishermen, while the hinterland of jungled foothills and the remote mountain plateaus provide refuge for an enormous variety of wildlife, including endangered species such as the orang-utan and the Sumatran rhino. Unfortunately, both these species are nearing extinction in the wild, though there are enough orang-utans left out there for the adventurous tourist to have chance sightings.

Every visitor will pass through Sarawak's state capital Kuching, and most will leave with an affection for this, one of Southeast Asia's most companionable cities. Close by are a range of national parks, each with a different topography and their own peculiar attractions, offering easy access to visitors. Further afield the mighty Rejang, Malaysia's longest river, leads into the heart of Borneo where traditional longhouses predominate. Today powerful launches have cut down the journey time from weeks to a matter of hours. Then there are the ancient cave paintings of Niah, the extraordinary secluded world of the Kelabit Highlands, and Gunung Mulu National Park, with its unique vertical landscape and a cave system of unprecedented scale (they say the Sarawak Chamber is large enough to hold 16 football pitches).

History

Until British 'adventurer' James Brooke appeared on the scene in 1841, Sarawak did not exist as a political entity. And yet there is evidence that people lived here as long as 40,000 years ago: the human skulls discovered at the Niah Caves in 1958 by Tom Harrisson – then Curator of the Sarawak Museum – are the oldest recorded in Southeast Asia (unless, of course, you count 700,000-year-old Java Man as human). Analysis of the skulls suggests an affinity with the Australo-Melanesian races, which points to the Penan tribe as the possible descendants of Borneo's first inhabitants (*see* 'Indigenous Tribes of Malaysia', p.40). A scattering of rock carvings, cave paintings and megaliths (such as the dolmens erected by the Kelabit, *see* p.351) provide further evidence of the prehistoric activities of indigenous tribes.

For many centuries the Sultan of Brunei had nominal control over the entire northern slice of Borneo. In fact 'Borneo' is probably a European corruption of the word 'Brunei'. By the 19th century the sultan's hold on the region was slipping, and when James Brooke turned up aboard his schooner *The Royalist*, the sultan enlisted his help to quell an uprising. In return, Brooke was granted land rights in the area surrounding present-day Kuching. So successful was Brooke at silencing disputes among fighting factions that in 1841 the sultan conferred the title of 'Rajah of Sarawak' upon the vainglorious Englishman.

Brooke maintained the peace by a mixture of heavy-handedness and clever politics; he appeased the Malays by offering lucrative positions within his administration, while protecting the tribespeople from piracy and subjugation by the Malays. When naturalist Alfred Russel Wallace visited remote longhouses in 1855 he noted the awe in which the White Rajah was held: 'Could he not bring the dead back to life? Was he not as old as the mountains?'

James Brooke was in fact only 38 when he became Rajah of Sarawak. He was born near Varanasi in India and enlisted in the army of the East India Company, having fled boarding school in England. He was wounded in the First Anglo-Burmese War and invalided out of the army. On inheriting a fortune, he bought himself a state-of-the-art yacht, which he armed to the hilt before setting off for Singapore and a voyage of adventure. He spent quite some time in the company of Raffles, founder of modern Singapore, and became fascinated by the concept of a colonial administration that would protect the trader while fostering native welfare.

By today's standards Brooke's 'divide and rule' policy, underwritten by the romantic ideal of the 'noble savage', is arcane to say the least. Each ethnic group had its alloted role; the Malays: administration; the Dyaks: military; and the Chinese: economic. Segregation was enforced; it was forbidden, for instance, for a Chinese to enter a longhouse without permission from the Rajah. Brooke believed that the values and traditions of the indigenous peoples should be upheld – primarily because, in their state of 'savagery', they were not ready to take on the ideologies of the civilized world.

Despite the contradictions of the White Rajah's benevolent autocracy, his dictum was a noble one: 'Sarawak belongs to the Malays, the Sea Dyaks, the Land Dyaks, the Kayans and all the other tribes, and not us. It is for them we labour, not ourselves.'

When James Brooke handed power to his nephew Charles Brooke in 1868, the territory under his control had expanded dramatically. James Brooke had been granted the new land by offering the Sultan of Brunei fifty per cent of any trade revenue. By 1905 Sarawak had achieved its present-day dimensions, leaving Brunei hemmed in against the coast.

Charles Brooke continued to rule in much the same vein as his uncle. He transformed Kuching into an elegant town, with street lighting and grand public buildings. Each morning, at 8am, he would cross the river from his residence in the Astana to the Court House, where he would dispense justice in person. According to his daughter-in-law Sylvia Brooke, the Rajah's government officers 'shivered in their shoes' in his presence. In her autobiography she describes her father-in-law as 'starkly supreme, gaunt and unapproachable... a stern figure with a hawk-like nose, one glass eye from which a constant trickle of water dripped onto his snow-white moustache, and a heart of stone'.

Relations between the Rajah and his daughter-in-law were frosty. At his lowest ebb he more or less disowned her husband Vyner – his eldest son – by announcing that his youngest son Bertram would be his heir. Nevertheless in 1917 it was Vyner Brooke who took the reins. He spent more time in England than Sarawak and was a compulsive womanizer, working his way through the wives of his officials. Still, when it came to governing Sarawak he upheld the principals of his father, employing a civil service to administer the realm in his absence.

By the mid-20th century, Sarawak was a true anachronism. In the age of democracy, Vyner Brooke's position as absolute ruler of his own private kingdom had no doubt become an embarrassment, and he was forced to work towards the goal of self-government for Sarawak. Shortly after the centenary of the Brooke dynasty in 1941, the Japanese occupied Sarawak and the Rajah fled to Australia. On his return in 1946 Vyner Brooke ceded power to the British Crown and – in the same year that Britain announced its intentions to grant independence to India – Sarawak became a British colony. Many in Sarawak were unhappy. There were riots and, in 1949, the new governor Duncan Stewart was murdered by anti-cessionists.

The ultimate fate of Sarawak had been shaped largely by the discovery of oil off the shore of Miri back in 1910. With these resources Sarawak became a prime candidate for inclusion in the Federation of Malaysia, when the concept was first discussed after Malaya attained independence in 1957. Sarawak, along with Sabah, Malaya and Singapore joined forces to become Malaysia in 1963. Brunei thought about it but, jealous of its own vast oil reserves, sat on the fence. With Singapore's Chinese majority loath to be dictated to by the Malay ruling party, Singapore soon pulled out of the Federation.

Indonesia vehemently opposed Sarawak's inclusion in the Federation and war broke out. Guerilla fighting ensued along the border and tens of thousands of Commonwealth soldiers were drafted in to help quell what became known as the *Konfrontasi* (Confrontation).

Kuching

'Kuching' is Malay for cat, and most histories of the state capital offer up quaint stories about James Brooke and a cat on the bank of the Sarawak River. More plausible origins of the name are a local, lychee-like fruit called *mata kuching* (literally 'cat's eyes') and – least exciting but most likely – *cochin*, a word for 'port' once used by traders across Indochina. Still, the cat theme has been absorbed into the psyche of Kuching and you'll find cat kitsch all over the place, from public sculptures to the city's very own Cat Museum.

Kuching came into existence in 1841 when Rajah James Brooke was granted land rights in the area (*see* 'History' above). He landed at a small riverine village known as Sarawak, which soon expanded to become his administrative capital. It remained a relatively small and unimposing place until the rubber boom in the first decades of the 20th century, which attracted immigrants from Hokkien Province in China.

Kuching is one of Malaysia's least demanding cities in which to spend any time – perhaps because it has the feel of a lively provincial town rather than a modern Asian city. A sense of colonial languor still hangs about the place, with its collection of indulgent colonial buildings set alongside stilted kampung houses on a slow bend of river. The centre is compact, the people are warm-hearted, and the coffeeshops plentiful, while the new Kuching Waterfront development is ideal for a safe evening stroll. The key to Kuching's charm is in large part the spirit of hospitality so integral to the culture of Borneo's indigenous peoples. Kuching is well located for practical purposes too. Ringed by National Parks and accessible longhouses, the city is a great place from which to make forays into the wilds.

Kuching Waterfront and Chinatown

New arrivals, with preconceptions of Borneo firmly in mind, may be a little bewildered by Kuching Waterfront. Modern sculptures, musical fountains, landscaped gardens, dinky cafés – even an open-air theatre – take their places along this elegant kilometre-long esplanade. Ignore the creamy-brown river beyond the railings (and the beads of sweat developing at your hairline) and you might be in Europe.

Until the early 1990s this stretch of river was lined with Chinese godowns, where goods from upriver and from abroad were hauled ashore and sorted by merchants. Warehouses were demolished and land reclaimed from the river to build the Waterfront, which has been a hit with locals ever since. Despite the changes, traditional *tambang* still ferry passengers across the water – locals to and from the Malay kampungs, and tourists to the orchid garden and the fort (*see* p.319). The *tambang*, Kuching's version of the Malay sampan, is a wooden boat with a pitched roof, a tiny motor at the stern and an oarsman who stands up front, his oars forming an X at the bow. Tempers have flared over the future of these pretty craft. Some talk of modern launches capable of ferrying motorbikes across the river; others point to the gondolas of Venice for affirmation, or to the 2000-plus *tambang* operators who will lose their jobs (they work shifts, operating 80 *tambangs* day and night).

In the Shadow of Darwin: Alfred Russel Wallace

Alfred Russel Wallace (1823–1913) is not a household name. And yet, independently of Darwin, he drew parallel conclusions on the theory of evolution. In fact it was Wallace who suggested to Darwin that he use the phrase 'survival of the fittest' to help explain the new theory to a disbelieving public.

Wallace spent eight years in Southeast Asia from 1854–62, exploring its remotest corners, collecting specimens (he is famous for bequeathing 125,000 specimens to the British Museum), and developing his theories on evolution and the geographical distribution of animal species. His best-known work, *The Malay Archipelago* (*see* Bibliography), remains a wonderfully readable piece of travel writing and natural history, with clear and candid observations about the people and places he visited alongside interpretations of his research findings.

His greatest legacy is the Wallace Line, a transitional zone which runs between Bali and Lombok, and over which very few animal species have crossed. Species to the east of the line – formed by a deep water channel – have evolved independently of those to the west. Many thousand of years ago, when sea levels were lower, the archipelago of islands to the west of the Wallace Line was moulded together as one land mass, allowing for the transmigration of species. But throughout this period the Wallace Line sealed Australasia from the Asian landmass, leaving creatures such as the marsupials to evolve in their own eccentric manner.

It is possible to hire a *tambang* for about RM30/hour for a tour up and down the river, past a string of Malay kampungs. If you prefer to cruise along the river in a large boat with karaoke facilities, then board the *Equatorial* for the 'Sarawak River Cruise' (*two or three sailings each day from the Waterfront; adult RM35, child RM20*).

Up towards the Wet Market stands the Waterfront's most prominent structure, the **Square Tower**. A diminutive fort in its own right, the tower was built in the same year and in the same style as Fort Margherita across the river. It stands on the site of the original wooden fort, built by James Brooke and razed in 1857 during a gold-diggers' rebellion. It is thought that the tower was built to hold prisoners, though it saw more use as a dancing hall for colonial administrators and their wives.

Towards the opposite end of the Waterfront is the **Chinese History Museum** (*open Sat–Thurs 9–6; free*), set in the old Chinese Chamber of Commerce. Most of Kuching's first-generation Chinese left their homeland with dreams of returning to their families one day with new-found fortunes. This was the common dream in the poverty-stricken southern provinces of China, and by the turn of the 20th century there was a saying that, for every ten Chinese who emigrated, three would die, six would never escape their destination, and one would return home with his fortune. This one-room museum details the harsh conditions under which so many Chinese fled their homeland in search of better times – often to find equally arduous lifestyles awaiting them at the other end. But there were success stories too, as this tiny museum recounts. It is well worth popping inside, if only for a break from the heat.

Getting There

Kuching International Airport is about 10km south of the city. There are regular **flights** to and from all major West Malaysian airports. Within East Malaysia there are connections with Kota Kinabalu, Miri, Sibu, Bintulu, Labuan and Mukah (Twin Otter service). There are also irregular flights to destinations in Indonesia, Philippines and Australia.

Most people will arrive in Kuching by air: domestic flights within Sabah and Sarawak are cheap and the road network in Sarawak is not extensive. For those who want to slog it out overland, however, there are plenty of **bus** services between the main towns. These leave from the express terminal at Mile 3 on Jalan Penrissen.

As an alternative to catching a bus, a daily **speed-ferry** service operates between Kuching and Sibu (4hrs). Ferries leave from the jetty at Pending, 7km east of Kuching.

Getting Around

You can walk right across the centre of Kuching in about 20mins and this is the way most people move about. Kuching has its own so-called 'city tram', which is actually a tourist **bus** that takes in the main sights in and around town. The bus leaves hourly from 10–4 and 7–9, departing from the Visitor Information Centre on Padang Merdeka. The taxi rank is situated next to the wet market. To order a **taxi** by phone call **t** 082 480 000/082 348 898. For **car hire** try Pronto Car Rental, 98 Jalan Padungan, **t** 082 236 889.

Pretty 'Lipton Tea' sampans – known locally as *tambangs* – can be hired for river tours. They are also the means of crossing from the Square Tower on Main Bazaar to Fort Marguerita, the Orchid Garden and the Astana.

Pronto Car Rental, 98 Padungan Road, **t** 082 236 889, **f** 082 236 889. Good-value car rental. They will deliver the car and pick it up from your hotel.

Tourist Information

Visitor Information Centre, Padang Merdeka, **t** 082 410 944, **f** 082 256 301, open Mon–Fri 8–6, Sat 8–4, Sun and hols 8–3. An excellent information centre with plenty of literature and helpful staff. The centre also serves as the National Park and Wildlife booking office, which issues visitor permits for the state's National Parks (if you visit the parks as part of an organized tour, the agents should arrange permits themselves). On the Waterfront is the Sarawak Tourist Association, **t** 082 240 620, open Mon–Thurs 8–12.45 and 2–4.15, Fri 8–11.30 and 2.30–4.45, Sat 8–12.45, which can provide information and help with bookings. Get hold of a copy of the free *Official Kuching Guide*, an excellent 70-page pamphlet on the city and its attractions with comprehensive listings. Copies are available from the tourist offices.

Tour Operators

Unlike in West Malaysia, the best (and often only) way of visiting many of the sights is with the help of a tour operator. Kuching has many to choose from and the best are ethically-sound, slick operations with well-informed guides. All offer tours across the state.

Borneo Adventure, 55 Main Bazaar, **t** 082 245 175, **f** 082 422 626, *www.borneoadventure.com*. This tour operator sets the standard in Borneo, with numerous awards for responsible tourism

Set back from the Waterfront is **Main Bazaar**, Kuching's oldest street. Today it is lined with attractive Chinese shophouses, some owned for generations by the same family, others converted into showrooms and offices for antiques dealers, handicraft stores and tour operators. Parallel to Main Bazaar is Lebuh Carpenter and, adjacent to that, Lebuh China. This is the heart of Chinatown, a zone of small traders, traditional coffee shops, and well-preserved shophouses from the late 19th century. Under the order of the rajah, they were built of brick and *belian* (ironwood) after a large fire in and quality of service. Their established tours, which take visitors well off the tourist trail, benefit local communities (many of whom are vulnerable to abuse from irresponsible operators). They also have a wide network of contacts for organizing tailor-made tours. One of their latest ventures, in association with the Orangutan Foundation UK, is the Red Ape Trail (*www.redapetrail.com*), an arduous 11-day trek into one of Borneo's few remaining orang-utan habitats. Much of the proceeds go towards community-based conservation projects.

Borneo Inbound Tours and Travel, 98 Main Bazaar, **t** 082 237 287/082 233 354. Offers exclusive tours to Tanjung Datu National Park, at the western tip of Sarawak, with guided treks and a homestay programme at Kampung Melano.

Borneo Interland, 63 Main Bazaar, **t** 082 413 595, **f** 082 411 619, *www.bitravel.com.my*. Offers a wide range of tours in Sabah and Sarawak.

Borneo Transverse, 15 Jalan Green Hill, **t** 082 257 784, **f** 082 421 419, *www.borneotransverse.com.my*. A long-standing operator with a good range of tours.

CPH Travel Agency, 70 Padungan Road, **t** 082 243 708, **f** 082 424 587, *www.cphtravel.com.my*. As one of the first Borneo travel agencies, this lot call themselves 'the Borneo Travel Pioneers'.

Where to Stay

Luxury–Expensive

Crowne Plaza Riverside, Jalan Tunku Abdul Rahman, **t** 082 247 777, **f** 082 425 858, *cprk@po.jaring.my*, *www.ichotelsgroup.com*. A plush 5-star hotel with a large adjoining business centre and shopping mall with cinema complex. Rooms are large, with views over the riverfront. There's a good outdoor pool, tennis and squash courts, a big fitness centre and three restaurants.

Expensive

Hilton Kuching, Jalan Tunku Abdul Rahman, **t** 082 248 200, **f** 082 428 984, *infokuching@hilton.com*, *www.hilton.com*. One of Kuching's most expensive hotels and possibly its best, not least because of the wonderful river views. Rooms are spacious, there is a mediocre outdoor pool and a fitness centre. The Waterfront Café serves international dishes, while Toh Yuen serves Cantonese and Szechuan cuisine. There's also a Steakhouse, which surprisingly offers Kuching's finest dining. Bordering on the 'luxury' price category.

Merdeka Palace Hotel, Lorong Temple, **t** 082 258 000, **f** 082 425 400, *info@merdekapalace.com*, *www.merdekapalace.com*. A notch down from the Hilton, though it outdoes it in opulence, with a grand marble foyer and plummy atmosphere. Rooms have all the expected facilitites, plus there's a gym, swimming pool and sauna/steambath. Overlooking Merdeka Square, and right by the Sarawak Museum. Has six restaurants and bars, including a decent Italian restaurant and the Victoria Arms, an 'authentic' English pub.

Holiday Inn Kuching, Jalan Tunku Abdul Rahman, **t** 082 423 111, **f** 082 426 169, *hikmy@myjaring.net*, *www.ichotelsgroup.com*. Another huge hotel right on the riverfront just east of the centre of town. Rooms have views of the string of pretty Malay kampungs across the river. Facilities include seven food and drink outlets.

1884. **Tua Pek Kong** (1876) is the spiritual centre of Chinatown, and Kuching's oldest Chinese temple. It stands in a haze of incense at the eastern end of Main Bazaar, and is packed throughout the day with supplicants.

Head right to the eastern end of the Waterfront, past the dominating curve of the Hilton, and you reach the heart of Kuching's modern shopping district, full of malls and high-rise hotels. Hidden in the middle of it all is a fascinating Iban textile gallery, the **Tun Jugah Pua Gallery** (*Level 4, Tun Jugah Tower, Jalan Tunku Abdul Rahman*, **t** *082*

Expensive–Moderate

Harbour View Hotel, Lorong Temple, **t** 082 274 666, **f** 082 274 777, *sales@harbourview.com.my*, *www.harbourview.com.my*. Rooms in this business-class hotel are in good condition and have views over the river, probably offering the best value in town. Café Harapan downstairs serves a buffet of Malay/Chinese staples at reasonable prices.

Moderate

Borneo Hotel, 30 Tabuan Road, **t** 082 244 122, **f** 082 254 848. Some of the rooms are beginning to look like they need an overhaul, but this friendly hotel provides good value and service compared to many of the other options. Large doubles have air-con, coffee-making facilities, mini-bar, TV and phone.

Telang Usan Hotel, Jalan Ban Hock, **t** 082 415 588, **f** 082 425 316, *www.telangusan.com*. Though this family-run hotel doesn't look much from the outside, the interior is adorned with the art and crafts of the Kenyah tribe of the Orang Ulu. By far the most popular of the mid-range options in Kuching, with facilities including mini-bar, en suite bathrooms and TV.

Kingwood Inn, Jalan Padungan, **t** 082 330 888, **f** 082 332 888, *kingwd@tm.net.my*. This is a solid mid-range business hotel just outside the town centre. Facilities include mini-bar, TV, modem socket and a swimming pool.

Inexpensive

Goodwood Inn, 16–17 Jalan Green Hill, **t** 082 244 862, **f** 082 235 690. One of a crop of inexpensive hotels on Jalan Green Hill. Though fairly stark, all rooms have air-con, TV and phone.

River View Inn, 22–23 Jalan Green Hill, **t** 082 412 551, **f** 082 256 302. Another acceptable option on Jalan Green Hill. Don't count on a river view, though.

Diocesan Rest House, St Thomas Cathedral, Jalan Tun Haji Openg, **t** 082 414 027. Attractive, airy rooms in a wooden house beside the cathedral. Facilities are basic and rooms are often occupied by visitors on church business. Still, this is probably the best budget option.

Eating Out

Locals are obsessive in their love of Sarawak *laksa*, the traditional Borneo breakfast. Once you've had a bowl or two yourself, it's not hard to understand why. Large quantities of coconut cream combine with lemon grass, tamarind, garlic, chilli and shrimp paste to form a robust and spicy soup, into which strips of chicken, omelette, prawns, beansprouts and *bee hoon* noodles are thrown. Coffee shops are the places to track down a good *laksa*; locals all have their coveted favourite.

Most meals in Malaysian Borneo are accompanied by a side dish of jungle fern. This healthy staple comprises the young shoots of various types of widespread indigenous ferns, usually fried up with garlic and oyster sauce. Other specialities include *umai*, the Melanau equivalent of *ceviche* (a salad of raw fish and shallots doused in lime juice and chilli), and the Iban specialities *pansoh manok* and *lemang*, chicken and glutinous rice respectively, cooked in sections of bamboo over an open fire.

One of the first ports of call for a meal in Kuching is usually one of the food centres, where a range of cuisines can be sampled. Within walking distance of the riverfront is

239 672; open Mon–Fri 9–12 and 1–4.30; all visitors must call in advance). The gallery is run by a charitable foundation established in 1985 to help record and preserve Iban folklore, culture and the arts. The status of an Iban woman within her community was determined by her ability to weave *pua*, decorative pieces of cotton fabric used for ritual purposes or as clothing, with anthropomorphic designs inspired by dreams. The finished article is a statement of the relationship between the weaver and the spirits. Cotton was grown specially for the purpose and natural dyes were used to the **Topspot Seafood Centre** (above the car park at Taman Kereta, Jalan Padungan), where dozens of hawker stalls present mouth-watering displays of fresh fish and seafood alongside other Southeast Asian dishes, all at cheap prices. Other popular food centres include the **Chinese Food Centre** on Jalan Carpenter and the **Open-Air Market** (now covered) on Jalan Market.

Expensive

The Steakhouse, Hilton Kuching (*see* above). Despite its uninspiring name, this restaurant has a new-found reputation as one the city's best spots for 'international' cuisine. Beef comes in a number of guises, from carpaccio to pan-seared or roasted. And it's not all meat: the fish dishes are put together with a good deal of invention too.

The Junk Restaurant, 80 Wayang Street, **t** 082 259 450. Fusion cooking in a Chinese setting. Pleasant nostalgic décor, with potted palms crowding the entrance. An eclectic and somewhat baffling menu, including grilled rainbow trout, fish and chips and lamb shank alongside teriyaki chicken and tempura crab salad. Large portions and not bad value (bottom end of this price category).

Moderate

Denis' Place, Lebuh Wayang (corner with Main Bazaar). Set in a restored Chinese shophouse and aimed unambiguously at tourists, this is an atmospheric little restaurant with Western dishes (delicious burgers and chips) and local options too. Come here for the desserts in particular.

Benson Seafood, Jalan Abell. Set behind the moorings of Kuching's seagoing fishing fleet, this open-sided restaurant is well positioned to pluck some of the best fish and seafood. Dining is informal – plastic tables and chairs – but the food is exceptional. A little upriver from the centre of town, and well known.

Jojo Seafood Centre, Ground Floor, Twin Centre, 2.5 mile, Rock Road (near the 3-mile bus terminal), closed Mon. If you happen to be nearby, this local Chinese restaurant is well known for the quality of its offerings. Good value.

Tapanga Tree, Taman Kereta, Jalan Padungan. A trendy restaurant with a bar-terrace, serving the requisite fusion cuisine alongside traditional dishes of Sarawak.

Cheap

Some of the best food in Kuching is found among the dozens of coffee shops or at hawker stalls within food centres (*see* above). A few other options are listed below.

Life Café, 108 Jalan Ewe Hai. A great little noodle restaurant, designed in the style of a Chinese teahouse. The extensive range of teas, coffees and juices are complemented by the likes of claypot noodles and wonderful Chinese dumplings (pork or vegetable). Wide range of vegetarian options.

Choon Hui Café, Jalan Ban Hock (next to Grand Continental). Not exactly in the centre of town, but this humble-looking coffee shop is worth tracking down for its Sarawak *laksa*, which many think is the best in Kuching. Come early for breakfast and wait for a table.

Satay Stall (a.k.a. 'Next to Nelson's', *see* Shopping), off Jalan Wayang. Another good breakfast spot if you want to do as the locals do. As well as satay by the dozen, this food stall is known for its *mee jawa*, a spicy noodle dish not unlike spaghetti in tomato sauce – if you ignore the kick.

Zhun San Yen Vegetarian Restaurant, Jalan Green Hill, open daily 7–7. A cosy neighbourhood restaurant where beancurd

create the earthy tones typical of authentic Iban textiles. The whole process, which is an integral part of Iban ritual and taboo, is known as *ikat* weaving.

Colonial Kuching

The strip of town that runs from the Court House past the Padang, as far as the Sarawak Museum and Reservoir Park, is often referred to as the Colonial Quarter and soya is resurrected as 'lemon chicken' and 'sweet and sour pork'. Good value and tasty, with helpful owners.

Nightlife

While Kuching is not the liveliest of places by night, many of its residents – notably the Iban – are partial to a drink or three. Combine this predilection with Sarawak's famous hospitality, and you have a good night ahead of you if you veer towards the right places. Many locals drink and socialize during the evenings at their favourite food stall or coffee shop, most of which stock beer. Bear in mind that many of the bars, clubs and karaoke lounges (if you are so aligned) don't get going properly until the early hours.

De Tavern (Jalan Borneo, behind the Hilton), a Kuching institution run by a companionable Kayan, is a good place to sample *tuak*, the famous and fiery rice wine of tribal Borneo. Upstairs another family-run pub called **The Royalist** – this one Iban, and decidedly English in theme (*The Royalist* was the ship which carried James Brooke to Sarawak) – competes at raucous hospitality. At the eastern end of the Waterfront is **Khatulistiwa**, a lively bar in the round with views over the water. The club upstairs plays house and techno at weekends. **The Eagle's Nest** (Jalan Bukit Mata Kuching) is a popular hangout with expats and locals alike, with pool tables, DJ and a selection of beers and wines, while **Peppers** at the Hilton is another popular bar and club. The beer-garden terrace attached to the **Tapanga Tree** (*see* Eating Out) is a good spot for an evening drink, with snacks served up from the restaurant kitchen and views over the city.

Shopping

Kuching is a dream for souvenir-hunters. Shops here are packed with the sort of items coveted by ethnic stores throughout the West. The town is a repository for tribal handicrafts, though prices are bumped up considerably: haggling is acceptable. For the bargains you will need to head upriver and buy direct from the **longhouses** – though even here (unless you go remote), they often know the value of the ringgit in a Western pocket, and charge accordingly. Remember to get a licence from the curator of the Sarawak Museum if you want to come home with antiques of any sort.

Contemporary and tribal-influenced fine art is on sale in numerous galleries across town. The most popular handicrafts to be picked up include elaborate hornbill carvings (traditionally used in ritual), blowpipes, woven mats and baskets and *pua*, the famous hand-woven Iban textile (*see* p.30). Many of the best handicraft shops congregate along Main Bazaar. Two of the best are **Nelson's Gallery** and **Atelier Gallery**, which has a massive collection of handicrafts, furniture and antiques. **Galeri M**, in the lobby of the Hilton (and at the smaller showroom on Main Bazaar) is the place to find paintings by local artists. **Saracraf** (Ground Floor, Sarawak Plaza, opposite Holiday Inn) is another handicrafts centre that was set up by the state government to encourage fair compensation for the upriver craftsmen and women who supply Kuching's growing handicrafts industry.

The main general shopping centres are concentrated just east of the Waterfront, near the Holiday Inn. These include the Crowne Plaza Riverside and Cineplex, Sarawak Plaza and Tun Jugah.

(though 'Brooke Quarter' would be more fitting: technically, Sarawak was a colony only between 1946 and 1963).

The **Court House** was built in 1873 under the rule of Charles Brooke. A shady verandah runs round the front of the building, though the highlight is the ironwood roof engraved with tribal designs. For nearly a century the building served as government offices and as a venue for state functions. Outside the Court House stands the plain stone Charles Brooke Memorial, erected in 1924. Charles was by all accounts a true Brit of the Empire (despite the fact that Whitehall turned its nose up at Sarawak as a possible colony during the Brooke era). Stern and unapproachable, Charles would rise at first light each day, proceed to the Court House to hear local cases and, true to his role as despot, dispense justice as he saw fit.

Further down, on the opposite side of the road is Kuching's grandest building. Though it only served as the **General Post Office**, it was built in 1931 to outlandish scale, with towering Corinthian columns, decorative friezes and a massive pediment. There are plans to put the building to more appropriate use as the new Sarawak Art Museum.

Beyond the green stretch of the *padang* is the famous **Sarawak Museum** (*Jalan Tun Abang Haji Openg, open daily 9–6; free*), first stop for most tourists. It was the great naturalist and explorer Alfred Russel Wallace (*see* 'In the Shadow of Darwin', p.312) who encouraged Rajah Charles Brooke to establish an ethnographical and natural history museum in Kuching back in 1891. The museum was a hit with locals from the start and was only superseded in its ability to rouse wonder by the towering wireless mast that was erected towards the end of Charles Brooke's rule: some thought the mast was a ladder from which they might spy God.

A series of high-profile curators have left their mark on the Sarawak Museum, including Tom Harrisson, the talented eccentric (*see* 'In the Shadow of Darwin', p.312) who discovered 40,000-year-old human remains in the Niah Caves. The museum serves as the perfect introduction to the state, and it is well worth spending an hour or two absorbing the displays before heading upriver to the longhouses. Though the collection is extensive, don't expect anything on the scale of a major museum in the West.

Today the museum is divided in two; the original building, designed in the style of a Normandy villa, holds key exhibits from the original collection, including a grisly array of stuffed 'specimens' contributed by Wallace. There are some fascinating old photographs, a large collection of antique wood carvings and a reproduction of the interior of an Iban longhouse. High up on the walls is a reproduction of a Tree of Life mural spotted by one of the curators in a remote Kenyah longhouse. The new wing contains a reconstruction of the Niah Caves (*see* pp.342–3), documentation of the history of Sarawak and a collection of archaeological finds. At the time of writing, the new wing was closed for renovation.

In the grounds of the museum are landscaped gardens, a little aquarium (free) and the Heroes' Memorial, commemorating the dead of the Konfrontasi and World War II. Inland from the museum is **Reservoir Park**, an attractive urban park built around a reservoir, and the towering **Civic Centre**, which looks more like a water tower and offers the best views in Kuching.

Back near the *padang* is the rather ugly **St Thomas's Cathedral**, behind which stands Kuching's oldest building, the **Bishop's House**. This was home to Reverend Thomas Francis McDougall, the Anglican 'bishop' appointed to Kuching. Thanks to the missionary work begun by Rev. McDougall, many of Sarawak's indigenous people count themselves as Christians today. In fact, there are more Christians in East Malaysia than Muslims.

Across the River

Across the river from the Court House stands the understated **Astana**, residence of the White Rajahs from 1870, when Charles Brooke built the palace as a bridal gift to his new wife. Sylvia Brooke, always forthright with her opinion (especially when it came to matters concerning her stern father-in-law) described the palace as a 'fantastic medley of beauty and bad taste'. Today the building serves as the official residence of the Head of State and is not open to the public. Beside the Astana is the **Kuching Orchid Garden** (*open Tues–Sun 10–6; free*), a floral extravaganza. The seven-acre plot is packed with orchids – 80,000 of them, with more than 100 species on display.

Further east stands Kuching's most prominent building, **Fort Margherita**, built in 1879 by the second Rajah and named after his wife. An English Renaissance-style castle with crenellated towers, it was built to defend Kuching from pirates who dared to probe the Sungai Sarawak (though it never saw any action). The fort now houses the **Police Museum** (*open Tues–Sun 10–6; free; bring passport to gain entry*), a small exhibition of weapons, with a replica opium den and a few grim displays on the different types of punishment meted out by the Brookes.

Kampung Boyan is the first of eight Malay kampungs slung out along the bank of the Sungai Sarawak, just upriver from the fort. There are plans to build another esplanade here, on a smaller scale but similar concept to the Kuching Waterfront. Until then the traditional Malay *rumahs* of these villages – all wood and stilts – can be enjoyed in their original setting.

Inland from the river is Petra Jaya, Kuching's new town. There is nothing much of interest here, unless you happen to be a lover of cats. The **Cat Museum** (*DBKU building, open Tues–Sun 9–5; free*), which claims to be the only of its kind in the world, traces the history of humankind's fondness for the feline species, from Ancient Egypt through to modern times. Cat-inspired art in every conceivable medium is scattered throughout the museum.

Markets and Mosques

The life and soul of Kuching remains Jalan Gambier and the **Wet Market**, which was left untouched by the development of the Kuching Waterfront. The road is lined with stallholders selling fish, fruit, vegetables and spices. In the late 19th century prosperous Chinese traders built their houses facing the river on Gambier Road. Trade continues to this day, though on a smaller scale, with most of the ocean-going vessels docking further downstream.

Running parallel with Jalan Gambier is Lebuh India, a pedestrian street with archways at either end. Goods from the shophouses, mainly clothes and textiles, spill out onto the street. The Indians who inhabit the area are mainly descendants of those brought over in the early 20th century to work at the docks. Halfway down the street a dim passageway opens out into **Masjid India**, Sarawak's oldest mosque, constructed with nipah palms in 1837 by immigrant Indian Muslims. From early times, Malays came to worship here too, and the mosque still provides a night's sleep for

Muslim traders of any race who are away from home. From the outside the frontage of the mosque looks like just another shophouse; yet come Friday, the congregation inside swells to nearly 2000.

Just west of Jalan India is the 'Open Air Market', a busy collection of hawker stalls gathered beneath a single roof. Further west still are the gilded cupolas of the **Masjid Kuching**, formerly the State Mosque (Masjid Negara), built in 1968 on the grounds of an old Malay cemetery. The impressive new State Mosque, its interior cooled by Italian marble, is situated across the river at Petra Jaya in a complex that includes a new library and a lake.

The nearby **Islamic Museum** (*Jalan P. Ramlee, open Sat–Thurs 9–6; free*) houses eight themed galleries surrounding a courtyard. The museum tackles the development of Islamic culture both in Sarawak and further afield, with an eclectic collection of ceramics, Islamic manuscripts, decorative arts and early scientific instruments such as astrolabes.

For the uninitiated, Kuching's **Sunday Market** is a great introduction to the state. Late on Saturday afternoon, stalls appear between Jalan Satok and Jalan Rubber to the southwest of Masjid Kuching. A large percentage of the stallholders are Bidayuh women selling fruit and vegetables (much of which is unrecognizable to the Western eye), but there are cheap handicrafts to be found as well as food stalls, live animals and other jungle produce. The market runs from Saturday afternoon through to about midnight, then from dawn on Sunday until midday.

Around Kuching

The relatively small crescent of land that constitutes southwest Sarawak is dotted with national parks and – unlike the rest of the state – is served by a good network of roads. There are enough sights and activities in the southwest to keep the visitor locked in and around Kuching for a week or two at the least.

Semenggoh and Annah Rais

This tiny reserve is Sarawak's oldest, constituted as the Semenggoh Forest Reserve in 1920 by Rajah Vyner Brooke. Today it is known primarily for the **Semenggoh Wildlife Rehabilitation Centre** (*open daily 8–12.30 and 2–4.30; orang-utan feeding times 9.30–10.30 and 2.30–3.30, adm adult RM3, child RM1.50*), which offers the chance of seeing rehabilitated orang-utans in their natural environment. The centre was established in 1975, with the aim of rehabilitating confiscated orang-utans, gibbons, sun bears and hornbills into the Semenggoh Forest Reserve, which covers an area of 650 hectares. The programme was successful, and all the orang-utans confiscated have been rehabilitated. In 1996 the orang-utans began breeding in the wild and there were soon concerns that the population would outgrow the Reserve. In 1999 a number were relocated to the Matang Wildlife Centre (*see* p.324), at the edge of the much larger Kubah National Park, and this is where the rehabilitation programme will continue.

The success of the programme at Semenggoh means that orang-utan sightings here are not guaranteed, unlike at the Sepilok Rehabilitation Centre in Sabah (*see* p.380). If enough trees are fruiting within the reserve, the orang-utans don't bother turning up at feeding time. Semenggoh is situated 20km south of Kuching; most people visit as part of a tour, though taxi drivers will be happy to make the return journey, of course. Bus number 6 stops outside the gate.

There are a number of Bidayuh longhouses south of Semenggoh that are set up to receive visitors. Because they are the most accessible longhouses from Kuching, they are used to the daily flow of tour groups. **Annah Rais** is the largest and most visited of the Bidayuh settlements, situated at the foot of Gunung Penrissen near the border with Kalimantan. For the purposes of tourism, the community has agreed not to modernize the two longhouses; though what you see is hardly authentic, it provides a wonderful insight into the traditional lifestyle of the Land Dyaks, as they were known during the Brooke dynasty.

The Bidayuh traditionally lived in the foothills, away from the river systems (where their old enemies the Iban ruled the roost). They are masters with bamboo, constructing strong (but precarious-looking) bamboo bridges all about the hills. Because of the terrain, the Bidayuh longhouse often consists of more than one building, all linked by raised boardwalks. The focal point is the ceremonial house known as the *baruk*, where enemy skulls are hung. Today most of the Bidayuh have left their longhouses to settle in and around Kuching.

Santubong Peninsula

The Santubong Peninsula, also known as the Damai Penisula, has become one of Sarawak's prime tourist spots: Damai Beach, in the shadow of Gunung Santubong 35km north of Kuching, is one of the state's only accessible sandy beaches. The beach resorts here are popular, as is the Sarawak Cultural Village, which is worth a visit however strong your misgivings – for this is no ordinary cultural village (*see* p.322). Pepper plantations and Malay fishing kampungs (including Santubong itself) punctuate the approach to the peninsula: Buntal in particular has developed a name among Kuching folk for its seafood restaurants.

The peninsula is Sarawak's richest archaeological site, thanks in large part to Gunung Santubong, a solitary peak which rises 823m from the sea and has acted as a navigational beacon for millennia. Archaeological evidence suggests Santubong may have played an important role in the international trade network linking West Asia and China. The remains of numerous 10th-century iron foundries were discovered in the 1960s by Tom Harrisson (*see* p.309), along with Tang and Song Dynasty ceramics, glass beads, rock carvings and Buddhist and Hindu artefacts. At Bongkisam a Buddhist-Hindu temple was excavated and linked to the *Candi* architecture of the Bujang Valley in West Malaysia (*see* p.205). The sandy sweep of Damai Beach,

Getting There

Regular local buses serve Santubong from Kuching. A taxi costs around RM35 one way. The journey takes around 45mins.

Where to Stay

Expensive

Holiday Inn Damai Lagoon, next to Sarawak Cultural Village, **t** 082 846 999, **f** 082 846 777, *hirdbo2@po.jaring.my*, *www.ichotelsgroup.com*. The smaller of the two Holiday Inn resorts, with its own private cove and a massive 'lagoon'-style pool with swim-up bar. Rooms both in main building and in chalets are spacious with wooden floors and four-star facilities. There are tennis courts, watersports facilities and a fleet of minibuses on hand for sightseeing trips. Frequent promotions offer great value.

Holiday Inn Damai Beach Resort, **t** 082 846 900, **f** 082 846 901, *hirdlbsc@po.jaring.my*, *www.ichotelsgroup.com*. Much larger than its sister resort next door and a touch plusher, though the former has the edge for its setting. The attractive chalets here are based on Bidayuh roundhouses. There are tennis courts, two pools and more kids' facilities than next door.

Moderate

Permai Rainforest Resort, **t** 082 846 487, **f** 082 846 486, *www.permairainforest.com*. At the foot of Gunung Santubong and aimed mainly at incentive groups, with a wide range of activities on offer, from mountain biking and abseiling to orienteering and canoing. There is an assault course too. Ten air-conditioned treehouses provide the most interesting accommodation.

Nanga Damai, Jalan Sultan Tengah, **t** 016 887 1017, **f** 082 414 802, *www.nangadamai.com*. This 'luxury homestay' offers excellent value, with three double rooms equipped with air-con, fridge, phone, TV and wonderful views. There is a swimming pool and gym too. Not suitable for children.

where today's visitors sun themselves, served long ago as an open-air market for barter trade.

By the 1500s Santubong had become an important trading post within the domain of the Sultan of Brunei. James Brooke, the first White Rajah, is said to have been particulary fond of the peninsula: he had a holiday bungalow built here, which was in turn used by naturalist Alfred Russel Wallace on a research trip (*see* p.312).

The **Sarawak Cultural Village** (*www.scv.com.my, open daily 9–5.15; adm adult RM45, child RM22.50*) surrounds a small man-made lake at the foot of Gunung Santubong. It is worth visiting for the setting alone, though the seven traditional houses (a Bidayuh longhouse, an Iban longhouse, an Orang Ulu longhouse, a Melanau *rumah tinggi*, a Malay townhouse, a Malay coastal house and a Chinese farmhouse), provide the perfect introduction to multi-ethnic Borneo. The cultural village sells itself as a 'living museum', with many of the staff living on site. The houses, which are constructed with traditional materials, are staffed by locals who demonstrate traditional crafts and pursuits, from weaving and instrument-playing to top-spinning and cooking. There's even a Melanau sago-processing hut, and an Orang Ulu blacksmith who works his bellows on-site. Look out for the swirling murals in the Orang Ulu longhouse, the work of famous Kenyah artist Tusau Padan. A cultural show – more pantomime than culture – is performed in the auditorium twice a day (11.30 and 4.30). You won't miss much by avoiding it.

Gunung Santubong itself can be scaled in 5–7 hours (to the summit and down again). The trail, which begins from the Santubong Mountain Trek Canteen (not far from the cultural village) is very steep in parts, with rope ladders for assistance.

The mouth of the Sarawak river, just off Santubong Peninsula, is home to the Irrawaddy dolphin, a rare species which inhabits the brackish waters of estuaries: dolphin-spotting trips can be arranged by most tour operators in Kuching.

Bako National Park

This remarkable little National Park, at the tip of a separate peninsula to the east of Santubong, is home to seven distinct ecosystems and a great concentration of wildlife, including the preposterous-looking proboscis monkey, once known by the Malays as *orang belanda*, or 'Dutchman', for its pendulous nose and pot belly.

Bako offers a wonderful chance of spotting wildlife. Many of the animals here have become relatively accustomed to the presence of the binocular-wielding ape: Bako has been a national park since 1957 (the first in Sarawak) and is only ten square miles in size. Seventeen well-tended trails offer everything from a half-hour stroll to a two- or three-day trek. Park headquarters provides plenty of information, from trail maps to a video documentary about the park.

The Paku and Delima trails, to the north and south of park HQ respectively, pass through mangrove forest before climbing inland into dipterocarp jungle. Several

Getting There

From Kuching catch bus no. 6, or take a taxi, to Kampung Bako, about half an hour away. From the village jetty you then need to charter a *sampan* (RM40 for up to seven passengers) for the 30min boat journey out of the mouth of Sungai Bako and to the National Park headquarters. Wear waterproofs for the boat journey: the bay is shallow for miles and rippled with waves. The small sampans only run at high tide, so ask at one of the tourist information centres in Kuching before you set off. Bad weather may also prevent the boatmen from venturing out into the bay. If you do end up stuck at Kampung Bako for any length of time, take advantage of the little riverside restaurants: the village is renowned for its *belacan*, the shrimp paste which forms the basis of a Malay diet.

Tourist Information

To avoid delays and ensure that you have somewhere to stay, it is best to check high-tide times and book accommodation in advance at one of Kuching's tourist information centres. The Park HQ itself provides a wealth of information, including a small exhibition and a documentary video. Entry permits for the park (*RM10*) can be purchased at Park HQ.

Where to Stay and Eat

The Park Headquarters, situated on a strip of cleared palm-fringed land behind the main beach, offers a range of accommodation from dorm beds to fully equipped lodges. The lodges (*RM75*) contain two fan-cooled bedrooms and a large kitchen, with fridge and stove. You can rent out one of the rooms (*RM50*), a bed in the hostel (*RM15*), as well as tents for overnight treks (*RM8*).

The canteen is open 7am–9pm and serves cheap rice and noodle dishes. The attached shop sells tinned food, drinks and other supplies. Be sure to lock any food away in your rooms: the resident macaques have learned how to open unlatched windows.

troupes of proboscis monkeys (*see* 'The Proboscis Monkey', p.387) inhabit these mangroves, where they feed almost exclusively on the young leaves of mangrove trees. The best time to catch sight of these rare animals is just after dawn or in the early evening before dark.

Five secluded beaches reward those who tackle some of the longer trails within the park. The closest, Teluk Paku, is only an hour away and most of that is on the flat. Much more rewarding, however, is to climb up into the heath forest that covers the higher ground, then descend to the beautiful twin bays of Teluk Pandan. When you emerge from the half-light of the lowland rainforest into the heath forest, or *kerangas* (an Iban word denoting land not fertile enough for rice), the contrast couldn't be more startling. *Kerangas* has the feel of temperate heathland, though the sun beats down relentlessly and plantlife such as orchids and carnivorous pitcher plants cling to the stunted trees or eke out an existence between great slabs of pockmarked limestone. Birds twitter from tree to tree and are easy to spot because of the sparsity of undergrowth up here. An amazing 150 species of bird have been recorded within the boundaries of the park.

Tougher trails climb to hilltops within the park, such as Bukit Gondol or (closer by) Bukit Tambi. Another trail crosses the *kerangas* to reach the Tajor waterfall. The water here is dyed the colour of black tea by the surrounding peat bog, though it is perfectly pure and delightfully cool for bathing. The longest trails strike out for the eastern-most beaches of Teluk Limau and Teluk Kruin. Tackling these requires a night in the forest (or on one of the beaches, if you're confident of the high-tide mark).

As well as proboscis monkeys, the park is home to gentle silver leaf monkeys and a plague of crab-eating macaques, who supplement their seafood diet by scavenging from tourists. Back at park HQ, those who leave doors and windows unlocked are sure to receive unwanted visitors. To prevent frightening showdowns with these brave little animals, avoid staring directly at the larger male monkeys (an act that will be read as a challenge and be followed by demonstrations of bravado). The largest animal to frequent park HQ is the Borneo bearded pig, an enormous tusked beast unique to Borneo and nonchalant in the presence of humans.

Kubah National Park

With so many options for day trips around Kuching, not many people make it to Kubah National Park. Which is a blessing for those that do: the spine of hills that converge on Gunung Serapi (911m) has one of the richest varieties of orchids and palms in Borneo, and is alive with birds and animals, including rehabilitated orang-utans.

The **Matang Wildlife Centre** now plays host to a rehabilitation programme first set up at Semenggoh back in 1975 (*see* p.320). Rescued and confiscated animals, including many endangered species, are kept in a series of large enclosures. Those animals that complete the rehabilitation programme are released back into the wilds of the Kubah National Park (where they have more space to roam than at Semenggoh).

Getting There

Park HQ is only 30mins from the centre of Kuching and is served by bus no. 11 (though this is not a very regular service so check return times before departure). Matang is set on its own on the other side of the park, and is not accessible by public transport. If you don't have your own transport, this means RM35 one-way for a taxi, or visiting as part of a tour. The entrance fee for the park is RM10, from either entry point.

Where to Stay

Both Park HQ and Matang Wildlife Centre offer accommodation in the form of hostel beds and chalets (RM15–150). Park HQ also offers double-storey bungalows with verandahs, two bedrooms, kitchen, air-con, TV and hot water (RM180). Book rooms or beds in advance at one of Kuching's information centres.

The staff at Matang keep a close track on released orang-utans and can suggest trails where you may have a chance of spotting them. If you come across orang-utans in the wild, remember to keep a respectful distance and not to loiter too long in their presence. Despite their gentle reputation, orang-utans are territorial animals who will put up a fight if intruders fail to move on in good time.

The Pitcher Nature Trail is a two-hour loop that provides a wonderful introduction to the variety of rainforest vegetation. It climbs into a patch of *kerangas* forest, where pitcher plants grow in abundance, before descending into classic dipterocarp jungle where the old giants of the forest stand 250ft tall. The final stretch demonstrates the huge variety of palms for which the national park is famous.

The Sungai Buloh trail leads through towering stands of bamboo to a peaceful waterfall (*buloh* means bamboo in Malay). Another, the Ulu Rayu Trail (3–4 hours), leads across the spine of the hill range, linking Matang with the **Park Headquarters** on the eastern flank of Kubah National Park. This is the starting point for the trail to the summit of Gunung Serapi (6 hours return).

Gunung Gading and Tanjung Datu

Just outside the predominantly Bidayuh town of Lundu lie the jungled slopes Gunung Gading, gazetted as a national park in 1983, and scene of fierce fighting during the Konfrontasi with Indonesia in the 1960s. The main attraction here – and the primary reason for the park's status – is the abundance of endangered Rafflesia plants, which produce the world's largest flower.

The Rafflesia was first brought to scientific attention by naturalist Joseph Arnold, who spotted one while out walking with Stamford Raffles, founder of Singapore. He unabashedly named it *Rafflesia arnoldii*. These bizarre plants, fleshy and pungent, bloom only once a year, and the single flower they produce survives only a few days before it rots into the undergrowth. Their chief fame is their size, with each flower growing up to a metre in diameter. The Rafflesia is unlike any other plant: it has no leaves and no roots, but lives as a parasite on a specific vine native to the primary forests of Southeast Asia. For most of the year only the bud is visible. Then, the thick blood-red petals unfurl and send forth the reek of decay, attracting bluebottles who pollinate the flowers.

Getting There

Gunung Gading National Park is 80km west of Kuching, near the town of Lundu. There is no road bridge across the Lundu River so cars are ferried across during daylight hours. Be prepared to wait, as queues can develop, particularly at weekends. For those without their own transport, the Sarawak Transport Company (STC) run bus services between Kuching and Lundu.

Getting to Tanjung Datu from Kuching requires a 3hr journey by car to Sematan, followed by a 1hr boat trip to Kampung Melano. Most people visit the national park as part of a tour with Borneo Inbound (*see* 'Tour Operators', p.313).

Information

It may be worthwhile to call the Gunung Gading Park HQ in advance, to check whether or not there are any Rafflesia in bloom (**t** 082 735 714). If you intend to stay overnight, then be sure to book in advance at the Tourist Information Centre in Kuching.

For visits to Tanjung Datu, contact Borneo Inbound (*see* 'Tour Operators', p.313), the only operator to offer tours here. If you prefer to visit independently, speak to staff at one of Kuching's tourist information centres.

Where to Stay

The Gunung Gading Park HQ provides high quality accommodation in attractive wooden chalets. Hostel beds go for RM15/person or RM40/room (four beds), while a whole chalet costs RM150 (three bedrooms, two bathrooms, a fully-equipped kitchen).

The only accommodation available to those visiting Tanjung Datu National Park is a homestay programme at Kampung Melano (*see* above). This can be arranged through Borneo Inbound Tours and Travel (*see* p.313 for details). Alternatively, contact the Kuching office of the Fisheries Development Authority (2nd floor, Bangunan Bank Negara, Jalan Satok, Kuching, **t** 082 245 481, **f** 082 256 871).

Though the Rafflesia is rare today, the Gunung Gading National Park provides the ideal home, with more than 200 Rafflesia plants within its boundaries. Luckily for the tourist, the park authorities keep track of which flowers are flowering and when. For a small fee, a guide will lead you to a flowering plant, pointing out dormant buds (some the size of footballs) along the way. A number of trails can be tackled without a guide, including the Rafflesia Boardwalk which loops through a creek tangled with vines and past a series of labelled trees, before turning back to park HQ. Another trail climbs to the former British base near the summit of Gunung Gading (965m).

The park headquarters is situated just outside the town of Lundu, beside delightful Kampung Seling, an idyllic congregation of houses on stilts set around the Church of St Francis (clapboards, corrugated iron and a cross of light bulbs atop a tiny bell tower). Lundu itself, a sleepy, not-unattractive town, gets its name from *ikan lundu*, a species of catfish that congregate near the mouth of the Sungai Lundu once a year for a frenzy of mating – so many of them that their whiskers show above the water.

North of Lundu a track leads down to Siar Beach, one of many beautiful stretches of sand that characterize the far western coastline of Sarawak. At present these beaches are untouched by tourism. Further along is Pandau Beach, a popular spot with locals for swimming.

Follow the westbound road from Kuching as far as it goes, and you end up in Sematan, a small fishing port frequented by Indonesian fishermen and timber barges. From here it is possible to charter a speedboat (or hitch a ride on one of the local fishing boats) to picturesque Kampung Melano, which sits in a bay next to the **Tanjung Datu National Park**. The park was opened to the public in 1998 and, at only 13 sq km, is the smallest in Malaysia. Due to rough seas, Tanjung Datu is inaccessible during the wet season (October–March). A number of short trails loop between the park's pristine beaches; others climb the flanks of a steep ridge that leads out towards the promontory. The beaches at Tanjung Datu are nesting sites for olive ridley and hawksbill turtles, while just offshore is Sarawak's only accessible coral reef.

Because the park is still in its infancy as a tourist destination, visitor numbers are restricted and there are no park facilities. A homestay programme has been established at Kampung Melano, a tiny Malay village of pepper farmers and fishermen. (Melano, which means 'sugar palm', has no relation to the Melanau tribe.) Traditional stilted houses are scattered among the coconut palms and wooden fishing boats are hauled up onto the beach. Everywhere, pepper is laid out on tarpaulins to dry in the sun. Inaccessible by road, the village has hardly changed in generations. The easiest way to visit Tanjung Datu is with Borneo Inbound, the only operator to run tours to the national park (*see* 'Tour Operators', p.314).

Batang Lupar to Batang Ai

East of Kuching the Batang Lupar winds its way inland past the 'city' of Bandar Sri Aman towards the huge Batang-Ai hydro-lake. Its tributaries include the Skrang, the Lemanak and the Batang Ai itself, all dotted with Iban longhouses, many of which can be visited.

Simmanggang was the original name of Bandar Sri Aman, renamed 'City of Peace' in honour of the agreement signed between the Malaysian government and communist insurgents in 1976. It is a quiet place that tourists tend to pass through en route to longhouses further upriver. However, many of the tour operators will stop by at the riverfront to catch the famous **tidal bore**, which at certain times of year is said to roar upstream at speed, wreaking havoc along the banks. The bore occurs daily at high tide, though it is often no more than a passing ripple. Though the Batang Lupar is well over a kilometre across at its mouth, it narrows sharply, forcing the incoming tide into a wall of water that rolls 70km upriver, peaking at Sri Aman.

Somerset Maugham immortalized the event in his story *The Yellow Streak*, written after he almost drowned when the bore caught his boat unawares. He was paying a visit to Rajah Vyner Brooke, then stationed at the fort in Simmanggang. His oarsmen – prisoners of the Rajah – were unable to control the narrow boat, which capsized and left the sickly writer flailing.

Times when the bore passes Sri Aman are posted on a board at the waterfront. April is the high season for bore-spotting. The best place to view the event is from the raised verandah of the Buddhist temple, which is a pleasant enough spot in itself, with wonderful views downriver.

The Longhouse Experience

A longhouse is a tribal village under one roof. A covered gallery known as the *ruai* runs the length of the building, backed by a long line of living quarters. Behind the *ruai* is the open verandah, where pepper, rice or other crops are left to dry. Different tribes build longhouses according to their own traditions, and to suit their particular environment – though all are raised on piles and constructed (traditionally) of local materials such as rattan, bamboo, *belian* hardwood and *attap*. Notched logs serve as steps that lead up to either end of the *ruai*. The size of a longhouse is measured by the number of 'doors' leading off the *ruai*, which in turn corresponds to the number of families in the community (anything from a dozen to over a hundred, in some cases). Smoke-dried, rattan-bound skulls, which are usually hung from the rafters of the *ruai*, form the centrepiece of any longhouse. These relics from the head-hunting era were the focal point of tribal ritual, endowing the longhouse with their protective presence.

There are nearly 5,000 longhouses in Sarawak alone. Those longhouses commandeered by tour operators may come across as museum pieces, relics from the past, but for many of Sarawak's rural people the longhouse remains the preferred way of life – not only for its practical advantages, but because it is integral to the ritual element of tribal culture. Life within a longhouse is governed by a code of behaviour known as *adat*, whose laws are bound up with the will of the spirits. Though the majority of longhouse dwellers have converted to Christianity, the ritual element of their old animist beliefs remain fundamental to day-to-day life. In the old world of boundless rainforest and tribal warfare, the longhouse was the firm heart of the community, engendering a powerful sense of place. Even in modern times, with the young seeking prosperity in the cities or abroad, most return whenever they can – to recount their stories and give something back to the community. Though longhouses are often situated deep within the rainforest, the tradition of *bejalai* (a long, coming-of-age journey expected of young men) ensures that these communities have never been strangers to the outside world.

One thing all longhouses have in common is a tradition of hospitality – which goes hand in hand with the concept of *bejalai*. Guests are welcomed on the *ruai*, where they are entertained by the headman and his family. The traditional welcome ceremony, known in Iban as *miring*, comprises dancing, offerings of food and the free flow of rice wine (*tuak* in Iban or *borak* in Orang Ulu dialects). It is almost a crime to

Head inland on the Lupar and you eventually run up against the vast Batang-Ai lake, part of the hydroelectric complex which provides power for much of the state. Right around the edge of the lake the weathered tops of trees poke through the surface of the water – an eery reminder of the 90 sq km of forest that was flooded in 1986 when the lake was formed. Still, the lake is well stocked with fish, attracting Brahminy kites and kingfishers in their dozens, both of which can be spotted perched on tree tops or diving for fish.

leave Sarawak without *tuak* having passed your lips. Guests are usually invited to sleep on the *ruai*, though a number of tour operators offer clients the privacy of a separate guesthouse.

Iban longhouses are the most commonly visited by tourists. These are always built along the banks of a river (the Iban were the 'Sea Dyaks' after all). Bidayuh longhouses are situated inland and are unique in containing a separate ceremonial house (*baruk*), an octagonal building where enemy skulls are hung, guests are entertained and young men sleep at night. Orang Ulu longhouses are more permanent structures than their Iban counterparts, sometimes double-storey, and always more ornate, with carvings on the piles and colourful Tree of Life murals on the walls.

Woodcarving is a revered skill among the men of any longhouse community, just as weaving and beadwork expertise is a skill coveted by the women. Those longhouses accustomed to tourists will usually transform the *ruai* into a mini-market at the drop of a hat, offering handicrafts for sale, from *ikat* weavings and blowpipes to masks, basketry and beads.

Longhouse Etiquette

If you visit a longhouse independently, it is important to understand something of longhouse etiquette (an important feature of any close-knit community). Interestingly, there is no word for 'hello' in most of the tribal languages of Sarawak. Those visiting as part of a tour should be given plenty of guidance by the tour operator.

- Never enter a longhouse unannounced; always ask the permission of the headman, or *Tuai Rumah*, before heading inside.
- Remove shoes before entering a family room (*bilik*), or an area of the *ruai* laid with mats. More often than not, shoes are not worn at all in a longhouse, and are left at the entrance to the *ruai*.
- If you bring gifts, give them straight to the headman to distribute, rather than doing so yourself (even to children).
- Accept food and drink with both hands. If you want to decline the offer of food or drink, touch the edge of the plate or glass with your right hand, rather than holding up your hands or pushing it away.
- When bathing in the river, keep as covered-up as possible (nudity is not acceptable). Members of the opposite sex are usually expected to bathe separately.

The Longhouses

In many ways the Skrang, which leads into the Lupar just upriver from Sri Aman, is the Iban heartland. In the battle of Batang Marau (1849), Rajah James Brooke massacred around 1,000 Iban warriors from the Skrang region. As a reward for his deeds, Brooke was ceded the Second Division of Sarawak by the Sultan of Brunei (the Iban of these parts had developed a fearsome reputation as head-bagging pirates).

Where to Stay

Expensive

Hilton Batang-Ai Longhouse Resort, **t** 083 584 388, **f** 083 584 399, *www.hilton.com*. In a wonderful setting on the edge of the Batang-Ai lake, this place bills itself as 'luxury longhouse-style accommodation'. Other than the fact that rooms are lined up in long single-storey buildings, there's not much here to remind you of a longhouse; and if it really is luxury that you're after, bear in mind that there are no baths, no room service and only one place to eat. Still, the hotel is perfectly placed for visits to longhouses or treks into the surrounding jungle. Jungle walks with eccentric in-house guide, Winston, are certainly to be recommended. With the exception of the Sarawak *laksa* (which is heavenly), food at the Nanga Mepi restaurant is below par for a Hilton. Facilities include a decent outdoor pool and tennis courts.

Borneo Adventure Lodge, Nanga Sumpa (contact Borneo Adventure in Kuching at 55 Main Bazaar, **t** 082 245 175, **f** 082 422 626, *www.borneoadventure.com)*. The lodge was built with local materials in 1995 by members of the Nanga Sumpa longhouse community. Few concessions have been made to comfort, but that is part of the experience. The wooden building forms a square around the buttresses of a giant dipterocarp tree. Screens and curtains separate rooms, with bamboo mats (and thin mattresses) for beds. Mosquito nets and oil lamps are provided. In the morning you will awake to birdsong and the snuffling of pigs. The food, cooked by members of the longhouse, is substantial and delicious. You can only stay at the lodge as part of Borneo Adventure's 'Ulu Ai' package, which costs approximately RM800/person for 3days/2nights including all food, transfers and a trip upriver to a local waterfall. The trip includes a traditional Iban lunch of fish, chicken and glutinous rice cooked in sections of bamboo over an open fire. The fish is caught en route and the bamboo prepared as the fire warms; it will probably be the best meal you've ever eaten out-of-doors.

Iban longhouses along the Skrang – and to a lesser extent the Lemanak – have been visited by organized tour groups since the 1960s. Some of these communities have come to rely on tourists as their primary source of income. As a result, much of what you see is staged; those looking for an 'authentic' longhouse experience would do better to visit one of the lesser-known regions.

If you do visit a longhouse as part of a tour – as opposed to visiting independently on the back of an invitation – you won't do much better than **Nanga Sumpa**, an Iban longhouse situated 1.5 hours upriver from the Batang-Ai lake, not far from the border with Kalimantan. The setting is wonderfully remote: the longboat journey begins by crossing the Batang-Ai lake and passing through patches of hill paddy and pepper plantations, before the river narrows and the primary rainforest closes in overhead.

The first thing you notice on arrival is that this longhouse community has not yet relinquished its traditional lifestyle. More importantly, the whole setup is a template for responsible tourism. The tour operator works hand-in-hand with the community, careful to minimize the disruption to their daily lives. Despite new sources of livelihood, the community has been careful not to neglect traditional sources of income and sustenance (farming and fishing). The project is managed by a committee of longhouse members, and a lodge has been built with local materials so that visitors don't have to sleep in the *ruai*. Numbers of visitors are strictly limited, so that the longhouse is never overrun. Since the late 1980s, when the tourism project first got underway, the number of 'doors' in the longhouse has extended from 24 to 28: a sure sign that the project has proved a success (when you consider the general trend of shrinking longhouses).

The tour to Nanga Sumpa is run by Borneo Adventure (*see* opposite; *also see* 'Tour Operators', p.313). They also run tours into the nearby (and little visited) **Batang-Ai National Park**, home to a healthy population of wild orang-utans. An arduous trek along the 'Red Ape Trail' has been established in association with the Orangutan Foundation. Led by Iban guides, participants head deep into the Batang-Ai national park in search of orang-utans, gibbons and other creatures of the rainforest. The tour, which can last up to two weeks, includes visits to the Nanga Tibu and Nanga Sumpa longhouses. All proceeds go towards community-based conservation projects.

The Rejang

The Batang Rejang is Malaysia's mightiest river, tumbling 640km from its source in the mountainous forests near the border with Indonesia, all the way down to its mangrove-lined delta beyond Sibu. For many centuries the river has served as a highway into the heart of Borneo. North of Sarikei, a Malay town famed for its pineapples, the Rejang splinters into a maze of brackish channels inhabited by the Melanau. The habitat is ideal for the cultivation of the sago palm, staple diet of this water-bound people. The middle reaches of the Rejang are dominated by the Iban, who pushed upriver in the middle part of the 19th century, forcing Orang Ulu tribes such as the Kayan and Kenyah deeper into the forest. The Pelagus Rapids, a furious 2km-stretch of white water, came to form the natural barrier between the warring tribes. Nineteenth-century Chinese traders pushed inland as far as the small town of Kapit, the Rejang's upriver trading centre – though they have always formed the minority, with the Iban constituting 80% of the town's population. The Orang Ulu dominate Belaga, a sleepy trading post upriver from the Pelagus Rapids.

In traditional dugouts, upriver boat journeys once took many weeks. Today the navigational skills of tribal boatmen are employed aboard powerful launches capable of reaching speeds of 70kph, all the while negotiating rapids and avoiding mud flats and stray rafts of timber. These boats provide quick access to more remote quarters of Sarawak; they are a modern lifeline for inhabitants of the upper reaches of the Rejang, and a handy means of access for the independent tourist.

Sibu

With a population of a quarter of a million at the last count, Sibu is Sarawak's second city. It has been the trading centre of the mighty Rejang River since the White Rajahs began shaping present-day Sarawak. Along today's waterfront, boats of every kind shunt against one another as they offload their wares. Upriver from the esplanade a long line of signboards advertise the destinations of passenger launches

– slim-lined speedboats powered by V12 engines, which roar up and down the length of the Rejang dodging longboats and timber rafts.

Most visitors barely scratch the surface of Sibu, en route to quieter upriver destinations, and the town has acquired a reputation for its rough edges and lack of charms. Nevertheless Sibu compares favourably to many of Malaysia's trading centres. Year by year it smartens its image, with bursts of greenery appearing all about town and a growing awareness of its cultural heritage. With the steady injection of funds (largely on the back of timber profits), Sibu is in the midst of a planning overhaul designed to transform the town into a so-called 'garden city'.

History

Sibu first emerged on the site of a Melanau longhouse; just south of Sibu the Rejang splinters into dozens of separate channels which form its lower delta, heartland of the Melanau tribe. By the mid-19th century the Iban had pushed into the region from their stronghold on and around the Batang Lupar. When the Third Division of Sarawak was officially created in 1873, Sibu (named after a native rambutan known in Iban as *buah sibua*) became its centre. An influx of immigrants from Hokkien stamped their mark on the settlement in its early years. They were soon followed by the Cantonese, who made

Getting There

Sibu's airport is 23km east of the city centre. There are regular flights between all the main airports in Sarawak and Sabah, as well as a daily service to KL. The MAS office is at 61 Jalan Tunku Osman, north of the Padang. To and from Kuching, it is also possible to travel by speed ferry (4hrs), docking at the new River Express Terminal beside the esplanade. Buses from Kuching take 7hrs, and at RM35, are only half the price of a flight and not much cheaper than catching the ferry.

Information

The Visitor's Information Centre (32 Jalan Cross, **t** 084 340 980, open Mon–Fri 8–5, Sat 8–12.30) is staffed by a friendly and helpful team, who can provide information and advice about the whole state.

Where to Stay

Expensive

Premier, Sarawak House, Jalan Kampong Nyabor, **t** 084 323 222, **f** 084 323 399. Probably Sibu's top hotel, as the name would like to suggest. 4-star facilities with spacious rooms, some with views of the river. Situated above a shopping centre and cinema.

Tanah Mas Hotel, Block 5 Jalan Kampoung Nyabor, **t** 084 333 188, **f** 084 333 288, *tanahmas@po.jaring.my*. International-class hotel with 120 rooms and an outdoor pool. Peppers Café downstairs is often packed.

Moderate

Kingwood Hotel, 12 Lorong Lanang 4, **t** 084 335 888, **f** 084 334 559, *kingwood@tm.net.my*. An enormous hotel set right on the waterfront, with rooftop swimming pool, gym and sauna facilities. Despite the low rates this is a 4-star hotel and the best deal in town.

Li Hua Hotel, Jalan Maju, **t** 084 324 000, **f** 084 326 272. This hotel sits behind the esplanade, offering views of the river and enjoys a rooftop mini-pool. Handy for catching a launch upriver. Promotions bring prices down into the inexpensive category.

Inexpensive

Hotel Zuhra, 103 Jalan Kampung Nyabor, **t** 084 310 711, **f** 084 320 712. A good-value, friendly mid-range hotel overlooking the *padang*, a success of their pepper plantations. But it was the Foochow Chinese who were to have the greatest influence on Sibu. The first group arrived in 1901, with the financial assistance of Rajah Charles Brooke, who saw great potential in the legendary work ethic of the Chinese. Sibu soon became known as 'Little Foochow', with the latest influx making a success of their pepper plantations and paddy fields. They soon turned their hands to rubber, and finally, timber. Today Sibu is home to more millionaires – all timber *towkays* – than anywhere else in Sarawak.

The Sights

The waterfront, a hive of activity day and night, forms the focal point of Sibu. In 1987 the eastern stretch was graced with a lengthy **Esplanade**. At the western end stands a graceful seven-tiered **pagoda**, built in 1989 on the site of an old temple. This remains Sibu's primary landmark. A climb to the top of the pagoda provides a good impression of the town's present-day dimensions.

If you only do one thing in Sibu, then wander round the wonderful ***pasar malam***, held every evening off Jalan Market and lined by old Chinese shophouses. The food stalls are particularly enticing. The main day markets, including Sibu Central Market, are just east of here along the Lembangan River (no more than a narrow water

and away from the seedy side of town. Rooms are all in a good state of repair and have air-con, TV, phone and hot water.

Sarawak Hotel, 34 Jalan Cross, **t** 084 333 455. Another decent value mid-range hotel closer to the heart of town, with good-sized rooms and similar facilities to the Zuhra (though the Zuhra has the edge, not least because it is quieter).

Phoenix, 1-3 Jalan Kai Peng, **t** 084 313 877, **f** 084 320 392. At the top end of this price category, offering reasonable value for money; rooms are sizable and have air-con, TV, phone and hot water. Situated in a quiet patch of town near the Zuhra.

Budget

Hoover House, Methodist Church, Jalan Pulau, **t** 084 332 491. This Methodist guesthouse is the best of a bunch of grim budget options. Rooms are well cared for and there is a locker room for longterm storage.

Eating Out

Because Chinese dominate Sibu, there are dozens of coffee shops serving the likes of Foochow noodles and pastries. If you want unlimited choice (Chinese, Malay, Muslim Indian) head for the hawker centre above the **Sibu Central Market**. Meanwhile the daily ***pasar malam*** on Jalan Market has dozens of wonderful food stalls serving ready-cooked seafood, satay, stuffed dumplings, crispy duck and cakes, though there's nowhere to sit.

One of the city's most popular places to eat is the **Hai Bing Coffeeshop**, situated behind the esplanade. It serves a huge range of local Chinese specialities and has seating both outside and in an air-conditioned restaurant. At the other end of the esplanade is the **London Café**, an incongruous place that serves up 'Western' food. **Peppers Café**, in the lobby of the Tanah Mas Hotel (*see* above), is always packed with business lunchers. The menu covers Western, Malay and Chinese food and there's a daily buffet.

If you happen to be north of the *padang*, there's a row of decent, cheap food stalls on Jalan Tuanku Osman. Further along the same road is **Aloha Corner**, a popular restaurant that serves a wonderful *laksa*. Next door to the Zuhra hotel is the **Nur Islamic Café**, serving typical *mamak* cuisine (Indian Muslim), including great *roti canai*. Back on the waterfront, opposite the local bus station, is the **To-Eat Bakery**, which serves a good range of bread, cakes and biscuits.

channel that soon disappears underground). The **Lembangan Market** is the place to go for jungle produce: everything from the ubiquitous jungle fern to unrecognizable fruits and animals like flying foxes, snakes and turtles.

The only other tourist attraction is the **Sibu Civic Centre Museum** (*open Tues–Sat 3–8, Sun 9–12 and 2–8; free*), situated 3km north of the town centre. Exhibits include a decent collection of 10th–12th-century white ceramics, a reproduction of an Iban longhouse, old photographs and a shabby menagerie of stuffed animals.

Sibu **Town Square** is impressive, if only for its scale, with floodlights raised on four pylon-like structures. The town council is clearly serious about transforming Sibu into a 'garden city': there are plans to build a lake garden on a 50-acre plot in front of Sibu General Hospital, and to extend the town square westwards all the way to the riverfront, with gardens, walkways and ponds.

Kapit and Upriver

The Kapit Division is Sarawak's largest, a vast upriver territory of rainforest run through with river systems and hill ranges. Any trip along the Batang Rejang reveals that logging is the primary earner up here; along this silt-rich river innumerable rafts of timber – each log marked with its credentials – are borne downstream to the sawmills. The tropical hardwoods, so dense that they sink in water, are transported on Chinese barges.

Kapit itself is the Division's capital, a seemingly inconsequential town on the south bank of the Rejang, beyond the smaller trading posts of Kanowit and Song. A few blocks of Chinese shophouses cater for the logging camps and surrounding longhouse communities. Each day tribal women set off from their longhouses to sell their produce at Kapit's central market or to stock up on provisions from the predominantly Chinese-run shops. Others come to spend their wages in the brothels and karaoke bars, or to catch up with friends outside coffee shops.

Fort Sylvia is the showpiece of a town otherwise devoid of architectural interest. Kapit first emerged as a small administrative settlement for officials of the Brooke government. Chinese *towkays* soon took hold and the settlement expanded. The fort was constructed entirely of *belian* hardwood by Rajah Charles Brooke in 1880. It was defended by large cannons on the ground floor and smaller ones on the first floor, their muzzles protruding through sliding hatches. Meanwhile gun barrels poked through the line of small diamond-shaped holes which run round the walls of the fort. The fort's primary purpose was to prevent the Iban from penetrating any further upriver into Kayan and Kenyah territory. However, it was not until 1924 that a treaty was finally 'signed' between the warring tribes. A peace ceremony was conducted in front of the fort. Rajah Brooke addressed the crowds in Iban. A pig was slaughtered and its blood sprinkled on the assembled leaders as an everlasting pact between the tribes.

The fort was renovated in the late 1990s by the Tun Jugah Foundation and now contains a museum *(open Tues–Sun 10–12 ans 2–5; free)*, with a history gallery, a textile gallery, weaving and handicraft workshops, and an amber gallery (a massive amber

Getting There

There is no road access to Kapit, and the nearby airstrip is for non-commercial use only. The regular express boats that ply the Rejang between Sibu, Song and Kapit are the only means of access. The journey takes around 3hrs and services run between 6am and 2.30pm daily. The one-way fare from Sibu to Kapit is around RM18.

There are two MAS Twin Otter flights each week between Belaga and Bintulu (Wednesday and Saturday, RM40 one-way). There is one daily express boat service from Kapit to Belaga, which leaves at 9am (4–5 hours, RM25). When the water level is low, boats may not be able to pass the Pelagus Rapids. All other destinations, including longhouses on the Sungai Baram or along tributaries of the Rejang, are accessible by longboat only.

Information

Visitors who wish to travel up the Baleh River, or beyond the Pelagus Rapids on the Rejang, need to obtain a permit from the Resident's Office in Kapit before setting out. The office is situated on the first floor of the State Government Complex. Passports are required and the permit is free of charge.

Tour Operators

Kapit Adventure Tours, 1st Floor, 11 Jalan Tan Sit Leong (on the east side of the square). The only tour company based in Kapit, with registered guide Tan Teck Chuan. Most of the hotels in Kapit can also arrange trips to longhouses near Kapit.

Where to Stay

Kapit has a handful of inexpensive hotels and guesthouses, most of which verge on the grim side of acceptable. The only resort upriver on the Rejang is the Regency Pelagus, set at the foot of the Pelagus Rapids and affiliated with a good range of longhouses.

Expensive

Regency Pelagus Resort, **t** 084 799 051, **f** 084 799 050, *pelagus@tm.net.my*, *www.theregencyhotel.com.my/pelagus* (Sibu Office, Sibu Airport, **t** 084 307 746, **f** 084 307 749; KL Office, **t** 03 2715 7927, **f** 03 2715 7921). Forty guest rooms – some with air-con others without – are lined up in an attractive longhouse-style building at the foot of the Pelagus Rapids. The setting is remote and magnificent, with banks of steaming rainforest on either side of the river. The building incorporates local carvings and

deposit was unearthed at a nearby coalfield, including the largest single piece of amber ever found). Spot the 'high water' marks recorded on the side of the fort, and you begin to understand why longhouses are raised so high off the ground on stilts.

For the tourist, Kapit acts as a springboard for independent visits to surrounding Iban longhouses or for trips upriver into Orang Ulu territory. The most commonly visited longhouse is **Rumah Seligi**, situated 10km away and accessible by road – though having come as far as Kapit, it makes more sense to strike out for the more traditional longhouses further up the Rejang, or on **Batang Baleh**, a major river that branches eastwards from Kapit as far as the Indonesian border. For a foretaste of travel along the Baleh, read Redmond O'Hanlon's hilarious travel narrative *Into the Heart of Borneo*, in which he describes his journey to the source of this river in the early 1980s.

The **Pelagus Rapids** are situated an hour north of Kapit by speedboat. For centuries they formed an effective barrier between the Lower and Upper Rejang, enabling the Orang Ulu (literally 'upriver people') to keep the territory-hungry Iban at bay. Only with heavy-duty, modern outboards can boats blast their way up the 2.5km stretch of latticework into its entirely wooden structure. Rooms are spacious, with handcrafted furniture and local rattan mats scattered about. All have en suite bathrooms with hot water, and balconies overlooking either the river or the forest behind. Out of sight behind the main building is a swimming pool. The open-sided restaurant, which overlooks the river, serves up a range of cuisines, including Iban specialities such as *pansoh manok* (chicken cooked in bamboo). The resort's main attractions are its tours to seven surrounding longhouses, including a Orang Ulu settlement where five elaborately designed burial poles, or *klierieng*, can be seen (*see* p.337). There are a number of trails surrounding the resort, which can be tackled independently or in the company of the excellent on-site guide Nyaring Bandar.

Inexpensive

Greenland Inn, Lot 463, Jalan Teo Chow Beng, Kapit, **t** 084 796 388, **f** 084 796 708. This is the best hotel that Kapit itself has to offer. Rooms are spacious and clean, with attached bathrooms, hot water, TV, fridge and phone. Near the top end of this price category.

New Rejang Inn, 104 Jalan Teo Chow Beng, Kapit, **t** 084 796 600, **f** 084 799 600. Good-value hotel, with facilities including fridge, TV and hot water. A little sterile, but friendly and helpful staff.

Hotel Belaga, 14 Main Bazaar, Belaga, **t** 086 461 244. Reasonable fan-cooled rooms, all with attached bathrooms, above a popular coffee shop. Generally seen as the best of Belaga's three hotel options.

Eating Out

In Kapit, the **food stalls** at the west end of town, beyond the temple, are as good a spot as any for a simple dinner, with satay and *roti canai* in abundance. The **Soon Kit Café**, round the corner from the New Rejang Inn, is the most popular noodle restaurant in town. They also serve good chicken rice. The **Ung Tong Bakery**, one block west of the town square, serves a wonderful selection of freshly baked breads, buns and doughnuts for about 50 sen apiece.

Chuong Hill Coffeeshop, opposite the jetty, is the best place to pass time while waiting for your boat. Excellent coffee and snacks such as Chinese dumplings are served at traditional marble-top tables.

Eating out in Belaga is limited to a handful of coffee shops, most without menus (eat the special).

rapids. When the water level is high, the 'white water' gives way to whirlpools and a deceptive maelstrom of currents which rage silently beneath the surface, each year taking their toll on unwary boatmen. In the days of paddle power, boatmen were forced to haul their boats ashore and drag them overland from one end of the rapids to the other. The well-beaten path they used runs along the bank to this day, with 21 wooden footbridges crossing streams and inlets.

At the foot of the rapids is the Pelagus Resort (*see* 'Where to Stay', p.335), from where the path is accessible. The resort provides the best alternative for those without the time to arrange their own longhouse visits on the Rejang. A series of jungle trails loop out from the longhouse-style buildings of the resort into some pristine tracts of rainforest. A study of Bukit Raya, the hill across the river from the resort, identified 711 species of tree in the space of a single hectare: an astounding indication of the biodiversity of Borneo's rainforests, especially when you consider that the whole of North America can lay claim to only 171 indigenous trees. The on-site guide is on hand to point out creatures of the forest, elusive to the untrained eye. The odd scorpion or snake is sure to feature, as is the Rajah Brooke birdwing butterfly and the Borneo horned frog, whose nightly croaks sound like the sinister cackles of a man. Those looking to hone their jungle survival skills will be delighted to learn that the ubiquitous cicada is perfectly edible, as is the prickly stick insect which, when fried, tastes very much like a prawn cracker.

Nearby longhouses include **Rumah George** (Iban longhouses are generally named after the headman), a small and idyllic setup on a tributary of the Rejang, and Rumah Punan Bah, a well-known Orang Ulu longhouse upriver from the rapids. Visit Rumah George during the day and the longhouse will be virtually deserted, its members working their plots of hill paddy. Only the likes of Mano will be present, a stately man in his eighties covered from head to foot in tattooes (signifying worldliness and achievement). On a typical day he spends his time threshing rice and looking after his great-grandchildren, who race up and down the verandah between dips in the river. Meanwhile, in the shelter of an outbuilding, Mano's brother caulks a longboat with the sticky orange resin of a local tree, and on the *ruai* (covered verandah) their wives weave ceremonial *pua* and baskets.

Rumah Punan Bah is famous for its five *klirieng*, traditional burial poles of which only 20 remain in the whole of Sarawak. Each pole is carved from a single *belian* tree and embellished with elaborate designs, with the bones of aristocrats stored inside a hollowed chamber. The tribe of this longhouse adhere to their own peculiar religion, a blend of animism and Christianity, in which the *manang*, or medicine man, holds great influence.

Belaga

Continue upriver from the rapids and you arrive eventually at **Belaga**, quintessential bazaar town of the interior. Here various Orang Ulu tribes convene to barter their wares and socialize. A few well-established Chinese *towkays* provide modern essentials, such as kerosene and shotgun cartridges. Their ancestors first appeared in Belaga at the turn of the 20th century, attracted by the lucrative trade in jungle produce for the Chinese market – aromatic woods, resins and aphrodisiacs such as rhino horn and the gall bladders of monkeys. The small market town soon came to serve as an administrative outpost of the Brooke government.

Of course, Belaga is not the place it once was. As late as the 1960s it took the best part of a month to travel from Kuching to Belaga – under-powered boats being the only means of transport. Today an airstrip links Belaga with Bintulu, providing access in tiny Twin Otter aircraft, while logging roads link the town with Tubau, just a few hours upriver from Bintulu.

The controversial **Bakun Dam** project changed the face of this remote district of Sarawak for good. The plan, given the go-ahead by ex-Prime Minister Mahathir in the early 1990s, was to build a dam big enough to supply energy for the whole of Sarawak, with 700 sq km of rainforest earmarked for flooding. The region's inhabitants – 10,000 Orang Ulu from the Kayan, Kenyah, Lahanan, Ukit and Penan tribes – were forced to abandon their longhouses and set up home at the Sungai Asap resettlement scheme 120km away. Although those displaced received compensation – they are no doubt wealthier: one government statistic points out that the number of washing machines owned by the community has risen from seven to seventy-seven – most rue the fact that their traditional lives have been shattered.

The economic crisis of 1997 put the Bakun Dam project on hold, and future plans for the hydroelectric plant were scaled down. Still, those who lost their homes are not permitted to return by the government, their land effectively bought from them through compensation.

Coastal Sarawak: Mukah to Miri

From the Melanau stronghold of Mukah, as far as the oil town of Miri, the long central stretch of Sarawak's coastal region is often overlooked by tourists. With the exception perhaps of the Niah National Park – where visitors are treated to caves of gob-smacking proportions complete with prehistoric cave paintings – the attractions in this region have yet to hit the mainstream. Which is half of the appeal. Where previously visitors were expected to make their own arrangements, tour operators and homestay programmes now offer greater accessibility.

Mukah

Mukah is the heartland of the Melanau, a people who have lived for many centuries among the mangroves and sago palms of Borneo's north coast, a watery world crisscrossed with shallow channels, walkways and stilted homes. Traditionally known as seafarers, sago farmers and fishermen, the Melanau influence stretches from the delta of the Batang Rejang as far as present-day Miri.

This region was once known as Melano, and was a vassal state of Majapahit – an empire ruled by the Hindu kings of eastern Java – before being assimilated by Brunei some time in the 13th century. The land around Mukah was the last place ceded to the White Rajah by the Sultan of Brunei (in 1860). In those days it was a treacherous sliver of coastline, prone to attacks from the interior by Iban head-hunters, and from the open ocean by pirates of the Sulu archipelago. This constant threat of invasion resulted in the striking defensive architecture of the Melanau: their multistorey longhouses – known as 'tall houses' – were raised on stilts 20–30ft from the ground, with retractable, notched logs serving as stairways.

After centuries of close contact with the Malays of Brunei, the Melanau gradually abandoned their tall houses in favour Malay-style kampung houses. Many turned to Islam, though the ritual elements of their traditional beliefs, a form of animism known locally as Liko, are performed to this day.

Many Melanau have long since moved to the larger towns, and modern Mukah is something of a backwater. The centre of Mukah itself holds little appeal – a dusty grid of shophouses resembling that of any other small Malaysian town. It is in adjoining **Kampung Tellian**, a pretty Melanau water village, that traditions are best preserved.

Over a century after the last Melanau tall house was destroyed by fire, villagers have constructed a replacement on the same site. **Lamin Dana**, as the new tall house is known, is part of a remarkable community project aimed at reviving the flagging traditions of the Melanau. It serves on the one hand as a living museum and homestay programme (*see* 'Where to Stay', below), and on the other as a repository of Melanau customs: an open platform in front of the tall house serves as a stage for traditional dances and music recitals, while local craftsmen are encouraged to leave their handicrafts here for sale to tourists – anything from conical sunhats made from the leaves of sago palms to sago-pith carvings and musical instruments.

From Lamin Dana, visitors (who at the time of writing were few and far between) can arrange longboat tours of the water village, which is divided into Kampung Tellian Tengah (Catholic) and Kampung Tellian Ulu (Muslim). Rafts of sago logs line the narrow water channels, where they are left to soak for three months, filling the air with a peculiar stench – not unpleasant and reminiscent of hops. The soaking encourages the cultivation of plump sago worms, a Melanau delicacy eaten either live, fried or steamed. Here and there among the stilted houses are sago-processing plants, where circular saws are used to pulverize the sago wood, before sending it down a shoot, through a fine sieve, and into a submerged trough where the sago flour settles. Each plant is worked by one or two men, who walk about on submerged planks, ankle-deep in the peat-black water. A few still process the sago the old way – by trampling it underfoot.

Getting There

Three kilometres outside town is Mukah's airstrip, served by flights from Kuching. Otherwise there are daily buses from Sibu and Bintulu.

Where to Stay

Inexpensive

Lamin Dana, Kampung Tellian Tengah, Mukah, **t** 084 871 543/019 260 6931/082 241 735, *www.lamindana.com* (*see* main text, above, for full description). A homestay programme in the heart of the water village, offering simple fan-cooled rooms on the upper floor of a Melanau tall house. Bathrooms with hot showers are separate. On the ground floor is a display of Melanau handicrafts and musical instruments. Breakfast, which is included (*see* below), is served in an open-sided restaurant among potted plants on the river's edge. Highly recommended.

Eating Out

Lamin Dana, details as above. If you are staying at Lamin Dana, don't hesitate to eat your meals here too: the cooks are excellent. Breakfast is a hearty affair with doughnuts, glutinous rice with coconut, banana bread, pancakes rolls, tea and coffee. Lunch might consist of black pomfret steak in a sweet-and-sour sauce with jungle fern and rambutan, while dinner is sure to feature a Melanau speciality: catch of the day smoked before your eyes in the attached smokehouse. Breakfast, lunch and dinner for two costs RM60.

Nibong House Seafood Restaurant, Jalan Orang Kaya Setia Raja (10mins walk from centre on foot: ask in town for directions), **t** 018 680 5540. An atmospheric little restaurant with high ceilings and walls decorated with conical hats, shells and fan coral. Serves up the full range of local specialities including *umai*, a tangy Melanau version of *ceviche* (slivers of raw fish, onion, chilli, lime) which comes accompanied by a bowl of sago pellets in place of rice. Fresh fish and seafood dominate the menu. Two dressed crabs cost RM12.

It is a timeless scene, if you ignore the satellite dishes and mobile phones. All along the narrow waterways are glimpses of everyday life: men line-fishing in pairs, bicycles clattering along wooden walkways, children swimming, their parents tending potted plants on verandahs. Meanwhile stork-billed kingfishers perch on wooden poles, herons lurk on landing platforms, swifts scoot about thinning the air of mosquitoes, and Brahminy kites survey the scene from on high, waiting for the return of the fishing boats.

Lamin Dana becomes a hive of activity during the annual Kaul festivities, an extravaganza of games, dancing and ritual. The festival celebrates the end of the monsoon (late March/early April) and is an offering to the spirits of the sea, in advance of the main fishing season. Most Melanau are Muslim or Catholic nowadays, but all still celebrate Kaul. Up to 15,000 people gather on the beach near Mukah, where the Bapa Kaul, leader of the ceremony, scatters rice to the spirits in front of the *seraheng*, the totemic symbol of the Kaul. A flotilla of decorated fishing boats gather offshore, while young Melanau men take part in games, the highlight of which involves the *tibou*, a 30ft-high swing with a liana rope dangling adjacent to a broad ladder. The men fling themselves from the ladder and cling together in a clump on the liana, as many as eight at a time.

Bintulu and Similajau National Park

Bintulu is a fast-growing industrial town on the coast midway between Miri and Sibu. In 1975 it was no more than a Melanau fishing village with a fearsome name ('Bintulu' is thought to be derived from *meta ulau*, Melanau for the place where enemy heads were smoked). Then a huge pocket of natural gas was discovered just offshore. Now Bintulu has a population of more than 100,000 and is proud to be home to the world's largest liquefied natural gas (LNG) production facility.

There is little of interest in the town itself, though you can gauge the true extent of Bintulu's transformation by catching a *tambang* (river bus) to Kampung Jepak, a Melanau fishing village across the Batang Kemena. Spread out on stilted platforms, small fish and shrimps are baked dry beneath the sun to be used in Bintulu *belacan*, a fiery shrimp paste thrown into virtually every local dish. In Kampung Jepak the traditional cottage industries of the Melanau continue undaunted by the progress of big sister across the water – which is pushing for city status by 2020.

The primary attraction of the Bintulu Division is the **Similajau National Park**, a coastal reserve gazetted in 1978, though it was only opened to the public in 1995. Thirty kilometres of rocky promontories and beaches, golden and undefiled, are backed by *kerangas* and mixed dipterocarp forest. Pitcher plants, orchids and a slender tree nicknamed 'Malaysian ginseng' for its medicinal properties are found here in abundance. Like Bako, more than 150 species of bird have been recorded within the park, including migratory water birds such as the highly endangered Storm's stork. Mammals are thinner on the ground than at Bako – the park is only

Getting There

Bintulu's airport is right behind the town centre itself (a larger one is being built out of town), with regular flights to and from Kuching, Sibu and Miri. There are also twice-weekly flights to Belaga on the Batang Rejang. The town is situated on Sarawak's coastal trunk road, so is easily accessible by bus and taxi too.

Similajau National Park is situated 30km north of Bintulu. The only way to reach the park headquarters is by car or taxi (RM40–50 one-way).

Where to Stay

Expensive–Moderate

Regency Plaza Hotel, 116 Taman Sri Dagang, Jalan Abang Galau, **t** 086 335 111, **f** 086 332 742, *hotel@plazabintulu.com.my*, *www.theregencyhotel.com.my*. Situated beside the airport. Décor is based on the motifs of Sarawakian *pua* textiles and rooms are spacious and comfortable. Frequent promotions offer excellent value for money. Facilities include a gym and rooftop pool.

Moderate–Inexpensive

Riverfront Inn, 256 Jalan Sri Dagang, **t** 086 333 111. Bintulu offers a lot of crusty mid-range hotels in the centre of town, of which this is probably the best: clean, quite smart and right on the waterfront.

Royal Hotel, 10–12 Pedada Street, **t** 086 332 166. A reasonable alternative to the Riverfront Inn though slightly tattier. Rooms are all en suite, with air-con, TV, phone and fridge.

Similajau National Park

Park headquarters offers hostel accommodation and a range of fan-cooled chalets ranging in price from RM50–150. A bed in the hostel costs RM15.

Eating Out

Bintulu is a good place to sample Melanau specialities such as *umai*, a tangy dish served cold and consisting of raw fish, lime, chilli and onion. Bintulu is also known for its *belacan* (spicy shrimp paste), which is used in Malay and Melanau cooking and as an accompaniment to dishes such as Sarawak *laksa*. There are simple Chinese and Muslim Indian restaurants all about town. A wide range of local specialities are on offer each evening at the *pasar malam*. For fresh fish and seafood, head out to the seaside stalls at Pantai Ria, 2km out of town.

1.5km in width, after all – though 24 species have been recorded, including gibbons, banded langurs and, of course, crab-eating macaques.

The park's highlight, if they can be called that, are its crocodiles, of which there are two species, the Malayan false gharial (generally harmless) and the estuarine crocodile (generally dangerous). The crocs are found mainly around the mouth of the Sungai Likau, so avoid paddling in the shallows at this point. Warning signs are posted at danger spots, and no crocodile attacks have yet been reported. Boats can be hired after dark for a touch of crocodile-spotting by torch light. The other reptiles of note that frequent the park are green turtles, which come ashore to lay their eggs, mainly between May and September.

There is an information centre at park headquarters and a range of places to stay. A series of trails provide easy access to the park, from Golden Beach (a beautiful stretch of sand 3hrs from park headquarters) to the Selunsur Rapids (2hrs away).

Niah Caves National Park

The **Great Cave** at Niah is the site of perhaps Southeast Asia's greatest archaeological find, one to rival even the discovery of Java Man. In 1958, Tom Harrisson, archaeologist and curator of the Sarawak Museum, unearthed a 43,000-year-old human skull buried beneath 8ft of petrified guano near the cave entrance. Where Java Man was an example of a *Homo erectus*, this skull belonged to a *Homo sapiens sapiens*, one of our own, a discovery that turned previous theories about the origins and transmigration of modern man on their heads.

Further excavations revealed that the Niah caves had seen the presence of humans from this point right up until the modern day. Sophisticated cave paintings were found and hundreds more human burials were exhumed, some from as recent as the 1400s. The later the burial site, the more sophisticated were the artefacts found alongside the bones – revealing mankind's cultural development in snapshots, over the course of tens of thousands of years. Animal bones were discovered, including the remains of giant pigs, oversize predecessors of animals still hunted today. Other remains proved to be those of animals long extinct. Recent archaeological research using radiocarbon dating has confirmed many of Harrisson's original theories and found **Deep Skull** (as the relic is now known) to be 4,000 years older than the original estimate.

Though no longer inhabited, these caves are of commercial importance for their guano and edible birds' nests, formed by the saliva of the male swiflet. Until only a few decades ago the swiflet population of the Great Cave was said to exceed the entire human population of Sarawak. From as early as the 8th century, men have scaled slender poles to scrape nests from the roof of the Great Cave, often hanging precariously up to 200ft from the cave floor. The nests were stripped of feathers and exported to China, where a sackful could fetch a small fortune. The same is true today (a kilo of high-grade nests sells for US$1,000). Collecting rights are held by the local Punan, original inhabitants of the area and possible descendants of the original cave dwellers.

Getting There

Niah Caves National Park is 110km south of Miri and a little further north of Bintulu. There are regular buses from both towns (around 2hrs), as well as share-taxi services, though most visit the caves with the help of tour operators. The buses drop passengers at Batu Niah. Longboats or taxis make the 3km journey between here and park headquarters.

Information

Visitors need to register at park headquarters before proceeding to the caves. A small exhibition provides extensive information about the archaeological discoveries at Niah.

Where to Stay

A hostel and various well-appointed chalets (some with air-con) provide a good range of accommodation options at Niah. Rates range from RM15.75–157.50. For reservations contact the National Parks & Wildlife Booking Office, c/o Visitors' Information Centre, Jalan Melayu, Miri, **t** 085 434 184.

Though the caves themselves cannot quite match those at Mulu (indeed no cave system in the world can match Mulu for geological grandeur), it is a wonder that the Niah National Park doesn't see more visitors. Park facilities are excellent, and access to the caves is made easy by a 3km plankwalk through primary forest. In addition to the caves, two jungle trails lead up Bukit Kasut for views across the rainforest canopy. A small exhibition displays replicas of Deep Skull and some of the cave paintings.

From park headquarters visitors are ferried across the small Sungai Niah to the start of the plankwalk. Throughout the day, guano collectors pass by lugging 30kg sackloads in the direction of the river, where the guano is graded and sold as fertilizer for pepper plantations. The plankwalk passes between giant-buttressed *tapang* trees and padanus plants. Walk quietly and you may spot all sorts of wildlife along the way, from flying lizards and tree nymph butterflies to giant squirrels, monkeys and hornbills. After about an hour, the trail climbs up to **Traders' Cave**, a rock overhang beneath which the collectors used to conduct their business. The hardwood structures within the cave once served as traders' huts and are thought to be at least 100 years old.

The gaping entrance to **Great Cave** (250m by 60m) is approached from the north, and it is only possible to appreciate the scale of the cave mouth from inside. Just within stands a reconstruction of the original hut used by Tom Harrisson during the initial excavations. Behind this, a network of bamboo poles rise like a series of ships' masts in the direction of the roof. In places the slippery floor is covered with guano several metres in depth, and crawling with cockroaches and earwigs. A further kilometre of plankwalk continues into the deeper recesses of the cave, climbing small mountains of guano, where collectors work by the light of paraffin lamps. The path enters a number of other cave chambers, including Moon Cave, a natural circular passageway, before emerging into the light of a small gorge.

The **Painted Cave** lies twenty minutes beyond this point on a steep incline. Further archaeological discoveries were made here by Harrisson, notably a collection of boat-shaped wooden coffins and, most important of all, a series of cave paintings daubed onto one of the walls with red haematite. The 1,200-year-old paintings depict warriors, fantastical beasts and funerary boats manned, presumably, by the dead. Don't expect anthing on the scale of Lascaux or Altamira. At one time a large tree shaded the entrance to the cave. When it fell the extra light caused the paintings to fade, making them very hard to decipher, particularly from behind the protective fence (which prevents visitors from getting within several metres of the wall). Head as far left as possible for the clearest images.

Miri

Miri is not the place it was. Hardened expats and locals reminisce about a bullish boom town growing fat on oil, a place with a rough edge and a nightlife to rival anywhere in Borneo. But things have quietened down in recent years – many of Miri's hotels, bars and restaurants are closing their doors as the fortune-seekers move on

Getting There

Miri's busy little airport is 8km outside the town centre, with flights to Kuching, Sibu, Bintulu, Mukah and Labuan. MAS also run 18-seater Twin Otter planes from Miri to many interior destinations, including Bario, Mulu, Marudi, Long Bang, Long Lellang and Limbang. Long-distance buses serve Kuching, Sibu and Bintulu, while local services head for the Lambir Hills National Park and the Niah caves. The bus station is beside the Visitor Information Centre off Jalan Padang. Buses also head for Bandar Seri Begawan in Brunei, though the convoluted journey involves two river crossings.

Taxis from Miri to the Lambir Hills National Park cost approximately RM25 one-way. Buses between Miri and Bintulu also pass by the park headquarters (RM2.50 one-way).

Information

Visitor Information Centre, 452 Jalan Melayu (at the south end of town), **t** 085 434 181. This large, well-stocked tourist office is a good source of information and advice about onward travel.

Where to Stay

Expensive

Miri Marriott Resort & Spa, Jalan Temenggong Datuk Oyong Lawai, **t** 085 421 121, **f** 085 421 1099, *www.marriott.com*. Situated along from an attractive beach fringing Miri, this is the town's top hotel, with most rooms in attached 'chalets' set around gardens. The highlight is the enormous pool, which attracts Miri's expat community. There are also three food outlets.

Moderate

Grand Palace Hotel, Jalan Miri Pujut, **t** 085 428 888, **f** 085 427 777, *www.grandpalacehotel.com*. A business hotel 2km north of the town centre, offering large rooms, with a small pool and a fitness centre.

Dynasty Hotel, Jalan Pujut Lutong, **t** 085 421 111, **f** 085 422 222. Probably the most comfortable option in the town centre, with clean but spartan rooms in a block.

Inexpensive

Luak Bay Lodge, 13, Lot 211, Jalan Pantai, Luak Bay (6km from Miri airport), **t** 012 870 0191, *www.kelabit.net* (on the accommodation page). A wonderful homestay environment

and the Bruneians begin to look elsewhere for their thrills. The oil is still flowing but not at the same rate (all the inland wells are running dry), and the 1997 economic crisis has taken its inevitable toll.

Miri's one piece of history (oil-related, of course) presides over the town centre from **Canada Hill**. Known as Grand Old Lady on the Hill, she stands about 50ft tall, is built of *belian* ironwood and has the honour of being the first and longest serving of Miri's oil platforms, built in 1910. A small museum is due to open beside the platform, from where there are views south over palm-oil plantations to the distant rainforest, and views north over Miri itself and the South China Sea. The road up Canada Hill passes a small shanty-town, home to newcomers (mainly illegal Indonesians) who are looking for work on the oil platforms.

For tourists, Miri is the staging post for journeys up the Baram or into the northeast interior of Sarawak. There is not much to do in town, other than wander round the local markets or shop for supplies and souvenirs (Wisma Pelita near the bus station has a good selection). The intrepid could pay a visit to the Malay/Melanau water village, which encroaches on the Sungai Miri from the east side of town.

in the suburbs of Miri. Hosts David Bennett, a Kiwi pilot for Sarawak's Rural Air Service, and his wife Pauline, a Kelabit from a longhouse in Bario, make their guests feel completely at home in their detached house with wraparound garden. They are very knowledgeable about interior travel in Sarawak and are more than happy to help arrange trips to any of the longhouses. *At the time of going to press, Luak Bay Lodge was set to close, with a new lodge due to open shortly; check the website for details.*

Telang Usan Hotel, 2.5km Airport Road, **t** 085 411 433, **f** 085 419 078, *www.telangusan.com*. An unusual 50-room hotel showcasing Orang Ulu artwork and offering spacious though cluttered rooms in a hotch-potch of styles. Business-class facilities and an in-house travel agency.

Treetops Lodge (Siwa Guesthouse), Lot 210, Siwa Jaya, **t** 085 482 449. A 12-bed longhouse-style guesthouse set in two acres of fruit gardens near the Lambir Hills National Park (20mins drive from Miri centre). Basic accommodation with a quirky homestay feel and a 15ft pool with decking.

Miri Hotel, 47 Brooke Road, **t** 085 421 212, **f** 085 412 002. Centrally located business-class hotel offering small, spick-and-span rooms at a good price (RM69 for a double) – a big step up from places charging RM10-15 less.

Lambir Hills National Park

At park headquarters there are air-con and fan-only chalets (RM100 and RM50) for those who want to stay overnight. To book, contact park headquarters on **t** 085 491 030, or Miri National Parks Booking Office on **t** 085 434 184.

Eating Out

Miri has plenty of **hawker stalls** and coffee shops serving the usual staples, but the real treat here is the fresh fish and seafood. **Apollo Seafood**, Jalan Yu Seng Selatan, is an open-sided restaurant right in the centre of town and probably Miri's most popular place to eat. The speciality is fish grilled on a banana leaf and served with local *belacan*. **Maxim's Seafood Centre** outside town (Jalan Miri Pujut) gives Apollo's a run for its money, with a similar menu of fresh seafood options. If you are staying at the Miri Marriott, head across the road to **Tanjung Seafood** for your fresh fish and seafood experience. Try the ten-inch tiger prawns. If you're staying around Jalan Brooke, then track down the **Nice Taste Café and Steakhouse**, which lives up to its name.

The **Lambir Hills National Park**, situated along a sandstone escarpment 30km to the south of Miri, makes a worthwhile day trip. The authorities claim that the forest here is the most species-rich on the planet. It is the site of ongoing botanical research and is popular at weekends with locals, who head for the park's numerous waterfalls to eat their picnics. More arduous trails lead deeper within the park boundaries and to the summit of Bukit Lambir (465m). With the exception of the summit trail, all trails are well marked and can be tackled without a guide. Within a kilometre of the park headquarters, a 40m-tall tree tower allows visitors to get in amongst the tree canopy. A little beyond here, the Latak Waterfall plunges 25m into a clear, deep pool – a good spot for a swim.

The Northeast Interior

Some of the least spoilt areas of Sarawak can be found in the northeast, around Brunei's meandering border and up in the Tama Abu mountain range. Historically as well as topographically, the region is dominated by two rivers, the Limbang and the Baram, which spill into Brunei Bay and Luak Bay respectively. This corner of Sarawak is the realm of the Orang Ulu, with the Kayan and Kenyah tribes dominating the mid reaches of Sungai Baram, and the Kelabit holding reign over the remote highlands.

For centuries, the Orang Ulu of these parts have paid little attention to political delineations, resolutely unfazed by the claims and demands of sultans and White Rajahs. Even today the region retains its self-sufficiency and relative inaccessibility. Which is half of the attraction for modern visitors. High up on a mountain plateau, the beautiful **Kelabit Highlands** (*see* p.351) is a world unto itself. Water buffalo plough fields of wet paddy and megaliths lie scattered about the hillsides, providing insights into the distant history and customs of the hospitable Kelabit people. The region's premier attraction, however, is the cave system and dramatic limestone scenery of the **Gunung Mulu National Park** (*see* below).

Marudi is the largest settlement along the Sungai Baram. In the days before an airstrip was built at Mulu, tourists would pass through Marudi en route to the national park. Today few visitors pay much attention to the town, though it remains an important trading post for upriver longhouse communities. A faithful reconstruction of **Fort Hose** stands on the hilltop. The original fort, built in 1901, burned to the ground during a fire early in the 1990s. Dr Charles Hose, after whom the fort was named, was one of the better known Residents to serve under Rajah Charles Brooke. He was a keen naturalist and anthropologist, though he was famed across the state principally for his great size.

Inland from Marudi, off a tributary of the Baram, is the **Loagan Bunut National Park**, newest and least visited of Sarawak's gazetted parks. It is accessible by boat from Marudi, though a new section of road now links the park with Miri. This 650-hectare natural lake rises and falls with the seasons and is particularly rich in aquatic life and birds. At the peak of the dry season, the lake often dries completely, leaving its resident fish to eke out a crowded existence in swampy pools, or simply to flounder on the cracked mud. Dry season is thus a time of plenty for the aquatic birdlife, as it is for the local Berawan, who have exclusive rights to fish on the lake. Over generations, the Berawan of Loagan Bunut have perfected a unique fishing technique known as *selambau*, whereby fish are harvested as they embark on their seasonal migrations in and out of the lake. A simple hostel provides accommodation for visitors.

Gunung Mulu National Park

Visitor numbers to the Mulu National Park have soared since UNESCO named it a World Heritage Site in 2000. It is the largest of Sarawak's national parks, covering more than 500 sq km of virgin rainforest with a biodiversity that has inspired decades of scientific research. It is Mulu's astonishing geological features, however, that make the park unique. Concealed deep within its mountainous terrain is one of the world's great cave systems, threaded with some 600–800km of cave passages, only thirty per cent of which have been explored to date. Within this underworld, the planet's largest known cave chamber was found, measuring 600m by 415m (a space large enough to contain 16 football pitches or park 40 Boeing 747s, so the brochures claim).

In addition to cave exploration, the park offers some great trekking terrain. **Gunung Mulu** itself (2376m) was first scaled in 1932 by Antarctic explorer Edward Shackleton and a support group of Berawans. It remains a challenging trek to this day, though a gentler route to the summit has since been found. For many, Mulu's highlights are the steep climb up to the **Pinnacles** – 45m-tall limestone spikes that pierce through the jungle canopy on the upper slopes of Gunung Api – and the dusk-time exodus of over a million bats from the mouth of Deer Cave, a spectacle that lasts up to an hour and resembles a plume of black smoke against the paling sky.

The Gunung Mulu National Park falls within the ancestral homeland of the Penan and the Berawan tribes; the last remaining nomadic Penan still live in and about the

Getting There

Access to Gunung Mulu National Park is by air from Miri and Kuching. It is possible to make the journey by bus and boat, though less practical (time-consuming and more expensive). There are two scheduled flights a day from Miri, and one from Kuching, using either 50-seater Fokker Friendships or 18-seater Twin Otter planes. To book contact MAS, 239 Haluman Kabor, **t** 085 414 144. To ensure the safe passage of the 2–3 million bats which stream out of Deer Cave at sundown, no planes are allowed to land or take off later than 4.30pm.

Information

Fees for boats and guides at Mulu can be prohibitively expensive if arranged independently. Most visitors therefore resort to using tour operators, who can tailor a package to your needs, book flights and accommodation and obtain entry permits. For tour operators *see* p.313–4, or contact Miri's Visitor Information Centre, 452 Jalan Melayu, Miri, **t** 085 434 184, **f** 085 434 179. The following website is a good resource: *www.mulupark.com*.

Where to Stay

Royal Mulu Resort, **t** 085 790 100, **f** 085 790 101, *sales@royalmuluresort.com*, *www.royalmuluresort.com*. Set aside from park headquarters on the banks of the Sungai Melinau, offering luxury accommodation in longhouse-style buildings on stilts. 4-star facilities, with a swimming pool and Berawan staff who can arrange activities within the national park.

Park Headquarters, c/o Visitor Information Centre, 452 Jalan Melayu, Miri, **t** 085 434 184, **f** 085 434 179. The standard of accommodation here is particularly good for a national park. At the top end is a single air-conditioned chalet with two bedrooms (each en suite), lounge, dining room and kitchen (RM225). There are two 'longhouse' buildings, each with four en suite rooms with air-con (RM100 for a double), plus a further ten rooms in the 'rainforest cabins' without air-con (RM50). Otherwise, there is the 18-bed hostel with shared facilities and lockers (RM18). Within the park itself are a number of camps, offering a roof over your head (dormitory-style accommodation beneath an open-sided building), shared bathrooms and cooking facilities.

Eating Out

Just across the footbridge from park headquarters, on the banks of the Sungai Melinau, is a small restaurant serving beer and cheap local dishes. There is usually no menu: you get whatever is in on that particular day (which will always include jungle fern. To the chagrin of the owner, a new café with greatly superior offerings has opened recently at park headquarters. Café Mulu offers set meals and an à la carte menu each day, with local specialities like *laksa*, and Western alternatives such as pancakes, tuna mayonnaise sandwiches and banana smoothies. Camping provisions can be bought from the shop beside Cafe Mulu.

park boundaries, safe from the encroachment of logging companies. When the airstrip was first built beside park headquarters, and plans to transform the park into a mainstream 'ecotourism' destination were set in motion, there were outcries from the indigenous communities, for whom the caves and surrounding jungle were sacred sites. By 1993 heated exchanges between the two sides were commonplace. One slack-mouthed government official publicly referred to the Berawan as 'squatters' – which was met with a wry challenge from Berawan leader Thomas Ngang: 'If we are squatters, then drop myself and the Chief Minister inside the Mulu caves and let us see who finds his way out first'.

Today many of the Berawan and settled Penan are employed at park headquarters, mainly as guides and boatmen. Having given up their land, they at least want to see a little of the booty – which is one reason for the obligatory (and overpriced) boat journey that tourists are forced to take if they want to link up with the Melinau Trail.

The Caves

Eighteen caves in total have been surveyed and made accessible for caving or research purposes, though reaching some of these requires climbing equipment and considerable expertise. Mulu's four 'show caves', all of which lie within a few kilometres of park headquarters, are lined with plankwalks and lighting, though a torch is still necessary in parts.

The closest is **Deer Cave**, linked to park headquarters by a 3km boardwalk, which crosses an area of peat swamps and alluvial flats. The gaping mouth of Deer Cave dominates the entire vertical flank of a mountainside, and is a fitting entranceway into Mulu's subterranean world. Once inside, the ceiling reaches well beyond the range of flashlights, in parts nearly 200m above the cave floor. Just under a kilometre of boardwalk follows a route through the cave, passing the 'Garden of Eden', an errant patch of rainforest that survives on a shaft of sunlight where the cave roof has collapsed. Between 5pm and 7pm on dry evenings a large proportion of Deer Cave's resident bats – in excess of two million of them (*see* 'Bat Facts' opposite) – stream from the cave mouth for a night of feeding. It is thought that they travel all the way to the coast and back each night in search of food. The best place to observe the spectacle is from the bat observatory, a covered pavilion several hundred metres beyond the entrance to the cave.

Just round the corner from Deer Cave is **Lang's Cave**, smallest of the show caves and a natural gallery of stalactites, stalagmites and rimstone pools – the whole scene glowing pearly white among angled spotlights. Because the ceilings are low-slung and the passageways narrow, Lang's Cave is a good place to get up close with the various species of bat that inhabit the Mulu Caves. Look out for carnivorous cave crickets too (they feed on swiflet eggs, navigating in the dark with the help of 15cm-long antennae) and cave racers, harmless snakes which feed on bats.

Just off the Sungai Melinau north of park headquarters is the entrance to **Clearwater Cave**, which, at 107km, is the longest cave in Southeast Asia. It was carved into existence over the course of several million years by the passage of water: the

Bat Facts

Being furtive cave dwellers (on the whole) and creatures of the night, bats have an understated role in the ecosystem of our planet. They inhabit every region of the globe, with the exception of the North and South Poles. Of the world's 4,800 species of mammal, more than 1,000 of these are bats, ranging in size from 6ft (the wingspan of a large fruit bat, or flying fox) to that of a human thumb-tip (the bumblebee bat). The majority of bats feed on insects, though about a quarter favour fruit, while five per cent hunt birds, fish and small mammals. The infamous South American vampire bat, of which there are three species, is an oddity with its predilection for blood. A bat's wing consists of a thin layer of skin stretched across a bone structure that resembles that of the human hand. All bats have good vision ('blind as a bat' is a misnomer) and many can navigate in pitch darkness with the aid of echo location. Most live for between 15 and 20 years.

Mulu has a metropolis-sized population of bats, with more than 27 species making their homes in its caves. The most common is the wrinkle-nosed bat – it is this species which streams from the mouth of Deer Cave each evening. They live in complex communities, with males and females occupying separate roosts. Young bats are raised in large nurseries; being mammals, bats give birth to live pups which are breastfed for a number of weeks. While their parents are out feeding, the pups remain huddled in their nurseries for warmth. The bats of Mulu play a vital role in dispersing the seeds of fruiting trees and culling the insect population – to the extent that mosquitoes are barely noticeable within the national park.

porous bedrock of the Mulu mountains absorbs rainwater, which finds its way through subterranean channels down to the river. In fact, a small river passes through Clearwater Cave itself, bubbling up from underground to form a tributary of the Sungai Melinau.

It is possible to trek to the entrance of Clearwater Cave, though most arrive by longboats, which pull up at the river bank near where the subterranean tributary bubbles to the surface. The water here is turquoise and startlingly clear (hence the name), filtered by a mountain range of porous limestone. Hundreds of Rajah Brooke birdwing butterflies flit about at the foot of a 200-step stairway that leads up to the cave entrance. Along the way, rare orchids – unique to this very spot – cling to the rockface, along with unusual single-leaf plants (*monophyllaea glauca*) which bloom tiny, delicate flowers. Within the cave is a chamber draped with limestone formations. A separate path leads down to a bridge across the underground river, which becomes a torrent after heavy rainfall. With much expense, and a fair amount of red tape to hurdle, it is possible to travel upriver by longboat along this subterranean waterway – in true Vernean spirit.

A little downriver from Clearwater Cave, but beyond the ramshackle Penan settlement, is **Wind Cave**, which is usually visited en route to the former. Inside are many impressive limestone formations, particularly in the 'King's Room' where the stalactites and stalagmites are illuminated with spotlights. The cave gets its name from the constantly perceptible breeze that blows from the direction of the cave mouth. Which, incidentally, provides a handy cave survival tip: to find your way out, follow the direction from which the wind is coming. If you can't tell, then check which way the stalactites are slanting.

Many more caves are accessible to those with the inclination for adventure caving, including the mighty **Sarawak Chamber** itself. Bear in mind, however, that the journey to the Sarawak Chamber involves a hard trek, a wade through chest-deep water and some serious rock climbing.

Treks

One of Mulu's most popular treks is the climb to the **Pinnacles**, near the summit of Gunung Api (1732m). These dramatic spikes of limestone are, in a sense, the Mulu cave system showing its face to the sky. Like the caves, they have been sculpted by the action of water over millions of years. The regular downpour of tropical rain has sharpened the stone into knife-like ridges.

Though the return journey from the Melinau Gorge Camp to the Pinnacles can be completed in a single day, this is a strenuous climb, in parts near-vertical. Towards the end of the trail, aluminium ladders breach gaps in the rock or ease the route up sheer rockfaces. No special skills are needed for the ascent, but the trail is a fair definition of hell for those with a fear of heights. Like the Pinnacles themselves, the rocks all about the upper reaches of the trail are razor-sharp, forcing climbers to watch carefully where they put their hands. For those who make it, the rewards from the viewpoint make the exertions worthwhile. It is as if a large area of rainforest has been stabbed through with rocky knives.

A trip to the Pinnacles is usually undertaken as part of a three-day trek. The journey begins with a longboat from park headquarters to a landing point known as Long Berar. The boat trip takes between one and three hours, depending on the level of the river. From Long Berar the trail cuts through level jungle for 2–3 hours before emerging into a clearing beside the river, where the Melinau Gorge camp (Camp 5) is situated. Twenty minutes upriver from the camp by foot, there is a wonderfully clear, natural pool in which to swim – though mind the leeches, which will be waiting to pounce at the river bank. The trek to the viewpoint on Gunung Api, at an altitude of 1200m, begins next morning at first light, with groups of average fitness returning to Camp 5 by mid–late afternoon.

Across the small footbridge in front of Camp 5 is the start of the **Head-hunters' Trail**, so called because Kayan raiding parties were said to use the route to reach the Sungai Limbang, dragging their boats overland from the Melinau Gorge to Sungai Terikan. Today tourists can use the route to get as far as **Limbang** town itself, a journey involving a two-day trek and two longboat jouneys. The little-visited Limbang region of Sarawak extends like a finger into Brunei, almost as far as the capital Bandar Seri Begawan (BSB). Limbang is a Malay-dominated trading town just 12km or so by road from BSB.

Another popular challenge is to conquer the park's namesake, **Gunung Mulu** itself (2376m). Four camps are staggered along the trail, which begins at park headquarters. Most people spread the journey over a leisurely four days. Though it is not quite the slog that Lord Shackleton faced when he conquered the peak back in 1932, much of the trail is steep and demands a reasonable level of fitness. Part of the route follows the 'southwest ridge', discovered in the 1920s by a Berawan rhino hunter called Tama Nilong. It was he who led Shackleton to the summit a decade later, and should rightly be credited as the first person to reach the peak.

The mountain is a favourite haunt of hornbills, eight species of which inhabit Gunung Mulu National Park. Their 'took-took' cries can often be heard along the trail, as can the beating of their broad wings. As the trail ascends the mountainside, the limestone bedrock is replaced by sandstone, and the giants of the mixed dipterocarp forest give way to the more stunted trees of the moss-abundant montane forest. From the craggy peak itself there are magnificent views across wide areas of the park.

The Kelabit Highlands

The Kelabit Highlands straddle the Tama Abu mountain range, which runs alongside the Indonesian border southeast of Brunei. **Bario** sits in the heart of the Kelabit territory, hidden from the world in a great bowl of mountains. It is the highest settled community in Borneo, with a number of longhouses scattered about a fertile plateau of paddy fields, irrigation ditches and grassy knolls. The surrounding jungle is run through with tiny brooks which merge to form the headwaters of the Sungai Baram. Outside visitors cannot fail to be enchanted by the otherworldliness of Bario and the beauty of its setting – a beauty recorded over the centuries in local songs, one of which recounts the pioneering journeys of distant ancestors, describing the highlands as '... the place where the wild waters tremble/Up to the edge of the moon'.

No one knows quite how many centuries the Kelabit have inhabited the area, but it is long enough for the growth of a sophisticated culture, and for the perfection of advanced techniques of irrigation and rice cultivation (Bario rice is much prized across Southeast Asia). The Kelabit are unique among the people of Borneo for their use of megaliths. Dolmens and carved rocks – monuments to the dead – lie scattered about the surrounding hillsides, and, on special occasions, a U-shaped swathe of jungle is cut into a distant ridge. Hemmed in by the mountains, such gaps were thought to allow the safe departure of the spirits of the dead. Or perhaps they were simply landmarks, pieces of art. At any rate, a team of chainsaw-wielding Kelabits decided to mark the year 2000 in just this fashion.

The arrival in 1944 of British soldier and archaeologist **Tom Harrisson** had a lasting effect on the Bario community. He has gone down in Kelabit legend as the man who fell from the sky: with a team of British and Australian commandos, he parachuted into the Highlands and succeeded in rallying the Kelabit against the occupying Japanese forces. He remained for months at a time, befriending the people and studying their culture (*World Within: a Borneo Story* is a wonderfully eccentric and erudite account of his times). Harrisson went on to become curator of the Sarawak Museum, before making ground-breaking discoveries at the Niah Caves (*see* p.342).

After the war, European missionaries recognized Bario as a ripe picking ground and converted many of the Kelabit to Christianity. Elderly members of the community, some of whom remember Harrisson with fondness, still rise before dawn to gather for prayers, which are spoken aloud in long incantations while a minister strums his guitar. The *tubung*, a thick bamboo drum, is beaten at 5.30 each morning as the call to prayer.

For the visitor, Bario is like no other place on Earth. It is both civilized and anachronistic. When not speaking their own tongue, the people converse in an outdated English, elegant and measured. Conversation revolves around the unhurried telling of stories. Men are 'fellows', not guys or blokes, and greetings are replaced by a simple description of the journey that has just been undertaken. In spite of their pride in traditions and the isolation of their existence, the Kelabit are nevertheless a forward-thinking people: they even have their own website (*www.kelabit.net*), where you find an appeal for the contribution of words towards the first English–Kelabit dictionary, alongside news items ('preparations for rice planting are underway').

Each day the major event in Bario is the arrival of the 18-seater plane. Half the village turns up to greet the new arrivals, or buy coffee for the pilot. The days slide gently into one another and most evenings there are dinner invitations to honour. If someone returns from a successful hunting trip, then you can be assured of a boozy barbecue that lasts well into the night, the men of Bario huddled under the stars nibbling on mouse deer or wild boar, the women nattering indoors.

Getting There

The only way to get to Bario – unless you want to trek for 7–10 days from Marudi, which can be arranged – is to fly from Miri. There are two flights daily on 18-seater planes. Because Bario sits in a plateau surrounded by a ring of mountains, landing on the small airstrip can be a tricky manoevre: when it is overcast, pilots need to wait for a hole in the clouds before they can descend. Seats on the tiny Twin Otter aircraft often get booked up by locals, so plan in advance, and bear in mind that planes may not be able to land if conditions are not suitable (it is fairly common for planes to turn back for Miri). By the same token, return dates must be flexible too: if the incoming plane doesn't land, you'll have to stay another night. On landing at Bario, immediately book a seat for the return flight, even if you have already done so in Miri.

Tourist Information

There is no tourist information facility in Bario, nor are there any banks – so bring all the cash you will need. Tour operators do offer trekking packages in and around Bario, though treks can be easily arranged at any of the guesthouses or longhouses (this way, the money goes back to the community too). Officially, visitors to the Kelabit Highlands need to get hold of a permit in Miri, though in practice no one bothers. Ask at the Miri's Visitor Information Centre (*see* p.344). David and Pauline Bennett, who run the Luak Bay Lodge homestay in Miri (*see* p.344), are a wealth of information on Bario and are always happy to help with arrangements: Pauline is herself a Kelabit from Bario while David is a pilot for MAS's Rural Air Service.

Where to Stay

Inexpensive–Budget

Bario Asal, Bario. David Bennett (**t** 012 870 0191, *see* 'Luak Bay Lodge' p.344) can make all the necessary arrangements for staying at Bario Asal, which is Bario's main longhouse:

Like many of Borneo's tribal peoples, the Kelabit are great fans of excess. They pride themselves on their gargantuan appetites, and it is seen as a great dishonour if a guest refuses food. The Kelabit appetite for indulgence is best represented by the *irau*, a great party which lasts several days and serves multiple functions; the celebration of a wedding or a wake, perhaps, and the consolidation of accumulated debts. Whatever the occasion, an *irau* is a show of wealth. *Borak* (rice wine) is brewed to sate the thirst of hundreds or thousands of guests, while chunks of buffalo flesh simmer in trough-like cauldrons.

Kelabit longhouses are often named after streams, or *pa*, (hence Pa Umor, Pa Ukat, Pa Dalih). They differ from other longhouses in their construction; as well as the common verandah on which guests are traditionally entertained, part of the living quarters at the back of the longhouse is open-plan too. A long line of fireplaces – one for each family – run down the centre of the second gallery, the roof blackened from years of cooking. Like the Kayan, Kelabit society is hierarchical, with those of higher 'class' living nearer the centre of the longhouse. Despite such distinctions, for a Kelabit to demean another on the grounds of his class is considered to be the worst possible insult.

Modern Bario comprises six distinct communities which are dispersed across the plateau. A tiny row of shops beside the old airstrip form the centre of activity. The **Bario Asal** longhouse itself is situated at the west end of the valley. Dirt tracks and trails lead up into the hills from all directions, providing wonderful trekking territory.

he was adopted into the longhouse community when he married a Kelabit. Alternatively, ask for Peter Matu on arrival; he is one of Bario Asal's residents and has set aside two double rooms within his own living quarters for guests. Meals are taken around the stove with the rest of the family. An unforgettable experience, though certainly rawer than staying at one of the purpose-built lodges.

Gem's Lodge, near Pa Umor. No phone. This beautiful lodge was built recently on the banks of a small river just south of the Pa Umor longhouse, 5km from Bario. Ask for Jaman Riboh, who runs the operation. Rooms are neat but basic, and the setting is wonderful, though remote. Jaman's wife provides the meals while Jaman himself is a guide.

De Plateau Lodge, Bario, **t** 019 855 5491, *deplateau@hotmail.com*. An attractive, open-plan (yet cosy) home in the Bario valley owned by Douglas Munney Bala and his wife. Attractive furnishings and simple guest rooms.

Tarawe's, Bario. The longest running of Bario's lodges, near to the shops and run by John Tarawe and his English wife. The lodge serves as something of a meeting place and is a great place to come for information or advice.

Bariew Lodge, Bario. No phone. Not so characterful as the other lodges, but with a few more facilities, such as hot water, bikes for hire, laundry and free tea/coffee. Run by Reddish Aran and his wife.

Eating Out

Two basic cafés are the sum of Bario's food scene. They serve up basic meals depending on what ingredients are available. Guest lodges and longhouses, true to the Kelabit spirit of hospitality, will make sure guests are well fed. Jungle fern and wild boar are sure to feature.

A number of routes can be tackled independently, such as the level path to **Pa Umor**, about an hour's walk east of Bario. There is a pretty wooden church here beside the old missionaries' airstrip, now a meadow. From Pa Umor there are plenty of trails up into the mountains, or even across the border into Kalimantan, which is only a few kilometres away. One of the trails leads past a stone chair carved by the headman of Pa Umor as a memorial to his father. He came across the smoothed stone while bathing in the river, and had it moved to its present position as part of a ceremony on the death of his father.

Close to Pa Umor is a salt spring, still worked by the Kelabit. In past times salt was of great commercial importance, serving as a unit of currency among the Kelabit; the grey salt is boiled from the muddy water of the spring and sold on to other upriver tribes (who would otherwise be forced to travel as far as the coast to barter for this commodity). Bario salt was particularly prized for its high iodine content (hence the grey colour) and used as a cure for goitre.

All of the lodges in and around Bario can arrange guides for ambling day trips to week-long treks. Peter Matu of Bario Asal has built a hunting lodge in the jungle (he calls it Brigadoon Jungle Hut), where guests can spend a night. The round trip from Bario Asal passes by a number of secluded longhouses (Pa Derung and Pa Ramapoh) and a waterfall known as Ruab Pa Ramapoh.

Bario is not the only place in the Kelabit Highlands with its own airstrip, and this means that one-way treks between distant longhouses are a possibility for those of a hardy disposition. The other airstrips are located at Long Banga and Long Lellang to the south, and Ba Kelalan and Long Semado to the north. Along the way, the Highlands are dotted with the longhouses and settlements of the Kenyah, the Saban and the Penan tribes, as well as the Kelabit.

Sabah

18

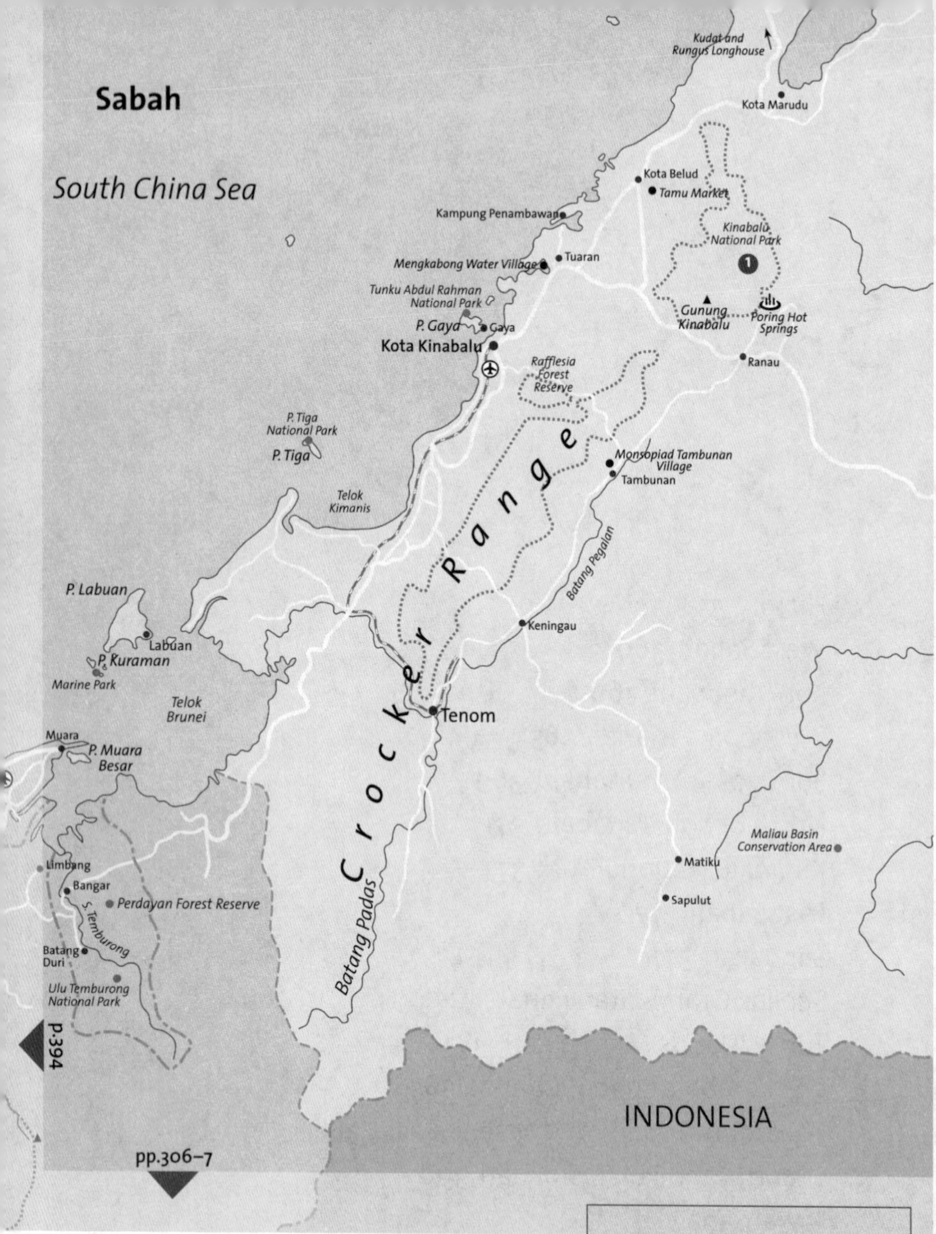

p.394
pp.306–7

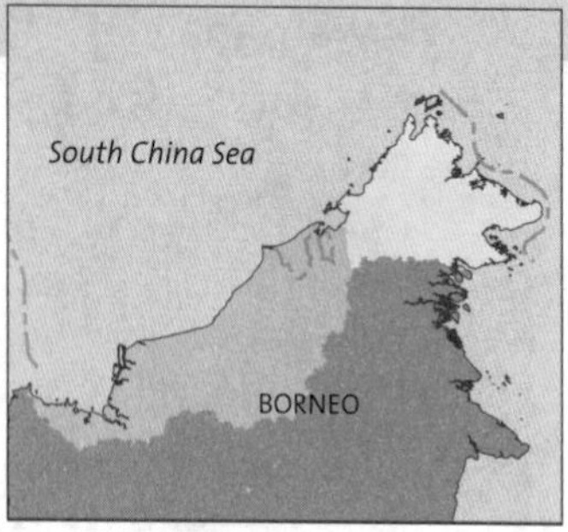

Highlights

1 Kinabalu National Park, home to the tallest mountain between New Guinea and the Himalayas

2 Sepilok Forest Reserve and Orang-Utan Sanctuary

3 Pulau Sipadan – enjoy the exhilaration of the 680m vertical drop-off at this world-class dive site

4 The Kinabatangan Wetlands – one of the best places to see wildlife in Southeast Asia

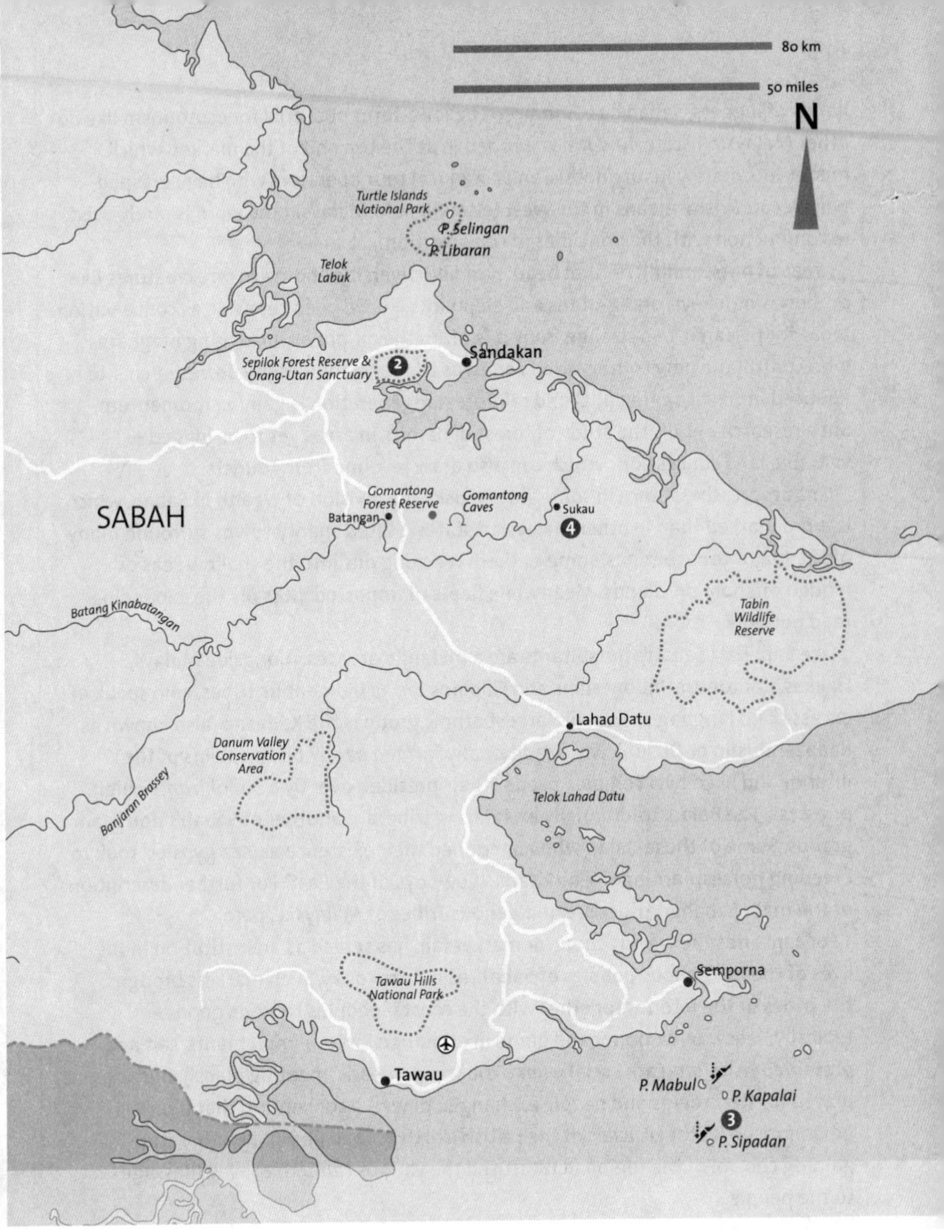

Sabah is Malaysia'a Wild East, complete with 'cowboys' and a frontier mentality. It attracts visitors primarily as an adventure destination; many come to climb Mount Kinabalu, the highest peak between the Himalayas and New Guinea. Others come for the wildlife, or to explore Malaysia's remotest and least spoilt nature reserves. More still head for the Celebes Sea and some of the world's best dive sites.

Sabah's riches are its timber resources, ancient hardwoods which sustain diminishing tracts of species-rich rainforest. Despite decades of destruction at the hands of loggers, Sabah has embraced the long-term potential for ecotourism like no other Malaysian state. And it has jumped in at the top end of the market, which means lots of new luxury hotels, and slick local tour operators who have grasped what 'ecotourism' means in the West (elsewhere in Malaysia the word is rarely used in conjunction with the principles of conservation).

Areas of outstanding natural beauty and biodiversity – home to rare creatures like proboscis monkeys, orang-utans and elephants – have been set aside as conservation areas for research. In a strange irony it is often the all-powerful logging magnates who control the new conservation zones: as timber resources dry up, research into Reduced Impact Logging (RIL) and rainforest regeneration is gaining momentum. Such research entails the study of forest dynamics in areas yet to be logged – valuable land concessions which can also draw revenue from tourists.

This progressive stance in some ways masks the division of wealth in Sabah, which is more marked than in other Malaysian states. Stilted shanty towns surround many of the major conurbations, some of them reaching out into the shallow seas or hidden offshore on islands. Meanwhile fleets of imported 4X4s ply the expanding road network.

Like Sarawak, Sabah's inhabitants are a melange of races. Alongside Malays, Hakkas, Cantonese, Indonesians and Filipinos are 32 indigenous tribes, who speak in excess of 50 languages. Sabah's largest ethnic group is the Kadazan (also known as Kadazandusun or Dusun), who traditionally farmed paddy on the plains of the interior and lived by a complex set of rituals presided over by a *bobohizan*, or high priestess. The Bajau, traditionally a seafaring tribe, are another of Sabah's dominant groups. Some of those Bajau who abandoned their existence as 'sea gypsies' took to breeding horses, earning the nickname 'Cowboys of the East'. For further descriptions of the main Sabahan tribes *see* 'Indigenous Tribes of Malaysia', p.40.

For centuries the weekly *tamu*, or market fair, has served as an institution in the lives of the indigenous peoples of Sabah, as it does today. Such markets brought the tribes of the interior together with the coastal peoples to trade goods – typically beeswax, camphor and game in exchange for iron implements, salt and preserved fish. *Tamu* are social events too (*tamu* means 'meeting place'); musicians played for the crowds and people exchanged news – a convention that didn't go unnoticed by the officials of the British North Borneo Company, who, after gaining control of the region in 1881, used the various *tamu* to convey messages to the people.

History

Prior to the founding of the British North Borneo Company in 1881, the region passed hands between the sultans of Brunei and Sulu – though the indigenous tribes rarely acknowledged their overlords. In 1846 the Sultan of Brunei ceded Pulau Labuan to the British East India Company, who were drawn to the island's rich coal deposits. But it was Englishman Alfred Dent and Austrian business associate Baron von

Overbeck who recognized the commercial potential of mainland North Borneo, as the region was then known. They secured the territory in 1878 by offering to pay handsome annuities to the sultans of Sulu and Brunei, who had long squabbled over territorial boundaries. Dent bought von Overbeck's share in the venture, then founded the British North Borneo Company, gaining the immediate protection of the British Crown.

The company floundered in its early years, relying heavily on the age-old export of jungle produce to China, before rubber and tobacco were planted and timber exported. Unlike the administration in Sarawak, the Company struggled to gain the recognition and the loyalty of the local people. The underhand tactics used to recruit indigenous labourers for the estates did not help matters: typically, the estate manager would send his recruiter to hang about popular gambling dens, where he would offer sums of money to those who squandered their own – in exchange for periods of indentured labour. Neither did the Company show any regard for ancestral land rights, and when the administrators attempted to impose taxes on the indigenous tribes, they soon had a rebellion on their hands. Bajau leader Mat Salleh gathered his supporters about him and, catching the Company off guard, sacked the settlement on Pulau Gaya (just off modern-day KK), before going on to rout the arsenal in Kudat. The Bajau leader eluded Company forces until January 1900, when he and many of his supporters were rounded up and killed. To this day Mat Salleh is regarded as a martyr among Sabahans.

One of the few relics of the days of the British North Borneo Company – Allied bombs during the World War Two laid waste to the architecture of Sabah's main towns – is the short stretch of railway that runs between Kota Kinabalu and Tenom on the west coast. The original plan had been to link Sandakan with the west coast, but funds ran dry.

North Borneo suffered at the hands of the Japanese during World War Two, with the immigrant Chinese communities on the receiving end of violent discrimination (the British North Borneo Company had encouraged the immigration of Hakkas and Cantonese to work on rubber and tobacco estates). It is the infamous Death March, however, that serves as the lasting record of wartime cruelty. In September 1944, nearly 2,500 Allied POWs were forcibly marched with scant supplies between Sanadakan and Rantau, a journey of more than 200km which claimed the lives of all but six of the POWs.

Following the war, North Borneo served as a British colony until 1963, when it became part of Malaysia and was renamed Sabah. Persistent underfunding has since soured relations between KL and the local government in Sabah. Islamic propaganda is not well received in Malaysia's only state with a Christian majority, while profits from Sabah's lucrative timber trade find their way almost exclusively to the federal pot.

West Sabah

Kota Kinabalu

Kota Kinabalu, referred to more commonly as KK, gained city status in 2000 and is Sabah's fast-growing state capital. Despite its colonial heritage, the city is not much to look at. Allied bombing during World War Two levelled the entire town, and it was later rebuilt in concrete with streets arranged in a grid. The old **post office building**, which now houses the tourist information centre, and the **Atkinson Tower**, a 1902

Getting There

KK's busy airport is 6km from the centre of town, with flights to and from Labuan, Lahad Datu, Sandakan, Tawau and Kudat in Sabah, plus KL and Johor Bahru and all the main airports in Sarawak. There are also direct international flights to Singapore, Hong Kong and Manila.

The long-distance bus station is a busy coach park on Jalan Tunku Abdul Rahman dotted with ticketing huts. Air-conditioned coaches leave for all destinations in Sabah, though be prepared for the onslaught of touts when you approach.

Sabah has one short stretch of railway track between Tanjung Aru (just south of KK) and Tenom via Beaufort. Old steam engines make the journey once a day (*see* p.364).

Information

The tourist offices in Sabah are generally slicker operations than those elsewhere in Malaysia, providing plenty of information and advice. **Tourism Malaysia**, 1 Jalan Sagunting, Ground Floor, Uni Asia Building, **t** 088 248 698/088 242 064, **f** 088 241 764, is stocked with brochures and staff are helpful; **Sabah Tourism Promotion Corporation**, 51 Jalan Gaya, **t** 088 212 121, **f** 088 212 075, is equally useful. The official website of the Sabah Tourism Board has lots of useful information about the state (*www.sabahtourism.com*).

Tour Operators

Travel in Sabah is virtually impossible without the use of tour operators. Even if you do manage to visit sights independently, the costs involved are likely to be much greater than paying for an all-in-one package. Most operators are happy to tailor your trips to your liking. Tours to all destinations in Sabah can be arranged in Kota Kinabalu. Listed below are some of the better tour operators with offices in Kota Kinabalu.

Borneo Adventure, 5th Floor, Room 509–512, Gaya Centre, **t** 088 238 731, **f** 088 238 730, *infokk@borneoadventure.com*, *www.borneoadventure.com*.

Borneo Eco Tours, Lot 1, Pusat Perindustrian Kolombong Jaya Mile 5.5, Jalan Kolombong, **t** 088 438 300, **f** 088 438 307, *www.borneoecotours.com*.

Borneo Divers, 9th Floor, Menara Jubili, 53 Jalan Gaya, **t** 088 222 226, **f** 088 221 550, *diving@bdiver.po.my*.

Borneo Wildlife Adventure, 1st Floor, General Post Office Building, **t** 088 213 668, **f** 088 219 089, *bwa@tm.net.my*, *www.borneo-wildlife.com*.

Coral Island Cruises, Tours & Travel, 10th Floor, Wisma Merdeka, Jalan Tun Razak, **t** 088 223 404, **f** 088 272 404, *www.coral-island-cruises.com*.

KK Tours& Travel, Lot 32, Block F, Lintas Square, **t** 088 238 480, **f** 088 238 268, *kktours@tm.net.my*, *www.kktours.com*.

Sipadan Dive Centre, 11th Floor, Wisma Merdeka, Jalan Tun Razak, **t** 088 240 584, **f** 088 240 415, *sipadan@po.jaring.my*, *www.sipadandivers.com*.

Wildlife Expeditions, Tanjung Aru Resort (Shangri-La), **t** 088 246 000, **f** 088 231 758, *www.wildlife-expeditions.com*.

memorial to the settlement's first District Officer, are the only buildings to have survived from the colonial era.

After a rebellion in 1897 by the legendary Mat Salleh resulted in the sacking of Pulau Gaya, the British North Borneo Company relocated its west-coast headquarters to the mainland, naming the settlement Jesselton after the Deputy Manager Sir Charles Jessel. The site on which Jesselton was founded was originally a tiny village called Api-Api (Fire Fire), probably because it was so frequently torched by passing pirates. Tobacco and rubber estates were planted inland and a railway line (*see* 'North Borneo Railway', p.364) was constructed to transport goods from the interior. Plans to link the

Where to Stay

Listed below are hotels in and around Kota Kinabalu. Those in the city centre itself are functional and patronized largely by local businessmen. The best resorts are situated along the coast both north and south of the city. The area has a good range of upmarket hotels, with not so many mid-market and budget options.

Luxury–Expensive

Tanjung-Aru Resort (Shangri-La), **t** 088 225 800, **f** 088 217 155, *tah@shangri-la.com*, *www.shangri-la.com*. A luxury resort on a small cape south of KK, with a glorious free-form pool and impeccable service. Between the main building and the sea is a wide 25-acre stretch of gardens with views across to Pulau Mamutik. Facilities include tennis courts, a kids' centre and pitch and putt. There is only one small patch of beach, which is a shame. Peppino's, one of six bars and restaurants, serves some of the best Italian food in Sabah.

Sutera Harbour, 1 Sutera Harbour Boulevard, **t** 088 318 888, **f** 088 317 777, *www.suteraharbour.com*. With almost a thousand rooms and several hundred acres of land, this must be one of the largest resorts in Southeast Asia. The complex includes a 27-hole golf course, a 100-berth marina, 16 bars and restaurants, a spa and two separate wings of rooms, the Pacific Wing (business) and the Magellan Wing ('leisure'). The resort even operates its own railway line (*see* North Borneo Railway p.364). Being so large there is rather an impersonal feel to the place, but all your needs are sure to be met. The club rooms and suites are beautifully furnished with motifs taken from indigenous art. All the facilities of a 5-star resort can be expected.

Nexus Karambunai Resort, Karambunai Peninsula, near Kampung Bikasan, **t** 088 411 222, **f** 088 411 020, *reservation@nexusresort.com*, *www.nexusresort.com*. The most beautiful setting of all Sabah's beach resorts, with more than 3,000 acres of land comprising a large lagoon and 6km of wide powder-sand beach backed by jungle. The rooms, which are set in double-storey villas, are spacious and stylish (particularly those in Borneo Villa with a sea view). The Royal and Presidential suites come with their own private swimming pools and gardens. There's a watersports centre at the lagoon, three pools, a 75-acre nature park on the hillside, an immaculate golf course and horses for rides along the beach. Noble House serves expensive Cantonese food, and Olives specializes in Mediterranean cuisine. A regular shuttle (free) offers daily services to and from Kota Kinabalu itself (a 40-minute journey).

Rasa Ria Resort (Shangri-La), Pantai Dalit, Tuaran, **t** 088 792 888, **f** 088 792 777, *rrr@shangri-la.com*, *www.shangri-la.com*. A good match for the Nexus Karambunai, and just north along the coast. It has all the same facilities and features, minus the lagoon, but with the addition of a few resident orang-utans, who live in the attached 65-acre nature reserve. For a fee, guests can watch the animals at feeding time. Peperoni's serves excellent pizzas from a wood-fired oven, while a chic new restaurant named Coast is set in its own railway with Sandakan – then capital of North Borneo – never came to fruition through lack of funds. After the withdrawal of the Japanese at the end of World War Two, North Borneo became a Crown colony and Jesselton replaced Sandakan as the capital. It was renamed Kota Kinabalu on becoming part of the Federation of Malaysia in 1963.

Today KK is one of Malaysia's most ethnically diverse cities, a fact reflected in the broad range of cuisines on offer at hawker stalls and coffee shops. The city centre is dominated by a monotone collection of concrete complexes, built on reclaimed land and home to offices, shopping centres and apartments. **Jalan Gaya** is modern KK's

octagonal, glass-walled building beside the beach. The cuisine at Coast is described as California, with a dab of Mexico and Asia. Rooms are attractive and spacious, though not quite up to the standard of those at the Nexus.

The Jesselton, 60 Jalan Gaya, **t** 088 223 333, **f** 088 240 401, *jesshtl@po.jaring.my*, *www.jesseltonhotel.com*. A boutique hotel in the town centre with a British Raj theme – right down to porters in pith helmets and a black London cab parked out front. The 31 rooms are rich in wood tones while the suite comes complete with roof terrace and fish pond. The attached Gardenia Restaurant serves good British and Continental favourites and has a decent wine list.

Moderate

Hyatt Regency Kinabalu, Jalan Datuk Salleh Sulong, **t** 088 221 234, **f** 088 218 909, *hyatt@hyattkk.com.my*, *http://kinabalu.regency.hyatt.com*. Occupying one of the largest buildings in the centre of town, with 290 rooms and 4-star facilities, including three restaurants, an outdoor pool and a fitness centre.

Hotel Capital, 23 Jalan Haji Saman, **t** 088 231 999, **f** 088 237 222. A central option at the lower end of this price category, with large doubles. All rooms have decent en suite bathrooms, TV and minibar. Very functional and good value but lacking character.

Langkah Syabas Beach Resort, Kinarut, **t** 088 752 000, **f** 088 752 111, *lsr@po.jaring.my*. Located 25mins south of KK in the village of Kinarut. A number of detached and semi-detached chalets surround a pleasant swimming pool. All chalets have air-con, TV, fridge and tea/coffee-making facilities. Other facilities include a library and video room and a nearby horse-riding centre. A mid-market alternative to the nearby Tanjung Aru Resort.

Inexpensive

Kinabalu Daya Hotel, Lot 3 Block 9, Jalan Pantai, **t** 088 240 000, **f** 088 263 909. A good-value, modern, clean mid-range option in the centre of town with air-con, TV, phone and hot water in all rooms.

Mandarin Hotel, 138 Gaya Street, **t** 088 225 222, **f** 088 225 481. A great-value, modern six-storey hotel in the centre of KK, with sizable rooms in good order and very helpful staff.

Seaside Travellers' Inn, KM20, Jalan Papar, Kampung Laut, Kinarut, **t** 088 750 555, **f** 088 750 479. Set right on the beach at Kinarut, facing Pulau Dinawan, 25mins south of KK. Rooms are plain and functional and there is a swimming pool. The deluxe rooms have TV, air-con and hot-water showers, while the standard rooms are fan-only.

Budget

Farida's B&B, 413 Jalan Saga, Mile 4.5, Likas, **t** 088 428 733, **f** 088 424 998, *faridabb@tm.net.my*, *www.homeaway.com.my*. A friendly homestay set in a garden compound in a northern suburb, 6km from the centre of KK. Farida offers a range of options from dormitory beds to doubles with air-con. She can also help arrange tours to nearby sights.

most appealing street, lined with restaurants and Chinese apothecaries; every Sunday it is closed to traffic and transformed into a lively open-air market, a weekly event that goes back to colonial times when Jalan Gaya was the centre of activities in Jesselton. Towards the street's northern end stands the old post office, living proof that the modern city does indeed have something of a past.

Just inland from Jalan Gaya looms **Signal Hill**, which once served as a navigation aid for approaching ships. Today the hill provides a bird's-eye view of KK's drab centre and the contrasting beauty of its aquamarine bay dotted with the tropical islands that form the **Tunku Abdul Rahman Park** (*see* p.365).

Backpacker Lodge, Lot 25, Lorong Dewan, Australia Place, **t** 088 261 495, *backpackerkk@yahoo.com*. Offers clean segregated dorms for RM18 per bed, and one double room for RM40. A reasonable breakfast included in the price.

Eating Out

Malay, Indonesian, Filipino, Chinese, European and Sabahan cuisine can all be sampled in Kota Kinabalu if you know where to look. Many of the best upmarket restaurants are those belonging to the major hotels. Notable examples include **Coast** and **Peperoni's** at the Rasa Ria, Peppino's at the Tanjung-Aru, and **Noble House** at the Nexus (*see* under 'Where to Stay' for descriptions).

Among the many local specialities is *hinava*, a type of pickle traditionally used by the Dusun to preserve fresh meat and fish. One of the favourite *hinava* recipes combines fresh mackerel with chillies, shallots, ginger, lime juice and grated mango stone. Another Dusun favourite is a rich chicken soup cooked in rice wine. A less appetising Murut speciality is *jaruk*, fresh game stuffed inside a section of bamboo with salt and cooked rice, all of which is left to 'ferment' for several months. Strangely, Sabah is a good place for fresh temperate vegetables, such as asparagus, sweet peas and shiitake, oyster and abalone mushrooms, all of which grow on the slopes of Mount Kinabalu.

Many of Sabah's peoples have a seagoing heritage, and this is reflected in the state's love for seafood. Restaurants worth tracking down include **Ocean Seafood Restaurant** (4 Lorong Api-Api), an *attap*-roofed structure overlooking the sea, which bills itself as a 'seafood village'. Inside, crustaceans and fish eye you from dozens of tanks – just so you know how fresh your dinner will be. Otherwise try **Port View Restaurant** (1st Floor, Lot 16, Jalana Haji Saman) or **Kampung Nelayan Floating Seafood Market Restaurant** (Taman Tun Fuad, Bukit Padang), which sits in the middle of a pond in the botanical gardens.

For Chinese food, a good mid-range choice is **Canton House** (70 Jalan Gaya), which serves delicious crispy duck. There is a large menu of rich Nyonya specialities at the **Rasa Nyonya Restaurant** (50 Jalan Gaya). If noodles are your thing, try the **Tenom Laksa and Noodle House** (Lot 72, Block I, Ground Floor, Lintas Square).

All about town are inconspicuous coffee shops, which are often the best places to sample local Sabahan cuisine, as well as staple rice and noodle dishes. After 5pm every day **Sedco Square** (Jalan Kampung Air) transforms into a lively hawker centre and is one of the best places to taste local dishes. A good place for a cheap lunch is the food centre inside the **Wisma Merdeka** building, which offers a wide choice throughout the day.

Borneo's only Spanish restaurant can also be found in Kota Kinabalu: **Olé** (Lintas Plaza, near the State Museum) is as authentic as it gets with paella, gazpacho, tapas, lamb shank, stuffed quail and sangria all featuring on the menu. The other place in town for Mediterranean cuisine is **Little Italy** (Ground Floor, Hotel Capital). It is run by an Italian family who claim to import most of their ingredients from Italy.

Two markets dominate the waterfront. Fishermen unload their daily catch behind **Central Market**, where piles of fruit, vegetables, fish and game exchange hands throughout the day. Close by is the **Filipino Market**, where hundreds of cramped stalls, run mainly by Filipinos, sell handicrafts from both Sabah and the Philippines – everything from baskets to wall hangings and cheap, cultured pearls.

Though tourist attractions in Kota Kinabalu itself are few and far between, the **Sabah Museum** (*Jalan Muzium,* ***t*** *088 253 199; open Sat–Thurs 9–5, adm RM5*) is certainly worth a visit. It is situated just south of the centre, not far from the ornate State Mosque. The unusual concrete building in which the collection is housed was inspired (so they say) by the design of the traditional Rungus longhouse. The museum attempts to replicate the success of the Sarawak Museum and the Cultural Village at Santubong. A number of galleries showcase the ethnography and natural history of the region, with a decent collection of ceramics, costumes and photographs – and a few human skulls too, swiped from the shoulders of their owners in the days before colonial influence. Outside in the Heritage Village are reconstructions of the traditional dwellings of the people of Sabah, set within a botanical garden.

Further south still is a tiny peninsula known as Tanjung Aru, dominated by a large beach resort. The Tanjung Aru station is the start of the line for the **North Borneo Railway** (***t*** *088 263 933, www.northborneorailway.com.my; departures 10am Wed and Sat; fare RM180, including 'tiffin' lunch.*), built originally for the transportation of goods from the interior to the harbour at Jesselton. For local people, the line remains the only means of transport to remote villages on the route to Tenom. For the pleasure of tourists (no one else would pay the exorbitant fee), the Sutera Harbour Resort operates a restored Vulcan steam engine, which, every Wednesday and Saturday, chugs through villages, paddy fields, rubber plantations and mangrove swamps between Tanjung Aru and **Papar**. It is a leisurely and picturesque journey that includes a stop at the Kinarut Tien Shi Buddhist Temple and time to wander about the market at Papar. Lunch is served in tin 'tiffin carriers' at carefully laid tables in true colonial style.

The **Kota Kinabalu Bird Sanctuary** (*off Jalan Buki Bendara, Likas,* ***t*** *088 246 955; open Tues–Sun 8–6; adm RM10*), just to the north of the city centre in Likas, is becoming increasingly popular with visitors. This 24-hectare patch of mangrove forest is an important feeding ground for many migratory birds, as well as resident species (sandpipers, plovers, redshanks, purple herons, kingfishers and green pigeons all frequent the sanctuary). All over the place, crabs and mudskippers side-step and sloop about in the mud. A boardwalk winds through the mangroves via a hide.

In the region of **Likas Bay** two swanky buildings provide stark contrast to the bedraggled stilt villages which dominate the outskirts. The cylindrical, glass-fronted **Sabah Foundation Building** stands alone and thirty storeys high on the north lip of the bay. It is one of only four buildings in the world to be supported by high-tensile steel rods which run through the centre of the building. Architects liken the structure to that of a tree, with each floor 'dangling' off a central support. The upper floors of the building house the offices of the Chief Minister.

At the opposite end of the bay stands the beautiful **Likas Mosque**, with its ornate sky-blue dome and four minarets, the whole ensemble rising dreamily out of a moat. Between the two buildings clusters of impoverished stilt villages inhabit patches of stagnant land. Before the state government embarked on its project of large-scale land reclamation, these were attractive water villages that reached out into the bay.

West Coast Islands

As diving destinations, the islands off Sabah's west coast do not compare to those in the Celebes Sea – with the exception perhaps of Layang-Layang. But as examples of tropical islands they all fare well – endowed as they are with powdery white sand lapped by clear blue water. Those islands nearest to KK (forming the Tunku Abdul Rahman National Park) are often overrun at weekends, while the Pulau Tiga National Park is rarely visited by tourists and has been set aside primarily for marine research. Pulau Labuan, officially an 'International Offshore Financial Centre', is something of an anomaly within the Malaysian Federation, with close links to Brunei.

Pulau Layang-Layang, one of the disputed Spratly Islands, lies almost 300km north of Kota Kinabalu and is fast gaining a reputation among divers. Not so long ago Layang-Layang was no more than a submerged coral atoll. The artificial island built in its midst is now home to a dive resort, a Malaysian army base and a huge nesting colony for migratory birds, including brown-footed boobies, crested terns and swallows (*layang* is Malay for swallow). For the purposes of diving, visibility is as good as it gets in the surrounding waters (up to 60m), and the atoll has earned the no-nonsense nickname 'Big Fish' for the amount of pelagic species typically encountered at its wall dives. A huge lagoon, 20m deep provides great opportunities for macro-diving, while right round the edge of the atoll – which measures 7km by 2km – is a sheer wall that drops 2,000m to the ocean bed. Manta rays, turtles, hammerhead sharks, leopard sharks and the odd silvertip shark reward those partial to big fish. For information and reservations contact the Layang-Layang Island Resort (KL office: 12 Jalan Yap Kwan Seng, Kuala Lumpur, **t** 03 2162 2877, **f** 03 2162 2980, *layang@po.jaring.my*, *www.layanglayang.com*).

Tunku Abdul Rahman National Park

After a few hours pounding the streets of KK, dry-mouthed and weary, the sight of a scattering of beach-rimmed islands across the water is enough to send most visitors scurrying in the direction of the ferry terminal. The five small islands that form the Tunku Abdul Rahman National Park remain remarkably unspoilt, considering their proximity to KK: speedboats make the 10-20 minute journey throughout the day and visitor numbers are high, particularly at weekends. For many the TAR experience is the primary reason for stopping by at the state capital. However, illegal dynamite fishing has laid waste to much of the coral that surrounds the islands and serious divers are likely to be somewhat disappointed. Whale sharks frequent the islands from November to January, when accumulations of plankton attract clouds of krill.

Getting There

Speedboat ferries to the all of the islands in the TAR National Park leave on demand throughout the day from the main ferry terminal at the northern end of Jalan Pantai. Numerous operators run ferries, so hunt around for the best deal and remember to organize a pick-up time for the return journey.

Where to Stay

Expensive–Moderate

Gayana Island Eco-Resort, Pulau Gaya, **t** 088 245 158, **f** 088 264 460, *info@gayana-resort.com*, *www.gayana-resort.com*. The resort comprises 22 comfortable *attap*-roofed chalets which are linked by walkways and extend over the water on stilts. The water below is shallow and clear, the sea bed littered with sea cucumbers and starfish. The restaurant serves sumptuous seafood feasts. Attached to the resort is a reef rehabilitation centre with a coral and giant clam nursery, along with a small exhibition.

Manukan Island Resort, Pulau Manukan, c/o Sutera Harbour, **t** 088 318 888, **f** 088 317 777, *www.suterasanctuarylodges.com.my*. At present a number of timber chalets offer units with communal sitting rooms, shared bathrooms and air-con, though plans are afoot to further develop the resort. The chalets offer plenty of room and come with small balconies. Other facilities include a swimming pool and badminton courts. Particularly popular with locals.

The largest of the islands is **Pulau Gaya**, which holds a prominent place in the history of the state. In the days before Jesselton (now KK) came into being, the island served as the west-coast headquarters of the British North Borneo Company. The administrators lived an uneasy existence alongside a Bajau water village, and it wasn't long before Mat Salleh and his Bajau followers torched the Company settlement. That was 1897 and – aside from the appearance of a resort – the island has changed little since, with the water village still huddled about a promontory. The interior of the island is cloaked in jungle and mangrove forest, accessible via a network of trails. Attached to the resort (*see* above) is a coral reef rehabilitation centre with a small exhibition.

Just off the western corner of Gaya is tiny **Pulau Sapi**, an islet popular with picnickers. If you can beat the crowds, it is easy to appreciate the popularity of the main beach where wide stretches of sand are shaded by casuarinas. The shallow channel that separates the two islands makes an excellent spot for a lazy swim, and there are changing facilities and a café for freshening up afterwards.

Boomerang-shaped **Pulau Manukan** is home to park headquarters and is the most developed of the islands after Gaya, with a large resort and 'jogging' trails leading into the forested interior. Like all of the islands, it is ringed by beautiful beaches. Just south of Manukan are the least-visited islands, **Pulau Mamutik** and **Pulau Sulug**, both of which offer some of the park's best snorkelling sites.

Pulau Tiga National Park

Pulau Tiga means 'island of three', though years of erosion have worn down Pulau Kalampunian Besar to no more than a sand spit, while Pulau Kalampunian Damit (also known as Pulau Ular, or 'snake island') is an isolated rock ruled by a seething mass of sea snakes.

Getting There

Reaching the islands requires a 90min car ride from KK to Kuala Penyu on the Klias peninsula, followed by a 30min boat journey. Transfers can be organized by the Pulau Tiga Resort (*see* below).

Where to Stay

Expensive

Pulau Tiga Resort, c/o 11th Floor, Wisma Merdeka, Jalan Tun Razak, KK, **t** 088 240 584, **f** 088 240 415, *pultiga@tm.net.my*, *www.pulau-tiga.com*. The resort offers 'humble but comfortable' chalet accommodation, built for minimal impact on the surrounding forest. Deluxe chalets have air-con, fridge and hot water, while standard chalets are fan-only. A decent range of food is provided by the Pulau Tiga Restaurant, which nestles among the giant banyan trees. The resort also has diving facilities. A two-day/one-night package ex-KK, including transfers, meals and park entrance, costs approximately RM300/person.

Pulau Tiga itself is the largest in the group. Like its neighbours, it too is in constant flux due to volcanic activity. On a geological timescale, these islands are relative newborns, formed by the expulsion of sediment from a 'mud volcano'. In various places about the island, thick mud still oozes from geothermal vents.

Pulau Tiga was gazetted as a national park in 1985, both for its unusual geological features and for its wildlife. The islands are home to rare proboscis monkeys and megapodes, unusual ground-dwelling birds that nest exclusively on volcanic islands, burying their eggs in ash or decomposing vegetation or sun-warmed sand. A megapode looks somewhat like a chicken and mews like a cat. **Pulau Kalampunian Damit** is home to the park's other wildlife oddity, the yellow-lipped sea krait. This is the world's largest sea snake, with venom twice as potent as that of the king cobra. These yellow-and-black-banded snakes are amphibious, feeding on eels and returning to land to digest food, slough their skin, mate and lay eggs.

The national park was set aside largely for the purposes of scientific research and, until 2000, was rarely visited by tourists. Then came reality TV series 'Survivor', which used Pulau Tiga as its desert-island location. On the back of new-found publicity, a chalet complex has been built and tourist numbers are on the rise, not least for the novelty factor that the island served as a TV set. Props from the series have been salvaged for the delectation of visiting fans.

Several miles of hiking trails loop about the island, providing access to numerous secluded beaches. One trail leads to a 'mini mud volcano', where, like the Survivor contestants, you too can indulge in a natural mud bath. Guided boat tours to Snake Island can also be arranged; on any given day several hundred sea kraits are likely to be coiled beneath the sun, fat on eels.

Pulau Labuan

Pulau Labuan is a strange place. Lumped together with Sabah when the Federation of Malaysia was created in 1963, it is now a duty-free island under the direct governance of Kuala Lumpur. It has a largely Bruneian Malay population (Labuan guards the Brunei Bay), closely followed in numbers by the Kedayan, a tribe that

Getting There

There are regular flights to Pulau Labuan from KL, KK, Kuching, Miri and Bandar Seri Begawan. Express ferries also link Labuan to Brunei, Limbang and KK.

Tourist Information

Tourism Malaysia (corner of Jalan Dewan and Jalan Berjaya, **t** 087 423 455) provide good brochures and maps. The tourism authority's website is a decent source of information too (*www.labuantourism.com.my*).

Where to Stay

Expensive

Sheraton Labuan, Jalan Merdeka, **t** 087 422 000, **f** 087 422 222, *www.sheraton.com/labuan*. Labuan's most expensive international-class hotel, situated in the business district and overlooking the harbour. The whole hotel is done out in opulent décor to match the 5-star facilites, which include a pool with swim-up bar and good European and Chinese restaurants.

The Waterfront, Jalan Wawasan, **t** 087 418 111, **f** 087 413 468. Another 5-star hotel with good rates and an obscenely large palm-fringed pool. The hotel manages the marina, with berths of its own and yachts to charter for luxury cruises about the South China Sea.

Manikar Beach Resort, Jalan Bunga Mawar, **t** 087 418 700, **f** 087 418 740. Labuan's only beach resort situated at the island's northern tip. A free-form pool runs down to a cleaned, raked beach, while rooms offer plenty of space and paved balconies overlooking 15 acres of gardens.

Moderate

Mariner Hotel, Jalan Tg. Purun, **t** 087 418 822, **f** 087 418 811. Offers good-value rooms north of the *padang*. Mini-bar, air-con and hot water in all of the rooms, with a coffeeshop and frequent promotional discounts.

Hotel Global, Jalan O.K.K. Awang Besar, **t** 087 425 201, **f** 087 425 180. In very good order with all the expected 3-star facilities. Towards the west end of town.

Inexpensive

Victoria Hotel, Jalan Tun Mustapha, **t** 087 412 411, **f** 087 412 550. One of Labuan's long-standing low-end hotels, with modest rooms that come with air-con and hot water.

Federal Hotel, Jalan Bunga Kasuma, **t** 087 411 711, **f** 087 411 337. All rooms have air-con, TV, phone mini-bar, tea/coffee-making facilities, though rooms are small and a little lustreless.

Eating Out

Hawkers set up stall along Jalan Muhibbah during the evenings, providing a wide range of cheap meals and snacks. The town centre is scattered with Chinese coffee shops, *mamak* stalls (Muslim Indian) and the odd South Indian restaurant. Seafood is Labuan's speciality, with **Portview Restaurant** (Jalan Merdeka) and **Mawilla II** (Jalan Tanjung Purun) leading the way, alongside the upmarket hotel restaurants. The **Emperor Restaurant** in the Sheraton Labuan is the place to go for top-class Chinese cuisine, while the Sheraton's **Victoria Brasserie** is recognized as one of the best for European cuisine. **Bunga Mas Restaurant** at the Manikar Beach Resort offers the widest choice of cuisines, with seating inside and out.

claims Javan origins. It sells itself as a haven for shoppers, tourists and banks, and has several high-rise, steel-clad buildings to match the image.

But the Labuan economy never really took off in the way the government had hoped. The island remains the pressure valve on prohibition-bound Brunei, with liquor stores and brothels doing all the good business. Despite a remarkably colourful history, and the enthusiasm of Labuan's tourism authority, there is limited appeal for the casual visitor, unless wreck dives are on your agenda.

Labuan has been a place of strategic importance throughout its history. The British East India Company rushed to its shores in 1846, when they discovered that the island concealed coal deposits. They managed to prise Labuan from the hands of the Sultan of Brunei and set up a fuel station for British steamships. The fledgling settlement was named Victoria. After British North Borneo was demarcated in 1878, Labuan slipped into the backwaters, coming to prominence only during World War Two, when it served as the headquarters of the Japanese occupation.

Unfortunately, Labuan has little to show for its colonial past. A tall red-brick structure known as The Chimney is one of the few remaining colonial buildings. For years it was thought that it served as some sort of chimney for the coal industry, but in recent years archaeologists have ruled that out by pointing to the lack of soot deposits. Some now believe it was a ventilation shaft, others that it was some sort of shipping beacon.

Other tourist attractions include a small bird park, with a collection of Bornean species cooped up in a series of domed cages, and the landscaped gardens of Peace Park, memorial to the losses of the war. The Financial Park Complex stands as the symbol of modern Labuan, a futuristic steel and glass structure stacked full of shopping arcades and offices. Of more interest is the water village of **Kampung Patau-Patau**: inhabited by Bruneian Malays, it predates anything else on the island.

A group of islets to the south of the main island form the **Labuan Marine Park**, where fishing and anchoring are banned in attempts to protect the coral. A few of the islands offer secluded beaches and good snorkelling. Four wrecks in the waters around Labuan – two of them from the war – make Labuan one of Asia's leading wreck-dive destinations.

South of Kota Kinabalu

The southwest region of Sabah, though little visited by tourists, has a surprising amount to offer, from the mountain valleys farmed by the Kadazan and Murut people to the fireflies and proboscis monkeys of the Klias Wetlands and the white-water rapids of Sungei Padas. Though limited and basic accommodation is available, all of the following destinations can be visited on lengthy day trips from Kota Kinabalu.

Just south of Kota Kinabalu the coastal highway forks to climb the Crocker Mountain Range and descend into the valley of Sungei Pegalan and the Kadazan heartland around Tambunan. En route to Tambunan, and easily accessible from KK, is the **Monsopiad Village** (*open daily 9–6; adm RM25; for information contact Borneo Legend, Myths & Tours,* ***t*** *088 761 336, www.monsopiad.com*), a living museum run by the descendants of legendary warrior Monsopiad himself. The museum consists of a reproduction of a traditional Kadazan village, set on the banks of the Sungei Moyong, with cultural performances held in the main hall. A 'house of skulls' displays what are supposed to be the grisly trophies of Monsopiad, who is best known for his success at swiping enemy heads. As well as the main hall, there is a rice granary and Monsopiad

House itself, which contains handicraft, medicine and cookery displays. A restaurant serves up traditional Kadazan dishes.

From the turning for Monsopiad Village, the main road passes through the Christian township of Donggongon, before climbing into the Crocker Range and crossing the Sinsuran Pass (1,649m), beyond which lies the **Rafflesia Forest Reserve** (***t*** *087 774 691; open daily 8–5, closed for lunch; adm free*). Trails lead into the forest where Rafflesia plants bloom year-round, and a small but thorough exhibition provides information about this the world's largest flower (*see* p.325 under 'Gunung Gading' for more on the Rafflesia). Bear in mind that each flower blooms for only five days of the year, so sightings cannot be guaranteed. The Rafflesia Forest Reserve is part of the larger Crocker Range National Park, which, at the time of writing, has no visitor facilities.

Until the British built a railway line as far as Tenom (*see* below), the Crocker Range provided a natural boundary between the coastal people and those of the interior. Beyond the mountains lies the fertile valley of Sungei Pegalan, heartland of the Kadazan who, a few centuries back, gave up their hunter-gatherer lifestyle to become settled agriculturalists. **Tambunan** is the valley's first settlement, a small unprepossessing town surrounded by a plain of paddy fields and bamboo stands. It was here that folk hero Mat Salleh met his death at the hands of the British in 1900. Just outside town, in the middle of a paddy field, is a small concrete memorial, built on the site of the rebel's besieged fort.

Some way downriver from Tambunan is **Keningau**, capital of Sabah's old Interior Division. Today it serves mainly as a logging centre and a meeting place for the Kadazan and Murut peoples of the interior. The main road continues south as far as **Tenom**, heartland of the Murut, and end of the line for the North Borneo Railway, which cuts back across the mountains to the coast. The town itself is predominantly Chinese. The majority of the Murut live in surrounding villages and longhouses, where they tend orchards (Tenom is said to produce the best durians in Sabah) and farm soya, tobacco, hill paddy and cocoa. Murut festivities traditionally centre around the *lansaran*, a wooden platform with bamboo 'springs' that serves as a kind of antiquated bouncy castle on which up to forty people at a time can dance. A good example of a *lansaran* survives in Kampung Kemabong, around 20km south of Tenom.

The railway line from Tenom follows the course of the fast-flowing Sungei Padas as far as **Beaufort**, a sleepy town named after one of the governors of the North Borneo Company. It sits on the flood plain of the river and many of its shophouses are raised from the ground on stilts or concrete plinths. Between Tenom and Beaufort lies the **Padas Gorge**, where the Sungei Padas becomes a torrent of white water. A number of KK-based tour operators run rafting and kayaking trips through the gorge.

Eventually the Sungei Padas winds its way into a swampy delta west of Beaufort known as the **Klias Wetlands**, a mangrove reserve rich in wildlife. Riverboat safaris into the swamps from Kota Klias offer the chance of spotting proboscis monkeys, silver langurs and, after dark, fireflies – though the wildlife experience cannot be compared to that at Sukau in east Sabah.

North of Kota Kinabalu

The coastal road stretches north from Kota Kinabalu as far as Kudat, near the northernmost tip of Borneo, a corner of Sabah lately reconceived by the authorities as a tourist destination (the current chief minister hails from these parts). The area is home to the Rungus people, many of whom still live in longhouses. Their comely traditional dress – for women, body-hugging black skirts and black strapless bodices, beads and brass jewellery; for men, handwoven shirts with geometric motifs, cummerbunds, baggy trousers and colourful headdresses – has been hijacked by Sabah Tourism as the state costume (for the purposes of brochures, at any rate).

En route to Kudat, the coastal road passes the Mengkabong Water Village and the Kota Belud Tamu (weekly open market), two places commonly visited on day trips from Kota Kinabalu. The Bajau Laut, known in the West as 'sea gypsies', inhabit water villages right around Sabah's coast, though most commute inland to earn a living (in the past it was said of the Bajau Laut that they only stepped on dry land to bury their dead). **Mengkabong**, which stretches out across the estuary near the market town of Tuaran, has been adopted by tour operators as a show village. To get a more authentic picture of a traditional Bajau water village, head through the swampland and paddy fields north of Tuaran to Kampung Surusop, from where it is possible to catch a boat to **Kampung Penambawan**. Little has changed over the decades at Penambawan; each day *ikan bilis* is laid out to dry on the boardwalks, while many of the stilted houses still sport *attap* roofs.

Sabah's best known *tamu* is held every Sunday in a rural setting just outside the town of **Kota Belud**, a Bajau stronghold renowned for its horse breeders. This open-air market goes back many centuries, and still serves its function as a meeting place for local Bajau, Kadazan and Irranun. Goods and gossip are exchanged, local cuisines sampled and, from the direction of a small bandstand, music drifts across the whole colourful scene. Items for sale range from embroidered cloth, sarongs and jeans to herbal medicines, blowpipes, rattan baskets and electrical goods. Handicrafts go for a fraction of the price they are sold for in Kota Kinabalu. In an adjacent field, horse and buffalo traders parade their goods.

In May or June each year the *tamu besar* is held, Borneo's largest gathering of its kind, with festivities spread over three days. Bajau horsemen exhibit their skills dressed in embroidered shirts and colourful headdresses, their bare feet in brass stirrups; prize cocks are pitted against one another; buffaloes are raced; dances are staged; and rice wine is drunk freely.

From Kota Belud the road cuts north into the Kudat peninsula, with the sock-shaped bay of Teluk Marudu to the east. This is Rungus territory. There are more than 200 Rungus longhouses scattered about the peninsula, many of them built in the traditional way, with sloping, nipa-thatched roofs and bamboo flooring buffed smooth by the passage of bare feet over the years. Of the few that have consciously opened their doors to tourists, **Kampung Bavanggazo** provides overnight accommodation (a mattress and mosquito net) and the villagers will go out of their way to showcase their cultural heritage. Head off the beaten track, and the longhouse experience can be very different; with the spread of palm-oil plantations, many Runggus have been forced off their land, and poverty is a marked problem in the region.

Two other Rungus longhouse communities, **Kampung Gombizan** and **Kampung Sumangkap**, have opened their doors to tourists and are well worth a visit. Both have reinvented themselves on a 'one village, one trade' basis, with Gombizan exclusively producing honey, and Sumangkap manufacturing hand-beaten ceremonial gongs. The beekeepers of Gombizan use bellows to smoke bees from their hives, before collecting the sodden honeycomb. At Sumangkap the whole village resounds with hammer blows as various metal alloys are beaten into shape. The ceremonial gongs are sold on to other longhouses.

Kudat

Kudat itself sits in the mouth of Teluk Marudu, surrounded by coconut groves. It has a history of influence from Celebes (now Sulawesi) and the Philippines, with traders from both frequenting its markets. Kudat became the first capital of British North Borneo in 1881, but retained that status for only two years, after failing to develop as a commercial centre – either because of hostility from the nearby Spanish, who controlled the Philippines, or because of the constant threat from pirates (the sheltered coves of Teluk Marudu served for centuries as a stronghold for Bajau and Irranun marauders).

Today Kudat is a quiet place – deadly quiet at times, despite the chief minister's efforts to unveil the town as a tourist destination. The new Kudat Esplanade provides a wide and pleasant promenade for evening strolls, though with the lack of crowds it can have the feel of an empty parking lot. Nevertheless Kudat is a friendly and amenable place (the Rungus are renowned for being good-natured and hospitable), and the fish market is the cheapest in Sabah. Bobbing in the water in front of the Esplanade are a handful of fish farms, their net tanks linked by precarious

Getting There

There are flights from KK to Kudat on Monday, Wednesday and Saturday. Regular buses and minibuses ply the route between KK and Kudat, though the nearer you get to Kudat, the less frequent are the bus services. To be able to explore the area freely it is necessary to have your own transport or to visit as part of an organized tour.

Where to Stay

Two of Sabah's best hotels, the Nexus Karambunai Resort and the Rasa Ria Resort, both run free shuttle services to and from the state capital and are therefore listed under the KK listings (despite being nearer to Tuaran).

Moderate

Kudat Golf & Marina Resort, Kudat, **t** 088 611 211, **f** 088 611 311, *kgmr@po.jaring.my*, *www.kudatgolfmarinaresort.com*. Offers a number of sterile though functional rooms, a decent enough restaurant, a small pool, a little-used marina and a basic golf course. Though somewhat uninspiring, this is the only accommodation in Kudat itself, bar a few budget rooms in the town centre.

boardwalks. Ask the proprietors and they will be glad to let you look into the nets or feed the fish (sharks, red snappers, lobsters and more).

Kinabalu National Park

Sabah's topography is dominated by Gunung Kinabalu (4,101m), a lone giant which stands head and shoulders above the rest of the Crocker Range. It is the tallest mountain between New Guinea and the Himalayas, its summit an unearthly massif of granite that has been pushed through the sandstone of the Crocker Range within the last million years – a fact that makes Kinabalu the world's youngest non-volcanic mountain. The last ice age carved a smooth plateau into the barren rock near the summit, leaving only the jagged peaks that look so foreboding in profile. Until recent times Sabah's indigenous population kept well clear of the mountain as a mark of respect to the spirits of the dead, who were thought to populate the mist-shrouded summit.

The Kinabalu National Park was declared a World Heritage Site in 2000, in recognition of the park's remarkable variety of flora. Locals claim that the mountain, and its forested slopes, form the most biodiverse patch on the planet. And they certainly have a case for their claims; the park's biodiversity spans the familiar giants of the lowland dipterocarp forest, through the oaks and chestnuts that dominate the montane forest, to the higher conifer and rhododendron forests. Above the tree line, plants more commonly associated with alpine meadows, such as buttercups, eke out an existence alongside necklace orchids – natural garlands made up of delicate, white flowers. Many species are unique to Kinabalu. And not just plant species; the Kinabalu friendly warbler (so named because of its habit of hopping about in front of Kinabalu's first climbers) and the Kinabalu mountain blackbird are found only on these slopes. Virtually all of Borneo's animal species live within the boundaries of the park, though the summit trail is so well trodden that they are rarely spotted by climbers.

Sir Hugh Low, a colonial administrator on Pulau Labuan, was the first to climb Kinabalu. The year was 1851 and he managed to recruit a team of 42 Kadazan porters, against their better judgement. At first they refused, believing the summit to be out of bounds to the living: the name Kinabalu is derived from *aki nabalu*, Kadazan for 'mountain of the dead'. After much negotiation, they agreed to climb the mountain on the condition that they be allowed to appease the spirits by making a sacrifice. A white cockerel was promptly slaughtered and, along with seven eggs, offered up in a ceremony officiated by a *bobohizan*, a Kadazan high priestess.

The rituals may have kept the spirits at bay, but they didn't grant Low passage to the summit itself, now called Low's Peak in spite of the failed attempt. Botanist John Whitehead was the first to reach the summit, in 1888.

Today Kadazan guides and porters move up and down the mountain on a daily basis, and the ritual sacrifice has become an annual event.

Getting There

Park headquarters is situated just off the KK–Sandakan highway, two hours beyond KK. Buses bound for Ranau leave KK's main bus station every other hour between 7am and 4pm, passing the entrance to Park Headquarters en route. Taxis charge RM15 per person for the journey (providing they can fill the car).

Information

Visitors who plan to head up the Summit Trail need to register at park headquarters before making the ascent. A permit fee of RM50 is charged per person. Those aiming to climb beyond Laban Rata are obliged to hire a registered guide (if you only go as far as Laban Rata you can climb independently). Guides charge approximately RM60 for the round trip (payable by the whole group of up to six). Guides and porters must be booked in advance through the Sabah Parks Head Office, Lot 3, Block K, Sinsuran Complex, Kota Kinabalu, **t** 088 212 719, **f** 088 221 001, *info@sabahparks.org.my*, *www.sabahparks.org.my*.

Attached to the park headquarters office is a shop stocked with a good range of books about the national park. Maps are available for free, as are slide shows held once daily (check with the authorities for times).

Where to Stay

All accommodation within Kinabalu National Park is managed by Sutera Harbour.

Expensive–Inexpensive

Kinabalu Park Accommodation, **t** 088 889 086, **f** 088 889 091, *info@suterasanctuarylodges.com*, *www.suterasanctuarylodges.com*. Spread around park headquarters are ten separate hostels and lodges offering varying degrees of comfort, from dormitory bunks to suites

Summit Trail

The very least that climbers deserve for their efforts is that moment of epiphany, when they stand astride Low's Peak with the world laid out at their feet and views as far as the Philippines. Kinabalu, however, spends much of the day lost in thick cloud – the presence or absence of which can make the difference between a day of unrewarded pain and the experience of a lifetime.

For this reason most climbers aim to reach the summit at sunrise, when the mountain is most likely to be free of cloud (on an average day the clouds appear at around 10am). Typically, day one is spent climbing to the base camp at Laban Rata. Day two begins at around 3am with the final climb to the summit, before the descent back down to park headquarters. The climb requires no special skills, though those without a moderate level of fitness are likely to suffer. A second night at Laban Rata makes things much easier on the limbs, and the slower pace will help prevent altitude sickness.

The Summit Trail begins at Timpohon Gate, 4km from Park Headquarters, at an altitude of around 1,500m. A board lists record times for the ascent: the fastest have made it to the summit and back in well under three hours. Each year, the Kinabalu Climbathon brings athletes from round the world to compete on the slopes of the mountain. Having completed the climb yourself, it's enough to make you look upon athletes with reverence ever after.

An endless staircase of gnarled roots leads climbers towards the first shelter, after which point the cloud forest begins, a world of twisted trunks, orchids, mosses and with king-size beds, fireplaces, kitchens and sitting rooms. Bookings should be made well in advance if visiting during peak season or at weekends.

Mesilau Nature Resort, **t** 018 281 3733, **f** 018 281 0977, *info@suterasanctuarylodges.com*, *www.suterasanctuarylodges.com*. Situated at an elevation of 2,000m among montane forest on the eastern flank of Kinabalu with views of the dramatic east ridge (a sight that makes the mountain look both inhospitable and inaccessible). There is a resthouse with around 100 beds, which go for RM30 each per night, along with eight separate and spacious lodges, each with either two or three bedrooms, bathroom, a kitchen and lounge. The resort has its own restaurant built over a mountain stream. The Mesilau Trail, which begins near the resort, links up with the Summit Trail.

Poring Hot Spring & Nature Reserve, **t/f** 088 878 801, *info@suterasanctuarylodges.com*, *www.suterasanctuarylodges.com*. Like elsewhere in the park, there is a wide range of accommodation on offer at Poring Hot Springs, from plots in the campsite, to basic hostel accommodation and private lodges.

Inexpensive

Laban Rata, **t** 018 281 4907, **f** 018 281 8239, *info@suterasanctuarylodges.com*, *www.suterasanctuarylodges.com*. The Laban Rata Resthouse and five separate huts provide accommodation for climbers right on the tree line of Gunung Kinabalu (all building materials were carried by porters along the Summit Trail). Beds get booked up fast, so book in advance. A room in the resthouse is infinitely preferable to a bed in one of the huts, none of which have heating or hot water. The resthouse has both – a real comfort when night-time temperatures push freezing. Sleeping bags are provided. The restaurant serves decent buffet food, drinks and snacks. Sunrise from the verandah is breathtaking.

ferns. *Nepenthes lowii*, or Low's pitcher plants, begin to appear after the second shelter. The nourishment that the peculiar pitcher plant gains from its diet of insects enables it to live off very poor soils. Kinabalu Park is home to the the Rajah Brooke pitcher plant, largest of the species. British Consul-General Spencer St John, who accompanied Sir Hugh Low on a second expedition up the mountain in 1858, claimed to have found one containing four litres of water and a drowned rat.

Bamboos begin to appear above the third shelter, where Kinabalu friendly warblers often flit about the trail. At the fourth shelter, where wild raspberries grow in profusion, the vegetation changes abruptly, with more visible rock and stunted trees such as the tea tree. Rhododendrons also proliferate, each species blooming at different times of year, their trunks bleached and windswept as if frozen in mid-action.

At the Paka Shelter, the sixth, a half-hour trail leads to a rock overhang known as the Paka Cave and famous as the place where Hugh Low and Spenser St John camped out before the final push to the summit. Today's base camp is situated a little higher at Laban Rata, where a resthouse and a scattering of mountain huts cling on to the steep rock face which marks the tree line. Laban Rata is a corruption of a Kadazan word meaning 'place of sacrifice', for it was here that the first climbers stopped to sacrifice their cockerel and seven eggs.

Above Laban Rata, the going gets tougher, with stretches of rope deployed to help climbers up the steeper slabs of granite. Eventually, the vegetation dies out completely, leaving nothing but vast fields of granite scooped smooth by ancient glaciers. At 3,800m, at the very limit of the vegetation line, is the last shelter, known as the Sayat-Sayat Hut after the shrubby tea tree. From here climbers ascend onto the granite massif proper, with dramatic peaks looming on all sides, St John's Peak and South Peak on the left, and the Donkey's Ears and the Ugly Sisters on the right (named, by the sounds of it, during a bout of altitude sickness). The summit itself, Low's peak, is not visible until the last section of the climb. The air up here is very thin, forcing climbers to slow the pace, while up on the exposed rock it can get very cold, with ice sometimes forming in pools. The summit itself is a scramble up a jumble of rocks to a narrow point, able to hold only a handful of people. To the west are views across the lowland plain and out over the South China Sea 50km away; to the northeast the rock face plunges down a full mile into Low's Gully, a treacherous and virtually inaccessible place that has claimed many lives over the years, and that was reached for the first time as recently as 1998.

Equipment

For most of the climb you'll be sweating in the heat, but at nearly 14,000ft, it can get very cold on the summit, with night-time temperatures often dropping below freezing. Gloves, hat, warm layers, waterproofs and high-energy food (chocolate, nuts, biscuits, glucose sweets) are essential. A supply of paracetamol is also a godsend for treating pounding, altitude-induced headaches. Be sure to wear comfortable shoes too – a good pair of trainers should be fine.

Fresh water is available at each of the mountain shelters, so there is no need to weigh yourself down with bottles. Bring enough for the final ascent to the summit from the Sayat-Sayat Hut. One litre should do. Other essential supplies include a torch with spare batteries (for the night-time ascent to the summit), high-factor suntan lotion and toilet paper. Sleeping bags are provided at the resthouse at Laban Rata. If you can't face carrying the supplies yourself, porters can be hired at park headquarters (they charge around RM6-10 per kilo).

Elsewhere in Kinabalu National Park

The main trail from Timpohon Gate is not the only route to the summit of Kinabalu. The Mesilau Trail begins 18km east of Park Headquarters, near the Mesilau Nature Resort (*see* p.375), meeting the Summit Trail at Layang-Layang (below the fifth shelter). It is a longer route, but is much quieter and provides a better introduction to the flora of the Kinabalu National Park. The trail scales two ridges before emerging into cloud forest, where the lucky few may spot Rajah Brooke pitcher plants, largest of the species.

The beautiful montane forest around park headquarters itself is laced with trails often overlooked by those who climb the mountain. The park office provides detailed maps that enable visitors to trek unaided; otherwise there is a free guided tour which sets off each morning at eleven o'clock. Just behind the main park headquarters building is the five-acre Mountain Garden, which showcases a range of trees and plants from across the park.

Many visitors pencil in a trip to **Poring Hot Springs** for the morning after the climb. These natural sulphur springs are included in the Kinabalu National Park, though they lie just east of the traditional park boundary. They are one of the rosier legacies of the Japanese occupation. The steaming water is piped into a series of tiled baths with cubicles large enough for two. A cool pool is provided as well, while deluxe cabins offer a lounge area, a jacuzzi, and privacy. The baths are set in a complex that includes a canopy walkway, a small butterfly farm and trails that lead to two waterfalls. The walkway passes between a series of towering *menggaris* trees and hangs 41m above the leaf litter, offering a monkey's-eye view of the rainforest. *Poring* is Kadazan for 'bamboo': the surrounding forest contains some magnificent stands of this giant grass, which can attain heights of up to 40m.

Around Gunung Kinabalu

The temperate flanks of Gunung Kinabalu are fully exploited by local market gardeners, who gather at market stalls along the KK–Sandakan highway to sell their fresh vegetables in the shadow of the mountain. The 'exotic' offerings include cabbage, cauliflower, broccoli, tomatoes and asparagus.

Nearby **Ranau** hosts a large *tamu* on Thursdays, described by locals as one of the major supermarkets of the interior. Ranau is better known as the final stop on the 'Death March' from Sandakan during World War Two, on which almost 2,500 POWs perished. A small memorial can be found behind the village of **Kundasang**, which is a hive of market-garden activity. For those wishing to pay their respects, the memorial at Sandakan provides a complete history of the event, with photos and quotes from the six survivors (*see* p.382).

East Sabah

Sandakan

Across Sabah's mountainous interior is the coastal town of Sandakan, which sits in the mouth of a shallow, island-studded bay, just 15 miles from the maritime border with the Philippines. After the devastation caused by Allied bombing raids during the war, the town holds little historical interest and isn't much to look at today – a fact which belies its prewar role as capital of North Borneo. For the casual visitor, Sandakan is no more than a staging post en route to some of Malaysia's premier wildlife destinations, namely Sepilok Orang-Utan Rehabilitation Centre, the Kinabatangan Wetlands, Turtle Islands National Park and the Danum Valley Conservation Area.

Sandakan's origins are immortalized in its name, which is Suluk for 'pawned place'. Back in the 1870s a Scottish adventurer called William Cowie was granted an island in the Sandakan bay by the Sultan of Sulu, in exchange for arms. After a destructive fire, the settlement was relocated to the site of the present-day water village Kampung

Getting There

There are eight daily flights from KK, and a less regular service from Tawau and Kudat. Express buses from KK (6hrs) drop their passengers at the terminal 3km out of town. Taxis from the terminal shouldn't cost more than RM6.

Information

Sandakan Tourist Information Centre, Wisma Warisan Building (beside the Sandakan Municipal Council), **t** 089 229 751. Newly opened with plenty of brochures and helpful staff.

Where to Stay

Moderate

Hotel Sandakan, 4th Avenue, **t** 089 221 122, **f** 089 221 100, *tengis@tm.net.my*. The town centre's only decent hotel, mainly patronized by visiting businessmen. Rooms are functional, if unexciting, with 3-star facilities. Good value with promotions. The main restaurant in the lobby serves decent buffet food, while upstairs there is a Japanese restaurant and a Chinese restaurant which serves dim sum, Cantonese and Szechuan cuisine.

Sabah Hotel, Km1 Jalan Utara, **t** 089 213 299, **f** 089 271 271, *www.sabahhotel.com.my*. Situated on the edge of town and surrounded by jungle, this is Sandakan's only 4-star hotel, complete with outdoor pool, fitness centre, tennis courts and four bars and restaurants. Some of the rooms are rather drably decorated.

Sanbay, Mile 1.5 Jalan Leila, **t** 089 275 000, **f** 089 275 575, *sanbay@po.jaring.my*, *www.sanbay.com.my*. A new 3-star hotel, also just outside town, with views of the bay and comfortable en suite rooms.

Moderate–Inexpensive

City View, Block 23, 3rd Avenue, **t** 089 271 122, **f** 089 273 155. Perhaps the best of the mid-range options, with spacious, bright and well-kept rooms, each with fridge and en suite facilities.

Hotel Ramai, Mile 1 Jalan Leila, **t** 089 273 222, **f** 089 273 231. Large, well-kept rooms with en suite facilities. Within walking distance of the town centre.

Inexpensive

Hotel Hung Wing, Block 13, 3rd Avenue, **t** 089 218 855, **f** 089 271 240. The best of a motley bunch. Some rooms have air-con, others are fan-only. All rooms are of a good size, clean and have attached shower cubicles.

Buli Sim Sim. Cowie named his new home Elopura (meaning 'beautiful city'), though the name that stuck was the less-than-glamourous Sandakan.

The settlement expanded and soon became the capital of British North Borneo, graced by a deep harbour, a sea bed rich in sea cucumbers and pearls, and a hinterland of unfelled timber and jungle produce. The resident Bajaus and Sulus stuck to the age-old professions of pearl diving, fishing and scouring the forests for camphor, beeswax and bird's nests, while the growing Chinese population grew fatter still on timber.

During World War Two, the Japanese established Sandakan's infamous POW camp, from where the Death March to Ranau was initiated. By 1946, when North Borneo became a British Crown colony, the town had been reduced to rubble and the colonial capital was moved to Jesselton (Kota Kinabalu). Sandakan was rebuilt along the same lines as KK – in regimental concrete – and soon regained its position as timber capital of North Borneo. By the 1970s locals claimed that their town had the country's greatest concentration of millionaires.

Eating Out

Restaurants are not so widespread in Sandakan as one might expect – though *kedai kopi*, serving cheap rice and noodle dishes, are not hard to come by. The food stalls in Central Market (or the more sanitized food stalls in Centre Point Plaza) are a good bet for cheap local food. The fish market in Sandakan is the largest in Sabah, and the seafood restaurants here stand out from the crowd. The food stalls and restaurants on Trig Hill, 2km outside town and with wonderful views over the bay, are some of the best places for a seafood dinner.

Expensive–Moderate

Palm Garden, Hotel Sandakan. A good Chinese restaurant in the centre of town. Serves delicious dim sum for breakfast and lunch, with a menu of Cantonese and Szechuan dishes for dinner.

XO Steakhouse, Hsiang Garden Estate, Jalan Leila. The leading 'Western' restaurant in Sandakan, with a good range of food, from grilled seafood to Australian steaks and a barbecue buffet.

Moderate

English Teahouse and Restaurant, 2002 Jalan Istana (next to the Agnes Keith House), **t** 089 222 544, **f** 089 222 545, *www.englishteahouse.org*. A delightful, if incongruous, teahouse perched on the hillside above Sandakan, with wide views across the bay. There is an immaculate croquet lawn, a tea garden, complete with pergola and wicker garden furniture, and waiters dressed in finery. All the while prewar music plays softly in the background. As well as scones and a range of teas served in bone china, there are other British staples such as fish and chips, bangers and mash, roast beef, and bread and butter pudding.

Supreme Garden Vegetarian Restaurant, Block 30, Bandar Ramai Ramai, Jalan Leila, **t** 089 213 292. The best vegetarian option in town, with steamboats and many familiar (though mock-meat) Chinese dishes.

Ocean King Seafood Restaurant, Batu 2.5, Jalan Batu Sapi, **t** 089 618 111. A well-known seafood restaurant outside town, built on stilts over the water.

Inexpensive

Restoran Habeeb II, Bandar Sibuga Jaya (opposite Hotel Sandakan). This is one of eight Habeeb restuarants in Sandakan, each serving good *mamak* (Indian Muslim) cuisine, from *roti canai* and *murtabak* to a range of curries.

Today, with much of the surrounding timber felled and exported, the millionaires have grown thin on the ground, while the cleared land has been planted with cocoa and that all-too-familiar monocrop, oil palm.

The Sights

Sandakan's historic heart is the adjoining water village of **Kampung Buli Sim Sim**, which predates the town itself. It was here that Scotsman Willie Cowie established his trading post in 1879. Visitors are welcome to stroll the *jambatan* (walkways) which reach out across the water, linking rows of stilted homes. One or two have opened their homes to visitors, with shells and other knick-nacks for sale. The water village forms the backdrop to the **Sandakan Town Mosque** a stark but eye-catching pyramidal building, with a long, pencil-thin minaret.

The waterfront **markets**, by far the most raucous in Sabah, form the focal point of the modern town centre. Wooden fishing boats line up at the quay having deposited their catch in the hour before dawn, while the fish market itself is a smorgasbord of culinary possibilities, from sharks and stargazers to sea cucumbers and sea horses.

The only remnants of Sandakan's colonial era are a church and a breezy colonial home, both on hills overlooking town. The Anglican church of **St Michael's and All Angels**, a pleasing, unornamented building of local granite, sits on a hill above the padang and dates back to 1893. Standing among the worn wooden pews, it is hard to imagine that outside lie the clear, warm waters of the Sulu Sea.

The **Agnes Keith House** stands at the top of Jalan Istana and serves today as a fine example of the colonial lifestyle. Agnes Keith, wife of Sandakan's 'Conservator of Forests', was a writer best known for her book *Three Came Home*, which tells of her ordeal in a Japanese prison camp (and was subsequently made into a film). She also wrote about Sabah in *Land Below the Wind*. The present house was faithfully rebuilt by the Keiths in 1946, after bombs flattened their original home. There are plans to convert the house into a museum. Nearby, cream teas are served at the English Teahouse and Restaurant (*see* 'Eating Out', p.379).

Sandakan's oldest building is the **San Sin Kung Temple**, built in the 1880s and dedicated to three deities, one of whom draws students around the time of exams (just as the fishermen prayed to the goddess Tin Hou for safe passage at sea, so scholars prayed to the Min Cheong Emperor deity for success in examinations). The red-brick temple sits on the edge of the padang. Much grander is the **Puu Jih Shih Buddhist temple**, built at great expense in 1987 on a hilltop south of Sandakan. The building is a blast of gold leaf and garish paint, with lanterns in their hundreds and dragons entwined about columns.

The well-tended **Sandakan Memorial Park** (Jalan Labuk, Taman Rimba) lies north of the town centre, on the site of the Sandakan POW camp established by the Japanese in 1942. It serves as a poignant commemoration of the atrocities suffered by the predominantly Australian POWs. A dark granite column marks the boundary of the POW camp and serves as the key memorial, while a Commemorative Pavilion tells the harrowing story of the prisoners, with the aid of photographs and eye-witness accounts from the survivors (only six of the 2,400 POWs brought to Sandakan survived the war). A recent overhaul of the memorial park was funded by the Australian government, and it is impossible to leave the park unmoved.

Sepilok Orang-Utan Rehabilitation Centre

Sepilok is the largest and oldest of the world's five orang-utan sanctuaries, and one of Sabah's most popular tourist attractions. The centre was established in 1964 as a sanctuary for confiscated orang-utans, many of whom had been captured by loggers and sold on as pets. The surrounding virgin forest has served well as a home for those orang-utans that successfully complete Sepilok's rehabilitation programme: since the 1930s the land had been protected as a site for scientific research, and when the centre opened in 1964, the 4,500-hectare plot was officially gazetted as the Sepilok Forest Reserve.

Orang-utans brought to Sepilok undergo a programme that can take years to complete. Like humans, orang-utans depend for their survival on acquired skills –

Getting There

Sepilok is 30mins from Sandakan by tour bus or taxi. Those travelling independently can get there on the regular 'Sepilok' bus which leaves from the bus stand next to Central Market in Sandakan.

Information

The RM10 entrance fee for Sepilok is payable in the office next to the information centre, where there is a small exhibition and a regular video screening about orang-utans. Feeding times 10am and 3pm, though these occasionally change, so it is best to check in advance. For further information contact the **Sabah Wildlife Department**, W.D.T. 200, Sandakan, **t** 089 531 180, **f** 089 531 189.

Where to Stay

Most people pay Sepilok a flying visit as part of a day trip from Sandakan or Kota Kinabalu. However there are a number of good places to stay in the vicinity of the rehabilitation centre, allowing for time to explore the forest reserve.

Expensive–Moderate

Sepilok Nature Resort, c/o Pulau Sipadan Resort & Tours, 484 Bandar Sabindo, Tawau, **t** 089 765 200, **f** 089 763 575, *info@sepilok.com*, *http://sepilok.com*. This resort offers comfortable chalet accommodation in a clearing at the edge of the Sepilok Forest Reserve. A line of wooden chalets linked by boardwalks meander about a pond. 150 species of orchid are tended within the extensive gardens. All chalets have air-conditioning and en suite bathrooms with bath and hot shower.

Moderate–Inexpensive

Sepilok Jungle Resort, **t** 089 533 031, **f** 089 533 029, *www.sepilokjungleresort.com*. A step down from the Sepilok Nature Resort in price and in appeal, though the setting is pleasant enough, with a large garden replete with flowers and fruit trees. There are a series of modestly furnished chalets as well as dormitory beds, and breakfast is included in the price.

Inexpensive

Sepilok Resthouse, **t** 089 534 900. Closest accommodation to the rehabilitation centre itself, with a small number of clean, simple rooms, some with air-con, others without.

Budget

Uncle Tan's, Mile 16, Jalan Gum Gum (5km from Sepilok), **t** 089 531 917, **f** 089 531 639, *www.uncletan.com*. Extremely popular among backpackers, Uncle Tan is best known for his tours into the Kinabatangan wetlands (*see* p.385). Accommodation is very basic (dorm beds), though all meals (breakfast, lunch, afternoon tea and dinner) are included in the budget rates – at the time of writing RM25/person.

skills which orphaned animals have been denied. In place of a mother-figure, trainers at Sepilok give their hairy young students lessons in climbing, foraging for food and nest-building (each night orang-utans build their own nest high in the tree canopy, where they sleep safe from predators).

There have been many success stories over the years, where released animals have been wholly integrated into the wilds once more, fending for themselves and mating with wild orang-utans. A large percentage of the orang-utan graduates, however, cannot so easily shrug off their years of close association with humans. These animals live out the rest of their lives in the semi-wild, returning to feeding platforms each day for an easy meal and a bit of familiar, human contact. It is this element of the programme that has ensured the centre's success with tourists, who are guaranteed sightings of semi-wild apes at allotted feeding times.

Man of the Forest

I soon found it necessary to wash the little Mias [orang-utan]. After I had done so a few times, it began to like the operation, and as soon as it was dirty would begin crying, and not leave off till I took it out and carried it to the spout, when it immediately became quiet, although it would wince a little at the first rush of cold water and make ridiculously wry faces while the stream was running over its head. It enjoyed the wiping and rubbing dry amazingly, and when I brushed its hair seemed to be perfectly happy, lying quite still with its arms and legs stretched out.

Alfred Russel Wallace, *The Malay Archipelago*, 1869

It is no coincidence that the Malay name for the *Pongo pygmaeus* (*orang utan*, or 'forest man') draws the red ape into close association with humankind. Distinct orang-utan populations have developed distinct 'cultures' – a phenomenon previously thought to be unique to man; the orang-utan can live for 60 years; it shares almost 97 per cent of our genes, and the female has a gestation period of almost nine months.

As far as Borneo's indigenous people are concerned, the animal has almost human standing. Iban folklore is full of anthropomorphized orang-utans. In one tale a female orang-utan comforts a woman in the throes of birth. In another, an old Iban warrior is reincarnated as an orang-utan: he appears in front of his bewildered son to explain that he can no longer live in the longhouse with his family, but must begin a new life in the forest. He asks that a special bond be observed between mankind and 'men of the forest' – a bond observed to this day by the Iban people.

Orang-utans are the largest tree-dwelling mammals: males have been known to weigh in at 130kg, females at up to 50kg. They are semi-solitary apes that feed on a wide range of fruit – durian is their favourite – supplementing their diet with bark,

With around 50,000 visitors each year, there are many who believe that this overdose of human contact can only hinder their progress. Indeed, there are times when Sepilok feels more like a zoo than a conservation project. Others believe that the popularizing of such sanctuaries serves the noble cause of spreading the word about the plight of the orang-utan, and the importance of bringing conservation issues to a wider audience.

One small but significant effect of the publicity attracted by Sepilok is the behaviour of local plantation owners. Orang-utans have an unfortunate fondness for the shoots of young oil palms; instead of shooting the animal that is munching away their investment (as was the traditional solution), owners of oil palm plantations are now getting on their mobile phones and asking rehabilitation centres like Sepilok, Semenggoh and Matang (or Wanariset and Tanjung Puting in Kalimantan) to deal with the pests.

There are two feeding platforms at Sepilok. Only the first, a ten-minute boardwalk from park headquarters, is open to the public. Feeding times are at 10am and 3pm, though the schedule can change, so check in advance. There is an information centre

leaves and the occasional insect. Every evening before sundown an orang-utan builds a new nest high in the tree canopy in which to spend the night.

Orang-utans are intelligent animals, proficient in the use of simple tools and with an ability to learn new skills and solve problems. Sticks stripped of their leaves are used to find food, to scratch backs or to clean teeth, while a carefully arranged umbrella of leaves and branches is used to shelter from the rain or sun. A game dubbed by researchers as 'snag-riding' has been observed in certain orang-utan populations: the animal rides a falling tree (one unable to sustain its weight), before grabbing a vine and swinging clear at the last moment. One female orang-utan was caught on film rowing herself and her baby across a stream in a dugout canoe. No one had taught her how to do this; she had learned by watching people.

In 1990 there were an estimated 180,000 orang-utans left in the wild. By 2000 that number had dropped to between 10,000 and 25,000. Wild orang-utans are on course for extinction within the next decade. Though hunting remains a problem, it is unprecedented habitat loss that has been the undoing of the red ape. Each animal needs 1,000 acres of virgin forest – rich in fruiting trees – in which to survive. Because orang-utans are the slowest-breeding primate, they are especially vulnerable; females give birth to one baby at a time, often with an eight-year gap between offspring, while young orang-utans spend up to 10 years in the company of their mothers.

Most wild orang-utans now live within protected reserves in Borneo and Sumatra. But these reserves are isolated pockets of jungle which do not allow for inter-breeding over long distances and the maintenance of a healthy gene pool. Meanwhile, hunting, the illegal activities of *garu* loggers (*garu* is an aromatic wood that fetches US$500 per pound in the Middle East) and the global demand for palm oil are hammering the final nails into the coffin of the wild orang-utan.

at park headquarters, with a small exhibition and a video about orang-utans, shown three times daily. It is not only orang-utans that Sepilok accepts for rehabilitation. Sun bears, cats and elephants have also been brought to the sanctuary, while two rare Sumatran rhinos have a permanent home here. These small, hairy rhinos were once so common that colonials were known to complain of them trampling their back gardens. They are now on the brink of extinction in the wild after decades of hunting (on the Chinese market their horns are worth more than their weight in gold, literally).

A number of well-marked trails lead deeper into the Sepilok Forest Reserve, taking in a range of forest habitats from classic lowland rainforest to mangrove forest and heath forest. These trails seem to open and close sporadically, so check in advance.

Turtle Islands Marine Park

The so-called Turtle Islands lie right on the Filippino border, 40km north of Sandakan. Formed by the accumulation of fine, coral sand on top of a series of rocky shoals and coral reefs, each island is circled by broad sandy beaches – ideal nesting

Getting There

Pulau Selingan is 40km north of Sandakan and accessible by speedboat as part of a tour package. The journey takes approximately 90mins.

Information

Visitors to Pulau Selingan need to obtain a permit from **Sabah Parks Head Office** (Lot 3, Block K, Sinsuran Complex, Kota Kinabalu, **t** 088 212 719, **f** 088 221 001, *info@sabahparks.org.my*, *www.sabahparks.org.my*). However tour operators should make all the necessary arrangements: the most cost-effective way of reaching the island is to sign up for an all-inclusive package with a tour operator (*see* 'Tour Operators' under Kinabatangan Wetlands, p.387, and Kota Kinabalu, p.360).

Where to Stay

Pulau Selingan is small and visitor numbers are restricted. There are only 14 rooms available on any given night, situated within three comfortable cabins. Rooms cost RM120/night. Most people sign up for an all-inclusive package with one of the Sandakan-based tour operators.

grounds for green and hawksbill turtles, who come ashore year-round to lay their eggs in the soft sand. Those islands on the Malaysian side of the border have been designated a marine park in recognition of their importance as breeding grounds. All three Malaysian islands have ranger stations and turtle hatcheries. One of the islands, **Pulau Selingan**, is accessible to the public.

For many centuries, turtle eggs were collected from this small archipelago and sold on at markets on the mainland – as they are by licensed collectors to this day (though not from those islands with hatcheries). Pulau Selingan is frequented mainly by green turtles, which lay their clutches year-round, though the peak period falls between July and October. The hatchery programme has proved to be a modest success, and visitors are virtually guaranteed a turtle sighting every night of the year.

Once a turtle has laid, park rangers retrieve the 80–100 eggs from the nest site and move them at once to the hatchery, where they are reburied to the correct depth and protected by lizard-proof wire mesh. After an incubation period of 40–50 days, the hatchlings dig their way out of the sand and paddle instinctively in the direction of the open water – or at least they would if they were not trapped behind wire fencing. So park rangers help the hatchlings on their way by releasing them onto the beach and keeping watch as they scramble towards the waves (turtle hatchlings, their shells still soft and fleshy, make a much-desired snack for monitor lizards, crabs and marine birds). Once in the water the dangers loom yet greater, and chances of survival are slim, with only one in a thousand hatchlings reaching maturity. Nevertheless each little turtle, pumped with the instinct to survive, swims for all it is worth in the direction of deeper water, where it depends for its survival on either the protective cover of a seaweed raft, or uncanny luck.

After sundown, visitors to Pulau Selingan sip tea at the resort café, flashlight at the ready, awaiting the signal that a turtle has landed. An unnecessary scramble then takes place as tourists are invited to run, thereby securing a ringside view of the beleaguered turtle. Flash photography is prohibited in the presence of the turtle, as are torches, though the rangers seem happy enough to flash their own beams about.

On land, a mature green turtle is an impressive, if cumbersome, sight. Its sheer bulk often comes as a surprise (these are no mere terrapins), as does its grunting resolve to get its trench dug, its progeny laid and its tracks covered, before defying gravity once more by hauling its dead weight back into the waves. If you find yourself face-to-face with a turtle underwater, these roles are uncannily reversed. The weightless reptile glides about with ease and grace, like a bird through air, no doubt eyeing your floundering presence with amusement. Green turtles can reach speeds of over 30km/hr underwater.

Once each tourist has had a chance to witness the efforts of egg-laying, the turtle is left to complete its motherly duty alone, and the visitors return to the hatchery. Here each visitor is allowed to handle a hatchling, brand new to the world, before accompanying the ranger down to the moonlit beach, where the seething clutch is released. Close at hand, a turtle hatchling is a most unreal creature, so perfectly formed, rubbery to the touch and with flippers that flap incessantly like the legs of a mechanical bath frog.

Whether or not you are interested in visiting a turtle hatchery, Pulau Selingan is a beautiful island in its own right, with a wraparound beach and warm, shallow waters ideal for swimming and snorkelling. The island is often inaccessible during the monsoon, which falls between October and February. Visitors can only visit Pulau Selingan with a permit from the Sabah Parks Head Office (*see* opposite) though tour operators should make the necessary arrangements.

The Kinabatangan Wetlands

At 560km, the Sungai Kinabatangan is Sabah's longest river, wending its convoluted path from deep inside the state's uninhabited interior to a swampy delta in the muzzle of Sabah (on a map Sabah clearly resembles a dog's head). Today the Kinabatangan is known primarily as one of the best places in Southeast Asia for spotting wildlife, though it has a long history of trade links with China: Kinabatangan means 'Chinese River'. Edible birds' nests from the Gomantong Caves (*see* p.386) were the primary draw, though ivory, beeswax and camphor were in large supply too, with the mighty Kinabatangan acting as the transport artery between the jungled interior and the Sulu Sea.

Records suggest that there was once a Chinese settlement in the area of **Sukau**, a riverine settlement named after a type of local rattan. Today the people who live along the banks of the lower Kinabatangan are known as Orang Sungei. They are a people of mixed ancestry who catch giant freshwater shrimps in rattan traps. Their women were once known across Sabah for their black magic; among Sabahan men, it has become a customary joke to ask a woman if she is from Kinabatangan before proceeding to chat her up.

Ironically, logging activities have played their part in making the lower Kinabatangan such a good place for spotting wildlife. With ever-greater tracts of forest wiped clean and replanted as oil palm, the wildlife has been funnelled onto

Getting There

The only practical way of visiting the Kinabatangan Wetlands is with a tour operator. Transfers from Sandakan or direct from KK are included in the package price. Sukau is approximately two hours southeast of Sandakan, with much of the journey on dirt tracks through palm-oil plantations.

Tour Operators

Below are the head offices of tour operators that offer packages to Kinabatangan:

Borneo Eco Tours, Lorong Bernam 3, Taman Soon Kiong, Kota Kinabalu, **t** 088 234 009, **f** 088 233 688, *info@borneoecotours.com*, *www.borneoecotours.com*.

Discovery Tours, Wisma Sabah, Jalan Haji Saman, Kota Kinabalu, **t** 088 221 244, **f** 088 221 600, *distour@po.jaring.my*.

S.I. Tours, Lot 1&2, 1st Floor, Sandakan Airport, **t** 089 673 502, **f** 089 673 788, *sitours@po.jaring.my*, *www.jaring.my/sitours*.

Uncle Tan's, Mile 16, Jalan Gum Gum (5km from Sepilok), **t** 089 531 917, **f** 089 531 639, *www.uncletan.com*.

Wildlife Expeditions, Wisma Khoo Siak Chiew, Sandakan, **t** 089 219 616, **f** 089 214 570, *www.wildlife-expeditions.com*

Where to Stay

All accommodation on the Sungei Kinabatangan is affiliated to respective tour operators. The most up-market place to stay is the **Sukau Rainforest Lodge** (contact Borneo Eco Tours or visit *www.sukau.com*), which has won international ecotourism awards for touches like solar-powered hot water and lighting powered by recycled cooking oil. The accommodation provided by S.I. Tours, Discovery Tours and Wildlife Expeditions is a step down in comfort and price, offering fairly rudimentary rooms (though all are en suite). **Uncle Tan's Wildlife Camp** is located deeper within the forest and further upriver. The camp offers very basic shared accommodation with good simple food thrown in. It has long been popular with backpackers and long-termers.

(or near to) the banks of the river. In the company of a guide, visitors are guaranteed to see proboscis monkeys at close quarters (*see* 'The Proboscis Monkey', opposite); these endearingly comical, grunting and, let's face it, ugly creatures inhabit the mangrove trees which line the smaller tributaries of the Kinabatangan.

Meanwhile, a series of majestic oxbow lakes form oases for a whole range of fish and animals, from otters and giant catfish to birds like the sinuous oriental darter (otherwise known as the snakebird) and the rare Storm's stork. Eight species of hornbill, including the rhinoceros hornbill, inhabit the Kinabatangan forest, and are frequently seen perched in pairs or crossing the river in formation. Orang-utans too are often spotted building their nightly nests high in the tree canopy, while a significant population of elephants make this the best place in Borneo for spotting these animals in the wild.

Though it is possible to visit the Kinabatangan on a day trip by boat from Sandakan, most people opt to join a tour and stay overnight in one of the lodges run by the various Sandakan-based tour operators (*see* above).

Tours to the Kinabatangan usually include a side trip to the **Gomantong Caves**, once accessible to Chinese traders via a tributary off the Kinabatangan. The goal of these traders was the lucrative supply of edible swiftlet nests found within this cave system. The nests are still harvested today by the same age-old methods. Highly skilled (and somewhat foolhardy) collectors scale a precarious network of rattan ladders which stretch 90m to the cave ceiling. Harvesting is closely regulated by the Sabah Wildlife Department and now takes place only twice a year (February to April and July to September). Less valuable black nests are harvested from the entrance cave, known as Simud Hitam, while white nests are sought out deeper within the Simud Puteh cave complex. Black nests are made from a mixture of swiftlet saliva and feathers, while white nests are pure saliva; the latter can fetch over US$1,000 per kilo. A troop of pig-tailed macaques, larger and more aggressive than their crab-eating cousins, often loiter about the cave entrance.

Southeast of the Kinabatangan wetlands, the 120,000-hectare **Tabin Wildlife Reserve** offers a truly unadulterated jungle experience. The Reserve was gazetted in 1984 but it was not until 2003 that it was opened to tourists. A new park headquarters has now opened its doors on the banks of the Sungei Lipad, complete with chalet and lodge accommodation. (For further information contact *Borneo Intra Travel, Level 1, Office 5, Airport Terminal 2, Kota Kinabalu,* ***t*** *088 260 558,* ***f*** *088 267 558, www.intra-travel.com.my.*)

Tabin is best known for its fragile population of Sumatran rhinos (approximately thirty individuals), though it is also home to Sabah's greatest concentration of elephants. Orang-utans, too, live here in relatively large numbers: with the Sepilok Forest Reserve reaching capacity, a proportion of those orang-utans that complete the rehabilitation process are set free at Tabin. As with all rainforest experiences,

The Proboscis Monkey

It is the appearance of the male proboscis monkey that often draws attention to this threatened species. With his potbelly, hooded eyes and low-slung bulbous nose, he looks more like a character off Spitting Image than a bona fide monkey. To the Malays, he was once known as *orang belanda*, or 'Dutchman', for his indulgent proportions.

The pendulous nose serves the male proboscis as the tail feathers serve a peacock: scientists believe the unusual feature evolved through 'sexual selection', the Darwinian theory for survival of the sexiest. The bigger the nose, the bigger the harem – for proboscis monkeys usually move about in troops of 10–30 with one male at the helm. With the responsibility of propagation firmly on his shoulders, the dominant male of each troop swings about with a permanent erection.

Proboscis monkeys are unique to Borneo, where they are found in isolated pockets among coastal mangroves and riverine forests. They are the world's largest monkeys, with adult males often exceeding 25kg in weight. They are excellent swimmers too, and will leap into water if threatened, often remaining submerged for 30 seconds. Like cows, proboscis monkeys spend most of their time feeding: 95% of their diet consists of leaves. And like cows, their paunches contain complex, multichambered stomachs designed to neutralize poisons present in the leaves they eat.

As is the case with many of Borneo's larger mammals, the proboscis is an endangered species. Estimates suggest 1,000 survive in Sarawak, 2,000 in Sabah, 10,000 in Brunei and a further 4,000 over the border in Kalimantan.

wildlife sightings should be seen as a rare treat, rather than a certainty. One of the reserve's highlights is a mud volcano with a diametre of 100m. The primordial ooze which bubbles forth is packed with minerals which attract the park's larger inhabitants – though the most you are likely to see is footprints.

The Danum Valley and Maliau Basin

South of the Kinabatangan is the huge bay of **Lahad Datu**, sprinkled with dozens of pristine and (as yet) inaccessible islands. The area has gained notoriety for its lawlessness over the past century, and modern pirates are still known to use the islands as shelter. The town of the same name – which means 'Prince's Town' – was once home to the Sultan of Sulu. After moving his base north into the present-day Philippines, he granted the town and its surrounding catchment to the British North Borneo Company. Today Lahad Datu is a centre for the timber, cocoa and rubber industries, and is of little interest to the tourist other than as a staging post on the bumpy journey to the Danum Valley.

The **Danum Valley Conservation Area** falls within the enormous Yayasan Sabah logging concession, which covers a large part of Sabah's uninhabited interior. A field centre was established in 1986 for the study of rainforest ecology – primarily with a view to understanding the impact of logging on the ecosystem and investigating processes of regeneration. Scientists from around the world have taken advantage of the facilities to study one of the world's richest stands of forest, identifying some 290 species of birds, 124 mammals and 72 reptiles in the process.

Getting There

The Borneo Rainforest Lodge is 100km inland from Lahad Datu, a 2–3 hour journey along bumpy logging tracks. Transfers from Lahad Datu airport (or from the town itself) are arranged by Borneo Nature Tours, the company that manages the lodge.

Information

Borneo Nature Tours, Block 1, Lot 6, 1st floor, Fajar Centre, Lahad Datu, **t** 089 880 207, **f** 089 885 051, *ijl@po.jaring.my*, *www.brl.com.my*.

Where to Stay

Luxury

Borneo Rainforest Lodge, c/o Borneo Nature Tours, **t** 089 880 207, **f** 089 885 051, *www.brl.com.my*. In a spectacular location on the inside bend of the Sungei Danum with a near-vertical bank of rainforest across the water. The 24-chalet complex is linked by walkways and constructed from local *belian* hardwood and river stones. Rooms are simple but very spacious, with hot water and large balconies that offer views across to the steaming rainforest canopy on the opposite bank. For the price you pay, the food it a little disappointing, but then the lodge is very much out on a limb. Very knowledgeable guides are available throughout the day for walks along the trails. Right next to the resort is a short nature trail with boardwalks, while the canopy walkway (*see* opposite) is just off the main drive on the way into the resort. Personal guides, and all meals, are included in the price.

A good distance from human habitation, and buffered by a belt of semi-logged secondary forest, the Danum Valley is one of the last great refuges for Borneo's big mammals – orang-utans, clouded leopards, elephants, Sumatran rhinos, *banteng* (wild ox) and five species of deer. The Borneo Rainforest Lodge, located deep inside the Conservation Area, offers visitors a little taste of this wonderful habitat. Highly knowledgeable guides offer nature walks along a network of trails that loop out from the lodge, which is located in a clearing on a bend of the Sungei Danum. A large number of orang-utans (of the wild, rather than rehabilitated, variety) live in the surrounding canopy, and there is said to be a high density of clouded leopards too, one of the red ape's few predators. But the Danum Valley will appeal most to bird watchers, who are likely to spot dozens of species in the space of a few hours – especially with the help of the lodge guides, who are able to identify virtually any bird by its song. Just up from the lodge is a short **canopy walkway**, and there are numerous waterfalls within easy reach.

The Danum Valley has not always been uninhabited. Several centuries ago a Sutpan longhouse sat opposite the site of the Borneo Rainforest Lodge. The Sutpan are an 'upriver' subtribe of the Kadazan. A 300-year-old burial site, easily accessible from the lodge, was discovered at the top of the steep hill overlooking the river. A huge *belian* coffin sits on a rocky outcrop. It is thought to belong to a Sutpan chief, his trusty blowpipe laid out inside the coffin, his sun-bleached bones to one side. Nearby are the small coffins of two children, both of whom are said to have died of chickenpox.

Deeper still within the Yayasan Sabah logging concession is the **Maliau Basin Conservation Area**, equidistant from Sabah's east and west coasts, and romantically referred to as 'The Lost World'. The basin forms a natural amphitheatre 25km across; its virtually unsurmountable walls reach 1,700m in places, their upper flanks lined with crevasses and coated with spongy moss, sometimes metres deep. It was once speculated that this self-contained ecosytem was formed by the impact of a huge meteorite, though it is now known that millions of years ago this area was a river delta. When sea levels dropped, the vast silt deposits were slowly weathered away, exposing an almost circular ridge of sandstone.

The Maliau Basin really is the stuff of legend, a 'lost world' alien to humans until 1988, when the first recorded expedition took place. Only 30 per cent of the region has since been explored. The forest here is rich in dipterocarp trees, fruit trees and legumes – and as a consequence is packed with wildlife, all of it blissfully unaware that the world beyond has been so ravished by man. The basin holds by far Sabah's highest density of primates and cats, while on its upper reaches, above the oaks and chestnuts and laurels, dozens of rare or previously unknown orchids have been recorded.

For the intrepid (and wealthy) tourist, expeditions into the Maliau Basin can be arranged. Contact Borneo Nature Tours several months in advance (*Block D, Lot 10, Ground Floor, Sadong Jaya Complex, 88100 Kota Kinabalu,* **t** *088 267 637,* **f** *088 251 636, www.brl.com.my*).

Semporna and Pulau Sipadan

The sprawling fishing town of **Semporna** sits on the southeast tip of Sabah. It exists half on land and half at sea, with clusters of stilted buildings extending over the water. Alongside Semporna's resident Chinese and Malays, the town has a large, transient population of Filippinos, Bajau Laut and Suluk tribespeople. Beyond the busy market, the water is a constant melee of boats – simple wooden *jongkong*, modern speedboats, even seagoing dugouts and the occasional *lepa-lepa* (impossibly small houseboats, with *attap* roofs and stabilizing bamboo floats).

Beyond Semporna, shallow waters extend in all directions, allowing for the mirage-like appearance of elaborate *kelong* fish traps and stilted homes, their skeletal

Getting There

Pulau Sipadan is an hour's boat ride south of Semporna. The only access to the island is through tour operators and dive resorts. Transfers are included in the price of a dive package. See below for contact details.

Where to Stay

In preparation for Sipadan's pending designation as a UNESCO World Heritage Site, all accommodation on the island was closed down and dismantled in 2005. Now, the nearest accommodation is on the island of Mabul and the sand bar of Kapalai. The closest of the dive resorts is only a few minutes by speedboat from Sipadan.

Mabul and Kapalai

Expect a fairly upmarket experience on both Mabul and Kapalai. All-inclusive packages cover air and boat transfers from Kota Kinabalu, food and drink (non-alcoholic) and a set number of dives each day. Snorkellers are also welcome at a reduced fee (the excellent visibility and easily accessible reefs make snorkelling here a memorable experience). Listed below are the best of the resorts (each of which takes marine conservation very seriously). There are no budget options.

Luxury–Expensive

Sipadan-Kapalai Dive Resort, c/o 484 Bandar Sabindo, P O Box 61120, Tawau, **t** 089 765 200, **f** 089 763 563, *info@sipadan-resort.com*, *www.sipadan-resort.com*. An upmarket chalet complex standing entirely over water beside the Kapalai sand bar, which is a 15-minute boat ride from Pulau Sipadan.

Borneo Divers Mabul Resort, c/o Menara Jubili, 53 Jalan Gaya, Kota Kinabalu, **t** 088 222 226, **f** 088 221 550, *information@borneodivers.info*, *www.borneodivers.info*. Spacious, comfortable chalets set on a long white-sand beach on Mabul. There's an E6 film-processing service for underwater photographers.

Sipadan Water Village Resort, c/o TB226, Lot 3, 1st Floor, Wisma MAA, Town Extension 2, Tawau, **t** 089 752 996, **f** 089 752 997, *info@swvresort.com*, *www.swvresort.com*. Also on Pulau Mabul, but set on stilts above the water and slightly more upmarket.

Semporna

There is limited good-quality accommodation in Semporna and most people pass straight through. The two most promising options are listed below.

Moderate–Budget

Dragon Inn, Waterfront, PO Box 168, Semporna, **t** 089 781 088, **f** 089 781 559. On stilts above the water beside the waterfront tourist office. Offers a range of decent quality accommodation from dorm beds to air-conditioned doubles.

Inexpensive–Budget

Seafest Inn, Jalan Kastam, Pulau Bajau, Semporna, **t** 089 782 366, *seafestinn@hotmail.com*. The simple rooms and dorms at this Australian-run place have satellite TV and en suite facilities.

silhouettes etched at intervals on the horizon. A peppering of shoals and islands provide shelter for those Bajau Laut who continue to live the semi-nomadic, waterborne lifestyle for which they earned the title 'sea gypsies'.

Tourists who find themselves in Semporna usually have one goal in mind – to jump aboard a launch and head out to **Pulau Sipadan**, widely recognized as one of the world's top dive sites. The tiny island (you can walk round its circular beach in less than half an hour) is situated 35km south of Semporna above the cobalt-blue depths of the Celebes Sea. It is Malaysia's only oceanic island, formed by the accumulation of corals on the summit of an extinct underwater volcano.

Green and hawksbill turtles glide about Sipadan's waters in such obscene numbers that they become part of the marine flora. And this abundance is the rule rather than the exception; more than 3,000 species of fish have been classified in Sipadan's waters. According to the WWF, no other place known to man has more marine life.

Sipadan's top attraction is its most accessible one; for a glimpse of what all the fuss is about, all you need do is strap on a mask and kick off from the island's main beach. Just a few metres out, the rich coral bed plunges 680m to the sea floor, forming what has become a legendary wall dive. Five metres below the drop-off point is an underwater cavern, complete with a labyrinth of passageways and the scattered bones of turtles that have drowned, unable to find their way out. Right round the island, named dive sites offer their own peculiar coral formations or cruising grounds. Schooling barracuda and big-eye trevally provide one of the highlights, but pelagics such as manta rays, hammerhead sharks and whale sharks are often sighted too.

A picture-perfect beach runs right round Sipidan's oval circumference. The densely forested interior is home to monitor lizards, coconut crabs, fruit bats and – considering the island covers only 35 acres – a staggering 47 species of birds.

Pulau Sipadan was popularized in 1989 by oceanographer Jacques Cousteau, who famously described the island's underwater world as 'an untouched work of art'. It can no longer be described as untouched, though the island has since been designated a marine reserve, and visitor numbers are restricted to 80 at any one time. Recent developments have seen Sipadan placed on UNESCO's pending list for World Heritage Sites, and in 2005 all accommodation on the island was abandoned for conservation purposes.

Sipadan received a raft of unwelcome publicity in April 2000 when a group of Filippino separatists stormed the island and kidnapped 21 people, half of whom were foreign tourists. All were eventually released unharmed, and there is now (reassuringly) a constant police presence on and about the island.

Nearby **Pulau Mabul** sits in shallower water at the edge of the continental shelf, and has earned a name for itself as a top 'macro-diving' site. The 200-hectare reef which surrounds the island is rich in small marine life, from cuttlefish and harlequin shrimp to octopus, gobies, snake eels and even the occasional sea horse. The island is planted with coconut palms and is home to a number of Bajau fishermen and a few upmarket diving resorts. A further resort, built in the style of a water village, stands over the reef at **Kapalai**, a large sand bar in the waters between Mabul and Sipadan.

Tawau

Tawau sits across from Indonesia on the sock-shaped bay of the same name, rightdown in the southeast corner of Sabah. Before the British North Borneo Company got their hands on it in 1878, Tawau was a Bajau fishing village under the control of the Sultan of Sulu. The British then squabbled with the Dutch over possession of the village, before transforming the place by planting hemp and tobacco and making use of its deep harbour.

Today there is a large Indonesian and Filippino presence in town, mainly barter traders and migrant labourers looking for work at the port or on the plantations. Tawau likes to see itself as Cocoa Capital of Asia, though like elsewhere in Malaysia, oil palm has begun to dominate. The hinterland is characterized by rich volcanic soil, providing high yields for plantation owners. Smallholdings of rubber, coprah, hemp and coffee are common, while logging continues where land has yet to be cleared.

Divers travelling from the west coast to the islands off Semporna will flash through town after landing at Tawau airport. Beyond stomping around the clamorous markets, or tracking down some good cheap seafood, there is not much in Tawau to detain the casual visitor. However, for those with a little time on their hands, the **Tawau Hills Park** offers a number of well-marked trails through forested volcanic terrain. The park is an hour north of Tawau, covering a 28,000-hectare expanse of rainforest and rugged peaks. It was gazetted in 1979 to protect the water catchment of the Semporna peninsula. Mysterious white monkeys, yet to be properly identified (though scientists suspect they may be albino red-leaf monkeys), are occasionally spotted within the park boundaries. Though there are a few accessible waterfalls, some hot springs and basic accommodation facilities, the park is rarely on the itinerary of tour operators and receives few foreign visitors.

Getting There

Nine daily flights from KK land at Tawau's airport just north of town. There are good road links with Semporna, Lahad Datu and Sandakan, with minibuses leaving throughout the day. Tawau acts as a border town with Indonesia, and there are numerous ferry services from the main wharf to Tarakan in Kalimantan.

Where to Stay

Expensive–Moderate

Belmont Marco Polo, Jalan Clinic, PO Box 1003, **t** 089 777 988, **f** 089 763 739. This busy hotel is Tawau's best, catering almost exclusively for businessmen. The 150 rooms are spacious and come complete with 4-star facilities.

Moderate–Inexpensive

Merdeka Hotel, Jalan Masjid, **t** 089 776 655, **f** 089 761 743. A few steps down from the Belmont Marco Polo in price and appeal, but reasonable value nevertheless; rooms all have en suite facilities and air-con.

Eating Out

Tawau is known widely for its cheap seafood, which can be found in abundance at the waterfront and around the town's three markets. Otherwise try:

Moderate–Inexpensive

Kublai Chinese Restaurant, Belmont Marco Polo Hotel (*see* above), **t** 089 777 988. A huge Cantonese restaurant inside Tawau's principal hotel.

Brunei

19

Brunei

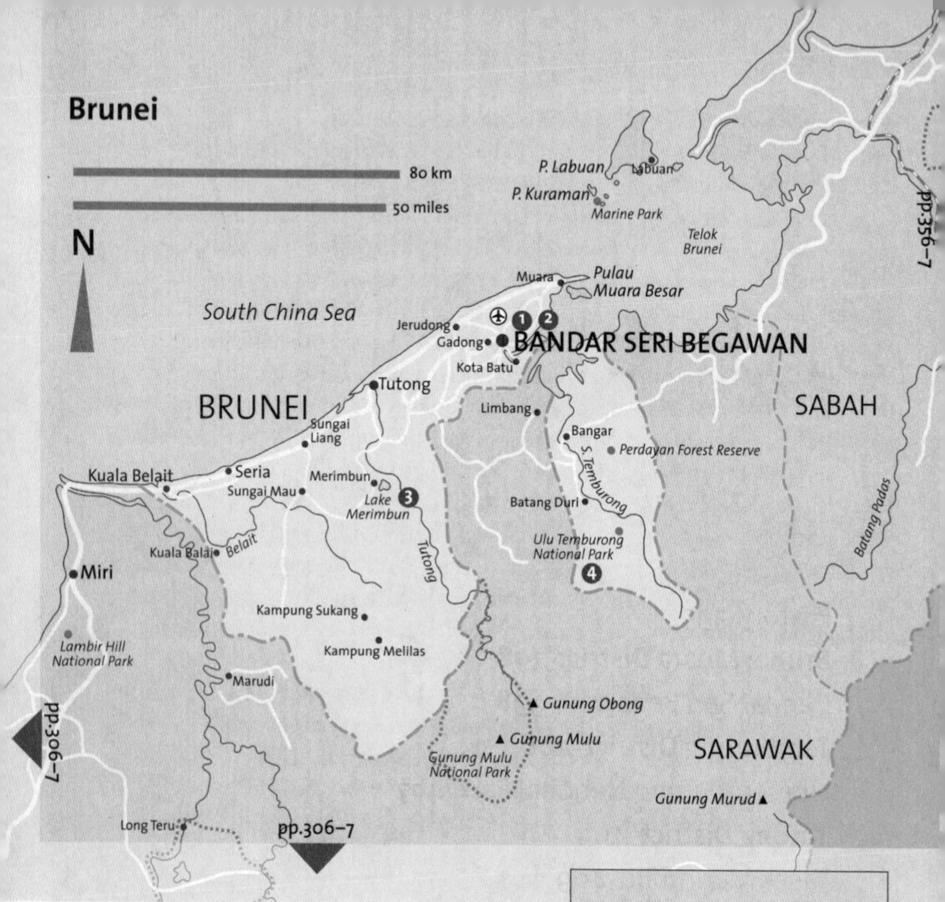

Highlights

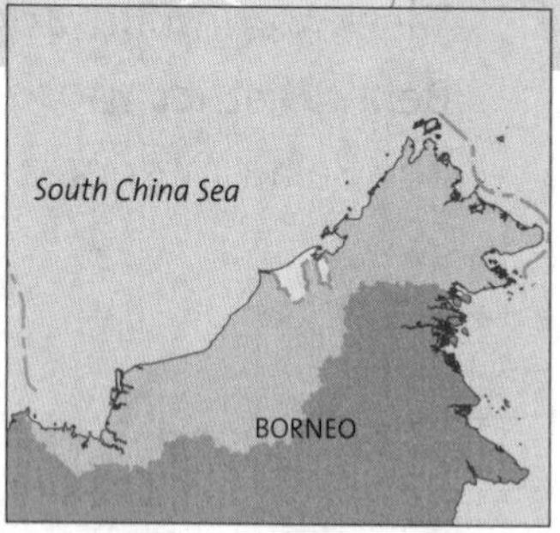

1 Kampung Ayer, one of the largest water villages in the world, on the fringes of Brunei's capital.
2 Masjid Omar Ali Saifuddien – one of the finest-looking mosques in Southeast Asia
3 Tasek Merimbun – a freshwater lake and wetlands system, home to rare wildlife including clouded leopards
4 Ulu Temburong National Park – uninhabited, unscathed by logging and boasting a fine canopy walkway

On first impressions, the tiny oil-rich sultanate of Brunei hardly looks like a very promising destination. If you're not put off by the strict prohibition on alcohol, you're probably wary of the comparatively high prices and the lack of tourism infrastructure. The latter is set to change (as Brunei looks to diversify its oil-reliant economy), though for many visitors Brunei's peace and quiet are its principle charms.

More often than not, Brunei serves merely as a stepping stone to Sarawak and Sabah. But for those who take the time to delve a little deeper, Brunei can provide a safe, easy introduction to the island of Borneo as a whole.

Though few people know much about the country itself, everyone has heard of the Sultan of Brunei – for a time the world's richest man. His family, who have ruled over Brunei for six centuries, once controlled much of Borneo and the Sulu archipelago (indeed, the name 'Borneo' is a derivation of 'Brunei'). Pirates, the Sulu kings and the British all played their parts in reducing Brunei to its present size (barely larger than the English county of Hampshire). Today, Brunei is a quiet, contented little place. Bruneians, on the whole, are happy with their lot; they are among Asia's most affluent citizens, they pay no taxes, while cars and housing are heavily subsidized. In any case, protest is not in their blood – Bruneians are (and have always been) subjects of a monarchical autocracy.

One problem looms for Brunei: the nation's precious oil reserves are set to dry up by 2020. The Asian Financial Crisis of 1997 was a wake-up call for the government, focusing attention on Brunei's newly fragile economy. The result is a more outward-looking government, with the first moves towards democracy set in motion, and a new focus on finance and ecotourism as future revenue earners.

A few days is enough to see the best of what Brunei has to offer. Kampung Ayer, a huge water village attached to the capital Bandar Seri Begawan, is the principle attraction. There are a couple of impressive mosques to visit and Iban longhouses to track down, while sightings of rare proboscis monkeys along the banks of Sungai Brunei are guaranteed. Brunei's pristine rainforest is its trump card. Thanks to the government's reliance on oil, logging has hardly touched the country, around three quarters of which lies beneath virgin jungle.

History

The earliest mention of Brunei is found in Chinese records dating from AD 473, by which time the settlement had developed into a trading centre for seafarers on the route between China and India. Archaeological finds indicate a much longer history, with evidence that coastal areas of Brunei have been inhabited continuously since Neolithic times. Between the 7th and 13th centuries, Brunei served first as a vassal state of Srivijaya, then of the Majapahit Empire – both Hindu-Buddhist kingdoms that boomed in turn on the back of regional trade with China and India.

Because of its strategic location and its wealth of natural resources, Brunei – or 'Poli', as it was known at the time – soon flourished as a collecting point for much-coveted jungle products such as sandalwood, beeswax, birds' nests, turtle shells, sago and camphor (Borneo camphor was once prized more highly than gold). Along with the trade in commodities came a great mix of cultures and ideologies, with Islam first establishing a foothold in the late 14th century. In 1405, ruler Awang Alak Betatar embraced Islam to become Sultan Muhammad Shah, the founder of a dynasty which survives to this day.

Brunei's so-called Golden Era came in the reign of Sultan Bolkiah (1485–1524), a time when Brunei effectively controlled the whole of Borneo, as well as parts of the modern-day Philippines. During Bolkiah's reign, Brunei was a populous, cosmopolitan place, with traders from right across Asia making their homes on the banks of the Brunei River. The sultan himself, who loved to travel, earned himself the nickname 'Nakhoda Ragam' (the 'Singing Captain') – he always announced his arrival with song and the beating of the royal drums.

Europe Takes Note

By the end of Sultan Bolkiah's reign Brunei had achieved great wealth, and it wasn't long before the little entrepôt caught the attention of the European powers. Antonio Pigafetta, the diarist aboard the Magellan voyage of 1521, was astounded by the wealth of the court and the size of Brunei's water village (he estimated the population to be more than 100,000).

Later centuries saw the gradual decline of Brunei, first at the hands of Sulu (the Sulu archipelago is today part of the Philippines), then in the face of colonial intrusions, with the Dutch, the British, the Portuguese and the Spanish all vying for control of the hugely lucrative spice trade. As the centuries passed, Brunei's vast territories were whittled away; in the 17th century, Brunei's northeastern territory (the area of modern-day Sabah) was snatched by Sulu. Two centuries later, and the dynasty of 'White Rajahs' (*see* p.306) in neighbouring Sarawak was almost the death knell for Brunei. In exchange for military help in 1841, Brunei ceded the territory around present-day Kuching to English adventurer James Brooke. With every decade (and with the growing influence of the Brooke dynasty) Brunei's borders were cut back to their present-day dimensions. Brunei's complete disappearance was prevented only by formal measures taken by the British: in 1888 Sir Hugh Low instigated the treaty by which Brunei became a British Protectorate. Further protection came in 1906, when the sultan accepted a British Resident (under similar terms to the various sultans of Malaya).

Brunei's turning point came in 1929, when vast oil reserves were discovered at Seria. Since then, oil wealth has transformed and shaped the tiny nation. As well as making its rulers among the wealthiest men on Earth, the discovery shaped relations with neighbouring countries; at the time of the independence of Malaya in 1959, Brunei gave up its British Resident – but resisted the chance to become part of the Federation of Malaysia. Brunei's new constitution provided for a Legislative Council, though this lasted only three years: a revolt by the radical People's Party was put down with the aid of British Gurkhas, and the Legislative Council was disbanded.

The incumbent Sultan Bolkiah came to the throne in 1967 at the age of 21. For much of his reign, Brunei has functioned under authoritarian rule, with Britain responsible for foreign affairs and defence. Brunei (somewhat reluctantly) gained independence in 1984, though a new defence agreement with the British has allowed for the stationing of a Gurkha battalion at Seria. The first tentative move towards 21st-century democracy was instigated in 2004, with the appointment of a new Legislative Council.

Brunei Today

Bruneians have become accustomed to a high standard of living, but the last years of the 20th century were a tough time for Brunei's economy. By the turn of the century, the country's per capita GDP was barely half what it had been at the time of Brunei's independence. Falling oil prices, the Asian Economic Crisis of 1997, and the subsequent collapse of the country's largest non-oil company brought things to a head.

The company in question was Amedeo Development Corporation, owned and run by Prince Jefri, then Finance Minister and one of the sultan's brothers. Thanks largely to the prince's playboy lifestyle, the company had run up debts of $3.5 billion, and the prince was forced to resign as Finance Minister. A national scandal followed, with the sultan eventually suing his brother for embezzling billions of dollars from the Brunei Investment Agency, for which the prince had served as chairman. The case was settled out of court, but this didn't stop the international spotlight falling on Prince Jefri's extravagant lifestyle (the prince has four wives, 17 official children, and a penchant for Filipino and American beauty queens, who he used to fly in for his own pleasure). In August 2001, many of the prince's personal possessions were auctioned off by Amedeo's liquidator in attempts to appease out-of-pocket creditors. The lots included a F1-racing-car simulator and a set of gold-plated toilet brushes. The prince's other possessions include a 165ft yacht, called *Tits*, with two tenders – *Nipple 1* and *Nipple 2*.

Surprisingly, given Brunei's conservatism, Prince Jefri was always a popular figure among Bruneians. Over the years, his ambitious projects – under the guise of Amedeo – provided many jobs. The company's legacy is the area around Jerudong, where Amedeo built the world's most extravagant polo ground, the Jerudong Playground (a theme park complete with roller coasters) and the Empire Hotel & Country Club. The hotel alone was said to have cost an astonishing US$800 million – at the time, the most expensive hotel in the world.

In the last few years, Brunei's economy has picked up once more. It seems that the old complacency has been shaken off once and for all: the sultan has any number of projects in the pipeline in attempts to diversify the economy. His big plan is to transform Brunei into an 'Offshore Financial Haven', with a focus on 'Islamic' finance. He has also opened a huge container terminal at Muara port, in an attempt to take advantage of Brunei's location on the trade route between East and West. With such a high proportion of virgin rainforest left intact, ecotourism, too, is seen as a big revenue earner for the future.

The need to attract foreign investors and tourists has forced the sultan to pay attention to Brunei's international image. In September 2004, the first moves towards democracy were set in motion with the reopening of parliament (for the first time since independence). To all intents and purposes, Brunei remains a monarchical autocracy (political parties are not yet allowed). Nevertheless, a 45-seat legislative council has been called for, with 15 elected members. Elections are still pending.

The coming years are likely to see new areas of the country opening up to tourists. The recent economic crisis has also turned Brunei into a less expensive place to visit, with top hotels, in particular, offering excellent value for money. Still, tourism figures remain negligible, and many people feel this is likely to remain the case until the government eases laws on the prohibition of alcohol.

Brunei Muara District

Bandar Seri Begawan

Brunei's capital, Bandar Seri Begawan, has the feel of a quiet provincial town rather than a capital city. Most of the inhabitants live on its fringes – either in Kampung Ayer or in the suburbs – leaving the city centre itself strangely quiet. Bandar (as the town is commonly known) sits on a bend of the Brunei River, directly opposite and adjacent to a watery world of boardwalks and stilted homes. In many ways, it is Kampung Ayer (Malay for 'water village') that forms the real heart of the city. The quiet streets of downtown Bandar provide a stark contrast to the mayhem on Brunei River, where *tambang* (water taxis) roar back and forth day and night.

Indeed, Bandar only began to develop as a land-based settlement after the appointment of a British Resident in 1906. The British Residency itself was one of the first buildings to appear – the wooden building known today as Bubungan Dua Belas (*see* p.401). The sultan followed suit in 1909, building a palace on land for the first time in 500 years. The central grid of shophouses only began to take shape after the discovery of oil in 1929, while Bandar's best-known landmarks – the elegant Omar Ali Saifuddien Mosque and the Istana Nurul Iman – appeared in the 1950s.

Modern Bandar is bound on three sides by water, with the Sungai Brunei to the south, Sungai Kedayan to the west and the narrow Sungai Kianggeh to the east. The latter is lined with the market stalls of Tamu Kianggeh. The city centre is tiny; it can be crossed on foot in a matter of minutes, with the smart Yayasan Complex (a shopping centre) serving as the focal point. Many of the interesting sights, including the old British Residency, the tombs of two sultans, and the Brunei Museum, lie along the banks of the river east of town. Bandar's immediate suburbs – Gadong, Kiulap and Kampung Kiarong – lie northwest of the centre, across the Edinburgh Bridge, from where there are views across the water village to the gold dome of the Omar Ali Saifuddien Mosque. Kampung Kiarong is home to the even larger Kiarong Mosque, while the excellent *pasar malam* (night market) is the daily highlight in Gadong, the commercial centre. North of the Bandar lies the government complex, the underused National Stadium and the airport.

Kampung Ayer

The history of Brunei is largely the history of Kampung Ayer, the higgledy-piggledy network of homes, mosques, schools and shops raised on stilts above Sungai Brunei. With a population of around 30,000, Kampung Ayer is said to be the largest water village in the world – but it is only a shadow of its former self. Back in the 15th century, Kampung Ayer was the hub of an empire stretching across much of Borneo, Mindanao and the Sulu archipelago. When the Magellan expedition stopped by in 1521, the ship's diarist Antonio Pigafetta described Kampung Ayer as the 'Venice of the East'. Today, inhabitants are encouraged to leave the village and settle on land. As a result, the population is slowly dwindling.

Kampung Ayer is a blend of old and new, with modern sections of the village rising from the water on concrete piles, while older buildings stand on mangrove and ironwood posts, with walls of woven nipa palm. The village is self-sufficient, with shops, schools, mosques, homes – even fire stations and floating petrol stations (look for the Shell signs) – all accessible by boat or on the endless network of rickety boardwalks. Strangely, the water village is not officially part of the municipality of Bandar Seri Begawan. Instead, it retains the old system of *mukim*, or 'wards', with 42 separate units, each governed by a *tua kampung* (headman). Traditionally, each ward was associated with a particular cottage industry, and echoes of this are still evident, with the odd blacksmith, potter, silversmith or boat-builder still plying his trade.

To reach Kampung Ayer, jump aboard any of the *tambang* (water taxis), which pull up on the riverside just south of the Yayasan Complex. You can't miss them: the boatmen will all compete for your attention. For around B$20, you can expect a lengthy tour of the water village, as well as a trip upriver to catch a glimpse of the Istana Nurul Iman, the sultan's opulent palace (*see* p.401). It is also possible to combine the tour with a boat safari upriver to spot proboscis monkeys among the mangroves – a highlight of any trip to Brunei (*see* 'The Proboscis Monkey', p.387). To access the water village by foot, strike out along the boardwalk situated just west of the Yayasan Complex.

Downtown Bandar

The city centre is dominated by two structures – the Omar Ali Saifuddien Mosque and the **Yayasan Complex**. The latter is a smart shopping centre with colonnades and a central water fountain aligned for views of the mosque in one direction, and the river in the other. Directly east of the mosque is the padang, almost always deserted. Between here and the narrow Sungai Kianggeh tributary – site of the Tamu Kianggeh open-air market – is a small grid of shophouses. To the south, the waterfront stretches from the covered wet market to the edge of the mosque complex. A number of the main sights, including the Brunei Museum, are situated along the river, east of downtown Bandar (*see* 'East to Kampung Kota Batu').

Built in 1957 in classical Islamic style, the **Omar Ali Saifuddien Mosque** (*open to non-Muslims Wed–Sat 8–12, 2–3 and 5–6; compound open daily 8am–8.30pm; visitors must remove shoes and dress conservatively*) is Brunei's finest monument – an elegant structure set beside an artificial lake and, by night, illuminated in pale green light to dramatic effect. Occasionally, the lift that runs to the top of the 44m minaret is in operation (ask the warden). In the middle of the lake is a replica of a 16th-century *mahligai*, or royal barge, used on special occasions for Koranic recitals. The mosque itself incorporates stained glass and chandeliers from England, carpets from Arabia, marble from Italy and granite from Shanghai. The giant onion dome is decorated with a mosaic of gold-leafed Venetian glass. During construction, flakes of gold leaf were reported to have fallen from the dome. This was a time when Brunei's oil wealth was only beginning to transform the lifestyles of Bruneians. Novelist Anthony Burgess, who was a teacher in Brunei during the 1950s, describes in his autobiography how the falling gold was 'taken by the fisherfolk to be a gift from Allah'.

There is one museum in downtown Bandar, the **Royal Regalia Museum** (*Jalan Sultan, open Sat–Thurs 9–4.30, Fri 2.30–4.30; free*), which is something of a showcase for the sultan's outrageous wealth, set within an extravagant domed building north of the *padang*. The museum opened in 1992, the sultan's Silver Jubilee year, and the major exhibits relate to this event. The gigantic gold-leafed, winged chariot (upon which the sultan was paraded through town) almost defies belief for its size and kitsch-factor. The museum is stuffed to the hilt with grandiose kitsch of this sort, along with hundreds of photos, ceremonial costumes and a gallery charting the royal history of Brunei. Next door is the **Brunei History Centre** (*open Sat–Thurs 7.45–12.15 and 1.30–4.30*), which is more a research centre than a tourist attraction. Opposite the Royal Regalia Museum is the **Lapau di Raja** (*Royal Ceremonial Hall; closed to the public*), where the 1968 coronation ceremony took place.

About a kilometre north of the Royal Regalia Museum, off Jalan Tasek Lama (turn right opposite the Sultan Omar Ali Saifuddien College), is the **Tasek Recreational Park**, a small picnic area at the foot of a waterfall.

East to Kampung Kota Batu

Kampung Kota Batu, and the adjacent stretch of river, was the original site of Kampung Ayer, and it was here that Brunei lived out its heyday back in the 15th and 16th centuries. Jalan Kota Batu, the road that runs for several kilometres along the river bank, links the village with the centre of Bandar Seri Begawan.

The principal reason to head east to Kota Batu is to visit the **Brunei Museum** (*open Sat–Thurs 9–5, Fri 9–11.30 and 2.30–5; adm free*), home to an impressive collection of artwork and artefacts from the sultan's personal collection. The Islamic Gallery has pride of place, with a large collection of Korans, ceramics, jewellery, weapons and calligraphy dating back as far as the 9th century. A banner from 18th-century India is spread across one wall, depicting the entire Koran in minute calligraphy – a labour of faith for a single scribe. Other items to look out for include wonderfully preserved gold and silver jewellery dating back to the 7th century, a collection of miniature perfume bottles and a peculiar decorative wooden boot with compass. On the same floor is the Petroleum Gallery (of limited interest) and the Natural History Gallery, its glass cabinets full of musty, poorly stuffed birds and animals.

Upstairs is the Traditional Culture Gallery, providing the rundown on old Malay customs. Exhibits include handcrafted kites, spinning tops (*gasing*), board games, traditional dress, *keris* (ceremonial daggers) and *bedok* (call-to-prayer drums). Next door, the Archaeology and History Gallery provides a thorough introduction to the history of Brunei and Borneo from Neolithic times. A final gallery is reserved for temporary exhibitions. The museum is accessible by taxi or alternatively by Eastern Line buses (Nos. 11 and 39), which run every half-hour from the main bus terminal in Bandar.

Down the hill from the Brunei Museum on the riverfront is the **Malay Technology Museum** (*same opening hours Brunei Museum*), which presents a series of dioramas depicting stilt-house building, boat building and fishing techniques, along with displays of *songket*-weaving and metalwork. Upstairs there are examples of indigenous dwellings, blowpipes, rattan fish traps and other traditional implements.

Follow the road back towards Bandar Seri Begawan, past the tombs of two of Brunei's greatest sultans – Sultan Syarif Ali (1426–32) and Sultan Bolkiah (1485–1524) – and you come eventually to the old British Residency, known today as **Bubongan Dua Belas** (*open Sat–Thurs 9–4.30, Fri 9–11.30 and 2.30–4.30; adm free*). Built on the hillside overlooking Kampung Ayer, Bubongan Dua Belas (which means 'Twelve Roofs') celebrated its centenary in 2006, making it Brunei's oldest surviving building. Today it is home to a small and rarely visited 'Relationship Exhibition', with maps, charts and old letters celebrating the ties between Brunei and the United Kingdom.

Next door to the old residency, a staircase leads up to the **Bukit Subok Recreational Park**, which offers the best views across Bandar and the water village. A series of steep stone staircases and wooden boardwalks, linked by viewing towers, climb the face of the wooded hill.

A little further along Jalan Residency, on the edge of Bandar Seri Begawan itself, is the **Arts and Handicraft Centre** (*open Sat–Thurs 7.45–12.15 and 1.30–4.15; adm free*), which lays on workshops for young Bruneians in an attempt to preserve traditional Malay skills (mainly *songket*-weaving, *keris*-making and brass casting). There is a modest shop on the first floor selling handicrafts, jewellery, traditional clothing and other gifts. Behind the Arts and Handicraft Centre is a small art gallery with exhibits by local artists.

West to the Istana

Jalan Tutong, the main road out of downtown Bandar, passes over the Sungai Kedayan tributary at Edinburgh Bridge, before veering southwest along the course of the Brunei River. The road passes by the Institute of Islamic Studies and a polo field, before reaching the heavily guarded fringes of the **Istana Nurul Iman**, home to the Sultan of Brunei. With a ludicrous 1,778 rooms, the palace is one of the world's largest buildings, comparable in size to the Palace of Versailles. The main dining room seats five thousand people, while the sultan's legendary collection of cars (he collects them like stamps) is housed in a vast underground car park beneath the palace. The only concession to traditional architecture is a sweeping Minangkabau-style roof. The palace is closed to the public – unless you happen to be around during His Majesty's Birthday festivities in July, when the grounds are opened briefly to visitors.

The best vantage point for glimpses of the palace are from the river; boatmen on the waterfront in downtown Bandar will happily oblige curious tourists. If you make

Getting There

The Brunei International Airport is located 10km north of the city centre. During daylight hours, there are regular shuttle buses between the airport and the bus station on Jalan Cator in Bandar Seri Begawan. This bus station is also the arrival point for buses from Sarawak and other parts of Brunei. A taxi from the airport should cost no more than B$20 (more after dark).

Getting Around

The centre of Bandar Seri Begawan is barely a kilometre across and the easiest way of getting around is **on foot**. Metered **taxis** can be flagged down or booked by phone on **t** 222 2214. Fares are set at B$3 for the first kilometre, then B$1 for every subsequent kilometre (fares rise 50 per cent after dark). **Water taxis** ply the river day and night, ferrying passengers about the water village. Fares can range from B$2 to B$15 depending on the length of the ride. To catch a water taxi, wait at the waterfront just south of the Yayasan Complex. The Brunei Museum and the suburb of Gadong are accessible on Central Line **buses**, which depart from the main bus station on Jalan Cator. Buses for other destinations in Brunei Muara District also leave from this station. If you intend to explore Brunei Muara in any detail, it is best to hire a car; try Avis (6 Haji Daud Complex, Jalan Gadong, Bandar Seri Begawan, **t** 242 6345) or Qawi Enterprise (P.O. Box 1322, Gadong, **t** 234 0380).

Tourist Information

The most helpful resource is the **Tourist Information Centre** (General Post Office Building, on the corner of Jalan Sultan and Jalan Elizabeth Dua, **t** 222 3734; open Mon–Sat 8–12 and 2–4.30), with knowledgeable staff who can provide brochures, lists of hotels, car rental companies and tour operators. They also provide copies of the useful *Explore Brunei* visitor's guide. The headquarters of **Brunei Tourism** (Ministry of Industry and Primary Resources, Jalan Menteri Besar, **t** 238 2822, *www.tourismbrunei.com*) is located among the government offices north of the city centre.

Tour Operators

Tour operators provide the easiest way of exploring Brunei, taking care of permits and travel arrangements, where necessary. Because tourism is still in its infancy in Brunei, you are very unlikely to find yourself in a large tour group (often, you will have a guide and driver to yourself). The Tourist Information Centre can provide a comprehensive list of tour operators based in and around Bandar Seri Begawan. A number are also listed on the tourist board's website (*www.tourismbrunei.com*). The following tour operators in particular can be recommended:

Mona Florafauna Tours, Ground Floor, Yayasan Complex, Bandar Seri Begawan, **t** 223 0761, *mft@brunet.bn*.

Freme Travel Services, Wisma Jaya, Jalan Pemancha, Bandar Seri Begawan, **t** 223 4277, *www.freme.com*.

Sunshine Borneo Tours, No.2, Simpang 146, Jalan Kiarong, Bandar Seri Begawan, **t** 244 1791, *www.exploreborneo.com*.

Where to Stay

Brunei t (+673, no local codes)

Given the relatively small number of visitors Brunei receives each year, the range of

it this far in a water taxi, ask the boatman to steer round the edge of the palace grounds and into the mouth of **Sungai Damuan**, where you are likely to catch glimpses of proboscis monkeys (*see* 'The Proboscis Monkey', p.387). These peculiar primates can be seen munching leaves in the mangroves at the edge of **Pulau Ranggu**, a small island in the river. Opposite the island is the **Taman Persiaran** accommodation is understandably limited. There is very little aimed at the tourist (as opposed to the business traveller). One exception is the Empire Hotel & Country Club, Brunei's only beachside hotel and one of the world's most luxurious resorts. There are few budget options.

Luxury

Empire Hotel & Country Club, Jerudong BG3122, **t** 241 8888, *www.theempirehotel.com*. It is almost worth stopping by the Empire Hotel even if you are not staying there – just to see what a US$800 million hotel looks like. The central atrium soars 80 metres to an ornate ceiling held in place by giant marble pillars; the Presidential Suite (the size of a moderate house) boasts its own indoor pool with a built-in cinema screen that glides down from the ceiling; there's an 18-hole Jack Nicklaus golf course, a multiscreen cinema complex, a sports club with squash and badminton courts, a watersports centre, a children's club with water slide, and seven restaurants. Standard rooms all have balconies and bathrooms with walk-in showers and baths for two. There is a free shuttle service in and out of Bandar Seri Begawan four times daily. It is definitely worth checking for promotions, which often have rooms going for a fraction of the rack rates.

Expensive

Sheraton Utama Hotel, Jalan Tasek Lama, Bandar Seri Begawan, **t** 224 4272, *www.sheraton.com/utama*. The top hotel within Bandar Seri Begawan itself, with large rooms, an outdoor swimming pool, two restaurants and a health club with spa treatments. Each of the rooms has internet access (chargeable). The waterfront is a 10-minute walk away.

The Centrepoint, Abdul Razak Complex, Gadong, **t** 243 0430, *www.arhbrunei.com*. Situated several kilometres beyond the city centre, in the suburb of Gadong. There's no pool or fitness centre, but in every other respect the hotel matches the Sheraton for luxury. Frequent promotions can see the rates almost halved.

Moderate

Orchid Garden Hotel, Lot 31954, Simpang 9, Kampung Anggerek Desa, Jalan Berakas, **t** 233 5544, *www.orchidgardenbrunei.com*. This is the nearest hotel to the airport, so handy for stopovers. Offers comfortable rooms with 4-star facilities, including high-speed internet access, two restaurants, a pool and a spa.

Brunei Hotel, 95 Jalan Pemancha, Bandar Seri Begawan, **t** 224 2372, *www.bruneihotel.com.bn*. Situated right in the centre of Bandar Seri Begawan, close to the Sungai Kianggeh market. Each of the 65 rooms has satellite TV, mini-bar and en suite bathroom. There's a restaurant, but no pool.

Inexpensive

Terrace Hotel, Jalan Tasek Lama, Bandar Seri Begawan, **t** 224 3554, *www.terracebrunei.com*. The best-value hotel in the capital, with 80 plain en suite rooms, each with TV, kettle and safe. There's a nice outdoor pool, a restaurant and a karaoke lounge. The waterfront is 10 minutes away by foot.

Jubilee Plaza Hotel, Jalan Kampung Kianggeh, Bandar Seri Begawan, **t** 222 8070, *jubilee@brunet.bn*. In a fairly quiet location off a side road, 10 minutes' walk from the waterfront. Rooms are functional, with TV, mini-bar and attached bathroom. Breakfast and airport transfers are included in the price, making this a good-value option.

Damuan, a kilometre-long park which runs along the river bank and also serves as a vantage point for monkey-spotting. Within the park are sculptures from each of the ten ASEAN nations.

For the best chance of spotting proboscis monkeys, book a tour with one of the many Bandar-based tour operators. The boatman will cut the engine and paddle your

Budget

Voctech International House, Jalan Pasar Baharu, Gadong, **t** 244 7992, *voctech@brunet.bn*. The best budget option, with spacious, clean rooms, each with TV and fridge. A real bonus is the nearby *pasar malam*, where you can find good, cheap local food. The city centre is 3km away.

Pusat Belia, Jalan Sungai Kianggeh, Bandar Seri Begawan, **t** 222 3936, *jbsbelia@brunet.bn*. Brunei's only youth hostel, providing clean four-bed dorms, and a swimming pool! Just five minutes from the waterfront in downtown Bandar.

Eating Out

Brunei offers the same variety of cuisine as neighbouring Malaysia, from Malay, Chinese and Indian, to Japanese, European and fusion cuisine. The quality of the food is almost universally excellent, and though the restaurants are considerably more expensive than those in Malaysia, the food stalls still offer excellent value for money.

The ***pasar malam*** (night market) in the suburb of Gadong is the best place to sample cheap, local Malay food. Satay, grilled meats, rice and noodle dishes, fruit juices and coconut-based Malay sweets are laid out at hundreds of stalls from 5pm onwards each day. In the city centre itself, the **Tamu Kianggeh** (the market stalls alongside Sungai Kianggeh) offers a smaller variety of the above on certain days. Otherwise, try the **Padian Foodcourt** (1st floor, Yayasan Complex; open daily 9am–10pm), which is great for cheap local food and drink, as well as Indian, Thai and Indonesian staples. There are also a handful of stalls set on the waterfront beside the Temburong jetty, which turn out *roti kosong* (the same as *roti canai*), *nasi campur* and *teh tarik*.

In the suburbs of Gadong and Kiulap, there are numerous food courts set inside the shopping malls. These offer hawker-style food covering the range of Asian cuisines. The food court on the top floor of **The Mall** in Gadong is the biggest of them.

Bars, it goes without saying, are non-existent in Brunei, where **alcohol** is prohibited. That is not to say that non-Muslims are banned from drinking alcohol altogether. If you have brought your allowance of alcohol with you through customs, some top-end hotels and restaurants will let you drink it with your meal. Otherwise, you will be restricted to drinking in the privacy of your hotel room.

There are plenty of restaurants to choose from in and around Bandar Seri Begawan, though they seem to come and go with great frequency.

A selection of favourites follows.

Expensive

Zaika, G24, Block C, Yayasan Complex, Bandar Seri Begawan, **t** 223 0817. 'Zaika' means 'fine dining' in Urdu, and this is some of the finest dining you'll get in the city centre. That's not to say it's stuffy or overly formal. A vast menu of excellent North Indian cuisine is served up in tranquil, wood-panelled surroundings strewn with antiques. Recommended.

I-Lotus Restaurant, 28 Spg 12–26, Perumahan Rakyat Jati, Rimba Gadong (just past Tungku Link), **t** 242 2466. Has the reputation of being one of Brunei's best restaurants. A little out of the way, but this place is certainly worth the trip. Serves a wide range of Nyonya, Chinese and Thai dishes, with frequent steamboat promotions. Take a taxi (you won't find the restaurant on your own).

Li Gong, Empire Hotel & Country Club, Jerudong, **t** 241 8888 ext.7329. Superlative

tambang quietly into the mangroves for the best views. Mono Florafauna Tours (*Ground Floor, Yayasan Complex, Bandar Seri Begawan,* ***t*** *223 0761, mft@brunet.bn*) is the only operator to *guarantee* sightings.

Chinese cuisine, set in a pavilion surrounded by koi ponds. The menu reads like a map of China, with specialities from every province. Stop by on Wednesdays for an all-you-can-eat buffet, or Thursdays for steamboat. Be sure to book in advance. *Closed Mon.*

Spaghettini, Empire Hotel & Country Club, Jerudong, **t** 241 8888 ext.7368. An Italian trattoria, complete with Italian chef and an authentic, wood-fired oven for pizzas. Bring your own wine (if you declared it at customs).

Moderate

RMS Portview Seafood Restaurant, Jalan MacArthur, Bandar Seri Begawan, **t** 223 1466. Set right on the waterfront, with a formal restaurant upstairs serving Thai, Japanese and Chinese cuisine. Excellent steamboats. Downstairs is a café serving cheaper Western and local cuisine.

Hua Hua, 48 Jalan Sultan, **t** 222 5396. One of the best Chinese restaurants in town, serving a wide variety of well-priced dishes, including excellent dim sum.

Ahan Thai, Ground Floor, Jubilee Plaza, Jalan Kampung Kianggeh, Bandar Seri Begawan, **t** 223 9599. This place has the air of a fast-food restaurant, though the food is excellent – Thai favourites, such as tom yam soup and chilli squid.

Escapade Sushi, Unit 4–5, Block C, Abdul Raza Complex (opposite Centrepoint Hotel), Gadong, **t** 244 3012. Perch on a stool and eat sushi from a conveyor belt.

Inexpensive

Seri Indah, Jalan MacArthur, Bandar Seri Begawan, **t** 224 3567. A simple *mamak* (Indian Muslim) restaurant serving delicious *roti kosong* and *teh tarik*. Situated opposite the waterfront wet market.

C.A. Mohamed, Unit 202, Yayasan Complex, Bandar Seri Begawan, **t** 223 2999. A no-nonsense local restaurant set upstairs in the Yayasan Complex, and serving inexpensive Malay and Indian staples.

Popular Restaurant, Unit 5, Ground Floor, Norain Complex, Bandar Seri Begawan, **t** 222 1375. The name says it all; a simple place serving North and South Indian cuisine, all of it delicious.

Shopping

With the excellent range of goods and cheap prices of neighbouring Malaysia and Singapore, Brunei's shopping opportunities are a disappointment. Which probably explains why shopping trips to Miri are so popular with Bruneians (well, that and the lure of sex and alcohol). Still, prices compare well with the West, and you'll have no problems finding luxury and branded items in the shopping malls.

The smart **Yayasan Complex** is the main shopping mall in downtown Bandar, complete with department store, supermarket, small boutiques and restaurants. Gadong, 3km outside Bandar, is the principal shopping centre, with numerous malls to choose from, including **Gadong Centrepoint** and **The Mall**, both of which are open late into the night.

A limited range of traditional handicrafts are available from the **Arts and Handicrafts Centre** on Jalan Residency (*see* p.401), with textiles, brassware, silverware and *keris* (traditional Malay daggers) all on sale. The upmarket hotels also sell gifts and handicrafts at hyped prices. To skip the middleman, browse the various outdoor markets. The biggest of them is the **weekly tamu** outside Tutong (*see* p.409), though Tamu Kianggeh in Bandar Seri Begawan has the odd item for sale, too.

Elsewhere in Brunei Muara District

Within **Brunei Muara District** (smallest of Brunei's four districts), visitors rarely stray beyond the capital itself. For those with time on their hands, there are various minor attractions worth tracking down.

The commercial heart of the capital lies in its nondescript suburbs, several kilometres northwest of the town centre. Nowadays, the main hubbub of activity is **Gadong**, a grid of modern shophouses, offices and department stores. This is where Bruneians come to shop; the only real attraction for visitors is the excellent ***pasar malam*** (night market), where Malay sweets line up alongside endless varieties of satay, which sizzle on charcoal grills. Bruneians roll in each night in their 4x4s, pick up their dinner, then drive home (consequently, there are no tables for dining on site). The market stalls open daily from late afternoon until midnight, or later.

Just south of Gadong, and its adjoining suburb of Kiulap, is the impressive National Mosque, known to locals as **Masjid Kiarong** (*the official name is Masjid Jame'Asr Hassan al Bolkiah; open Sat–Wed 8–12, 2–3, 5–6 and 8–9.30; closed to non-Muslims during certain religious festivals*). With its 29 intricate cupolas and four towering minarets, this is certainly the grandest mosque in Brunei, built in 1992 to celebrate the sultan's Silver Jubilee – though the Omar Ali Saifuddien Mosque in the city centre remains the nation's iconic monument.

Brunei Muara's other attractions line up along its coastline. Near the small coastal village of **Jerudong** are the fruits of Prince Jefri's extravagant business ventures (*see* 'Brunei Today', p.397) – the Empire Hotel & Country Club (one of the world's most lavish hotels) and the **Jerudong Playground** (*open Wed–Fri and Sun 5pm–midnight, Sat 5pm–2am; admission B$15 adults, B$5 children*). The latter is a peculiar collection of fairground attractions and roller coasters, eerily quiet for most of the year. Not to be missed if you happen to have children in tow.

The main coastal highway runs east from Jerudong as far as **Muara** itself, a small port at Brunei's northernmost tip. Along the way, the highway passes alongside two small forest reserves, **Bukit Shahbandar Reserve** and the **Hutan Berakas Forest Reserve.** Both contain a network of paved trails through the forest, and are popular with joggers and cyclists. A wooden observation tower marks the high point of Bukit Shahbandar, while Hutan Berakas is characterized by *kerangas*, or heath forest, where carnivorous pitcher plants grow in abundance. The forest runs down to a long sandy beach lined with casuarinas, where locals come to swim. Another beach popular with Bruneians is **Pantai Muara**, a 4km stretch of sand north of the town of Muara.

Temburong District

Temburong is the sleepy, barely inhabited finger of land that lies east of the Malaysian territory of Limbang. Virtually the entire district is forested, and this is the principle attraction for visitors. The highlight is the Ulu Temburong National Park – a match for any of Malaysia's national parks, and yet rarely visited, thanks to Brunei's sketchy tourism infrastructure. The few inhabitants of Temburong are a scattered population of Malays and indigenous tribespeople, mainly Iban and Murut.

Bangar (as opposed to Bandar) is the administrative centre, though it's little more than a village with a jetty, a resthouse, a government office and a handful of coffee shops. Speedboats, or 'flying coffins' as they are known locally, arrive at the jetty from

Bandar Seri Begawan, a thrilling 45-minute journey through a maze of mangrove channels inhabited by proboscis monkeys and dotted with ramshackle kampungs.

Twenty minutes east of Bangar, by road, is the **Peradayan Forest Reserve**, which contains a small forest recreation park with picnic tables and a series of trails into the jungle, one of which leads to a viewpoint on the summit of Bukit Patoi. Most visitors head south to the better equipped, and wilder, Ulu Temburong National Park (*see* below).

En route to the national park, the southbound road passes by a handful of kampungs and longhouses – not the traditional *attap*-roofed dwellings, but their contemporary equivalent, with mod cons and car-parking bays beneath. The largest is a 16-door Iban longhouse, situated at **Kampung Sembiling**. If you are passing by as part of an organized tour (which is invariably the case), you will have the chance to stop off and poke around the longhouse. If anyone is home, they will invite you into their private quarters for a glass of *tuak* (rice wine) and a bite to eat.

The road peters out as it reaches **Batang Duri**, which means 'Spiky Hamlet' after the wild durian trees that grow hereabouts. From here, indigenous longboats ferry visitors up the Sungai Temburong to the Ulu Temburong National Park, a wonderful ride into little-visited virgin rainforest.

Ulu Temburong National Park

The Ulu Temburong National Park is part of the remote **Batu Apoi Forest Reserve**, which occupies the southern half of Temburong District. This is pristine jungle territory, unscathed by logging and uninhabited. There are no roads, and access to the park is by longboat. Despite decent facilities and easy access, the national park is visited by only a handful of tourists each year. Which can be part of the appeal – more likely than not, you'll have the trails to yourself. The highlight is undoubtedly the **canopy walkway**, which stands 50m tall and is set on a hilltop, with serene views across virgin forest as far as the eye can see. A trip to Ulu Temburong is worth it for this view alone.

The rainforest here is known for its unusual biodiversity, thanks to work carried out at the Belalong Rainforest Field Studies Centre, which is situated within park boundaries. Insects, in particular, are found here in as yet unmatched numbers (one scientist identified more than 400 species of beetle on a single tree). As is always the case in the rainforest, wildlife is very hard to spot, though with a good guide, sightings are assured. The huge rhinoceros hornbill is commonly seen gliding across the river, its occasional wing beats audible across great distances. Pygmy squirrels are common, as are flying lizards and Wallace's flying frogs. Wild boar, mouse deer and gibbons are also present in large numbers (though less commonly seen).

The canopy walkway is linked with **park headquarters** by 7km of wooden boardwalks. The terrain here is steep and rugged, so a moderate level of fitness is required. Climbing to the foot of the canopy walkway is sweaty work in itself, with almost a thousand steps leading to the summit of the hill. The walkway is set

Getting There

The trip to Ulu Temburong starts with a journey by speed-ferry from the jetty on Jalan Residency, Bandar Seri Begawan, to Bangar (daily every half-hour 7.45–4; 45mins journey time; B$6 one-way). From the jetty in Bangar, it's a 20-minute taxi ride south to Batang Duri. The last leg of the journey is completed by longboat via Sungai Temburong to park headquarters (90mins; B$60 per boat – though travel costs will be included in the price if you use a tour operator). During the dry season (which peaks in July and August), the water levels can get very low, making the journey upriver fairly arduous. Travel arrangements can be made by all the Bandar-based tour operators.

Tourist Information

It is possible to visit the Ulu Temburong National Park independently, though there is little point in doing so; you will save no money, and will need to make all travel arrangements yourself. You will also need to get hold of a travel permit in advance from the Forestry Department (Ministry of Industry and Primary Resources, Bandar Seri Begawan BB3910, **t** 238 1687/238 1013, *forestrybrunei@hotmail.com*). Entering the national park without a permit carries a jail sentence. All of the tour operators based in the capital offer tours to Ulu Temburong. Most people opt for a day trip, and these can be booked with as little as a day's notice. The tour operator will take care of all travel arrangements and obtain a permit on your behalf. At park headquarters, there is a small exhibition, and a registration office, where visitors must sign in and pay a B$5 entrance fee.

Where to Stay

Most people visit Temburong District on day trips, but for those who want to stay over, there is (limited) accommodation. Indigenous **longhouses** are an option, though be sure to follow the correct etiquette if you turn up unannounced (*see* p.329). Two longhouses in particular (Amo C and the Kampung Sembiling longhouse, both Iban) offer informal homestays. For a nominal sum of money, meals are provided and mattresses are laid out on the *ruai* (common verandah). Arrangements can be made by tour operators in Bandar. Otherwise, contact the Tourist Information Centre. The only other accommodation in Temburong is as follows:

Government Resthouse, Jalan Batang Duri, Bangar, **t** 522 1239 (*moderate–inexpensive*). Simple, functional rooms and chalets situated five minutes (by foot) from the jetty in Bangar.

Ulu Temburong National Park, c/o Tourist Office, General Post Office Building, corner of Jalan Sultan and Jalan Elizabeth Dua, Bandar Seri Begawan, **t** 222 3734 (*inexpensive*). At park headquarters, there is plenty of clean, basic accommodation in chalets linked by boardwalks. Most people visit the national park on day trips, and accommodation for longer stays is generally arranged by the tour operator.

between soaring aluminium towers, with a series of step ladders providing the only access (vertigo sufferers beware). Up on the walkway, orchids and epiphytes can be seen clinging to the upper branches. Down below is the confluence of the Sungai Temburong and the Sungai Belalong, while thickly forested hills roll away in all directions.

From the canopy walkway, the trail of boardwalks continues as far as Sungai Apan, a narrow stream several kilometres upriver. A short walk upstream brings you to a lovely little waterfall, with a plunge pool deep enough for bathing in (depending on the time of year). A series of ropes lead round the edge of the waterfall to a second tier of falls.

Though few visitors stray off the boardwalks, there is plenty of scope in Ulu Temburong for longer treks, either using park headquarters as a base, or camping at night in the rainforest. The most challenging trail is the week-long trek to the top of **Bukit Pagon** (1843m), which sits on the border with Sarawak. Contact the tourist office, or one of the tour operators, to make arrangements.

Tutong District

Much of Tutong District – the strip of territory that follows the course of the Tutong River west of Brunei Muara – lies under the cover of virgin forest, with a scattering of small-scale plantations tucked away behind the coastal strip. The coastal highway passes by the district capital, **Tutong**, a sedate little town on a bend of the Sungai Tutong, with little to detain the visitor.

Just outside Tutong, to the north, is the **Taman Rekreasi Sungai Basong**, a forest recreation park complete with picnic tables, jogging paths and ponds. West of here is Pantai Tutong, a sandy beach which becomes **Pantai Seri Kerangan** (literally, 'Unforgettable Beach'), a sandy spit dividing the Sungai Tutong and the South China Sea. Locals come here to swim, fly kites and relax (the beach is regularly cleaned of debris). **River tours** along the Sungai Tutong can be arranged by Ilufah Leisure Tours (**t** 223 3524, *ilufah_tours@brunet.bn*). The boat weaves upriver through the mangroves and past numerous Malay and Dusun villages. Monkeys are common here, while estuarine crocodiles can sometimes be spotted basking on sandbanks.

Tasek Merimbun

The only real diversion for visitors in Tutong District is Tasek Merimbun, a snaking lake surrounded by dense jungle. The region is traditionally home to Dusun tribespeople, though since the lake and surrounding forest were set aside as a nature reserve, only a handful of Dusun remain. The **Tasek Merimbun Heritage Park** encompasses the lake and its surrounding habitats – wetlands, peat-swamp forest and lowland dipterocarp forest. It is a beautiful spot, rich in wildlife, with boardwalks leading across the peat-black water of the lake to a small island, where Bruneians come at weekends to fish. A number of unique species have been discovered in the area, including the white-collared fruit bat. Clouded leopards (Borneo's largest cat) and crocodiles are also present here (signboards on the island warn visitors to keep an eye out for crocodiles). A short 'Botanical Trail' leads through the forest beside the lake, and local Dusun guides can be hired for longer treks. There is a small visitor centre beside the lake, with accommodation in a handful of chalets (usually booked out by research groups). Kayaks can also be hired.

There is no public transport to Tasek Merimbun, so the only way of getting there is by taxi or hire car (which may well work out cheaper than a taxi). To reach Tasek Merimbun from Bandar Seri Begawan, take the old Tutong Road, which runs parallel and to the south of the new coastal highway. At mile 18, take the left fork signposted for Lamunin. Beyond Kampung Lamunin itself, follow signs for Tasek Merimbun. Journey time is 90 minutes or less.

Belait District

Belait District is the source of Brunei's oil wealth, and home to a sizable expatriate population of British and Dutch (thanks to the presence of Shell). Since the discovery of oil at Seria in 1929, Belait's coastal strip has developed beyond recognition, with oil refineries and 'nodding donkeys' (small, land-based oil wells) dotting the landscape. Inland, Belait remains virtually unscathed, with vast tracts of virgin rainforest inhabited only by a scattering of indigenous tribespeople – predominantly Iban and Dusun. Before the discovery of oil, the coastal strip was dominated by swamp-land and mangrove forests, a topography which caused considerable difficulties for oil prospectors. Even as late as the 1950s, much of the region was impassable. Novelist Anthony Burgess, who taught in Brunei during the late 1950s, tells in his autobiography of a near scrape with death when his car was caught by the incoming tide in Belait District. His wife saved the day by swimming to a local village for help, braving crocs along the way.

Brunei's oil industry developed around the town of **Seria**, once nothing more than open swampland. Today it is a truly surreal place, with a motley population of expat oil workers and their families, Chinese shopkeepers, indigenous tribespeople, a few Malays and a garrison of Gurkhas (the sultan pays the British government handsomely for the Gurkhas to be stationed here, as a means of protecting Brunei's precious oil supply). The town is strung out along the level coastal plain, with 'nodding donkeys' visible above neat rows of residential bungalows, and open fields of mowed grass speckled white with egrets.

There's one visitor attraction in Seria, the **Oil & Gas Discovery Centre** (*OGDC;* ***t*** *337 7200; open Tues–Thurs 9–5, Fri 10–12 and 2–6, Sat–Sun 10–6; adm B$5*), which provides the rundown on oil production as well as some fun exhibits for kids, including a gyroscope and a bed of nails. On the edge of town is the **Billionth Barrel Monument**, which speaks for itself.

West of Seria is the district capital, **Kuala Belait** (known to Bruneians simply as 'KB'). Again, it is a fairly uninspiring place, centred around a grid of shophouses, where the expat oil workers come to do their shopping. Kuala Belait also serves as the border town with Sarawak, Malaysia, and as a departure point for the interior of Belait District via Sungai Belait. River boats leave for Kuala Balai (*see* below) from behind the market building on Jalan Pasar.

The Belait Interior

Few people venture into the interior of Belait, though the region is earmarked by the government as a future ecotourism destination. As such, a few of the tour operators based in Bandar Seri Begawan are beginning to put together itineraries into the Belait interior. (Independent travel upriver in this region is difficult, and is certainly not cost-effective.)

Jalan Labi

The easiest route into the interior of Belait is via **Jalan Labi**, a road which cuts south from the coastal highway at Kampung Lumut, near the border with Tutong District. A mile or so along Jalan Labi is the **Sungai Liang Forest Reserve**, a well-established 'forest recreation park' with picnic shelters, ponds and a network of decent trails into the surrounding forest. On the nearest hilltop is a treehouse, providing views across the reserve. A few hundred yards from the entrance to the Sungai Liang Forest Reserve is the Forestry Department building, with a small 'Palmetum' and a forestry museum – the **Muzium Perhutanan** (*open Mon–Thurs and Sat 8–12.15 and 1.30–4.30*), set in a two-roomed bungalow.

Beyond here, Jalan Labi cuts through remote rainforest in the direction of Kampung Labi, passing another forest reserve along the way – the 270-hectare **Luagan Lalak Recreation Park**, which is part of the Labi Hills Forest Reserve. This area was once the focus of speculative oil drilling (indeed, that is the reason the Labi Road was built in the first place). Luagan Lalak is an area of swampland which turns into a lake during the monsoon season. A short boardwalk provides access to part of the lake.

Kampung Labi itself is situated 40km inland, a tiny settlement ringed by small-scale fruit plantations. Beyond here, the road becomes a dirt track, providing access to a number of Iban longhouses. The largest is the 12-door **Rumah Panjang Mendaram Besar**. A nearby trail leads to a large waterfall (ask at the longhouse).

The dirt track continues for around 15 kilometres, as far as a smaller longhouse called **Rumah Panjang Teraja**. The six families who live here are largely self-sufficient, cultivating their own paddy, fruit and vegetables, and rearing pigs and chickens. The longhouse is situated near the foot of **Bukit Teraja** (442m), with a 90-minute trail leading to the summit. Orang-utans have been spotted along the trail, though the journey is worth it for the views alone, which stretch as far as Gunung Mulu (*see* p.346) in Sarawak.

Sungai Belait

An alternative route into the interior is via Sungai Belait, a long river which snakes inland from its estuary at Kuala Belait (*see* above) as far as the southern hills bordering Sarawak.

An hour upriver from the district capital (Kuala Belait), is the tiny riverine settlement of **Kuala Balai**. Before the ascendancy of Kuala Belait as an oil town, Kuala Balai was the only settlement of any size to be found in the region. The inhabitants, known as 'Belait Malays', are descended from both Malays and indigenous tribes-people. Like the Melanau people of Sarawak, the Belait Malays relied almost exclusively on traditional sago processing. Today, the population has dwindled almost to nothing, though two simple sago-processing plants remain. The main focal point today is a reconstruction of a traditional stilted longhouse on the banks of the river – the work, ironically, of Raleigh International. Just down the river from the longhouse is a small box on stilts containing 20 human skulls – victims of long-dead indigenous headhunters.

Further longhouses – mainly Iban – can be found along the upper reaches of the Sungai Belait. Though it is possible to reach these from Kuala Balai, the journey takes many hours, and it is quicker to join the river instead at Kampung Sungai Mau, which is accessible via the Labi Road. Beyond this point, the region is known locally as **Ulu Belait**, or 'Upriver Belait'.

Two hours beyond Kampung Sungai Mau is **Kampung Sukang**, a community of Dusun and Punan tribespeople who have adapted to life in a hamlet (the Punan are traditionally nomadic hunter-gatherers). They now farm hill paddy, though traditional hunting methods (blowpipes with poison arrows) are still used.

Several hours beyond Kampung Sukang is **Kampung Melilas**, a collection of Iban longhouses on the banks of the river. The small community here has developed a thriving cottage industry in traditional basketry and textile weaving. Trips to one of these longhouses can sometimes be arranged by tour operators, along with treks into the surrounding rainforest (where hot springs and waterfalls can be found). The journey upriver as far as Kampung Melilas depends very much on the level of the river; during the dry season, villagers themselves are sometimes marooned for weeks on end.

Singapore

20

Singapore
DUNEARN ROAD
BUKIT TIMAH ROAD
STEVENS ROAD
SCOTTS ROAD
CLEMENCEAU AVENUE NORTH
NS21 Newton
Goodwood Park Hotel
Tanglin Club
CENTRAL EXPRESSWAY
EMERALD HILL ROAD
Cuppage Terrace
Tang's
PERANAKAN PLACE
ORCHARD ROAD
NS22 Orchard
ORCHARD BOULEVARD
TANGLIN ROAD
CUSCADEN ROAD
Singapore Botanic Gardens
TOMLINSON ROAD
EXETER ROAD
Post Office
KILLINEY ROAD
Singapore Tourist Board
RIVER VALLEY ROAD
KIM SENG ROAD
JIAK KIM ST
N
250 metres
250 yards

Sri Srinivas Perumal Temple
Mustafa Centre
Syed Alwi Rd
Farrer Park Field
Rochor Canal
Sri Veeramakaliamman Temple
Serangoon Road
Veerasamy Road
Jalan Besar
Rochor Canal Road
Victoria Street
North Bridge Road
Hajjah Fatimah Mosque
Istana Kampong Glam
Pahang Street
Beach Road
Upper Dickson Road
Dickson Road
NE7 Little India
Buffalo Road
Little India Arcade
Perak Road
Abdul Gaffoor Mosque
Kandahar St
Baghdad Street
Tekka Centre
Bukit Timah Road
Mayo Street
Arab Street
Sultan Mosque
Bussorah Street
Sungei Road
Rochor Canal Road
Albert Street
Albert St
New Bugis Street
EW12 Bugis
Bencoolen Street
Istane Park
Middle Road
Liang Seah St
Waterloo Street
Singapore Art Museum
Purvis St
Beach Road
Suntek Towers
1
2
3
4
5
Seah St
Victoria Street
Raffles Hotel
Orchard Road
NS24/NE26 Dhoby Ghaut
Fort Canning Road
Singapore History Museum
Bras Basah Road
Suntek City Mall
Temasek Blvd
Raffles Boulevard
Er Road
Oxley Rise
Clemenceau Avenue
National Museum Shop
North Bridge Road
NS25/EW13 City Hall
War Memorial Park
Stamford Road
Fort Canning Arts Centre
Armenian Street
ACM Armenia Street
Singapore Flyer site (Opening 2008)
Raffles Avenue
Yd Road
St Andrews Cathedral
St Andrews Road
Connaught Drive
Esplanade Drive
Esplanade – Theatres on the Bay
The Battle Box
Hill Street
Coleman St
Padang
Singapore Philatelic Museum
City Hall
Colombo Court
Marina Bay
Fort Canning Park
High Street
Supreme Court
River Valley Road
Mohamed Sultan Road
Parliament House
Victoria Theatre & Concert Hall
Asian Civilisations Museum
Fullerton Road
Unity Street
Clarke Quay
Empress Place
Anderson Bridge
Robertson Quay
Sir Stamford Raffles Landing Site
Cavenagh Bridge
NE5 Clarke Quay
Robertson Walk
Nanson Rd
Singapore River
Fullerton Square
One Fullerton
Merchant Road
Boat Quay
North Canal Road
Chulia Street
Clifford Pier
NS26/EW14 Raffles Place
Avelock Road
Upper Cross Street
Chin Swee Road
Eu Tong St
NE4 Chinatown
Far East Square
Mohamed Ali Lane
Mosque Street
Cross Street
Sri Mariamman Temple
Club Street
Temple St
Trengganu Street
Smith St
Amoy Street
Boon Tat Street
Robinson Road
Sago Street
Ann Siang Hill
Ann Siang Road
Thian Hock Keng Temple
Keong Saik Road
URA Gallery
EW16/NE3 Outram Park
Teck Lim Road
Maxwell Road
Neil Road
Duxton Rd
Tanjong Pagar Road
EW15 Tanjong Pagar
East Coast Parkway
Nson Road
Prince Edward Road

Singapore has done things backwards. In the space of only a few decades the little city-state has leapfrogged into the developed world, leaving a cultural deficit that has come to plague its image. In recent years, however, the authorities have begun to take note of Singapore's rich ancestral heritage and throw up modern spaces for the performing arts. The foreign media may scoff at the ruling party's top-down approach, but it seems to have worked. No longer can it be said of Singapore that shopping is the only approved outlet for expression; funds sourced by the new Ministry of Arts are being ploughed into a commendable line-up of museums, while the unveiling of a world-class arts centre and the easing of censorship have helped jump-start a mini-renaissance in the city.

Still, it cannot yet be said that Singapore is in vogue as a tourist destination. There is the sense, in some circles, that it remains uncool to admit a fondness for the city – a city where government initiatives have included the Smile Campaign, the Courtesy Campaign, and the Speak Good English Campaign. But that doesn't stop people coming in their droves, particulary as a stopover en route elsewhere. They zip about on the city's seamless transport system, they wander the shops, they enjoy the food, the museums, the gardens. Then they leave, quietly impressed.

The feeling that Singapore and its people have been straitjacketed by draconian social policies is at the heart of the image problem. The country's unprecedented climb to prosperity has been achieved at a cost – a cost which ex-Prime Minister Lee Kuan Yew famously dismissed: 'When you are hungry, when you lack basic services, then freedom, human rights and democracy do not add up to much.' Now that Singaporeans have all that they want, these costs are being addressed, particularly by the younger generation.

Whatever your opinion of Singapore, there can be no denying that it packs some punch as a modern-day tourist destination. For a start, it is arguably the culinary capital of Asia, with wonderful street food and an exciting range of restaurants serving the gamut of world cuisine. It is a surprisingly green place too, fully worthy of its tag line 'Garden City of Asia', with dozens of immaculate gardens to explore and even a patch of virgin rainforest full of monkeys and birdlife. And of course, Singapore is a great place to shop, an example of consumer mechanics at its smoothest, a place where brand names flex and bargain-hunters strut. In such a well-oiled machine as Singapore, visitors can expect exceptional standards of service and comfort. All in all, the city-state makes the ideal base for forays into Southeast Asia.

History

Singapore's distant history remains uncertain. According to the 17th-century *Sejarah Melayu* ('Malay Annals'), a Sumatran prince founded a settlement on the island some time around AD 1299. On landing, the prince spotted a lion and named the settlement 'Singapura' (derived from the Sanskrit for 'lion city'). What a lion was doing on a tropical island is anyone's guess – most assume the animal was actually a tiger, though lions were certainly more widespread in those days.

As early as the 14th century Singapore, or Temasek as it was then known, was notorious for its pirates. The narrow strait of water that splits Sentosa Island from

Sir Thomas Stamford Raffles

Appropriately, Thomas Stamford Raffles (1781–1826) was born aboard a ship, in the Caribbean. Little is known of Raffles' father, though one thing is certain – he could not afford a formal education for his son. Raffles compensated by studying hard in his spare time. At 14 he secured himself a position as a junior clerk for the East India Company. His single-minded determination saw him bound up the career ladder. He was posted to Penang as Assistant Secretary and, in a matter of months, mastered the Malay language and undertook a frenzied study of the people of Malaya – knowledge that was to make him indispensible to the Company. When the British wrested Java from Dutch control in 1811, Raffles was made Lieutenant Governor of Java, where he fought hard against the trade in slaves. A few years later he was promoted to Governor of Bencoolen (Sumatra).

Raffles became obsessed with the idea that a strategic port – ideally one at the southern approach to the Straits of Melaka – would secure British domination of Southeast Asia. This conviction did little more than raise eyebrows, and when Raffles landed on Singapore in January 1819, he did so without the authority or backing of either the East India Company or the British Crown. With diplomatic sleight of hand, he established a port on the island, and by 1824, Singapore was firmly in British hands. Raffles' move was beginning to look like a masterstroke.

Raffles was one of those rare and enviable men who managed to fit two or three lives into his own short lifespan (he died at 45). As well as single-handedly establishing the British as the leading in power in Southeast Asia, he was a fervent naturalist and historian, publishing a *History of Java* to critical acclaim and employing teams of botanists and zoologists to help him collect specimens. Many of the region's animals and plants were named by Raffles himself, including the Latin names for sun bear, silver leaf monkey, crab-eating macaque, and of course 'Rafflesia', the world's largest flower (*see* p.325). Like naturalist Alfred Russel Wallace, Raffles had a penchant for exotic pets. His favourite, so they say, was a Malayan sun bear, which sat with his children at dinner and ate mangoes off a plate. On a return trip to England, Raffles founded the Zoological Society and the London Zoo.

Raffles will be best remembered as a benevolent imperialist – one who fought for the welfare of indigenous peoples. He shunned the aloof approach to imperial domination by immersing himself in indigenous culture and establishing a meritocracy. His example was the inspiration for later imperialists, notably the Brookes – 'White Rajahs' of Sarawak. But Raffles goes down in history primarily as the founder of modern Singapore, the official starting point of the island's history (the dominant Chinese would rather not acknowledge the island's Malay origins).

Singapore was known to Chinese traders as 'Dragon Teeth Strait', for this very reason. Archaeological clues about Temasek's old settlements are thin on the ground; the best finds to date are a few pieces of jewellery crafted by goldsmiths of Java's Majapahit empire, unearthed near Fort Canning in 1928. The jewellery dates from the 14th century, at a time when a succession of Malay kings are thought to have ruled the island. The first of the kings, it is supposed, was Paramaswara, who based himself on the island briefly in the 1390s, before moving on to found the Sultanate of Melaka. By the turn of the 15th century the tiny kingdom appears to have been wiped from the map – probably as a result of conflicts between the rival powers of Majapahit and Siam.

A few centuries in the doldrums followed. Generations of Malay Orang Laut ('men of the sea') are thought to have frequented Singapore's shores during this time. They lived ghostly lives on the fringes of terra firma, building stilted settlements beyond the mangroves – immune (through destitution) to pirates.

When Sir Thomas Stamford Raffles (*see* p.417) appeared on the scene in 1819, Singapore was an island of little consequence at the tip of Malaya, densely jungled and home to no more than 150 semi-nomadic Orang Laut. Having consolidated power in India, and set up trading posts in Penang and Melaka, the British were in need of a new outpost – one which could command the southern approach to the Straits of Melaka, through which all trade between India and China must pass. Raffles, then Governor of Bencoolen (Sumatra), recognized Singapore's strategic potential, and set about securing the island. He struck a deal with a local chieftain and, with characteristic cunning, decided to recognize the Sultan of Johor's elder brother as the rightful ruler – thus usurping Dutch claims to the island (the reigning sultan was under the thumb of the Dutch and in no position to strike a deal himself).

A snubbed brother found his revenge, and Raffles realized a dream. He laid down a town plan and declared Singapore a free port (which it remains to this day). By 1824 the East India Company had acknowledged that Raffles was on to a good thing; the new sultan was duly brushed aside and the island ceded to the British.

Despite his prominent standing in Singapore, Raffles spent a total of only nine months in his new settlement, which was administered first from Bencoolen, then from Penang. The port boomed from the start. It soon became a vital crossroads for traders and their incumbent cultures – a halfway house between the great empires of Asia. Within a single year Singapore's revenue exceeded its administrative costs. Immigrants from China, Malaya, India, Siam, Java and the Arab world flocked to the island, lured by its free port status and by Raffles' policy of equality for all before the law. Singapore began to drain trade from Dutch ports, where heavy taxes and harsh laws prevailed – and the balance of power in Southeast Asia shifted in favour of the British. In 1827 Singapore became part of the Straits Settlement, a British administrative zone which united Singapore, Penang and Melaka.

By the time naturalist Alfred Russel Wallace visited in the late 1850s, Singapore had become the 'great commercial emporium' that Raffles had hoped for and predicted. 'The harbour is crowded with men-of-war,' noted Wallace, 'and trading vessels of many European nations, and hundreds of Malay praus and Chinese junks, from vessels of several hundred tons, down to little fishing boats and passenger sampans; and the town comprises handsome public buildings and churches, Mahometan mosques, Hindu temples, Chinese joss-houses, European houses, massive warehouses, queer old Kling and China bazaars, and long suburbs of Chinese and Malay cottages.'

As the Chinese population grew, so did the prevalence of secret societies. Each dialect group fell under the power of a 'Captain China', who in turn liaised with the colonial officials. Feuds were frequent and fierce – on one occasion 600 were killed over a dispute about the price of rice. Gambling and opium dependency took hold, thanks largely to the British, who farmed out monopolies among the wealthy Chinese merchants. Practical lawlessness prevailed until Singapore was made a British Crown Colony in 1867.

By the end of the century, Singapore had become the world centre of rubber and tin distribution. Henry Ridley, the first Director of the Singapore Botanic Garden, was the pioneer of the rubber industry in Southeast Asia. He had rubber seedlings shipped over from Brazil (the rubber tree is indigenous to South America) and spent decades testing their agricultural worth, convinced of rubber's potential as the future cash crop for British Malaya. With the advent of the motorcar, Ridley's dreams were realized and the industry boomed.

Singapore continued to prosper, until the Great Depression of the 1930s took its toll on exports. Then came the Japanese occupation; and everything changed in an instant. In February 1942 Japanese forces attacked from Malaya, and Singapore fell without much of a fight. Winston Churchill called it one of Britain's worst ever military capitulations: the British forces had anticipated an attack from the south and had concentrated their fire power at Fort Sentosa, leaving the northern approach from Malaya unprotected.

Singapore was renamed Syonan-To (Light of the South), local time was advanced to match Tokyo time and the calendar changed to match the Japanese year. Europeans were herded to the infamous Changi Prison (*see* p.456), and Chinese were executed in their thousands. In the eyes of Singapore's residents, the British had abandoned them in their neediest hour. After the Japanese surrender in 1945, a path towards self-rule was struck at once.

Independent Singapore

In May 1959, after a decade of social tension fuelled by communist guerilla activities in Malaya (a period known as the Emergency – *see* p.20), the independent State of Singapore came into existence, headed by Prime Minister Lee Kuan Yew of the People's Action Party (PAP). Lee Kuan Yew, a Straits Chinese educated at Cambridge and fluent in Mandarin, Hokkien, Malay and English, was to prove himself a shrewd politician. He believed that Singapore was too small, and too poor in natural resources, to survive on its own at this stage. So he began at once to negotiate with Kuala Lumpur. In August 1963, Singapore became part of the newly formed Federation of Malaysia – a federation which came into being primarily for the very purpose of absorbing Singapore.

However, political and racial differences between Singapore and Kuala Lumpur were further exacerbated by the Indonesian Konfrontasi (armed confrontation) against the formation of Malaysia. Tensions ran high, and a call for racial equality from Chinese-dominated Singapore proved the last straw for the Alliance government – whose politics were based on ethnic alignment and 'positive discrimination' in favour of Malays, rather than a cross-race social and economic policy. Fear from extremists in KL that Singapore's leaders were plotting to seize control of Malaysia prompted Prime Minister Tunku Abdul Rahman to take drastic action. With little warning, in August 1965, he announced the expulsion of Singapore from the Federation.

Singapore's new status as an independent republic was viewed as a potential disaster by PAP leader Lee Kuan Yew. Economic growth became a matter of urgency. The Jurong swamp in the southwest of the island was drained and turned into a vast industrial estate; incentives were offered to private capital; tough labour legislation was pushed through; and state-controlled social policies were rigorously pursued. Singapore was developed as a secular, multiracial state with English adopted as the first language. Within a decade, to the surprise of many, the city-state had become an economic heavyweight – making up for its lack of natural resources by concentrating on financial services, electronics, rubber distribution, food processing and oil refineries.

On paper Singapore is governed as a democracy, adopting the Westminster model, with elected members of parliament and electoral divisions. Governments are elected for five-year terms. A President is also elected by the populace, though his role is largely ceremonial. Like the parliamentary model, the legal system mirrors that in Britain, with a Supreme Court and (supposed) independence of the judiciary. However, the drive that transformed Singapore into Southeast Asia's leading economic power came at a price; despite appearances, a mild authoritarian streak runs through the government of Singapore, with the ruling PAP controlling the press, enforcing strict censorship, playing a hand in the outcome of important court proceedings, and pressing legal suits on anyone who dares to voice political opposition with any degree of vehemence. The PAP call it paternalism.

In 1990 Prime Minister Goh Chok Tong took the reins on Lee Kuan Yew's retirement. He has seen Singapore through its toughest test to date – the Asian economic crisis of 1997, the post-9/11 fallout, and the SARS epidemic, which all contributed to a slump in GDP. A new and welcome drive to 'pursue the subject of fun' and to develop the arts is beginning to change the face of Singapore.

The Colonial Centre

Singapore's colonial quarter is centred around the Padang, that rectangle of close-cropped lawn held close at heart by colonials across the old British Empire. West of the Padang, the land rises towards the gardens and green spaces of Fort Canning; while to the south, Parliament House, the Victoria Concert Hall, Empress Place and the Supreme Court huddle among the trees opposite Boat Quay. North of the Padang are some of Singapore's architectural landmarks, from the beautiful Chijmes complex and the classical-Baroque building of the Singapore Art Museum, to the towering Swissotel Stamford and, of course, the venerable Raffles Hotel itself.

The colonial quarter forms the heart of downtown Singapore, an area easily explored on foot and endowed with a healthy dose of museums and open spaces: the authorities have purposefully set aside the quarter as a 'place of government, culture and recreation', slapping conservation orders on anything with the vaguest whiff of history about it.

Around the Padang

The **Padang** was known as 'the Plain' to 19th-century colonials, who used it for parades and games (that nostalgic clonk of leather on willow), and also as a place to stretch legs, exchange gossip and get a breath of sea air – before land reclamation, the Padang fronted the Straits of Singapore. Flanking the Padang to the south is the **Singapore Cricket Club** (1852), a wonderful example of breezy, tropical architecture with its domed clock tower, neoclassical pediments and endless verandahs. On the other side of the Padang, across half a kilometre of grass, is the Singapore Recreation Club, built in chagrin by the Eurasians who were refused membership at the élite Cricket Club. Both clubs are still up and running (strictly members only), and the Padang stills serves as a cricket pitch (and a bowling green and rugby sevens pitch).

Arranged around the Padang are a crescent of buildings designed to make the British administrator feel at home. **St Andrew's Cathedral** (1861) is a full-blown neogothic affair complete with slender steeple and flying buttresses. It was built by Tamil convict labourers shipped specially from India. The walls of the cathedral achieve their brilliance with the aid of *madras chunam*, an Indian plaster, combining egg, lime, sugar and water, that has been soaked in coconut husks.

South of the cathedral stand **City Hall** and the **Supreme Court**, both built between the wars to stately effect, with a dramatic flight of steps and Corinthian pillars respectively. The Supreme Court was formerly the famous Hotel de l'Europe, whose drawing rooms were the stomping ground and inspiration of Somerset Maugham. High Street, Singapore's first road, separates the Supreme Court from **Parliament House** (1827), one of Singapore's oldest colonial structures, though the building has since undergone much renovation. It was built initially as a home for a wealthy merchant by George Coleman, the settlement's appointed architect. After Independence, the building was extended to serve as the debating chamber for Parliament. In 2003 Parliament House reopened as **The Arts House** (*open Mon–Fri 10–8 and Sat 11–8*). The old debating chamber, with its high-backed chairs, has been left intact, with only a simple stage added. Instead of political debate, the building now hosts plays, art films and concerts. Next door is the **Victoria Concert Hall and Theatre** (1862), which, until Theatres on the Bay appeared on the scene in 2002 (*see* p.429), was Singapore's premier arts venue. It is still home to the Singapore Symphony Orchestra.

Asian Civilisations Museum

At the southernmost limit of the colonial quarter, opposite Boat Quay, stands **Empress Place**. Named after Queen Victoria (Empress of India), the Palladian building was constructed in 1867 by convict labour and served as government offices right up until 1988. Since then it has undergone major renovation and the building now houses the new wing of the **Asian Civilisations Museum** (*ACM, 1 Empress Place,* **t** *6332 7798; open Mon 1–7, Tues–Sun 9–7, open until 9pm on Fri; adm S$5, concession S$2.50, free Fri after 6pm*), which opened its doors in 2003 to become Singapore's flagship museum. This is a good starting point for new arrivals to Singapore, offering an excellent introduction to the city-state, its diverse ethnic make-up and wide ancestry. In keeping with Singapore's love of gadgetry, a range of hi-tech techniques have been employed to keep museum-goers' boredom threshold at bay.

Empress Place was already earmarked as the flagship site for the ACM when the first wing of the museum opened its doors on Armenia Street in 1997 (the latter now focuses exclusively on all things Peranakan). Within Empress Place, ten thematic galleries explore the ethnology of Southeast Asia, China, India and the Islamic world. The museum's stated aim is to help educate Singaporeans about their ancestral cultures; and it does so with the help of video projections, singing voices, interactive exhibits and clever use of light and shadow. Up the broad staircase from the entrance lobby is the small Singapore River Interpretive gallery, with wide views across the river itself. The story of this waterborne marketplace is told by former inhabitants, with the aid of old photographs and film – including some fascinating footage of the Singapore Sea Regatta, with *sampan panjang* race boats competing for prize money, and locals attempting to remove a flag from the end of a slippery pole extended high over the river.

The ACM's most comprehensive collection, the Southeast Asian section, is particularly strong on textiles and gold jewellery, with some spectacular gold Minangkabau headdresses, festooned with gold-foil flowers, and some Javanese earrings from as early as the 3rd century, forged in designs that are still used to this day. Other interesting exhibits include a human skull carved with Dyak designs by the head-hunters of Borneo; some ornate Vietnamese water puppets; and some buffalo bones inscribed with the archaic script of the Batak community of Sumatra. The bones were used as amulets in rituals orchestrated by a *datu*, or magician-priest. The *datu* was the only member of the community able to write the unique script. Accompanying the bones is a *pustaha*, a wooden book used by the *datu* to record myths, medicines and magical spells.

The China Gallery, which leads on from Southeast Asia, traces the development of Eastern religions and explores the Imperial system. The 'Immortals Drinking Cards' is one of the more unusual exhibits to look out for. Illustrated in the early 19th century, these albums contain 48 leaves depicting Taoist immortals pulling comical facial expressions. They were subsequently mass-produced onto wooden blocks, providing an elaborate form of spin-the-bottle for the drinking parties of the Chinese literati.

A huge, pink sandstone archway provides a grand entrance to the South Asia Gallery – which explores the ancient sciences, performing arts and architecture of India and Sri Lanka – while upstairs in the Islamic Gallery, projections of mosque architecture work together with a soundtrack to recreate the experience of being inside a variety of mosques. For those weary on their feet, there are cushions on which to lie back and sample Islamic music through headphones.

Around Fort Canning Park

Until the Fort Canning Reservoir was dug in 1926, the gentle rise to the west of Hill Street held the secrets of Singapore's distant history. Workers stumbled upon one of Singapore's few archaeological hauls – a collection of 14th-century gold jewellery thought to have originated from the Majapahit Empire in Java, and confirming claims in the *Malay Annals* that the 14th-century kings of Singapore (then Temasek) ruled over the Malay world.

Before Raffles appeared on the scene, the hill was known to local Malays as 'Forbidden Hill' (Bukit Larangan) – forbidden out of respect for the royal tomb of Iskandar Shah, last of Singapore's Malay rulers. Iskandar Shah went on to found Melaka and establish the first sultanate on the Malay peninsula (*see* p.127). There is indeed a tomb on Bukit Larangan, but it is unlikely to be that of a Malay ruler who spent his last years in Melaka. Nevertheless, when Raffles ordered locals to clear the forest here (he had decided that the hilltop, raised above the torpid heat of the harbour, would be a nice place for his home), they refused to set foot on the sacred hill. Unmoved, Raffles ploughed ahead, renaming the mound Government Hill and constructing his official residence alongside Singapore's first botanic garden.

Raffles hilltop home has since disappeared, but the royal tomb – known as the **Keramat Iskandar Shah** and housed in an elaborate wooden shelter – still attracts offerings from locals to this day. The Raffles Terrace marks the site of the old residence, with a replica of the flagpole up which the Union Jack was raised each day. Close by is the settlement's first Christian cemetery, full of the souls of those struck down by tropical disease.

Government Hill became Fort Canning Hill in 1861, when a fort was constructed on the site of Raffles old home. Again, little of this defensive structure has survived, give or take the fort gate and the odd crumbling wall. Today, the park attracts visitors mainly as a respite from the city's sunbaked streets. A network of footpaths, shaded by enormous fig trees and flame-of-the-forest, weave about the hillside and around the reservoir. A surprising number of tropical birds – orioles, kingfishers, bulbuls, barbets – flit about the foliage (mosquitoes drone about in fair numbers too, so bring insect repellent).

A small **Spice Garden** pays tribute to Raffles' early botanic garden, where experimental cultivation of spices such as nutmeg and cloves took place. Nearby, the small **Archaeological Dig Exhibition** marks the site of recent excavations, where local ceramics and Yuan Dynasty porcelain and stoneware were uncovered, reconfirming Temasek's importance in the 14th-century Malay world. **The Battle Box** (*open Tues–Sun 10–6; adm S$8/5*) is a small museum housed in the military bunker complex used during World War Two. The bunkers, situated nine metres underground with 26 separate rooms and corridors, were earmarked as Britain's Far East Command Centre when war broke out.

The hill's modern focal point is the **Fort Canning Arts Centre**, which was arms store and barracks to the British in World War Two. Theatre Works, the Singapore Dance Theatre and a cooking academy called 'at-sunrice' are now resident in the building (*see* under 'Entertainment', p.448, for booking details). A graceful stretch of lawn slopes down from the arts centre to a large stage, where most performances take place. 'Ballet Under the Stars' is one of the venue's most popular events, attracting picnicking expats in their droves, and evoking an atmosphere not unlike that at summertime concerts in the gardens of London's Kenwood House.

At the foot of Fort Canning Park are the National Archives and the **Singapore Philatelic Museum** (*23 Coleman Street; open Tues–Sun 9–7, Mon 1–7; adm S$3/2*), which is of more than passing interest, even to those without the slightest concern for stamps. The permanent gallery tells the story of Singapore – through stamps – and runs visitors through the stamp-making process. There is even a 'Be a Stamp Booth' which allows children (and adults) to print stamps sporting their own portraits. One gallery exhibits stamps from right across the globe, and there are also regular temporary exhibitions.

Across the road from the Singapore Philatelic Museum is the **Armenian Church of St Gregory the Illuminator**, which sits at the southern end of Armenia Street. The church is small (it has a capacity of fifty) but exquisitely formed and sits in a peaceful garden that acts as a buffer to the surrounding clamour of Singapore. Like St Andrew's Cathedral, it was designed by official colonial architect George Coleman and completed in 1835 – making it Singapore's oldest church. With its simple colonnade and wide pediments, it has the feel of a classical villa, and is said to have been influenced by London's St Martin-in-the-Fields. The church was funded by the small but significant Armenian population, best represented by the Sarkies brothers, who founded Raffles Hotel.

Also on Armenia street is **The Substation** (*45 Armenia Street*, **t** *6337 7535; free entry*), a modern arts centre situated in a disused power station and host to some of Singapore's more daring contemporary art exhibitions – mainly displaying the work of up-and-coming local artists. The Substation is a multidisciplinary arts centre, and often has overlapping performances and screenings by repertory theatre groups, musicians and contemporary film-makers.

At No.39 is the **ACM Armenia Street** (*Asian Civilisations Museum I*, **t** *6332 3015; open Mon 1–7, Tues–Sun 9–7, open until 9pm on Fri; adm S$3/1.50, free Fri after 6pm*). Now that much of the ACM's growing collection is housed permanently at Empress Place (*see* p.421), the original Armenia Street wing of the museum is focusing its attentions on Peranakan culture. The collection is housed in the old Tao Nan School, a tropical-style neoclassical building from 1910. Peranakan is a Malay term meaning 'born locally', and the distinctive Peranakan culture derives from intermarriages between the various ethnic groups of Singapore and the Malay Peninsula – though it usually refers specifically to the so-called Straits Chinese, or 'Babas and Nyonyas', those Chinese who intermarried with the Malays yet retained much of their ancestral heritage. Rich Peranakan dishes derived from a combination of Chinese and Malay influences is an interesting feature of Singapore's cuisine (*see* 'Peranakan Cuisine', opposite).

Peranakan Cuisine

If Singapore can be said to have a cuisine that is all its own, some might point to the Straits Chinese and their Peranakan, or 'Nyonya', food, an exotic fusion of Malay and Chinese influences. Peranakan recipes have been honed over the generations – and toyed with by different families in different ways, so that there is no such thing as a definitive recipe for any one dish. However, lengthy preparation is one thing all Peranakan dishes have in common. The secret ingredient in a good deal of Peranakan cuisine is *rempah*, a long list of spices hand-milled by pestle and mortar (using a machine creates a very different result, according to chefs in the know). Many dishes are made rich and creamy with coconut milk, while delicious cakes and puddings are a traditional way to round off a meal.

Just as Peranakans themselves are seen as a dying breed (the march of global culture is making sure of that), their cuisine is teetering too. Traditionally, it is the mum or grandma of the family (a 'Nyonya' is a Straits Chinese woman) who holds all the secrets, and this has not encouraged young restaurateurs to come forward – you can more or less count Singapore's Perenakan restaurants on one hand. Dig your chopsticks in before it is too late.

As a dedicated Peranakan museum, ACM Armenia Street is the first of its kind in the world. The museum has an ongoing programme of noteworthy temporary exhibitions, and a permanent collection which draws on 19th- and early 20th-century artefacts from both sides of the Straits of Melaka. Despite absorbing influences from the Malays, the Europeans and the Indians, the Peranakans retained Chinese rites and customs dating from the Ming Dynasty. By the turn of the 20th century the Peranakans of Singapore had become known as the 'King's Chinese' for adopting traits of British culture – some would say to a sycophantic degree. Still, it helped many of them to achieve key posts within the administration and to accumulate extraordinary wealth, allowing for patrons of the culture to foster Peranakan concerns and traditions.

With the recent reshuffle of Singapore's national museums, the **National Museum of Singapore** (*93 Stamford Road, closed until sometime in 2007 for redevelopment*), which sits at the foot of Fort Canning Park to the north, has taken something of a back seat. From its inception in 1887 right up until 2003, this was Singapore's flagship museum, called first the Raffles Museum, then the National Museum. But its ethnology collections have been plundered by the new Asian Civilisations Museum, and the present collection is being rejigged to tell the story of Singapore's political and social history. In mid-2003 the museum was closed for extensive redevelopment, with the official re-opening due some time in 2007.

Raffles Hotel and Around

That Singapore is a relatively new place goes some way towards explaining why it is a late 19th-century hotel that steals the historical limelight. After the Suez Canal had opened up trade and independent travel between Europe and the East, a group of brothers from Armenia had the genius to corner the luxury accommodation market – at a time when luxury hotels did not exist in the Far East. Martin Sarkies and his brother Tigran set out from their home in Persia to establish the Eastern & Oriental Hotel in Penang. In 1887, on the back of roaring success in Penang, Tigran bought a second hotel in Singapore, a modest bungalow on the seafront by the name of **Raffles**. He soon expanded the premises, and the Raffles legend was nudged into being.

Early guests included Joseph Conrad and Rudyard Kipling, neither of whom were particularly taken by what the hotel had to offer: Kipling famously denounced the hotel by writing, 'feed at Raffles, stay at the Hotel de l'Europe'. Service improved dramatically after extensions were built in 1899. The new Grand Dining Room was grand indeed – it could seat 500 with room to spare – and the legends began circulating once more. One of the more outlandish tales takes the Billiard Room as its setting: it was here, apparently, among the low-slung lamps and rectangles of felt, that Singapore's last surviving tiger was shot dead. How a tiger got past the doormen in the first place was never explained by the management.

The early decades of the 20th century were the hotel's heyday, its suites booked round the year by celebrities and royalty. Electric fans were installed and running hot water plumbed into every guest room (both relative novelties at the time), and the world's first Singapore Sling was knocked up by barman Ngiam Tong Boon (in 1915). The Raffles institution imploded with the Japanese occupation during World War Two and never really managed to get back on its slippered feet – until 1987 that was, when the crumbling edifice was saved from the demolition gang by a conservation order. Though the porticoed building is immaculate once more, many have complained that the restoration of the building was too heavy-handed; but then that has been the way with every one of Singapore's conservation projects. Luxury and service have become the bywords once more, with two members of staff for every guest, impeccable antique-lavished suites and manicured courtyard gardens. But no more is Raffles only a hotel; it is at the top of everyone's sightseeing wish list, and it is a brand, with its own shopping arcade, souvenir industry and memorabilia museum.

The Bras Basah Road, which cuts northwest from Raffles Hotel until it meets up with Orchard Road, is flanked by several other Singapore landmarks. The nearest, perhaps aptly, is a shopping centre. The **Raffles City** complex, a behemoth dreamed up by architect I. M. Pei (of Louvre fame), dwarfs its namesake across the road. Along with a posh multistorey shopping mall, it contains Southeast Asia's tallest hotel. Further along is a daintier consumer haven known as **Chijmes** (pronounced *chimes*), packed full of boutiques, bars and restaurants. The rambling neogothic building is one of Singapore's architectural highlights. It dates from 1854, when it opened as the Convent of the Holy Infant Jesus. Today its sunken courtyards and less-than-holy cloisters make for an atmospheric amble, even if the idea of shopping holds little appeal. At night Chijmes comes into its own, with subdued lighting and a collection of choice bars, clubs and restaurants.

A few blocks up the road, the **Singapore Art Museum** (*open Mon–Sun 10–7, Fri open until 9; adm S$3/1.50; free guided tours available*) completes the triumvirate of museums administered by the National Heritage Board (along with the Asian Civilisations Museum and the National Museum of Singapore). The galleries are housed within the former St Joseph's Catholic Boys School, a classical-Baroque building from 1867, its interior knocked through to create some highly effective gallery spaces. Venture inside the old school chapel to see the window above the altar. The original stained-glass window was removed for safekeeping before the Japanese occupation, and it hasn't been seen since. The replacement, by a local artist, is made from great chunks of recycled glass and aluminium; look carefully, and the lines of aluminium can be seen to depict Christ on the Cross and Mary holding the infant Jesus.

Within the museum's climate-controlled galleries is the world's largest collection of 20th-century Southeast Asian art. But that is not to say it is large on the scale of Western galleries: both permanent and temporary exhibitions are easily explored within an hour or so. A good deal of the paintings combine the influences of Chinese brushstroke painting and European late Impressionism. Ask for one of the free guided tours, which serve as an excellent introduction.

The 'Waterloo Arts Belt' is the label hopefully applied by the tourist authorities to the area around **Waterloo Street**, which runs northeast of the Singapore Art Museum as far as the pedestrian zone of Bugis Village. The enclave is better known both as a place of worship and for its seedy past. A church, a synagogue, a Hindu temple and a Buddhist temple can be found along the length of Waterloo Street, while New Bugis Street is the sanitised reincarnation of Singapore's old transvestite pick-up ground, complete with street market, pubs and restaurants. Still, it can't be denied that a fair number of arts venues line up along Waterloo Street, from the Singapore Calligraphy Centre and the Action Theatre, to the YMS Arts Centre and Sculpture Square – an exhibition space housed in a former neogothic chapel.

The area to the east of the Raffles Hotel, beyond the open space of War Memorial Park, is dominated by a glut of business hotels and the **Suntec Centre**, which was built according to the principles of geomancy and feng shui: the ring of modest modern buildings (which house offices and a shopping mall) were built to resemble the forearm of a man, complete with four fingers and a thumb.

Singapore River

The mouth of the Singapore River was where it all started; a marble statue of Sir Thomas Stamford Raffles on the north bank of the river marks the site where Singapore's founder first landed. The waters here were once a raft of lighters and bumboats engaged in a hubbub of commercial activity – a stark contrast to today's squeaky-clean waterway, plied only by tour boats and backed by skyscrapers. Stand on Elgin Bridge and face eastwards for a view that provides a neat visual summary of modern Singapore: on the south bank, the heavily restored shophouses and godowns

The Singapura Cat

In cat circles, Singapore has become associated with the dainty ivory-coloured mog known locally as the *Kucinta*, or 'love cat', or less glamorously, 'drain cat'. To breeders in the West it is known as the much-prized Singapura cat (a single animal can fetch US$4,000 in the States). The breed is said to have emerged on the banks of the Singapore river, before making a home for itself in the city's extensive system of monsoon drains.

In the early 1990s the Singapura cat began to make a name for itself as an authentic natural hybrid. However, the drain cat's roots are not so earthy as some breeders would have us imagine: an American breeder, then resident in Singapore, is suspected of having created the mysterious breed by mixing Burmese- and Abyssinian-type cats. The myth of the Kucinta has now been largely discredited – though not by Singapore's town planners, who have immortalized the animal with a sculpture at the foot of Cavenagh Bridge.

of Boat Quay dwarfed by the glittering skyline of Raffles Place and the financial district; on the north bank, the stately ensemble of architecture that once housed the colonial administration.

Boat Quay was completed in 1842 and soon became the trading hub of Singapore. Throughout daylight hours deckhands shouldered gunny sacks along a maze of gangplanks which linked the quay with its shifting flotilla of boats. The wealthier Chinese *towkays* muscled their way into prime position on the riverfront, believing it to be a propitious spot to build their shophouses and godowns: the quay was shaped like the belly of a carp. Today this motley assembly of shophouses has become a neat crescent of seafood restaurants in pastel hues, with tables, chairs and sun canopies lined up along the waterfront. One or two converted bumboats offer boat rides out of the mouth of the Singapore River and into Marina Bay.

The pedestrianized waterfront of Boat Quay extends from Elgin Bridge as far as **Cavenagh Bridge**, passing Fernando Botero's wry sculpture of a squat bird and Chong Fah Cheong's *First Generation*, a collection of children in bronze leaping into the river. Look out too for a sculpted family of Singapura cats, a breed supposedly unique to Singapore (*see* 'The Singapura Cat', above), and Salvador Dali's *Homage to Newton*, which stands in the UOB Plaza, just back from the waterfront. Cavenagh Bridge (Singapore's only suspension bridge) was built from Glasgow steel in back in 1869, at which time it linked the government offices on the north bank with the commercial quarter on the south. Today it serves as a footbridge linking Boat Quay with the waterfront on the north bank, where the excellent Asian Civilisations Museum, Parliament House and the Raffles Landing Site are congregated (*see* 'Colonial District').

Adjacent to Cavenagh Bridge is **The Fullerton**, which stands out as one of Singapore's more dramatic riverside buildings, its entire circumference lined with Doric pillars. It was built in 1928 on the site of Fullerton Fort, which once defended the mouth of the Singapore river. The building served for years as the post office headquarters, before recent conversion to an upmarket hotel. A subterranean walkway leads from the hotel to **One Fullerton**, new location of the 70-tonne **Merlion** statue – a state symbol dreamt up by the tourist board back in the 1960s. One Fullerton plays host to a line of waterfront restaurants and cafés, all with views across the waters of Marina Bay, into which the strange lion-fish spews forth a high-powered jet of water.

Just south of here rise the steel and glass towers of **Raffles Place**, the number-crunching nucleus of Singapore's financial district. In fact, Raffles Place has always been Singapore's commercial nucleus; back in the 19th century, it served as the nerve centre of the trading port, a district packed with warehouses, ships' chandlers and money-changers (hence Change Alley). **Clifford Pier** extends into Marina Bay from here and serves – as it always has done – as the major berthing and departure point for the passenger ships that enter Marina Bay.

Across the water from the financial district, on the north side of Marina Bay, are the glittering domes of the **Esplanade – Theatres on the Bay**. This is Singapore's latest symbol of progress, a world-class arts centre combining practicality with that added 'wow' factor we have come to expect of modern architecture. Seen across the water of Marina Bay, the theatres bring to mind the Syndey Opera House, though with their metallic shells and curves, they perhaps have more in common with Bilbao's Guggenheim Museum. The Esplanade project was a key element in the government's plan to transform Singapore into a 'city for the arts', and it certainly goes some way towards shedding such epithets as 'dull' and 'sterile', so often applied to Singapore. Designed by British architect David Staples, the theatre and concert hall are both sealed within domes of glass, which are in turn clad in an armour of aluminium plates. Though the plates may seem to be arranged for aesthetic effect, each is angled perfectly to reflect the full glare of the sun as it makes its path across the sky, while allowing plenty of natural light to penetrate the glass. The effect is eye-catching to say the least, and the buildings have already earned nicknames, such as 'Bug-Eyes' and 'The Durians'. Disappointingly, the real inspiration for the design is said to be a pair of old microphones.

The theatre and concert hall, complete with 4,889-pipe Klais organ, host regular international performances, while free outdoor music and dance recitals are hoped to spark local interest in the performing arts. The **Jendela Visual Art Space** (*open Tues–Fri 11–8.30, Sat–Sun 10–8.30; adm free*) is a small art gallery housed within the complex, which also includes an outdoor theatre, a recital studio, a library and the Esplanade Mall, with various food outlets. The Marina Promenade runs east along the waterfront from about a mile, alongside sculpture gardens. It is here that a towering observation wheel called the **Singapore Flyer** is set to open in late 2008. It is being touted as a 'bigger and better' version of the London Eye. Across the main road from the Theatres on the Bay are the shady walkways of the Esplanade Park, which flanks the Padang and was once studded with colonial mansions.

Back along the Singapore River, upriver from Boat Quay, is the self-styled 'riverside village' of **Clarke Quay**, named after Singapore's second governor. In the early 1990s huge sums of money were ploughed into the conservation of the old godowns that lined the river bank at this point. The result is a mildly pleasant, if theme-park-like, collection of floating (and land-bound) restaurants, bars, food stalls, and gift shops. The weekend flea market is one of the highlights.

The conservation project extends upriver as far as **Robertson Quay**, where the DBS Arts Centre puts on plays performed by the Singapore Repertory Theatre. An interesting diversion at Robertson Quay is the **Singapore Tyler Print Institute** (41 Robertson Quay, **t** 6336 3663, *www.stpi.com.sg*), a non-profit organization dedicated to printmaking and paper-based art. The Institute serves as a gallery for temporary exhibitions, a printmaking workshop and a paper mill.

Orchard Road

If there is one name other than Raffles that people associate with Singapore, it is Orchard Road. It is the city's commercial artery, an example of consumer mechanics at its smoothest, where brand names flex and shoppers strut (this is Singapore's people-watching promenade). Innumerable department stores stand in line, stocked with the latest gadgetry and dangling their lures in front of a year-round stream of browsers. Shoppers don't want for choice on Orchard Road. But if you are familiar with city life, there will be little about the 2km stretch of stores to hold the attention for long – unless, that is, you happen to want the latest digital camera or a marked-down designer handbag, and even then, prices are nothing to shout about.

Orchard Road was once just that, a road through an orchard. It is hard to imagine now, but only a matter of decades ago fruit trees, nutmeg and pepper plantations lined its flanks, their branches meeting overhead. As the settlement grew, the road became an important thoroughfare linking the colonial residential districts of Tanglin and Holland Park with the former commercial centre at Raffles Place. It was a lace pedlar by the name of Tang who foresaw the street's potential. He took a long hard look at the daily stream of wealthy commuters, and in 1958 built his own modest department store, Singapore's first. Tang's is still there today, and it is said to be Singapore's busiest, though it competes with more than sixty others of its kind.

If you can look beyond the shopfronts, there are one or two historical distractions to break the monotony. Near the east end of Orchard Road, behind a grand entranceway complete with guard boxes, stands the **Istana**, home to SR Nathan, the current President of Singapore (a largely ceremonial post). This was once the official residence of the British Governor of Singapore, a handsome neo-Palladian palace built in 1869. The grounds, and of course the building, are closed to the public, except on five public holidays, when people queue at the gates (passport in hand if foreign) for the privelege of wandering the grounds. The President himself usually makes an appearance, to the sound of a brass band blasting its mayhem across the landscaped lawns.

The area to the east of the Istana is known as **Dhoby Ghaut** after the Indian washermen (*dhoby*) who once lived here. In the heat of the sun they congregated on the banks of the Stamford River where they laid washing out to dry. The narrow river once ran alongside part of Orchard Road, and now passes unnoticed beneath the ground.

Further along, traditional shophouses survive on Cuppage Terrace and **Emerald Hill Road**, which cut north from Orchard Road and Peranakan Place respectively. When British planter William Cuppage died in 1872, his land was bought up by wealthy members of the Straits Chinese community; a number of their Perenakan-style shophouses survive on Emerald Hill Road, with characteristic ornamented shutters and *pintu pagar* – saloon-style swinging doors. Most have been adapted to house restaurants and offices.

Towards the west end of Orchard Road, Scott's Road climbs a gentle hill topped by what looks suspiciously like a Germanic castle, complete with Rhineland turret. Now the luxury **Goodwood Park Hotel**, the building was built by Singapore's German community in 1900 to serve as the Teutonia Club. This area remains Singapore's clubland, with the American Club and **Tanglin Club** across the road. The latter was founded in 1865 on the site of an old orange grove and quickly established itself as an exclusive haunt of the British.

Singapore Botanic Gardens

The Singapore Botanic Gardens, west of Orchard Road, have matured into one of the world's leading horticultural centres, and are a highlight of any visit to Singapore. The first botanic garden was established in 1822 by Raffles himself in the grounds of his residence on Government Hill (now Fort Canning Park). For seven years, he used the garden to experiment with crops and spices with a view to large-scale cultivation. The present gardens opened with the same aims in 1859 and played a ground-breaking role in the development of horticulture and agriculture in Southeast Asia. In 1877 rubber seedlings were shipped over from Brazil, via London's Kew Gardens. After a decade of research Henry Ridley, the first Director of the Singapore Botanic Garden, grew obsessive about the potential of rubber as cash crop for British Malaya – so obsessive that he earned himself the nickname 'Mad Ridley': when in Malaya, he was

Vanda Miss Joaquim Orchid

Singapore's national flower, a splay-petalled purple and white beauty, was named after Miss Agnes Joaquim, budding gardener and eldest daughter of an Armenian immigrant. As the popular story goes, in 1893 she stumbled across the flower nestled in a clump of bamboo at the bottom of her garden. In her excitement, she rushed straight to Henry Ridley, director of the Botanic Gardens, with her find.

However, Miss Joaquim was a keen horticulturalist who won frequent prizes for her entries at Singapore's annual flower show. The writings of Henry Ridley confirm that Miss Joaquim did not in fact 'stumble across' the flower, but produced it herself by crossing two common hybrids – which makes her achievement all the greater: she was the first person in the world to produce a Vanda hybrid. Miss Joaquim's flower was later adopted as the Singapore national flower for its outstanding beauty. She lies buried in the tranquil graveyard of the Armenian Church, Armenia Street.

known to carry seeds in his pocket at all times, with a view to handing them out to any farmer he happened to stumble across. With the advent of the motorcar, Mad Ridley had the last laugh, and rubber went on to became Malaya's primary earner.

Research continues at the Singapore Botanic Garden to this day, with a focus on the hybridization of orchids. The varied and often stunning gardens extend over 52 hectares and include a visitor centre, herbarium, ginger garden, orchid garden, three lakes and a small patch of untended rainforest. Free open-air concerts are held at Symphony Lake on a weekly basis.

The Botanic Gardens are within walking distance of the Orchard Road, though plenty of buses head in the direction of the main entrance beside the visitor centre. The shortest route by foot is to head for the Tanglin Gate entrance (walk up Tanglin Road, which leads on from Orchard Road, then cut right onto Napier Road). The gardens are open daily from 5am until midnight and entry is free (though there is a S$2 charge for the orchid garden). For further information contact *Visitor Services Desk, 1 Cluny Road,* **t** *6471 7361,* **f** *6473 7983*.

Chinatown

Of the world's many Chinatowns, there can be few quite so polished as Singapore's. With its spotless streets and newly painted façades, it has the feel of a museum piece, and it is not unusual to encounter more tourists than Chinese among the 'five-foot ways'. What marks the district out is its architecture; the streets form a gallery of shophouse styles, from the plain but functional 19th-century shophouse to later, more elaborate styles with neoclassical and Art Deco influences. The whole enclave is dwarfed by the intimidating ensemble of high-rises that form Singapore's nearby financial district.

Few of Chinatown's shophouses serve the purposes for which they were first built: they became prime real estate after a conservation order was placed on the district in 1987 and surplus residents were moved to housing developments elsewhere on the island. In the intervening years Chinatown has transformed itself from the run down, overpopulated epicentre of all things Chinese, to the heritage showpiece of a modern city. Restaurants and boutique hotels now predominate, though there are still a good few Chinese medicine halls, traditional *kopitiam* (coffee shops) and sundry stores stacked high with pungent, dried goods. Enough of the past has survived – or been restored – to make for a good day's wanderings.

Chinatown was built in four stages, the first instigated by Sir Stamford Raffles himself when he drew up his town plan in 1828. Many of the streets were laid on a grid, and at the suggestion of Raffles, all were fronted by the now commonplace 'five-foot ways' – extended, five-foot-wide verandahs that run in front of the terraced buildings to protect shoppers from the sun and rain.

The first of the enclaves to appear were Telok Ayer and Kreta Ayer, which straddle South Beach Road. Further south, Bukit Pasoh and Tanjong Pagar are split by Neil

Road. Each of the four enclaves has its own character and traditions, though their peculiarities are mainly historical.

Telok Ayer

When Raffles first designated ethnic enclaves in Singapore, a small village south of the river called Telok Ayer was earmarked as the new Chinese quarter. Much land has been reclaimed from the bay since those times, but back in the 1820s Telok Ayer sat right on the coast. The beachfront (marked by present-day Telok Ayer Street) became the centre of Singapore's trading activities and the landing point for a steady flow of Chinese immigrants.

Some of the first to arrive were the Hokkien, and they set about building the **Thian Hock Keng Temple** (158 Telok Ayer Street), Singapore's oldest Chinese temple. It started out in 1821 as a simple 'joss house' dedicated to the Taoist goddess of mariners: new arrivals would make their way here to give thanks for safe passage. By 1842, the present building had been completed, with a statue of the goddess shipped specially from China along with the ornamental stonework and granite pillars. The temple complex also makes use of Delft tiles from Holland and Scottish ironwork. The three-tiered pagoda houses ancestral tablets. Three sculptures in the Telok Ayer Green next door depict the story of early Chinese and Indian immigrants.

Oddly the Thian Hock Keng temple is flanked by South Indian places of worship: Telok Ayer quickly became Singapore's trading centre and, though Raffles designated an Indian enclave north of the river, a growing number of South Indians muscled in on the action at Chinatown. The **Nagore Durgha Shrine** just to the north of Thian Hock Keng appeared in 1828, its neoclassical balustrades at ground level topped by the features of a miniature Islamic palace and flanked by two small pagoda-like minarets. The shrine served Singapore's South Indian Muslims, as did the simple Al-Abrar Mosque to the south, built around 1850.

The Telok Ayer District of Chinatown is best known today for the upmarket bars and restaurants around **Club Street**, which have become popular evening haunts of Singapore's expat community. The street was named after a gentlemen's club established in 1891 by a Peranakan millionaire. At the north end of Club Street is Far East Square, also gentrified, and bordered on two sides by a pedestrian mall.

Back on the Telok Ayer side of South Bridge Road, at Nos. 267–271, is Eu Yang San, a well-known Chinese medicine hall situated in three Art Deco shophouses adjacent to Temple Street. Inside, top-grade ginseng, dried herbs in jars, birds' nests, powdered pearls and shrivelled animal parts, such as deer's penis and monkey's gallstones, await the sick and needy. Better-known remedies include Tiger Balm, an ointment that 'works where it hurts' with the aid of a cocktail of herbs and oils, from camphor and peppermint to cloves and menthol. One of Singapore's home-grown cure-alls, Tiger Balm is now big business, having caught on round the world (*see also* 'Haw Par Villa', p.458).

Kreta Ayer

Across South Bridge Road from Telok Ayer is the heart of modern Chinatown, named after the ox-drawn water carts that moved back and forth from Spring Street, one of the settlement's few sources of fresh water. This area of Chinatown is in many ways the least authentic but the most pleasurable to walk round, with its pedestrianized streets, trinket stalls and heavily restored shophouses prettified by lanterns and a wash of pastel colours. A good place to start is pedestrianized Pagoda Street and the **Chinatown Heritage Centre** (*48 Pagoda Street, **t** 6325 2878; open daily 10–7; adm S$8.80 adult, S$5.30 child*), a well-organized and fascinating introduction to Chinatown and its early settlers. The hardships awaiting newcomers to Singapore are not washed over, with sections on opium dens, secret society feuds, prostitution and gambling. One of the three shophouses occupied by the Heritage Centre has been transformed into a painstaking reproduction of the cramped living quarters of a 1950s shophouse.

Next to the souvenir shop on the ground floor, and affiliated to the Heritage Centre, is a 'traditional' *kopitiam* (coffee shop) complete with marble-top tables and not-so-traditional coffees (lattes and cappuccinos feature on the menu). More authentic versions of the *kopitiam* can be found elsewhere in Chinatown. The Chinese acquired a taste for coffee from the resident Europeans and the first Chinese coffee shops began appearing early in the 20th century. Owners often roast their own coffee, blending it with a little vegetable oil and serving it sweet and milky. Traditional tea shops can also be found in Chinatown, particularly on Mosque Street (which runs parallel to Pagoda Street). A few of these serve as gentlemen's clubs (though they open their doors to the public). Instead of coffee, green tea and pricier yellow tea are washed back by the potload, with 'tea eggs' served as snacks (eggs hardboiled in green tea).

Street vendors line **Trengganu Street** each day, drawing the tourist crowds with reproduction goods alongside exotic fruit, waxed duck and printed T-shirts. At the end of Trengganu Street is the **Chinatown Complex**, an unsightly concrete market where the click of abacus beads is still a common sound among the stalls. Along with general stalls selling any number of things from mahjong sets to silk pyjamas, there is a large wet market where the local Chinese come to buy their meat and fish. On the south side of the market is a permanent durian stall with tables for consuming the pungent 'king of fruits' on site.

In front of the Chinatown Complex is **Smith Street**, also known as 'Food Street' – come six o'clock, the road is closed to traffic and hawker stalls, tables and chairs spill onto the tarmac. The full range of Chinese cuisines is on offer, from Teochew, Szechuan and Cantonese to the Malay-Chinese cross-cooking of the Peranakan community (*see* 'Peranakan Cuisine', p.425). On the corner of Smith Street and Trengganu Street stands Lai Chun Yuen, an old Cantonese opera house.

Tiny **Sago Street**, named after the sago-processing plants that once operated here, was better known for processing the dead, with makeshift hospices and funeral parlours along its length. A couple of shops still sell the papier-mâché models used in Chinese funeral ceremonies. The models are symbolic of the wealth of the deceased: burning them is thought to transfer that wealth into the next life.

Strangely, the main architectural landmark in Chinatown's heartland is the Hindu **Sri Mariamman Temple** on South Bridge Road. The original wooden temple was built in 1827 by South Indian immigrants, and dedicated to the goddess with the power to cure epidemics (Mariamman). The impressively garish *gopuram* (the tower above the main entrance) is sculpted with more than seventy different deities on five tiers. Inside the main shrine the ceiling is splashed with vivid friezes depicting the Supreme Being in his many guises. Devotees' faith is tested in the sternest way each year at the Thimithi festival, when supplicants perform a 'fire-walking' ceremony by walking (skipping rather) barefoot over red-hot coals.

Bukit Pasoh and Tanjong Pagar

Chinatown's southern enclaves appeared in the early 1900s when the populations of Telok Ayer and Kreta Ayer had reached bursting point. Bukit Pasoh is home to dozens of Chinese clubs and clan associations, some housed in elaborate Art Deco buildings and most lined up along Bukit Pasoh Road itself. The Keong Saik Road is traditionally associated with streetwalkers and matchbox rooms rented by the hour – though since the turn of the new millennium the street's seedy past has been turned to the advantage of a trendy hotel or two.

The Keong Saik Road arks uphill as far as Neil Road and Tanjong Pagar, the last section of Chinatown to be built, and the first to be preserved. Tanjong Pagar, which is Malay for 'Cape of Stakes', was once home to a village of Malay fishermen, whose wooden fish traps probably earned the cape its name – though there is also a legend about swordfish propelling themselves nose-first from the sea, and villagers defending themselves with stakes.

During the 19th century the fertile land here was used by colonial settlers to establish fruit and nutmeg plantations. By the early years of the 20th century Tanjong Pagar became a transport hub of sorts – for this was the base of most of Singapore's rickshaw pullers. Dragging rickshaws barefoot along the streets was seen, understandably, as the last rung on the social ladder, and the life expectancy of the rickshaw puller was short: most had opium habits and were indebted to creditors.

Today Tanjong Pagar is another place altogether, full of upmarket teashops, pubs screening Premiership football and craft galleries patronized by wealthy expats. Those interested in Chinatown's urban development, past and future, can visit the **URA Gallery** (*45 Maxwell Road, open Mon–Fri 9–4.30, Sat 9–12.30; adm free*), round the corner from the popular Maxwell Food Centre. Detailed models of the city show how the urban landscape has changed over the years, as well as detailing future plans to reclaim more land from the sea, doubling the size of the downtown area in the process.

Little India

Where Chinatown has sold a part of its soul to tourism fever, Little India is true to its roots. Crossing the Rochor Canal onto Serangoon Road is a little like leaping across the Bay of Bengal. Heady aromas of incense, jasmine garlands and spices mingle with the beats of Bollywood and the bright flash of saris.

Unlike Chinatown, the present location of Little India is not the one Raffles first designated for the Indian community. When he landed on the Singapore River in 1819, he had with him a trusty entourage of Indian assistants, who became the island's first Indian settlers. At Raffles' behest, they took up residence mainly on Chulia Street (near Raffles Place) and on High Street, just north of the river. European settlers began using the land around present-day Little India as an escape from the bustle of downtown Singapore, building country houses here and a race course. Some say it was the race course that drew Indians to the area – the British used Indian convict labour to clear the ground. Whatever the reason, by the latter half of the 19th century Indians had begun settling here, some operating brick kilns, others rearing cattle and buffaloes, encouraged by the presence of grazing grounds and a steady supply of water.

As Singapore grew, so did the need for a growing workforce of manual labourers, and the British shipped across a steady supply of Indian convicts, who formed chain gangs to work on such national monuments as St Andrew's Cathedral and the Istana. Those convicts who had served their term were given the option of settling in Singapore or returning to their homeland. Most decided to stay. They were joined by a growing rush of Indian merchants, and Little India evolved into the self-sufficient enclave it remains today.

The **Zhujiao Centre** (also known as Tekka Centre) marks the southern reach of Little India and forms its densest collection of market stalls. Piles of fish and row upon row of butchered carcasses present macabre scenes at the wet market, while upstairs, antiques dealers specialize in brassware, tailors display colourful fabrics and sundry stalls sell spices and cheap everyday items. The modern Zhujiao Centre stands on the old grazing grounds of Singapore's Indian buffalo farmers – hence Buffalo Road, which runs alongside the building.

Tourists may feel more at home across the road in the **Little India Arcade**, set in a rectangle of restored shophouses and stocked with craft shops, Indian confectioners, Ayurvedic herbalists, spice shops and sari stalls. Jasmine garlands for Hindu devotees are on display here, and a number of henna body artists are available on demand too.

Busy Serangoon Road forms the spine of Little India, though the warren of smaller streets to the east provide their fair share of sights and tastes. Look out for traditional Indian goldsmiths or fortune-tellers armed with a deck of cards and a visionary parakeet. Upper Dickson Road is lined with brightly painted shophouses and some excellent South Indian restaurants. One block south, Dunlop Street cuts east as far as the Abdul Gaffoor Mosque and the Church of True Light – the latter serving the Chinese Christian community. Though most of Little India's inhabitants are Hindu, a fair few are

Muslim – as is evident from the popularity of *mamak* cuisine which spills over from the Kampung Glam area (look out for men in songkoks flinging dough (to make *roti prata*) and 'pulling' tea (to make *teh tarik*). Most worship at the newly renovated **Abdul Gaffoor Mosque** (first built 1910), with its delicate minarets and glass cupola.

The small **Veeramakaliamman Temple** on Serangoon Road – dedicated to Hindu goddess Kali, consort of Shiva, and identifiable by its lavish *gopuram* – is one of Singapore's busiest Hindu places of worship, frenetic on holy days (Tuesdays and Fridays) and popular with Little India's transient population of contract labourers from India and Bangladesh. Further along the Serangoon Road, past the Mustapha Centre (Singapore's cheapest shopping mall – great for electrical items), stands the **Sri Srinivasa Perumal Temple**, which holds pride of place as the focal point of Singapore's Thaipusam celebrations. The bulk of the temple was built in 1855, though the convoluted five-tier *gopuram* – Singapore's tallest – was built in 1979 with funds donated by one of Little India's home-grown millionaires. If your visit coincides with the annual Thaipusam festival in January, be sure to pay the temple compound a visit, and prepare yourself for *kavadi*, the Hindu term for ceremonial body piercing. After a month of fasting and abstinence, devotees work themselves into a trance-like state and, as a sign of their faith, push skewers and barbs through their skin and cheeks. Remarkably, they feel no pain, nor do their wounds draw blood. Mornings are the best time to visit Hindu temples: most close their doors to the public in the afternoon.

Race Course Road runs parallel to Serangoon Road and leads up to Farrer Park, where 19th-century colonials staged polo matches and raced their horses. Two notable Buddhist temples can be found at the northern end of the road, the pretty **Leong San Temple** – its tiled roof adorned with golden dragons – and the **Sakya Muni Buddha Gaya Temple**, otherwise known as Temple of a Thousand Lights. Thai monk Vutthisasara, who died in 1976, made the latter his life's work, providing two impressive focal points for prayer: a piece of bark prised, so they say, from the Buddha Tree (under which the One found enlightenment 2,500 years ago), and – in typical Thai style – a gargantuan seated buddha, 50ft tall and weighing more than 300 tonnes. Ringing the statue are a thousand light bulbs, illuminated every time a visitor makes a donation of S$5 or more.

Kampong Glam

Kampong Glam was around well before Raffles got his hands on Singapore in 1819. Back then it was a Malay fishing village named after the *gelam* tree, the sap of which was used by fishermen to caulk their boats. It sat at the mouth of the Rochor River; land reclamation has since shunted the district well inland.

With diplomatic sleight of hand, Raffles decided to recognize the Sultan of Johor's elder brother as the rightful ruler. He had him shipped to Singapore from his home in Riau, proclaimed him sultan – in exchange for jurisdiction of Singapore – and installed him at Kampong Glam for his own safekeeping (back in Johor the sultan-proper was by now after his brother's scalp).

Getting There

By Air

Arriving in Singapore by air is a breeze: Changi Airport, which sits on reclaimed land on the east side of Singapore, is acknowledged as the most efficient airport in the world. The island's underground system now stretches as far as the airport, which means you can be in downtown Singapore within half an hour. Plenty of taxis and buses make the journey too. See the 'Travel' chapter for more information about flights.

By Rail

Singapore is the end of the line for the KTMB, Malaysia's rail network (*www.ktmb.com.my*). There are regular daily services to and from the major west-coast towns of Malaysia, and less regular services along the 'Jungle Railway' (*see* p.280), which runs through Malaysia's interior as far as Tumpat, near Kota Bharu. The rail network also extends across the border into Thailand, making it possible to catch a train from Bangkok to Singapore. If you want to do this journey in style, then take the Eastern & Oriental Express (Singapore **t** (65) 6392 3500, UK **t** 0845 077 2222, USA **t** 1 800 524 2420, *www.orient-express.com*), which extends the 2,000km journey over three days, with stops along the way.

By Bus

In effect, Singapore is part of the Malaysian bus network, so arrival in Singapore from Malaysia is a straightforward procedure by road. With the recent opening of the 'Second Link', Singapore now has two land-bridge connections with Malaysia. Most people still cross into Singapore on the Causeway, which links the Malaysian city of Johor Bahru with the north end of Singapore. The longer 'Second Link' connects the west side of Singapore with Geylang Patah, to the west of Johor Bahru.

Getting Around

Singapore has an excellent public transport system, while traffic is kept to a minimum by heavy import duties on private cars. Virtually every corner of the island is now accessible on public transport.

For the purposes of the visitor, it is the state-of-the-art Mass Rapid Transit rail system, otherwise known as the **MRT**, that proves the most useful (by comparison, the London Underground is like a network of sewers). Five lines crisscross the city centre, sending spokes out into the suburbs, one of which becomes the **LRT** (Light Transit Railway). MRT trains run every few minutes from 6am to midnight. Fares can be bought for individual journeys at ticket machines, though the handiest way to get around is to buy an Ez-link Card (*www.ezlink.com.sg*), which costs S$15 ($5 of which serves as a deposit on the card). Bizarrely, the cards can also be used to buy a meal at McDonalds.

Singapore's **bus system**, predictably, is comprehensive, timely and efficient, with services anywhere you a likely to be heading. Ez-Link cards can be used to buy tickets (*see* above); otherwise you'll need to drop the exact fare in the box. For more information about services, contact the Singapore Bus Service (SBS; **t** 1800 767 4333, *www.sbstransit.com.sg*). The **SIA Hop-On** is a half-hourly tourist bus which plies the central sights from 8.30am to 7pm.

Taxis are also plentiful. They can be hailed, or you can wait in a queue at the designated taxi ranks. Journeys within downtown Singapore will cost no more than a few dollars (though after midnight there is a 50 per cent surcharge). Extra baggage also entails a surcharge. To call a cab, try CityCab on **t** 6552 4525.

Information

For more practical information about Singapore, see the general 'Travel' chapter (pp.68–74) and the 'Practical A-Z' (pp.76–88).

The main Singapore Visitors' Centre is situated at the head office of the **Singapore Tourist Board** (STB), 1 Orchard Lane, freephone **t** 1800 736 2000, *www.visitsingapore.com*. Open Mon–Fri 8.30–5, Sat 8.30–1.

There are three others dotted about town: **Singapore Visitors Centre** @ Suntec City, 3 Temasek Boulevard, Suntec City Mall, freephone t 1800 332 5066. Open daily 8–6.30.

Singapore Visitors Centre @ Liang Court, Level 1, Liang Court Shopping Centre, 177 River Valley Road, t 6336 2888. Open daily 10.30–9.30.

Singapore Visitors Centre @ H2o Zone, 160 Orchard Road, H2o Zone, freephone t 1800 738 8169. Open daily 11–8.30.

Where to Stay

When you cross the border from Malaysia, hotel rates take an inevitable jump – though for a developed city-state like Singapore, there are some great bargains to be had, mostly at the top end of the range. Those hoping for a good spread of budget options are likely to be disappointed. Most of the inexpensive hotels are located in Chinatown and Little India. Unless the Sentosa Resort tickles your fancy, all of the viable options are situated in downtown Singapore (there are several hotels in the East Coast Park area, but they're not up to much).

All rates are exclusive of taxes. Promotional rates, which are often available, can sometimes half the published price. Ask before paying the full whack.

Colonial District

Luxury

Raffles Hotel, 1 Beach Road, t 6337 1886, f 6339 7650, *singapore-raffles@raffles.com*, *www.raffleshotel.com*. A hotel that needs little introduction and remains Singapore's choicest accommodation. Guests enjoy 'an experience of absolute comfort and old world opulence', though this is very much a brand-led establishment that relies more on the voyeurism of the tourist than the guests themselves. All 104 rooms are suites, with high ceilings, luxurious bathrooms and period furnishings. The suites are arranged in four wings around courtyard gardens of frangipani. There are themed Personality Suites (Conrad, Maugham, Chaplin, to name a few); suites aimed at business clientele (with separate offices); and three palatial Grand Hotel Suites, with two bedrooms, dining room, parlour, pantry, verandah and ludicrous price tags. Rates start at S$650. (*See* p.426 for a description of the hotel's illustrious history.)

Inter-Continental, 80 Middle Road, t 6338 7600, f 6338 7366, *singapore@interconti.com*, *www.intercontinental.com*. A luxurious hotel in a winsome block of restored Peranakan shophouses, with unique touches that may come as a surprise in a chain hotel like this. Different themes mark out some of the rooms, with two floors dedicated to all things Peranakan. Other floors focus on elegant European furnishings. Facilities include a gym, spa and rooftop pool, and there are top Mediterranean, Cantonese and Japanese restaurants to choose from.

Raffles the Plaza, 80 Bras Basah Road, t 6339 7777, f 6337 1554, *emailus.plaza@raffles.com*, *www.rafflestheplazahotel.com*. Across the road from Raffles proper, this modern hotel is located next to the enormous Raffles City shopping mall. Rooms here are supremely comfortable, with huge beds and bathrooms. The hotel shares facilities, including two pools and the Amrita Spa, with the Swissotel Stamford next door.

Luxury–Moderate

Swissotel The Stamford, 2 Stamford Road, t 6338 8585, f 6338 2862, *emailus.singapore@swissotel.com*, *www.swissotel-thestamford.com*. Once the tallest hotel in the world, on a clear day the loftier rooms at the Stamford offer views across to Malaysia and Indonesia. The hotel rises above the Raffles City Shopping Complex and offers remarkably low rates for some of its rooms, which range widely in price. There is a well-known spa, two pools and more than ten bars and restaurants to choose from, with cuisines from across the world. The 1200 rooms come with broadband connectivity, 4-star facilities, neutral décor and marbled bathrooms.

Moderate

Metropole Hotel, 41 Seah Street (on corner of Beach Road and Seah Street), t 6336 3611, f 6339 3610, *metropole@metrohotel.com*, *www.metrohotel.com*. A 50-room hotel right next to Raffles and very good value considering its location. Rooms are spacious, if plain and tending towards the musty, with attached bathrooms, fridge and TV.

Inexpensive

Hotel Bencoolen, 47 Bencoolen Street, **t** 6336 0822, **f** 6336 2250, *bencoolen@pacific.net.sg*, *www.hotelbencoolen.com*. A solid and inexpensive option just north of the colonial district and east of Orchard Road (equidistant from most of Singapore's downtown quarters). Rooms are fairly stark, though quite spacious. The selling point is a jacuzzi pool on the terrace.

Orchard Road

Luxury

Goodwood Park Hotel, 22 Scotts Road, **t** 6737 7411, **f** 6732 8558, *enquiries@goodwoodparkhotel.com.sg*, *www.goodwoodparkhotel.com.sg*. A smart but quirky hotel set in the old Teutonia Club, a gabled, colonial structure from 1900. Rooms are characterful, decorated in neutral colours and smarter than outside appearances suggest. Eight bars and restaurants are located off the corridors which sweep round the low-rise building. Facilities include two pools and a gym.

The Singapore Marriott, 320 Orchard Road, **t** 6235 5800, **f** 6735 9800, *http://marriott.com*. On the corner of Orchard Road and Scotts Road, near some of Singapore's famous expat clubs. Its defining feature – an unusual pagoda roof perched atop what is otherwise a plain tower block. This is a 5-star hotel which lays its focus on the six executive floors. Rooms are refurbished regularly in understated tones.

Four Seasons, 190 Orchard Boulevard, **t** 6734 1110, **f** 6733 0682, *www.fourseasons.com*. A little more intimate than the other monster hotels in this district, and with all the comfort you would expect of a 5-star property, including almost a two to one staff-guestroom ratio. The sports facilities are exceptional – two pools (one for lazing, the other for lengths), a well-equipped spa, a golf simulator and four tennis courts, including two floodlit indoor courts.

Grand Hyatt Singapore, 10 Scotts Road, **t** 6738 1234, **f** 6732 1696, *reservations.sg@hyattintl.com*, *www.singapore.hyatt.com*. A reasonably swanky business hotel with a big range of facilities, from air-conditioned squash courts to spa and attractive courtyard gardens. Rooms are spacious, with simple décor and paintings by a local artist. A step up in price gets you digital flat-screen TVs and broadband internet access.

Expensive

Traders Hotel, 1A Cuscaden Road, **t** 6738 2222, **f** 6831 4314, *thssales@traders.com.sg*, *www.shangri-la.com*. A straightforward Shangri-La business hotel with 550 rooms, situated at the west end of Orchard Road. There is a good pool and gym, but nothing to mark out the rooms. Promotions (which sometimes bring suites down to S$250) make this hotel worth looking at.

Copthorne Orchid, 214 Dunearn Road, **t** 6415 6000, **f** 6250 9292, *rsvn@copthorneorchid.com.sg*, *www.copthorneorchid.com.sg*. A reasonably priced hotel northwest of Orchard Road, on the main route into downtown Singapore. Rooms are very spacious with low-key décor and floral designs. Facilities include an outdoor pool and heath centre.

Moderate

Orchard Hotel, 442 Orchard Road, **t** 6734 7766, **f** 6734 8595, *enquiry@orchardhotel.com.sg*, *www.orchardhotel.com.sg*. With the same ambience and facilities as pricier hotels on Orchard Road, this one is quite a bargain. All standard rooms have been refurbished, and there's a gym and a pool – with waterfall.

Sha Villa, 64 Lloyd Road, **t** 6734 7117, **f** 6736 1651, *shavilla@sha.org.sg*, *www.sha.org.sg*. One of its kind for hotels in the Orchard Road area. The setting is a whitewashed colonial-style villa, with porte-cochere. Most rooms are spacious, with wall hangings, wooden floorboards and a good range of facilities (though no pool or gym). Be warned, though: Sha Villa is the 'learning school' of the Singapore International Hotel and Tourism College – so all staff are students. In practice, this often means excellent service.

Inexpensive

Metropolitan YMCA, 60 Stevens Road, **t** 6839 8313, **f** 6235 5528, *hotel@mymca.org.sg*, *www.mymca.org.sg*. Not your average youth hostel. There's a pool and all rooms are large and air-conditioned, though a little spare. Well situated on the cusp of the colonial district and a mere skip from the Orchard Road.

Singapore River

Luxury

The Fullerton, 1 Fullerton Square, **t** 6733 8388, **f** 6735 8388, *reservation@fullertonhotel.com*, *www.fullertonhotel.com*. The latest 5-star addition to Singapore's hotel quota, set in the historic Fullerton building, a neoclassical extravaganza. Rooms, restaurants and bars are elegantly furnished and overlook either Marina Bay or the Singapore River. No great surprises inside, but the hotel has a prime spot at the mouth of the Singapore River, next to Boat Quay, opposite the Asian Civilisations Museum and close to the financial district and Esplanade.

Ritz Carlton, 7 Raffles Avenue, **t** 6337 8888, **f** 6337 5190, *www.ritzcarlton.com*. Situated close to the Theatres on the Bay, and overlooking Marina Bay itself, in an appealing multistorey block designed by American architect Kevin Roche. There are more than 600 guest rooms, all of them spacious. The marbled bathrooms are the highlight; a four-square-metre window allows guests to lie back in their bath and look out across the cityscape or the Singapore Strait. The hotel has the largest collection of artwork of any hotel in Singapore, with more than 4,000 pieces, including works by Andy Warhol and Frank Stella. There's a fully equipped fitness centre, a spa, a tennis court and a pool.

Expensive

The Gallery Hotel, 76 Robertson Quay, **t** 6849 8686, **f** 6836 6666, *general@galleryhotel.com.sg*, *www.galleryhotel.com.sg*. The first of a new breed of 'hip' hotels to open in Singapore, set in a postmodern block with irregular windows and a glass-walled pool, which juts out from the side of the building (and offers the unlikely experience of vertigo while swimming). Facilities include free internet access, gym, four restaurants, two bars and the Liquid Room dance club. Not exactly cosy, but most people stay for design features such as sensors in the rooms which light your path to the bathroom at night.

Swissotel Merchant Court, 20 Merchant Road, **t** 6337 2288, **f** 6334 0606, *emailus.merchantcourt@swissotel.com*, *www.swissotel.com*. On the banks of the Singapore River at Clarke Quay. Rooms are smart and well-equipped. There's a free-form pool on the rooftop. One of the highlights is the Amrita Spa, with nine private treatment rooms. This is a reasonable alternative to the Singapore's luxury options.

Novotel Clarke Quay, 177A River Valley Road, **t** 6338 3333, **f** 6339 2854, *info@novotelclarkequay.com.sg*, *www.novotelclarkequay.com.sg*. A business-orientated hotel beside Boat Quay. All rooms have PCs with broadband access and marble bathrooms with shower and separate bath. Look out for substantial promotions.

Chinatown

Expensive

Amara Singapore, 165 Tanjong Pagar Road, **t** 6879 2555, **f** 6224 3910, *singapore@amarahotels.com*, *www.amarahotels.com*. Situated at the southern edge of Chinatown in the financial enclave, with a large outdoor pool, tennis courts and a fitness centre with sauna and jacuzzi. Rooms on upper floors are in much better condition and offer views over Chinatown. Very much a business hotel.

Expensive–Moderate

Berjaya Hotel, 83 Duxton Road, **t** 6227 7678, **f** 6227 1232, *berhotel@singnet.com.sg*, *www.berjayaresorts.com*. Though this remains one of Chinatown's priciest hotels, it has seen better days, as the slipping rates indicate. It is characterful though, with a pleasant courtyard and good rooms – hence its popularity as an alternative to business hotels in the nearby financial district.

Inexpensive

1929 Hotel, 50 Keong Saik Road, **t** 6347 1929, **f** 6327 1929, *www.hotel1929.com*. This unique hotel, named after the year it was built, occupies a row of shophouses on the Keong Saik Road. Despite remarkably low rates, it is the only one of Singapore's upcoming establishments that fits the label 'hip hotel'. Marimekko fabrics, sky lights and Pizaza mosaic tiling give rooms a bright feel, despite limited space. Amenities include broadband access, flat-screen TVs, CD players and shower heads the size of dinner plates. Old photos of colonial Singapore line the corridors, and on a roof terrace is a mosaic-lined jacuzzi pool. The attached restaurant Ember is fast gaining a reputation for itself too.

The Royal Peacock, 55 Keong Saik Road, **t** 6223 3522, **f** 6221 1770, *rpeacock@singnet.com.sg*, *www.royalpeacockhotel.com*. Situated in a row of Chinese shophouses, this is a slightly smarter version of the Keong Saik Hotel next door. Rooms are decorated in rich tones, but don't expect much space: cramped living quarters are a characteristic of shophouses and the rooms in this hotel are no exception.

Keong Saik Hotel, 69 Keong Saik Road, **t** 6223 0660, **f** 6225 0660, *keongsaik@pacific.net.sg*. Offers tiny, wood-adorned rooms in a row of converted shophouses. The hotel certainly has character, though its reputation as a past brothel lingers somewhat.

Chinatown Hotel, 12–16 Teck Lim Road, **t** 6225 5166, **f** 6225 3912, *enquiries@chinatownhotel.com*, *www.chinatownhotel.com*. In a pretty section of restored shophouses off the Keong Saik Road, with Corinthian pillasters and louvred shutters. The forty rooms come with TV, air-con, bureau and shower room. As with all the hotels in this little enclave of Chinatown, the new 1929 Hotel has somewhat stolen its thunder.

Damenlou Hotel, 12 Ann Siang Road, **t** 6221 1900, **f** 6225 8500, *www.damenlou.com*. One of Chinatown's most popular inexpensive hotels, set in a row of shophouses and featuring a roof garden and a range of small, neat rooms (though the cheaper ones are a little worn and over-cramped).

The Inn at Temple Street, 36 Temple Street, **t** 6221 5333, **f** 6225 5391, *theinn@singnet.com.sg*, *www.theinn.com.sg*. Set in a series of restored shophouses in the heart of Chinatown. All rooms, though small, are furnished with Peranakan antiques alongside the usual mod cons. A great-value choice for its setting alone.

Budget

Cozy Corner Hotel, 5 Teck Lim Road, **t** 6225 4812, **f** 6225 4813. Favoured by backpackers in the Keong Saik area of Chinatown, where S$50 gets you a decent, simple room with en suite bathroom. There are locker facilities and booking services.

Little India

Moderate

Albert Court Hotel, 180 Albert Street, **t** 6339 3939, **f** 6339 3252, *info@albertcourt.com.sg*, *www.albertcourt.com.sg*. A boutique hotel just across the Rochor Canal from Little India. Built to blend into a block of restored shophouses, with Peranakan touches throughout and comfortable rooms. Floral teak mouldings and china tea sets in the rooms help this place stand out from the crowd. A new extension with 50 guest rooms is arranged around a covered courtyard. With promotional rates, this is one of Singapore's best-value choices.

Moderate–Inexpensive

The Claremont, 301 Serangoon Road, **t** 6392 3933, *www.claremont.com.sg*. A brand-new hotel on the main drag in Little India, opposite Mustapha Mall. Rooms are spick-and-span with en suite facilities, TV, tea/coffee facilities, offering comfort and good value – promotional rates are in the inexpensive category, though they are likely to rise as the hotel establishes itself.

Inexpensive

Perak Lodge, 12 Perak Road, **t** 6299 7733, **f** 6392 0919, *reservations@peraklodge.net*, *www.peraklodge.net*. This guesthouse is the best in Little India, with comfortable modern rooms that are immaculately kept (you hardly notice how small they are, and the fact that most of them lack windows). There's a pleasant breakfast area with newspapers and a fish pond. The staff are welcoming and helpful and have earned a visitors' book full of compliments.

Classique Hotel, 240 Jalan Besar, **t** 6392 3838, 6392 2828, *reservations@classiquehotel.com.sg*, *www.classiquehotel.com.sg*. One of Singapore's best-value hotels, with sizeable, well-kept rooms decorated with warmth. There's a fridge in every room and the en suite bathrooms have bathtubs.

Budget

Little India Guesthouse, 3 Veerasamy Road, **t** 6294 2866, **f** 6298 4866, *vietsing@singnet.sg.com*, *www.singapore-guesthouse.com*. Certainly one of the better no-frills guesthouses in Little India. Bare rooms with tiled floors all have (noisy) air-con, though bathroom facilities are shared. Because some of the rooms have large ventilation slats, street noise can be a problem at night.

Sentosa Island

Luxury

The Sentosa Singapore, Sentosa Island, **t** 6275 0331, **f** 6275 0228, *dos@beaufort.com.sg*, *www.thesentosa.com.sg*. Formerly called the Beaufort, this hotel has jumped a notch in appeal after a major revamp. Situated on a hill on the east side of the island, with comfortable rooms, 18-hole golf course and views across the Singapore Straits. The highlight is Spa Botanica, set in tropical gardens with mud pools, 'meditation labyrinth' and Turkish-styled steam pools. The Garden Villas, with two bedrooms, are set in their own gardens with private pools. Tanjong Beach is just down the hill. Infinitely preferable to the ugly 5-star Rasa Sentosa Resort at the other end of the island.

Budget

NTUC Sentosa Beach Resort, Sentosa Island, **t** 6275 1034, **f** 6275 1074. This cheap option provides chalet accommodation and describes itself as a '5-star budget resort', whatever that means. Still, facilities aren't bad for the price: rooms have air-conditioning and en suite bathrooms, and there's a pool too. The karaoke room can get a bit raucous.

Eating Out

If you want to explore the gamut of Asian cuisine, there is probably no better place in the world to do so than in Singapore. Food – the making of it as well as the eating of it – is the national pastime. In Britain, people look to the clouds for small talk; in Singapore, they compare notes on favoured hawker stalls. The dominant cuisines are Chinese, Indian and Malay, or homebred combinations of the three (*see* 'Peranakan Cuisine', p.425), though there are plenty of European restaurants to choose from too. East-West fusion cuisine is the latest fad – brave and curious concoctions served, more often than not, in minimalist spaces that resemble design showrooms more than restaurants.

Any food odyssey in Singapore should begin by weaving a path between the city's ubiquitous hawker centres (food courts), where the best creations are to be found. (Food courts are scattered right across Singapore; even shopping centres have their own sanitized versions.) Traditionally, hawker centres are functional places. Stallholders sweat over woks inside rented cubicles. Customers sit on plastic chairs at trestle tables. Food is cheap and ambience is not a consideration. Thanks to the hygiene police, modern stalls are a far cry from the traditional roadside hawkers from which they derive, but the offerings are just as varied and the standard of food is just as high: top hawkers become minor celebrities with queuing customers and handsome turnovers.

Another place to look for authentic local cuisine is at the *kopitiam*, traditional Chinese coffee shops, many of which serve their own snacks and signature dishes. Singapore has its fair share of upmarket restaurants too. The greatest concentration of these can be found along the waterfront (Boat Quay, Clarke Quay, One Fullerton, The Esplanade); on Club Street in Chinatown; within the former convent known as Chijmes; and in Holland Village, outside the centre.

Hawker Centres

Maxwell Food Centre, on the corner of South Bridge Road and Maxwell Road. Singapore's best-loved hawker spot, which has been forced to smarten its act a little in recent years. Baffling choice; ask someone on the next table what they recommend.

Newton Circus, Scotts Road. Open more or less 24 hours and used to tourists (don't pay more than you should). A favourite with locals too.

Lau Pa Sat Festival Market, junction of Robinson Road and Boon Tat Street. Means 'old market' in Hokkien: it goes back to 1822. Good range of local favourites.

Chinatown Complex Hawker Centre. Great selection of Chinese hawker fare in scruffy surroundings.

Chinatown Food Street, Smith Street. Around 20 kiosks spill their tables and chairs across the road after six. Aimed at tourists, but tasty nonetheless.

New Bugis Street. A good range of Asian hawker fare, in New Bugis Street's revamped open market.

Little India Arcade. There's a small food centre in this arcade, where you can sample Indian food in all its wonderful variety.

Prima Taste, One Fullerton. Come here for the sophisticated hawker experience, with views across the water and a good range of traditional hawker food – at inflated prices.

Shopping Centres. Virtually all of the shopping malls have their own sanitized hawker centres, each providing a delicious spread of choices from across Asian cuisine. Prices are inflated but still very reasonable. Try the ground floor of the Meridien Centre, at the east end of Orchard Road, the food centre at bottom of Bugis Mall, the Picnic Food Court in Scotts Shopping Centre, the food centre in Takashimaya (Orchard Road), or the Water Court in Raffles City.

Chinese

Expensive

Imperial Herbal Restaurant, Metropole Hotel, 41 Seah Street, **t** 6337 0491. Tastier than it sounds, but not for the faint-hearted. And don't read 'herbal' in the Western/organic/vegan sense; the menu includes crocodile and scorpion. There's a resident physician who will help put together a meal based on any ailments you wish to dream up. A simple herbal soup will do just fine, thank you.

Jade, The Fullerton, 1 Fullerton Square, **t** 6877 8188. Probably Singapore's smartest Chinese restaurant, with the advantage of an extensive wine list. Classic dishes (such as shark's fin and suckling pig) often with a European-influenced twist.

My Humble House, The Esplanade, **t** 6423 1881. Progressive Chinese fusion cuisine, with pride of place inside the aluminium-shelled Theatres on the Bay complex. And there's no little irony in the name: this is an achingly trendy place with draped fabrics all over the interconnected rooms, origami, clever lighting and high-backed chairs.

Ming Jiang Sichuan, Goodwood Park Hotel, **t** 6730 1756. Top-notch Szechuan cuisine in the Teutonic surrounds of the Goodwood Park Hotel. Huge quantities of duck, noodles, sea bass, prawns and spit-roast suckling pig (you can order them whole).

Imperium, 01–07 Ngee Ann City, 391 Orchard Road, **t** 6733 9833. Traditional Chinese cuisine from across the Provinces. Excellent dim sum and lobster. Formal setting.

Moderate

Lingzhi Vegetarian Restaurant, Far East Square, **t** 6538 2992. Classic Chinese dishes that will have you coming back for more – and not a bit of meat or fish in sight, despite what the menu says (it's all mock meat cleverly crafted from soya).

Empire Cafe, Raffles Hotel, 1 Beach Road, **t** 6337 1886. Considering the setting (Raffles), the prices here are not bad at all, and neither is the food. The café takes the theme of a traditional *kopitiam*, with tiled walls, marble-top tables and plenty of teak. Classic *kopitiam* dishes, such as Hainanese chicken rice, *laksa* and *roti prata* are served.

Fatty's, Burlingon Complex, 175 Bencoolen Street, **t** 6338 1087. Serves excellent Cantonese cuisine in a frenetic atmosphere: this place has become a bit of an institution among Singaporeans.

Grand City Chinese Restaurant, 02–19 Raffles City Shopping Centre, **t** 6338 3622. Excellent Cantonese food, with Peking duck, plenty of seafood, a good variety of dim sum and wonderfully tender beef. Queues develop at lunch times.

Crystal Jade Palace, 04–19 Takahimaya Shopping Centre, 391 Orchard Road, **t** 6735 2388. A hugely popular Cantonese restaurant, with a couple of other branches about town. Noted for its dim sum and seafood, though the menu is exhaustive. Quality of service sometimes dips when the place is packed, and waits can be long.

Long Beach Seafood Restaurant, 1018 East Coast Parkway, **t** 6445 8833. Singaporeans flock here for the fresh fish and seafood. The choice is huge and the house speciality is peppered crab.

Inexpensive

Great Wall Noodle House, 36 Temple Street. Adjoined to the Temple Inn. Delicious homemade noodle dishes – mainly Hokkien yellow noodles. You can watch the cooks stretching the noodles through the glass partition that separates the kitchen from the seating.

New Flavour Gourmet (signboard also says 'Famous Hong Kong Dim Sum'), 76-78 Smith Street. A well-known little spot for cheap dim sum, usually closed by 12 noon. Great for a mid-morning pick-me-up.

Ci Yan Organic Vegetarian Health Food, 2 Smith Street, **t** 6225 9026. The name says it all. Informal, with cheap set meals at lunch time.

Armenia Street Kopitiam, 34 Armenia Street, **t** 6339 6575. An informal coffee shop opposite the ACM Armenia Street, which draws the crowds at lunch time for its famous *char kway teow* and *wanton mee*.

Indian

Expensive

Vansh, 01–04 Singapore Indoor Stadium, 2 Stadium Walk, **t** 6345 4466. Just east of downtown Singapore. 'Vansh' means 'next generation' in Hindi, and this place lives up to its name, with 'Modern Indian' cuisine and décor to match, from sunken seating and soft lighting to an open-kitchen concept. Indian tapas are offered as starters, while food straight from the belly of the tandoor oven, or from the teppan hotplate, make up a good deal of the mains. Vegetarians are well catered for. Completely unauthentic, but modish and hip, with food to match.

Moderate

Mango Tree, 1000 East Coast Parkway, **t** 6442 8655. Being on the beach at the East Coast Park, seafood is a primary item on the menu of this popular restaurant, which specializes in dishes from Kerala and Goa. Prawns with coconut-based curry, garlic crab, green mango curry and lots of tasty naan breads. Highly recommended.

Inexpensive

Komala Vilas, 76-78 Serangoon Road, **t** 6293 3544. This simple unassuming South Indian restaurant, up and running since 1947, has become an institution in Singapore. They put together just about the best vegetarian *thali* in Southeast Asia (a *thali* comprises a range of vegetable curries and condiments served with rice on a banana leaf).

Muthu's, 76 Race Course Road, **t** 6293 2389. One of the most popular curry houses along Race Course Road, which used to be known as 'Curry Row'. Specialities include fish-head curry, crab massala and chicken biryani. You often have to wait for a table.

Tandoori Restaurant, 320 Serangoon Road, **t** 6294 2232. Acknowledged by some as the best North Indian cuisine in Singapore. The menu will be familiar to Brits. At the north end of the Mustapha Mall on Serangoon Road.

Gokul, 19 Upper Dickson Road, **t** 6396 7769. A great new vegetarian restaurant on one of Little India's most appealing side streets. There is a long menu of 'Asian fusion' dishes and a daily all-you-can-eat buffet – all of it vegetarian and wonderfully spicy.

Woodlands, 12 Upper Dickson Road, **t** 6297 1594. A cheap and popular option for *thalis* and vegetarian curries.

Zam Zam, 699 North Bridge Road, **t** 6298 7011. One of Singapore's longest established Muslim Indian restaurants, renowned for its *murtabak* – a kind of pancake-omelette stuffed with a range of savoury fillings.

Malay/Indonesian/ Nyonya

Expensive–Moderate

The Blue Ginger, 97 Tanjong Pagar Road, **t** 622 3928. Singapore's best-known Peranakan restaurant, with a forward-looking attitude (the owner calls his cuisine 'Modern Peranakan'). The menu features *assam puteh*, a Peranakan version of *tom yam* soup, and in the desserts section, a take on the refreshing Malay snack durian *chendol* (a bowl of flavoured crushed ice with red beans and jelly). Presentation is key here.

Moderate

Rendez-Vous, Hotel Rendez-Vous, 9 Bras Basah Road, **t** 6339 7508. This long-term favourite, which specializes in Sumatran *nasi padang* (rich curries with rice), has established itself as a Singapore landmark. Well worth a visit.

House of Sundanese, 55 Boat Quay, **t** 6534 3775. One of a chain of no-nonsense Indonesian restaurants (the other two are in Suntec City and East Coast Road) serving the likes of barbecued chicken with side dishes loaded with *sambal*. A rare laid-back choice along Boat Quay.

Bumbu, 44 Kandahar Street, **t** 6392 8628. A beautifully restored shophouse in the Arab quarter. In the upstairs dining rooms are marble-top tables, antiques and sepia photos of languishing colonials. The food is Indonesian with Thai touches.

Moderate–Inexpensive

Belachan, 10 Smith Street. A well-priced Nyonya restaurant with surprisingly delicate tastes. Fragrant, infused pork and chicken, and delicious Peranakan desserts such as sago pudding and *pulot hitam*, 'black rice'.

Inexpensive

Islamic Restaurant, 797 North Bridge Road, **t** 6298 7563. Singapore's oldest Muslim eatery, opened in 1921 and still run by the same family. A wide choice of curries from beef *rendang* to Madras mutton and chicken *sambal*, plus *murtabak* and *roti prata*.

Sabar Menanti, 5 Kandahar Street, **t** 6293 0284. The place to come for Malay curries, which are ladled out in vast quantities at lunchtime, along with glasses of *teh tarik* – sweet enough to make you wince.

Japanese

Expensive

Aoki, 02-17 Shaw Centre, Scotts Road, **t** 6333 8015. Backed by the Les Amis Group (who own Les Amis and Au Jardin), this top class and very expensive restaurant serves the gamut of Japanese cuisine, from sushi and sashimi through *yakimono* grilled dishes and tempura to udon noodle dishes. The slivers of *wagyu* sirloin, which is billed at S$135, must be worth their weight in gold. Crisp, elegant surroundings, and an extensive wine list.

Ikukan, 23 Mohamed Ali Lane, **t** 6325 3362. Modern Japanese cuisine, just off Club Street, specializing in *yakatori* (charcoal grilled dishes), with sashimi and some interesting Japanese-European combinations.

Chikuyotei, The Mandarin Singapore, 333 Orchard Road, **t** 6738 1990. On the 5th floor of the Mandarin hotel and famed for its *unagi*, Japanese eel, and freshly prepared sushi. The set lunch is reasonably priced.

Moderate

Sakana, 01–04 Liang Seah Street, **t** 6336 0266. Focuses on the food, rather than the setting, which is a good thing if you want a no-nonsense Japanese feast with a range of sakes to choose from – all without breaking the bank.

Inexpensive

Sushi Don, B1-01 Funan The IT Mall, 109 North Bridge Road. A chain of conveyor-belt sushi restaurants, with a number of outlets dotted about town. If you are used to Yo Sushi! from back home, the setup will be familiar, but the sushi here is a good deal fresher.

Thai and Vietnamese

Expensive

IndoChine, 49B Club Street, **t** 6323 0503. This place maintains a good reputation in

Singapore and has become a stalwart of Club Street. The menu is full of inventive dishes from the Indochina region (Laos, Vietnam, Cambodia, Thailand) – all in the sort of ambience you'd hope for. Artwork and artefacts all over the place. A second branch of IndoChine has opened recently at the Asian Civilisations Museum (1 Empress Place), where there are wonderful views over the Singapore River to Boat Quay.

Patara, 163 Tanglin Road, 03–14 Tanglin Mall, **t** 6737 0818. Sophisticated Thai cuisine, with plenty of seafood and all the traditional dishes – green and red curries – along with a few oddities, such as 'Thai taco'. Also has a branch in Swissotel, The Stamford.

Moderate

Yhing Tai Palace Restaurant, 36 Purvis Street, **t** 6337 9429. Authentic Thai dishes served in a soothing setting within a restored shophouse on Purvis Street. Try the crab cakes served in their own shells.

Inexpensive

Naam The Thai Restaurant, 02-22 Plaza Singapura, 68 Orchard Road, **t** 6339 9803. A casual Thai restaurant – great as an interlude to shopping the Orchard Road, with affordable Thai dishes including mango salad, chicken green curry, seafood *tom yam* and baked buttered pomfret.

International and Fusion

Expensive

Les Amis, 02–16 Shaw Centre, 1 Scotts Road, **t** 6733 2225. Likes to see itself as Singapore's most sophisticated restaurant, in a sparse classical setting with 17 tables, two of them in private dining rooms. The cuisine is Modern French. Fresh truffles, pigeon and chocolate soufflé are typical of the exquisite offerings here. Les Amis also has the best wine list in Singapore, with over 1200 labels to mull over.

Pierside Kitchen & Bar, Unit 01, One Fullerton, **t** 6438 0400. Pierside is the place to be seen. There are views from the tables across Marina Bay to the Espanade. The interior design is cool and spare, with lots of blond timber and carefully placed white cuboids. The adjoining bar provides communal benches for 'camaraderie and canoodling'. Cuisine is European fusion with a focus on seafood: snapper pie or stuffed baby squid and eggplant paella. Wines from around the world.

Au Jardin, Botanic Gardens, **t** 6466 8812. This sister restaurant to Les Amis has the advantage of a wonderful setting: a 1920s colonial mansion surrounded by the exotic greenery of the Singapore Botanic Gardens. There are only 12 tables, all above the bar on the first floor, with views across the gardens. The restaurant features French classics and set *menus dégustation* of six, seven or twelve courses. Come hungry.

Equinox, 70th Floor, Swissotel The Stamford, 2 Stamford Road, **t** 687 3322. Both cuisine and décor are a confused hotchpotch of East and West, the former sometimes excellent, other times less than inspiring. However, 70 floors up, it's hard to notice anything other than the staggering views.

La Smorfia, 36 Purvis Street, **t** 6338 4322. An Italian seafood restaurant situated in a gentrified row of restored shophouses near Raffles. Offers a full range of fresh seafood, plus homemade pasta and lamb shank, with Italian wines.

Restaurant 360, No.02 One Fullerton, **t** 6220 0055. A painfully trendy component of Singapore's new waterfront. Furnishings are as eclectic as the menu, with Arne Jacobsen-like leather sofas, Indian teak and Greek marble. Chilean cod, Australian yabbie and Calvados soufflé are some of the items on the menu, best decribed as Modern European fusion. The attached glass-walled club, Centro, has become the place to be.

Moderate

The Marmalade Pantry, Palais Renaissance, 390 Orchard Road, **t** 6734 2700. This bistro is about as modish as you get, with a small menu of Modern European dishes, cakes and tarts, and minimalist décor – hand-glazed tiles, mirrors, expanses of stainless steel and chocolate-brown sofas. Doubles up as an outlet for Harvey Nichols food products.

Ember, 1929 Hotel, Keong Saik Road, **t** 6347 1928. One of a growing breed of new-fangled 'fusion' restaurants in Singapore,

Ember is commendable for its very reasonable prices. Cuisine here is described as Modern European with a Japanese twist – from simple dishes like fish and chips with tartare sauce or *escargots* on toast, to pan-roasted quail with creamed sweetcorn and madeira juice. Retro-chic décor, excellent value for money, and very much in vogue.

Beaujolais Winebar, 1 Ann Siang Hill, **t** 6224 2227. This small wine bar is a popular place with expats for dinner. Excellent goat's cheese salad, decent banger's and mash and other hearty pies, plus a good wine list. Soothing candlelit feel.

Las Pampas, 36 Club Street, **t** 6325 3360. A predominantly Brazilian bar and restaurant specializing in *rodizio* – lashings of skewered meat. French and Spanish dishes also feature on the menu (foie gras, paella, gazpacho).

Lazy Gourmet, 1 Scotts Road, 02–10 Shaw Centre, *www.lazygourmet.com.sg*. Heavenly delicatessen, full of rich man's snack food and attached to a large wine cellar. Same management as Les Amis and Au Jardin.

Original Sin, Block 43, Jalan Merah Saga, 01–62 Chip Bee Gardens, Holland Village, **t** 6475 5605. Vegetarian Mediterranean cuisine serving (mainly) the expat community of Holland Village. Outdoor and indoor dining, with a range of dishes likely to get meat-eaters, as well as veggies, drooling. There aren't too many vegetarian restaurants in Singapore, so this one is often booked up.

The Garlic Restaurant, 01–13 Esplanade Mall, **t** 6835 7988. A mix of Western, Thai and Chinese cuisine, best visited for the novelty value only. Every dish has one thing in common; this place is strictly for garlic lovers only – though the garlic ice cream may be taking things a little too far.

Entertainment and Nightlife

With the appearance of a world-class arts centre, in the form of the Esplanade – Theatres on the Bay, there's muffled talk about a mini-renaissance in Singapore. Though neither the arts scene nor the nightlife are a patch on most other world cities, things have certainly come on in leaps and bounds over recent years. Every area of the arts is represented in some way. Though there's not much of a live music scene, there's a fair deal of contemporary theatre and dance – if you look for it. Bars are certainly not thin on the ground, and new clubs seem to be opening every month.

The hottest strip for bars and nightclubs is the Mohamed Sultan Road, near Robertson Quay. Other places to head for include Club Street in Chinatown, Emerald Hill off the Orchard Road, Chimjes in the colonial district, and on the river, Boat Quay, the Esplanade, One Fullerton and the formulaic bars of Clarke Quay. As one might expect, the upmarket hotels house a fair share of Singapore's drinking establishments. For some of the better choices see the listings below.

For listings of up-and-coming events try *The Straits Times* newspaper, *The Arts Magazine*, or flick through the hip and exhaustive *I-S Magazine*, or *Juice*, both of which are free and distributed in cafés across town.

Venues for the Performance Arts

Tickets for most events are available through SISTIC (**t** 6348 5555, *www.sistic.com.sg*). Venues include:

Esplanade – Theatres on the Bay, 1 Esplanade Drive, **t** 6828 8389, *boxoffice@esplanade.com*, *www.esplanade.com*. Wonderful new concert hall, theatre, studios and outdoor performances spaces.

Victoria Concert Hall and Theatre, 11 Empress Place (buy tickets through SISTIC). Home to the Singapore Symphony Orchestra, who play here weekly.

Fort Canning Arts Centre, Cox Terrace (buy tickets through SISTIC). Theatre Works, the Singapore Dance Theatre and a cooking academy called 'at-sunrice' are resident here.

DBS Arts Centre, 20 Merbau Road, **t** 6733 8166, *venue@srt.com.sg*, *www.srt.com.sg*. Home of the Singapore Repertory Theatre.

The Substation, 45 Armenia Street, **t** 6337 7535, *admin@substation.org.sg*, *www.substation.org*. Nurtures up-and-coming contemporary artists and performance artists.

Bars

Long Bar, Raffles Hotel Arcade, Level 2, 1 Beach Road, **t** 6331 1612. A Raffles institution: barman Ngiam Tong Boon knocked up the world's first ever Singapore Sling at this very bar back in 1915. Apparently, today's hard-worked barmen sling together more than 2,000 of these sickly cocktails every day. The quirk of throwing peanut husks onto the floor continues to this day – enjoy it with abandon. Alternatively head for the Bar & Billiard Room for a martini (there's a choice of over 70). Singapore's last tiger was purportedly shot dead right here, among the billiard tables.

Harry's Bar, 28 Boat Quay, **t** 6538 3029. Live jazz and blues every day, along with happy hours and pub food, has made upmarket Harry's a popular place along the Boat Quay strip. If you have expat phobia, this is not for you (it was recently voted the top hangout for expats). The new, slick Harrys@The Esplanade (Esplanade Mall) vows to nurture the best jazz, blues and R&B.

No.5 Emerald Hill, 5 Emerald Hill, **t** 6732 0818. A cocktail bar in the popular watering-hole area of Emerald Hill, just off the Orchard Road. Set in a restored Peranakan shophouse.

Ice Cold Beer, 9 Emerald Hill Road, **t** 6735 9929. Naff name but after pounding the pavement on Orchard Road, it catches your attention. Serves a wide range of lagers, ales and stout. Regularly catches the eye of members of the expat community too.

Que Pasa, 7 Emerald Hill, **t** 6235 6626. Spanish wine bar stocked with good wines and port. Not bad tapas either.

Barrio Chino, 60 Club Street, **t** 6324 3245. Club Street's cosy salsa stop. Serves some interesting cocktails.

Beaujolais Wine Bar, 1 Ann Siang Hill, **t** 6224 2227. Tiny atmospheric little bar with a long wine list and a decent menu too.

New Asia Bar & Grill, 71st and 72nd Floor, Swissotel The Stamford, **t** 6837 3322. Singapore's most spectacular bar, its floors sloping 20 degrees in the direction of huge windows with glittering views across the cityscape. If you prefer comfy sofas and the scent of cigar smoke, descend one level to City Space.

Altivo Bar, 109 Mount Faber Road, **t** 6270 8223. Beside the Mount Faber cable-car station, with views across to Sentosa and retro styling. Come evening, the disco beats swing louder.

Metz, Gallery Hotel, 76 Robertson Quay, **t** 6887 2490. Ultra trendy, minimalist, 'NYC-style metropolitan' bar with a five-piece band.

Embargo, 01–06, One Fullerton, **t** 6220 6556. Sofas and soft lighting and open spaces provide the setting for drum 'n' bass and chill out tunes. Fresh fruit cocktails are the house speciality.

Bar Opiume, 1 Empress Place, **t** 6339 2876. Vodka and *prosecco* are the drinks of choice at Bar Opiume, which overlooks the Singapore River. Crystal chandeliers and buddha statues are offset with leather couches and lit blue-glass tables. Strangely, the bar professes to recreate the ambience of Singapore's bygone opium dens.

Balaclava, 01–01B Suntec City, 1 Raffles Boulevard, **t** 6339 1600. A popular new bar where chill is the operative word; designer armchairs are strewn about and, just in case you get a little bored with the live jazz, each table has its own TV, which can be tuned into news and cartoons.

Clubs

Zouk, 17 Jiak Kim Street, **t** 6738 2988. The leading light of Singapore's clubland, and it still has the edge, mainly because of its glowing international reputation (that its website – *www.zoukclub.com* – has had more than three million hits gives some idea of its popularity). Five bars and plenty of floor space provide the setting for the club's world-class DJ line-up.

Centro, 02–02, One Fullerton, **t** 6220 2288. Singapore's current hotspot, attracting international DJs. 20,000 sq ft of dance space and views over the water. Progressive house and techno.

The Liquid Room, Gallery Hotel, 76 Robertson Quay, **t** 6333 8117. Attracts the young and the rich. Designed to feel like an ex-industrial space. Has Singapore's top DJs queuing for a set. Trance, progressive house and techno.

Milieu, 2/F Peranakan Place, 180 Orchard Road, **t** 6738 1000. An old Peranakan building full of plush sofas, and with a dose of minimalism. The resident DJ is ex-Zouk. House.

Brix, B/1 Grand Hyatt Singapore, 10–12 Scotts Road, **t** 6416 7108. A basement club with a wine bar and a whisky bar. There's often a live band. Salsa night on Mondays, with free lessons. Jazz, soul, funk and R&B (and salsa).

Madam Wong's, 12 Mohamed Sultan Road, **t** 6738 4024. One of the old-timers on the Mohamed Sultan strip, and still going strong. Young crowd. Retro and top-40.

dbl o, 11 Unity Street, Robertson Walk, **t** 6735 2008. Pronounced 'double-oh', trendy, towering ceiling, three bars. Top 40s and retro.

Ministry of Sound, The Cannery, Clarke Quay, **t** 6235 2292, *www.ministryofsound.com.sg*. The world's biggest Ministry of Sound establishment, with 40,000 sq ft of genre-specific rooms to cater for all tastes.

Shopping

Now we get to the meat of things Singaporean. If you want to fill a suitcase with consumer goods, you're in the right place but Singapore is no longer the bargain basement it used to be. Even with electrical goods – for which Singapore is well known – you rarely make much of a saving nowadays. And despite its reputation, the Singapore shopping experience can be bewildering and humdrum; many downtown streets are wall-to-wall shopping malls, which breeds monotony. There are few specific enclaves for shoppers, so if you are after something in particular, you have to cover a lot of ground if you want to compare and contrast. Still, the patient shopper is unlikely to be disappointed.

Orchard Road, often referred to as Singapore's 'Fifth Avenue', is the place most shoppers home in on, lined as it is with no fewer than 60 department stores – expect mainstream offerings, blazing brand names and nothing too quirky. The Tanglin Mall has a good collection of antiques shops. To find the bargains you need to veer off mainstream limits. At the Mustapha Mall in Little India, for example, you can usually find a cut-price counterpart for the same electrical item bought on Orchard Road.

Of course, the ethnic enclaves of Little India and Kampung Glam are great for textiles, silk stores, batiks, basketry, gold jewellery and handicrafts, while Chinatown still nurtures the odd traditional medicine hall and porcelain outlet. There is a flea market at Clarke Quay on Sundays.

The tourist board offers a deluge of literature for the prospective shopper, listing all of the malls and many of the shops. For more considered listings get hold of free monthy magazines such as *Where*, *I-S Magazine* or *Juice*.

A few of Singapore's more unusual shops are listed below:

C K Collection, 586 Serangoon Road. No, not Calvin Klein but a musty shop in Little India full of bric-a-brac and a sizable collection of antique fans, including a Thomas Edison fan dating from 1886 – thought to be the most valuable fan in the world.

Kazura, 755 North Bridge Road. A traditional perfumery in the Arab quarter. The scents are customized in-store from essential oils.

Yue Hwa Chinese Products, 70 Eu Tong Street. The place to come for all things Chinese, from porcelain, jade, jewellery and musical instruments to furniture, embroidered textiles and medicinal herbs.

Eu Yang San, 267–271 South Bridge Road. A well-known Chinese medicine hall situated in three Art Deco shophouses in Chinatown. Inside, top-grade ginseng, dried herbs in jars, birds' nests, powdered pearls and shrivelled animal parts, such as deer's penis and monkey's gallstones, await the sick and needy.

Katong Antique House, 208 East Coast Road (**t** 6345 8544, by appointment only). A jumble of Peranakan antiques and memorabilia in an old shophouse in Katong, and owned by an authority on Peranakan heritage.

The village soon expanded to become the Malay quarter and, as time progressed, more specifically the Islamic quarter (many of Singapore's Malays later moved to Geylang Serai; *see* p.456). Wealthy merchants from the Arab world were drawn to Kampong Glam, and the quarter's simple mosque grew in both size and popularity. Today, the **Sultan Mosque** is Singapore's principle Muslim place of worship, large enough to hold more than 5,000 worshippers at a time. The present building was completed in 1928, funded by Singapore's Muslim community, and designed by an Irishman who combined Saracen and Mogul themes with a few quirky touches of his own: look closely at the base of the huge gold dome, where a ring of glass bottles give off a pleasing glint.

Arab Street forms the heart of the Kampong Glam area and is the place to come for one of Singapore's alternative shopping experiences. Five-foot ways are stacked high with goods from the Arab world, Malaysia and Indonesia – silks, lace and batiks, traditional perfumes, wickerware, brassware, jewellery, rattan and basketry. Shop as if you were in the Middle East: haggle hard for the going rate. And be sure to stop by at one of the many informal cafés – there are few better ways to recharge than by washing down a couple of *roti prata* with a *teh tarik* (sweet frothy tea) – *roti prata* are Indian Muslim pancakes known as *roti canai* in Malaysia, at once crispy and chewy, and served with a choice of curry sauces.

Close to the Sultan Mosque, on North Bridge Road, is the **Istana Kampong Glam**, historic seat of Singapore's Malay royalty until 2000, when the heirs apparent were thrown out and the *istana* was shut down for renovation work. The present building appeared in 1840, a simple tropical colonial mansion, plain from the outside and a fitting unregal home for a royal line that sold out to Raffles. There are plans to transform the building into a museum.

Other spots to track down include **Bussorah Street**, once dilapidated and now a pedestrianized strip lined with palm trees and conservation properties; the pretty Malabar Jamaath Mosque on the corner of Jalan Sultan and Victoria Street; and the **Hajjah Fatimah Mosque**, home to Singapore's very own leaning tower – its church-style spire tilts a noticeable six degrees to one side. The mosque is one of Singapore's oldest, built in 1845. It was funded by, and named after, a formidable businesswoman from Melaka.

Beyond the City

Singapore is tiny (only 42km across) and its transport system efficient, so exploring beyond the city centre is fairly effortless – in fact few of the sights are more than a matter of minutes away. Much of the outlying land is dominated by housing developments; since independence, city dwellers have been encouraged to relocate, each family provided with its own subsidized apartment. Surprisingly for a place so densely populated, there is no shortage of green spaces beyond city limits.

The South

Just south of downtown Singapore is **Sentosa Island**, and below that a constellation of islets which line up like stepping stones across the Singapore Straits – the latter rarely visited by tourists. Formerly a British army base, Singaporeans have since adopted Sentosa as their island playground, flocking at weekends to its artificial beaches and themed attractions. Recent years have seen the island a little down-at-heel, with a number of its attractions past their prime or quietly mouldering their way to oblivion. But things are set to change. Three billion Singapore dollars are being invested in Sentosa in the years leading up to 2012.

The face lift has begun already; an all-important dose of the hi-tech has wrested a few of Sentosa's ageing attractions into the new millennium, while new restaurants and luxury resorts (*see* listings) are hoped to provide an injection of 'class' into an island previously developed with such garish abandon. 'Rejuvenation' is set to split the island into three zones – beach zone, entertainment zone and green zone, catering for the pleasures of lazing, playing and escaping. Reclaimed land at the east of the island is being developed into Sentosa Cove, with golf course, marina and luxury apartments. Despite investment, the experience remains – and is set to remain – synthetic. But put haughtiness to one side, avoid weekends, and there is fun to be had on Sentosa. Particularly if children are involved.

There is a S$2 entrance fee to get onto the island, along with separate fees for each attraction: a family trip to Sentosa can wind up being an expensive day. Package tickets covering different sights can save money. A monorail, soon to be revamped, eases the journey between sights.

The beaches on the south flank of Sentosa, complete with soft, imported sand and California-style lifeguard chairs, hardly look authentic. However the wide sands are great for sunbathing while the lagoon, calm as a pond, makes for safe clean swimming. A nature trail leads through the interior of the island (it comes as something of a surprise that seventy per cent of Sentosa is covered in secondary forest). Wild macaques, pumped with bravado, hunt for tourist scraps, pitcher plants hunt flies and around 30 species of birds rid trees of their fruit.

Sentosa's one piece of history, **Fort Siloso** (*open daily 10–6; adm S$8/5*) is situated at the western tip of the island. The fort, a collection of battlements and underground tunnels, was built by the British in the 1880s to protect the Singapore harbour. Unfortunately it was on the wrong side of the island when Singapore needed it most: when the Japanese invaded in 1942 they did so from Malaya. The whole fort – its command post, guardroom, magazine, tunnel complex, barracks, cookhouse, laundry, tailor's shop and assault course – is open to the public and brought to life with sounds, smells and wax models with plummy voices.

Underwater World (*open daily 9–9; adm S$19.50/12.50*) is certainly worth a visit. A series of aquariums take visitors on a journey from the shallows to the ocean depths passing, along the way, through an 83m acrylic tunnel, above which predators such as bamboo sharks, white-tip sharks and eagle rays glide among marine turtles and shoaling fish. At allotted times each day, a brave member of staff dons a wet suit and joins the fish to feed them by hand. Many of the fish are happy enough to breed; a display of live bamboo-shark eggs is backlit to reveal wriggling embryos at various stages of their development. A shallow touch pool encourages visitors to stroke starfish, stingrays and small sharks. The ticket for Underwater World also allows admission to the **Dolphin Lagoon** (*open daily 10.30–6; performances at 1.30, 3.30 and 5.30*), where humpbacked dolphins perform tricks for the crowds – a sure hit with the children.

Other attractions include **Butterfly Park & Insect Kingdom** (*open daily 9–6.30; adm S$10/6*), **Images of Singapore** (*open daily 9–7; adm S$10/7*) – an extensive, hi-tech history of Singapore from the 14th century to the present – and **Cinemania** (*open daily 11–8; adm S$ 12.50/8*), an artificial reality ride through a haunted mine in computer-synchronized seats (bizarre and typically Singaporean). One new and exhilarating attraction is the **Luge & Skyride** (*open Mon–Thurs 10–6, Fri–Sun 10–7; adm S$8*), described as 'part go-cart, part-toboggan, pure excitement'. A chairlift ferries people to the top of the run.

A popular means of getting to Sentosa is via the **cable car** (*operates 8.30am–11pm; adm S$9.90/4.50*) which links the island with the World Trade Centre (a mighty shopping centre and ferry terminal) and Mount Faber, a small hill offering views across downtown Singapore and Keppel Harbour.

South of Sentosa are in excess of forty islands, a few of which are accessible by ferry services from the World Trade Centre. **Kusu Island** ('Turtle Island') is the most popular, not least for its legendary origins. A beneficent turtle is said to have turned itself into an island to save two shipwrecked sailors, a Malay and a Chinaman. During the ninth lunar month, thousands of Singaporeans – both Chinese and Malay – make an annual pilgrimage to Kusu, where they pay homage at respective shrines for prosperity, good health and happiness.

The North

North of downtown Singapore, beyond the immediate sprawl of suburbs, is the green core of the island, a patch of forest punctuated by reservoirs. Just west of the reservoirs, the forest rises to Singapore's highest point, Bukit Timah (163m). The area serves as part of the island's all-important water catchment area. Despite high annual rainfall, Singapore is nevertheless obliged to top up its supplies by piping fresh water from across the Johor Straits, a predicament that provides an endless source of wrangle between the governments of Singapore and Malaysia (the Malaysians, a little green at the progress of their diminutive neighbour, take full advantage by charging rates deemed appropriate for a nation of such enviable economic standing).

Bukut Timah is also the last refuge for Singapore's wildlife – or what little remains of it. Back in 1854, naturalist Alfred Russel Wallace (*see* 'In the Shadow of Darwin', p.312) spent months collecting insects on Bukit Timah. He got his hands on more than

700 species of beetle, many of which were new to science at the time. 'In all my subsequent travels in the East,' he writes of Bukit Timah, 'I rarely if ever met with so productive a spot'. In those days tigers still roamed Singapore's forests; Wallace noted that 'they kill on average a Chinaman a day'. While out collecting, Wallace was more concerned about the many carefully concealed tiger pits, 20ft deep and with sharpened stakes at their base.

The 81-hectare **Bukit Timah Nature Reserve** is all that remains of this pristine habitat. The parks board is fond of claiming that the reserve is home to more species of plantlife that the entire North American continent. Though many of the animal species have disappeared, the reserve is home to monkeys, flying lemurs, lizards, pangolins, pythons, plenty of birds and insects by the million. As if taking revenge for being driven out of the city, mosquitoes drone about in ravenous fury – visitors are advised to douse themselves in repellent. There are plenty of hiking trails, including one to the summit of Bukit Timah, and a couple of mountain-biking tracks. The reserve is open daily from 7am to 7pm and is accessed from the Upper Bukit Timah Road. The visitor centre is serviced by plenty of buses (*SBS No.160; TIB Nos. 65, 75, 171, 173, 184, 852, 961*).

One noteworthy diversion just east of Bukit Timah is the **Sun Yat Sen Nanyang Memorial Hall** (*12 Tai Gin Road, across the expressway from Tao Payoh MRT station; open Tues–Sun 9–5; adm S$3/2*), an elegant villa built by a wealthy Chinese merchant in the 1880s. Between 1906 and 1908 the villa was used as a safe house by republican leader Sun Yat Sen, who came here to plot the downfall of China's Qing Dynasty. Sun Yat Sen was installed as China's first President, albeit briefly. The villa now houses an exhibition devoted to the man who came to be known in China as 'Father of the Revolution'.

At the northern reaches of the reserve is the **Singapore Zoological Gardens & Night Safari** (*80 Mandai Road, **t** 6269 3411, **f** 6367 2974; zoo open daily 8.30–6, adm S$15/7.50; night safari open daily 7.30–midnight, adm S$20/10*). The zoo is set among secondary forest on a 28-hectare promontory surrounded by the waters of the Seletar Reservoir. Concern for animal welfare is high on the agenda and the zoo uses an 'open concept', with plenty of space and carefully researched techniques for containing the 2,800 animals – instead of containing the gibbons within cages, for example, a moat is used to define the boundary; gibbons have an aversion to water and would rather stay within the enclosure than escape across the tree canopy. Other animals, such as marmosets, tamarins and silver leaf monkeys, are free to roam as they please, happy to make the zoo grounds their home. The positive effect of these concepts is evident in the success of the zoo's breeding programme. Recent additions to the zoo include an enclosure for pygmy hippos, complete with glass-walled pool for viewing the animals as they swim, and a 50-strong troop of hamadryas baboons with an adjoining replica village from Ethiopia's Rift Valley.

The Night Safari covers 40 hectares of secondary forest split into eight geographical zones, which can be explored by tram or on foot. Three quarters of the animals on view are endangered species and all are housed in spacious, naturalistic enclosures,

the boundaries of which are largely hidden under cover of night. The whole setup is well conceived, though don't expect to be able to suspend disbelief. The 45-minute tram ride is accompanied by a commentary.

At the northwest tip of Singapore is one of the island's best-kept secrets, the 130-hectare **Sungei Buloh Wetland Reserve** (*301 Neo Tiew Crescent,* **t** *6794 1401; open daily 7.30am–7pm; adm S$1/50 cents*). The mouth of the Sungei Buloh, sheltered by mangroves, was farmed for prawns until the area was set aside as a reserve in 1989. Large numbers of migratory birds use the wetlands as their refuelling and breeding grounds. Small-clawed oriental otters have been observed, as have horseshoe crabs and archerfish, insectivores who catch their unwary prey by squirting jets of water. Keep an eye out, too, for golden web spiders, which spin enormous webs and can attain a leg-span of up to 50cm. A 500m boardwalk leads from the visitor centre across the tranquil Sungei Buloh (from where there are views across to Johor in Malaysia), past a mangrove arboretum and round a series of freshwater ponds once used by prawn farmers, now a wildlife haven. On weekdays you may have the reserve to yourself. Expect clouds of mosquitoes.

The East

When the value of real estate in Kampong Glam began to rocket in the early decades of the 20th century, many of the Malays relocated to **Geylang Serai** and **Katong**, east of the city centre. The original inhabitants were descendants of Malay fishermen, who inhabited a water village at the mouth of the Singapore River – until Raffles moved them on. Today these districts are largely residential, with the Geylang Serai Market providing residents with a one-stop source of provisions. During Ramadan, Malay hawkers set up a legion of stalls at the market to deal with the nocturnal hunger pangs of fasting Muslims.

The only conscious tourist attraction at Geylang Serai is the **Malay Village** (*open daily 10–10*), which provides a lame introduction to Malay culture and a glut of neglected souvenir stalls. A little to the east, Geylang Serai blends into Katong, known in the past for its wealthy Eurasians and Straits Chinese. A handsome terrace of lovingly restored Peranakan (Straits Chinese) houses can be found at the junction of Joo Chiat Road and Koon Seng Road (from the Malay Village head south down Joo Chiat Road). For a real insight into Peranakan heritage visit Peter Wee's **Katong Antique House** (*208 East Coast Road, t 6345 8544, by appointment only*), established in 1971. The exuberant owner is a true guardian of all things Peranakan and his house is a jumble of antiques and memorabilia.

Just south of Geylang Serai and Katong is the **East Coast Park**, a 5km strip of reclaimed land with gardens and recreational facilities such as a children's water park, tennis courts, a driving range and a windsurfing centre. The whole length of East Coast Park is fronted by a beach (the soft sand was snatched from a few choice Indonesian islands).

Changi, which occupies the eastern lobe of Singapore, is known nowadays for its slick, world-beating airport. Those who have read James Clavell's novel *King Rat* will know the name for other reasons; the notorious Changi Prison was where Allied POWs were incarcerated during the Japanese occupation of World War Two. Until the 1930s, when the British established a military base here, the area was covered in rainforest. It was a fairly isolated spot, and it suited the Japanese as the ideal place in which to herd, and subsequently abuse, the 85,000-strong members of the Allied forces and Singapore's Caucasian population. The **Changi Chapel and Museum** (*1000 Upper Changi Road North, open 9.30–4.30; adm free*) is a stirring memorial to the sufferings, the faith and the solidarity of those held by the Japanese. The centrepiece is a reconstruction of the Changi Chapel itself, a simple wooden structure with an *attap* roof built by the POWs themselves. Inside the stark museum the story of suffering is told through photographs, personal accounts and artwork, including the 'Changi Murals', a series of colourful paintings by a British POW, based on New Testament stories. By a strange irony, a Japanese school stands opposite the museum.

Modern Changi Village is a popular escape for Singaporeans, who come for picnics on the Changi beach (a small memorial here marks the site where hundreds of POWs were massacred by the Japanese). The **food centre** near the Changi Point jetty (mainly seafood and Malay dishes) is another draw. Specialities here include *otah* – mackerel, coconut, spices and flour mashed together into a thin slab and cooked in a pandanus leaf – and *nasi lemak*, the traditional Malay breakfast of coconut rice with fried peanuts, crispy anchovies, cucumber, hard-boiled egg and a slop of *sambal* sauce. An unassuming stall called International Nasi Lemak has gained a name for itself across Singapore, attracting by far the longest queues at lunch time.

From Changi Village bumboats putt-putt across the Serangoon Harbour to delightful **Pualu Ubin**, an island strewn with old prawn farms, flooded quarries and pockets of rainforest. Think Sentosa, and Pulau Ubin is its direct opposite (though plans for extending the island's recreational facilities are likely to transform its present laid-back mood; there's already a holiday resort).

Weekenders visit Pulau Ubin for a dose of kampung lethargy – a drawn-out seafood lunch in the compound of one of the teetering kampung houses, among begging dogs and dust-pecking chickens. Or they fill a water bottle and saddle up on one of the mountain bikes ranked near the jetty; the island is laced with tracks and quiet metalled roads ideal for leisurely exploration by bike. During the week, the island is deadly quiet and it makes for a peaceful day's retreat from downtown Singapore. There's little to do, other than pedal about the roads or stare out to sea from one of the cafés near the jetty.

Pualu Ubin was once home to several thousand villagers of Malay and Indonesian descent, though today only a few hundred remain. A fair part of the structure of modern Singapore was dug out of the bedrock of Pulau Ubin. 'Ubin' is Malay for granite, and the island is pock-marked with old quarries where stone was sourced for the causeway linking Singapore with Malaysia, among other construction projects.

The West

Out west, beyond the expat stronghold of Holland Village and the residential district of Bukit Timah, lies **Jurong**, the engine of Singapore's economic might. A grey-tinted landscape of industrial estates surrounds the enormous container port, where a legoland of giant boxes stand in piles among the yellow necks of cranes (Singapore is the world's busiest seaport after Rotterdam).

But **Jurong** is not all cranes and concrete. To offset the grey with a little green, a series of gardens and visitor attractions have been built inland from the industrial estates. Jurong Lake lies south of the residential district of Jurong West New Town. Chinese and Japanese gardens face one another from islands within the lake, while the popular **Singapore Science Centre** (*15 Science Centre Road,* **t** *6425 2500; open*

Tues–Sun 10–6; adm S$6/4) provides hands-on fun for children – unsuspecting that they are being taught something in the process. The centre has been around for decades, though a recent multi-million-dollar revamp has brought exhibits right up-to-date. Displays, which cater for a range of age groups, range from a dome full of hatching chicks, to exhibitions on aviation, biotechnology and the 'eco-friendly car'. At the 'Omni-Theatre', filmic panoramas of natural wonders such as the Grand Canyon are shown on a hemispheric screen five storeys high. Attached to the Science Centre is Snow City, where dreams come true for children of the tropics: snowball fights are staged, and there's a slope for tobogganing and skiing.

On the edge of the Jurong Industrial Estate is the excellent **Jurong Bird Park** (*2 Jurong Hill, **t** 6265 0022; open daily 9–6; adm S$14/7*), home to more than 8,000 birds and 600 species. A series of aviaries display birds from across the world in varying environments. The penguin enclosure is one gigantic freezer, complete with snow and several hundred happy penguins, while inside the walk-in Waterfall Aviary, 1,500 birds from Africa fly free. The nearby **Jurong Reptile Park** (*241 Jalan Ahmad Ibrahim, **t** 6261 8866, open daily 9–6; adm S$7/3.50*), home to crocs, snakes and komodo dragons, is less well-kept.

Not far from the West Coast Park, on the Pasir Panjang Road, is the extraordinary **Haw Par Villa** (*262 Pasir Panjang Road; open daily 9–7; free*), kitsch home of the Haw brothers, who became two of Singapore's wealthiest men back in the 1930s – thanks to their cure-all, Tiger Balm. Seven pagoda-like structures stand in the grounds – known as 'Tiger Balm Gardens' – while clusters of statuettes and figurines depict stories from ancient Chinese mythology. Plays and puppet shows are sometimes staged at the villa.

Language

The official language in Malaysia is Malay (or Bahasa Malaysia, as it is properly known). In Singapore, English, Tamil and Mandarin all have equal status. English is widely spoken in Malaysia; it is the common means of communication between the different races, who speak dozens of languages between them. The main Chinese dialects spoken are Cantonese, Hokkien, Hakka, Teochew and Hainanese, while the Indians speak Tamil, Malayalam, Hindi, Punjabi, Telegu, Gujarati and Urdu, depending on their roots. Then there are all the indigenous languages, with Iban widely spoken in Sarawak and Kadazan in Sabah (in Sabah alone there are in excess of 50 different dialects spoken).

Bahasa Malaysia differentiates the Malay spoken in Malaysia from that spoken in Indonesia, which is known as Bahasa Indonesia. They are basically the same language, with minor differences. In Malaysia, you will often hear the Malay language referred to simply as 'Bahasa'. Malay has distant origins as the language of trade in the Malay archipelago. Its ancestor was the language of Srivijaya, the empire which dominated the Malay world between the 7th and 13th centuries AD (see pp.7–8). In its time, Malay has absorbed influences from Arabic, Sanskrit, Portuguese, English and several Chinese dialects. Classical Malay was written in the Jawi script, an adaptation of the Arabic script. Malay as we know it today evolved out of the pidgin Malay spoken among traders.

For English speakers in particular, Malay is an easy language to pick up. Malay has borrowed plenty of words from English (*teksi*, *tren*, *restoran* are common examples), while the grammatical structure of the language is basic; there are no articles, nouns have no gender, verbs have no tenses and plurals are constructed simply by saying a word twice (man is *orang*, men is *orang-orang*). Syntax is similar to English, with a subject-verb-object structure. Adjectives are usually placed after their corresponding noun ('bus station' is *stesen bas*).

Pronunciation

Like English, modern Malay uses the Latin alphabet, and spellings are phonetic. So Malay is spoken pretty much as it is written. Most vowels are pronounced as you would expect, as are most of the consonants.

Vowels to look out for include 'i', pronounced 'ee' (*pisang*, or 'banana', is pronounced *pee-sang*) and 'u', pronounced 'oo' (*buku*, or 'book', is pronounced *boo-koo*). Consonants to remember are 'c', which is pronounced 'ch' (*cantik*, or 'beautiful', is pronounced *chan-tik*) and sy, pronounced 'sh' (*syariah*, or 'Islamic law', is pronounced *sha-ree-ah*). Consonants on the end of words are often silent. *Tidak*, the word for 'no', sounds more like *tee-da*, though the final vowel is short and sharp.

There are no hard-and-fast rules for where stress should fall in words, though more commonly than not it falls on the penultimate syllable.

Body Language

After shaking hands, Malays will usually place their right hand on their heart as a sign of respect and warm feeling. It is good practice to follow suit. Handshakes in Malaysia are gentle brushes of the palm; avoid the hand-crushing technique. In the strict Muslim states, it is considered inappropriate for members of the opposite sex to shake hands.

Pointing with your index finger is also a social faux pas in this part of the world. Instead, point by placing your thumb on the middle knuckle of your index finger.

Avoid losing your temper in Malaysia, especially in petty situations; showing your anger is is equivalent to losing face, and will probably hinder your cause.

Useful Words and Phrases

yes *yah*
no *tidak* (tee-da)
Please *Tolong*
Thank you *Terima kasih*
You're welcome *Sama-sama*
Hello *Helo*
Good morning *Selamat pagi*
Good afternoon *Selamat tengahari*
Good night *Selamat malam*
Goodbye (if you're leaving) *Selamat tinggal*
Goodbye (if you're the one staying) *Selamat jalan*
See you later *Jumpa lagi*
Bon appétit *Selamat makan*
Excuse me/I'm sorry *Maaf*
I don't understand *Saya tidak faham*
I don't know *Saya tidak tahu*
I want *Saya mahu*
I don't want to *Saya tidak mahu*
Do you speak English? *Adakah anda berbahasa Inggeris?*
Please speak slowly *Tolong cacap perlahan sikit*
Help! *Tolong!*
How much does it cost? *Berapa?*
What's your name? *Siapa nama anda?*
My name is *Nama saya*
How are you? *Apa khabar?*
I'm fine thanks *Khabar baik*
Where do you come from? *Dari mana*
I come from *Saya dari*
May I/Can I? *Boleh?*
It doesn't matter *Tak apa*
good/nice *bagus*
not good *tidak baik*
I'm lost *Saya sesat*
What? *Apa?*
When? *Bila?*
Where? *Di mana?*

Numbers

zero *kosong*
one *satu*
two *dua*
three *tiga*
four *empat*
five *lima*
six *enam*
seven *tujuh*
eight *lapan*
nine *sembilan*
ten *sepuluh*
eleven *sebelas*
twelve *dua belas*
thirteen *tiga belas*
fourteen *empat belas*
fifteen *lima belas*
sixteen *enam belas*
seventeen *tujuh belas*
eighteen *palan belas*
nineteen *sembilan belas*
twenty *dua puluh*
thirty *tiga puluh*
one hundred *seratus*
two hundred *dua ratus*
one thousand *seribu*
two thousand *dua ribu*
one million *sejuta*

Days

Monday *hari Isnin*
Tuesday *hari Selasa*
Wednesday *hari Rabu*
Thursday *hari Khamis*
Friday *hari Jumaat*
Saturday *hari Sabtu*
Sunday *hari Ahad*
holiday *cuti*

Time

What time is it? *Pukul berapa?*
It's three o'clock *Pukul tiga*
day *hari*
week *minggu*
month *bulan*
minute *minit*
hour *jam*
today *hari ini*
tomorrow *besok*
yesterday *kelmarin*
morning *pagi*
afternoon *tengahari*

evening *petang*
soon *sekejab lagi*
later *kemudian*

Travel Directions

left *kiri*
right *kanan*
straight ahead *terus*
corner *simpang*
traffic lights *lampu isyarat* (lahm-poo ee-shah-raht)
road *jalan*
street *lorong*
highway *lebuh raya*
north *utara*
south *selatan*
east *timur*
west *barat*
opposite *berlawanan*
next to *sebelah*
near *dekat*
Where is the (bus station)? *Di mana (stesen bas)?*
Is it far? *Ada jauh?*

Transport

airport *lapangan terbang*
train station *stesen tren/ stesen keretapi*
bus station *stesen bas*
bus stop *perhentian bas*
taxi *teksi*
boat *bot*
ship *kapal*
rickshaw *beca*
bicycle *basikal*
car *kereta*
motorbike *motosikal*
service station *stesen minyak*
petrol *minyak/ petrol*
exit *keluar*
ticket *tiket*
one-way *sehala*
return *pergi-balik*
economy class *kelas ekonomi*
second class *kelas dua*
first class *kelas satu*
timetable *jadual*
When does (the train) leave? *Bila (tren) berangkat?*
How much is the ticket? *Berapa tiket?*

Accommodation

hotel *hotel*
guesthouse *rumah tetamu*
room *bilik*
bathroom *bilik air*
hot water *air panas*
drinking water *air minum*
fan *kipas*
bed *katil*
mosquito net *kelambu*
pillow *bantal*
sheets *cadar*
towel *tuala*
soap *sabun*
toilet paper *tisu tandas*
window *tingkap*
clean *bersih*
noisy *bising*
Do you have any rooms available? *Ada bilik yang kosong?*
How much is it per night? *Berapa harga satu malam?*
Can I see the room? *Boleh saya melihat bilik itu?*
I'd like a room for one person *Saya mencari bilik untuk seorang*
I'd like a room for two people *Saya mencari bilik untuk dua orang*
Do you have a room with a double bed? *Ada tak bilik yang ada katil besar?*
Do you have a room with two beds? *Ada tak bilik yang ada dua katil?*
I'm leaving today *Saya berangkat hari ini*
Please can you call me a taxi *Tolong panggilkan teksi*

Shopping

shop *kedai*
bank *bank*
bookshop *kedai buku*
chemist *farmasi/ apotik*
supermarket *pasaraya*
department store *pusat membeli-belah*
market *pasar*
night market *pasar malam*
What time does it open? *Pukul berapa buka?*
What time does it close? *Pukul berapa tutup?*
I want to buy... *Saya mahu beli...*
Do you have any...? *...ada tak?*
How much is it? *Berapa?*

I'm just looking *Saya nak tengok saja*
It's too expensive *Mahalnya*
Can you lower the price? *Boleh kurang?*
Can I pay by credit card? *Boleh bayar degan kad kredit?*

Health

hospital *hospital*
chemist *farmasi/ apotik*
doctor *doktor*
fever *demam panas*
diarrhoea *cirit-birit*
headache *sakit kepala*
medicine *ubat*
I'm sick *Saya sakit*
I'm pregnant *Saya hamil*
I'm asthmatic *Saya sakit lelah*
I'm diabetic *Saya sakit kencing manis*
Call an ambulance! *Panggil ambulans!*

Food and Drink

(*See* also 'Food Glossary', pp.62–5)

food *makan*
drink *minum*
chicken *ayam*
pork *babi*
beef *daging*
mutton *biri-biri*
goat *kambing*
fish *ikan*
squid *sotong*
prawn *udang*
lobster *udang karang*
crab *ketam*
egg *telur*
beans (*also* nuts) *kacang*
vegetable *sayur*
vegetables only *sayur saja*
bean curd *tahu*
rice *nasi*
noodles *mee*
bread *roti*
banana *pisang*
coconut *kelapa*
salt *garam*
sugar *gula*
fried *goreng*
grilled/barbecued *bakar*
boiled *rebus*
steamed *kukus*
drinking water *air minum*
tea *teh*
sweet, milky cappuccino-style tea *teh tarik*
tea with milk (usually condensed) *teh susu*
black tea *teh kosong*
black coffee *kopi-o*
white coffee (usually with condensed milk) *kopi susu*
beer *bir*
Iban rice wine *tuak*
palm-tree spirit *todi*
fruit juice *jus*
Indian yoghurt drink, often with added fruit *lassi*
young coconut (served with a straw) *kelapa muda*
ice *ais*
breakfast *makan pagi*
lunch *makan tengahari*
dinner *makan malam*
restaurant *restoran*
food stall *gerai*
night market *pasar malam*
bill *bil*
menu *menu*
fork *garfu*
knife *pisau*
spoon *sudu*

Further Reading

Travel

Bird, Isabella, *The Golden Chersonese* (1883, reprinted Könemann, 2000). Epistolary account of a woman's intrepid travels through the Malay States in 1879. Packed with detail.

Gullick, J. M., *They Came to Malaysia: A Travellers' Anthology* (Oxford University Press, 2001). An eye-opening collection of extracts and accounts from colonial administrators, writers and visitors to Malaya between 1811 and Independence.

Hanson, Eric, *Stranger in the Forest* (1988, reprinted Methuen 2001). Tale of an epic journey across the Bornean rainforest, in the company of the nomad Penan.

Hope, Sebastian, *Outcasts of the Islands: The Sea Gypsies of Southeast Asia* (HarperCollins, 2001). The author recounts the time he spent living with a Bajua Laut family off the east coast of Sabah. The Bajau Laut are sea nomads who live on their boats and scrape a living as fishermen.

King, Victor, *Best of Borneo Travel* (Oxford University Press, 1993). A compilation of 19th-century travel accounts.

O'Hanlon, Redmond, *Into the Heart of Borneo* (Penguin, 1985). Hilarious, crisply written romp through the Bornean jungle to the summit of a mountain near Sarawak's border with Kalimantan.

Theroux, Paul, *The Great Railway Bazaar* (Hamish Hamilton, 1975). Theroux sets off round the globe by train, with a chapter covering the route between Bangkok and Singapore.

Young, Gavin, *In Search of Conrad* (Penguin, 1992). Journalist and travel writer Gavin Young traces Joseph Conrad's footsteps round Asia, revealing an obsessive passion for Conrad's work.

History

Andaya, Barbara and Andaya, Leonard, *A History of Malaysia* (Palgrave, 2001). The most up-to-date of the recent histories of Malaysia, with good coverage of the pre-colonial Malay world. Not quite as readable as some of the other histories, but quite comprehensive.

Hoyt, Sarnia Hayes, *Old Malacca* (Oxford University Press, 1992). A well-written introduction to Melaka, from its origins as a fishing kampung through the Portuguese, Dutch and British influences, with a brief chapter on Melaka today.

Hsü, Marco, *A Brief History of Malayan Art* (Millennium Books, 1999). Traces the art of the Malay Peninsula, from indigenous art and Malay crafts, to the colonial influence and the modern-day art scene, small as it is. Illustrations throughout.

Hughes, D. R., *The Peoples of Malaya* (Eastern Universities Press, 1965). Deals fairly briefly with the cultures of the Malays, the 'aborigines' and the Chinese of the old Malaya.

James, Harold and Sheil-Small, Denis, *The Undeclared War* (Leo Cooper, 1971). The first thorough account of the Confrontation, when the British sent troops to deal with Indonesian insurgents between 1962 and 1966.

Kennedy, J., *A History of Malaya* (Macmillan, 1970). A well-written and very readable history of Malaya.

Milton, Giles, *Nathaniel's Nutmeg* (Sceptre, 2000). The story of nutmeg, featuring the spice-producing islands of South East Asia during the 16th and 17th centuries, and centring on the exploits of Nathaniel Courthope, an employee of the East India Company, who for five years defended the tiny island of Rum against Dutch opposition.

Osborne, Milton, *Southeast Asia: An Introductory History* (George Allen & Unwin, 1983). A broad introductory history to the whole region.

Ryan, N. J., *The Cultural Heritage of Malaya* (Longman, 1962). Outlines the cultural heritage of the Malays, Indians and Chinese of Malaya.

Smith, Colin, *Singapore Burning: Heroism and Surrender in World War II* (Viking, 2005; reprinted Penguin 2006). The definitive book on the event that Winston Churchill described as 'the worst disaster and largest capitulation in British history'.

Suárez, Thomas, *Early Mapping of Southeast Asia* (Periplus Editions, 1999). A beautiful book, which recounts the story of how Southeast Asia was mapped, in cartographic terms and as a literary and imaginative concept. Full of early maps and charts.

Turnbull, C. Mary, *A Short History of Malaysia, Singapore and Brunei* (Graham Brash Singapore, 1981). A thorough introduction to the history of the region, and quite readable. Coverage up to the late 1970s.

Fiction

Aw, Tash, *The Harmony Silk Factory* (HarperPerennial, 2005). A promising debut novel set in Malaysia's Kinta Valley during World War Two. The story of anti-hero Johnny Lim is told by three separate narrators, including Johnny's wife Snow and a creepy English aesthete. The first section of the novel brilliantly evokes 1940s Malaya.

Burgess, Anthony, *The Malayan Trilogy* (Vintage, 1996). This trilogy of novels, first published between 1956 and 1959, provides an accurate and very funny glimpse of post-war Malaya in the 'Emergency' years leading to independence. Burgess himself worked as a schoolteacher in Kuala Kangsar during the 1950s.

Carey, Peter, *My Life as a Fake* (Faber and Faber, 2003). A literary thriller set mainly in the Kuala Lumpur of the 1940s; a vivid evocation of the city.

Clavell, James, *King Rat* (reprinted Flame 1999). This bestselling novel is set in Singapore's notorious Changi prison during the Japanese occupation.

Conrad, Joseph, *Lord Jim* (1900, reprinted Penguin Classics 2000). One of Conrad's masterpieces, *Lord Jim* follows the story of a man who seeks redemption in Malaya after deserting ship. Conrad also set a number of his short stories in the Malay Archipelago, including 'Lagoon', the first story he ever wrote.

Farrell, J. G., *The Singapore Grip* (1978, reprinted Phoenix 1996). This long novel (Farrell's last) is set on the eve of Singapore's fall to the Japanese; the decadent colonial lifestyle of the Blackett family is about the meet its end.

Fauconnier, Henri, *The Soul of Malaya* (1930, limited availability). An in-depth, semi-fictional look at Malaya from the perspective of a rubber planter.

Maugham, Somerset, *Maugham's Malaysian Stories* (Heinemann, 1969) and *Maugham's Borneo Stories* (Heinemann 1976). Quintessential colonial literature. These easy-reading stories delve deep into the everyday lives of British colonials in Malaya and Borneo.

Theroux, Paul, *Saint Jack* (Penguin, 1976) and *Collected Stories* (Hamish Hamilton, 1997). *Saint Jack* tells the story of an American pimp and ships' chandler in Singapore; *The Consul's File* is a collection of short stories set in rural Malaya (now out of print but available in the Collected Stories).

General

Allen, Charles (editor), *Tales from the South China Seas* (Futura, 1984). The stories and lives of the British in Southeast Asia during the first half of the 20th century. A fascinating insight into the colonial existence, gleaned after more than 500 hours of recorded interviews. (The stories were originally broadcast on Radio 4 as oral history documentaries.)

Auger, Timothy (editorial director), *The Encyclopedia of Malaysia* (Didier Millet, 1998). The most comprehensive reference work on Malaysia, with 15 volumes, each highly illustrated, covering everything from history and environment to religions, architecture and the performing arts.

Brooke, Sylvia, *Queen of the Head Hunters* (Sidgwick and Jackson 1970). Candid and entertaining autobiography of the wife of Vyner Brooke, the last 'white rajah' of Sarawak.

Buruma, Ian, *God's Dust: A Modern Asian Journey* (Phoenix, 2000). A unique and insightful look at the cultural and political moods of Burma, Thailand, Malaysia, Singapore, Taiwan, South Korea and Japan, with a focus on how the modern world has impacted upon age-old traditions. Very readable.

Chapman, Spenser, *The Jungle is Neutral* (reprinted Lyons Press 2003). A survival account set in the jungles of Malaya during the Second World War.

Craig, Jo Ann, *Culture Shock* (Times Books International, 1979). A thorough, if outdated, look at the customs of Malaysia and Singapore.

Evans, Ivor H. N., *Among Primitive Peoples in Borneo* (1922, reprinted Oxford University Press 1990). An ethnographer and museum curator in British Malaya, Evans offers some fascinating snippets on the lives and cultures of the Dusuns and Bajau of British North Borneo (now Sabah).

Harrisson, Tom, *World Within: A Borneo Story* (1959, reprinted Oxford University Press 1986). A highly eccentric and erudite account of Harrisson's time in the remote Kelabit Highlands of Sarawak during the time of the Japanese Occupation. A talented archaeologist and ethnologist, Harrisson parachuted into the Highlands to help organize resistance against the Japanese forces. The book provides a detailed look at the Kelabit people and their customs.

Keith, Agnes, *Land Below the Wind* (Ulverscroft, 1969). Agnes Keith lived in Sandakan, Sarawak, during the 1930s and this book records her impressions of the cultures and natural environment of the region, winning her brief acclaim back in the States.

Medway, Lord, *The Wild Mammals of Malaya* (Oxford University Press, 1969). Coverage of 200 of Peninsular Malaysia's wild mammals, with colour plates.

Raslan, Karim, *Ceritalah: Malaysia in Transition* (Times Books International, 1996). A collection of the author's weekly essays for *The Sun*, a Malaysian newspaper, providing a glimpse of the modern Malaysian identity.

Tay, Lillian (editor), *80 Years of Architecture* (PAM Publication, 2000). A look at Malaysia's modern architecture. More images than text.

Wallace, Alfred Russel, *The Malay Archipelago* (1868, reprinted Periplus 2000). A ground-breaking work of natural history, and a wonderful piece of travel writing too, with clear and candid observations about the people and places he visited alongside interpretations of his research findings. Independently of Darwin, Wallace drew parallel conclusions on the theory of evolution.

Index

Main page references are in **bold**. Page references to maps are in *italics*.

Borneo Adventure.
BORNEO